Turfgrass Soil Fertility and Chemical Problems: Assessment and Management

R.N. Carrow, University of Georgia

D.V. Waddington, Pennsylvania State University

P.E. Rieke, Michigan State University

Ann Arbor Press

Chelsea, Michigan

Ann Arbor Press
310 North Main Street
P.O. Box 20
Chelsea, MI 48118
www.sleepingbearpress.com
Ann Arbor Press is an imprint of Sleeping Bear Press

Printed and bound in the United States.
10 9 8 7 6 5 4 3 2 1

Library of Congress Cataloging-in-Publication Data

Carrow, Robert N.
Turfgrass soil fertility and chemical problems : assessment and management / Robert N. Carrow, Donald V. Waddington, Paul E. Rieke.
p. cm.
Includes bibliographic references (p.).
ISBN: 1-57504-153-7
1. Turfgrasses—Fertilizers. 2. Turf management. 3. Soil chemistry. 4. Soil fertility. I. Waddington, D.V. (Donald V.) II. Rieke, Paul E. III. Title

SB433 .C3244 2001
635.9′64289—dc21

2001022858

Acknowledgments

The authors wish to acknowledge contributions of those individuals who provided advice, encouragement, and guidance during the preparation of this book.

Special thanks for the patience and encouragement of our spouses and to the several secretaries for their skillful assistance. Thanks to John H. Detrick, former Vice President of Pursell Technologies, for providing review and information related to turfgrass fertilizers; Dr. Ann M. Wolf, Director of Agriculture Analytical Services Laboratory, Penn State University, for review and comments on soil and tissue analyses; Dr. Richard H. Fox, Professor of Soil Science, Penn State University, for sharing his knowledge on soil chemistry and fertility; and Dr. D.D. Warncke, Michigan State University, for information on organic soils.

Thanks also are expressed to many other colleagues, industry representatives, and turf managers who over the years have freely shared information regarding soil chemistry and fertility problems and management of turfgrass soils.

About the Authors

Robert N. Carrow is Professor of Crop and Soil Science at University of Georgia. His degrees are from Michigan State University (B.S. in 1968; Ph.D. in 1972). He has held research and teaching positions in turfgrass science at the University of Massachusetts (1972–1976) and Kansas State University (1976–1984) prior to his turfgrass science research position at the University of Georgia (1984–present). Dr. Carrow has concentrated his research emphasis on: (a) soil chemical (nutrients, acidity, salinity) and soil physical (compaction, oxygen, drought) stresses, and (b) traffic stresses (compaction, wear) on turfgrasses.

He has served in many professional turfgrass manager and scientific society responsibilities. Dr. Carrow is a Fellow of the American Society of Agronomy and is Vice President of the International Turfgrass Society.

Donald V. Waddington is Professor Emeritus of Soil Science at Pennsylvania State University. He received his Ph.D. from the University of Massachusetts in 1964, and M.S. from Rutgers University in 1960, and a B.S. from Penn State in 1953. Following graduation he served for 2 years in the U.S. Army, and worked in the fertilizer industry for 2 years. He taught and conducted research in the turfgrass programs at the University of Massachusetts (1960–1965) and at Penn State (1965–1991). He continued his activities for several years following retirement. He served as visiting scientist and taught in the turfgrass management program at Mississippi State University during the spring semester in 1997 through 2000. He has conducted research dealing with soil-related problems on turfgrass areas. Topics included N-source evaluation, soil test calibration, soil modifications and playing surface characteristics of sports fields. His teaching assignments have included courses in beginning soils, soil physics, soil physical properties on turf, turfgrass nutrition, weed control in turf, and turfgrass management.

He has served in many turfgrass industry and professional society offices and committees. His contributions have been recognized by various awards and honors including Fellow in the American Society of Agronomy, the Fred V. Grau Turfgrass Science Award from the Crop Science Society of America, and the Dr. William H. Daniel Founders Award from the Sports Turf Managers Association.

Paul E. Rieke is Professor Emeritus of Crop and Soil Sciences Michigan State University. His degrees are Ph.D. from Michigan State University in 1963, and M.S. and B.S. from the University of Illinois in 1958 and 1956, respectively. He joined the faculty at M.S.U. in 1963 and retired in 1999. His research program has concentrated on cultivation, topdressing, and fertilization of turfgrasses. For 20 years he coordinated the turfgrass extension program at M.S.U. His teaching included courses in beginning soils, soil management, and turfgrass soil management, the latter having been taught to over 1600 students.

Dr. Rieke has served the turf industry and professional societies in a number of capacities. Among recognitions for Dr. Rieke's contributions as a turfgrass scientist are: Fellow of the Crop Science Society of America; Green Section Award and Piper and Oakley Award from the U.S. Golf Association; Distinguished Service Award from the Golf Course Superintendents Association of America; and Honorary Membership in Turfgrass Producers International.

Preface

The Challenge

Fertilization is one of the three major management practices on turfgrasses, along with irrigation and mowing. Without a sound plant nutrition/soil fertility program, turfgrasses will not sufficiently respond to other management inputs, and fertilization plays a major role in stress tolerance of grasses. Also, adequate fertilization is essential for a healthy plant in integrated plant/pest management protocols.

Developing sound turfgrass fertilization programs, however, is becoming more complex because: (a) there is a heightened awareness that fertilizer applications must be made in a manner to protect water quality and the environment; (b) a greater number of species and cultivars are available, each with specific nutrient responses or requirements; (c) the diversity of sports turf uses, where high quality demands, close mowing, intensive traffic, and seasonal use patterns require site-specific fertilization; (d) additionally, site-specific management is increasingly necessary as turfgrasses are established on poor soils (e.g., excessively acid, salt-affected, low cation exchange capacity, poorly drained, etc.) and where effluent or poor quality irrigation water is used; (e) fertilization is important for environmental, traffic, and pest stress tolerances as well as recovery; (f) the great diversity of turfgrass fertilizers and amendments with differing characteristics can cause confusion; and (g) the necessity of utilizing and properly interpreting soil, tissue, and water quality test information in development of fertilization regimes.

Our Approach

Several *foundational principles* were used to guide the authors in the development of this book.

- *To use a field problem approach.* Soil fertility/plant nutrition courses are seldom taught from a field problem perspective. Instead, the scientific principles are presented but not applied to common field problem situations.
- *To incorporate both scientific principles and practicum.* Arising from a scientific understanding of a field problem should be practical management recommendations (i.e., practicum). *Scientific principles* are necessary to understand specific problems and to comprehend the logic behind practical recommendations or management options. Developing effective management strategies to address a specific soil fertility/chemical problem requires that we understand the primary problem, and not just secondary symptoms. *Practicum or practical recommendations* are to guide turfgrass managers as they consider various management options—i.e., to provide them with the practical information to make wise management decisions.
- *To compile into one source* all the information required to *identify* (assessment) and *manage* soil fertility/chemical *problems.*
- *To use an international approach* that incorporates problems that occur outside of North America, and metric units as well as English units.

Our Goals

- *To provide current turfgrass managers* a practical, science-based, single-source information package to assist in their fertility management challenges.
- *To provide a "textbook" for the next generation of turfgrass managers.* It is our hope that more turfgrass soil fertility courses will be developed as part of 2-year, 4-year, and graduate turf programs that will: (a) use a field problem solving orientation, and (b) incorporate the "practicum" along with the scientific principles.

May the Lord bless each turf manager as they pursue a productive career in Turfgrass Management and Science!

Contents

Part I. Introduction

Part II. Soil Chemical Properties and Problems

Part III. Fertilizers and Fertilization

Appendixes

Turfgrass Soil Fertility and Chemical Problems: Assessment and Management

Part I

Introduction

Chapter 1

Soil and Soil Related Problems

THE AREAS OF EMPHASIS IN THIS BOOK are turfgrass plant nutrition, soil fertility, and soil chemical problems; more specifically:

1. *Plant Nutrition,* which includes

    - essential plant nutrients
    - functions of nutrients
    - nutrient deficiency symptoms and problems
    - nutrient toxicity or excess problems
    - assessing plant nutrient status

2. *Soil Fertility,* which entails

    - nutrient forms and reactions in the soil
    - factors affecting soil nutrient availability
    - assessing soil nutrient status
    - characteristics of fertilizers
    - practical guidelines for developing agronomically and environmentally sound fertilization programs

3. *Soil Chemical Problems.* Beyond the deficiency or excess/toxicity of essential plant nutrients, there are certain soil chemical constraints that may limit turfgrass growth or cause management problems. Understanding and managing these constraints are part of the overall nutritional program for a particular turfgrass site. These are:

    - low nutrient holding capacity (cation exchange capacity or CEC) in the soil
    - low soil pH (acid) problems
    - high soil pH (alkaline, calcareous) problems
    - salt induced problems (saline, sodic, saline-sodic conditions)
    - influence of soil microbial populations and biologically derived biochemicals on plant nutrition and soil chemical properties
    - unique soil chemical problems such as waterlogged soils, presence of pollutants, and organic soils

Fertilization guidelines are presented for each essential nutrient within their particular chapter. But, the last chapter (Chapter 19, Developing Fertilizer Programs) focuses on development of an overall fertilization program that incorporates all necessary nutrients.

Soil is the reservoir for water and the source of most of the essential nutrients for turfgrass plants, yet soil problems that hinder turfgrass growth may seem nebulous and mysterious to the grower. Reasons for this are diverse. Soils are normally out-of-sight and even when we view a soil, nothing spectacular appears to be occurring. But, in reality, very complex and dynamic activities are constantly in progress. Unfortunately, when turf managers have studied Soil Science, classes have focused on fundamental theory and terminology with little emphasis on application to real-world problems of turfgrass culture and environmental issues that confront growers in the field.

Our approach in this book is to focus on field problems—those situations that adversely affect turfgrass growth and development, or contribute to environmental concerns. In Chapter 1, an overview is given of *primary soil fertility and chemical problems.* Additionally, each problem is indexed in Table 1.1 to a specific chapter that contains detailed discussion of the problems, causes, and preventative/corrective measures. Thus, the user need not read the book in chapter order, but can go directly to those sections related to a specific problem.

Some of the soil fertility and chemical constraints listed in Table 1.1 are not widespread within the United States but are very important on a worldwide basis—such as aluminum toxicity under excessive acidity (pH <5.0).[4] We have attempted to write this book from a *world view* by presenting problems that occur in turfgrass field situations regardless of the world location and by presenting both English and metric units. Additionally, for salt-affected soils, the Australian classification system is presented along with the widely-used U.S. Salinity Laboratory system.

It is assumed that most readers have a basic background in Soil Science; therefore, our book is not written to be a basic soils textbook.[1] Instead, we emphasize the practical management of specific field problems. However, fundamental principles and terminology are addressed within each chapter as they relate to the chapter topic. A basic science appreciation of plant nutrition and soil fertility/chemistry will greatly enhance understanding of why different nutrient management practices are used. Additional, selected references that address turfgrass fertility and soil chemical problems include Beard,[2] Waddington,[6] and Waddington et al.[7]

I. WHAT IS A SOIL?

COMPONENTS THAT MAKE UP A SOIL are very different in physical, chemical, and biological properties, and thus contribute to great diversity among soils. *Components* include:

- *Mineral (inorganic) constituents*—when inorganic constituents are classified solely on physical size, they are categorized as clay, silt, sand, gravel, and stones. However, great chemical diversity is found among the inorganic materials. What are identified as clay particles in a particle size analysis may, in fact, consist of many different types of clay and numerous precipitated inorganic compounds associated with the clay. Among the associated inorganic chemicals are various salts, Fe and Al oxides, calcium carbonate, gypsum, sodium carbonate, calcium phosphates, and many other compounds.
- *Organic matter*—Organic materials range from fresh, undecomposed debris to well-decomposed humus, as well as considerable organic compounds in the bodies of the living soil microorganisms and macroorganisms and turfgrass roots. In most turfgrass soils, part of the organic matter may not be directly in the soil, but on the soil surface as *thatch*, a mixture of living and dead organic matter that may also contain some mineral constituents. If the thatch contains appreciable mineral matter, it is called a *mat.*

Table 1.1. Primary soil fertility and chemical problems and chapters dealing with their nature, identification, causes, and corrective/preventative measures.

Primary Soil Chemical Problem or Condition	Commonly Associated Nutrient Deficiencies[a]	Commonly Associated Nutrient/Element Toxicities or Excessive Levels[b]	Relevant Chapters
1. Nutrient deficiencies	Any essential nutrient	–	2, 3, 10–14
2. Nutrient imbalances	(K, Mg, Ca), (Fe, Mn)	Na	2, 3, 10–14, 16
3. Low CEC (cation exchange capacity)	K, Mg, Mn, N	Na, total soluble salts	4
4. Moderate acidity (pH 5.0–6.5)	Mg, K, P	–	5
5. Excessive acidity (pH 3.5–5.0)	P, Mg, K, Ca, N	Al, Mn, H	5
6. Acid sulfate soils (pH 1.5–3.5)	P, Mg, K, Ca, N	Al, total soluble salts, Na, Mn	5
7. Acidic thatch (pH <5.5)	N, Fe, P, K	–	5
8. Alkaline soil (no free $CaCO_3$)	Fe, Mn, Zn, P	B	6
9. Calcareous soil (free $CaCO_3$)	P, Fe, Mn	B	6
10. High P fixing soils	P	–	11
11. Salt-affected soils			7, 8
• Saline	K, Mg, Ca, P, Mn, NO_3^-	High total salts, Na, Cl, B, SO_4	
• Sodic	Soil O_2, Ca, Mg, K	Na, Cl, B, OH, Al	
• Saline-sodic	K, Mg, Ca, P, Mn, NO_3^-, low soil O_2	High total salts, Na, Cl, B, SO_4	
12. Waterlogged (reduced conditions, nonacid sulfate soils)	low soil O_2, N	Methane (CH_4), ethylene (C_2H_4), Fe, Mn, H_2S, organic acids	15, 16
13. Soil pollutants	Varies	Heavy metals, herbicides, other	16
14. Organic soils	P, K, Mg, Zn, Cu, Mn, B	Mn, Fe	16

[a] Commonly associated nutrient deficiencies in turfgrass situations. Deficiencies may be due to low levels of a particular nutrient in the soil, or in some cases, a deficiency induced by a high level of another element.

[b] Commonly associated nutrient/element toxicity or excessive levels that occur in turfgrass situations. These may differ for other crops. Excessive levels of a nutrient/element may induce a deficiency of another nutrient.

- *Biological entities*—Turfgrass soils are often rich in microorganisms, worms, mollusks, anthropods, vertebrates, and nonturfgrass plants. The actual constituents in these biological components, as well as their activities within the soil, are important.
- *Pore space*—The voids within the physical matrix of the soil play essential functions in water retention and movement, gas exchange, and channels for root growth. Larger pores (>0.10 mm diameter) are called *macropores*, *aeration pores*, or *noncapillary pores*. Pores of <0.10 mm diameter are termed *micropores, capillary pores*, or *moisture retention pores*.

A person's concept of soil depends upon their background. For example, when "soil" is mentioned, differing concepts occur in the minds of a scientist, a highway or construction engineer, a turfgrass manager, a pedologist (one who studies soil development and classification), or an environmental ecologist, but the basic principles are still the same. Turfgrass science and culture has benefited from the study of soil: (a) by scientists investigating soil formation and soil classification; (b) more recently by scientists who determine the role of soil in environmental issues, such as pesticide/nutrient fate, wetlands, runoff, and erosion; and (c) by scientists and growers who view soil as it relates to growth of higher plants. Also, concepts of soil mechanics used by engineers have been valuable in their relationship to soil physical properties of turfgrass soils.

Thus, one general definition of soil may not suit all needs or concepts. However, a simple definition could be the unconsolidated mineral and organic matter on the immediate earth surface that serves as a medium for plant growth. This definition can be refined, depending on the need. Three major concepts of soil are presented in the following sections—soil as it forms, soil as a component of the environment, and soil as a medium for plant growth.

II. SOIL FORMATION AND CLASSIFICATION

A. Soil Formation Processes

AN APPRECIATION OF THE CONCEPT OF SOIL FORMATION aids turfgrass managers in understanding (a) how soils are dynamic over both long and short periods, and (b) how different chemical and physical properties evolve in soils. In nature, formation of a soil is the result of five major factors: parent material, climate, vegetation and other living organisms, topography or relief, and time. Different relationships among these five factors can produce soils that vary dramatically in their characteristics.

As consolidated rocks begin to disintegrate, soil formation begins. The initial parent material may be volcanic rock, granite, limestone, sandstone, or other rocks. Parent material can also be unconsolidated deposits laid by water (alluvial), gravity (colluvial), wind (loess), and glaciers. Organic matter (organic soils) and volcanic materials (ash, lava) can also serve as parent material.

The climatic forces of temperature and rainfall have a major influence on weathering rates, minerals, and vegetation. Soils in warm, humid regions are substantially different in profile development, chemical properties, and clay types, compared to soils in warm, arid climates. Tropical soils are often acid, bases are highly leached, kaolinitic (1:1 lattice silicate clay) clays dominate, iron and aluminum oxides are common, and organic matter content is reasonably good where vegetation covers the soil. In contrast, hot, dry climates often evolve soils that are alkaline, contain base cations, are low in acid cations, contain 2:1 silicate clays (since silica doesn't leach as much as in tropical regions), and are low in organic matter.

Vegetation and other organisms, such as small animals and microbes, are important in both quantity and type for soil formation. Climates that produce abundant vegetation result in large additions of organic matter and nutrient recycling. Two major types of vegetation are forests and grasses. Grasslands normally contain significantly more organic matter than forest soils with more uniform distribution throughout the soil profile. Both living and dead (decomposed) organisms can play an important role in soil structure development and stability.

Topography directly influences water runoff and infiltration, erosion that removes topsoil, and the location where suspended materials and water are deposited. Thereby, soil formation is affected. The vegetation present on a site is also often a function of topography due to water availability, drainage, slope, and radiation (angle toward or away from the sun).

Soil formation requires time for several processes to occur: (a) additions to the soil including water and dissolved minerals, sediments, organic matter, energy from the sun; (b) losses from the soil such as water by evapotranspiration, runoff, percolation or leaching; gaseous losses of N, O_2, and CO_2; soil by erosion; energy by radiation; and minerals and colloids by leaching; (c) translocation of materials within the soil profile including clays and organic colloids, sesquioxides, nutrients, salts, and mixing of soil by animals; and (d) transformations within the soil such as clay formation, humus formation, reduction in particle size as particles weather, and structure development.

As soil formation processes continue, layers that have distinct properties start to appear within the soil. These layers are called *horizons* and all horizons in a vertical section of soil form the *soil profile.* The *master horizons* are defined by the *Glossary of Soil Science Terms*[5] (U.S. Soil Classification System) as:

O horizons—Layers dominated by organic material.
A horizons—Mineral horizons that formed at the surface or below an O horizon that exhibit little or none of the original parent material structure and: (a) are characterized by an accumulation of humified organic matter intimately mixed with the mineral fraction and not dominated by properties characteristic of E or B horizons; or (b) have properties resulting from cultivation, pasturing, or similar kinds of disturbance.
E horizons—Mineral horizons in which the main feature is loss of silicate clay, iron, aluminum, or some combination of these, leaving a concentration of sand and silt particles of quartz or other resistant materials.
B horizons—Horizons that formed below an A, E, or O horizon and are dominated by obliteration of all or much of the original rock structure and show one or more of the following:

- illuvial concentration (accumulation) of silicate clay, iron, aluminum, humus, carbonates, gypsum, or silica, alone or in combination;
- evidence of removal of carbonates;
- residual concentration of sesquioxides;
- coatings of sesquioxides that make the horizon's color conspicuously lower in value, higher in chroma, or redder in hue than overlying and underlying horizons without apparent illuviation of iron;
- alterations that form silicate clay or liberate oxides, or both, and that form granular, blocky, or prismatic structure if volume changes accompany changes in moisture content; or
- brittleness.

C horizons or layers—Horizons or layers, excluding hard bedrock, that are little affected by pedogenic (soil formation) processes and lack properties of O, A, E, or B horizons. The material of C horizons may be either like or unlike that from which the soil presumably formed. The C horizon may have been modified even if there is no evidence of pedogenesis.
R layers—Hard bedrock including granite, basalt, quartzite and indurated limestone or sandstone that is sufficiently coherent to make hand digging impractical.

Transitional horizons can also be designated when a horizon contains properties of both the overlying and underlying horizons. These are listed by combination of the primary horizons (i.e., AB, BC, etc.). Subordinate distinctions, such as By (y = accumulation of gypsum), are used to identify other characteristics. Twenty-four subordinate terms are presently used as defined in the *Glossary of Soil Science Terms.*[5]

A basic understanding of soil formation and terminology assists turfgrass managers in recognizing how and why *soils vary in the vertical direction.* The "soil" on a site is not just the top horizon but also underlying horizons that can influence turfgrass rooting depth in response to subsoil chemical (pH; Al, Mn toxicities; nutrient deficiencies; salt problems) and physical (soil strength; O_2 status; water status) properties. For recreational turfgrass sites, it is not unusual to modify the original soil or to create a whole new soil (and soil profile, i.e., horizons) with the desired chemical and physical properties. Or, because of extensive soil movement during construction some areas become devoid of topsoil, leaving compacted subsoils for turf establishment.

B. Classification of Soils

Soil characteristics also *vary on the horizontal or landscape plane.* Determination in the field of important soil characteristics and boundaries of similar soils is used to classify soils and develop soil descriptions. The basic (lowest) classification of a soil is the *soil series,* which is a group of soils with similar profile characteristics and parent material. Profile characteristics used for classification include color; contents of clay, iron oxides, aluminum oxides, and organic matter; pH; presence of salts; and percent base saturation. Also, the presence of certain diagnostic horizons in the surface or subsurface of the soil aids in classification. Examples of diagnostic horizons are spodic (subsurface accumulation of Fe and Al oxides and organic matter) and histic (surface horizon of very high organic matter, wet during parts of the year).

Soils within a series can be subdivided into *soil phases* when there is an important difference in surface texture, depth, slope, erosion, stoniness, or soluble salts. Thus, a soil in the Cecil series can be designated at the soil phase level as a Cecil sandy loam, 3 to 5% slope. The basic soil mapping unit is the soil phase. In older classification systems, the term *"soil type"* was used instead of "phase."

In addition to the soil series, there are five higher soil classification levels as indicated in Table 1.2 for the example of a Cecil soil common in the Piedmont region of the USA. The soil orders, which contain soils with broadly similar characteristics, is the broadest classification category. There are 12 *soil orders* under which all soils are grouped: Alfisols, Andisols, Aridisols, Entisols, Gelisols, Histosols, Inceptisols, Mollisols, Oxisols, Spodosols, Ultisols, and Vertisols. Other countries also have similar soil classification systems to categorize soils into major groups.

C. Soil Surveys and Maps

Classification of soils in the field allows soil to be mapped into units having similar physical, chemical, and biological aspects; and based on these aspects projected uses or suitabilities of the soil can be listed. Many countries have developed soil maps. Within the United States, the mapping units are soil series and phases. Soil surveys are often conducted on a relatively small area basis and soil phases are delineated on an aerial photograph.

A detailed survey includes discussion on the soil capabilities and limitations for agricultural, recreational, wildlife, and engineering uses. Soil surveys can be very useful to turfgrass managers. Prior to development of a site, considerable information can be gleaned on suitability of the site for a projected use. After site development, soil surveys continue to provide much informa-

Table 1.2. Soil classification orders and the classification of a Cecil series soil.

Soil Level	Example [a]
Order	Ultisol
Suborder	Udults
Great Group	Hapludults
Subgroup	Typic Hapludults
Family	Clayey, kaolinitic, thermic
Series	Cecil

[a] U.S. soil classification (taxonomy) system.

tion on soil properties unless the soils have been dramatically altered. In the United States, soil surveys are available through the U.S. Department of Agriculture.

On many established turfgrass areas, the natural soil profile is often altered. Sometimes a complete man-made profile is developed, such as on golf greens. This would then alter the accuracy of a soil survey.

III. SOIL AND THE ENVIRONMENT

THE SECOND CONCEPT OF SOIL that is useful to the turfgrass manager is *soil as an active agent in the environment.* Soils have a major impact on environmental issues such as wetlands, runoff, leaching, water quality, water conservation, remediation of contamination, pesticide/nutrient fate, sediment control, wind erosion, and use of soils in waste treatment methods.

Chemical, physical, and biological properties of a soil determine the movement, retention, and activity of components in the soil such as water, an element in water, or a pesticide in the soil. Understanding these properties is a prerequisite for making wise management decisions relative to the environment. Society increasingly is demanding substainability of natural resources in contrast to the mining of water and soil. Thus, turf managers are called upon to continue to be proactive environmentalists.

In this book, an environmentally positive approach has been incorporated. Relevant environmental issues are addressed in pertinent sections of chapters. Management considerations and recommendations are also made from a proenvironment stance. Most turfgrass growers are used to thinking of their site, as well as adjacent areas, as a system where many potential interactions between system components are possible. This concept is elaborated on in the next section.

IV. SOIL AND TURFGRASS CULTURE

VIEWING THE SOIL FROM THE PERSPECTIVES of soil formation or environmental concerns provides only a partial understanding. Turfgrass growers are ultimately interested in using the soil as a medium for turfgrass culture.

Turfgrasses in a particular ecosystem are influenced by many factors that will determine their persistence and vigor. Many of these factors are soil based (Figure 1.1). Soils have chemical, physical, and biological properties that may be either beneficial or detrimental to turfgrass growth.

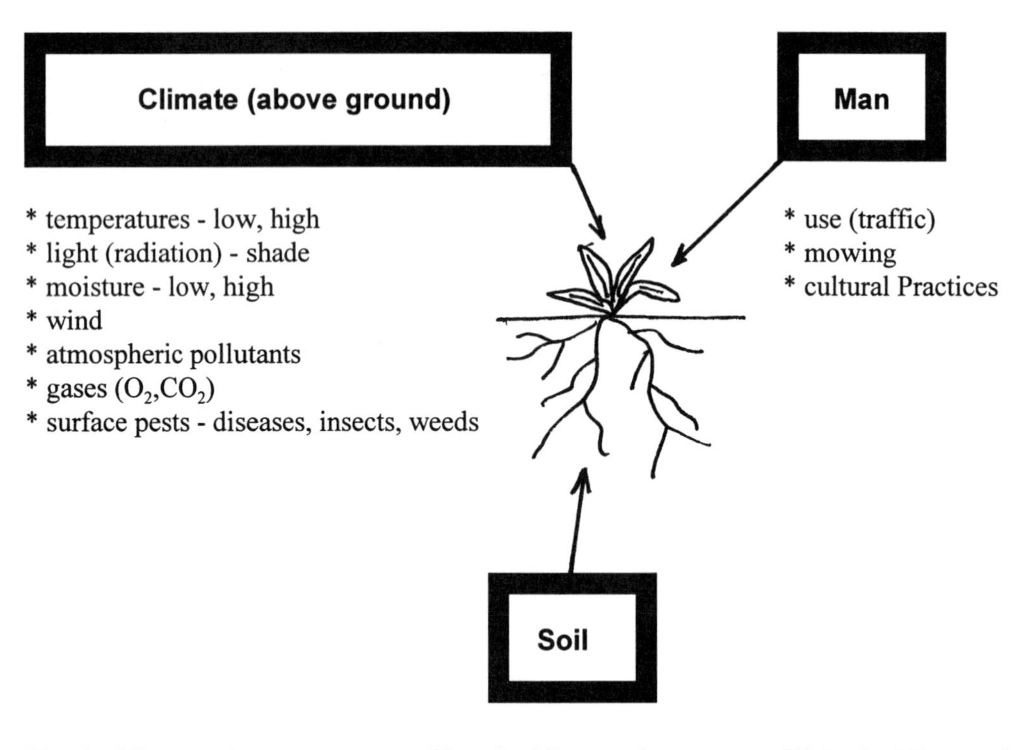

Physical Properties
* low moisture
* excessive moisture
* macro/micro pore distribution
* O_2 and CO_2 contents
* other gases
* soil strength
* low temperature
* high temperature
* soil stability
* thatch

Chemical Properties
* pH
* Al, Mn toxicities
* nutrient deficiencies
* nutrient imbalances
* total salts
* salt toxicities
* low CEC
* heavy metals
* toxic substances
* calcareous soils

Biological Properties
* microbial types
* microbial population levels
* microbial population balances
* insects
* nematodes
* weeds
* animals

Figure 1.1. The Turfgrass System: plant-soil-climate-man (after Duncan and Carrow[3]).

Man affects the *turfgrass system* (Figure 1.1) in several ways: (a) through use of the site, which imposes traffic stresses such as wear and soil compaction; (b) by mowing, which differs from other cultural practices because it is done so the turfgrass can be used for recreational, functional and/or aesthetic purposes; and (c) by all other cultural practices that are conducted to improve some potentially adverse component in the turfgrass system. For example, irrigation is applied to provide adequate water, while drainage techniques are incorporated to prevent excess water. Cultivation provides temporary macropores for water drainage, gas exchange, and rooting. Fertilization is a means to adjust nutrient levels and balances. Pesticides are used to control specific harmful pests.

A major factor in successful turfgrass culture is the ability to identify what components within the system are problems that limit turfgrass growth or utilization. Primary soil problems

Table 1.3. Primary soil physical field problems.

Physical Problem
Fine-Textured Soils (High Silt/Clay)
1. Excessive quantities of silt and clay
2. Soil compaction – surface, subsurface
3. Presence of layers – surface, subsurface[a]
4. Salt affected soil
a. Saline – salt induced drought
b. Sodic – soil structure, permeability
c. Saline/sodic – soil structure, permeability, and salt induced drought
5. High water table/excess water
6. Improper contouring for surface drainage
7. Low water content (drought)
8. Uneven or unstable soil surface
9. Thatch[b]
Coarse-Textured Soils (High Sand)
1. Excessive sand content (low water-holding capacity)
2. Presence of layers – surface, subsurface
3. Hydrophobic condition
4. Salt affected sands
a. Saline – salt induced drought
b. Sodic – soil structure and permeability
c. Saline/sodic – soil structure permeability, and salt induced drought
5. High water table/excess water
6. Improper contouring for surface drainage
7. Hard sand surfaces
8. "Soft" or unstable sand surfaces
9. Thatch[b]
Organic Soils
1. Subsidence, wind erosion
2. Drainage, water table

[a] There are a number of specific types of layers that can occur in turfgrass soils.
[b] Thatch is listed under soil physical problems since the primary influence of thatch is often physical in nature. Thatch could also be listed in soil biological problems.

caused by adverse soil chemical, physical, and biological properties are listed in Tables 1.1, 1.3, and 1.4, respectively. This approach—of identifying specific soil problems that constrain turf growth and then targeting management to alleviate the problem—is illustrated for management of root systems in Chapter 3, Section II, Managing Root Development and Viability.

As stated earlier, the emphasis of this book is to provide a comprehensive presentation of soil fertility/chemical constraints to turfgrass shoot and root growth. Detailed cultural recommendations and approaches are provided. These are based on the current scientific understanding. In some cases where limited research has been conducted, guidelines are based on research information from other crops.

V. REFERENCES

1. Basic soil science textbook. Most college level soil science textbooks published in many countries provide an excellent discussion of terminology and the fundamental principles.

Table 1.4. Primary soil biological field problems.

Biological Problem
1. Microbial population levels/activity—adequate levels
2. Microbial population balances—beneficial versus pathogenic
3. Improper levels of biochemicals (biostimulants, hormones, etc.)—those produced by soil organisms, secreted by roots, or added as an amendment
4. Insect populations and balances
5. Weeds
6. Algae, moss
7. Nematode populations and balances
8. Soil animals

2. Beard, J.B. 1973. *Turfgrass: Science and Culture.* Chapter 10 (Soils). Englewood Cliffs, NJ: Prentice-Hall, Inc.
3. Duncan, R.R. and R.N. Carrow. 1999. Turfgrass molecular genetic improvement for abiotic/edaphic stress resistance. In D.L. Sparks, Ed. *Advances in Agronomy,* Vol. 67, pp. 233–305. New York: Academic Press.
4. Sanchez, P.A. and T.J. Logan. 1992. Myths and science about the chemistry and fertility of soils in the tropics. Chapter 3. In R. Lal and P.A. Sanchez, Eds. *Myths and Science of Soils in the Tropics.* Madison, WI: Soil Sci. Soc. Amer. Pub. 29, SSSA.
5. Soil Science Society of America. *Glossary of Soil Science Terms.* 1997. Madison, WI: Soil Science Society of America.
6. Waddington, D.V. 1969. Soil and soil-related problems. In A.A. Hanson and F.V. Juska, Eds. *Turfgrass Science, Agronomy Monograph No. 14.* Madison, WI: American Society of Agronomy.
7. Waddington, D.V., R.N. Carrow, and R.C. Shearman, Eds. 1992. *Turfgrass, Agronomy Monograph No. 32.* Chapters 6 (Salinity and Turfgrass Culture), 9 (Effects of Traffic on Turfgrass), 10 (Soils, Soil Mixtures, and Soil Amendments), and 11 (Nutritional Requirements and Fertilization), Madison, WI: American Society of Agronomy.

Chapter 2

Plant Nutrition

DEVELOPMENT OF A GOOD FERTILIZATION PROGRAM requires that we understand plant nutrition and soil fertility. *Plant nutrition* focuses on nutrient-plant interactions. In this chapter, an overview of basic plant nutrition topics is discussed, such as:

- essential nutrients
- plant uptake of nutrients by roots
- foliar uptake of nutrients
- nutrient losses from plants
- an overview of nutrient deficiencies and toxicities
- nutrient and disease relationships

Soil fertility is focused on nutrient-soil interactions that influence nutrient availability and uptake, leaching, volatilization, fixation, denitrification, soil nutrient forms and conversions, and related areas. Readers are referred to Chapters 4–9, 15, and 16 for soil fertility and soil chemical problems. In Chapters 10 to 14 essential nutrients are discussed in detail with soil fertility, plant nutrition, and practicum aspects incorporated.

I. ESSENTIAL NUTRIENTS

TURFGRASS PLANTS MUST SYNTHESIZE OR MANUFACTURE hundreds of complex organic compounds from 17 nutrients (Table 2.1). These nutrients are *essential mineral elements or nutrients* because they satisfy at least one of three criteria (Marschner[6]):

- The turfgrass cannot complete its growth cycle without the mineral element.
- The element performs a function that cannot be done by another element.
- The nutrient is directly involved in plant metabolism or required for an essential metabolic reaction.

Essential nutrients are often classified as *macronutrients* or *micronutrients* (trace elements) based on the quantity required for growth (Table 2.1). Macronutrients are used at 0.1 to 6.0% by dry weight of tissue, while micronutrients are <1.0 to 500 ppm concentrations (1 ppm = 1 mg kg^{-1}). Macronutrients are often involved in the structure of molecules, which accounts for the larger quantities required. Micronutrients generally serve catalytic or regulatory roles.

Carbon (C), hydrogen (H), and oxygen (O) are the essential nutrients required in the greatest quantity because C and H are present in all organic compounds of turfgrasses and O is in most. These are the *basic nutrients*.

Table 2.1 Essential nutrient elements, plant available forms, and concentrations in shoot tissues.

Nutrient	Chemical Symbol	Plant Available Form	Concentration by Dry Weight in Plants	Common Sufficiency Range[a]	Frequency of Deficiency in Turfgrasses	Mobility in Plant
MACRONUTRIENTS (essential)			(%)	(%)		
Basic nutrients						
Carbon	C	CO_2	45	–	Sometimes[c]	–
Hydrogen	H	H_2O	6	–	Sometimes[c]	–
Oxygen	O	CO_2, O_2	45	–	Sometimes[d]	–
Primary Nutrients						
Nitrogen	N	NO_3^-, NH_4^+	2.0–6.0	2.8–3.5	Common	Mobile
Phosphorus	P	$H_2PO_4^-$, HPO_4^{-2}	0.10–1.0	0.20–0.55	Sometimes	Mobile
Potassium	K	K^+	1.0–3.0	1.5–3.0	Sometimes	Mobile
Secondary Nutrients						
Calcium	Ca	Ca^{+2}	0.30–1.25	0.50–1.25	Rare	Immobile
Magnesium	Mg	Mg^{+2}	0.15–0.50	0.15–0.50	Sometimes	Mobile
Sulfur	S	SO_4^{-2}	0.15–0.60	0.20–0.50	Sometimes	Somewhat mobile

MICRONUTRIENTS (essential)			(ppm)[b]	(ppm)		
Iron	Fe	Fe^{+2}, Fe^{+3}, Fe-Chelates	100–500	50–100	Common	Immobile
Manganese	Mn	Mn^{+2}, Mn-Chelate	20–500	20–100	Sometimes	Immobile
Zinc	Zn	Zn^{+2}, $ZnOH^{+}$	20–70	20–55	Rare	Somewhat mobile
Copper	Cu	Cu^{+2}, $Cu(OH)^{+}$, Cu-Chelates	10–50	5–20	Rare	Somewhat mobile
Molybdenum	Mo	MoO_4^{-2}, $HMoO_4^{-}$	1–8	1–4	Rare	Somewhat mobile
Boron	B	H_3BO_3, BO_3^{-3}	5–50	5–60	Rare[e]	Somewhat mobile
Chlorine	Cl	Cl^{-}	1000–2000	200–400	Never	Mobile
Nickel	Ni	Ni^{+2}	1–10	<1	Never	–
OTHER BENEFICIAL NUTRIENTS (not essential)						
Sodium	Na	Na^{+}	<0.50%	NA[f]	NA[f]	Mobile
Silicon	Si	$Si(OH)_4$	1–3%	NA	NA	Immobile
Cobalt	Co	Co^{+2}	<0.3 ppm	NA	NA	–
Selenium	Se	SeO_4^{-2}	<1 ppm	NA	NA	–

[a] Sufficiency ranges are only general. They can vary with species and cultivars within a species. Specific ranges have not been developed for most turfgrass species and cultivars.
[b] 1% dry weight = 10,000 ppm on a weight basis; 1 ppm = 1 mg kg^{-1} dry weight.
[c] Drought stress limits root uptake of water and induces stomatal closure that limits CO_2 intake.
[d] Oxygen deficiency for respiration can occur under compacted or waterlogged conditions.
[e] Boron toxicity is sometimes observed, and is much more probable than B deficiencies.
[f] NA = not applicable.

Nitrogen (N), phosphorus (P), and potassium (K) are termed *primary nutrients* since these are the most common fertilizer needs. *Secondary macronutrients* are calcium (Ca), magnesium (Mg), and sulfur (S). Micronutrients, so named because they are used in low quantities, are Fe, Mn, Zn, Cu, Mo, B, Cl, and Ni.

Other elements that are nonessential are listed as *beneficial elements* because they may benefit some plants. For example, silica (Si) is useful to rice in preventing lodging and as a barrier to certain fungal pathogens. It is possible that tissue rigidity produced by Si could impact wear tolerance to turfgrasses. Also, sodium (Na) may produce positive growth responses in very salt-tolerant *(halophytes)* turfgrass species.

The 17 essential nutrients in Table 2.1 can be found in many different chemical forms in nature. Plants, however, take up nutrients only as rather simple molecules or in elemental form. Total soil content of a particular nutrient is not an indicator of plant availability, since it may be present in complex inorganic or organic forms the plant cannot use. Fertilizer forms of a nutrient must be already in a chemical state where it is plant-available or they must be transformed to an available state by chemical or biochemical (by microorganisms) activity.

Turfgrass nutrition is the subject of a 1992 review article by Turner and Hummel.[7] Handreck and Black[3] also provide a good discussion of plant nutrition of turfgrasses and ornamentals.

II. NUTRIENT UPTAKE

NUTRIENT ACQUISITION BY PLANT ROOTS involves several complex processes for nutrients to come into contact with roots, move from the root surface into the xylem, and then be transported to shoot tissues. Excellent books that cover this broad subject in considerable detail have been written by Barber[1] and Marschner.[6]

A. Nutrient Movement from Soil to Roots

Plant available nutrients consist of ions in the soil solution, cations on the clay and organic matter cation exchange sites, anions on the anion exchange sites (minor in most soils), nutrients contained in relatively soluble minerals, ions released from organic matter by decomposition, ions in organic chelates, and ions contained in applied fertilizers. These aspects of soil fertility will be discussed in later chapters on individual nutrients (Chapters 10 to 14). For nutrient uptake to occur, plant available nutrients must come into contact with the root surface. Three processes can be involved: (a) root interception; (b) mass flow of ions within the soil solution; and (c) ion diffusion in the soil solution.

Root growth and extension into new areas of the soil mass markedly increase nutrient availability as new roots contact more soil solution in the pore spaces and more clay or organic matter surfaces. Enhancement of maximum root growth and viability (health) is an essential component of a good soil fertility program. Factors that limit rooting are covered in Chapter 3, Enhancing Turfgrass Nutrient-Use Efficiency. Root hairs dramatically enhance the effective soil volume contacted by primary and lateral roots. Additionally, the mycorrhizae (an association of roots and fungi that is mutually beneficial) around root surfaces enlarge contact volume. Mycorrhizae are especially important for enhanced P uptake in very low P soils. Root exudates of carbohydrates and other compounds not only enhance mycorrhizae but also can increase nutrient dissolution from soil minerals and enhance ion chelation.

The soil solution moves through macropores (infiltration, percolation, and drainage processes), micropores (retained water), and water films around particles (capillary movement).

Nutrients can move along with the water to root surfaces. Mass flow of water in the micropores and water films is enhanced by evaporation and transpirational water losses. But, as water is extracted from the soil by root uptake in response to transpiration, water movement becomes increasingly slower, thus reducing the influence of mass flow on nutrient uptake.

Diffusion of nutrients in the soil solution is for short distances around the root (<1 cm) and in response to concentration gradients. As root uptake occurs, a gradient is normally established for diffusion to the root from ions in solution. Diffusion of nutrients also occurs from high concentration areas around fertilizer particles to lower concentration areas in the soil solution. With soil drying, diffusion pathways become more restricted. Diffusion increases with soil temperature at about twofold for every 10°C (18°F) increase.

B. Root Uptake Mechanisms

Nutrient uptake by turfgrass roots from the soil solution or colloid surfaces involves a number of transport processes. Nutrient transport across the plasma membrane of root cells is especially complex. An excellent overview of membrane transport principles is provided by Hopkins,[4] while Marschner[6] and Jacoby[5] also give good reviews of the subject.

Intercellular spaces (between cells) of root epidermis and cortex cells create a volume where nutrients can enter the root by *simple diffusion* (movement of a molecule from high concentration to low concentration without crossing a membrane) (Figure 2.1). This volume is called *apparent free space* (AFS). The AFS is part of the plant *apoplasm* which includes all of the intercellular spaces and outer cell walls of root or shoot tissue. Since the cell walls contain carboxyl groups ($R\text{-}COO^-$), some positively charged ions, especially Ca^{+2}, entering the AFS are electrostatically attracted to these negatively charged sites and are restrained from free diffusion. However, most ions can move from the soil solution into the AFS by diffusion until the *Casparian band strip* in the endodermis is reached. This band contains hydrophobic fatty acids and alcohols that physically plug the intercellular spaces. Nutrients must then cross cell plasma membranes to reach the xylem vessels for transport to the shoot tissues. Nutrient uptake by simple diffusion within the AFS does not require a metabolic energy source.

The *plasma membrane* surrounds the cell *protoplasm*, which consists of the *nucleus* (genetic control center of the cell) and *cytoplasm* (all other cell organelles and constituents of the protoplasm, excluding the nucleus) (Figure 2.2). While the plasma membrane physically limits cell protoplasm, it also controls passage of materials into cells and is selectively permeable. Since nutrients must be taken across root cell plasma membranes, nutrient uptake is strongly influenced by *membrane transport mechanisms.* Three basic membrane transport modes are *membrane diffusion, facilitated diffusion,* and *active transport.*[4] These processes function in shoot cells as well as root cells.

Membrane diffusion is diffusion of a substance across the plasma membrane or other membranes. The plasma membrane consists of proteins and lipids with some carbohydrates. The most abundant lipids are *phospholipids* that have two hydrophobic (water repelling) hydrocarbon tails that are nonpolar and a hydrophilic (water loving) polar group. In an aqueous medium, a *bilayer* forms as the hydrophobic tails orient in the interior and the hydrophilic groups orient outward toward the water. The resulting bilayer membrane is impermeable to most polar molecules and is fluid but stable in nature. Proteins are embedded within and across the bilayers.

Most nutrient solutes are polar and do not cross the plasma membrane by membrane diffusion. The exceptions are O_2, CO_2, and NH_3. Water, a highly polar molecule, also freely crosses by diffusion, probably due to its small size and neutral charge.

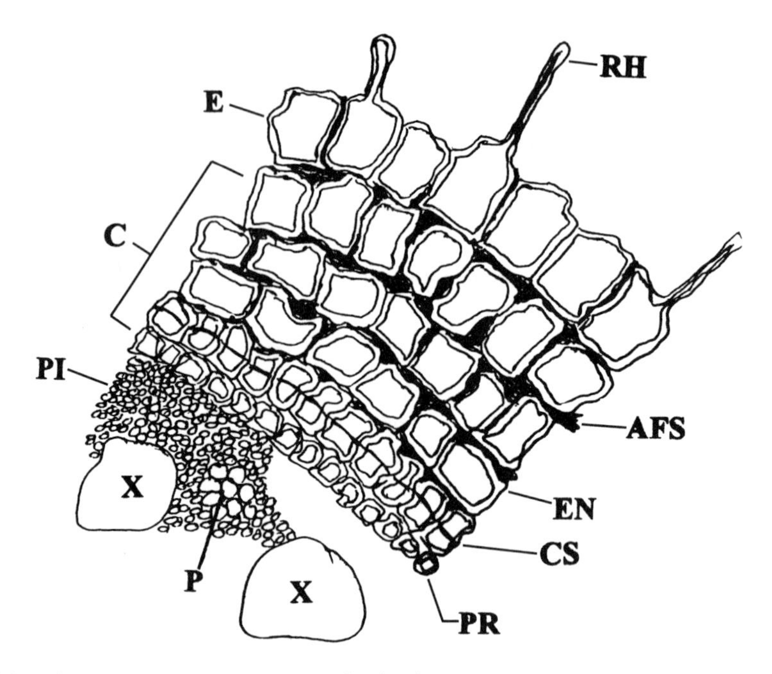

E, epidermis, some cells have **root hairs (RH).**
C, cortex cells are parenchyma cells.
AFS (dark areas), intercellular spaces and outer cell wall surfaces outside the Casparian strip. Called AFS **(apparent free space).**
EN, endodermis, the innermost layer of cortex cells. This contains the **Casparian strip (CS),** a waxy band that inhibits simple diffusion of water.
PR, pericycle, a single layer of cells just within the endodermis. Lateral roots can arise from this layer.
X, xylem, vascular tissue that conducts water and nutrients to the shoots.
P, phloem, vascular tissue that conducts sugars and solutes through the plant, including from shoots to roots.
PI, pith cells.
Stele, is the endodermis, pericycle, and vascular tissues (xylem, phloem) and pith cells.

Figure 2.1. Cross section of a turfgrass root.

Facilitated diffusion allows charged ions and solutes to diffuse across the lipid bilayer membrane through certain *transport proteins* embedded in the membrane. Either a higher concentration for uncharged solutes across the membrane or a higher electrochemical charge for charged ions can provide the gradient for transport. The transport proteins are embedded across the bilayer which allows nutrients to diffuse within the protein media and remain soluble; whereas in the lipid environment they would be insoluble and hydrated ions would be repelled by the hydrophobic interior. As with membrane diffusion, facilitated diffusion is a *passive process* that does not require direct input of metabolic energy—instead a concentration or electrochemical gradient from one side to the other side of the membrane provides energy for transport.

One type of transport proteins is *channel proteins* that form water-filled, charged channels extending across the membrane. Depending on ion charge and hydrated size, channel proteins are selective for specific ions such as K^+, Ca^{+2}, Cl^-, and organic ions. Channel proteins can

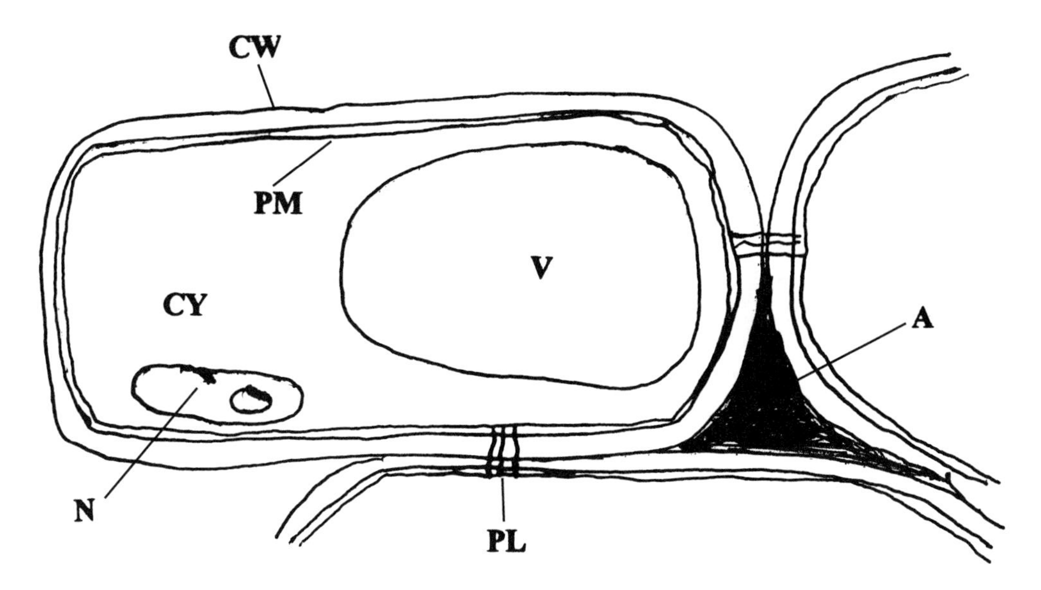

CW, cell wall
PM, plasma membrane surrounds the **protoplasm** which consists of the nucleus and cytoplasm
CY, cytoplasm contains all cell organelles and constituents except the nucleus. These include vacuoles, mitochondria, chloroplasts, endoplasmic reticulum, Golgi bodies, vesicles, lysosomes, ribosomes
V, vacuole cavity that contains cell sap
A, apoplasm space between cells
N, nucleus with nucleolus
PL, plasmodesmota linking adjacent cells

Figure 2.2. Diagram of a plant cell.

facilitate rapid diffusion of large quantities of charged solutes or ions across membranes, such as K^+ movement in stomata guard cells. Additionally, channels may be gated (i.e., be either open or closed) in response to electrical membrane potentials of a certain magnitude, presence of a particular ion, or other stimuli.

Active transport requires input of metabolically derived energy, usually from ATP hydrolysis, and is able to accumulate solutes in the cell against concentration or electrochemical gradients. Because they function against concentration or electrochemical gradients, carrier proteins are required in active transport either into or out of the cell. These carrier proteins are called *ion pumps* or *ATPase-protein pumps.* Active ion pumps are highly selective and can accumulate ions inside cells, limit uptake, or actively expel ions. Also, active ion pumps can control ion movement into and out of cell vacuoles. These aspects are particularly important in controlling ion toxicities or excesses (i.e., Na^+, Cl^-) as well as nutrient acquisition.

Once nutrients are released into the xylem sap, transport upward to the shoot tissues occurs. Within the shoot tissues the same transport mechanisms discussed for root uptake function to distribute nutrients to shoot cells, across plasma membranes, and within cells. Marschner[6] provides an in-depth discussion of these aspects of nutrient movement and the roles of root pressure and transpiration on xylem flow of nutrients.

C. Foliar Nutrient Uptake

While most nutrients are applied to the soil and taken up by the root system, *foliar uptake* can be useful in turfgrass culture. Nutrients applied to the foliage can enter leaves through cuticle pores or cracks and stomatal pores. Once inside leaves, nutrients enter the *apoplasm* (spaces between cells and the outer cell wall surfaces) or pass directly into cells through the plasma membrane. Those nutrients in the apoplasm may be translocated to other locations through the vascular system. Nutrients taken up by shoot cells ultimately must pass through the plasma membrane with membrane transport mechanisms similar to those discussed for roots. See Marschner[6] for a review chapter on foliar uptake.

Micronutrient application, especially Fe and Mn, is the most common use of foliar treatment for turfgrasses. Since micronutrients are required at low rates, they lend themselves to foliar application. Even when soil Fe is not limiting, foliar treatment, usually in conjunction with some N, is a common practice on high quality turfgrass sites to enhance color without promoting growth.

Other nutrients may be applied by foliar means in several situations:

- Spoon-feeding during high stress conditions to maintain optimum nutrient levels (N, K, Fe, Mn).
- When high rainfall and sandy soils cause excessive leaching potential (K, N, Mg).
- For N on golf course greens when the turf manager uses a light, frequent approach to N fertilization.
- When plant roots are lacking or not healthy. Cool-season turfgrasses exposed to prolonged indirect high temperature stress often exhibit few roots or low root viability and can respond to foliar application. Also, a seasonal influence may cause a temporary nutrient deficiency during cool periods such as spring root dieback of warm-season grass roots, early spring P deficiency on bentgrasses, and Fe deficiency on zoysiagrasses in cold, wet springs.
- When a turfgrass manager has the equipment and selects foliar treatment as a means of application rather than granulars.
- As a method of applying any micronutrient when it is deficient. Folair treatment is also a means of assessing whether a turfgrass is deficient in a particular micronutrient based on turf response after foliar treatment of a small test area. Rates and procedures for assessing a potential deficiency of various micronutrients by foliar application to a small area are found in Chapter 14.

A true *foliar feeding* requires a low volume of water (<1 gal per 1,000 ft^2; <4 L per 100 m^2) so that most of the water and nutrients remain on the foliage (Table 2.2). Most often this is accomplished by use of a sprayer in conjunction with fungicide, herbicide, or plant growth regulation applications. Liquid lawn care companies use spray trucks and apply through a hose and various types of nozzles. Since lawn care companies usually apply 0.33 to 1.0 lb N per 1,000 ft^2 (0.16 to 0.49 kg N per 100 m^2) per treatment, a higher volume of water is required to remove most of the nutrients (salts) from leaf tissues, while still leaving some for a foliar feeding and rapid response. Nutrients washed off are available for root uptake. Thus, 3 to 5 gal H_2O per 1,000 ft^2 (12 to 20 L per 100 m^2) are typical of lawn care situations, while golf course and sport field managers often use 1 to 3 gal H_2O per 1,000 ft^2 but lower nutrient rates per application.

Fertigation, the application of nutrients through the irrigation system is used on some golf courses and other recreational sites. Nutrients are proportioned at the desired rate and injected into irrigation lines for delivery. It is not unusual for this type of application to be referred to as

Table 2.2. Liquid delivery of nutrients to turfgrasses.

Liquid Application Type	Volume of Water		Quantity of N	
	gal per 1,000 ft^2	liters per 100 m^2	lb N 1,000 ft^2 [b]	Comments
Foliar	<1	<4	0.05–0.15	95–100% on foliage
Lawn care	3–5	12–20	<1	50–70% on foliage
Drench or fertigation	>25[a]	>102	0.10–1.0	98–100% into soil

[a] 25 gal H_2O per 1,000 ft^2 = 0.04 inch water per 1,000 ft^2.
[b] 1 lb N per 1,000 ft^2 = 0.49 kg N per 100 m^2.

"foliar feeding" when it is really a *drench* where a high volume of water is used to wash nutrients off the leaves and into the soil for root uptake (Table 2.2). Fertigation is liquid delivery but not liquid or foliar feeding. It does allow for frequent and low rate applications of nutrients to be applied.

The greatest potential problem of true foliar feeding is *fertilizer burn* or leaf tissue damage. For turfgrasses, damage appears to be due to nutrients (salts) drying on leaf surfaces and then dehydrating or desiccating adjacent cells as salts compete for the water. High concentrations of some nutrients at leaf tips can also damage tissues without apparent desiccation but due to cell toxicities. In either situation, injury is reduced by using low nutrient rates or increasing water volume to wash nutrients off leaves. Other potential problems of foliar feeding are: (a) low uptake rates due to thick cuticles; (b) rapid drying before uptake can occur; (c) limited retranslocation from leaves to stem, crown, lateral shoots and roots. Transport of Ca, Fe, and Mn in the phloem from shoots or sheath tissues to roots is limited but other nutrients can move upward (xylem) or downward (phloem) easily; (d) removal from leaf surfaces by runoff, washing, or volatilization. Volatilization of N as ammonia from urea or ammonium carriers is possible from leaf surfaces, especially with rapid drying before N is taken into leaves; and (e) foliar applied nutrients may be removed by mowing before uptake or translocation from the leaf tissue.

III. NUTRIENT LOSSES FROM PLANTS

Once nutrients are taken up by turfgrass roots or have been applied to the foliage, nutrient losses from the plant are possible. In most cases, any lost nutrients are deposited into the soil and may be taken up again. Nutrient removal directly from the plant is possible by: (a) clipping removal; (b) root exudates; (c) washing off leaf surfaces; (d) leaching from shoot tissues; (e) volatilization from leaves; and (f) nutrients in guttated water.

When turfgrasses are mowed, the clipped leaves contain nutrients. On a dry weight basis, clippings may contain 2 to 6% N, 0.10 to 1.00% P, and 1.00 to 3.00% K (2–6% N, 0.23 to 2.29% P_2O_5, 1.20 to 3.60% K_2O). If clippings are deposited onto the soil, they act as a slow release fertilizer and nutrients are eventually available for plant uptake when the organic compounds decompose. Turfgrasses grown on fine-textured soils, where leaching from the soil is limited, especially benefit from nutrient enrichment by clipping addition, and annual N needs can often be reduced by 10 to 35% after 1 or 2 years of returning clippings to a new site. Grasses grown on sandy soils also benefit from returned clippings but leaching losses of more mobile nutrients (N, K) from the soil could occur. If clippings are removed, additional fertilizer is required to compensate for these losses. For example, P and K soil tests in particular could be reduced to deficiency levels in some soils by routine removal of clippings.

Another significant loss of nutrients from plants is by secretion from roots in the form of individual nutrients or as components of carbohydrates (sugars), organic acids (citric, malic acids), amino acids, mucilage, and other compounds. Turfgrass roots may secrete into the rhizosphere as much as 10 to 30% of total carbohydrates produced by photosynthesis. Secreted nutrients may be taken into the plant again, used by rhizosphere microorganisms, lost from the system by leaching, or precipitated as minerals.

In reality, secreted nutrients and compounds usually enhance nutrient availability and soil fertility. This enhancement is achieved by (a) increasing the volume of soil contacted by roots and associated rhizosphere organisms which are supplied food by the exudates; (b) maintaining a nutrient-rich environment in the organic-rich microenvironment surrounding roots as nutrients are incorporated into microbial organic compounds and protected from leaching or soil chemical immobilization; and (c) certain acidic secretions may increase release of P from soil minerals or act as chelating agents for micronutrients.

Washing of nutrients off leaf surfaces and leaching of some nutrients by rain or irrigation from leaves are minor means of removal from plants. With turfgrasses, these nutrients are washed into the soil and usually become available for root or microbial uptake.

Volatilization from leaf surfaces was discussed in the previous section. Except for lawn care liquid applications where higher N rates may be applied with appreciable quantities left on leaves, volatilization from leaves is minimal. However, N volatilization from soil and possibly thatch surfaces after fertilization can be substantial at times, up to 25% of applied urea N under optimum conditions for such losses.

IV. NUTRIENT DEFICIENCY, SUFFICIENCY, AND TOXICITY

A. Basic Principles

MOST NUTRIENTS HAVE SEVERAL IMPORTANT FUNCTIONS within the plant. When the nutrient level in plant tissue is low enough to induce a 10% growth reduction, this nutrient concentration (in the tissue) is called the *critical concentration*[4] or *critical level* (Figure 2.3). Nutrient concentrations below this value are in the *deficiency range* since growth is limited by lack of the nutrient. The curve illustrated in Figure 2.3 is general in nature and the shape may change considerably for individual nutrients, soil conditions, or grasses.

Above the critical concentration is the *sufficiency range* where additional applied nutrient does not increase growth beyond 10%. Some people denote a *luxury consumption range* where plant nutrient level exceeds what is needed to achieve maximum growth but without any obvious detrimental effects. The idea of luxury consumption deals only with growth and not physiological health. For example, potassium tissue levels adequate for maximum turfgrass wear tolerance or cold/heat/drought hardiness may be above that considered as sufficient for growth.

Toxic concentrations of a nutrient where growth declines is potentially possible for all nutrients. But toxicities are more common for micronutrients than macronutrients. An example of a macronutrient toxicity is when K tissue levels are sufficiently high to cause tissue desiccation of leaf tips as a salt.

B. Carbon, Hydrogen, and Oxygen

The essential nutrients required in the greatest quantity (C, H, O) are basic inputs in the *photosynthesis process:*

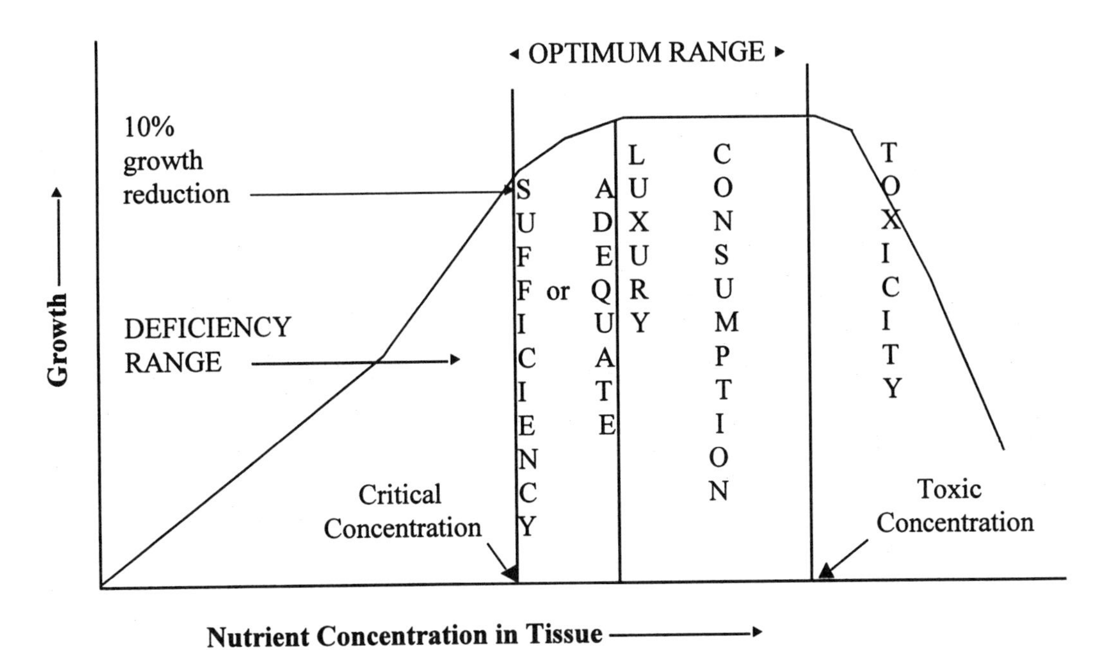

Figure 2.3. Turfgrass growth as a function of nutrient concentration in tissue.

$6\ CO_2$ *carbon dioxide – from air*	+	$6\ H_2O$ *water – from air*	+	light *red, blue wavelengths*	+	chlorophyll *pigments*	→
$C_6H_{12}O_6$ *carbohydrates (sugars)*	+	$6\ O_2$ *oxygen*					

Carbon (C) and oxygen (O) are supplied to the plant through leaf stomata as CO_2 from the air that contains 0.032% or 320 ppm CO_2, while hydrogen (H) is derived from splitting the water (H_2O) molecule taken up by the root system. The O_2 is evolved by splitting of the water molecules. Carbohydrates produced from the photosynthesis process are used: (a) in respiration to provide readily available energy for plant metabolic processes; (b) as basic building blocks for all other organic molecules such as proteins, enzymes, lipids, hormones, etc., necessary for growth and cell function; and (c) as storage carbohydrates necessary for dormancy periods and recovery from injuries.

Since *photosynthate (i.e., carbohydrates) production* is essential for immediate energy needs of plant cells and as building blocks for new compounds in growth and development, providing sufficient C, H, and O for maximum photosynthate production is necessary. Insufficient C, H, or O leads to reduced growth and at the worst, carbohydrate starvation.

Deficiency of C and O uptake can be caused by drought stress resulting in partial or full stomatal closure, thereby limiting CO_2 uptake. In this instance, CO_2 is not truly limited in the atmosphere but within the plant it becomes deficient. Sufficient water to meet the H needs in photosynthesis is almost always adequate even in a drought stressed plant since the quantity of H_2O used in photosynthesis is much less than for transpirational cooling.

Maximum CO_2 uptake and fixation can be limited by deficiencies of nutrients necessary for photosynthesis reactions or for chlorophyll, either as a structural component of chlorophyll or as a nutrient used during chlorophyll synthesis. These include deficiencies in N, Fe, S, Mg, and Mn. Adequate light intensity and quality (i.e., red and blue photosynthetically active radiation) are also needed to maximize CO_2 fixation into carbohydrates during the daylight hours.

Respiration, which must occur in all living cells (shoot and root) for the whole 24-hour daily period also requires C, H, and O. The C and H are provided in the form of sugars or carbohydrates from photosynthesis. The reactive O_2 in respiration comes from above- and belowground atmospheres. A simplified form of the respiration equation follows:

$C_6H_{12}O_6$	+	$6\ O_2$	+	$6\ H_2O$	$\longrightarrow$
carbohydrates – from photosynthesis		*oxygen – from air and soil air*		*water – from soil*	*carbon building blocks as 3C and 4C compounds*

$6\ CO_2$	+	$12\ H_2O$	+	Energy *transferred to ATP – adenosine triphosphate, a mobile energy form*
carbon dioxide		*water*		

Oxygen aboveground (21% O_2) is never limiting except possibly by a long-term ice cover. However, deficient O_2 levels in the soil are common for turfgrasses and are associated with: (a) lack of O_2 diffusion or mass flow from the aboveground atmosphere into the soil caused by limited size and numbers of soil macropores (i.e., >0.10 mm diameter). Conditions that limit macropores are: soil compaction; structure deterioration by high sodium; naturally fine-textured soils that have poor structure development, especially within the B horizon; and lack of earthworms; and (b) saturation of micro- and macropores by excessive rain, flooding, a high water table, limited drainage due to low infiltration or percolation of water through a layer with very few or no macropores, or black layer formation which plugs soil pores. Deficient soil O_2 is evident by limited root uptake of water (wet wilt) and root death. Deficiency of soil O_2 is very serious in hot summer periods when turfgrass and microbial O_2 demands are high. When soil O_2 is limiting, some plants including grasses, obtain O_2 from air that enters plant tops and diffuses to the roots through *aerenchyma* (air spaces in root tissues). For most grasses, O_2 supplied by this method only maintains roots near the surface.

While C, H, and O are involved in many other plant processes, photosynthesis and respiration are foundational since these produce the building blocks to produce new tissues and energy for other processes. Thus, provision of adequate C, H, and O for these two reactions assures sufficient levels of these nutrients, as well as energy for other processes as long as the remaining 14 essential elements are in adequate supply.

C. Macronutrients and Micronutrients

Within Chapters 10 (N), 11 (P), 12 (K), and 13 (Ca, Mg, S), each of the macronutrients is addressed in terms of: (a) content in plant tissues and soil; (b) essential functional roles within plants; (c) deficiency symptoms; (d) factors that influence nutrient availability and, therefore, the occurrence of deficiencies or toxicities; and (e) practical guidelines on fertilization with each nutrient. For the micronutrients (Fe, Mn, Zn, Cu, B, Mo, Cl, Ni), these issues are presented in Chapter 14.

However, an *overview* of macronutrient deficiency symptoms and factors that induce deficiency or toxicity occurrences is given in Table 2.3 as an introduction to plant nutrition (Plate 1). Table 2.4 contains similar information on micronutrients.

V. NUTRIENT-DISEASE INTERACTIONS

OF PRIMARY INTEREST TO TURFGRASS MANAGERS as they apply a fertilizer is how the nutrient will influence turfgrass quality, growth, color, and stress tolerance. But, fertilization practices also affect pathogens, particularly when a nutrient is deficient or excessive (Table 2.5).

Nutrients may influence disease activity by: (a) enhancing growth of the pathogen population since disease organisms utilize the same essential nutrients as higher plants; (b) altering turfgrass growth to favor greater or lesser susceptibility to a disease infestation. For example, low N results in slow growth, senescence of leaves, and thin, weakened plants which are more susceptible to dollar spot, red thread, pink patch, or rust; (c) altering turfgrass tissues in a manner that makes the plant more prone to disease infection, such as succulent tissues, thin cell walls, thin cuticle wax layers, and low carbohydrate levels; (d) changing the microenvironment in a manner that favors or disfavors a pathogen population. Altered thatch or soil pH in response to a fertilizer application, for example, may affect pathogen activity; and (e) applied nutrients can influence nonpathogen populations that aid in suppression of a particular disease organism.

Thus, nutrient and disease interactions may be direct or indirect in nature, resulting in some relations that are strong, while others may be weak and inconsistent (Table 2.5).[2,7,8] Those relationships that are the most consistent and strongest are denoted in the table. Also, nutrient balance between N-P-K can affect some of these relationships. Especially at high N, adequate P and K are important. Nutrition alone is seldom sufficient to adequately control diseases but can be used in an integrated approach to disease management, such as with rusts, dollar spot, red thread, necrotic ring spot, summer patch, and pink patch. Thus, adequate nutrition and avoiding extreme deficiencies or excesses can be useful in an integrated approach *(IPM, integrated pest/plant management)* to manage diseases.

VI. REFERENCES

1. Barber, S.A. 1995. *Soil Nutrient Bioavailability: A Mechanistic Approach,* 2nd edition. New York: John Wiley & Sons, Inc.
2. Couch, H.B. 1995. *Diseases of Turfgrasses.* Malabar, FL: Krieger Publishing Co.
3. Handreck, K.A. and N.D. Black. 1994. *Growing Media for Ornamental Plants and Turf.* Randwick, NSW, Australia: University of NSW Press.
4. Hopkins, W.G. 1999. *Introduction to Plant Physiology,* 2nd edition. New York: John Wiley & Sons, Inc.
5. Jacoby, B. 1994. Nutrient uptake in plants. In M. Pessarakli, Ed. *Handbook of Plant and Crop Stress.* New York: Marcel Dekker, Inc.
6. Marschner, H. 1995. *Mineral Nutrition of Higher Plants.* New York: Academic Press.

Table 2.3. Factors that induce *macronutrient* deficiencies or toxicity/excess nutrient problems and typical deficiency symptoms. See respective chapter listed in the table for detailed discussion of fertility aspects.

Nutrient	Deficiency Occurrence	Toxicity or Excessive Occurrence	Deficiency Symptoms
N Chapter 10	N deficiency is associated with sandy soils; high leaching conditions from rainfall or irrigation; low organic matter content; clipping removal; loss by denitrification under anaerobic conditions such as waterlogged and compacted soils; low pH <4.8 inhibition of *Nitrosomonas* for nitrification; infertile soils.	Direct toxicity as a salt and/or excessive growth and tissue succulence related to excessive application of N as fertilizer or in effluent water.	Chlorosis or a gradual loss of green color that appears first on older (lower) leaves; reduced growth rate; senescence of lower leaves; loss of shoot density in response to loss of leaves, tillers, and whole plants; increase in low N diseases.
P Chapter 11	P deficiency is often greater on sandy, low CEC irrigated soils; under low pH (<5.5) due to fixation with Fe, Al, Mn; high pH (7.5–8.5) from fixation with Ca; soils containing hydrous oxides of Fe, Al, Mn or kaolinite fix P; soils high in clay content; during establishment due to high P demand and limited rooting; reduced uptake in cold soils; site receiving little or no P over several years; turf grown on subsoils or infertile soils; clipping removal.	Excessive P application may induce Fe deficiency under some conditions.	Reduced growth rate; dark green color, lower leaves may turn reddish at the leaf tips and progress down the blade; low density.
K Chapter 12	Deficiencies most likely under high rainfall or leaching; sandy or low CEC soils; acidic soils (pH <5.5); clipping removal; sites receiving high Ca, Mg, or Na additions; under high N fertilization; soils high in vermiculite, illite or smectite at high pH.	Excessive K can contribute to salinity stress; suppress Mg, Ca, or Mn uptake; cause fertilizer burn.	Interveinal yellowing of old leaves (lower) followed by dieback at the tip, scorching or firing at leaf margins; eventually total yellowing of the leaf blades including veins; weak, spindly turf; greater tendency to exhibit wilting and wear injury.

Ca Chapter 13	Deficiency most likely under acidic (pH <5.5) conditions on low CEC soils receiving high Na levels or with high Al, Mn or H; high leaching. True deficiencies most probable in the root rather than shoot tissues.	Excessive Ca can induce Mg, K, Mn, or Fe deficiencies.	Distorted appearance of new leaves; reddish brown to rose leaf blades; leaf tips and margins wither and die; stunted, discolored roots.
Mg Chapter 13	Mg deficiencies enhanced by acidic (pH <5.5) conditions, especially on sandy soils due to low CEC and high Al, Mn, H; under high Na, Ca, or K addition; high leaching.	Excessive Mg can induce deficiencies of K, Mn, Ca.	General loss of green color of older (lower) leaves progressing from pale green to cherry red with leaf margins exhibiting blotchy areas of red. Leaf veins remain green, some light yellowing striping between veins; leaves start to die.
S Chapter 13	Deficiencies of S are often associated with soils low in organic matter; sandy, low CEC soils; high rainfall and leaching; areas not receiving atmospheric S additions; under high N with clipping removal.	Excessive S applications can cause foliar burn; induce extreme acidity on soils not buffered by free $CaCO_3$; contribute to black layer under anaerobic conditions.	Reduced shoot growth rate; yellowing of new leaves with leaf tips and margins showing symptoms first; older leaves may show symptoms later in the interveinal areas.

Table 2.4. Factors that induce *micronutrient* deficiencies or toxicity/excess nutrient problems and typical deficiency symptoms. See respective chapter listed in the table for detailed discussion of fertility aspects.

Nutrient	Deficiency Occurrence	Toxicity or Excessive Occurrence	Deficiency Symptoms
Fe Chapter 14	Deficiencies are most likely at pH >7.5; under poor rooting; excessive thatch; cold and wet soils; under high soil P, especially at high pH; on high pH calcareous soils in arid regions; irrigation water high in HCO_3^-, Ca, Mn, Zn, P, or Cu; low organic matter soils; heavy metals from some sewage sludges.	High foliar Fe can blacken leaves and, if sufficiently excessive, cause tissue injury; can induce Mn deficiency; acidic, poorly drained soils can produce toxic levels of soluble Fe for roots.	Interveinal yellowing of new leaves (upper); leaves turn pale yellow to white; thin, spindly leaves; eventually older leaves exhibit chlorosis; turfgrass stand has mottled appearance with some areas exhibiting symptoms while others do not.
Mn Chapter 14	Deficiencies are associated with high pH, calcareous soils; peats and muck soils that are at pH >7.0; dry, warm weather reduces Mn availability; high levels of Cu, Zn, Fe, Na, especially on leached, low CEC soils.	Toxicity to roots can occur in acid soils of pH <4.8; anaerobic soils, especially if acidic; high Mn levels can induce Ca, Fe, and Mg deficiencies; Si and high temperatures increase plant tolerance to Mn toxicity.	Reduced shoot growth rate; small, distinct greenish-gray spots starting on youngest leaves; progresses to interveinal yellowing with veins green to light green; leaf tips may turn grey or white and exhibit drooping or withering. Turf stand may appear mottled.
Zn Chapter 14	Deficiencies more common on alkaline soils; high levels of Fe, Cu, Mn, P, or N; high soil moisture; cool, wet weather and low light intensity; highly weathered acid soils.	Some municipal wastes may be high in Zn. High Zn may cause chlorosis by inducing Fe or Mg deficiencies.	Chlorotic leaves with some mottled, stunted leaves; leaf margins may roll or appear crinkled; symptoms most pronounced on young leaves.
Cu Chapter 14	Deficiencies are more often observed on organic soils due to strong binding of Cu; heavily leached sands; high levels of Fe, Mn, Zn, P, and N; high pH.	Toxic levels can occur from some sewage sludges or pig/poultry manures; use of high Cu content materials.	Yellowing and chlorosis of leaf margins of youngest to middle leaves; white to bluish leaf tips that wither, turn yellow, and die; stunted growth, leaves roll or twist.

B Chapter 14	High pH can induce deficiencies, especially on leached, calcareous sandy soils; high Ca can restrict B availability; dry soils; high K may increase B deficiency on low B soils.	B toxicity is much more likely than deficiencies due to irrigation water high in B; soils naturally high in B; overapplication of B; use of some compost amendments.	Young leaves exhibit leaf tip chlorosis followed by interveinal chlorosis of young and older leaves; leaves curl; roots stunted and thick; plants may appear bushy or rosette in appearance.
Mo Chapter 14	Deficiencies are usually on acid, sandy soils; acid soils high in Fe and Al oxides; high levels of Cu, Mn, Fe, S suppress uptake.	Mo toxicities are important for grazing animals and are associated with high pH soils that are wet.	Similar to N with chlorosis of older leaves and stunted growth. Some mottling and interveinal yellowing of leaves.
Cl Chapter 14	Cl uptake is suppressed by high NO_3^- and SO_4^{2-}.	Cl is a component of many salts that can be directly toxic to leaf tissues and roots; more often it reduces water availability by enhancing total soil salinity.	Deficiency symptoms not described on turf but other plants exhibit chlorosis of new leaves; wilting, especially at leaf margins; leaf curling; eventually necrosis.
Ni Chapter 14	Conditions associated with Ni deficiency are not clear due to the rare occurrence of Ni deficiency.	Ni toxicity can arise from use of some high Ni sewage sludges.	Deficiency symptoms not described on turf. Barley shows partial chlorosis as interveinal yellowing followed by necrosis; failure of leaf tip to unfold.

Table 2.5. Common turfgrass disease interactions with nutrients and pH. Strong relationships are denoted by an asterisk.

High Level Favors[a]	Low Level (Deficiency) Favors[a]
NITROGEN	
– brown patch (*Rhizoctonia solani*)* – pink snow mold – Fusarium patch (*Microdochium nivale*)* – gray snow mold (*Typhula* spp.)* – stripe smut (*Ustilago striiformis*)* – flag smut (*Urocystis agropyri*)* – gray leaf spot (*Piricularia grisea*)* – *Pythium* spp. – yellow tuft (*Sclerphthora macrospora*) – copper spot (*Gloeocercospora sorghi*) – spring dead spot (*Leptosphaeria* spp., *Gaeumannomyces* spp., *Ophioshaerella* spp.) – leaf spot (*Drechslera* spp., *Bipolaris* spp.)*[b] – net blotch (*Drechslera distoyoides*) – take-all patch (*Gaeumannomyces graminis*)*[b]	– anthracnose (*Colletotrichum graminicola*)* – dollar spot (*Sclerotinia homeocarpa*)* – red thread (*Laetisaria fuciformis*)* – pink patch (*Limonomyces rosiepellis*)* – rusts (*Puccinia* spp.)* – necrotic ring spot (*Leptosphaeria korrae*)* – summer patch (*Magnaporthe poae*)* – melting out (*Drechslera poae*)*[b] – leaf spot (*Bipolaris sorokiana*)*[b] – leaf blotch (*Drechslera cynodontis*)[b] – red leaf spot (*Drechslera erythrospila*)[b] – Helminthosporium brown blight (*Drechslera siccans*)[b] – take-all patch (*Gaeumannomyces graminis*)*[b]
PHOSPHORUS	
	– damping off (*Pythium* spp.) – take-all patch – pink snow mold (*Microdochium nivale*)
POTASSIUM	
– brown patch – pink snow mold	– spring dead spot – leaf blotch – take-all patch – red leaf spot – crown and root rot (*Helminthosporium* spp.) – dollar spot – red thread

CALCIUM	– red leaf spot – Fusarium blight (*Fusarium* spp.) – Pythium blight – red thread
SULFUR	– take-all patch – pink snow mold
IRON	– pink snow mold
MANGANESE	– take-all patch
pH – pink snow mold* (pH >6.5) – summer patch* (pH >6.0) – take-all patch* (pH >6.5) – spring dead spot (pH >5.3)	

[a] Compiled from Turner and Hummel,[7] Vargas,[8] and Couch.[2]

[b] Leaf spot and take-all diseases are listed under both low and high N. Differences exist among specific pathogens, effect of time of N application, and recommendations of individual pathologists.

7. Turner, T.R. and N.W. Hummel, Jr. 1992. Nutritional requirements and fertilization. In D.V. Waddington, R.N. Carrow, and R.C. Shearman, Eds. *Turfgrass. Agronomy Monograph No. 32.* Madison, WI: Amer. Soc. Agron.
8. Vargas, J.M., Jr. 1994. *Management of Turfgrass Diseases.* Boca Raton, FL: CRC Press, Inc./ Lewis Publishers.

Chapter 3

Enhancing Turfgrass Nutrient-Use Efficiency

THE PRIMARY REASONS TO FERTILIZE A TURFGRASS STAND ARE: (a) to eliminate nutrient deficiencies; (b) correct any nutrient imbalances; and (c) provide acceptable turfgrass quality, shoot density, color, physiological health, and growth rate for the particular site and use. Secondary goals are to minimize management costs and potential environmental problems, especially on sensitive sites where environmental considerations are of high concern. Enhancing *turfgrass nutrient-use efficiency* is important for all of these issues—i.e., turfgrass responses, economics, and environmental.

Nutrient-use efficiency in the broadest definition implies a high degree of uptake and utilization of nutrients from the soil as well as applied fertilizer. Components of efficient nutrient uptake and use are:

- Management to reduce unnecessary losses, especially through leaching and runoff.
- Recycling nutrients.
- Managing root development and viability for efficient uptake of nutrients.
- Grass selection and development for high nutrient use efficiency.

I. MINIMIZING NUTRIENT LOSSES

REDUCING THE POSSIBILITY OF NUTRIENT LOSSES FROM A SITE is especially important for environmental reasons because once a nutrient moves beyond the intended site it may be considered a pollutant. Of most concern are N, especially as NO_3^- in water, and P. High NO_3^- in groundwater can be a health hazard, while NO_3^- and especially P, contribute to eutrophication in water bodies and wetland features. When considering a turfgrass plant growing in a volume of soil, a nutrient may become unavailable for plant uptake by leaching, runoff, volatilization, denitrification, erosion, clipping removal, or fixation in soil mineral or organic constituents into an unavailable form. Reducing the extent of these processes will improve nutrient availability.

A. Leaching

A nutrient is considered "leached" once it moves beyond the turfgrass root system. Movement of nutrients beyond the root zone is usually as a form dissolved in the soil solution. However, particle migration in high sand soils may move some nutrients are strongly adsorbed on clay or organic colloids. Soil nutrient mobility can be summarized as:

Relatively Mobile	*Relatively Immobile*
NO_3^-	$H_2PO_4^-$ (except in sands)
SO_4^-	K^+ (except in sands)
HBO_4^-	NH_4^+ (except in sands)
MoO_4^-	Ca^{++}
Cl^-	Mg^{++}
$H_2PO_4^-$ in sands	Fe^{++}
K^+ in sands	Mn^{++}
NH_4^+ in sands	Zn^{++}
	Cu^{++}

To reduce leaching loss of a nutrient generally requires a combination of several cultural practices. Common approaches are to: use slow-release nutrient forms; use a spoon-feeding approach to fertilization; enhance cation exchange capacity (CEC) of sands; promote deep root development and root viability; and adjust irrigation so that excessive water is not applied. Many of these management practices are discussed in later chapters and in the sections on individual nutrients.

B. Runoff

Nutrient runoff losses can be as dissolved constituents in surface runoff water, as nutrients in fertilizer particles, or as nutrients adsorbed to eroded mineral and organic materials. Generally, runoff losses are very low on turfgrass sites since a grass cover reduces water runoff, sediment movement, or fertilizer particle movement. Situations where runoff of nutrients may be more substantial would be during establishment when the soil is exposed; when a heavy rainfall immediately follows an application of fertilizer to a fine-textured or compacted soil with low infiltration; on sites with appreciable slopes, especially in conjunction with the previous conditions; and where surface water from adjacent land areas runs across the turf site.

On sites where grass is being established, measures to reduce runoff include: (a) use of mulches or soil stabilization chemicals until the grass is established; (b) applying water soluble fertilizers with enough water to dissolve and move them into the soil; (c) using erosion control practices and careful irrigation to avoid runoff; and (d) applying low rates of N and P in the seedbed followed by spoon-feeding of the young grass after emergence.

Additional practices on established turfgrasses are: (a) avoiding fertilization prior to anticipated heavy rains; (b) using a spoon-feeding philosophy rather than high, less frequent nutrient applications; (c) on sloped sites, applying a light irrigation to dissolve soluble nutrient forms or to wash slow-release forms off tissues into the soil or thatch surface; (d) maintaining a dense grass stand to retard water runoff; (e) using surface cultivation methods on sloped areas to enhance water infiltration; and (f) avoid throwing fertilizer onto hard surfaces (sidewalks, parking lots, etc.).

C. Volatilization

Volatilization of NH_3 (ammonia) from turfgrass leaf, thatch, and soil surfaces can be substantial under some conditions. This topic is also discussed in Chapter 10, Nitrogen. Factors favoring high volatilization are: (a) a high quantity of urea, regardless of surface soil/thatch pH; (b) a high quantity of NH_4^+ when surface soil/thatch pH is above pH 7.5; (c) soil/thatch pH above 7.5. High pH favors NH_3 formation. Urea hydrolysis results in soil solution pH increasing to above 7.0 and, therefore, volatilization may occur even on acid soils. But NH_4^+ forms only exhibit volatilization if pH is above 7.5, such as on calcareous soils; (d) NH_3 volatilization increases with temperature; (e) thatch can enhance volatilization due to high urease activity and maintaining a moist environment that encourages NH_3 losses; and (f) a moist thatch or soil surface.

Even with urea application, volatilization can be greatly reduced by an immediate irrigation to dissolve granules and move the urea into the surface soil zone. Sufficient water should be applied to avoid leaving the liquid urea on leaf and thatch surfaces. Other practices to minimize losses are: (a) use of slow-release N fertilizers (natural organics, synthetic organics, and coated ureas are not susceptible to volatilization); (b) use of fertigation, which generally applies sufficient water to move N into the soil; (c) avoiding applications on nonirrigated sites, especially with soil pH values above 7.5, when rainfall is not anticipated; and (d) avoiding urea application within several weeks following a lime application.

D. Denitrification

Gaseous loss of N from a turfgrass system as N_2O (nitrous oxide), NO (nitric oxide), or N_2 gases can occur under low aeration (anaerobic) conditions. Waterlogged and compacted soil sites especially favor denitrification. The topic is discussed in considerable detail in Chapter 10, Nitrogen.

E. Fixation

Nutrient fixation into inorganic or organic constituents in the soil that are highly insoluble or nondecomposable is another potential nutrient "loss" in terms of plant availability. All macro- and micronutrients except Cl^- are susceptible to fixation over time. In the chapters on each nutrient, soil factors that influence availability are presented. The one management practice that influences overall nutrient availability the most is soil reaction (pH) with a pH of 6.5 to 7.0 favoring the maximum availability of most nutrients in mineral soils.

F. Clipping Disposal

Clippings on a dry weight basis usually contain in the range of 2 to 6% N, 0.10 to 1.00% P, and 1.00 to 3.00% K, as well as other nutrients. When recycled by adding back into the sod, clippings may contribute 20 to 35% of annual N needs along with the other nutrients contained in the tissues. Thus, when feasible, clippings should be returned. They also contribute to soil organic matter while normally having negligible effect on thatch accumulation since clippings readily decompose. On closely mowed, dense turfgrass stands, clippings do not integrate easily into the grass but remain on the surface. This surface accumulation is unsightly, can restrict light, affect ball roll on greens, and may promote some disease infestations; thus, clippings are normally removed on close-cut turf. If excessive clippings occur on higher cut turf due to delays in mowing, removal is usually appropriate to prevent smothering of grass. With a compost facility on the site, clippings can be incorporated in the compost and recycled for later use.

II. MANAGING ROOT DEVELOPMENT AND VIABILITY

ROOT FUNCTIONS ARE TO PROVIDE:

- Anchorage for the plant.
- Absorption and translocation of water.

- Absorption and translocation of nutrients. If nutrients are not taken up into the plant due to lack of roots or unhealthy roots, any fertilization program will be inefficient.
- Synthesis and transportation of certain growth regulators (hormones) used in the whole plant. Cytokinins are the most widely recognized hormones synthesized in roots, but significant quantities of gibberellins and abscisic acid can also be produced.
- Serving as a sink for carbohydrates produced in the shoots. Not only do root cells require carbohydrates for food but considerable total carbohydrate (10 to 30%) produced by the plant can be excreted into the rhizosphere. However, roots do not serve as a major storage area for carbohydrate reserves.

Root system characteristics that influence their ability to absorb water and nutrients are: (a) Root systems are dynamic and change with environmental conditions, especially soil temperatures and moisture. Management practices targeted toward achieving maximum rooting must be timed to take advantage of natural root growth cycles; (b) depth and the extent of rooting is controlled by the genetic rooting capability, and genetic tolerances to any adverse soil condition. Important soil physical or chemical conditions that directly limit rooting are high soil strength, low soil moisture, low soil O_2, high or low temperatures, Al/Mn toxicities, and Na^+ toxicities; (c) rate of root extension or elongation is greatest when environmental and management conditions favor root growth and there is no soil factor limiting growth. For example, close mowing may limit rate of root extension and may even cause root dieback. Also, high soil strength reduces rate of growth; (d) roots per unit volume of soil. Grasses can differ in the number of roots per volume of soil or amount of root contact with the soil, which is especially important in sandy soils where unsaturated hydraulic conductivity (i.e., capillary water movement) is slow; (e) root hair numbers. Actively growing roots have more root hairs; (f) root viability. Roots may be present but not healthy, and, therefore, water and nutrient uptake are limited. Low soil O_2 and high soluble salts can reduce root viability as does high temperature stress on cool-season grasses; and (g) mycorrhizal relations between the plant and soil microorganisms may influence root activity.

For example, why does a bermudagrass exhibit a rooting depth of a few inches on a particular site when it has the genetic potential to develop a root system several feet deep? Numerous factors can limit actual rooting to much less than the genetic potential. Root limiting factors can be grouped into two categories: shoot (aboveground) and soil-related causes.[4,5]

Shoot Factors

The maintenance of an existing root system and growth of new roots depend on net food (carbohydrate) production. Carbohydrates are produced in the green shoot tissues by the photosynthesis process. Uses of carbohydrates are:

- Respiration, which breaks down complex carbohydrates into simpler compounds while releasing energy in a form that can be used to maintain the many plant biochemical processes.
- Providing the building blocks or compounds necessary for growth of new tissues, such as a leaf or a new root.
- Carbohydrate reserves necessary for dormancy periods and recovery from injuries.

Because carbohydrates are only produced in shoot tissues, these tissues have first priority for their use. Only if sufficient carbohydrates are manufactured to meet the maintenance respiration needs of all cells and the shoot growth needs will roots obtain sufficient carbohydrates for growth. Thus, anything that decreases photosynthesis, increases respiration, or encourages topgrowth at the expense of root growth will eventually reduce root growth, and if these trends are severe, they can cause root dieback.

Some aboveground factors (such as any type of mechanical, disease, or insect injury) can increase respiration rate, which causes greater use of carbohydrates, leaving less available for root growth. Increasing temperatures also dramatically increase respiration and carbohydrate depletion, while photosynthesis may also decline at high temperatures. Thus, indirect, high temperature stress is a main contributor to root deterioration of cool-season grasses during summer months.

Soil Factors

A host of soil conditions can limit rooting to less than a grass's genetic potential (Table 3.1). These can be categorized as soil physical, chemical, or biological in nature. Root limiting soil conditions can be a result of one or a combination of these factors. Two important points to consider about soil properties and root growth are:

- For most of the soil physical and chemical factors that restrict root growth (low soil O_2, high soil strength, acid soil complex stresses, soil drought, salt ion toxicity, and high soil temperatures for cool-season grasses), each species has a *genetic-based tolerance.*[4,5] Because there is diversity in these factors across genotypes of a species, it is possible for breeders to develop cultivars with broader tolerance to important root-limiting soil properties. For example, more Al-tolerant tall fescues could be developed for very acid, high Al situations found where the acid soil complex stress occurs. Genetic diversity to soil biological stresses, such as root diseases and nematodes, also is present within a species.
- Within the genetic tolerance range, *management practices* can often correct or minimize the adverse effects of a specific root limiting factor, such as cultivation to increase soil O_2 and reduce high soil strength, or liming to negate Al toxicity.

Maximum use-efficiency of existing soil nutrients and those applied as fertilizers depends on a deep, extensive, and viable root system. One can develop an excellent fertilization program but achieve few benefits for the plant if roots are limited or unhealthy. Thus, an essential component of a good fertilization program is to develop and maintain roots. *Six steps to maximizing turfgrass root growth and viability are:*

- Select species and cultivars that have high genetic-based tolerance to soil (edaphic) physical, chemical, and biological stresses (Table 3.1). Genetic-based tolerance to these stresses are more important than genetic-based inherent rooting depth when these stresses are present since deep rooting can only occur if the grass has tolerance to all of the stresses that are present. These issues and others that relate to grass-nutrient uptake efficiency are discussed in the next section on grass development.
- Maximize net carbohydrate production through providing shoot conditions favorable to produce sufficient carbohydrates for root development and maintenance. Especially important are: (a) adequate leaf area, i.e., proper mowing height, avoiding leaf tissue injury, etc.; (b) adequate chlorophyll, i.e., avoiding nutrient deficiencies or imbalances

Table 3.1. Primary soil stresses that limit root growth and viability (also see Table 3.3).

Soil Physical Properties[a]	Soil Chemical Properties	Soil Biological Properties
• Low soil O_2 • High soil strength • Soil drought • High soil temperatures[b] • Low soil temperatures	• Acid soil complex–nutrient deficiencies, element toxicities (Al, Mn), high soil strength (often) • Nutrient deficiencies (Ca, Mg, K, Mn, S, N, Fe) • Salt ion toxicities–Na, Cl, B • Toxins–heavy metals, herbicides, grasses under anaerobic conditions, allelopathy	• Root feeding insects • Nematodes • Root pathogens

[a] Field situations that cause root deterioration from soil physical conditions are associated with one or more of these factors. For example, soil compaction may result in low soil O_2 (wet), or high soil temperatures (dry) as well as high soil strength for root penetration.

[b] Can be direct injury to cool-season grass roots at the surface, or by high soil temperatures contributing to indirect high temperature stress and carbohydrate depletion, causing root dieback.

important for chlorophyll synthesis or activity (N, Fe, Mg, Mn, S, Cl); and (c) adequate light conditions.

- Avoid factors that cause unnecessary depletion of carbohydrates and, therefore, potential carbohydrate deprivation of roots. Scalping, excessive N, and overirrigation are the most usual causes. Adequate irrigation to allow for transpirational cooling and reducing indirect high temperature stress is also important. Cool-season grasses planted in warm climates can exhibit substantial root loss due to lack of adequate carbohydrates to sustain root tissues during the summer months. But this can occur with extended warm periods in cooler regions as well.
- Correct adverse soil physical conditions limiting root growth and viability.
- Correct adverse soil chemical conditions limiting root growth and viability.
- Monitor and correct biological agents that may injure roots.

These six steps for managing turfgrass root growth and maintenance will enhance both the fertilization and irrigation programs. One additional item is thatch control, when thatch becomes excessive. Even with good soil properties, an excessive thatch layer tends to result in roots growing in the thatch zone rather than growing into the soil.

III. GRASS DEVELOPMENT FOR NUTRIENT-USE EFFICIENCY

AS NOTED IN THE PREVIOUS SECTION, grasses can vary in their ability to obtain nutrients from the soil. Duncan and Baligar,[3] Duncan,[2] and Clark and Duncan[1] provide excellent reviews on nutrient-use efficiency mechanisms for plants in general (Table 3.2) and for individual nutrients. *Genotypic variations* (i.e., differences among cultivars or genotypes within a species) for the factors listed in Table 3.2 allow genotypes to be selected that have characteristics favorable for high nutrient uptake and use efficiency. Once efficient genotypes within a species have been identified for uptake and nutrient use efficiency of a particular nutrient, these can be the basic germplasm for further improvement. Also, identification of the most efficient genotypes within a species: (a) allows for research to identify the responsible mechanism or mechanisms

Table 3.2. Possible components for genotypic variations in plant nutrient efficiency requirements.[a]

I. *Acquisition from the environment*
   1. Morphological root features (root system efficiency)
      a. High root/shoot ratio under nutrient deficiency
      b. Greater lateral and vertical spread of roots
      c. High root density or absorbing surface, more root hairs, especially under stress
   2. Physiological efficiency mechanisms for greater ion uptake per unit root length
   3. Generation of reducing and chelating capacity compounds (i.e., for Fe)
   4. "Extension" of the root system by mycorrhizae
   5. Longevity of roots
   6. Ability of the roots to modify rhizosphere and overcome deficient or toxic levels of nutrients

II. *Nutrient movement across roots and delivery to the xylem*
   1. Lateral transfer through the endodermis
   2. Release to the xylem
   3. Control of ion uptake and distribution by either root or shoot systems, or by both
      a. Delivery to root or shoot under deficiency
      b. Overall regulation of nutrient uptake in intact plants and use on a whole-plant level

III. *Nutrient distribution within plants*
   1. Degree of retranslocation and reutilization under nutrient stress
   2. Release of ions from vacuoles under nutrient deficiency
   3. Natural iron chelating compounds in xylem
   4. Rate of leaf abscission and rate of hydrolysis (i.e., organic P)
   5. Capacity for rapid storage for later use when nutrient is available

IV. *Growth and metabolic efficiency under nutrient limitations*
   1. Capacity for normal functioning at relatively low tissue concentrations
   2. Nutrient substitutions (i.e., Na^+ for K^+)

V. *Polyploidy and hybridity levels*

[a] Source: Duncan and Baligar.[3]

accounting for the high efficiency of uptake or use; and (b) as mechanisms are known, the responsible genes may be located for further use in traditional and biotechnological plant improvement techniques.

However, a review of the potential components to plant nutrient efficiency in Table 3.2 indicates that the presence of an extensive, deep, and healthy (viable) root system is essential. In the previous section, management practices to maximize root development and viability were emphasized. Since there are only six direct soil physical and chemical characteristics that limit rooting, another approach (beyond management practices to improve nutrient use efficiency through better rooting) is to identify genotypes that exhibit genetic based tolerance to these six factors (Table 3.3).

Duncan and Carrow[4,5] provide insight into achieving the goal of developing genotypes within each species that have superior root systems based on high genetic tolerance to these soil factors. Identification of genotypes within a species that have high tolerance to a specific root limiting soil factor (for example, salt toxicity) allow the same benefits as noted above for nutrient-use efficiency mechanisms; namely:

- The mechanism or mechanisms responsible for the high tolerance can be determined. This is important since only the most tolerant genotypes will possess these mechanisms.

Table 3.3. Six primary soil physical and chemical constraints of rooting, associated field situations where the stresses are expressed, and relative importance (from Duncan and Carrow[5]).

Root Stress	Associated Field Problem Situations	Relative Importance of Stress: Turfgrasses, Warm-Season	Relative Importance of Stress: Turfgrasses, Cool-Season
High soil strength	Fine-textured soil Compaction Layers with few macropores Sodic soil Soil drought	very high	very high
Low soil O_2	Fine-textured soils Compaction High water table Poor surface drainage Layer impeding percolation Sodic soil	low	high
Acid soil root toxicities/deficiencies, D = deficiencies T = toxicities	Acid soil complex (T, D) • Al/Mn/H toxicities • nutrient deficiencies (Ca, Mg, K) • usually low organic matter[a] • usually high soil strength Moderately acid soil (D) Acid sulfate soil (T, D) Acid mine spoils (T, D)	high	high
Salt root toxicities/deficiencies	Sodic soil (T, D) • Na, Cl, B, OH toxicities • K, Mg, Ca deficiencies • high soil strength • low soil O_2 Saline soil (T, D) Saline-sodic (T, D)	high	high
Desiccation of root tissues	Soil drying	moderate	very high
High soil temperature	Direct high temperature root injury. Indirect high temperature[b] stress limits root development, maintenance, viability.	very low	very high

[a] High organic matter helps to alleviate the Al toxicity factor.
[b] Indirect high temperature stress is *the* major factor limiting cool-season grass adaptation into warmer temperature climatic zones because it determines carbohydrate status for maintaining root viability. It becomes a site-specific problem when site conditions inhibit canopy cooling. High root temperatures enhance indirect high temperature stress just as high aerial temperatures will.

- Once mechanisms are known, genes associated with or responsible for the mechanism response can be identified.
- Gene technology can then be focused on these genes for plant improvement of other genotypes.

For the turfgrass manager, the practical and immediate benefits of concentrating on *root improvement first* and then upon *enhancing other nutrient efficiency parameters* would be substantially greater water uptake efficiency (i.e., drought resistance) and ability to explore a greater volume of soil for nutrient uptake.

Hull and coworkers[6–9] have investigated the uptake kinetics and efficiencies of a limited number of genotypes for N, P, and K for certain cool-season grasses. As economic and environmental pressures continue, greater emphasis is anticipated on identifying and developing grasses with improved nutrient uptake and use efficiencies.

IV. REFERENCES

1. Clark, R.B. and R.R. Duncan. 1991. Improvement of plant mineral nutrition through breeding. *Field Crops Research* 27:219–240.
2. Duncan, R.R. 1994. Genetic manipulation. In R.E. Wilkinson, Ed. *Plant-Environment Interactions.* New York: Marcel Dekker, Inc.
3. Duncan, R.R. and V.C. Baligar. 1990. Genetics, breeding, and physiological mechanisms of nutrient uptake and use efficiency: an overview. In R.R. Duncan and V.C. Baligar, Eds. *Crops as Enhancers of Nutrient Use.* San Diego, CA: Academic Press.
4. Duncan, R.R. and R.N. Carrow. 1997. Stress resistant turf-type tall fescue (*Festuca arundinacea* Schreb): Developing multiple abiotic stress tolerance. *Inter. Turf. Soc. Res. J.* 8(Part I):653–662.
5. Duncan, R.R. and R.N. Carrow. 1999. Turfgrass molecular genetic improvement for abiotic/edaphic stress resistance. In D.L. Sparks, Ed. *Advances in Agronomy* Vol. 67, 233–305. San Diego, CA: Academic Press.
6. Jiang, Z. and R.J. Hull. 1998. Interrelationships of nitrate uptake, nitrate reductase, and nitrate use efficiency in selected Kentucky bluegrass cultivars. *Crop Sci.* 38:1623–1632.
7. Liu, H., R.J. Hull, and D.T. Duff. 1993. Comparing cultivars of three cool-season turfgrasses for nitrate uptake kinetics and nitrogen recovery in the field. *Inter. Turf. Soc. Res. J.* 7:546–552.
8. Liu, H., R.J. Hull, and D.T. Duff. 1995. Comparing cultivars of three cool-season turfgrasses for potassium uptake kinetics and potassium recovery in the field. *J. Plt. Nut.* 18(3):467–485.
9. Liu, H., R.J. Hull, and D.T. Duff. 1995. Comparing cultivars of three cool-season turfgrasses for phosphate uptake kinetics and phosphorous recovery in the field. *J. Plt. Nut.* 18(3):523–540.

Part II

Soil Chemical Properties and Problems

Chapter 4

Cation Exchange Capacity

I. THE PROBLEMS

CATION EXCHANGE CAPACITY (CEC)—a measure of the amount of cations that a soil can hold which are potentially exchangeable for plant uptake—is one of the most important chemical properties of soils (Brady,[2] Handreck and Black[3]). *Soils with low CEC often result in several problems:*

- Low cation retention enhances the potential for nutrient deficiencies of N as NH_4^+, K^+, Mg^{+2}, Mn^{+2}, Fe^{+2}/Fe^{+3}, and Ca^{+2}. Since many, but not all, soils with low CEC are sands with high water percolation rates, other nutrients like N, P, S, or B, which exist in anion forms, may also be leached. In these instances, low CEC is not the cause but instead high water percolation rates.
- Leaching potential increases for environmentally sensitive compounds such as pesticides that could be retained on CEC sites or otherwise sorbed on fine-textured soils.
- Total soluble salts can build up in low CEC soils and cause salinity problems since few salts are retained on CEC sites but remain in the solution phase or as soluble precipitates.
- Na can easily accumulate and dominate the CEC sites to create sodic or saline-sodic conditions, as well as create Na toxicity problems.
- pH can be easily altered with the use of some fertilizers, irrigation water, or effluent sources.
- Because of low CEC, there is little chemical buffering so nutrient balance can be readily changed.
- Nutrient monitoring and maintaining adequate nutrient levels are more challenging.
- Establishment of turfgrasses on these sites is often more difficult than on high CEC soils.

Prior to discussing management practices on low CEC soils, it is important to understand the concept of CEC and how CEC influences fertilization, nutrient retention/leaching, and soil buffering.

II. CONCEPT OF CATION EXCHANGE CAPACITY

MINERAL (INORGANIC) AND ORGANIC CONSTITUENTS OF SOILS are very diverse in chemical nature and size. Cation exchange capacity resides almost entirely within the smallest soil particles called *colloids,* which are smaller than 2 micrometers (μm, micron) in diameter. Because of their small size, colloids have very high surface area per unit mass, which along with their

Table 4.1. Cations and anions in soils.

Cations (+)		Anions (–)	
Al^{+3}	K^{+}	BO_3^{-}	NO_3^{-}
Ca^{+2}	Mg^{+2}	Cl^{-}	SO_4^{-2}
Cu^{+2}	Mn^{+2}	HBO_3^{-}	
Cu^{+}	Na^{+}	HCO_3^{-}	
Fe^{+3}	NH_4^{+}	$H_2PO_4^{-}$	
Fe^{+2}	Zn^{+2}	HPO_4^{-2}	
H^{+}		MoO_4^{-2}	

chemical structure, causes them to be highly active chemically. Additionally, colloids carry negative and some positive charges. For most soils, the net charge is predominately negative. Positively charged ions (*cations*) are electronically attracted to the negative charges on the colloids. Thereby, CEC is a measure of how many negatively charged sites a soil contains, or conversely, how many cations can be adsorbed by a soil.

Ions are individual atoms or groups of atoms that are either positively charged (*cation*) due to loss of electrons or negative (*anion*) by gain of electrons. Common cations and anions are presented in Table 4.1. All the cations listed in this table, except Al^{+3} and Na^{+}, are essential nutrients, and these cations are the chemical form necessary for plants to absorb the nutrient (H^{+} is taken up by plants, but the hydrogen source for carbohydrates is from splitting water molecules). Except for bicarbonate (HCO_3^{-}), the anions listed in Table 4.1 are essential nutrients.

Cations and anions can arise from several sources. As soil minerals dissolve, ions are released into the soil solution. This is the primary source of ions over long time periods, but important sources of ions for plant use include: ions carried in irrigation water; ions applied as fertilizers, lime, or associated with any material applied to the soil; and ions from organic matter as it decomposes.

Surrounding the colloids is a swarm of loosely attracted cations. These cations can be exchanged for cations in the soil solution or for H^{+} and other cations associated with roots. Thus, cations on the CEC of colloids serve as a "storehouse" of nutrients for plants.

A. Types of Soil Colloids

Layered Silicate Clays

Layered silicate clay minerals are the predominant colloids in many soils, especially in temperate climates. These are secondary minerals formed by alteration of existing minerals and by chemical formation over time. They have a crystalline, layer-like structure. Two basic components are: (a) the silicon-oxygen tetrahedron (four faced) where four oxygens are coordinated with each silicon; and (b) the aluminum octahedron (eight sided) where six oxygens and/or hydroxyls are coordinated with each aluminum. Each of these components forms sheets or layers. Clay types have a particular arrangement of these sheets, which is repeated in the layered structure of the clay. For example;

- 1:1 types have one silica tetrahedral for one alumina octahedral sheet. *Kaolinite,* the most common 1:1 clay, is highly weathered and common in subtropical to tropical regions.

- 2:1 types have crystalline units composed of an octahedral layer between two tetrahedral layers. Examples of these types are *smectites (montmorillonite), vermiculite,* and fine-grained *micas (illite).*
- 2:1:1 types are additional clay types but are similar to 2:1 clays except 2:1:1 types contain a hydroxide sheet. *Chlorites* are the most common.

Negative charges arise during formation of layer silicate clays when a cation is replaced by another cation of similar size but lower charge. This is termed isomorphic substitution. Typical substitutions are Al^{+3} for Si^{+4} and Mg^{+2} or Fe^{+2} for Al^{+3}. This negative charge does not change when soil pH is changed; it is called *pH independent.*

Some of the CEC sites (i.e., negative charges) do change as soil pH is altered. These are *variable or pH-dependent* charges and are associated with the "broken edges" of silicate clay layers. On these edges >Al-OH and >Si-OH groups are exposed. Under high acidity (i.e., low pH), the –OH group remains intact, but as pH increases, hydrogen dissociates from the –OH and a negative charge is formed.

$$> \text{Si-OH} \quad \rightarrow \quad > \text{Si-O}^- + \text{H}^+$$

Moderately acid	As pH increases

A second source of pH-dependent charge as pH increases is by removal of positively charged complex aluminum hydroxy ions. Blockage of negative charges by $Al(OH)_2^+$ ions occurs at low pH; thereby, they are unavailable for cation exchange. As pH is increased, $Al(OH)_2^+$ ions react with OH^- ions in the soil solution and form insoluble $Al(OH)_3$, which frees the negatively charged sites. Only about 5 to 10% of the CEC sites are pH-dependent on 2:1 clays. But 1:1 clays (kaolinite) may have 50 to 90% of the CEC sites as pH-dependent (see Table 4.4).

Iron and Aluminum Hydrous Oxides

Heavily weathered soils in subtropical and tropical regions are often dominated by iron and aluminum oxides such as goethite [$Fe_2O_3 \cdot H_2O$] and gibbsite [$Al_2O_3 \cdot H_2O$]. These oxides range from crystalline to amorphous in structure. Negative charges arise by dissociation of hydrogen from Al-OH and Fe-OH groups as pH increases, just as occurs in kaolinite. Also, freeing of CEC by precipitation of insoluble $Al(OH)_3$ as pH increases is prevalent on Fe and Al oxides.

Amorphous-Like Materials

Many volcanic soils contain allophane, an aluminum silicate that lacks a well-defined crystalline structure. Allophane plus other more amorphous silicate colloids can be found in many soils around the world. These are often called short-range order minerals because they lack crystalline structure. The CEC of amorphous-like minerals is pH-dependent by the same mechanisms present in kaolinite and Fe/Al hydrous oxides, dissolution of H from OH groups.

Organic Colloids

Humus is the fraction of soil organic matter that has undergone extensive decomposition and chemical alteration, including the synthesis of complex organic compounds. Further decomposition of the humus fraction is very slow. Of the total soil organic matter, humus comprises about 60 to 80% and can be further divided into the: (a) fulvic acid fraction (FA), which is soluble in dilute alkali and remains soluble upon acidification. The FA fraction is composed of low-molecular-weight organic compounds and polysaccharides; (b) humic acid fraction (HA), which is soluble in dilute alkali but precipitates upon acidification. *Humic acids* are intimately bound to clay minerals and are of higher molecular weight than FA; and (c) humin fraction, which is not dissolved with dilute alkali solution, is highest in molecular weight, and is most resistant to further microbial degradation.

Humus colloids have very high surface area and high CEC due to several functional groups; especially, carboxyl (–COOH) and hydroxyl (–OH) units associated with quinonic or phenolic rings and enolic hydroxyls, such as:

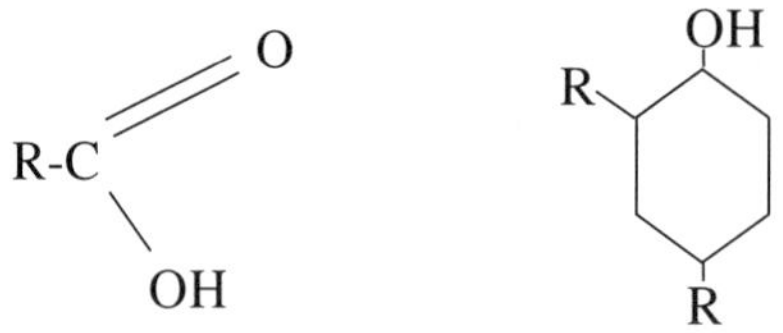

O
R-C
OH

OH
R
R

R = remainder of the humic compound

Carboxyl groups account for about 50% of the CEC in organic colloids.

The CEC of humus is pH-dependent because hydrogen dissociates from the carboxyl and hydroxyl groups as pH rises. For example, the CEC of organic colloids may increase by 10 to 30% per pH unit (i.e., pH 5.0 to 6.0) with the greatest change occurring at more acid pH levels.

In addition to CEC sites, micronutrient cations may bind with humus by several mechanisms that range from weak to strong attractions (Table 4.2). These reactions are discussed in greater detail in Chapter 16 on Unique Soil Problems (Waterlogged, Pollutants, Organic).

B. Expressing and Measuring CEC

Expression of CEC

Cation exchange capacity, as a measure of the total exchangeable cations that a soil can absorb at a given pH, is often expressed on a weight basis in terms of *milliequivalents per 100 grams dry soil.* One milliequivalent (m.e. or meq.) of a cation is the atomic weight of the cation in grams, divided by the number of positive charges on the cation, and then divided by 1,000. For example, 1 meq. weight of Ca^{+2} or H^{+} is determined by:

Ion	Atomic Weight	Milliequivalent Weight
Ca^{+2}	40	$(40 \div 2)/1,000 = 0.020$ gm Ca^{++}
H^{+1}	1	$(1 \div 1)/1,000 = 0.001$ gm H^{+}

One milliequivalent of CEC is equal to 6.02×10^{20} (i.e., 602,000,000,000,000,000,000) negatively charged sites that can attract cations. Thus, a soil with a CEC of 1 meq per 100 g dry soil would contain 6.02×10^{20} negative charge sites per 100 grams of dry soil.

Another CEC unit that may be used is centimoles per kilogram (i.e., cmol kg^{-1}) of soil, where:

$$1 \text{ cmol kg}^{-1} = 1 \text{ meq per 100 g dry soil.}$$

Table 4.2. Binding mechanisms for micronutrients on humus.

Binding mechanism =	Water Bridge ———	Electrostatic (Coulombic) ———	Coordinate Link ———	Chelate Ring
Bond strength =	Weak ———			Strong
Predominant micronutrient =	Mn^{+2}, Zn^{+2} ———			Fe^{+3}, Cu^{+2}

In soil test reports, CEC is normally reported as CEC, Cation Exchange Capacity, or Total Cation Exchange (TEC). Each of these terms has the same meaning and use the same units.

Measurement of CEC

To determine CEC, a sample is saturated with a cation that replaces into solution all the other cations on the *cation exchange (CE)* (Hendershot et al.[4]) sites. Then CEC is measured by either: (a) calculating the sum of all individual cations displaced from the CEC sites. These would include Ca^{+2}, Mg^{+2}, K^{+}, Na^{+}, H^{+}, Al^{+3}, Fe^{+2}, Fe^{+3}, and Mn^{+2}. This method is called a summation method and two common saturation chemicals are Ba^{+2} from $BaCl_2$ and NH_4^{+} from NH_4OAc (ammonium acetate); or (b) measuring the quantity of saturating cation absorbed in the CE sites by displacing it with another cation (displacement method).

The summation method provides not only total CEC but also percent saturation of each cation present on the CE sites, percent base saturation, and ratios of various cations. This information provides the basis for a soil test philosophy called *Basic Cation Saturation Ratio (BCSR)*, which is discussed in greater detail in Section IIIA. Summation of individual cations to determine CEC is illustrated in Table 4.3 for a soil with a CEC of 4.46 cmol kg^{-1}.

Since turfgrass managers may submit soil samples to university or commercial labs that are in different regions or countries, a knowledge of potential errors in CEC determination is useful. Error in CEC measurement can arise from dissolution of precipitated soluble salts, especially $CaCO_3$ or $CaSO_4$, by the extracting solution. The Ca or other cations that are dissolved cause CEC and the particular cation saturation level to be overestimated. For alkaline soils with appreciable free lime or gypsum, the use of an extracting solution buffered at a pH of 7.0 or 8.2 will decrease errors due to dissolution of these salts. Many soil test laboratories use a saturating solution of pH 7.0 to measure CEC but unless the solution is buffered (i.e., does not adjust to the actual soil pH) the above errors may occur.

In acid soils, it is best to use unbuffered saturating solutions that will adjust to the soil pH. Buffered solutions (i.e., maintained at pH 7.0 or other high pH level) in acid soils are less effective in removal of Al^{+3} and Fe^{+3} that may be present on the exchange sites. Also, pH-dependent CEC is more prevalent in acid soils, especially in the organic matter fraction, and a pH 7.0 buffered solution will overestimate actual CEC in the field. Thus, CEC is more accurate if measured at the same pH as in the field instead of in a buffered solution at pH 7.0 or 8.2. This overestimation of CEC by the use of a higher pH buffered solution is particularly a problem on soils containing considerable amorphous colloids.

The use of NH_4OAc on soils containing micas (illite) or vermiculites may result in CEC error. If NH_4^{+} moves into the interlayers and replaces K^{+}, CEC and percent K saturation are overestimated. However, NH_4^{+} may cause the edges of interlayers to collapse and prevent exchange of K^{+} from some CEC sites; thereby underestimating CEC and percent K^{+} saturation in some instances.

Table 4.3. CEC by summation of cations.

Cation	CEC Saturation cmol kg^{-1}	Percent
K	0.09	2
Ca	3.02	65
Mg	0.23	5
Na	0.70	15
H	0.28	6
Other	0.33	7
CEC =	4.46	100%

C. CEC of Soil Colloids and Soils

Soil Colloids and CEC

Various soil colloids differ markedly in total CEC and the percent pH-dependent (i.e., variable) CEC sites (Table 4.4). Values for CEC in Table 4.4 are based on pure colloid and at a pH of 7.0. Thus, CEC in all soil often arises from several sources.

Tropical soils are often acidic and have a higher percentage (60 to 80%) of pH-dependent colloid types (i.e., kaolinite, Fe oxides, Al oxides, amorphous minerals) than do temperate region soils (10 to 20%). As a result, tropical soils often have lower CEC and a greater amount of the CEC is pH-dependent than for temperate soils. However, many 2:1 clays with high CEC can be found in tropical regions, often intermixed with 1:1 clays and Fe/Al oxides.

Soil Texture and CEC

Soil texture classification is based on the percentage of sand, silt, and clay size particles in a soil. Clay particles less than 2 μm in diameter are colloids or colloidal in nature. Thus, as the percent clay content increases, CEC also increases. However, this relationship is influenced by the type of soil colloid (Table 4.5).

D. CEC of Roots

Carboxyl groups (–COOH) on plant roots are similar to carboxyl groups in humus and result in CE (cation exchange) sites on the root tissues. Grasses (monocots) have been found to exhibit CEC of 10 to 30 cmol kg^{-1}, while dicots have 40 to 100 cmol kg^{-1} of CEC. The root CE sites are not essential for ion uptake but binding of cations on root CE sites does increase their concentration at the root surface. Grasses are reported to preferentially absorb K^+ versus divalent cations on root CE sites, but Ca^{+2} is often the dominant cation. Replacement of Ca^{+2} on root CEC sites by Al^{+3} (highly acid soils) or Na^+ (highly sodic soils) can result in root deterioration.

III. IMPORTANCE OF CEC

A. Fertilization

CATIONS HELD ON THE CE SITES are exchangeable with those in the soil solution. For example, a Mg^{+2} on the colloid can be replaced by two H^+ so that the Mg^{+2} goes into soil solution.

Table 4.4. Cation exchange capacity of soil colloids and the percent pH-dependent CEC.

Colloid Type	Clay Layer Type	Cation Exchange Capacity[a] Total cmol kg^{-1}	pH-dependent %
Silicate Layered Clays			
Vermiculite	2:1	120–150	5–10[b]
Smectites (montmorillonite)	2:1	80–140	5–10
Fine-grained micas (illite)	2:1	20–45	5–10
Chlorite	2:1:1	20–40	15–25
Kaolinite	1:1	1–15	50–90
Fe and Al Oxides			
Goethite (Fe-oxide)	–	2–6	100
Gibbsite (Al-oxide)	–	2–6	100
Amorphous-Like Minerals			
Allophane	–	0–100	100
Organic Matter			
Humus	–	140–250	90–100
Thatch	–	120–160	90–100

[a] Since pH-dependent CEC can vary, total CEC is usually determined at pH 7.0, but this can overestimate actual CEC of acid soils.
[b] Expressed as percentage of the total CEC.

K^+ Mg^{+2} / K^+ Ca^{+2} [Soil Colloid] $+ 2 H^+ \rightarrow$ (soil solution) K^+ H^+ H^+ / K^+ Ca^{+2} [Soil Colloid] $+ Mg^{+2}$ (soil solution)

Cations in the soil solution are readily available for plant uptake, while cations on the CEC sites are considered moderately available. Cations are also present in various compounds within the soil that range from relatively soluble to very insoluble. Additionally, cations may be a part of the structural framework of clays, silts, sand particles, or humus. These structural cations are slowly to very slowly available for plant uptake. Thus, cations in soil solution and on CEC sites are the most available for turfgrass use, but cations in relatively soluble compounds and some structural cations also are nutrient sources. As an example, of the total K in a soil containing appreciable levels of K minerals such as micas and feldspars, the distribution would approach the following values:

- <1% K — in soil solution, readily available
- 1–2% K — on CEC, moderately available
- 1–10% K — in vermiculite, smectite, etc. lattices and relatively soluble compounds. Slowly available.
- 90–98% K — feldspars, micas, etc. Relatively unavailable over a growing season.

However, for a sand with low CEC and little organic matter, the distribution would approach 5 to 15% in soil solution and 85 to 95% on CEC or as precipitated soluble K forms.

Table 4.5. Cation exchange capacity as influenced by soil texture and colloid type.

Soil Texture	Cation Exchange Capacity cmol kg^{-1}
Sand (1 to 2 % organic matter by weight)	1–3
Sand (2 to 4% organic matter by weight)[a]	3–5
Sandy loam	3–10
Loam	7–16
Silt loam	10–25
Clay, clay loams (2:1 clay)	20–50
Clay, clay loam (kaolinite clay)	4–6

[a] A USGA golf green typically contains 1 to 3% organic matter by weight at time of construction.

Of the *total readily available cations* (soil solution plus cations on CEC sites), 1 to 10% is in the soil solution and 90 to 98% on the exchange sites. Thus, CEC sites are the major source of available cations for plants in most soils. Several factors influence the release of cations from the CEC as nutrients for turfgrasses.

First, the strength of cation absorption on CE sites on clays is proportional to the charge of the cation and hydrated ion radius in the order.

$$Al^{+3} > Ca^{+2} > Mg^{+2} > K^{+} = NH_4^{+} > Na^{+}$$

The H^+ ion is an exception due to its very small size and higher charge density; thus, it has an absorption strength between Al^{+3} and Ca^{+2}. For cations with the same charge, those with smaller hydrated radii are held the tightest.

Second, is the percent saturation of the CE sites by a nutrient. A cation is more readily exchanged if it is present at a higher percent saturation than at a low saturation level. Thus, if K^+ saturation is low, the addition of a K fertilizer will increase percent K saturation and, thereby, K availability. Also, adding a high concentration of a cation will result in it replacing other cations, even if they have a higher charge.

A third factor influencing cation availability to plants is the clay type. Clays with a higher charge density (i.e., CEC) may retain a nutrient much stronger than one with a lower charge density, even though both have the same percent saturation level. Thus, Ca^{+2} on kaolinite at 50% saturation may be as plant available as Ca^{+2} at 70% saturation on a smectite which has a higher charge density or CEC.

From the previous discussion, it should be apparent that CEC has a major influence on fertilization practices, and that through fertilization cation saturation percentages can be altered. In fact, a major soil test philosophy evolved from focusing only on the CEC sites; namely, the *"Basic Cation Saturation Ratio"* or *BCSR approach.* Three types of information are developed by the BCSR approach and used to make fertilization recommendations: (a) percent saturation level for each nutrient, which are then normally ranked from Very Low to Very High as to a desirable percent level; (b) nutrient ratios such as Ca:Mg, Ca:K, and Mg:K can be generated and ranked relative to a desirable ratio level; and (c) percent base saturation where the base cations are (Ca, Mg, K, Na). Again, this parameter can be ranked as to a desirable level. The pros and cons of BCSR versus the more traditional soil test philosophy of *SLAN (Sufficiency Level of Available Nutrients)* are discussed in the soil testing chapter (Chapter 9).

Table 4.6. Pounds of each cation required to fully saturate 1.0 cmol kg^{-1} of CEC to an acre furrow slice depth of 6 inches (assumed to weigh 2,000,000 pounds).[a]

Cation	Atomic Weight	Equivalent Charge	Weight	Pounds/Acre Equivalent to 1.0 cmol kg^{-1}
H	1	$^{+}1$	1	20
K	39	$^{+}1$	39	780
Ca	40	$^{+}2$	20	400
Mg	24	$^{+}2$	12	240
Na	23	$^{+}1$	23	460

[a] 1 acre = 2.47 ha; 6 inch = 15.2 cm; 2,000 lb = 908 kg.

Assuming that an acre-furrow slice (an acre to a plow depth of 6 inches) has a weight of 2,000,000 pounds, the pounds of each cation required to occupy 1.0 cmol kg^{-1} can be estimated (Table 4.6). These values can be used in determining amounts of fertilizer required to change the saturation percentage of a cation and also in determining lime requirement to reduce H^+ saturation percentage. If less than an 6 inch soil depth is to be treated, rates would require adjustment.

B. Nutrient Retention/Leaching

Nutrients that are retained on the CE of colloids have a degree of protection from leaching beyond the root system, loss by runoff, and in some instances volatilization. Soils with high CEC provide significantly more protection against leaching loss of cations.

Very sandy soil mixes used for golf greens and sports fields often exhibit low CEC such as 2 cmol kg^{-1} or less. These soils require careful attention to plant nutrient requirements, to nutrient levels and balances, and to environmental concerns about leaching.

C. Buffer Capacity

The ability of a soil to resist chemical change is called *buffer capacity*. Without buffer capacity, soil pH and factors influenced by pH (i.e., nutrient form, nutrient availability/levels, chemical composition of compounds, solubility of various compounds, bacteria populations, etc.) would rapidly change with the addition of rainfall, irrigation, and small quantities of chemicals.

The major buffering system on most soils is the CE sites. Hydrogen (H^+) ion activity in soil solution is what determines soil pH. However, added H^+ does not stay in the soil solution. Instead, most will exchange with another cation on the colloid surfaces, thereby buffering against rapid soil solution changes in pH.

A second buffering system occurs in soils containing *free* $CaCO_3$ (i.e., lime particles), which occurs naturally or may arise from lime application. Alkaline soils often contain free $CaCO_3$ that precipitated out during soil formation or remains as residual from the limestone parent material. Also, calcareous sands result from limestone parent material, coral parent material, and/or presence of seashell fragments in a quartz sand. These soils resist pH change since added H^+ reacts with $CaCO_3$ by the reaction;

$$CaCO_3 + 2H^+ \rightarrow \underset{(remainder\ in\ soil)}{CaCO_3} + H_2O + \underset{(gas)}{CO_2 \uparrow}$$

A very sandy soil with a low CEC may require a relatively small quantity of lime to increase pH from acid to neutral or a small quantity of elemental S to decrease pH from neutral to acid. Such responses would be the case where only the CEC buffer system is present. In contrast, the same soil, but with 10% free $CaCO_3$ by weight, would require several hundred pounds of elemental S per 1,000 ft^2 to reduce pH from alkaline to neutral in just the surface inch of soil. Buffering systems in soils are discussed in further detail in the chapters on soil reaction.

IV. MANAGEMENT OF LOW CEC SOILS

TURFGRASS MANAGERS WITH LOW CEC SOILS typically ask two questions: (a) how can CEC levels be increased; and (b) what management practices can be used to minimize the problems associated with these soils? The following sections deal with these practical questions.

A. Increasing CEC of a Soil

Several options are available to turfgrass growers to increase soil CEC. Generally, practices to enhance CEC are considered only when turfgrass soils have a CEC of less than 4 cmol kg^{-1}. However, on environmentally sensitive sites where runoff could be adverse, enhancement of CEC in the surface of the soil may be considered. Practices to increase CEC are as follows.

Adjust Soil pH

The CEC of many soils is pH-dependent (Table 4.4). If the inorganic colloids (clays) are kaolinite, Fe/Al oxides, or amorphous-like, then increasing the pH to 7.0 will provide near maximum CEC. As pH is increased from 4.5 to 7.0, CEC residing in these colloids may increase as much as one- or twofold with the greatest rise from pH 6.0 to 7.0.

Of greatest concern for turfgrass managers is low CEC in high sand content golf greens or sports fields. These sites often contain few inorganic colloids. Instead, CEC comes primarily from organic matter. In organic matter, essentially all the CEC sites are pH-dependent with a CEC increase of 10 to 30% per pH unit. Thus, if a golf green of pH 5.0 and CEC of 1.0 cmol kg^{-1} received lime to increase pH to 7.0, the CEC may increase to between 1.20 and 1.70 cmol kg^{-1}.

The most accurate laboratory determinations for CEC are in unbuffered saturating solutions that adjust to the current soil pH (an exception is when $CaCO_3$ is present; see section II.B). Determining CEC in a buffered solution at pH 7.0 will provide an estimate of near maximum CEC that would occur if the soil pH was adjusted to 7.0. A turf grower interested in obtaining a more precise pH-CEC relationship could request that a laboratory use the procedure for "pH-dependent AEC-CEC" detailed by Hendershot et. al.[4] This method accurately determines CEC over a wide pH range as well as anion exchange capacity (AEC).

Addition of Organic Matter as Composts or Organic Fertilizers

Addition of humus (well-decomposed organic matter) to a sandy soil can markedly increase CEC. As an example, assume a sandy soil has a CEC of 2.0 cmol kg^{-1} and contains by weight 1% humus which has a CEC of 150 cmol kg^{-1}:

- Since the humus is 1% by weight, it contributes $1/100 \times 150$ cmol kg^{-1} = 1.50 cmol kg^{-1} of CEC; thus, 1.50 cmol kg^{-1} of the total 2.0 cmol kg^{-1} CEC comes from the humus and 0.50 from inorganic sources (i.e., clays).
- If humus content was increased to 2% by weight, it would contribute $2/100 \times 150$ cmol kg^{-1} = 3.0 cmol kg^{-1} CEC.
- The total CEC is the sum of humus CEC plus CEC from the inorganic component; 3.0 + 0.5 = 3.5 cmol kg^{-1}; thus, there was an increase from 2.0 (original CEC) to 3.5 cmol kg^{-1} (i.e., a 75% increase in CEC due to the 1% added humus).

This example illustrates the influence that a well-decomposed organic matter (humus) can have on the CEC of a sandy soil. There are, however, some practical limitations.

During turfgrass establishment on a sandy site, organic matter is usually added. Specifications for golf greens or other sand fields could include the use of 1.0 to 3.0% by weight (5–15% by volume) of a well-decomposed organic matter mixed throughout the 12 inch (30 cm) root zone depth. A 2.0% by weight addition of organic matter to a 12 inch root zone mix would require about 1,840 lb per 1,000 ft^2 of organic matter (90,023 kg ha^{-1}). Inclusion of organic matter is primarily to provide CEC and moisture retention. As higher rates (especially above 4% by weight) of organic matter are added to a sand, adverse effects can develop; namely, reduced infiltration/percolation, excessive water retention, and low soil oxygen. Thus, there are practical limits on the quantity of organic matter that should be added to a sand, even in the establishment phase when native organic matter is low or nonexistent. However, the addition of an appropriate organic matter source at 1 to 3% by weight to a sandy soil provides CEC enhancement and other benefits during the establishment phase.

A number of organic matter sources can be used. But if increased CEC is a priority, the material should be well-decomposed and humus-like. Within peat types, decomposed peat (peat humus) would be the preferred form. Fibrous, less decomposed moss or reed-sedge peats can be used to add organic matter; however, they are less stable in the soil mixture and have lower bulk density values than decomposed peats. Thus, a greater volume is required with fibrous peats to obtain a desired weight percentage of peat in the soil mixture. Differences in organic matter content of various peats will also affect the amount required to obtain some level of soil organic matter content. Fibrous peats generally have higher organic matter contents than decomposed peats. Readers are encouraged to review Chapter 16, Unique Soil Problems (Waterlogged, Pollutants, Organic), for further details on organic sources and factors affecting organic matter decomposition.

On an *established* turfgrass site, such as a golf green, there are two potential sources for addition of organic matter to the soil: (a) organic matter produced by the plant, and (b) added organic matter through topdressing. Observation of what happens to the organic matter generated by the plant provides insight into whether adding organic matter as peat or compost in topdressing materials or organic based fertilizer may be beneficial for CEC enhancement in a mature turfgrass stand. There are three general cases that can occur with respect to organic matter content in sandy soils after the grass is well-established.

First, is the *organic matter equilibrium case* where organic matter remains relatively constant within the range of 2 to 4% by weight solely through the addition of organic matter from the turfgrass plant. This is often the case in *many warm to mild temperate climates*. In this situation, humus makes up about 60 to 80% by weight of the organic matter, and 2 to 5% of the humus may decompose each year. For example, for a sandy soil with 2% humus (3% total O.M.) by weight in the surface 6 inches (15.2 cm) and a bulk density of 1.50 g cm^{-3}, annual humus loss would be:

- Assuming the weight of soil per acre to a 6 inch depth is 2,000,000 lb (909,091 kg).
- 2,000,000 lb × 2/100 humus = 40,000 lb of humus per acre.
- 40,000 lb humus × 5/100 decomposition rate = 2,000 lb of humus lost per year per acre (2,240 kg ha^{-1}) or 46 lb per 1,000 ft^2 on a dry weight basis.

If organic matter is to remain constant in this soil, the turfgrass plant must produce sufficient organic matter to replace the 46 lb dry weight of humus per 1,000 ft^2 over the growing season. Recently dead turfgrass root tissues would be expected to decay in a ratio of about 25% of fresh weight becoming humus and the remainder evolved as CO_2 and H_2O. Thus, to obtain 46 lb humus per 1,000 ft^2 would require about four times this quantity of fresh organic material or 184 lb nondecomposed organic matter by dry weight produced each year per 1,000 ft^2. As an example of potential organic matter/humus production from a turfgrass system:

> A square yard (0.84 m^2) of washed sod (free of soil) cut at 0.15 inch (1.9 cm) weighs about 20 lb (9.1 kg) for a moist weight of about 2,222 lb per 1,000 ft^2 (1,089 kg per 100 m^2). On a dry weight basis, the sod would weigh approximately 560 lb (255 kg). As this 560 lb of dry weight, fresh organic matter is decomposed, about 140 lb per 1,000 ft^2 (68 kg per 100 m^2) of humus on a dry weight basis is formed. Also, a typical Kentucky bluegrass lawn has been estimated to add 130 lb root biomass per 1,000 ft^2 per year to the soil on a dry weight basis, while, for a sports turf, the annual additions of organic matter on a dry weight basis have been estimated to be 165 lb with about 72 lb being roots per 1,000 ft^2. These calculations illustrate that over a growing season an actively growing turfgrass sward can generate considerable organic matter and humus that is added to the soil.

Rate of decomposition of organic matter in the field depends on factors influencing the number and activity of microorganisms that degrade organic compounds; namely, soil temperature, moisture, pH, oxygen status, essential elements, and availability of a ready food source. In many climates, environmental factors are such that soil organic matter tends to reach an equilibrium of 2 to 4% organic matter content. For soils exhibiting consistent organic matter content in this general range, addition of more organic matter will not be particularly beneficial for CEC enhancement because: (a) the 2 to 4% organic matter will already provide reasonable CEC from the humus fraction; and (b) climatic conditions often allow the microorganisms to decompose the added organic matter back to the original equilibrium value; thereby, CEC enhancement is temporary.

The second case in sandy soils of organic matter status is the situation where native *organic matter levels equilibrate but at a low-level* of less than 2%. *In humid or arid subtropical and tropical climates* on sandy soils, long periods of high temperature can result in appreciable organic matter decomposition. Even the humus fraction decomposes at a more rapid rate, resulting in inherently low organic matter content. On these sites, the routine addition of compost and organic fertilizers may enhance CEC. But if the practice is stopped, organic matter tends to revert to the original low level.

Third, is where *soil organic matter tends to accumulate* in the *cool, humid areas* due to insufficient decomposition rates. Accumulation often occurs because of prolonged periods above 32°F (0°C) and below 55°F (12°C), such as Northern Europe, Canada, and the NW and NE United States. Cool season grasses continue to grow at above 32°F but soil microbial activity for organic matter degradation is low, between 32° and 55°F. In these climates, organic matter may accumulate to unacceptable levels, especially in very sandy root zone mixes. Turfgrass growers in such regions have at times experienced dissatisfaction with high sand green specifications where in practice, any sandy root zone mix expresses the same problem of excessive organic matter buildup—i.e., the problem is climate related and not associated with specifications.

In summary, with respect to organic matter addition for increasing CEC on very sandy soils: (a) during establishment a moderate to well-decomposed organic source added at 1 to 3% by weight (8 to 15% by volume) is often very beneficial. Organic matter sources should meet the desired particle size to meet physical soil properties; (b) addition of compost by topdressing to a mature turf for improved CEC status would be most successful in tropical or subtropical areas where native organic content levels remain low (<2% by weight). However, additions will need to be continued on an annual basis; and (c) mature turfgrasses in temperate and cool-humid climates may not benefit from addition of organic matter for CEC improvement because soil organic matter levels reach an equilibrium that is sufficient or excessively high.

Humic acid based fertilizers are sometimes applied to turfgrasses at rates well below that of organic composts. Some of these fertilizers are organic composts but with sufficiently high N or other nutrient levels to be marketed as organic fertilizers. Other materials are liquids or granules from mined humate deposits. Regardless of the source, single application rates are normally less than 20 to 30 lb of total material per 1,000 ft^2 (980 to 1,470 kg ha^{-1}) because the fertilizer nutrients limit the rate of application. To add 1.0% by weight of an organic compost to a 6 inch (15 cm) soil depth would, in comparison, require about 460 lb compost per 1,000 ft^2 (225 kg per 100 m^{2}). Thus, the contribution of humic or organic based fertilizers toward improved CEC in a sandy soil would be very small (i.e., < 5% of compost rates) at normal rates of treatment compared to the addition of a compost to enhance CEC. However, humic acid or organic fertilizers do add nutrients; they can have a chelation effect to improve micronutrient uptake; and other direct or indirect benefits (contain micronutrients or hormones) may occur to enhance turfgrass growth (see Chapter 15, Biochemical Aspects and Amendments).

Zeolite Incorporation

There are many natural and synthetic zeolites but the zeolite clinoptilolite has great potential for increasing CEC on high sand soils (Andrews et al.[1]). This mineral is a crystalline, aluminosilicate originally derived from volcanic rock. It has a structure with internal channels and voids in which water and cations are held. A high CEC (100 to 230 cmol kg^{1}) arises from isomorphous substitution of Al^{+3} for Si^{+4} in the crystal lattice. The selectivity order for cations on CEC sites is:

$$\text{(greatest) } K^+, NH_4^+ > H^+ > Na^+ > Ca^{+2} > Mg^{+2} \text{ (least)}$$

Zeolite has a high selective tendency for K^+ and NH_4^+. These cations, as well as other cations, can be retained on zeolite CE sites in the internal pores, which affords protection from leaching. Normally, specific bacteria oxidize NH_4^+ to NO_3^-, that has a higher leaching potential. In zeolite, the bacteria are unable to enter the internal pores and channels so NH_4^+ is retained for gradual release to plants. Zeolites can be amended with other nutrients to enhance nutrient characteristics (Andrews et al.[1]).

Clinoptilolite has high structural strength but some other zeolites are softer. Mined product can be crushed, milled, and screened to meet particle size standards used in golf green and sports field soil specifications. Deposits are found in the United States, Australia, Japan, and other countries. Calculations of the quantity of zeolite (or other amendments) to add to a root-zone medium prior to turfgrass establishment to increase CEC to a particular value are illustrated in the section "Guidelines for Increasing CEC by the Addition of Amendments" presented later in this chapter.

In an Australian study, the *expected* CEC from zeolite addition was about 30% higher than *laboratory* measured CEC values after zeolite was added. The laboratory methods commonly used to measure CEC in soil may underestimate zeolite CEC due to the internal pores and channels, which could prevent full exchange with the saturation cation. Thus, calculated CEC may be a better estimate of final CEC than the laboratory procedure.

At a CEC value of above 4 cmol kg^{-1}, the problems associated with low CEC in soils become minor. A good target for CEC enhancement by zeolite addition, or other CEC enhancement materials, therefore, is about 4 cmol kg^{-1}. To reduce costs the turf manager could incorporate sufficient zeolite throughout a shallow depth in the root zone mix, perhaps 2 to 6 inches (5 to 15 cm).

On established turfgrasses, zeolite could be incorporated into the topdressing sand, especially with aerification and working the material into the holes. Until more specific research on topdressing with zeolite is conducted, turfgrass managers may wish to consider about a 30% (by wt.) or less zeolite addition (i.e., 70% sand, 30% zeolite). At this ratio, the sand is still the predominant structural matrix to resist compacting forces.

When selecting a particle-size distribution for the zeolite, the USGA Green Section criteria for root-zone media or topdressing sand would apply. Where increased soil moisture retention is desired, particle sizes in the 0.105 to 0.50 mm diameter range can be used but saturated hydraulic conductivity (SHC) or infiltration may be reduced. Particles within the 0.25 to 2.00 mm range seem to enhance water holding capacity somewhat while still maintaining SHC. The increased water holding capacity of a zeolite amended soil may not result in an appreciable increase in plant available water. Much of the water is retained in relatively small pores and channels and apparently not readily released for plant uptake.

Some mined clinoptilolitic zeolite may contain high Na levels. These would require leaching to remove excess Na, especially for grasses with low salt tolerance. Where irrigation water is high in Na^+, the Na^+ may accumulate more easily in zeolite than in straight sand. This is due to the selective tendency of zeolite for Na^+ cations and the presence of channels and pores, which can protect Na^+ from easy leaching. However, research in Australia indicates that Na^+ does not easily replace K^+ from zeolite. Additional water beyond the normal leaching requirement for a sand may be required to remove Na^+, but this should not be a problem when a small quantity of zeolite (i.e., < 5% by wt.) is used and adequate K^+ is maintained.

Another potential nutrient problem with zeolite amended sand is low Mg^{+2} level. Zeolite has a low affinity for Mg^{+2} and this cation can also be easily leached from the sand component, especially when high K rates are applied. Additional Mg^{+2} applied two or three times per year as determined by soil testing may be necessary.

Coal fly ash has been converted to a zeolite by NaOH or KOH treatment at high temperatures. Zeolites formed by this process may contain high salinity, high Na, and potentially toxic trace elements. Particle size of the created zeolite is quite small and would require pelletizing, which may not provide a high structural or weathering strength. Any zeolite should be evaluated carefully to assure a high quality product that can be used on intensively maintained turf sites.

Addition of Calcined Clays or Diatomaceous Earth

The firing of various clays or diatomaceous earth at 1500 to 1800°F (815 to 982°C) results in inorganic materials that have high structural strength. These "calcined" materials are usually incorporated into a high sand mix for improved moisture retention. However, they do contain some CE sites and have internal pores and channels that assist in retaining nutrients.

Calcined clays, sometimes called porous ceramics, are reported to have CEC up to 33 cmol kg^{-1}, while calcined diatomaceous earth and noncalcined diatomaceous earth products range from 1.2 to 27 CEC cmol kg^{-1}. Due to much lower CEC than zeolite, more of these materials by weight would be required to significantly increase CEC. For example, it would require about five times by weight of a calcined clay with a CEC of 33 cmol kg^{-1} than a zeolite of CEC 165 cmol kg^{-1} to achieve the same CEC change in a mix.

These sand substitutes are sometimes used as topdressing materials, usually at 5 to 30% by weight of the topdressing media. At these rates some CEC enhancement would occur over time. If increasing CEC is an important goal, sand substitutes with high CEC or zeolite should be chosen. As with zeolites, no more than 30% by weight is recommended in mixes or in topdressing mixes to maintain sand as the primary matrix.

Natural Clays

Until about 1970, most USGA specification golf greens contained 2 to 3% by weight of a well-aggregated clay, which produced a final mix with 3 to 6 cmol kg^{-1} CEC. This was usually achieved by selecting a sandy loam soil with good structure and then amending with sand and organic matter to achieve the final mix. Care was taken to select a sandy loam with minimal silt content (0% would be best but very difficult to achieve). These greens had higher CEC, higher inherent nutrient levels, and were easier to manage during the grow-in period than greens without the "soil" component.

The change to two component green mixes (i.e., sand and organic matter) was due to economics and convenience, and not because of better agronomics. Good, consistent sources of sandy loam topsoil were often difficult to locate and costly. Many turf managers assume that the clay component was left out because of water drainage and aeration problems. This was not the case since well chosen and mixed components resulted in excellent physical properties. Thus, one approach to achieving adequate CEC is to revisit the practice of incorporating some well-aggregated clay into the mixes at establishment by using the "soil" component. Such mixes could still meet current USGA specifications of $< 3\%$ clay. Care should be taken not to pulverize these aggregates when handling or mixing components, nor when preparing a sample for the laboratory.

Economic considerations of omitting the clay component are often based on false economics. Certainly, a lower bid can be obtained for construction but long-term costs and problems remain. Also, the convenience aspect should be weighed in the light of what "a good specification" is intended to do. Good specifications limit choices, but for a better result. Limited choices often translate into higher initial cost and inconvenience but lower future management costs.

Resins

Synthetic ion-exchange resins have been available for 150 years but were not economically feasible. Most synthetic ion-exchange resins are solid organic polymers of styrene polymer cross-linked to divinylbenzene to achieve CEC levels of 100 to 500 cmol kg^{-1}. These can be manufactured to contain different macropore and micropore combinations with high internal porosity similar to zeolite. Some newer resins have a chain-like structure and are reported to have CEC levels up to 3,000 to 5,000 cmol kg^{-1}. Resins vary substantially in affinity for particular cations and effective pH range for release of cations.

Use of resins with appropriate chemical and physical properties for CEC enhancement is a possibility, especially where resins with very high CEC could be incorporated into an existing turf and if they did not readily decompose.. Resins may also find use as surface applied materials to limit chemical runoff. In this case a surface zone CEC of >4.0 cmol kg^{-1} would likely be desired. Interestingly, anion resins with strong affinities for NO_3^- are available. However, little research has been conducted on resins for turfgrass application, including research on effectiveness, longevity (weathering, mechanical stability), biological decomposition, etc.

Guidelines for Increasing CEC by the Addition of Amendments

The amount of amendment required to increase soil CEC by a given amount can be calculated if the following information is known:

(a) amount of CEC increase desired in cmol kg^{-1} (I)
(b) CEC of amendment (C)
(c) water content by weight of amendment
(d) dry weight of soil or sand being amended (S)
(e) dry weight of amendment required (A)

In the following equation, the unknown value is amendment required (A)

$$\frac{A}{S+A} \times C = I$$

The value of A/(S+A) represents the percentage (in decimal form) of dry amendment in the mixture. That value times the CEC of the amendment gives the increase in CEC due to the addition of the amendment. Assume that 31,000 lb (14,091 kg) of sand is to be amended with a zeolite having a CEC of 120 cmol kg^{-1} and negligible water content, and the increase in CEC desired is 3.6 cmol kg^{-1}. [The 31,000 lb sand value approximates the weight of a 4 inch (10 cm) layer over 1,000 ft^2 (93 m^2). With amendment additions an increase in volume will occur and be dependent on the nature of the amendment. Organic additions or fine clay materials or soils will have less effect than granular amendments because they will occupy some of the pores within the sand.]

Calculate A as follows:

$$\frac{A}{31{,}000+A} \times 120 = 3.6$$

where

$$\begin{aligned} 120\text{ A} &= 3.6\,(31{,}000 + \text{A}) = 111{,}600 + 3.6\text{A} \\ 116.4\text{ A} &= 111{,}600 \\ \text{A} &= 959 \text{ lb of dry amendment required} \end{aligned}$$

In cases where the amendment contains appreciable water, such as in peat and other organic sources, natural clays, and natural soils, the value of A must be corrected due to the water

Table 4.7. Effect of amendment CEC on the amount of amendment required to increase the CEC of a typical sand used for turfgrass root zones by 1, 2, 3, and 4 cmol kg^{-1}.

CEC of Amendment[a]	Increased (cmol kg^{-1}):	Amendment (dry weight basis) to be added to 31,000 lb[b] sand to obtain the following increases in CEC			
		1	2	3	4
		Pounds Amendment[c]			
10		3444	7750	13286	20667
20		1632	3444	5470	7750
40		795	1632	2514	3444
80		392	795	1208	1632
120		260	525	795	1069
160		195	392	592	795
200		155	313	472	633

[a] For other CEC values use this equation to determine amendment (A) required: A = (31,000 × CEC increase)/(CEC of amendment − CEC increase).
[b] 31,000 lb sand is approximately equivalent to a 4 inch depth over 1,000 ft^2 or 12.35 yd^3.
[c] For moist amendments, increase accordingly based on water content. 1 pound = 0.45 kg.

content. Because water content of these materials is reported on the dry weight basis, the corrected value for A can be obtained by multiplying A by one plus the decimal value of water content. For example, if an organic matter source contains 38% H_2O, multiply A by 1.38 to obtain the weight of moist amendment required.

The data in Table 4.7 can be used as a guide for determining the amounts of various amendments required for 31,000 lb sand, which is approximately equivalent to a 4 inch (10 cm) depth over 1,000 ft^2 (0.93 m^2) or 12.35 yd^3 (9.44 m^3).

B. Management Practices for Low EC Soils

At the beginning of this chapter specific nutritional problems were listed that are associated with low CEC soils. These included important issues such as low nutrient levels, rapid changes in nutrient levels or balances, leaching, salinity buildup, pH changes, difficulty in monitoring soil nutrient status, and establishment problems. A diversity of management practices, beyond practices to enhance CEC, are necessary to minimize these problems. More detailed information on many of these can be found in other chapters—for example, on salinity, pH control, soil testing, or specific nutrients. In this section, however, management problems and options will be presented in limited detail.

Nitrogen

Primary problems with N on low CEC soils are NH_4^+ leaching, maintaining adequate N levels for turfgrass growth, and N carrier effect on pH. Additionally, NO_3^- can easily leach on these high percolation rate soils. Cultural practices directed toward limiting N leaching and maintaining adequate N levels include:

- Use of slow-release N sources. The development of a wide variety of polymer-coated N fertilizers in recent years provides even greater choice in N sources, along with the natural organic, synthetic organic, and sulfur-coated products. Polymer (also called plastic or resin) coatings can be developed with a wide range of N release rates. And, multiple coating arrangements (polymer-coated urea, polymer/sulfur-coated urea) and a variety of materials being coated (urea, other N compounds) provide additional flexibility. These carriers, as well as other slow-release formulations, may allow increased use of slow-release N on high sand sites associated with low CEC.

- Spoon-feeding with quick-release N. Frequent N application but at low rates is a common practice to reduce leaching potential while maintaining adequate N. Sometimes slow-release N forms are applied at a moderately low "base level" and then supplemented by light applications of quick-release N, while other growers depend solely on quick-release N applications. On small sites, such as golf greens, applications may be through a sprayer. Larger acreage sites may be fertilized by granular materials. In some areas, fertigation is a popular option.

The influence of acidic N carriers, $(NH_4)_2SO_4$ and NH_4NO_3 especially, on decreasing soil pH within high sand greens can be corrected by changing carriers or light rates of lime application. If irrigation water is alkaline, use of an acidic N source aids in offsetting pH changes.

Potassium

The primary problems in K nutrition on low CEC sand soils are maintaining adequate K for drought, heat, and cold tolerance, and wear resistance; and avoiding excessive salinity from high K use. Potassium can be easily leached and, therefore, the soil test value often reads very low. Approaches to maintaining adequate K are:

- Use of slow-release K carriers. Slow-release K fertilizers are now available based especially on polymer coating technology as well as relatively insoluble potassium magnesium phosphates. These products should gain in popularity as growers learn appropriate rates and frequency of application. Application several times over the growing season is more likely to achieve adequate K than one heavier long-term application.
- Spoon-feeding K. Relatively frequent application of K at low rates can achieve adequate K, using the same approaches as for spoon-feeding of N.

In the mid-1980s, the practice of associating K application with N application was suggested for sites where heavy rainfall or irrigation caused K leaching and K soil test values were, thereby, low. On such sites, basing K fertilization on N application can help maintain adequate K. Potassium is applied as a spoon-feeding program whenever N is applied using a $N:K_2O$ ratio of about 1:1. The following adjustments may be considered (also see Chapter 10 and Chapter 12, Table 12.5):

- Use a 1:1.5 ($N:K_2O$) ratio for annual N rates of 1 to 3 lb N per 1,000 ft^2 (49 to 150 kg N ha^{-1}).
- Use a 1:1 ratio when annual N rates are 3 to 7 lb per 1,000 ft^2.
- Use a 1:0.75 to 1:0.50 ratio when annual N exceeds 7 lb per 1,000 ft^2 to avoid the potential for excessive salt buildup.
- In the summer months, apply K at 0.10 to 0.33 lb K_2O per 1,000 ft^2 spaced at two to four week intervals.

On sand soils with low CEC, salt levels can rapidly increase whenever rainfall or irrigation is insufficient for leaching. Potassium fertilizer sources are salts, and increased use of fertilizer K also enhances the possibility of salinity. In arid regions, turf managers may not apply sufficient irrigation for leaching of K and, therefore, soil test K levels may not be low, even on sandy soils. The above **N:K_2O recommendations are only for sites where K is leached**. For all other sandy soils, soil test extractable K is a better measure to base K fertilization. In humid climates, a prolonged dry period should signal the turf manager to test for total salts and reduce K use if salts are accumulating.

Another potential means of maintaining adequate K (and possibly other nutrients) is periodic application of polyaspartates. These are polymers of aspartic acid containing anion exchange and CEC of approximately 300 mol kg^{-1}. Nutrients are retained on the CEC sites of the polymer. Their mode of action is believed to be that they artificially act as extensions of the plant's root hairs. High nutrient content on the polymer results in transfer of nutrients to the roots. Absorption of monovalent cations (i.e., K^+, NH_4^+) appear to be enhanced. Since polyaspartates are biodegradable, application would need to be repeated periodically. Research on these materials to document these potential attributes under turf systems is very limited. Turf managers are encouraged to request research information that documents specific benefits of such products when considering their use.

Magnesium

Magnesium deficiency can easily occur on low CEC sands, especially if high K fertilization is practiced or high Ca and/or Na applications arise from the irrigation water. Even with soil pH values of 6.0 to 7.5, Mg deficiency can be present. Extractable Mg (a measure of the quantity of Mg) using a suitable extractant, such as Mehlich I or ammonium acetate, is a more reliable measure of plant available Mg than is percent Mg on the CEC sites or the use of Ca:Mg ratios based on percent of cations on the CEC.

If the extractable Mg level ranks as low, Mg should be applied. At pH of 6.0 or less, a dolomitic limestone (contains Mg) can be used at 5 to 10 lb limestone per 1,000 ft^2 (244 to 488 kg ha^{-1}). Otherwise, a Mg fertilizer containing at least 8% Mg can be applied at 2 to 4 lb product per 1,000 ft^2 several times per year with periodic soil testing to evaluate Mg level. Most Mg carriers, except dolomitic limestone, can cause foliar burn if applied at high rates or not immediately watered into the sward.

Calcium

Calcium deficiency on shoots of turfgrasses has not been reported in the scientific literature except in solution culture studies where Ca was omitted or where high Na or Al were present. Turfgrasses are very efficient in taking up Ca and the soil contains a number of compounds in which Ca is a constituent. Even very acid soils contain appreciable Ca. Thus, Ca application is very rarely needed because of a true Ca deficiency. Calcium compounds, however, are commonly used to adjust soil or thatch pH (lime), and to amend sodic or saline-sodic (gypsum) soils.

However, on low CEC sand soils receiving water high in Na and low in Ca (seawater irrigation, seawater blends, or salt spray, etc.), there are instances where Ca *as a nutrient* would be useful. It has been demonstrated that supplemental Ca can be beneficial for enhancing salt tolerance of other plants. Thus, some Ca fertilization could be considered if all the following conditions are present: irrigation water contains high Na but little Ca; the soil is sandy with low CEC; the salinity levels are sufficient to create stress on the plant. A suggested fertilization rate would be 5 to 10 lb $CaSO_4$ (gypsum) per 1,000 ft^2. In Chapter 13, Calcium, Magnesium, and Sulfur, additional uses of Ca are presented for sand sites.

Iron

On sandy, low CEC soils, Fe deficiencies can occur, especially if any of the following conditions are present: high soil pH; excessive applications of P or Mn; high levels of Ca or Zn from applied fertilizers or pesticides; and prolonged tropical, wet periods. Foliar application of Fe is the most common remedy.

Manganese

Manganese deficiency is fairly common on high sand soils with low CEC when in conjunction with: high Fe applications; high levels of Cu or Zn from pesticides; alkaline soil pH, especially with high Ca soil tests; clipping removal; and cool, moist weather. Foliar application of Mn or granular materials can be applied to correct any deficiencies.

Sulfur

Bermudagrasses grown on sandy soils with low organic matter content and under heavy N fertilizer regimes are most prone to exhibiting S deficiency. Sulfur can be applied as elemental S, $CaSO_4$ or by incorporating S containing N and K fertilizer carriers in the fertilizer program for a site.

More common than S deficiency is the problem created by use of S to reduce pH on low CEC, sand soils that do not contain free $CaCO_3$. The limited buffering capacity of these soils can allow pH to decrease dramatically if too much S is applied in the surface zone (i.e., 1 inch or 2.5 cm) where the turfgrass crown resides. Turf managers using S to reduce pH on these soils should monitor pH of the surface 1 inch (2.5 cm) every 6 months as well as from the usual 0 to 3 inch (0 to 8 cm) or 0 to 4 inch (0 to 10 cm) soil sampling depth.

Salt Related Problems

Since low CEC sands have limited buffering capacity, it requires much less total salts or Na to create saline or sodic soil conditions compared to soils with higher CEC. The most common problem is from high total salts causing a saline condition which limits water uptake and causes drought symptoms.

Since sands have a single grain structure without "aggregates" that can become deflocculated by high Na content, some turfgrass growers do not realize that high Na (i.e., sodic condition) can create poor physical conditions in a sand just as well as an aggregated soil. In an aggregated soil, Na disperses the clay colloids and, thereby, destroys structure, leading to poor water movement and aeration. While high sand soils may not contain appreciable clay colloids, they do contain organic matter particles of colloidal size that can be dispersed by Na. These colloids can start to migrate and accumulate at the depth of irrigation water penetration. In arid climates with rather standard daily irrigation, this colloid zone may eventually start to plug up the pores and lead to black layer development. Readers are referred to the chapters on salt affected soil problems and corrective practices for further information.

Monitoring Nutrient Status

Careful monitoring of nutrient status is very important on low CEC sands because nutrient levels and ratios change more rapidly than on high CEC soil, inherent nutrient levels are generally lower, frequent irrigation is practiced, and clippings are often removed. Additional information on this topic is found in the chapters on soil testing and tissue testing. Concerning soil testing and recommendations for sand soils, an understanding of BCSR versus SLAN soil testing philosophies is especially important.

Irrigation Scheduling

Irrigation practices on sandy soils have a major influence on the degree of nutrient leaching and retention, and on whether salt problems arise. In arid regions, salt problems are more prevalent, while in humid climates excessive leaching is more common. Attention to good irrigation practices will result in nutritional dividends.

V. ANION EXCHANGE CAPACITY

FOR MOST SOILS, NEGATIVE CHARGES THAT ATTRACT CATIONS account for over 95% of the charged sites, while positively charged sites for anion attraction are less than 5%. However, in the tropics some soils actually contain a net positive charge; i.e., anion exchange capacity is greater than CEC.

Positively charged sites can arise on kaolinite clays, iron hydrous oxides (goethite), and aluminum hydrous oxides (gibbsite) under very acid conditions. The exposed >Al-OH and >Si-OH edge groups of these minerals give rise to a net positive charge under extreme acid conditions:

$$\rangle \text{Al-OH}_2^+ \xleftarrow{+\text{H}^+} \rangle \text{Al-OH} \xrightarrow{-\text{H}^+} \rangle \text{Al-O}^-$$

Positive Charge	No Charge	Negative Charge
very low pH (acid)	*intermediate pH*	*high pH*

Thus, anion exchange capacity (AEC) is pH-dependent and decreases as soil pH increases. The same –OH group may be positive, neutral, or negative depending on pH. Total anion exchange capacity is normally no more than 5 cmol kg^{-1} even on soils with appreciable kaolinite clay or iron and aluminum hydrous oxides with very low pH. Humus may also contain some AEC under very low pH.

Anion exchange functions just as cation exchange except that the colloid charges are positive and the ions are negative (anions). When AE is present, it provides sites for important nutrient anions (such as NO_3^-, SO_4^{-2}) to be retained for plant uptake instead of being leached. When anions are leached they take cations with them, such as Ca^{+2}, Mg^{+2}, K^+, and Na^+. Thus, leaching of NO_3^- is detrimental because of environmental concerns, as a lost nutrient, and because of the loss of an associated cation.

Some anions, especially phosphates and molybdates, react quickly with iron and aluminum hydrous oxides (acid pH) or calcium (alkaline pH) to form insoluble precipitates instead of being attracted to AEC sites. Other anions (namely, NO_3^-, Cl^-, and BO_3^{-3}) do not directly form compounds with other soil constituents and AEC becomes a much more important means for these to be loosely retained in soils; the anion SO_4^{-2} can react with AEC sites but also with inorganic constituents (e.g., calcium) and organic matter. Thus, the *general mobility of anions in soil is:*

$$\text{Phosphates} < \text{Molybdates} < SO_4^{-2} = BO_3^{-3} < Cl^- < NO_3^-$$

(least mobile) *(most mobile)*

VI. REFERENCES

1. Andrews, R.D., A.J. Koski, J.A. Murphy, and A.M. Petrovic. 1999. Zeoponic materials allow rapid greens grow-in. *Golf Course Management* 67(2):68–72.
2. Brady, N.C. 1990. Soil colloids: their nature and practical significance. In *The Nature and Properties of Soils*. Chapter 7. New York: Macmillan Publishing Co.
3. Handreck, K.A. and N.D. Black. 1994. Clay and humus:soil colloids. In *Growing Media for Ornamental Plants and Turf.* Chapter 7. Randwick N5W, Australia: University of NSW Press.
4. Hendershot, W.H., H. Lalande, and M. Duquette. 1993. Ion exchange and exchangeable cations. pp. 167–176. In M.R. Carter, Ed. *Soil Sampling and Methods of Analysis.* Boca Raton, FL: Lewis Publishers.

Chapter 5

Soil pH Concepts and Acidity Problems

SOIL PH, ALSO CALLED *SOIL REACTION,* is probably the most commonly measured soil characteristic. It is essentially a measure of the acidity or alkalinity of the soil.[1] Specific problems associated with excessively acid and alkaline pH will be presented in greater detail later in this chapter and the following chapter. But in general, pH influences:

- nutrient availability and balances
- the potential for Al and Mn toxicities
- the activity of specific microbial populations and, therefore, the processes that they facilitate
- the quantity of lime or S to alter pH
- turfgrass vigor and persistence.

I. CONCEPT OF SOIL pH AND ACIDITY

A. Soil pH and Measurement

SOIL PH IS A MEASURE OF H ION (H^+) ACTIVITY <u>in the soil solution</u>.[5] Hydrogen ion content in the soil solution is called *active acidity* and is in equilibrium with H^+ ions on CEC sites or associated with other soil constituents. Thus, determination of pH of the soil solution is also a measure of soil pH.

The technical definition of pH is a numerical system of *acidity* or *alkalinity,* defined as the logarithm of the reciprocal of the H^+ activity in solution. Thus,

$$pH = \log\frac{1}{\left[H^+\right]} \text{ or } pH = -\log\left[H^+\right]$$

where the pH scale goes from 0 to 14, but for soils the common range is pH 4.0 to 10.2. A soil reaction of 7.0 is neutral where H^+ activity equals OH^- activity. Below pH 7.0 is the acid range with greater acidity as pH gets lower in number, while above 7.0 is the alkaline range, where alkalinity increases as pH increases. Within the acid range, acidic cations (H^+, Al^{+3}) dominate, while above pH 7.0 basic cations (Ca^{+2}, Mg^{+2}, K^+, Na^+) predominate and OH^- activity exceeds H^+ activity.

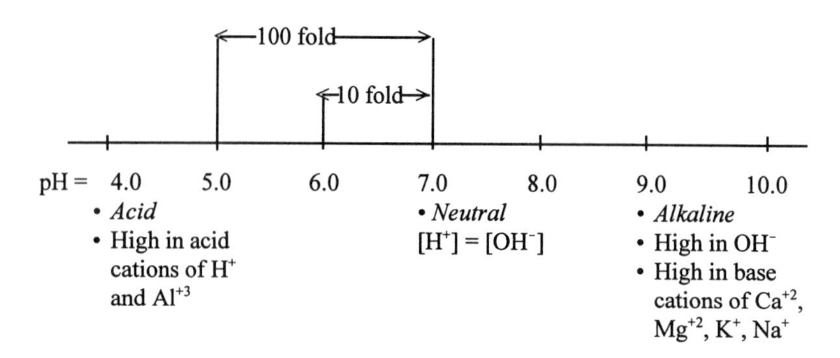

Since the pH scale is logarithmic, H^+ activity increases 10-fold from pH 7.0 to 6.0 but 100-fold from pH 7.0 to 5.0 and 1,000-fold from 7.0 to 4.0. Thus, small changes in pH between 4.0 to 5.0 can represent significant differences in H^+ activity.

In common laboratory procedures for determining soil pH, measured quantities of soil and distilled water are mixed by stirring, allowed to equilibrate for a prescribed time, and then measured for pH value by inserting electrodes so that they just penetrate the settled soil. The values are read on a pH meter. The most common ratios of soil to water used in pH measurements are 1:1 and 1:2. For instance: 5 g soil in 5 mL of water is a 1:1 ratio. In some cases the ratio represents volume mixtures, and 1 part soil and 2 parts water (both by volume) represents a 1:2 ratio. For calcareous soils, which contain free $CaCO_3$, more accurate pH determinations are obtained by stirring the mixture during measurement. However, noncalcareous soil samples should not be stirred at the measurement time.

In addition to pH measurement in water (at times presented as pH_w but usually as just pH), other solutions are sometimes used. One solution is 1 M *KCl* where the pH is listed as pH_K. In some soils low in salts, the supernatant may not clear by precipitation of soil particles, which induces an error in pH of 0.20 to 1.00 units. Using 1 M KCl eliminates this "suspension effect" and provides more stable pH values. However, pH_K values are often lower than pH_w especially in acid soils with low salts where pH_K is usually 1.0 unit less than pH. As soil pH increases, the disparity between these methods decreases.

A second solution used for pH is 0.01 M $CaCl_2$ and is listed as pH_{ca}. Use of 0.01 M $CaCl_2$ eliminates the suspension effect and is thought by some to be a more accurate measure of soil pH since it simulates the ionic strength of soil solution. When a soil contains significant soluble salts, pH_w and pH_{ca} are similar. Between pH_w 5.0 to 7.0, pH_{ca} values will be 1.2 to 0.8 units lower than pH_w. As pH_w falls below 5.0 or rises above 7.0, the two pH measurements become closer together. Usually, pH_{ca} values are slightly higher than pH_K.

Common reasons for pH values from the same site to vary from one year to another are:

- leaching and plant uptake of basic cations
- addition of an amendment that alters pH such as irrigation water, fertilizer, lime, or S
- production of strong acids during organic matter decomposition
- changing sampling depth
- using a laboratory that uses a different soil:solution ratio.

B. Soil Acidity

The majority of a soil's *total acidity* comes not from H^+ in soil solution but H^+ and Al^{+3} (with associated H^+) on the soil colloids. Exchangeable Al^{+3} is a primary source of H^+ and acidity in soils that are strongly acid (i.e., pH < 5.0). Such highly acidic conditions result in considerable soluble Al^{+3} that resides on CEC (cation exchange sites) and increases Al^{+3} in soil solution. When in soil solution, Al^{+3} ion attracts water (i.e., becomes hydrated or is hydrolyzed) and in the process creates free H^+ ions. To illustrate:

$$\underbrace{\boxed{\text{Soil Colloid}}^{-3}\ Al^{+3}}_{\text{clay or organic matter with CEC}} \leftrightarrow \underbrace{Al^{+3} + H_2O \rightarrow Al(OH)^{+2} + H^+}_{Al^{+3}\text{ in soil solution}}$$

Some *exchangeable H*$^+$ can also be present, especially at pH values of < 5.0, on CEC sites of soil colloids. Hydrogen ions from this source are far fewer than from Al^{+3} on CEC sites. This source of H^+ can be represented as:

$$\underbrace{\boxed{\text{Soil Colloid}}^{-1}\ H^+}_{H^+\text{ on CEC sites}} \leftrightarrow \underbrace{H^+}_{\text{(soil solution)}}$$

Considerable hydrogen in very acid soils (pH < 5.0) is tightly bound in organic matter and in clay structures; only a small quantity of the *bound H* is released into soil solution, especially from edges of clay crystals. For example

$$\text{Clay Al-OH Crystal} \rightarrow \text{Clay Al-O}^- + H^+ \text{ (soil solution) Crystal}$$

In moderately acid soils (pH 5.0 to 6.5), Al^{+3} becomes hydrated to form *hydrated Al cations,* which can reside on CEC sites and be in equilibrium with the soil solution.

$$\underbrace{\boxed{\text{Soil Colloid}}\begin{matrix}^{-2}\ Al(OH)^{+2} \\ _{-1}\ Al(OH)_2^+\end{matrix}}_{\text{Hydrated Al on CEC sites}} \begin{matrix}\leftrightarrow \\ \leftrightarrow\end{matrix} \underbrace{\begin{matrix}Al(OH)^{+2} + H_2O \rightarrow Al(OH)_2^+ + H^+ \\ Al(OH_2)^+ + H_2O \rightarrow Al(OH)_3 + H^+\end{matrix}}_{\text{Hydrated Al in soil solutions}}$$

The final H^+ source that can occur in 2:1 clays, especially vermiculite, is associated with hydrated Al ions that move into the clay interlayers. As pH increases, some of the *interlayer H* ions are released into soil solution.

The particular mechanisms accounting for H ions and acidity depend on the soil pH (Table 5.1). Since soil acidity can arise from different sources, *total soil acidity has been divided into*

Table 5.1. Sources of H^+ ions and soil acidity and their relative importance at different pH levels.

H^+/Acidity Source	Soil pH Range[b]		
	<5.0	5.0–6.0	6.0–7.0
Exchangeable[a] Al^{+3}	****	**	—
Exchangeable[a] H^+	**	*	*
Hydrated Al[a] Ions	*	****	***
Bound H, Al	*****	***	*
Interlayer H, Al	*	*	—

[a] These forms reside on the CEC sites and are in equilibrium with the soil solution levels.
[b] The more stars represent greater importance of the source.

three classes: (a) *activity acidity* due to H^+ in the soil solution. This is what is measured by a routine soil pH determination. Since soil solution H^+ can interchange with H^+ on CEC sites and reach a chemical equilibrium, a routine pH measurement is representative of the soil acidity level; (b) *salt-replaceable acidity* represents H^+, Al^{+3}, and hydrated Al cations that are on CEC sites, and can be easily replaced by other cations. Salt-replaceable acidity is often over 100 times greater than active acidity; and (c) *residual acidity;* this component represents bound H and Al as well as interlayer H and Al. If a soil has appreciable clay colloids or organic matter colloids, residual acidity can be greater than salt-replaceable acidity. The term *potential acidity* is sometimes used to denote the sum of salt-replaceable acidity and residual acidity.

While a routine pH determination indicates soil pH level, it does not provide sufficient information to determine the *lime requirement (LR)*—the quantity of lime to adjust acid pH to a specific level, usually pH 6.5 to the plow depth (6 inches, 15 cm). Lime requirement is based on neutralizing total acidity. To determine lime requirement, soil test laboratories use a buffer pH procedure to measure total acidity (see Section III.D).

Salt-replaceable and residual acidities are responsible for the *buffering capacity (BC)* of soils (in soils with free calcium carbonate, $CaCO_3$, an additional buffering system can operate). Buffer capacity is stability against rapid pH changes in soils and determines the quantity of lime or S to alter pH. At times the term buffering capacity is used in a wider sense than just pH to mean the ability of a soil to absorb nutrients and to minimize rapid chemical changes in the soil. In this meaning, buffer capacity is related to CEC and chemical composition of a soil.

I. IMPORTANCE OF SOIL pH

SOIL PH CAN INFLUENCE TURFGRASSES and other landscape plants by a variety of mechanisms (Delhaize and Ryan,[2] Foy[4]).

A. Nutrient Availability and Losses

Soil pH has a profound influence on nutrient availability (Figure 5.1). A change in soil reaction modifies the balance of cations on CEC sites, influences chemical forms, and alters microbial

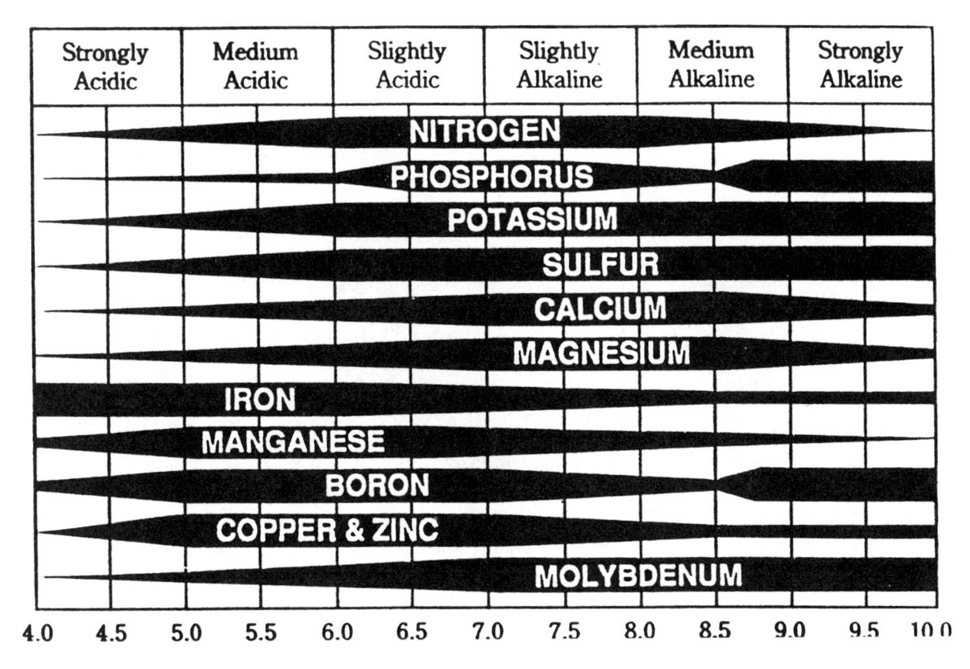

Figure 5.1. Influence of soil pH on nutrient availability. A wider band width implies greater availability for plant uptake (after E. Truog, 1947).[8]

activity associated with certain nutrients, such as N and S transformations. Nutrient availability is generally most favorable at pH 6.0 to 7.0 on mineral soils.

As pH becomes increasingly acid, nutrients most likely to be deficient are: N, P, K, Mg, and S. Calcium levels will decline but unless a salinity stress is present, Ca deficiency is very unlikely. With increasingly alkaline pH, Fe, Mn, P, and B are nutrients that may become deficient. Primary reasons for potential nutrient deficiencies under acid and alkaline conditions are listed in Table 5.2.

Soil pH can influence N losses by volatilization and denitrification. Under alkaline pH, N volatilization from applied N is much more likely than under acid conditions, especially for urea. Also, gaseous loss of N under poor aeration is greater at alkaline than acid pH.

B. Toxicities and Acid Soil Complex

At very acid pH (pH <4.8), certain chemicals (i.e., Al, Mn) become much more soluble and can be sufficiently high in soil solution to cause direct plant root toxicity. The most common toxicities to turfgrass roots are from high Al and Mn levels found in subsoils (and sometimes surface zones) of many cool, humid temperate soils, and humid subtropical and tropical soils. Often Al and/or Mn toxicities are in conjunction with other stresses; namely, deficiencies of Mg, K, Ca, or P, and high soil strength of nonexpanding kaolinitic clays and Fe/Al oxides. This complex of toxicities/deficiencies/high soil strength is called the *"acid soil complex."* Turfgrass species and genotype within a species can vary dramatically in tolerance to this complex of stresses. Turfgrass root growth is particularly inhibited by direct Al toxicity (brown, stunted roots), high soil strength for root penetration, and associated nutrient deficiencies.

Table 5.2. Primary reasons for soil pH to reduce nutrient availability of individual nutrients.

Nutrient	Soil pH	Reason for Potential Nutrient Deficiency[a]
N	Acid	Bacteria populations involved in nitrification (conversion of NH_4^+ to NO_3^- in the soil) decline so NH_4^+ accumulates but NO_3^- level is low. Less microbial N fixation.
P	Acid	Phosphate ions form insoluble chemical compounds with Fe, Mn, Al.
Ca, Mg, K	Acid	Fewer basic cations are present. They are replaced by H^+ and Al^{+3} on the cation exchange sites.
S	Acid	SO_4^{-2} ion may bind with Al and/or Fe oxides and kaolinite.
Mo	Acid	Relatively unavailable Mo compounds form at pH <5.0.
B	Acid	Relatively soluble at low pH but can be easily leached in acid sands.
P	Alkaline	Phosphate can form relatively insoluble compounds with Ca.
Fe, Mn, Cu, Zn	Alkaline	Form less soluble hydroxide and oxide forms.
B	Alkaline	Increasing amounts bound in clay colloids at higher pH.

[a] Strongly acid or alkaline conditions are more serious than less acidity or alkaline pH levels.

While high H^+ can be directly toxic to plant roots, Al and Mn toxicities normally occur before soil pH is sufficiently low to develop H^+ toxicity (pH <4.0), except in acid sulfate soils that are discussed later in this chapter. However, high H^+ concentration may adversely affect soil microorganisms. Iron toxicity is also possible under acidic, poorly drained situations.

C. Lime and Sulfur Requirements

Soil pH is an important factor in establishing how much lime or S will be needed to adjust initial pH to the 6.5 to 7.0 range. It will require more lime to adjust pH from 4.5 to 6.5 than from 5.5 to 6.5.

D. Influence on CEC

In Chapter 4, Cation Exchange Capacity, a detailed discussion of CEC is presented. In summary, many soils have a CEC component that does not vary as pH changes (pH independent CEC) and a component that is altered as pH changes (pH dependent CEC). Soils with the most pH dependent CEC contain Fe or Al hydrous oxides, allophane, kaolinite, or humus. Increasing pH of these soils from pH 4.0 to 5.0 up to pH 6.5 to 7.0 results in significant increase in CEC.

Conversely, acidification of soils containing pH dependent CEC results in a significant reduction in CEC. Thus, excessively acid soils containing these colloids cannot retain as many nutrients. However, excessively acid soils with 2:1 clay types do not exhibit loss of CEC since their CEC is pH independent.

E. Soil Microorganisms and Microbial Transformations

Soil reaction is a primary factor influencing population levels of specific soil microorganisms, whether beneficial or pathogens (see Chapter 15, Biochemical Aspects and Amendments). In general, total fungal populations remains relatively constant over a very wide pH range, but specific fungi species are favored by more narrow ranges. Total bacteria and actinomycete populations steadily decline at pH <5.5.

Chemical transformation of organically bound N into simple inorganic forms (NO_3^-, NH_4^+) that are available to plants is called *mineralization.* In the first stage, *ammonification,* soil microorganisms transform organic bound N into NH_4^+. *Nitrification* involves transforming NH_4^+ (ammonium ion) into NO_3^- (nitrate-N) by the following reactions:

$$\underset{\text{ammonium ion}}{2NH_4^+} + 3O_2 \xrightarrow[\text{bacteria}]{\textit{Nitrosomonas}} 4NO_2^- + 4H^+ + 2H_2O$$

$$2NO_2^- + O_2 \xrightarrow[\text{bacteria}]{\textit{Nitrobacter}} \underset{\text{nitrate ion}}{2NO_3^-}$$

Both ammonification and nitrification are suppressed as pH decreases below 5.5 with nitrification the most sensitive to pH reduction. Suppression of this transformation is due to reduced populations of the specific bacteria species involved.

Phosphorus held in organic matter can be mineralized by microorganisms into inorganic forms that are available to plants. This process is somewhat inhibited at low pH due to suppression of the microorganisms responsible for the process.

Thiobacillus spp. bacteria can transform reduced S forms into an oxidized form (sulfate, SO_4^{-2}) that plants can use. Also, microbial decomposition of organic matter can release organic S, which, upon mineralization, is a major source of plant available S. As pH declines, some *Thiobacillus* species involved in these processes decrease in number, while other species increase in number.

Many different types of soil microorganisms decompose organic matter. Bacteria and actinomycetes are particularly active in decomposing the more resistant forms of soil organic matter, while fungi are more active on the less resistant organic compounds. As pH decreases below pH 5.5, fungi dominate while bacteria and actinomycete populations decline. Thus, organic matter may accumulate in excessively acid soils. This problem of organic matter accumulation is especially acute in cool humid climates where cool soil temperatures reduce even the fungi activity.

If thatch pH is acid (pH <5.5), thatch accumulation may occur due to low microbial populations. Thatch pH is assumed to be near the soil pH; however, excessively acid thatch could occur:

- in humid climates with high rainfall
- from the use of acidifying N sources
- when S is being applied for pH reduction or to alleviate sodic conditions
- if irrigation water is naturally acid or has been acidified.

Thatch pH may also become more alkaline than the soil but high pH does not suppress total microbial levels, as does low pH.

Pathogenic microorganisms are influenced by soil and thatch pH but the association is complex, involving growth of the pathogen, initial infection, spread of the infection, growth and health of the host plant, and competition from other organisms (Table 2.6). There is limited evidence that low pH favors fusarium patch *(Microdochium nivale)* and brown patch *(Rhizoctinia solani)*. Alkaline pH may favor summer patch *(Magnaporthe poae)*, necrotic ring spot *(Leptosphaeria korrae)*, take-all patch *(Gaeumannomyces graminis)*, fusarium patch, and possibly spring dead spot (several organisms). Additionally, acidifying N-carriers have been reported to reduce the severity of fusarium patch, spring dead spot, take-all patch, and summer patch. For many diseases soil pH does not have a major influence on severity. Maintaining pH for a healthy turfgrass will assist in recovery of a grass from turf diseases.

Besides microorganisms, macroorganisms in soils are influenced by soil reaction. Many earthworm species prefer soils that are not too acidic.

F. Plant Community Composition

Plants differ in their tolerance to acid or alkaline soil reaction due to: (a) intolerance to high Al or Mn levels; (b) requirement for a high level of a particular nutrient, such as the high Fe need of azaleas (an acid-loving plant); (c) nutrient balances and levels at a particular pH range favorable to the plant; (d) nutrient deficiencies induced by pH, such as Fe deficiency at alkaline pH on some grasses, and (e) pH influence on mycorrhizae relations with a plant (Delhaize and Ryan;[2] Foy[4]).

Most turfgrasses do best at near pH 6.0 to 7.0, but many species such as *Cynodon* spp., can grow over a very wide pH range. Of particular importance in turfgrass culture is species and cultivar tolerance to the acid soil complex (see Section II. B) due to its prevalence around the world. In this case, tolerance normally involves tolerance to high Al and Mn; ability to grow and persist under low levels of basic cations and P; and the ability to develop and maintain a viable root system in high soil strength soils. Since these tolerance factors are subject to genetic control to a substantial degree, turfgrass breeders can select and breed for acid soil tolerance (see Chapter 3).

Species most tolerant to excessive acidity and alkalinity are listed in Table 5.3, but genotype tolerance with a species can vary substantially. It is important to note that because a turfgrass tolerates low pH does not mean that this is the optimum pH for growth. For example, creeping bentgrass *(Agrostis palustris)* can grow and persist better at pH 5.0 than can annual bluegrass *(Poa annua)*, but the optimum pH range for creeping bentgrass is 5.5 to 6.5. Also, control of a broadleaf or grass weed species by adjusting pH alone is seldom effective. In the preceding example, creeping bentgrass may obtain a slight competitive edge at pH 5.0 over *Poa annua*, but not enough to significantly impact the species dominance.

III. CORRECTION OF ACID SOIL PROBLEMS

A. Causes and Extent of Acid Soils

ACID SOILS (Dent;[3] Foy;[4] Sanchez and Logan[6]) can evolve through several processes: (a) as the result of leaching of base cations in humid, high rainfall climates; (b) by the action of acidic N sources, especially $(NH_4)_2\ SO_4$ and ammonium phosphates; (c) from overapplication of S; (d) by acid rain or acidic irrigation water; and (e) from waterlogging of soils rich in organic matter

Table 5.3. Turfgrass species most tolerant to soil pH extremes.

Soil Reaction	Cool Season Grass	Warm Season Grass
Excessive Acidity (pH < 5.0)		
Bentgrasses (*Agrostris* spp.)		
• creeping (*A. palustris*)	X	
• colonial (*A. tenuis*)	X	
• redtop (*A. alba*)	X	
• velvet (*A. canina*)	X	
Bermudagrasses (*Cynodon* spp.)		X
Carpetgrass (*Axonopus* spp.)		X
Centipedegrass (*Eremochloa ophiuroides*)		X
Fescues (*Festuca* spp.)		
• chewings (*F. rubra* var. *commutata*)	X	
• sheep fescue (*F. ovina*)	X	
• red fescue (*F. rubra*)	X	
• tall fescue (*F. arundinacea*)	X	
Seashore Paspalum (*Paspalum vaginatum*)[a]		X
Zoysiagrasses (*Zoysia* spp.)[a]		X
Excessive Alkalinity (pH > 8.0)		
Bermudagrasses (*Cynodon* spp.)		X
Blue grama (*Bouteloua gracilis*)		X
Buffalograss (*Buchloe dactyloides*)		X
Perennial Ryegrass (*Lolium perenne*)	X	
Seashore Paspalum (*Paspalum vaginatum*)		X
St. Augustinegrass (*Stenotophrum secundatum*)		X

[a] Some ecotypes are very sensitive to pH <5.0 but others are tolerant.

and dissolved sulfate that form sediments high in reduced sulfides, such as FeS_2 (pyrite). When drained, these sites become extremely acid with pH of 1.5 to 3.5; these are called *acid sulfate soils.*

The majority of acid soils are located in two broad zones: (a) the northern belt under humid, cold, or temperate conditions; and (b) the southern belt in humid, tropical climates. Within both zones, acid soils are most prevalent where soils formed in forest vegetation. Approximately 30% of the ice free land area is occupied by acid soils. Acid sulfate soils are found primarily in tropical coastal plain regions and tidal swamps to the extent of about 30 to 35 million acres (12 to 14 million ha) worldwide.

B. Acid Soil Situations

There are four acid soil situations that turfgrass managers may encounter during establishment of a turf or in mature stands:

- *Moderate soil acidity* (pH >5.0) in the surface and subsurface zones of upland soils. In this case, soil pH of the surface horizon is sufficiently acid to exhibit some of the problems associated with acidity but not Al, Mn, or H toxicities. This is the most common situation encountered in the USA (see Section IV).
- *Excessive acidity* (pH <5.0) in the surface and/or subsurface layers that results in Al, Mn, or H toxicities, (Sumner[7]). These soils often exhibit the "acid soil complex,"

especially in the B horizon, sufficient to inhibit root growth of acid sensitive plants (see Section V). Within the USA, excessive acidity is found in some Northeast, extreme Northwest, Appalachian region, and Southeast-Piedmont soils. However, this problem is very prevalent in many regions around the world.
- *Acid sulfate soils* where extreme acidity of pH 1.5 to 3.5 occurs throughout the profile (see Section VI) (Dent[3]).
- *Acidic thatch* where thatch pH is at <5.5. This is technically not a "soil" problem but is included because thatch becomes part of the growing media for the turfgrass (see Section VII).

Management practices unique to each situation will be discussed in the section specific to each problem. Before these are presented, however, the management aspects that are common to all acid situations will be discussed; namely, determination of lime requirement, characteristics of liming materials, and reaction of soils to lime application.

C. Determination of Lime Requirement

Lime requirement (LR) is the quantity of limestone ($CaCO_3$) required to increase the pH of an acid soils to a desired pH value to a plow depth (8 inch, 20 cm) (Lierop[5]). For a particular soil, LR depends on: (a) initial pH; (b) target pH (final pH desired) which is usually pH 6.5; and (c) buffer capacity (BC) of the soil. Buffer capacity is related to total CEC of clay and organic matter (i.e., salt-replaceable acidity) and the nature of the clay minerals (i.e., residual acidity) (see I.B, Table 5.1). Thus, to determine LR, the BC of a soil must be accurately measured.

The most accurate BC determination is by titrating a soil with: (a) a base, usually $Ca(OH)_2$, for acid soils and relating this to the increase in pH; or (b) an acid, such as HCl, for an alkaline soil and relating the quantity of acid required to reduce pH. The acid titration procedure is the best method to quantify BC of an alkaline soil and determine S requirement for pH reduction.

For acid soils, LR is usually not measured by the titration method due to time requirements. Instead an acid soil is equilibrated in buffered solution and the change in pH of the buffered suspension termed *buffer pH,* correlates with LR. Buffer pH differs from standard soil solution pH measured in water and has no meaning to the turf manager without a calibration curve. Some laboratories, however, report the buffer pH value on the soil test form.

Lierop[5] provides calibration information and detailed discussion on several *buffer pH methods.* The most common buffered solutions used to measure LR are: (a) SMP (Shoemaker, McLean, Pratt), which is especially accurate for excessively acid (pH <5.0) soils with high LR; (b) Woodruff single buffer; (c) new Woodruff single buffer (NW); (d) the Mehlich single buffer; and (e) Adams and Evans buffer.

Lime requirement methods have been developed for various types of soils: e.g., SMP for soils with significant exchangeable Al and high LR; the Woodruff for high organic content mineral soils such as found in the midwest United States; and the Adams and Evans for soils with low CEC and low LR [i.e., soils that are coarse-textured, low in organic matter, and containing clays that have relatively low CEC (kaolinite and Fe and Al oxides)]. If sandy, low CEC soils from sand or highly modified soils on turfgrass areas are sent to laboratories that routinely analyze higher CEC agricultural soil samples, they may not be tested with one of the more reliable LR methods for sandy, low CEC soils. The Yuan LR test is also reliable for sandy soils, but it utilizes two buffers and takes longer to run.

Routinely laboratories report the LR as pounds of $CaCO_3$ required per acre (or kg ha^{-1}) to adjust an 8 inch (20 cm) plow depth to the desired pH. There are situations where this rate may

Table 5.4. Neutralizing values of selected liming materials. Comparisons are based on pure material.

Material	Chemical Composition	Naturalizing Value (%)	Pounds Equivalent to 1 lb $CaCO_3$
Calcium carbonate, calcitic limestone	$CaCO_3$	100	1.0
Dolomitic limestone,[a] calcium magnesium carbonate	$Ca\ Mg\ (CO_3)_2$	109	0.92
Calcium hydroxide, hydrated, builders lime, slaked	$Ca(OH)_2$	135	0.74
Calcium and magnesium hydroxide, hydrated, slaked, builders lime	$Ca\ (OH)_2 + Mg(OH)_2$	152	0.66
Calcium oxide, burnt lime, quicklime[b]	CaO	179	0.56

[a] Domonitic limestone contains 35 to 46% $MgCO_3$.
[b] Not recommended for areas with a turfgrass stand due to extreme caustic nature.

be adjusted because the turfgrass grower desires to adjust pH of a different depth. Three examples are: (a) on moderately acid (pH >5.0) soils where only the surface horizon requires lime, LR can be adjusted to alter pH of just the surface 4 or 6 inch zone (10 to 15 cm); (b) on excessively acid (pH <5.0) soils with both surface and subsoil horizons requiring lime amelioration, LR may need to be increased to treat depths of 12 to 24 inches (30 to 60 cm); and (c) on acid sulfate soils (pH 1.5 to 3.5) which require lime treatment throughout the rooting zone. Also, the LR reported assumes a calcium carbonate equivalent (CCE) of 100. Applications of liming materials with a CCE value appreciably higher or lower than 100 should be adjusted accordingly. When a soil sample is submitted to a laboratory for LR determination, the turf manager should indicate that the sample is for turfgrass and indicate the soil depth for LR recommendations.

D. Liming Materials

Chemical Characteristics

Several *limestone materials* can be used to increase pH. These vary in chemical composition and are usually mined products that can contain some silicate minerals or other compounds. Lime requirement is given in terms of *calcium carbonate* which is given a relative neutralizing value of 100% (Table 5.4). Thus, if another material is selected the rate of application must be adjusted. For example, if the lime requirement was 50 lb per 1,000 ft^2 based on calcium carbonate, the use of $Ca(OH)_2$ (calcium hydroxide) with a higher neutralizing value (135%) would require 0.74 lb for every 1 lb of $CaCO_3$, or:

$$0.74 \times 50 \text{ lb } CaCO_3 = 37 \text{ lb } Ca(OH)_2.$$

Both hydroxide and oxide forms of lime are caustic to handle and can cause burn on turfgrasses if applied at too high a rate. Whenever these products are used, pelletized materials are best and residues should be immediately washed from leaf tissues. Applicators should avoid contact with eyes, skin, and clothes.

On highly acidic soils, total lime requirement may be over 100 lb per 1,000 ft^2 (4,900 kg ha^{-1}). All of the required lime can be applied at one time on a soil prior to turfgrass establishment and mixed to the desired depth. When a turfgrass is present, however, safe application rates per application are:

- $CaCO_3$ (fine) 25 to 50 lb per 1,000 ft^2, use <25 lb per 1,000 ft^2 on close-cut turf
- $Ca(OH)_2$ 5 to 10 lb per 1,000 ft^2
- CaO 2 to 5 lb per 1,000 ft^2

In all cases, irrigation should be applied to wash the materials off leaves. Applications can be repeated every few months to achieve the total LR.

Sometimes other materials are used as liming sources. Examples are:

- *Marl* or *bog lime* is a mined material from shallow deposits of soft calcium carbonates. These often contain organic matter or peat, seashells, and clays. Neutralizing value varies with purity but is often between 50 to 90%.
- Pulverized *sea and oyster shells* are very high in $CaCO_3$ but must be properly ground to an acceptable size.
- *Slags* are by-products of smelting operations and can have neutralizing values of 65 to 90. The Ca is usually derived from calcium silicate ($CaSiO_3$). When properly sized these can be acceptable liming materials and they often contain appreciable P and Fe.
- *Wood ash* is a mixture of carbonates/oxides/hydroxides of Ca, Mg, and K formed from burning of organic materials. Neutralizing value varies substantially from 5 to 50%.

For high quality turfs these sources are not normally recommended due to variability in chemical composition and particle size. They can be used as inexpensive liming sources if appropriately tested and the particle size is acceptable.

Physical Characteristics

In addition to chemical composition, particle size has a major influence on rate of neutralizing action. Since all liming materials are relatively insoluble compounds, finer particle size with high surface area increases dissolution rate in soils.

Limestone materials can be pulverized to an appropriate size. Fineness is measured by screening of lime particles where:

- No. 10 screen (sieve) has openings of 2.00 mm width
- No. 50 screen has openings of 0.30 mm width
- No. 60 screen has openings of 0.25 mm
- No. 100 screen has openings of 0.15 mm

For sites where a rapid pH change is desired, a good guideline is for all lime to pass a No. 50 screen and 70% through a No. 100. Where pH can change more gradually, limestone particles should all pass a No. 10 screen and 50% pass the No. 100. To illustrate particle size influence, it requires about 6 months to alter the pH of a silt loam soil from pH 4.5 to 7.0 with all limestone passing a No. 80 screen, but 18 months all passing a No. 50 screen.

State or governmental regulations exist concerning labeling of liming materials. For example, in Pennsylvania and other states in the northeastern region of the United States, the following rules and regulations are in effect:

1. Types
   Aglime materials must be labeled according to their type (i.e., limestone, hydrated lime, burnt lime, industrial by-products or marl and shells).

2. Elemental calcium and magnesium
   Aglime materials must be labeled as to the Total Calcium (Ca) and Total Magnesium (Mg) percentage by weight contained in the product. Oxide and carbonate guarantees may be stated following the elemental guarantee.

3. Fineness
   The label must state the classification (fine-sized, medium-sized, or coarse-sized materials) of the product and the minimum percentages by weight passing through the U.S. standard 20, 60, and 100 sieves. The classification must meet the minimum standards outlined by regulation (certain special limestone materials for lawn and garden have different quality standards). The following outlines the three groups based on fineness for agronomic liming materials:

   Fine-sized materials
   95% through a No. 20-mesh sieve
   60% through a No. 60-mesh sieve
   50% through a No. 100-mesh sieve

   Medium-sized materials
   90% through a No. 20-mesh sieve
   50% through a No. 60-mesh sieve
   30% through a No. 100-mesh sieve

   Coarse-sized materials
   All liming materials that fail to meet one of the above minimums for fineness.

4. CCE
   The label must state the minimum CCE (calcium carbonate equivalent) value of the aglime material.

5. Effective neutralizing value (ENV)
   The label must state the minimum ENV of the aglime material. [The ENV is a relative value that expresses soil acidity neutralizing capabilities of a liming material and is determined by using the calcium and magnesium oxide content and fineness. ENV is not utilized in Pennsylvania, but it is used by some other states of the region. The term is similar to "effective neutralizing power" (ENP)].

6. Moisture
   The label must state the maximum moisture content by weight of the material. A tolerance of 10% of the guarantee is set for moisture greater than what is stated on the label.

7. Dry-weight analysis
   The guarantees for elemental Ca and Mg, CCE, and ENV must appear on the label under the heading: "Guaranteed Dry Weight Analysis." If oxides and carbonates are guaranteed they should follow the elemental guarantee.

8. Tolerances
   A tolerance of 2% of the guarantee is allowed for the guaranteed minimum CCE value and minimum fineness value. All other guarantees are allowed a 10% tolerance range.

Finely ground limestone is sometimes pelletized for ease of application. The pellets quickly dissolve into individual, fine lime particles. Thus, *pelletized* lime reacts based on the size of the particles of lime within the pellets. For large turfgrass sites, bulk application of pulverized limestone is most economical. Aqueous suspensions of lime with water and attapulgite clay as a suspending agent can be used. These forms are called *fluid lime, aqua-lime,* or *liquid lime.* Particle sizes are usually able to go through a 100 mesh sieve and rates are only 1.0 to 2.5 lb $CaCO_3$ per 1,000 ft^2 (50 to 125 kg ha^{-1}). The kaolinitic conditioner may be objectionable on high sand soils where rapid drainage is a priority but not on other sites. Some producers add an organic chelating agent to aqueous mixtures to retain the Ca in a more active form instead of precipitating as a less soluble compound.

The term *"liquid lime"* is sometimes used to describe true solutions of $Ca(OH)_2$, CaO, or $CaCl_2$ (not a true "liming" material) dissolved in water. While $Ca(OH)_2$ and CaO are more soluble than $CaCO_3$, they still have relatively low solubility and only very minute quantities are present in solution. However, $CaCl_2$ has a high solubility but also a high foliar burn potential that limits quantities to 1 to 2 lb per 1,000 ft^2 (50 to 100 kg ha^{-1}). True liquid lime solutions have limited practical use in turfgrass culture as pH change agents.

E. Timing and Frequency of Application

Frequency of lime application depends on the presence of conditions promoting acidification such as rainfall, irrigation frequency, use of acidifying N sources, and low soil clay and organic matter contents. For most acid soils, liming may be required every 6 to 8 years, but can be as frequent as every 3 to 4 years on heavily leached sand sites or on excessively acid soils. A routine soil pH test every 2 to 3 years will aid in determining the correct frequency.

In climates where turfgrasses become dormant in winter months, late fall to early winter is a good time for lime application. Freezing and thawing will aid in working the lime into an established turf. Hydrated and oxide forms are best applied at this time if the turf is dormant and washed in by rain or irrigation. Lime can be applied at any time if recommended rates for established turfgrass are not exceeded, irrigation is used to remove leaf deposits, and stress periods are avoided. If an ammonia type N-carrier is being used, lime should not be applied until 10 to 14 days after fertilization or the fertilizer and lime could react to release toxic ammonia gas. Watering the N-carrier immediately into the turf will greatly reduce this potentially toxic reaction, which also results in much of the N being lost by volatilization.

F. Soil Reactions of Lime

Regardless of the chemical or physical form of lime used, the basic reactions in the soil are similar. Lime as $CaCO_3$ reacts as follows:

$$CaCO_3 + H_2O \rightarrow Ca^{+2} + HCO_3^- + OH^-$$

The Ca^{+2} ion can replace H^+ or Al^{+3} from CE sites, while the OH^- then reacts with H^+ to form H_2O or Al^{+3} to form Al $(OH)_3$ (gibbsite), an insoluble compound that precipitates (ppt) in the soil. These reactions can be represented by the following diagram:

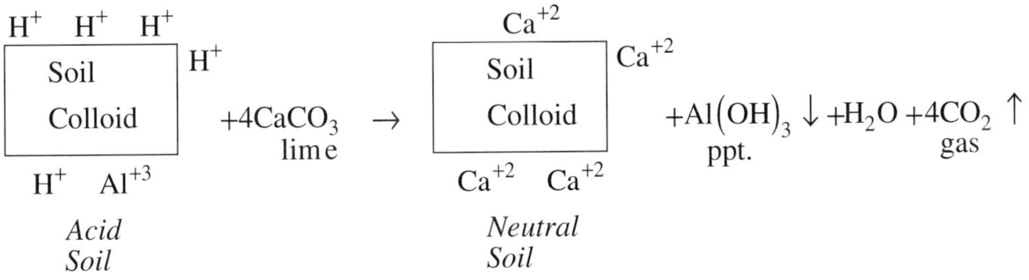

$$\underset{\textit{Acid Soil}}{\begin{array}{c} H^+ \; H^+ \; H^+ \\ \boxed{\text{Soil Colloid}} \; H^+ \\ H^+ \; Al^{+3} \end{array}} + \underset{\text{lime}}{4CaCO_3} \rightarrow \underset{\textit{Neutral Soil}}{\begin{array}{c} Ca^{+2} \\ \boxed{\text{Soil Colloid}} \; Ca^{+2} \\ Ca^{+2} \; Ca^{+2} \end{array}} + \underset{\text{ppt.}}{Al(OH)_3 \downarrow} + H_2O + \underset{\text{gas}}{4CO_2 \uparrow}$$

Over time the Ca^{+2} may be removed by leaching or crop use; thereby, lime would again be needed.

IV. MODERATE ACIDITY (pH >5.0) IN SURFACE AND/OR SUBSOIL HORIZONS

THE FOCUS OF THIS SECTION IS ON UPLAND SOILS with sufficiently acidic conditions in the surface horizon to demonstrate at least some of the problems associated with acid soils, but the surface and subsoil (B horizon) pH values are >5.0 and thus do not exhibit Al or Mn toxicities.

Within the tropics, 25% of the land area has been estimated to be constrained by surface soil acidity without Al or Mn toxicities (Sanchez and Logan[6]). Many subtropical, temperate-humid and cool-humid soils have excessive acidity in the surface, especially soils developed under forests.

The magnitude of problems associated with acid surface conditions depends on the degree of acidity and chemical composition of the soil. As pH becomes more acidic within the range of 5.0 to 6.5, problems most likely to occur are nutrient deficiencies (Mg, K, Ca, P), slower availability of N from soil N sources or N fertilizers, and reduced bacteria and actinomycete populations for organic matter/thatch decomposition. Turfgrasses grown on acid sandy soils are most likely to show nutrient deficiencies. As one or more of these problems are expressed, it often becomes economically beneficial to lime these sites.

For moderate acidity, lime requirement is often between 25 to 75 lb $CaCO_3$ per 1,000 ft^2 (1,200 to 3,700 kg ha^{-1}). If prior to establishment, all the lime can be applied and tilled into the soil to 4 to 8 inches (10 to 20 cm) depth. On an established turf, the guidelines in Section III.D can be followed for appropriate rates for a single application. Usually, one or two applications of lime applied over a season are sufficient to reach the total lime requirement.

Thus, correction of moderate acidity is achieved with lime application to the turfgrass surface, except for establishment when lime can be tilled into the soil. If acidic N sources or overapplication of S have contributed to acidity, turf managers should change to basic N sources and limit S applications. Also, fertilization to correct any pH-induced nutrient deficiencies would be necessary and should be based on soil test results. If thatch and/or soil organic matter have accumulated to levels that are detrimental, practices may be required to correct these problems. Subsoil lime treatment or selection of acid tolerant turfgrasses are usually not warranted for these moderately acid conditions.

V. EXCESSIVE ACIDITY (pH <5.0) IN SURFACE AND/OR SUBSOIL HORIZONS

In most humid cool temperate, subtropical, and tropical locations, high rainfall can leach base cations sufficiently to cause pH of <5.0. Additionally, the B horizon in many of these soils is not only at pH <5.0 but is also a zone of clay accumulation, especially nonexpanding clay types. Thus, the most prevalent turfgrass management problems demonstrated by these soils are: (a) Al and Mn toxicities to plant roots; (b) nutrient deficiencies of Mg, K, Ca, P, N, S, Mo, and B; (c) reduced populations of bacteria and actinomyctes that are important for organic matter/thatch decomposition; (d) earthworm activity is usually limited; and (e) the high clay content in the B horizon of many of these soils limits rooting due to high soil strength. All of these stresses combined are called the "acid soil complex" (Section II.B).

Approximately one-third of tropical soils (3.71 billion acres, 1.5 billion ha) are affected by sufficient soluble Al and/or Mn to be phytotoxic to most plant species. While the B horizons of many of these soils contain appreciable clay, the clays are predominately 1:1 (kaolinite) or Al/Fe hydrous oxides with substantial loss of pH dependent CEC at low pH. This contributes to very low basic cation (Ca^{+2}, Mg^{+2}, K^{+}) content in the subsoil, and Ca^{+2} deficiencies on landscape plants other than turfgrasses are common.

Surface and/or subsoil horizons with pH induced Al/Mn toxicities are less prevalent in humid, temperate climates than in subtropical or tropical areas. When Al/Mn toxicities occur in humid, temperate climates, 2:1 clay types usually dominate. These clays have CEC sites that are pH independent; thereby, CEC remains relatively constant, higher quantities of basic cations are present, and Ca^{+2} deficiency on landscape plants is not normally observed. Corrective practices for excessively acidic soils include one or more of the following (Foy;[4] Sumner[7]):

- alter the surface and subsoil pH with lime addition
- addition of gypsum materials
- addition of nutrients that are deficient
- change management practices contributing to acid conditions
- organic matter incorporation
- use of acid tolerant turfgrasses.

It is important to correct the subsoil problems as well as those of the surface horizon. Otherwise, turfgrass rooting will be limited to the surface zone and drought related problems will occur. Corrective measures are discussed in the following sections.

A. Lime Addition

Excessively acid soils will have high lime requirements. Mechanically mixing the required lime to a depth of 2 to 3 feet (0.6 to 0.9 m) will neutralize acidity in the surface and subsoil. This approach is effective but often impractical or not economically feasible. However, for new golf course construction and athletic sites, this approach should be seriously considered.

A potential problem with lime mixing is incorporation of clay from the B horizon into the A horizon, where the B horizon contains appreciably higher clay. This mixing could result in adverse soil physical properties at the surface. In this situation, lime can be mechanically mixed into the A horizon but injected into the B horizon. Various injection equipment has been developed for agronomic crops using: slit blades with lime suspensions applied in the slits; blowing lime into the soil behind a chisel plow; and injecting dry lime behind a chisel plow or slitter unit.

The Yeager-Twose Turf Conditioner is a cultivation unit developed for use on established turfgrasses. It has vibrating blades spaced about 6 inches (15 cm) apart and can penetrate to a depth of 7 to 8 inches (17 to 20 cm). A Top-Dresser attachment allows dry materials to be injected at the 7 to 8 inch depth. It can inject pelletized lime at 70 to 90 lb per 1,000 ft^2 (3,400 to 4,400 kg ha^{-1}) in one pass. Thus, this unit or any similar unit could be used to apply lime below the A horizon prior to turf establishment or under a sod.

For established turfgrasses, several surface applications of lime at 25 to 50 lb $CaCO_3$ per 1,000 ft^2 (1,200 to 2,400 kg ha^{-1}) are usually required to achieve the total lime requirement with 3 to 6 months between applications. Unfortunately, even after all lime is surface applied, it takes many years for lime to penetrate deeper into the profile. To alter the pH in the subsoil from surface applied lime requires the topsoil pH to achieve a pH of about 6.0 before HCO_3^- and OH^- ions are present as counter ions for Ca^{+2}. Calcium is much more mobile in the $Ca(OH)_2$ and $Ca(HCO_3)_2$ forms for movement into the B horizon than is Ca^{+2}.

Most rapid penetration occurs on sandy soils and Oxisols where the well aggregated Fe/Al hydrous oxides act like sands. On these soils, some lime may penetrate to 6 to 12 inches (15 to 30 cm) after 3 or 4 years but on finer textured soils movement to this depth may require 6 to 10 years. Thus, other methods beyond surface applied lime are normally used on excessively acidic soils, such as the Yeager-Twose Turf Conditioner mentioned above.

One important means to increase Ca^{+2} movement from surface lime applications into the subsoil is through the use of acidifying N fertilizers, such as NH_4NO_3 and $(NH_4)_2SO_4$. The basic reactions are:

$$NH_4NO_3 + 2O_2 \rightarrow 2HNO_3 + H_2O$$

$$CaCO_3 + 2HNO_3 \rightarrow Ca(NO_3)_2 + CO_2 + H_2O$$

Turfgrass roots take up more NO_3^- than Ca^{+2}. In the process of NO_3^- absorption, OH^- ions are exchanged from the roots to allow formation of $Ca(OH)_2$. Thus, the alkalinity (i.e., OH ions) formed in this process can neutralize H and Al in the subsoil. Mobility of $Ca(NO_3)_2$, formed by reaction of lime plus HNO_3, is much greater than $CaCO_3$.

Calcium nitrate applied to an acidic soil also neutralizes acidity in surface and subsoil horizons by the same mechanism. However, an acidic N carrier plus $CaCO_3$ neutralizes more rapidly because of the combined effects of $Ca(NO_3)_2$ formed from the N fertilizer plus $CaCO_3$ reacting as described in Section III.F.

When considering lime addition for amelioration of acidity in the surface and subsoil horizons of excessively acid soils, the following points should be considered:

- lime increases pH; converts toxic Al and Mn into less soluble and less toxic forms; adds Ca as a nutrient and Mg if dolomitic forms are used; and often increases availability of P, N, S, B, and Mo.
- mechanically mixing lime results in the most rapid pH increase to the depth of incorporation.

- when lime is applied to the soil surface or mixed only in the surface horizon, excessive acidity in the subsoil can still greatly limit rooting.
- when depending on movement of lime from the surface horizon into the subsoil for alleviation of subsoil acidity: (a) this works best on sandy soils and Oxisols (highly weathered tropical soils) where water can leach easily. On soils with low percolation, this process requires many years; (b) addition of an acidic N carrier will enhance movement of alkalinity; and (c) until the surface soil achieves a pH of about 6.0, little alkalinity in the form of OH^- or HCO_3^- will move into the subsoil to increase pH. To determine how liming treatments affect pH below the surface, soil samples can be collected from deeper depths, such as comparing 0 to 3, 3 to 6, 6 to 9, and 9 to 12 inches.

B. Gypsum and Phosphogypsum Addition

Since deep incorporation of lime is expensive and movement of surface applied lime is slow, the use of *gypsum* products for ameliorating acidic soils (surface and subsoil) has become increasingly popular (Sumner[7]). Gypsum materials are widely found in nature and can be mined. Examples are dehydrate, $CaSO_4 \bullet 2H_2O$; hemihydrate, $CaSO_4 \bullet 1/2\ H_2O$; and anhydrite, $CaSO_4$ forms. Also, several manufacturing processes create *phosphogypsum* (PG) or *flue gas desulfurization gypsum* (FGDG) as by-products. The presence of P and $CaFl_2$ in these materials is an additional benefit.

Gypsum, PG, and FGDG are much more soluble than limestone, and their use allows Ca to move more rapidly into the subsoil. Smaller particle size favors more rapid dissolution and gypsum by-products are often more soluble than mined materials.

While gypsum materials can move more rapidly than limestone through soil to amend the subsoil, the process will be increased by incorporation into the surface horizon and/or by deep injection. On established turfgrass, the Yeager-Twose Turf Conditioner with top-dresser attachment can apply 70 to 90 lb per 1,000 ft^2 (3,400 to 4,400 kg ha^{-1}) of pelletized gypsum to a depth of 7 to 8 inches (18 to 20 cm). For surface broadcast rates of gypsum materials over an established turfgrass, single applications are usually at 40 to 80 lb per 1,000 ft^2 (1,950 to 3,900 kg ha^{-1}). Applications can be repeated every 3 to 6 months. For an estimation of the total gypsum (or PG, FGDG) to apply:

- take the *lime* requirement for the surface 8 inch plow layer (20 cm) and multiply by 1.46. For example, if the lime requirement for the 8 inch plow layer was 200 lb $CaCO_3$ per 1,000 ft^2 (9,760 kg ha^{-1}), then the gypsum rate would be $1.46 \times 200 = 292$ lb per 1,000 ft^2. The basis for this is on the Ca content where $CaCO_3$ contains about 38% Ca while gypsum, PG, and FGSG contain 24 to 28% Ca.
- then adjust the gypsum rate based on soil depth to be amended. If a 16 inch total depth (41 cm) is to be amended, then twice the gypsum rate for an 8 inch depth would be needed.

When gypsum materials are incorporated into the surface horizon by mixing, the total quantity of material can be applied with the total determined as in the previous paragraphs. Excessively acid sands usually require 20 to 90 lb total gypsum per 1,000 ft^2; however, heavier soils may require 50 to 400 lb (2,440 to 19,500 kg ha^{-1}), depending on the soil type and depth of amelioration.

Since excessively acid soils require high lime or gypsum rates, the high Ca additions may induce Mg or K deficiencies. Use of dolomitic lime adds Mg but when gypsum materials are used, Mg and K fertilization may need to be increased and carefully monitored by soil testing. A nutritional benefit of PG or FGDG versus gypsum is their P content, a nutrient often deficient in excessively acid soils. Sometimes ordinary superphosphate (contains 50% gypsum) is incorporated with lime or gypsum to add P while also being high in Ca^{+2}.

When *gypsum* materials are added to excessively acid soils, the following *mechanisms* have been suggested for improving chemical conditions:

- "self-liming" effect where SO_4^{-2} exchanges for OH^- units on surfaces of Fe/Al hydrous oxides, allophane and 1:1 clays. This is followed by precipitation of exchangeable Al as follows:

$$\begin{matrix}\text{Fe, Al} \\ \text{Fe, Al}\end{matrix}\!\!>\!OH + Ca^{+2} + SO_4^{-2} \rightarrow$$

$$\begin{matrix}\text{Fe, Al} \\ \text{Fe, Al}\end{matrix}\!\!>\!SO_4^{-} + Ca(OH)_2 \rightarrow$$

Then,

$$\underset{\text{from CE sites}}{2Al^{+3}} + 3Ca(OH)_2 \rightarrow \underset{\text{precipitates, insoluble}}{2Al(OH)_3} + \underset{\text{goes onto CE sites}}{3Ca^{+2}}$$

- greater absorption of Al^{+3} from the soil solution due to increased negative charges on clay surfaces when SO_4^{-2} replaces OH^-
- precipitation of insoluble Al sulfates
- in the soil solution the ion pair $AlSO_4^+$ forms and remains in solution but is less toxic to plant roots than Al^{+3}. This mechanism probably operates only when SO_4^{-2} remains high in soil solution.

The net effect of these reactions to gypsum application is to: (a) decrease exchangeable Al^{+3}, an ion toxic to roots; (b) increase exchangeable Ca^{+2}; (c) enhance downward movement of Ca^{+2} because of the greater solubility of gypsum than limestone and presence of SO_4^{-2} as a counter ion; and (d) soil pH is not altered to a great extent with a small increase in some soils and a decrease in others. Initially, it would appear that $Ca(OH)_2$ in the "self-liming" mechanism should increase pH, but the OH^- are from clay surfaces and not as net additions. However, if pH is determined in $CaCl_2$ solution to minimize salt effects, pH_{ca} often increases 0.5 to 1.0 unit.

Since pH (as measured in H_2O) does not appreciably change after addition of gypsum materials, then CEC does not increase even if there are pH dependent charges. Also, improvements do not occur in nutrient availability (except Ca) or for enhancement of most microbial populations, as happens with liming where pH does increase.

C. Other Amendments

Incorporation of large quantities of organic matter (manures, chicken litter, sewage sludge, etc.) into the surface horizon of excessively acid soils aids in reducing toxic Al. This can be done with or without lime but better results would be expected with lime. Organic matter rates vary from 1,000 to 3,000 lb per 1,000 ft^2 (50,000 to 150,000 kg ha^{-1}) when applied before turf establishment. Apparently, soluble organic ligands leach into the subsoil and decrease exchangeable Al. Additional nutrients in the organic matter such as Ca, Mg, and K may also be beneficial.

Surface application or deep injection of deficient nutrients can improve crop response of excessively acid soils. This is often beneficial even if lime or gypsum has been used. Nutrients most likely to be deficient are Mg, K, P, and Ca.

D. Alter Practices Contributing to Acidity

Excessively acid soils are almost always the result of leaching of base cations due to high rainfall. However, some cultural practices may contribute to acidity. Acid forming N-carriers should not be used unless lime has been applied, in which case they actually enhance lime activity. Once pH has been adjusted to a desired range, acid N-carriers will cause pH to decrease if lime is not present. Basic N-carriers can add base cations and help maintain a higher pH.

Sometimes when turf managers are on a pH reduction program using S, a zone of excessively acid soil of 0.5 to 2.0 inches may form at the surface and cause root or crown injury. In this situation a light application of lime will correct the problem. Growers on an S program for pH reduction should monitor surface pH in separate soil samples from the routine testing depth of 3 to 4 inches, using the 0 to 1 inch (0 to 2.5 cm) zone for monitoring.

E. Use of Acid Tolerant Plants

The use of acid tolerant species and cultivars should be seriously considered on excessively acid soils (Delhaize and Ryan;[2] Foy[4]) (see II.F). This would include turfgrasses and other landscape plants. Turfgrass breeding/genetics efforts are being directed toward identifying and developing turfgrasses tolerant to acidity. In the Southeast (U.S.) Piedmont Region, this problem is common and approximately 30 to 40% of *Zoysia* spp. cultivars are acid intolerant; 10 to 20% of seeded *Cynodon* cultivars; 5 to 10% hybrid, vegetative *Cynodon* cultivars, and 30 to 40% of *Paspalum vaginatum* genotypes are intolerant. Due to severe root inhibition, intolerant grasses have poor drought resistance. Species most tolerant to excessive acidity are listed in Table 5.3; however, cultivar tolerance differences can be great within a species.

Establishing acid tolerant plants should not be the only practice on excessively acid soils. These plants may be able to tolerate higher Al or Mn levels but nutrient deficiencies can still inhibit growth. Thus, practices to reduce toxic ions and to increase surface and subsoil levels of deficient nutrients should be part of a long-range plan.

VI. EXTREME ACIDITY (pH 1.5 TO 3.5) OF ACID SULFATE SOILS

IN COASTAL PLAINS AND TIDAL SWAMPS, *pyrite* (FeS_2) can accumulate under waterlogged conditions where easily decomposed organic matter and a supply of sulfates are present (Dent[3]). As bacteria decompose the organic matter, sulfate ions are reduced to sulfides and iron transformed to the reduced state (Fe^{+2}), leading to FeS_2 formation. These sites are classified as acid sulfate soils and are estimated to cover 30 to 35 million acres (12 to 14 million ha) primarily in the tropics. Mine spoil soils can also be extremely acid due to the presence of FeS_2.

When acid sulfate soils are drained for development they become extremely acid as pyrite oxidizes to generate sulfuric acid. With pH at 1.5 to 3.5, Al toxicity is the primary chemical problem, but others include nutrient deficiencies (P, Ca, Mg, K) and salinity. Three general types of acid sulfate soils are:

- ripe acid sulfate soil where after drainage there is an irreversible loss of water and the soil becomes firm. Weathering and leaching has occurred to more than 3 feet (1 m).
- raw acid sulfate soil containing pyrite at shallow depths.
- unripe sulfidic soil that is still waterlogged.

Dent[3] provides an excellent discussion of further classifications of acid sulfate soils and reclamation strategies. Important factors to consider before reclamation are: quantity of pyrite present; location of pyrite in the soil profile; potential for leaching Al^{+3} from the profile; and potential for control of the water table. Some ripe acid sulfate soils that have been exposed to considerable weathering and leaching may be reclaimed using as little as 150 lb $CaCO_3$ per 1,000 ft^2 (7,300 kg ha^{-1}) while others may require many years of weathering and much higher lime.

Other factors to consider are: the influence of soil mixing and contouring of the landscape on movement of pyrite during reclamation; location of the water table; leaching ability (drainage capability); environmental fate of leachates; and nonuniformity of pyrite within the soil. Organic matter addition can help reduce soluble Al but should not be added until later in reclamation if it hinders initial leaching of Al. Conversion of these soils to an upland soil suitable to turfgrass growth can be very expensive. An economic evaluation based on sound understanding and knowledge of the factors influencing reclamation is a necessity before attempting drainage and earthmoving.

VI. ACIDIC THATCH (pH <5.5)

ACIDIC THATCH IS TECHNICALLY NOT A SOIL PROBLEM but is a turfgrass management problem. Thatch pH may not be the same as pH of the underlying soil. Factors that influence thatch pH are: magnitude of rainfall; pH and composition of irrigation (including effluent) water; and the type of fertilizers (i.e., acidic vs. basic N carriers); and recent lime or S applications. Most often acidic thatch with pH less than 5.5 occurs in regions of high rainfall that leaches bases from the thatch layer and with use of acidifying N-carriers.

The primary problem associated with acidic thatch is low microbial populations of bacteria and actinomycetes within the thatch. These organisms are important for breakdown of more resistant forms of organic matter. Thus, at low pH, thatch may accumulate due to low populations of these microorganisms.

A representative sample of the thatch layer can be submitted to a soil test lab for pH determination. The grower should note that the sample is thatch, high in organic matter, and pH should be determined using all the material (i.e., instruct the lab not to discard the organic fraction).

A light application of lime at 2 to 5 lb $CaCO_3$ per 1,000 ft^2 (98 to 245 kg ha^{-1}) is sufficient to increase thatch pH. Sometimes a rapid increase in thatch pH is desired to discourage algae or to inhibit disease activity of an unknown pathogen. For these purposes, 2 to 5 lb $Ca(OH)_2$ per 1,000 ft^2 will produce more rapid pH change. Normally, the $Ca(OH)_2$ is mixed with dry sand or applied through a sprayer as a suspension, followed by irrigation to remove $Ca(OH)_2$ from leaf tissues.

VIII. REFERENCES

1. Brady, N.C. 1990. Soil reaction: acidity and alkalinity. In *The Nature and Properties of Soils.* Chapter 8. New York: Macmillan Pub. Co.
2. Delhaize, E. and P.R. Ryan. 1995. Aluminum toxicity and tolerance in plants. *Plant Physiol.* 107:315–321.
3. Dent, D. 1992. Reclamation of acid sulphate soils. In R. Lal and B.A. Stewart, Eds. *Advances in Soil Science,* 17:79–122. New York: Springer-Verlag.
4. Foy, C.D. 1992. Soil chemical factors limiting plant root growth. In R. Lal and B.A. Stewart, Eds. *Advances in Soil Science,* 19:97–148. New York: Springer-Verlag.
5. Lierop, W. Van. 1990. Soil pH and lime requirement determination. In R.L. Westerman, Ed. *Soil Testing and Plant Analysis.* Chapter 5. Madison, WI: Soil Sci. Soc. of Amer., Inc.
6. Sanchez, P.A. and T.J. Logan. 1992. Myths and science about the chemistry and fertility of soils in the tropics. In R. Lal and P.A. Sanchez, Ed. *Myths and Science of Soils of the Tropics.* Chapter 3. Madison, WI: Soil Sci. Soc. Amer. Pub. 29, SSSA.
7. Sumner, M.E. 1995. Amelioration of subsoil acidity with minimum disturbance. In N.S. Jayawardane and B.A. Stewart, Eds. *Subsoil Management Techniques.* Boca Raton, FL: Lewis Publishers/CRC Press, Inc.
8. Truog, E. 1947. The liming of soils. pp 566–576. In Science in Farming. Yearbook Agr. 1943–1947. USDA. U.S. Gov. Print. Office, Washington, DC.

Chapter 6

Alkaline Soil pH Problems

IN CHAPTER 5, SOIL PH CONCEPTS AND ACIDITY PROBLEMS, certain pH related topics were discussed; namely, the concept of acidity and alkalinity; importance of pH on turfgrass culture, especially acid pH; and corrective measures for acidic soils. In this chapter, alkaline soils are the focus, where an *alkaline soil* is any soil with pH >7.0. One special class of soils that are often alkaline are salt-affected soils (saline, sodic, and saline/sodic). These soils, their problems and corrective measures, are the focus of Chapters 7 and 8; however, all other alkaline soil pH situations will be presented in the current chapter.

I. UNDERSTANDING ALKALINE SOILS

A. Formation

IN ARID AND SEMIARID REGIONS, base cations accumulate due to lack of leaching. This results in alkaline pH (typically between pH 7.3 and 8.5) as Ca^{+2}, Mg^{+2}, Na^{+}, and K^{+} dominate the exchange sites, while H^{+} ions are few and Al^{+3} and aluminum hydroxy ions are absent.

Alkaline soils can also result during soil formation from calcium carbonate parent material. These soils contain free calcium carbonate accumulation somewhere within the soil profile. If some calcium carbonate is retained in the surface horizon, then surface pH will be alkaline. Alkaline soils arising from this process can occur in humid as well as arid or semiarid locations.

Another example of alkaline soil formation is sands formed from coral. Such calcareous sands can be found in many humid as well as arid regions. Calcareous sands can also occur by mixing of seashell fragments into a quartz sand. Or, if a quartz sand or any soil is irrigated with water high in Ca^{+2}, Mg^{+2}, and HCO_3^- from a limestone aquifer, calcium and magnesium carbonates may precipitate and increase pH.

At pH 8.2 calcium carbonate can precipitate out of soil solution and a pH of 8.2 to 8.3 is a good indication that $CaCO_3$ is present. However, free $CaCO_3$ may be present in soils having a pH less than 8.2 averaged over the root zone depth or another depth of sampling. The specific localized soil zone containing $CaCO_3$, from solid applications or precipitation of dissolved material, can have a pH of 8.2, while the average pH over a soil sample depth may be less. An example of precipitation is caliche formation in the surface (1 inch, 2.5 cm) zone by calcium and magnesium carbonate deposition from irrigation water. Overliming is another potential cause of alkaline pH that could occur in a humid climate where acid soils are the norm. In well-mixed root zone mixes or recently cultivated soils, free $CaCO_3$ could be present but in small enough quantities that the pH could be <8.2.

B. Problems of Alkaline Soils

Fewer problems are associated with alkaline soils than excessively acid soils. The following turfgrass management problems are sometimes observed on alkaline soils (Christians;[2] Harivandi[3]): (a) P deficiency is common in alkaline soils, especially if Ca compounds, such as free $CaCO_3$ or $CaSO_4$ (gypsum), are abundant. Calcium reacts with P to form various calcium phosphates; (b) Fe and Mn deficiencies are often observed in alkaline soils, particularly on sandy soils. As pH increases, these ions are changed to their oxidized states and can form insoluble oxide and hydroxide compounds. Iron chlorosis on turfgrass grown on alkaline soils is perhaps the most common nutrition problem; (c) Zn deficiency can be a potential problem but is much less common than Fe or Mn deficiencies in alkaline soils. Application of high P to an alkaline soil can induce Zn or Fe deficiencies; (d) B deficiency is also possible as pH increases between pH 7.0 to 9.0. Boron is apparently bound or fixed in soil colloids at high pH; (e) Mo toxicity is a potential problem but very rare on turfgrasses at high pH; (f) calcite deposition at the surface, especially on sands, can potentially limit water infiltration.[1] However, this would occur only in arid regions; with irrigation water very high in carbonates and Ca/Mg; and over a prolonged time period; and (g) some pesticides are less effective at alkaline pH.

An alkaline soil may exhibit some of the nutritional problems noted above. However, many alkaline soils do not demonstrate any of these problems, due to inherently higher nutrient levels. Salt-affected alkaline soils exhibit certain soil chemical and physical problems in addition to the above nutritional stresses, but these will be presented in Chapters 7 and 8.

C. Classification

As noted before, any soil with pH > 7.0 is an alkaline soil. However, some alkaline soils are grouped into one of several categories based on chemical attributes other than pH (Nettleton[5]). Common problems encountered in alkaline soils, which were outlined in the previous section, can occur in any of the following soils. But some of the categories have unique management problems.

- *Alkaline soil without free $CaCO_3$* present in the surface horizon. Such a soil would not be buffered against chemical change by the presence of free $CaCO_3$.
- *Calcareous soil.* Contains sufficient free $CaCO_3$ and/or $MgCO_3$ to visibly effervesce when treated with 0.1 M HCl. These soils usually contain between 1 to almost 100% $CaCO_3$ equivalent. The $CaCO_3$ may arise naturally, be deposited from irrigation water, or arise from seashells mixed in the soil. This category includes calcareous sands formed by various means. Calcareous soils are most likely to exhibit the various nutritional problems, especially P and Fe deficiencies. These soils are very common soils in arid climates but can be found in any climatic zone.
- *Caliche* is a calcareous soil containing a zone near or at the soil surface of weakly to strongly cemented $CaCO_3$ and/or $MgCO_3$ precipitated from soil solution, usually as a result of irrigation water high in these carbonates. A newly formed caliche soil normally contains a low percentage of $CaCO_3$, while a strongly cemented layer denotes higher $CaCO_3$ and/or $MgCO_3$ content. If total carbonate content is low, many of the nutritional problems of more developed calcareous soils may be absent. The major problem arises from cementation impeding water infiltration and percolation. Sometimes black layer results from caliche formation deeper in the root zone.

- *Calcic soil* is a calcareous soil with a soil horizon of >6 inches (15 cm) containing >15% $CaCO_3$ equivalent and with at least 5% more $CaCO_3$ equivalent than the C horizon. Thus, calcic soils are calcareous soils with high $CaCO_3$ content and are likely to exhibit similar nutritional problems. The calcic horizon is normally very apparent.
- *Gypsic soil.* A soil with a gypsic horizon of >6 inches (15 cm) enriched in $CaSO_4$ to at least 5% more than the C horizon. Also, the product of the gypsic horizon thickness (in centimeters) times the $CaSO_4$ content (in g kg^{-1}) must exceed 1,500 g kg^{-1}. If cementation is strong, water percolation may be inhibited. As these soils are irrigated, high Ca and SO_4 salts can increase osmotic potential of the soil solution and restrict plant water uptake. Also, excessive Ca may cause deficiencies of Mg, K, Mn, Zn, and/or Cu. Water features may lead to potholes or dissolution areas as some of the $CaSO_4$ dissolves.

The remaining important categories of alkaline soils are listed but discussion of their problems and corrective measures is in Chapters 7 and 8.

- *Saline soil.* A soil with pH ≤8.5 and high total salts in relatively soluble form which adversely affect water uptake by many plants.
- *Sodic soil.* A soil often with pH >8.5 and high in exchangeable Na^+ percentage (15% or more of the CEC) that adversely affects soil structure and may be directly toxic to some plant roots.
- *Saline/sodic soil* has a pH <8.5, high total soluble salts, and a high exchangeable Na^+ content (15% or more of the CEC).

D. Should Alkaline pH Be Adjusted?

Nutritional stresses (deficiencies and imbalances) in alkaline soils (except for salt-affected classes) are less common compared to acid soils. Additionally, element toxicities in alkaline soils that limit rooting are very rare, in contrast to Al and Mn toxicities of excessively acid conditions. Alkalinity has much less impact on microbial populations, earthworms, thatch development, and plant community composition than acidity.

When a turfgrass manager has an excessively acid soil, there are sound agronomic reasons to alter (increase) pH by liming or use of other corrective alternatives. Whether to reduce pH in an alkaline soil, however, is not as clear, because: (a) many times nutritional problems associated with alkaline pH are not present; (b) even when nutritional problems are evident, the most economic approach may be adjustments in fertilization rather than pH reduction; and (c) the presence of even a small quantity of free $CaCO_3$ throughout the soil profile may make pH reduction impractical or not economically feasible.

However, in the case of caliche starting to form at the surface from $CaCO_3$ deposition, pH reduction to dissolve the caliche could be considered. Routine cultivation practices also aid in disrupting this physical barrier to water movement. As caliche accumulates, water infiltration and percolation can decline and nutritional problems are likely to appear. These responses are most obvious on sands in arid regions receiving frequent, year-around irrigation with water high in Ca^{+2}, Mg^{+2}, and HCO_3^- (Carrow et al.[1]). Even when caliche has already formed and these problems have appeared, pH reduction to eliminate the caliche over time may be beneficial along with cultivation. A thorough evaluation of pH, presence of free $CaCO_3$, and location of $CaCO_3$ within the soil profile will aid in determining whether pH reduction is feasible. Testing soil from various depths will be needed to determine where problems exist within the profile.

E. Assessing Alkaline Soils

Soil Reaction (pH)

Soil pH determined in a soil:water mixture is the sole chemical property used to identify a soil as alkaline with a pH >7.0 classified as alkaline. Measurement of pH is covered in Chapter 5.

Free $CaCO_3$ Content

A second important chemical property is the presence or absence of free $CaCO_3$. A soil with free $CaCO_3$ is termed calcareous and will exhibit greater buffer capacity against pH change such as with S addition.

The most accurate procedure for determining $CaCO_3$ is by titrating with an acid until the lime is dissolved. A laboratory can then calculate the quantity of free $CaCO_3$ present by weight loss or amount of acid required to neutralize the lime.

It requires 32 lb of S to neutralize 100 lb of $CaCO_3$. For a soil with 1% $CaCO_3$ in the surface 3 inches (7.6 cm):

- 3 inch zone of soil weighs about 1,000,000 lb per acre (1,120,00 kg ha^{-1}).
- 1% by weight of $CaCO_3$ is (0.01 × 1,000,000) = 10,000 lb $CaCO_3$ per acre = 230 lb $CaCO_3$ per 1,000 ft^2.
- to dissolve 230 lb $CaCO_3$ would require application of 74 lb S per 1,000 ft^2 (3610 kg S ha^{-1}).

Thus, a soil with even 2 or 3% $CaCO_3$ would require very high S application rates. On an established turf, elemental S is seldom applied at over 5 lb per 1,000 ft^2 twice per year (244 kg S ha^{-1}). In the example, it would require over seven years to apply sufficient S to neutralize 1% by weight of $CaCO_3$.

Reactions of S in the soil in the absence and presence of $CaCO_3$ are provided later in Section II.A. But it will suffice here to note that pH is not decreased on a permanent basis until all free $CaCO_3$ is dissolved. Or, to state it differently, pH reduction should not be attempted on an alkaline soil containing free $CaCO_3$. Possible exceptions are:

- Where $CaCO_3$ is localized in the surface 1 inch (2.5 cm) due to caliche deposition from irrigation water. The weakly to strongly cemented zone of caliche may be weakened or dissolved with S or other acidic compounds.
- Where a soil contains 1 or 2% by weight of $CaCO_3$ and a long-term S program is acceptable on established turf.
- In the case of a soil containing less than 2 to 3% $CaCO_3$ and sufficient S to neutralize, the $CaCO_3$ can be applied and tilled into the soil before turfgrass establishment.
- When the principal source of free $CaCO_3$ is from irrigation water and this can be offset by annual S addition or other alternative treatments. Sometimes when irrigation is initiated on a site, surface pH gradually starts to increase by alkaline irrigation water and $CaCO_3$ formation.

Adding an acid and observing whether effervescence occurs can be misleading for the example of $CaCO_3$ accumulation at the surface from irrigation water. Adding acid to a caliche soil at the surface may make it appear that considerable $CaCO_3$ is present when it is limited to a thin

Table 6.1. Approximate quantities of elemental S (99% purity) per 1,000 ft^2 to lower soil pH to 6.5 in the top six inches (15 cm) of soil.

Measured pH	Soil Texture		
	Sand to Loamy Sand	Loam	Clay or Organic Soil
	lb S per 1,000 ft^2		
8.5	30–50[a]	50–60	60–70
8.0	15–25	25–35	35–50
7.5	10–15	15–20	20–25
7.0	2–5	3–6	5–10

[a] 50 lb S per 1,000 ft^2 = 2,440 kg S ha^{-1}.

zone. Thus, evaluation for presence of $CaCO_3$ should involve location within the soil and percent content by zone (depth).

Sulfur Requirement

Total S requirement to reduce pH depends on initial soil pH, CEC of the soil, and quantity of $CaCO_3$ present. Assuming that no $CaCO_3$ is present, Table 6.1 lists approximate S needs. Since there isn't a specific soil test for determining S requirement, the quantity is estimated based on pH and soil texture, where texture is an indicator of CEC (Christians[2]; Harivandi[3]). The total quantity of S could be incorporated into the top 6 inches (15 cm) prior to establishment; but on a mature turf much less can be applied (see application guidelines later in this chapter).

When $CaCO_3$ is present, S requirement should be increased 130 lb per 1,000 ft^2 for every 1% $CaCO_3$ content across the 6 inches (15 cm). If 1 or 2% $CaCO_3$ is present in just the surface 2 inches (5 cm), such as a newly formed caliche layer, then S requirement should be reduced accordingly. In the case of 1% $CaCO_3$ in the surface 2 inches, 2/6 of 130 lb S would be 43 lb S per 1,000 ft^2. This example illustrates how S requirement to reduce pH multiplies rapidly with increasing $CaCO_3$ content.

Rates in Table 6.1 are for elemental S of 99% purity. These would need to be adjusted if less pure S or another acidifying material is used (Table 6.2). Approximate rate adjustments can be based on the pounds of material equivalent in acidifying potential to one pound elemental S (99% purity). Equivalent amounts of selected acidifying materials are shown in Table 6.3. Also, adjustments should be made if pH reduction is desired for less than the full 6 inch profile or to another target pH than pH 6.5.

II. AMENDMENTS AND APPROACHES TO pH REDUCTION

Various chemicals and application approaches have been used to reduce soil pH (Lubin;[4] Tisdale et al.[6]). Factors that influence choice of a chemical or application technique are:

- Cost of the product and application equipment. Depending on the product, application may be granular, suspension, or liquid.
- Bare soil or established turfgrass. Prior to turfgrass establishment, high rates of acidifying materials can be used. Where elemental S is used reduction in pH will be

Table 6.2. Chemicals used to acidify soils.

Material	Chemical Formula	Physical Form[c]
Aluminum sulfate	$Al_2(SO_4)_3 \cdot 18H_2O$	Granular
Ammonium polysulfide	NH_4S_x	Solution
Ammonium sulfate[a]	$(NH_4)_2SO_4$	Granular or solution
Ammonium thiosulfate	$(NH_4)_2S_2O_3+H_2O$	Solution
Ferrous sulfate	$FeSO_4 \cdot 7H_2O$	Solution
Lime sulfur (dry)[b]	CaS_x	Granular
Lime sulfur (solution)[b]	$CaS_5+Ca_2SO_4A5H_2O$	Solution
Phosphoric acid	H_3PO_4	Solution
Sulfur, elemental	S	Granular
Sulfur dioxide	SO_2	Gas→Solution
Sulfuric acid (100%)	H_2SO_4	Solution
Sulfuric acid (93%)	H_2SO_4	Solution
Sulfur-Bentonite	S+bentonite	Granular
Sulfur-Slurry	$S+H_2O$	Suspension
Urea-Sulfuric acid	$CO(NH_2)_2+H_2SO_4$	Solution

[a] Ammonium sulfate is a common granular N-fertilizer. It can also be formed by addition of NH_3 and sulfuric acid to irrigation water.
[b] Calcium polysulfide.
[c] Physical form normally used for soil acidification.

Table 6.3. Quantities of selected acidifying materials equivalent in acidifying potential to one pound (or 1 kg) of elemental S.

Material	Chemical Formula	lb (or kg) equivalent to 1 lb (or kg) S
Aluminum sulfate	$Al_2(SO_4)_3 \cdot 18H_2O$	6.9
Ammonium sulfate	$(NH_4)_2SO_4$	2.8
Ferrous sulfate	$FeSO_4 \cdot 7H_2O$	8.7
Lime sulfur solution (24% S)	$CaS_5+CaSO_4 \cdot 5H_2O$	4.2
Sulfur	S	1.0
Sulfuric acid (100% H_2SO_4)	H_2SO_4	3.0

slower than with materials such as sulfuric acid (immediate effect) or iron sulfate (hydrolys reaction), because time is needed for the microbial conversion of S to sulfuric acid. It may take several weeks or longer in cool conditions to notice the acidifying effect from S. Grasses could be seeded prior to the conversion. After turfgrass establishment or on a mature turfgrass, acidifying chemicals must be applied at low rates as granulars or as liquids/suspensions through sprayers or the irrigation system. Some chemicals may have too high a burn potential to use after turf is present. New materials to be applied to established turf should be evaluated on a small test area to assess burn potential before applying to large areas.

- Bicarbonates or carbonates in irrigation water. When bicarbonates (HCO_3^-) or carbonates (CO_3^{-2}) in irrigation water contribute to caliche buildup and pH increases, application of acidifying liquids/suspensions through the irrigation system can be used as corrective and/or preventative measures. However, since the caliche accumulation is primarily a physical problem (decreases infiltration) on high sand soils (i.e., greens), it may not be economical to acidify irrigation water over a whole golf course. Instead, elemental S or alternative approaches including application of acidic fertilizers, and cultivation of the greens may be better practices.

As each acidifying chemical is discussed, appropriate application techniques will be addressed. Chemicals used for pH reduction are listed in Table 6.2.

A. Elemental S-Based Sources

Formulations

Elemental S is the material most often applied for pH reduction due to its cost and effectiveness. Usually a high purity (85 to 99% S) formulation is used on turfgrasses, especially greens, to avoid impurities such as clay. Finely ground particles (passing at least a No. 80 sieve or 0.178 mm, but passing a No. 100 sieve of 0.150 mm width mesh is preferred) provide the fastest chemical reactions but are difficult to apply. Formulations are available where the fine particles are *pelletized* into water dispersible granules, or porous granules of S (termed *popcorn sulfur*), which are formed from molten S and water.

Sulfur and bentonite (90% S, 10% bentonite) have been blended. The bentonite imbibes moisture and speeds the conversion of S to SO_4^{-2}. Bentonite addition may be undesirable to sandy soils where high infiltration is desirable. Another formulation is *S-slurry* (S-suspension) where finely ground S is suspended in water along with 2 to 3% attapulgite clay. S-slurry can be directly applied to bare soil or be used as a suspension product on established turfgrasses.

Agricultural grade S is a mixture of particle sizes and is cheaper than finer grades. When elemental S is applied to a soil and mixed throughout the profile, this grade would be acceptable. For application to an established turfgrass, fine particle sizes or water dispersible pellets are preferred.

Application Guidelines

In Section I.E, determination of the total elemental S requirement to reduce soil pH and dissolve free $CaCO_3$ was discussed. During construction of a turfgrass site, the total S could be tilled into the depth desired for pH reduction. This procedure is the best option for rapid correction of pH. Formulations most likely to be applied would be agricultural grade S, finer grades of elemental S, S-bentonite, or S-slurry.

On established turfgrasses, relatively low *rates of elemental S* can be applied per application and on an annual basis. For golf greens the normal recommendation is 0.50 to 1.0 lb S per 1,000 ft^2 (24 to 48 kg S ha^{-1}) applied at three to four week intervals. Sulfur should not be applied during stress periods, such as the summer months, on bentgrass (*Agrostis* spp.) greens. Total annual S should be 10 lb S per 1,000 ft^2 (488 kg S ha^{-1}) or less on greens. Lower rates are recommended for high sand greens mixes with little or no $CaCO_3$ present. Sulfur should be immediately watered to remove residues from the foliage.

For higher mowed turfgrass sites, 2 to 5 lb elemental S per 1,000 ft^2 (98 to 244 kg S ha^{-1}) can be applied per application for an annual total of 10 lb S per 1,000 ft^2. As with golf greens, application should be avoided during stress periods. Irrigation to wash S from leaf tissues should be done immediately after treatment.

The main factor that limits the quantity of elemental S to be applied at a single date and over a season is the potential for excessive acidity developing in the surface 0.5 to 1.0 inch (12.5 to 25 mm) where the turfgrass crown is located. Several weeks are required for elemental S to be converted to H_2SO_4 (sulfuric acid). This process is normally gradual and irrigation or precipitation moves the H_2SO_4 deeper into the profile. However, a high rate of S can cause too much S conversion to H_2SO_4 at one time, resulting in excessive acidity in the surface 0.5 to 1.0 inch layer. Soil pH and/or thatch may decrease to within the pH 2.5 to 4.8 range where Al, Mn, and H toxicities develop and directly injure the lower crown and roots. Since this occurs well after application it is an insidious injury.

Any turfgrass managers attempting pH reduction or caliche removal with S should have a routine *pH monitoring program.* Two sets of soil samples are necessary. One set is sampling the surface 0 to 1.0 inch (0 to 25 mm) depth after discarding thatch; however, if the grass crowns are in the thatch, then it should be included as part of the 0 to 1.0 inch sample. If the thatch is 1 inch (2.54 cm) or more in depth, it may be sampled separately. A mat (thatch plus considerable soil or sand intermixed in the thatch) is considered as soil and should not be discarded. Soil pH should be monitored every three to six months, especially within the first two to three years of a program. Surface pH should not decline below 5.0.

The second pH sample is to the depth of routine soil test sampling; normally 0 to 3 or 0 to 4 inches (0 to 10 cm). Soil pH values will be an average pH across the depth of sampling and indicates the progress made toward bulk soil pH reduction. A sharp decrease in surface zone pH can easily be masked by pH averaged over a 0 to 4 inch sample. For example, overall pH may decrease from 8.1 to 7.8 but surface pH from 8.1 to 4.2.

If surface pH monitoring reveals an excessively acid pH, a light lime application of 2 to 4 lb $CaCO_3$ per 1,000 ft^2 (98 to 196 kg $CaCO_3$ ha^{-1}) or 2 to 3 lb $Ca(OH)_2$ per 1,000 ft^2 will often neutralize the acidity. Higher rates should be avoided since 0.32 lb S is required to dissolve every 1.00 lb $CaCO_3$ when the S program is resumed.

Granular S formations (pelletized, popcorn, or large mesh size particles) can be applied after core aeration and brushing or drag-matting of the core is completed. Using this practice does not mean that higher rates can be used. In fact, S is applied after these operations in order to prevent too much S accumulating in the coring holes. Accumulation of S particles or large S particles on the soil surface may eventually lead to a microspot of excessive acidity and injury to the turf.

Transformation of elemental S into H_2SO_4, the soluble and active form, is primarily by biochemical oxidation involving *Thiobacillus* spp. autotrophic bacteria. Thus, the rate of transformation depends on environmental factors influencing *Thiobacillus* activity; namely, available moisture, soil temperature, aeration, and nutrients.

Sulfur oxidation is maximum at soil moisture near field capacity and declines sharply in dry soil of about 50% field capacity. Thus, when S is added at high rates and mixed into a soil before turfgrass establishment, it is important to maintain adequate soil moisture for rapid S oxidation and pH reduction. Waterlogging or excessive moisture inhibits S oxidation since O_2 is required. Also, anaerobic conditions favor formation of reduced S forms such as FeS_2.

Soil temperature has a pronounced influence on S oxidation with little or no oxidation below 40°F (4.4°C). Oxidation rate increases to a maximum at about 86°F (30°C) and at above 130°F (55°C) ceases due to death of the bacteria. The optimum temperature range is 75 to 104°F (25 to 40°C).

Temperature, therefore, has a major influence on *time of S application* in temperate climates with early fall and midspring considered the best periods. A late fall or winter application can carry over with S oxidation starting in midspring, which may coincide with the S treatment of midspring to act as a double application rate. At least four weeks of favorable weather for oxidation should follow a treatment. Loss of turf due to excess acidity usually occurs during warm periods even though applications were made during cool weather.

Thiobacillus bacteria respond to the same nutrients as plants. When S is applied to an infertile soil before grass establishment, a complete fertilizer application can increase oxidation. Soil pH has only minor influence on oxidation, primarily because several species of *Thiobacillus* as well as some other microorganisms can oxidize S.

S Reactions in Soil

Biochemical oxidation in soil of elemental S into H_2SO_4 is by the reaction:

$$2S + 3O_2 + 2H_2O \xrightarrow{Thiobacillus} 2H_2SO_4 \rightarrow 4H^+ + 2SO_4^{-2}$$

The H and SO_4 ions result from dissociation of the sulfuric acid (H_2SO_4). These reactions are the same in noncalcareous and calcareous alkaline soils, but further reactions differ. For an alkaline soil that does not contain any free $CaCO_3$ (i.e., *noncalcareous soil*) the reaction is:

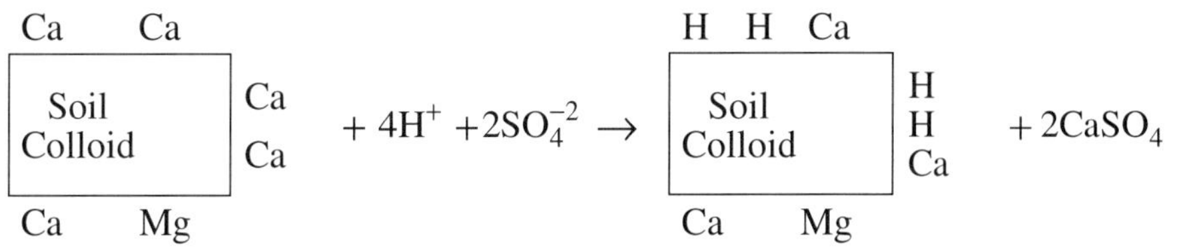

$$\begin{array}{c} \text{Ca} \quad \text{Ca} \\ \boxed{\text{Soil Colloid}} \begin{array}{l}\text{Ca}\\ \text{Ca}\end{array} \\ \text{Ca} \quad \text{Mg} \end{array} + 4H^+ + 2SO_4^{-2} \rightarrow \begin{array}{c} \text{H} \quad \text{H} \quad \text{Ca} \\ \boxed{\text{Soil Colloid}} \begin{array}{l}\text{H}\\ \text{H}\\ \text{Ca}\end{array} \\ \text{Ca} \quad \text{Mg} \end{array} + 2CaSO_4$$

The H^+ replaces Ca^{+2} from cation exchange sites on the soil colloids and Ca^{+2} then combines with SO_4^{-2} to precipitate out as $CaSO_4$ (i.e., gypsum). Since H^+ ions are added, pH decreases. The $CaSO_4$ can be leached deeper into the profile over a period of time.

In a *calcareous soil* the H^+ ions react with $CaCO_3$ instead of Ca^{+2} ions on the cation exchange sites. Only after $CaCO_3$ is dissolved will H^+ displace Ca^{+2} on the cation exchange and result in acidification. These reactions are:

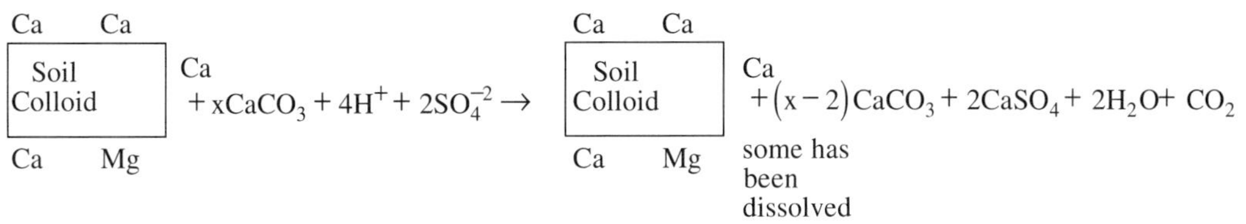

$$\begin{array}{c} \text{Ca} \quad \text{Ca} \\ \boxed{\text{Soil Colloid}} \; \text{Ca} \\ \text{Ca} \quad \text{Mg} \end{array} + xCaCO_3 + 4H^+ + 2SO_4^{-2} \rightarrow \begin{array}{c} \text{Ca} \quad \text{Ca} \\ \boxed{\text{Soil Colloid}} \; \text{Ca} \\ \text{Ca} \quad \text{Mg} \end{array} + \underset{\text{some has been dissolved}}{(x-2)CaCO_3} + 2CaSO_4 + 2H_2O + CO_2$$

This process continues as long as S is added until all $CaCO_3$ has dissolved. Note that H^+ reacts with one of the oxygen molecules in CO_3^{-2} to form water (H_2O) instead of replacing Ca^{+2} on the soil colloid. Once all $CaCO_3$ is dissolved the H_2SO_4 reacts the same as in a noncalcareous soil.

For pH reduction, it is the H^+ in H_2SO_4 that are the active ions. Without the addition of H ions, pH would not decrease. Thus, $CaSO_4$ is not effective for pH reduction since it does not result in added H^+ ions and it is an end product of acidification, acting as a sink for Ca^{+2} from soil colloids.

There is one situation where addition of $CaSO_4$ does reduce pH and that is on sodic soils. The mechanism will be discussed in detail in Chapter 8, but it is essentially by removal of OH^- ions that pH will decrease from pH 10.2 to 8.5. Further addition of $CaSO_4$ will not result in any further pH reduction.

B. Aluminum and Ferrous Sulfates

Aluminum sulfate reacts with water to produce H^+ ions by the reaction:

$$Al_2(SO_4)_3 + 6H_2O \rightarrow 2Al(OH)_3 + 6H^+ + 3SO_4^{-2}$$

The H^+ replaces Ca^{+2} and other basic cations on the soil colloids. Further, Al^{+3} can replace Ca^{+2} and contribute to pH reduction. This material should only be used on a bare soil prior to turfgrass planting. Ferrous sulfate reacts in a similar fashion to produce H ions:

$$FeSO_4 + 2H_2O \rightarrow Fe(OH)_3 + 2H^+ + SO_4^{-2}$$

C. Ammonium Sulfate

Ammonium sulfate is a common N fertilizer that has an acidifying effect on the soil, as does any N fertilizer containing NH_4^+, or producing NH_4^+ during mineralization (i.e., NH_4NO_3, urea, IBDU). Acidity (i.e., H^+) arises from the initial biological reaction in the formation of nitrate (NO^{-3}) from NH_4^+ (a process called nitrification):

$$2NH_4^+ + 3O_2 \xrightarrow[\text{bacteria}]{\textit{Nitrosomonas}} 2NO_2^- + 2H_2O + 4H^+ \ (\textit{acidity})$$

$$2NO_2^- + O_2 \xrightarrow[\text{bacteria}]{\textit{Nitrobacter}} 2NO_3^-$$

See Table 18.3 of Chapter 18 for acidifying effects of the N-sources.

The NH_4^+ content of ammonium sulfate prohibits its application at high rates before turfgrass establishment. But ammonium-based N sources can be incorporated into the routine N fertilization program of a site and will help: (a) offset pH increase from alkaline irrigation water; and (b) dissolve some surface zone $CaCO_3$. Every 4.76 lb of ammonium sulfate (i.e., 4.76 lb AS supplies 1.0 lb N) will neutralize about 5.35 lb $CaCO_3$, while every 3.03 lb ammonium nitrate (i.e., 1 lb N) neutralizes about 1.80 lb $CaCO_3$.

D. Sulfuric Acid

Sulfuric acid (H_2SO_4) provides rapid action when applied to a bare soil, since *Thiobacillus* bacteria do not have to oxidize it. Specialized application equipment is required to apply this strong acid.

More commonly on turfgrass sites, sulfuric acid is applied through the irrigation system on a routine basis for: (a) dissolving caliche in the soil surface; (b) prevention of caliche formation from irrigation water high in bicarbonates (HCO_3^-) or carbonates (CO_3^{-2}) by removal of these ions; (c) pH reduction; or (d) on sodic or saline-sodic soils for Na removal when in conjunction with a lime source (see Chapter 8).

Dissolution of existing caliche by H_2SO_4 is the same process as previously presented for elemental S once it was oxidized to H_2SO_4. Prevention of caliche formation can involve more than dissolving any current $CaCO_3$. Sometimes the irrigation source is high in HCO_3^- and/or CO_3^{-2}. These ions react with any Ca^{+2} and Mg^{+2} in the water to precipitate out as $CaCO_3$ or $MgCO_3$. Acidification of irrigation water by sulfuric acid reduces the HCO_3^- and CO_3^- to CO_2 which evolves off as a gas by the reactions:

$$HCO_3^- + \underset{\text{from } H_2SO_4}{H^+} + O_2 \rightarrow H_2CO_3 \rightarrow H_2O + CO_2 \uparrow$$

$$CO_3^{-2} + \underset{\text{from } H_2SO_4}{2H^+} \rightarrow H_2CO_3 \rightarrow H_2O + CO_2 \uparrow$$

When irrigation water contains Na^+, selective precipitation of Ca^{+2} and Mg^{+2} is especially serious since Na^+ remains to go onto CEC sites and a sodic condition may evolve.[1] But even without the Na^+, acidification of irrigation water could be used to eliminate caliche formation in some situations. If the caliche formation problem is only on high sand greens, acidification of irrigation water for a whole golf course for this purpose would not be warranted. It should be noted that caliche formation at the surface and reduction of water infiltration is primarily a problem when the following conditions occur together: high sand soil; unusually high Ca, Mg and HCO_3/CO_3; arid climate; and 12 month growing season. As discussed previously, other management approaches beyond water acidification can be used.

Sulfuric acid water treatment is a long-term process for soils containing free $CaCO_3$ and for water containing HCO_3^- or CO_3^{-2}. In contrast, noncalcareous soils irrigated with water free of these ions may exhibit pH reduction in one or two years. Once acceptable pH is achieved, acidification of irrigation water would not be necessary. Thus, the expense of adding an acid injection system to the irrigation system should be weighed in light of persistence of the particular problem on a site and alternative management options.

Irrigation water with appreciable bicarbonates typically has pH of 7.8 to 11.0. Sufficient sulfuric acid is added to adjust water pH to 6.5 to 7.0. At below pH 6.0, metal components of irrigation systems can be adversely affected. Instead of directly purchasing and handling H_2SO_4, another approach oxidizes elemental S in a generator system to form *SO_3 (sulfurous dioxide)*; and then by water addition, H_2SO_4 is produced and applied with irrigation.

E. Liquid N and S Materials

Several liquids containing various N and S forms are available for acidification purposes; primarily, *ammonium thiosulfate, ammonium polysulfide,* and *urea-sulfuric acid.* As with ammonium sulfate, the N content prevents use of these chemicals on a bare soil at high rates prior to turfgrass planting. Ammonium thiosulfate and ammonium polysulfide can be supplied by spray equipment as an acidification agent, but the toxic nature of sulfuric acid in urea-sulfuric acid mixture prohibits its use on mature turf unless diluted considerably by water.

All three materials could be injected through an irrigation system for acidification. Urea-sulfuric acid is sometimes used for this purpose and is also called *monocarbamide dihydrogen-sulfate*. As is true for any acid injection system, special precautions include: (a) storage and handling in appropriate containers due to their corrosive nature; (b) maintaining treated water above pH 6.0 to prevent corrosion of irrigation system components; (c) carefully monitoring for leaks; and (d) maintaining careful records of the quantity of N added since the N component contributes to the N fertilizer program.

F. Lime Sulfur

Lime sulfur (dry) and lime sulfur solution can be used for soil acidification, but primarily when a sodic or saline-sodic problem exists. The S must be oxidized prior to acidification. Calcium in CaS_x is beneficial in sodic situations, but in nonsodic alkaline soil, supplemental Ca is not necessary.

G. Phosphoric Acid

Phosphoric and *superphosphoric acids* can be injected into irrigation systems to decrease soil pH (Table 6.2). This approach, however, offers some problems beyond those of other acid injection systems such as: (a) the pH of the water must be maintained somewhat below 6.0 to prevent formation of insoluble phosphates in the irrigation lines. This is most likely to occur when irrigation water contains appreciable Ca or Mg. Corrosion of irrigation system metal components increases with acidity below pH 6.0 to 6.5; and (b) continual addition of P may result in excessive P accumulation, which can slowly leach over time if levels overload a soil's capacity to bind P. High P may induce Fe chlorosis, but only where pH remains alkaline. Also, high P may favor *Poa annua* encroachment.

III. ALTERNATIVES TO REDUCING pH

IN THE PREVIOUS SECTION VARIOUS AMENDMENTS AND APPROACHES for pH reduction and/or preventing caliche formation were outlined. It was noted that alkaline soils containing even a few percent $CaCO_3$ throughout the profile may not be candidates for pH reduction due to high cost or the long time required for effective results under an established turfgrass. However, many management problems associated with alkaline calcareous and noncalcareous soils can be treated by other means.

Prevention is feasible in some situations, especially when selecting mix components for golf greens, golf tees, or recreational fields. Sands should be evaluated for $CaCO_3$ content and any organic sources should be free of marl. If a good alternative sand is available, it would be preferable to a calcareous sand.

In terms of fertilization, P can be precipitated as various forms of calcium phosphates in alkaline conditions. It should be noted that the Bray P-1 extractant to estimate available P often underestimates P levels of calcareous soils. The Olsen bicarbonate extractant of Bray P-2 provides a more accurate measure of available P. If these tests indicate low P, application of P two or three times per year will provide sufficient P. Rates of P should be determined by recommendations from soil test results but splitting the annual P requirement into two or three applications will help maintain adequate P. During establishment or overseeding, supplemental P may be required.

Iron deficiencies can be corrected through foliar Fe at rates of 0.40 to 1.00 lb Fe per acre (0.012 to 0.023 lb Fe per 1,000 ft^2; 0.56 to 1.12 kg Fe ha^{-1}). Treatments can be repeated as needed with results lasting the longest in cool, dry weather and of least duration in warm, humid conditions. Some granular Fe materials provide good response but considerable variation occurs due to local climate and soil conditions. Demonstration trials at equal Fe rates on a particular site are beneficial in determining response to particular materials. On golf greens exhibiting chronic Fe deficiency, a periodic use of Milorganite® can assist. This material contains about 5% of a natural chelated Fe.

On calcareous sands a good micronutrient program is desirable based on soil and tissue tests to identify nutrients that may be limiting. Generally, on alkaline soils, these include Fe, Mn, Zn, and B (highly leached sands only). Caution should be observed with B so as not to develop a toxicity problem by overapplication. Micronutrient fertilization practices are addressed in greater detail in the chapters on plant nutrition, soil testing, and fertilization.

When caliche formation at or near the soil surface is reducing water infiltration and percolation, a good cultivation program can help maintain water movement. Potential methods are core aeration, solid tine coring (0.25 inch diameter, 6.3 mm), and high pressure water injection. For calcic and gypsic soils, thicker layers of >6 inches (>15 cm) of $CaCO_3$ or $CaSO_4$ may interfere with water movement. Deep cultivation techniques to penetrate through these layers may be useful.

Some information on turfgrass genotypic variation to Fe chlorosis has been published, especially for *Poa pratensis* and *Lolium perenne*. Certainly where Fe chlorosis is a chronic problem, exploring the use of a cultivar that does not easily exhibit Fe deficiency is worthwhile. Agencies or individuals conducting cultivar trails in regions where Fe chlorosis is a problem often can suggest tolerant cultivars.

IV. RELATED TOPICS

In this chapter the focus has been on alkaline soils, both calcareous and noncalcareous and pH reduction methods. However, S use and irrigation water treatment are sometimes required for problems not addressed in this chapter and this may cause some confusion. Our intention here is to point out these other situations but more detailed treatment is presented in the appropriate sections.

A. Additional Uses of S

In the current chapter, the use of S and S compounds was discussed for the purposes of:

- soil pH reduction
- dissolution of $CaCO_3$ and caliche from soil surfaces
- prevention of caliche formation.

However, S has other uses in turfgrass management and these include:

- S as a fertilizer when S is deficient (Chapter 13)
- S as an amendment for sodic and saline-sodic soils (Chapter 8). The same S compounds and methods of application (i.e., granular, through sprayers, injection into irrigation water) used for calcareous and noncalcareous alkaline soils apply to these salt-affected situations except that a lime source must be present to react with S to form gypsum.
- use of S to inhibit *Poa annua* invasion for certain ecotypes of this species (Chapter 13)
- use as a coating for sulfur coated urea fertilizers (Chapter 17).

B. Irrigation Water Acidification

Irrigation water acidification is one approach to pH reduction, dissolving free $CaCO_3$, and caliche prevention on alkaline soils.[1] In addition, irrigation water acidification with S based materials is a common practice on sodic and saline-sodic soils (Chapter 8). Reasons may include one or more of the following:

- to generate H^+ for replacement of Na^+ on CEC sites
- for generation of Ca^{+2} by gypsum formation when soils contain $CaCO_3$. The Ca^{+2} can then replace Na^+ on the CEC.
- to reduce HCO_3^- and CO_3^{-2} content in irrigation water that selectively precipitates Ca^{+2} and Mg^{+2} while leaving Na^+ to dominate the CEC.

V. REFERENCES

1. Carrow, R.N., R.R. Duncan, and M. Huck. 1999. Treating the cause, not the symptoms: Irrigation water treatment for better infiltration. *USGA Green Section Record* 37(6):11–15.
2. Christians, N.E. 1990. Dealing with calcareous soils. *Golf Course Mgt.* 58(6):60–66.
3. Harivandi, A. 1995. Sulfur, soil pH, and turfgrass management. *Golf and Sports Turf Australia* 3(Dec.):7–10.
4. Lubin, T. 1995. Controlling soil pH with irrigation water. *Golf Course Mgt.* 63(11):56–60.
5. Nettleton, W.D. 1991. *Occurrence, Characteristics, and Genesis of Carbonate, Gypsum, and Silica Accumulations in Soils.* Madison, WI: Soil Science Society of America. Special Pub. 26. SSSA.
6. Tisdale, S.L., W.L. Nelson, J.D. Beaton, and J. Havlin. 1993. Chapter 8. Soil and fertilizer sulfur, calcium, and magnesium. Chapter 10. Soil acidity and basicity. In *Soil Fertility and Fertilizers.* New York: Macmillan Pub. Co.

Chapter 7

Basics of Salt-Affected Soils

SALT-AFFECTED SOILS have excessively high total soluble salts or sodium (Na) levels and they are found on every continent with the highest concentration in Australia, North and Central Asia, and South America.* About 10% of the total land surface contains salt-affected soil and 1/3 to 1/2 of all irrigated land is influenced by salinity. Carrow and Duncan[3] provide a more in-depth discussion of salt-affected turfgrass areas and their management than allowed in Chapters 7 and 8.

I. CAUSES

SALT IONS MOST COMMON IN SALT-AFFECTED SOILS are Ca^{+2}, Mg^{+2}, Na^{+}, K^{+}, Cl^{B}, SO_4^{-2}, HCO_3^{-}, NO_3^{-}, CO_3^{-2} (at pH >9.0). These arise from dissolution of minerals, salts in irrigation water, added fertilizers and soil amendments, salts carried into the root zone by a high water table, flooding, salt water intrusion, and salt water spray.

Many arid and semiarid soils (especially at annual rainfall of <15 inches or 38 cm) are salt-affected due to insufficient leaching to remove salts that accumulate from weathering of minerals, groundwater, and rain. When these soils are irrigated, especially with poor quality irrigation water, salt-accumulation may escalate. In arid and semiarid climates, Na^{+} and sulfate salts (Na_2SO_4, K_2SO_4, $CaSO_4$, $MgSO_4$) usually dominate.

Coastal marshes and swamps contain high salt levels, especially Na^{+}, Cl^{-}, and SO_4^{-}, when soils are drained for development. Also, high water tables may allow salts to move into surface soils, such as along coastal wetlands and inland salt marshes. Sometimes irrigation in arid regions results in higher water tables that move salt into the root zone of plants on sites with poor internal drainage. On other coastal sites, salt water intrusion into the aquifer in response to excessive water removal by irrigation can reduce irrigation water quality or allow upward movement of salts in the water table.

Turfgrasses are increasingly irrigated with nonpotable water, in particular wastewater (Huck et al.[7]). Additionally, turfgrass managers are more frequently using drought resistant grasses, irrigating more judiciously, and irrigating deeper but less frequently. All of these practices are beneficial from the water conservation aspect but can accentuate salinity problems.

Placement of golf courses on coastal locations enhances the probability of salt problems through salt spray, periodic flooding, salt water intrusion, and poor irrigation water quality. Often the soils are sandy and can rapidly develop salinity problems. Thus, salt-affected soils for turfgrasses are becoming more common in all climates.

---

* Chapter 7 is based on material from Carrow and Duncan[3] by permission of the authors and publisher.

II. SALT RELATED PROBLEMS

ADVERSE ASPECTS OF SOIL SALTS ON TURFGRASS GROWTH may be by direct injuries or be indirect through effects on soil physical properties. Direct stresses include inducement of water deficits by high salt concentrations, ion toxicity, and ion (nutrient) imbalances. High Na^+ can destroy soil structure and, thereby, indirectly influence turfgrasses via low water infiltration, poor drainage, and low soil oxygen. Turfgrass species and cultivars within a species vary in tolerance to different salt injuries. This will be elaborated on later in the chapter.

Total salts and specific salt ions in irrigation water also affect turfgrasses as the salts influence soil salt status, and by direct contact on foliage of landscape plants. In this chapter, the emphasis will be on: (a) turfgrass management problems that arise from excessive salts in the soil or irrigation water; and (b) soil and water quality tests used to assess salt problems. In Chapter 8, Management of Salt-Affected Sites, both soil and irrigation water quality will be considered in developing management strategies.

A. Water Deficit

Salt-induced plant water stress is called *physiological drought.* High salt in the soil solution increases soil osmotic potential due to attraction of water to the solutes (salts). The water becomes less available for plant water uptake since its energy status is reduced—i.e., it is less free to move into plant roots. With less plant-available water, turfgrasses must be irrigated more frequently to avoid moisture stress. *Salt-induced drought stress is the most common injury from salts on plants.*

Limited water uptake and availability result in a number of plant responses. The most basic is reduced growth rate because cell enlargement requires adequate water. Other important responses are:

- increased wilting, leaf rolling, and leaf firing associated with water deficits
- greater potential for desiccation under drought stress
- reduced turgor of shoot cells and cell wall extensibility
- reduced leaf size and leaf area
- photosynthesis may decrease due to reduced leaf area and limited CO_2 exchange because of stomatal closure
- transpirational cooling may decline due to reduced water uptake and stomatal closure
- reduced cytokinin synthesis in turfgrass roots.

Thus, salt-induced water deficits cause immediate drought stress on turfgrasses and make them more susceptible to other stresses such as high temperature and wear.

The most prevalent field symptoms of salinity stress are those observed for drought stress. These include a bluish-green color; wilting; leaf rolling or folding; and eventually leaf firing. Thus, salinity stress has a major influence on turfgrass water relationship.

B. Ion Toxicity

Salt-induced water deficit is caused by high total salinity (i.e., total salts) without regard to the salt type. In contrast, *ion toxicity* is caused by specific ions that are toxic to root or shoot tissues of turfgrasses and other landscape plants. Usually Na^+ and Cl^- are the dominant toxic ions in soils, but B or an ion of B, HCO_3^-, and OH^- may be at toxic levels in some soils. Also, many trace elements can achieve toxic levels in certain situations. When total salts are high, the potential increases for a single specific ion to be high enough for a toxicity problem.

The above ions and trace elements may arise from several sources: (a) they may be at high level in a native soil due to lack of leaching and/or unusual mineralogy; (b) added through irrigation water, applied amendments, and applied fertilizers or pesticides; or (c) by atmospheric contamination, especially for trace elements. Toxicities may be expressed as direct toxicity to root tissues or by accumulation to toxic levels in shoot tissues by continual root uptake.

Accumulation of Cl^- in leaf tissues can lead to leaf burn and desiccation at 0.30 to 0.50% by dry weight in sensitive plants. Woody species are often most susceptible to Cl^- toxicity, while turfgrasses can tolerate higher Cl^- levels in soils. Removal of leaf tips, where Cl^- tends to accumulate, by mowing allows turfgrasses to tolerate Cl^- better than many other plants. Destruction of green tissues by Cl^- toxicity reduces photosynthesis capability.

Plants vary considerably in leaf Na^+ content that causes damage since Na^+ is accumulated within cell vacuoles and/or redistributed from new leaves to older leaves or sheath tissues. Thus, a leaf content that causes Na^+ damage depends greatly on species and even cultivars within a species. Many woody plants are relatively sensitive to Na^+ toxicity, and leaf tissue content of 0.25 to 0.50% Na^+ by weight can cause toxicity.

High Na^+, often in conjunction with Cl^-, can induce a number of detrimental responses in plants. In leaf and root tissues, Na^+ can accumulate in cell wall micropores (apoplasm) where carboxyl groups (R-COO^-) attract cations, especially Ca^{+2}. But high Na^+ can replace Ca^{+2} on root CE sites and cause root deterioration. In leaves, Na^+ accumulation leads to dehydration, reduced turgor, and death of cells. The most evident form of this injury is leaf burn at the tips or margin, but cell metabolic activity can be reduced even when leaf injury is not apparent. Woody species are especially sensitive since many accumulate Na^+ and Cl^- in their roots and lower trunk for several years and then may release these salt ions for movement into shoot tissues.

Besides the CE sites on outer cell walls, Na^+ can displace Ca^{+2} in cell walls and the plasma membrane. Cell membrane integrity can decline as Na^+ displaces Ca^{+2} and causes leakage of cell contents. Root cells are prone to this type of Na toxicity making them less viable for water and nutrient uptake. High salinity also enhances respiration, probably due to greater energy requirements to repair injured tissues, to secrete Na^+, or to compartmentalize Na^+. Increased respiration coupled with lower photosynthesis (due to water deficit) causes a significant decrease in net carbohydrate balance. This decrease is especially serious for root production and maintenance of root viability. Other adverse effects of Na^+ related to ion toxicity are a decrease in protein synthesis and altered hormonal activity where root produced cytokinin levels decrease but abscisic acid (ABA) increases.

Boron toxicity occurs in some salt-affected soils. This is most common in arid or semiarid soils and when the irrigation water is high in B. Injury from high B occurs as leaf margin or tip chlorosis. While Na and Cl toxicities are most often problems on woody species, B toxicity can occur on many plants. Leaf tissue content of B associated with injury varies from 100 to 400 mg kg^{-1} (ppm) dry weight with some plants tolerating 1,000 mg kg^{-1}. Grasses seem to tolerate soil B as high as 10 mg kg^{-1} since mowing removes leaf tip accumulations of tissue B; however, <1.0 mg kg^{-1} in the soil is appropriate for sensitive grasses or landscape plants.

Excessive soil HCO_3^- induces Fe deficiency on nongraminaceous species but has little influence on Fe in grasses. However, high soil HCO_3^- can inhibit root growth and cytokinin export to the shoot tissues where it is important for chloroplast development and protein synthesis.

In sodic soils, toxic levels of OH^- ions can be reached. High OH^- solubilizes certain organic compounds and inhibits root viability. Sodic soils with pH of 9.5 to 10.2 may have toxic OH^- levels.

C. Ion Imbalances

High levels of Na^+, Cl^-, and other ions in salt-affected soils can induce nutrient imbalances. Deficiencies of Ca, K, N (as NO_3^-), Mg, Mn, and P have been reported to be induced by high concentrations of certain salt ions. The degree of deficiency expression varies among plant species and within a species.

Calcium deficiency on turfgrasses is very rare; however, turfgrasses grown in salt-affected soils may be affected by low Ca^{+2} even if a true shoot deficiency is not observed. Sodium can displace Ca^{+2} from root cell membranes and reduce their integrity. Also, saline induced Ca^{+2} deficiency may reduce certain salt tolerance mechanisms such as ion exclusion and selective transport. Thus, added Ca^{+2} often improves the salt tolerance of plants, especially when high Na^+ is present.

Potassium uptake is depressed by high soil Na^+. Also, in the treatment of many salt-affected soils, high Ca additions are required which can induce K deficiency, as well as Mg deficiency. On recreational turfgrasses, K is important for wear tolerance as well as enhanced cold, heat, and drought resistances. Yet, caution is required in applying K because it contributes to total salinity and thus influences physiological drought.

Additional reading on salt-induced problems of water deficits, ion toxicity, and ion imbalances are Maas,[9] Marschner,[10] Pessarakli,[13] Harivandi et al.,[6] and Rhoades and Loveday.[14]

D. Soil Permeability

Soil permeability refers to the ability of water, oxygen, and roots to move within the soil macropores (pores > 0.10 mm diameter) for good turfgrass growth. A soil must have good soil physical conditions if it is to exhibit adequate permeability. In soils with high Na^+ content (sodic soils and sometimes saline-sodic) without adequate Ca^{+2} and Mg^{+2}, soil permeability decreases and several adverse soil physical conditions are exhibited, especially in soils with some silt and clay:

- Larger pores (macropores) are destroyed and small pores dominate.
- Pore continuity declines.
- Infiltration, percolation, and drainage decrease.
- Moisture holding capacity increases.
- Soil O_2 status decreases due to lower O_2 diffusion.
- Soil strength (hardiness) increases.

References related to salt-induced soil permeability problems are USSL,[18] Naidu et al.,[11] Pessarakli,[13] and Rhoades and Loveday.[14]

Sodium induces adverse soil physical responses as it replaces Ca^{+2} and Mg^{+2} on the clay CEC sites. Traditionally, a 15% exchangeable level of Na^+ (*ESP,* exchangeable sodium percentage) has been used to classify a soil as *sodic,* but no single value is adequate (USSL[18]). On fine-textured soils with 2:1 shrink-swell clay types, adverse effects may occur at ESP = 5 to 15%; on 1:1 clays (kaolintic types) that are not shrink-swell in nature, adverse effects may not

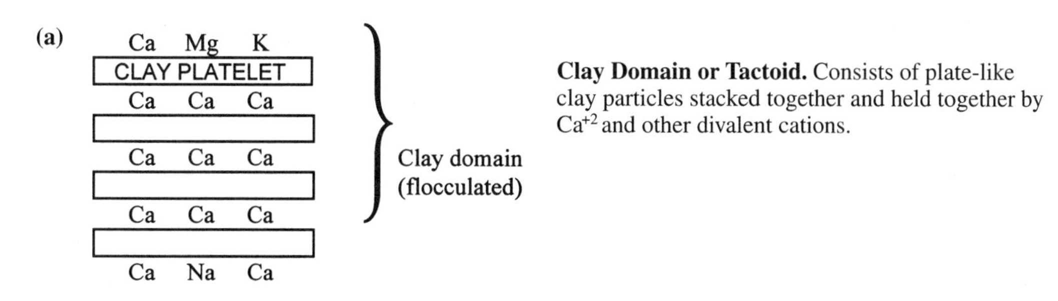
(a)
Ca Mg K
CLAY PLATELET
Ca Ca Ca
Ca Ca Ca
Ca Ca Ca
Ca Na Ca
Clay domain
(flocculated)
Clay Domain or Tactoid. Consists of plate-like clay particles stacked together and held together by Ca+2 and other divalent cations.

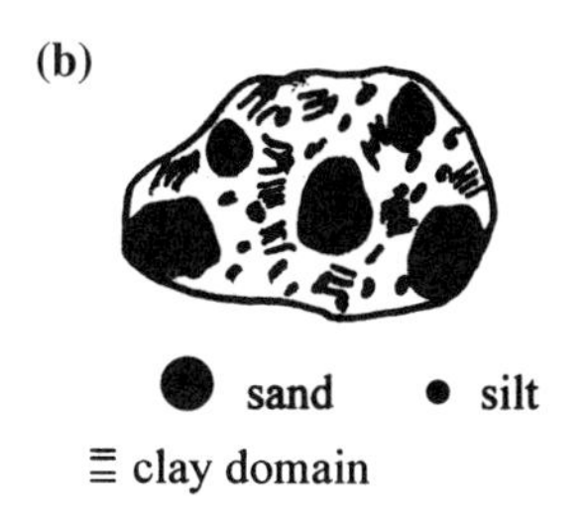
(b)
Soil Aggregate. Made up of clay domains, silt, and sand particles aggregated together by (a) Ca+2 holding clay platelets together in a domain, and (b) organic matter and Fe/Al flocculating together clay, sand, and silt particles into an aggregate.
sand
silt
clay domain

Figure 7.1. Illustration of (a) clay domain and (b) soil aggregate.

occur until >15% ESP; while sands may exhibit particle migration at 5 to 10% if the irrigation water is low in total salts.

Individual clay particles are plate-like and several plates may be stacked together in an arrangement called *domains* or *tactoids* (Figure 7.1). Divalent cations allow individual platelets to approach each other more closely than do monovalent cations (i.e., Na^+). Only as platelets come close together are they attracted to one another to form domains.

Domains can be further aggregated into larger structural units if the surface is dominated by divalent cations. The surface of domains consists of a *diffuse double layer* of electrical charges of the clay colloid and the swarm of ions (mainly cations) neutralizing the surface charges. Divalent ions are attracted much more than Na^+ to the clay surface charge and form a thinner diffuse double layer which allows domains to flocculate together. Also, the hydrated radius of Na is larger than Ca and tends to separate domains or platelets.

Aggregate units of several domains plus sand and silt particles can be joined together to form larger structural units or aggregates. Forces that bring smaller aggregate units together into larger aggregates include wetting and drying, freezing and thawing, root pressure, and tillage. Aggregates can be stabilized by organic matter gels and polysaccharides, Fe/Al/Mn oxides as cementing agents, and divalent or trivalent ions (Figure 7.1b).

When the percent Na^+ increases on the CEC sites of soil colloids, it first starts to dominate the diffuse double layer to make the layer thicker, thereby reducing the attractive forces between domains. *Aggregates deteriorate* into smaller units and *slake off* from the larger structural aggregate or unit (Figure 7.2). Since attractive forces between domains have been weakened, aggregates become susceptible to breakdown from wetting and air entrapment "explosion" as well as traffic and water droplet impact. Aggregate deterioration and slaking can start at ESP values well below the traditional ESP of 15%.

At somewhat higher Na^+ levels, a second process occurs. Sodium ions start to enter between domain platelets and replace the divalent cations. Attractive forces between platelets decrease since Na^+ does not allow platelets to be as close together. Thus, clay domains swell upon

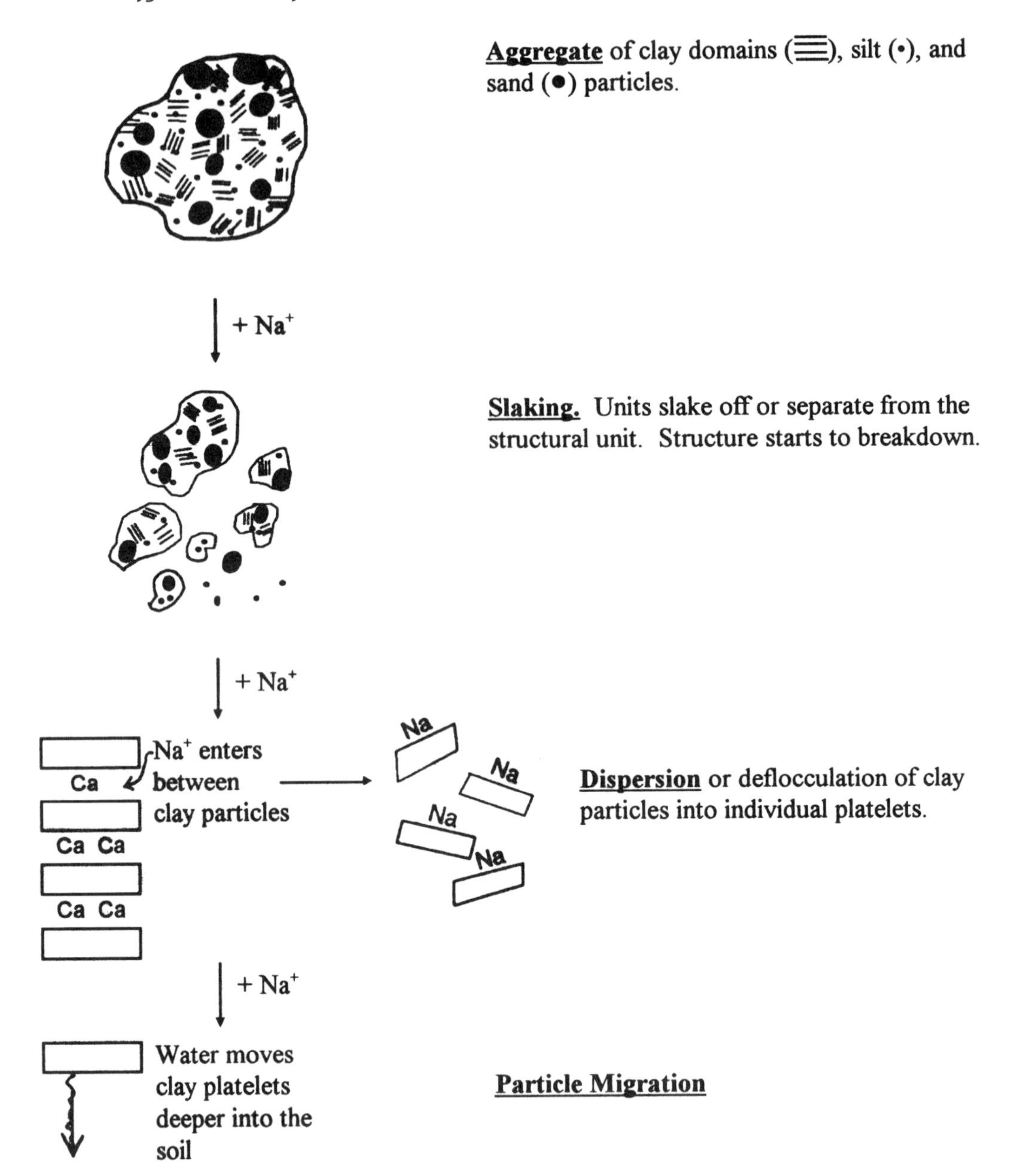

Figure 7.2. Soil structure deterioration by excess Na^+ resulting in slaking, dispersion, and particle migration (from Carrow and Duncan[3]).

wetting, attraction between platelets within a domain declines, and *platelets* (i.e., individual clay particles) *are dispersed.* This process essentially destroys the remaining structural units.

On sandy soils, a third process can occur. Colloid size *particles* can easily *migrate* in sands by water movement and plug pore channels as particles lodge at pore interfaces or connecting channels (Figure 7.2). Organic colloids, as well as clay colloids, are often present in sodic sands and may even be the dominant colloids on high sand content soils. Organic colloids also can migrate and plug pore channels to reduce water percolation. Sands with ESP >15 would be most susceptible but this process can occur at much lower ESP levels.

III. CLASSIFICATION OF SALT-AFFECTED SOILS

A VERY BROAD DEFINITION OF SALT-AFFECTED SOILS would include calcareous, gypsum enriched (gypsic) and acid-sulfate conditions as well as the traditional saline, sodic, and saline-sodic soils. In Chapters 7 and 8, the concentration will be on saline, sodic, and saline-sodic situations which are the "traditional" meaning of salt-affected soils. The other salt problem soils are discussed in detail elsewhere in this book.

Two soil based criteria traditionally are used to classify salt-affected soils (a) total soluble salt concentration, and (b) the quantity of exchangeable Na^+. Soil pH is often also listed but not used in the U.S. Salinity Lab[18] classification scheme, which is the most prevalent classification. Total soluble salt concentration is measured by *electrical conductivity of a saturation extract (ECe)* of soil. As total salt concentration increases, ECe also increases. High salinity or total soluble salts is at ECe >4 dSm^{-1}.

Sodium status in recent years has usually been determined by *sodium adsorption ratio (SAR)* where

$$SAR = \frac{Na}{\sqrt{(Ca + Mg)/2}}$$

The cation concentrations are determined in a saturation paste extract and are in $mmol_c\ L^{-1}$ or $meq\ L^{-1}$. As Na^+ concentration increases, SAR increases. It should be noted that extractable levels of N, Ca, and Mg using different soil test extractants than the "saturated paste extract" cannot be used to calculate SAR.

Instead of SAR as a measure of soil sodium status, *exchangeable sodium percentage (ESP)* was initially used and still is by many labs, where:

$$ESP = \frac{\text{Exchangeable Na } (100)}{\text{Cation Exchange Capacity}}$$

Exchangeable Na is the quantity of Na^+ on the CEC in units of cmol kg^{-1} or meq per 100 g. The CEC consists of all exchangeable cations on the soil CEC sites.

Later in this chapter, these three soil chemical measurements (ECe, SAR, ESP) will be elaborated upon. But the above information is sufficient to understand classification of salt-affected soils.

The most widely used system for classifying salt-affected soils is the one developed by the U.S. Salinity Laboratory[18] and is used in this book. This scheme consists of three classes: saline, sodic, and saline-sodic (Table 7.1) based on soil conditions in the surface horizon.

In recent years, there has been interest in redefining the *sodic* category into several subclasses, especially in Australia (Sumner[17]) (Table 7.2). This has resulted because of several factors: (a) the recognition that Na^+ can cause adverse effects on soil physical properties at levels well below the classic ESP level of 15—which is really the upper end of a continuum of

Table 7.1. U.S. Salinity Lab classification of salt-affected soils (USSL[18]).

Soil Class	Old Name	Total Soluble Salt Status	Sodium Status[a]		
		ECe, Electrical Conductivity[b] (dSm^{-1})[c]	ESP, Exchangeable Sodium Percentage (%)	SAR, Sodium Absorption Ratio	Soil pH
Saline	White Alkali	≥4.0	<15	<12	<8.5
Sodic	Black Alkali	<4.0	≥15	≥12	>8.5
Saline-Sodic	–	≥4.0	≥15	≥12	≤8.5

[a] SAR is determined in a saturated paste extract.
[b] ECe = electrical conductivity from a saturated paste extract.
[c] 1.0 dSm^{-1} (decisiemen per meter) = 1.0 mmho cm^{-1} (millimho per centimeter).

Table 7.2. The proposed Australian classification system for salt-affected soils uses the criteria of (a) soil pH, (b) ECe vs. TEC, and (c) SAR (1:5 soil to water extract) (Naidu et al.[11]).

Class	Soil pH	Total Soluble Salt Status		Sodium Permeability Hazard[a]	
		ECe vs. TEC[b] d Sm^{-1}	Approx. ECe	Aust. 1:5 (soil:water) extract SAR	ESP %
Saline	<8.5	ECe>TEC	≥4	<3	<6
Sodic					
• Alkaline sodic	>8.0	ECe<TEC	<4	≥3	≥6
• Neutral sodic	6.0–8.0	ECe<TEC	<4	≥3	≥6
• Acidic sodic	<6.0	ECe<TEC	<4	≥3	≥6
Saline sodic	8.5	ECe>TEC	≥4	≥3	≥6

[a] Australian classification system is based on SAR determined from a 1:5 ratio of soil:water which gives a much lower SAR reading than the USSL where a saturated paste extract is used. Approximate conversions are: SAR(1:5) of 3 ≈ SAR (USSL) 5.7 (see Table 7.4).
[b] TEC = threshold electrolyte concentration, which is the concentration of cations in the soil solution that causes a clay to flocculate or aggregate together.

Na saturation levels that cause structural breakdown on most soils. Part of the reason Na^+ can produce measurable adverse effects at lower ESP, particularly on infiltration/percolation, is because structure deterioration from high Na^+ involves several processes—aggregate breakdown by slaking, swelling of clay, and colloid dispersion. Aggregate breakdown by slaking can initiate in many soils at ESP near 5%; (b) other factors besides ESP, such as clay type and percent of clay content, influence the value of ESP at which structure deterioration starts to decline. Australian sodic soils tend to have higher clay contents than U.S. sodic soils that the U.S. Salinity Laboratory used to develop their classification scheme. The Australian soils are sometimes more sensitive to structural breakdown at lower ESP values than the ESP ≥15% baseline; and (c) ESP values in the U.S. Salinity Lab procedure have often been determined with tap water that contained higher cation concentrations than normal for many Australian locations. The higher total cations result in a higher ESP before adverse structural responses are observed.

Another change in classification has been to rely more on the SAR (from saturated paste extract ions) rather than ESP value, which was the initial factor used. The ESP procedure depends on an accurate determination of cation exchange capacity (CEC) which is pH dependent. If CEC is determined at laboratory pH different from field pH, the CEC value could be misleading. Also, in salt-affected soils, some of the cations not associated with CEC may be dissolved and reported as CEC and, again, cause error.

The USSL[18] classification system is most widely used and other classification systems, such as the Australian scheme (Naidu et al.[11]) are still in a formulation stage. Since an alternative classification for salt-affected soils has not been agreed upon, some guidelines for assessing whether a soil may express sodic problems are:

- The Australian classification is based on use of much more dilute soil to water ratio (1:5) compared to the saturated paste extract (about a 1:1 ratio). Thus SAR values are lower. Approximate conversions are : SAR (1:5) of 3 = SAR (saturated paste, USSL) of 5.7 (see Table 7.2).
- An important factor influencing clay dispersion is the *threshold electrolyte concentration (TEC)* of the soil solution, which is measured by ECe. Each soil has a particular TEC at which the clay flocculates or aggregates together. It is often based on the electrical conductivity (ECw) of the irrigation water since ECe at the soil surface is similar to ECw under irrigated conditions with leaching. The basic relationship of ESP and TEC is that a soil with high ESP (>15) may not exhibit clay dispersion if TEC is sufficiently high. Conversely, a soil with low ESP (well below 15, even down to ESP of 2 to 6) can demonstrate clay dispersion by the Na^+ if the TEC is low, such as in rain or very pure water.
- When the predominant clays are kaolinite or Fe/Al hydrous oxides, effects of Na^+ on water percolation generally agree with traditional ESP guidelines for sodic soils. However, other clay types (montmorillonite, vermiculite, illite, or mica) are more sensitive to Na^+ and often exhibit problems at ESP about 6.
- Sandy soils contain larger pores and water moves through at a higher velocity than fine-textured soils. Thus, clay dispersion and migration in sands can occur at relatively low ESP. In arid regions, where a sand may naturally contain some Na^+ to give an ESP of 6 to 10, irrigation with relatively pure water may cause clay dispersion, but irrigating with a water with salt levels above the critical TEC may result in no clay dispersion. In humid climates, irrigating a sand soil with water containing appreciable Na^+ may induce clay dispersion at ESP well below 15. When clay or organic colloids disperse in a sand, particle migration and possible plugging of pores deeper in the profile are probable. This is most likely to occur during the grow-in period.

Each type of salt-affected soil has certain characteristics and problems associated with it. The three major types are summarized in the next section.

A. Saline Soil

A saline soil is a nonsodic soil containing *high total soluble salts* sufficient to adversely affect the growth of most plants. Soluble salts (Table 7.1) are at ECe ≥4.0 dSm^{-1} and Na status at ESP <15% (SAR<12). Saline soils usually have pH between 7.0 to 8.5 but acidic pH can occur in some situations, usually on sands. An older term for saline soils is *white alkali* since a white crust of salt often occurs by salt deposition as water evaporates from bare soil surfaces (Plate 7). These soils have the same structure and permeability as they would if soluble salts were not present or were leached. The salts do not contribute to poor soil physical properties. Instead, primary problems associated with saline soils are:

- Reduced water uptake due to high soil salt content. These salts attract water and reduce water availability for plant uptake. High soil osmotic potential from the salts causes physiological drought.
- Ion toxicity to shoot and/or root tissues may occur depending on the specific chemistry of the soil salts and applied irrigation water. Toxicity is most often from high Na or Cl but can arise from B, HCO_3, or SO_4.
- Ion imbalance leading to nutrient deficiencies can occur in some soils, such as deficiencies of Ca, K, NO_3, Mg, Mn, or P.

While ECe $\geq$4.0 dSm^{-1} is used as a threshold value for a saline soil based on most plants being adversely affected by this salt level, salt-sensitive plants may be injured below this value and salt-tolerant plants may tolerate much higher levels. As with all classes of salt-affected soils, criteria used are most related to common agronomic crops. In nature, there is a continuum of crop tolerances to total salts, specific ion toxicities, and ion imbalances.

While soil laboratory procedures are used for classifying salt-affected soils, there are soil and plant symptoms that may suggest saline conditions. On bare soil, the appearance of a whitish crust due to salt accumulation as water evaporates is a common observation. Also, salt layers or lens may be evident in the soil profile.

The most common plant symptom is wilt even when the soil appears to have adequate moisture. In addition to wilt, the turfgrass may appear bluish-green and in serious cases leaf firing may appear. Salt-induced wilt is a result of high soil osmotic potential from salts and may be enhanced by ion toxicity to roots. Black and deteriorated roots, especially on salt sensitive landscape plants, are typical. Other plant symptoms may be leaf tip or margin burn on trees and ornamentals and nutrient deficiencies induced by high salinity.

B. Sodic Soil

A sodic soil contains *sufficiently high exchangeable* Na^+ (i.e., on CEC sites) to adversely affect soil structure of most soils and ultimately crop growth. The ESP $\geq$15% (SAR $\geq$12) indicates the predominant influence of Na but total salts are relatively low at ECe <4.0 dSm^{-1}. High Na^+ can cause high OH (alkalinity) and pH is >8.5 and can exceed 10.0. The OH ions arise from hydrolysis of Na_2CO_3 and Na on the CEC complex:

$$2Na^+ + CO_3^{+2} + H_2O \rightleftarrows 2Na^+ + HCO_3^- + OH^-$$

or

$$\begin{array}{c} Na^+ \\ \boxed{\begin{array}{c}\text{Soil}\\ \text{Colloid}\end{array}} \\ Na^+ \end{array} Na^+ + H_2O \rightleftarrows \begin{array}{c} H^+ \\ \boxed{\begin{array}{c}\text{Soil}\\ \text{Colloid}\end{array}} \\ Na^+ \end{array} Na^+ + Na^+ + OH^-$$

High pH can solubilize some of the organic matter which tends to accumulate at the surface as water evaporates. Due to the dark appearance from the organic coatings, sodic soils were once called *black alkali* soils (Plates 2 and 3).

The most prevalent problems on sodic soils are:

- Poor soil permeability or structure resulting from breakdown/slaking of structural units; swelling and dispersion of colloids (clay and organic matter colloids); and colloid migration in sandy soils to cause plugging of pores. Structure breakdown greatly inhibits water movement into (infiltration) and through the soil (percolation).
- Ion toxicities, especially Na and Cl but also B, HCO_3, OH, and Al, can occur in some soils.
- Ion imbalances, particularly Ca, Mg, and K deficiencies. Calcium is rarely deficient on turfgrasses, but under high Na, it may be deficient within root tissues. However, application of gypsum would provide ample Ca.

Field symptoms indicating presence of sodic soils include (a) the distinct black color from dissolution of some of the organic matter and deposition over the surface of soil particles; (b) physical properties indicative of poor permeability such as low water infiltration/percolation/drainage, low O_2 when moist, and high soil strength when dry; (c) a putty-like and sticky consistency for loams and clay loams when they are moist due to dispersion of particles that cause them to move more easily; (d) absence of aggregation in the profile when the soil is moist (upon drying, cracking or clods may occur from shrinking); and (e) the presence of slick spots in low areas that appear black and oily when wet.

Plant symptoms typical of sodic conditions are: (a) poor root growth and viability. Roots are often black, thin, and spindly. This can arise from low soil O_2 and/or Na toxicity to root tissues as well as OH or Al toxicities. Lack of adequate root growth is often expressed by frequent drought stress symptoms; and (b) foliar leaf toxicities from Na, Cl, or B and foliar deficiency symptoms related to Na-induced Ca, Mg, and/or K deficiencies.

C. Saline-Sodic Soil

Saline-sodic soils contain *high total salts* (ECe $\geq$4.0 dSm^{-1}) that adversely affect the growth of many plants. Also, *high exchangeable Na^+* is present (ESP $\geq$15% or SAR $\geq$12); however, the high total salts aid in counteracting the effects of Na^+ on structure. High total salts maintain a high TEC that inhibits clay dispersion. As long as TEC is high, structure will be the same as any similar soil that is unaffected by salts. However, if the salts are leached at the surface by rainfall or irrigating with a water source low in salts, a saline-sodic soil can start to convert to a sodic condition. The first symptoms would be reduced water infiltration. As salts are leached from deeper in the profile, water percolation also declines. To prevent this occurrence, Na must be replaced by Ca during salt removal by leaching.

The primary problems of a saline-sodic soil are the same as a saline soil, especially reduced water uptake from high soil osmotic potential. If total soluble salts decline without replacement of exchangeable Na by H or Ca, the physical problems associated with a sodic condition start to become evident. Field and plant symptoms vary, depending on which of the above situations are prevalent but symptoms observed for a saline soil are most common.

IV. ANALYSIS OF SALT-AFFECTED SOILS

A. Measurement of Total Salts (Salinity) in Soil

Laboratory

TRADITIONALLY, SALINITY (i.e., total soluble salts) in soils has been measured by *electrical conductivity of a saturated soil-water paste extract (ECe)* in a laboratory procedure where water is added to a soil until it becomes uniformly saturated; allowed to equilibrate for several hours; then the soil solution is extracted by vacuum; and the solution containing any salts is analyzed for ECe (USSL[18]). The ECe values are usually reported in units of dSm^{-1} (decisiemens per meter) or mmhos cm^{-1} (millimhos per centimeter) where:

$$1 \text{ dSm}^{-1} = 1 \text{ mmhos cm}^{-1} = 0.1 \text{ Sm}^{-1}$$

Salinity determined by saturated paste extract is more predictable of field conditions than are more dilute extraction ratios of 1:1 or 1:5 (soil:water) used by some laboratories. Since almost all salinity-crop tolerance data reported in the literature are based on this procedure, ECe is the standard. The salt concentration in ppm or mg L^{-1}, is usually listed as *TDS (total dissolved salts)* or *TSS (total soluble salts)* on a soil test report and is related to ECe by:

$$\text{TDS (in ppm or mg L}^{-1}) = \text{TSS} = 640 \times \text{ECe}$$

For soils containing appreciable gypsum, the relationship is:

$$\text{TDS} = 740 \times \text{ECe}$$

Since ECe is based on a saturated soil condition, *actual* salt concentrations in the field will be higher because the soil is not saturated; therefore, actual EC of the soil will be higher. This results from salts becoming concentrated as soil moisture is depleted. *Actual EC of the field soil water (ECsw)* is related to ECe by:

$$\text{ECsw at field capacity} \approx 2 \times \text{ECe}$$

$$\text{ECsw at permanent wilt point} \approx 4 \times \text{ECe}$$

Laboratory determined ECe is used: (a) to classify saline, sodic, and saline-sodic soils; (b) to diagnose the severity of the salinity hazard; and (c) to select plant species and cultivars that will tolerate the salinity hazard on the site. Maas[8,9] has classified crop tolerance to salinity using the ECe criteria listed in Table 7.3. Classification is based on the *threshold ECe,* which is the maximum soil salinity that does not reduce yield below that achieved under nonsaline conditions. In Chapter 8 the relations between plants and threshold ECe are discussed in greater detail and grasses are classified as to salinity tolerance.

Field Measurement

Salinity varies by depth, from location to location within a site, and over time in response to irrigation and rainfall. Field mapping of salinity is possible and will likely become a more

Table 7.3. Classification for crop soil salinity tolerance as measured by electrical conductivity of a saturated soil paste extract (ECe) for nongypsiferous soils (Maas[9]).[a,b]

Crop Soil Salinity Tolerance	ECe for Yield Reduction	
	0% Yield Reduction[c]	50% Yield Reduction
	dSm^{-1}	
Very sensitive	<1.5	1.5–5.0
Moderately sensitive	1.6–3.0	5.1–10.0
Moderately tolerant	3.1–6.0	10.1–15.0
Tolerant	6.1–10.0	15.1–21.0
Very tolerant[d]	>10.0[d]	>21.1

[a] ECe can also be used as an approximate guideline to Na and Cl toxicities since most salts contain high Na and Cl. Thus, a plant moderately sensitive to soil salinity can be considered moderately sensitive to Na and Cl ions when more specific data are not available.

[b] Nongypsiferous soil does not contain gypsum. For gypsiferous soils, plants will tolerate ECe of approximately 2 dSm^{-1} higher than the above table values. When developing the saturated paste extract, gypsum will dissolve sufficiently to increase ECe by about 2 dSm^{-1}.

[c] The maximum ECe within each tolerance class is called the *"threshold ECe"* which is the maximum soil salinity that does not reduce yield below that achieved under nonsaline conditions.

[d] It should be noted that some turfgrass species can tolerate much higher salinity levels. This traditional classification scheme presents problems on how to further classify grasses >10.0 dSm^{-1} tolerance.

common practice. As a general rule in saline soils under irrigated conditions, salinity increases linearly (approximately) in fine-textured soil with depth and exponentially with depth in sandy soils. However, in a sandy golf green or athletic field with drainage tiles at a depth of 16 to 24 inches (40 to 60 cm), salinity would not increase by depth as much as without drainage or with deeper tiles. Drainage barriers, such as a fine-textured B horizon of higher clay content, enhance salt accumulation.

One approach for field appraisal is to estimate ECe from *electrical conductivity of a saturated soil-paste (ECp)*. Extraction of the soil solution for ECe is accurate but more time-consuming than directly measuring ECp in a saturated soil-paste (i.e., the soil solution is not extracted in this case). Rhoades and Miyamoto[15] provide a detailed discussion and procedure for determining ECe from ECp. Commercial field units consisting of a conductivity meter and cell are available for rapid measurement of ECp and conversion factors for estimating ECe. These units are very portable and suitable for lab, office, or field (Carrow and Duncan[3]).

More expensive techniques for measuring *bulk soil electrical conductivity* (ECa) by depth and location include (a) time-domain reflectrometry which can simultaneously determine water content and ECa, (b) four-electrode sensors, and (c) electromagnetic induction sensors (Rhoades and Miyamoto[15]). In each method, ECa can be used to estimate ECe if soil water content is known.

B. Determination of Sodium Status in Soil

Assessing Na status of a soil is to determine the *"sodium hazard"* or potential for structure to deteriorate in response to high Na. The term *"permeability hazard"* is also used since water permeability and infiltration decline as structure breaks down. Traditionally Na status in soils has been measured by the *exchangeable sodium percentage (ESP)*

$$ESP = \frac{\text{exchangeable Na on CEC sites (100)}}{\text{cation exchange capacity}}$$

where the units of exchangeable Na and CEC are cmol kg^{-1} or meq per 100 g. The sum of all exchangeable cations represents CEC. This method does not consider the quantity of Ca and Mg relative to Na that are present.

To consider Ca and Mg content in the soil and because it is easier to accurately measure than ESP, a second characteristic to assess soil sodicity is now commonly used, the *sodium adsorption ratio (SAR);*

$$SAR = \frac{Na}{\sqrt{(Ca + Mg)/2}}$$

where Na, Ca, and Mg concentrations in soil solution from the saturated paste extract are in meq L^{-1} or mmol L^{-1}.

Sodium adsorption ratio is related to ESP. ESP can be estimated from SAR for soil solutions obtained from saturated soil paste extracts by

$$ESP = \frac{1.475\ (SAR)}{1 + 0.0147\ SAR}$$

The relationships between ESP and SAR are presented in Table 7.4 for procedures used in the U.S. Salinity Laboratory.[18]

In Australia, the more dilute 1:5 (soil:water) extract is used for either ESP or SAR. When using the 1:5 extract, the relationship is:

$$ESP = 1.95\ (SAR) + 1.8$$

As noted earlier, when discussing classification of sodic soils, structure deterioration can start at ESP (or SAR) values well below the ESP $\geq$15 (or SAR $\geq$12) used to categorize a soil as sodic. Thus, Table 7.5 contains expanded guidelines for assessing potential permeability (i.e., reduced infiltration and percolation) problems associated with Na.

As the footnote in Table 7.5. indicates, the use of soil ESP and SAR values to determine sodium hazard (i.e., potential for water infiltration and percolation problems due to structure deterioration) is best assessed in conjunction with irrigation water quality information (see Section 7.V, Irrigation Water Quality Analysis). Irrigation water quality of very high purity (ECw <0.5 dSm^{-1}) causes Na-induced permeability problems to be exhibited at lower ESP and SAR than if water is of average quality. When irrigation water contains excessively high salts (ECw >3 d Sm^{-1}) and appreciable Ca and Mg are present in the water along with Na, permeability problems may not appear until higher ESP or SAR are reached.

The procedures for determining ESP and SAR are laboratory based and accuracy depends on obtaining representative soil samples. To monitor changes over time, samples must be col-

Table 7.4. Conversions of SAR from the saturated soil paste extract (USSL[18]), SAR by the 1:5 soil to water ratio used in Australia (Naidu et al.[11]), and ESP values for salt-affected soils.

SAR Criteria[a]			
USSL Saturated Paste Extract	Aust. 1:5 (soil:water)	Corresponding ESP %	Comments
5	2.6	6.9	
5.7	3.0	7.7	Lower limit for sodic soil in Australian system
10	5.7	12.9	
12	6.8	15.0	Lower limit for sodic soil in USSL system
15	8.4	18.1	
20	10.8	22.8	
25	12.9	27.0	

[a] In this book, SAR values are based on the saturated soil paste extract procedure since it is the most widely used procedure.

Table 7.5. General soil ESP and SAR guidelines for permeability problems from sodium, assuming intermediate irrigation water quality.[a]

	Degree of Permeability Problem from Na[a]		
Soil Parameter	None	Increasing	Severe
ESP (%)	<3.0	3.0–15.0	>15
SAR	<2.1	2.1–12.0	>12

[a] *If irrigation water quality is very pure* (ECw of <0.50 dSm^{-1}), then permeability problems may occur at values lower than listed above (see Figure 7.3). For example, a soil with ESP of 10 might exhibit a severe permeability problem. In contrast, *an irrigation source unusually high in salts* (ECw >3 d Sm^{-1}), including appreciable Ca and Mg, may not cause severe permeability problems until at ESP of 20–25.

lected from the same locations and depth. There is not a field-based method for measuring these soil parameters.

C. Specific Ion Toxicity in Soil

Some constituents of soil salts (Na, Cl, B, HCO_3, OH) may be toxic to certain plants. Soil levels can be determined by the appropriate soil test. Toxicities may be directly on root tissues or more often shoot tissues are adversely affected when certain ions accumulate in the shoot. Many times grasses are more tolerant to toxic ions than are other landscape plants. Toxic ion tolerance of trees and shrubs should be carefully evaluated when selecting plant material.

Sodium (Na) can be directly toxic to roots, especially with repeated drying cycles when Na is concentrated and tissue dehydration enhanced. Even without tissue dehydration, high Na can replace Ca in root cell walls and cell membranes and cause membrane leakage. Accumulation of Na within root tissues can lead to root toxicity, especially in salt-sensitive woody species. Another form of Na toxicity arises from Na accumulation in shoot tissues at leaf margins and tips. This causes tissue dehydration and death. Mowing of grasses often removes some of the salt, but when accumulation occurs in lower leaves, these may senesce and die. Since Na is usually the predominant salt in high salinity situations, plants exhibiting sensitivity to high salinity often are sensitive to high Na. This may not always be true since osmotic effects of high salinity and toxic effects are different. Nevertheless, ECe guidelines for grasses and other plants serve as an approximate guide to both Na toxicity tolerance and total salinity tolerance (Table 7.3) (Maas[8,9]).

Chloride (Cl) is an essential micronutrient required in small quantities by plants, but some plants are sensitive to excessive Cl. Ocean water contains appreciable Cl and salt spray, ocean water irrigation or flooding may result in Cl accumulation. Maas[8] provides an extensive listing of crop sensitivity to Cl in soil solution. Maximum soil Cl concentrations in saturated soil extracts without yield loss for selected grasses are:

Grass	Cl^- (mg kg^{-1})
Crested wheatgrass	1,050
Tall fescue	1,400
Perennial ryegrass	1,925
Bermudagrass	2,450
Fairway, crested wheatgrass	2,625

Woody plants are more sensitive to Cl than most nonwoody plants. As with Na, Cl is often a predominant ion in high salinity situations and the salinity tolerance of plants based on ECe (Table 7.3) provides an approximation of Cl tolerance in the absence of more specific data on Cl.

Boron (B) can reach toxic levels in arid regions where leaching is limited. It is generally not a problem in humid climates unless the irrigation water contains high B or excessive B fertilizer has been applied. Maas[8] provides suggested guidelines for B content in soils (Table 7.6). Mowing aids in B removal from grasses, especially if clippings are removed, but B is an important concern for other landscape plants.

Bicarbonate (HCO_3^-) toxicity has been reported for some plants but tolerance limits for most plants are not known. Dallisgrass (*Paspalum dilatatum*) has exhibited toxicity at 420 mg kg^{-1} of soil solution HCO_3^-. High HCO_3^- is primarily a problem due to precipitating Ca and Mg as insoluble carbonates while leaving soluble Na, rather than a toxicity.

On highly sodic soils, hydroxyl (OH^-) ions can form. These soils exhibit pH of 10.0 to 10.2. Roots can be damaged by high OH. Tolerance to OH of grasses has not been studied but grasses that tolerate excessively sodic soils are likely to possess some tolerance.

D. Soil Nutrient Status

Since high Na^+ and Cl^- can induce nutrient imbalances or deficiencies, a good soil test program to determine nutrient status is important on salt-affected soils. The most important soil chemical factors to test for in addition to ECe, SAR or ESP (for sodium hazard), and other toxic ions are:

- soil pH. Sodic soils are likely to have soil pH of >8.5 and as high as 10.2.
- presence of free $CaCO_3$. This influences the choices of treatment on sodic soils.
- extractable or plant available levels of Ca, Mg, K
- percent saturation of the cation exchange capacity sites by Ca, Mg, K, Na, H, Al
- Mn soil levels
- extractable P

In the sections on plant nutrition and soil testing, these parameters are discussed in detail.

Table 7.6. Boron soil levels and plant tolerance before yield starts to decline (Maas[8]).

Sensitivity Class	Soil B ($mg\ kg^{-1}$)[a]	Examples
Very sensitive	<0.5	Lemon citrus
Sensitive	0.5–1.0	Fruit trees
Moderately sensitive	1.0–2.0	Many vegetables
Moderately tolerant	2.0–4.0	Kentucky bluegrass
Tolerant	4.0–6.0	Alfalfa
Very tolerant	6.0–10.0	Most grasses

[a] B concentration in saturated soil paste extract.

V. IRRIGATION WATER QUALITY ANALYSIS

IRRIGATION WATER QUALITY has the most influence of all management inputs on the future salinity status of a soil. In the previous section, focus was on measuring the soil for various chemical components. Measurement of soil salinity parameters (ECe, ESP, SAR) is important for: (a) determining current conditions; and (b) monitoring changes over time. Measurement of irrigation water quality, however, aids in predicting future problems from total salinity, sodium hazard, toxic ions, and nutrient additions. Also, management options depend on water quality. For example, irrigation programming can be markedly influenced by water constituents. When irrigation water contains high salt content, the quantity of water applied may need to be increased to produce greater leaching.

Many of the same constituents determined in soil analyses are measured in irrigation water. However, extraction techniques or dilution ratios of soil:water are not a concern in water analyses since total constituents are determined. Chemical components are reported in different units by various laboratories. Table 7.7 contains units and conversion factors that are normally used.

A. Measurement of Total Salts (Salinity) in Water

In irrigation water, total salinity is determined by measurement of *electrical conductivity of the water (ECw)*. Normally, ECw is reported in units of dSm^{-1} or mmhos cm^{-1}. Also, total salinity can be reported in terms of *total dissolved salts (TDS)* where ECw data are transformed to TDS in ppm or mg L^{-1} by:

$$\text{TDS (in ppm or mg L}^{-1}) = 640 \times \text{ECw (in dSm}^{-1}\text{ or mmhos cm}^{-1})$$

Some laboratories use 700 instead of 640. The type of salt or salts in the irrigation water influences which number to use. *Seawater* has an average ECw of 54 dSm^{-1} or 34,560 ppm total dissolved salt and a conversion factor of 744. For sodium chloride, 640 is a good conversion and 700 is a compromise between these values.

Since standard terminology is not practiced, laboratories may use different terms. Terms with the same meanings are:

- TDS (total dissolved *salts*)
- TSS (total soluble salts)

Table 7.7. Units and conversion factors commonly used in reporting irrigation water and soil test analyses.

Units of Measure

- ppm (parts per million)
- mg L^{-1} (milligram per liter)
- mg kg^{-1} (milligram per kilogram)
- dSm^{-1} (decisiemen per meter)
- mmhos cm^{-1} (millimhos per centimeter)
- cmol kg^{-1} (centimole per kilogram)
- $cmol_c$ kg^{-1} (centimole charge of saturating ion per kilogram). This is used for reporting exchangeable ions on CEC sites.
- mmol kg^{-1} (millimole per kilogram)
- meq L^{-1} (milliequivalents per liter)

Conversions

- 1 dSm^{-1} = 1 mmhos cm^{-1} = 1,000 μmhos cm^{-1}
- 1 ppm = 1 mg kg^{-1} = 1 mg L^{-1}
- Convert ppm or mg L^{-1} to dSm^{-1}
  ppm (0.0016) = dSm^{-1}
  mg L^{-1} (0.0016) = dSm^{-1}
- Convert dSm^{-1} to ppm or mg L^{-1}
  dSm^{-1} (640) = ppm
  dSm^{-1} (640) = mg L^{-1}
- Convert ppm to meq L^{-1}
  Divide ppm of ion by its equivalent weight.
  Equivalent weights are: Ca^{+2} (20), Mg^{+2} (12.2), Na^{+} (23), K^{+} (39), HCO_3^{-} (61), CO_3^{-2} (30), SO_4^{-2} (48), Cl^{-} (35.4).
  Example: 100 ppm Ca/20 = 5 meq L^{-1} of Ca

Guidelines for ECw as a measure of potential total salinity hazard for an irrigation water are in Table 7.8 with the USSL[18] guidelines more conservative than those of Westcot and Ayers.[19] Comparison of soil ECe values that adversely affect plant growth (Table 7.3) reveals higher values than ECw in Table 7.8. This is because continuous use of irrigation water of ECw >0.75 dSm^{-1} has the potential to cause salt accumulation in the soil and result in high soil ECe. Thus, the irrigation water classification in Table 7.8 is predictive of future soil salinity problems.

B. Sodium Hazard (Permeability) in Water

High Na content of irrigation water is the primary cause in development of sodic or saline-sodic soils on irrigated sites. Sodium concentration plus the quantity and type of other salts in irrigation water has a major influence on: (a) surface water infiltration and movement in the soil since these affect soil permeability at the surface and deeper in the profile; (b) the quantity of irrigation water required to leach excessive Na and other salts; (c) whether irrigation water treatment is required; and (d) choice of corrective management options.

The traditional means of assessing Na status is to determine the quantity of Na, Ca, and Mg in irrigation water and report it as the *SAR_W (Sodium Adsorption Ratio)*

$$SAR_W = \frac{Na}{\sqrt{(Ca + Mg)/2}}$$

Table 7.8. Total salinity (i.e., total salts, salinity hazard) classification guidelines of irrigation water based on ECw and TDS (total dissolved salts).

Salinity Hazard Class	Comments	Westcot and Ayers[19]		USSL[18]	
		ECw dSm^{-1}	TDS ppm	ECw dSm^{-1}	TDS ppm
Low	Low salinity hazard, no detrimental effects on plants or soil buildup are expected.	<0.75	<500	<0.25	<160
Medium	Sensitive plants may show salt stress; moderate leaching prevents soil salt accumulation.	0.75–1.50	500–1000	0.25–0.75	160–500
High	Salinity will adversely affect most plants. Requires selection of salt tolerant plants, careful irrigation, good drainage, and leaching. Soil amendments such as gypsum may be necessary.	1.50–3.00	1000–2000	0.75–2.25	500–1500
Very High	Generally unacceptable except for very salt tolerant plants, good drainage, frequent leaching, and use of amendments.	>3.00	>2000	>2.25	>1500

with ion concentrations in the water reported as meq L^{-1} or mmol L^{-1}. If water analysis data are presented in ppm or mg L^{-1}, the conversion formula (Table 7.7) is:

$$\text{meq } L^{-1} = \text{ppm (or mg } L^{-1}) \div \text{equivalent weight}$$

A low content of Ca and Mg in relation to Na causes deterioration of soil structure and colloidal dispersion at the surface. Thus the relative quantities are important.

Since high total electrolyte concentration in irrigation water can counteract the adverse effects of high Na in water (i.e., swelling, dispersion of colloids), SAR_W is best used in conjunction with EC_W data (Figure 7.3). Two important aspects are illustrated in Figure 7.3: (a) when irrigation water is very low in salts (EC_W <0.5 dSm^{-1}), permeability problems can arise at the soil surface even at low SAR_W (1–10 meq L^{-1}); and (b) at high EC_W (>3 dSm^{-1}), the high electrolyte concentration can aid in maintaining permeability even though the SAR_W is high (15 to 30 meq L^{-1}). This concept was discussed in the sections on soil SAR and irrigation water EC_W, along with the importance of threshold electrolyte concentration.

Where HCO_3^- or CO_3^{-2} concentrations in irrigation water are high, these ions react with Ca and Mg to precipitate $CaCO_3$ and $MgCO_3$, thereby leaving Na to dominate. While Na_2CO_3 can form, it is much more soluble than $CaCO_3$ or $MgCO_3$ and leaves soluble Na^+ to interfere with soil physical conditions. The SAR_W is adjusted to account for HCO_3 and CO_3 and is called the *adjusted* SAR_W (*adj* SAR_W). Laboratories normally do the conversion from SAR_W to adj SAR_W.

There are two means of adjusting SAR. One uses the formula

$$\text{adj SAR}_W = \text{SAR}[1 + 8.4 - pH_C]$$

$$= \text{SAR}(9.4 - pH_C)$$

where pH_C is a theoretical, calculated pH of the irrigation water in contact with lime and at equilibrium with soil CO_2. The tables and calculation for adj SAR_W are given by Ayers and Westcot,[2] Westcot and Ayers,[19] and Carrow and Duncan.[3]

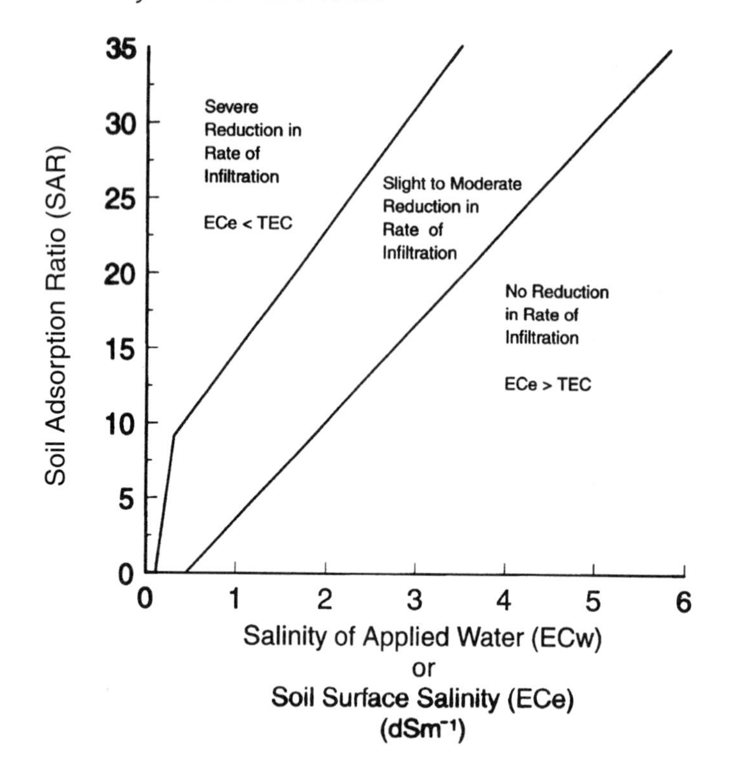

Figure 7.3. Relative rate of water infiltration as affected by salinity and sodium adsorption ratio. The SAR is of irrigation water (SAR_w) or soil (SAR). The salinity is of the irrigation water (EC_w) or soil (ECe) as determined by an extract from a saturated soil-water paste. TEC = threshold electrolyte concentration at which clays will flocculate (adapted from Oster and Schroer[12]).

The pH_C value is indicative of whether lime will dissolve as water percolates through the soil. A pH_C >8.4 indicates a tendency to dissolve lime in the soil while <8.4 suggests lime precipitation. Some individuals apply these guidelines to assess the potential for irrigation system scaling by lime deposition.

In recent years, the adj SAR has been calculated by a second method that does not use the pH_C value. Instead, the actual Ca concentration in the irrigation water that is used for the SAR_W equation is substituted for by an "equilibrium Ca concentration." The resulting SAR is then denoted as the "adj SAR" (Hanson et al.[4]).

Researchers have noted that the actual Ca concentration in the soil solution may be higher or lower than the Ca concentration in irrigation water. The actual or "equilibrium Ca concentration" differs because lime precipitation or dissolution can alter Ca in the soil solution. Precipitation of Ca is undesirable because this Ca cannot replace exchangeable Na. To determine an estimated equilibrium Ca concentration, some irrigation water consultants use the ratio of $[HCO_3]/[Ca]$ in meg L^{-1} as well as the ECw value. Tables for calculating adj SARw by this method are presented by Hanson et al.[4]

The SAR_W guideline ranges in Table 7.9 can be used for adj SAR_W, including those based on clay-type. As with SAR_W, adj SAR_W is best used with EC_W information and adj SAR_W can be substituted for SAR_W in Figure 7.3.

Table 7.9. Sodium hazard (permeability) guidelines of irrigation water based on SAR_W and adj SAR_W criteria. SAR_W is preferred when HCO_3^- (<2.0 meq L^{-1}, 120 mg L^{-1}) and CO_3^{-2} (<0.5 meq L^{-1}, 15 mg L^{-1}) are low, but adj SAR_W should be used at higher HCO_3^- and CO_3^- concentrations. Guideline ranges are the same for both SAR_W and adj SAR_W.

Na Hazard Classification	SAR_W or adj SAR_W (meq L^{-1}) of Water		Comments on Na Hazard
USSL Classification[18]			
Low	<10		Can be used to irrigate almost all soils without structure deterioration. Salt sensitive plants may be affected.
Medium	10–18		Appreciable Na permeability hazard on fine-textured soils with high CEC. Best used on coarse-textured soils with good drainage.
High	18–26		Harmful levels of Na accumulation on most soils. Will require intensive management-amendments, drainage, leaching.
Very High	>26		Generally not suitable for irrigation except at low to medium soil salinity levels. Requires intensive management.
Based on Clay-Type Classification[2]			
None	<6	Montmorillonite	Generally no Na hazard unless EC_W is very low.
	<8	Illite	
	<16	Kaolinite	
Possible	6–9	Montmorillonite	Possible problem unless a Ca source and some leaching is used.
	8–16	Illite	
	16–24	Kaolinite	
Probable	>9	Montmorillonite	Requires intensive corrective measures to use.
	>16	Illite	
	>24	Kaolinite	

Another criterion for determining Na hazard (permeability) problems from irrigation water besides the SAR_w and adj SAR_w methods is *Residual Sodium Carbonate (RSC)*, which is defined as

$$RSC = (CO_3 + HCO_3) - (Ca + Mg)$$

where ion concentrations are expressed in meq L^{-1}. This value indicates the quantity of Ca and Mg versus CO_3 and HCO_3. A negative RSC denotes that Ca and Mg exceeds CO_3 and HCO_3; thus, Na buildup is unlikely. When RSC value is positive, Na accumulation is possible (Table 7.10 has guidelines) and recommendations are given for: (a) quantity of gypsum (100%) to add per acre-foot of water. Gypsum supplies additional Ca to reduce Na accumulation on CEC sites and it can be added through the irrigation water or directly to the soil. Multiplication of the RSC value by 234 gives the gypsum requirement in pounds 100% gypsum per acre-foot of water. In the metric system, RSC × 86 = kg of gypsum per 1,000 m^3 water; or (b) quantity of 90% sulfuric acid required per acre-foot of water to neutralize the CO_3 and HCO_3 in the irrigation water by acid treatment.

Table 7.10. Sodium hazard (permeability) of irrigation water based on RSC, Residual Sodium Carbonate, guidelines (Harivandi[5]).

RSC Value ($meq\ L^{-1}$)	Na Hazard
<0 (i.e., negative)	None. Ca and Mg will not be precipitated as carbonates from irrigation water; they remain active to prevent Na accumulation on CEC sites.
0–1.25	Low. Some removal of Ca and Mg from irrigation water.
1.25–2.50	Medium. Appreciable removal of Ca and Mg from irrigation water.
>2.50	High. All or most of Ca and Mg removed as carbonate precipitates leaving Na to accumulate. How rapidly Na buildup occurs depends on Na content of the water.

The RSC does not contain Na in its formula but is widely used as a measure of sodium hazard for irrigation water. If not reported on a water analysis report, it is easily calculated from Ca, Mg, CO_3, and HCO_3 contents in $meq\ L^{-1}$ units.

C. Specific Ion Toxicity in Water

Irrigation water, especially some effluent sources, may contain ions that are potentially toxic: (a) to foliage of plants that water directly contacts; (b) to shoot tissues as ions are taken up by roots and accumulate in leaves; or (c) within root tissues, especially as ion concentrations in soils increases over time with irrigation. Turfgrasses are generally less sensitive to these toxicities than are other landscape plants.

The ions that most often cause toxicity problems are Na, Cl, B, HCO_3, and pH (i.e., OH ions). Table 7.11 provides guidelines for toxicity problems both from soil accumulation over time as well as from more immediate direct foliage injury on sensitive plants as a result of overhead irrigation. Residual chlorine can arise in treated wastewater due to chlorine disinfection and may cause foliage damage on some sensitive plants.

Trace elements in irrigation water may result in toxicity problems over time as they accumulate. Westcot and Ayers[19] compiled guidelines for Na, Cl, and B concentrations, and suggested maximum concentrations of trace elements in water that would allow long-term irrigation without toxicity problems. Soils vary substantially in ability to fix or tie up elements into less available forms. However, the guidelines of Table 7.12 are based on avoiding excessive buildup. They may be exceeded on a short-term basis but long-term irrigation with water containing higher concentrations should be avoided.

D. Nutrients and Other Considerations

Sources of irrigation water are very diverse, such as groundwater wells; lakes, reservoirs or ponds; rivers or streams; effluent (wastewater, reclaimed, regenerant) water that can range from secondary to advanced treatment to grey water (wastewater generated by residences from dish and wash water). Constituents in irrigation water that are of concern and vary from source to source are:

- *Biological Material That May Affect Turfgrass Stands.* These include nematodes, weed seeds, algae, and fungal spores.

Table 7.11. Guidelines for interpretation of irrigation water quality with respect to (a) soil accumulation, and (b) direct foliage injury from overhead irrigation (after Westcot and Ayers[19]).

Potential Toxicity Problem	Units	Degree of Restriction on Use for Sensitive Plants		
		None	Slight to Moderate	Severe
Soil Accumulation and Root Problem[a]				
Na	SAR	0–3	3–9	> 9
	mg L^{-1} (ppm)	0–70	70–210	> 210
Cl	meq L^{-1}	0–2	2–10	> 10
	mg L^{-1}	0–70	70–355	> 355
B	mg L^{-1}	0–1	1–2.0	> 2.0
Direct Foliage Injury				
Na	meq L^{-1}	0–3	> 3	
	mg L^{-1}	0–70	> 70	
Cl	meq L^{-1}	0–3	> 3	
	mg L^{-1}	0–100	> 100	
HCO_3[b]	meq L^{-1}	0–1.5	1.5–8.5	> 8.5
	mg L^{-1}	0–90	90–500	> 500
Residual Chlorine	mg L^{-1}	0–1	1–5	> 5
pH (i.e., OH^-)	pH	< 8.4	–	> 9.0

[a] Toxicity may occur as a direct root tissue injury or from ion uptake, translocation, and accumulation in shoot tissues, where injury then occurs.
[b] HCO_3 on foliage is primarily unsightly deposits.

- *Total Suspended Solids.* Presence of sand, silt, clay, or organic particles suspended in the water. These may clog the delivery system as well as lead to sealing of the soil surfaces. If the water is discharged into aquatic environments, sludge and anaerobic conditions can develop.
- *Biodegradable Organics.* These include organic compounds, such as carbohydrates, fats, and proteins that undergo biological decomposition when discharged into the environment. This can lead to depletion of dissolved oxygen in the water. This is determined by methods to measure *biochemical oxygen demand (BOD)* and *chemical oxygen demand (COD).*
- *Stable Organics* (Refractory Organics). These include phenols, certain pesticides, and chlorinated hydrocarbons that resist chemical degradation in conventional wastewater treatment. They may present a potential environmental hazard to plants, animals, or humans.
- *Human Pathogens.* Certain pathogens (bacteria, viruses, or parasites) may be disease organisms. These are determined by measuring indicator organisms such as *total and fecal coliform bacteria.*
- *Residual Chlorine.* In wastewater, most chlorine is combined with organics (i.e., termed combined chlorine or residual chlorine) rather than being free or available chlorine that could cause foliage injury to some crops. Residual chlorine is of some concern if chlorinated organics are toxic in nature.

Detailed discussions of the above aspects are found in the books by Asano et al.[1] and Snow,[16] which focus on the use of wastewater for irrigation purposes. Irrigation sources that may change over time, especially effluent, should be tested on a regular basis for chemical constituents.

Table 7.12. Recommended maximum concentrations of trace elements in irrigation waters for long term use (Westcot and Ayers[19] and Harvandi[5]).

Element	Recommended Maximum Concentration[a] (mg L^{-1})	Remarks
Al (aluminum)	5.0	Can cause nonproductivity in acid soils (pH <5.5), but more alkaline soils at pH >5.5 will precipitate the ion and eliminate any toxicity.
As (arsenic)	0.10	Toxicity to plants varies widely, ranging from 12 mg L^{-1} for sudan grass to less than 0.05 mg L^{-1} for rice.
Be (beryllium)	0.10	Toxicity to plants varies widely, ranging from 5 mg L^{-1} for kale to 0.5 mg L^{-1} for bush beans.
Cd (cadmium)	0.01	Toxic to beans, beets, and turnips at concentrations as low as 0.1 mg L^{-1} in nutrient solutions. Conservative limits recommended because of its potential for accumulation in plants and soils to concentrations that may be harmful to humans.
Co (cobalt)	0.05	Toxic to tomato plants at 0.1 mg L^{-1} in nutrient solution. Tends to be inactivated by neutral and alkaline soils.
Cr (chromium)	0.1	Not generally recognized as an essential growth element. Conservative limits recommended because of lack of knowledge on toxicity to plants.
Cu (copper)	0.2	Toxic to a number of plants at 0.1 to 1.0 mg L^{-1} in nutrient solutions.
F (fluorine)	1.0	Inactivated by neutral and alkaline soils.
Fe (iron)	5.0	Not toxic to plants in aerated soils, but can contribute to soil (iron) acidification and loss of reduced availability of essential phosphorus and molybdenum. Overhead sprinkling may result in unsightly deposits on plants, equipment, and buildings.
Li (lithium)	2.5	Tolerated by most crops up to 5 mg L^{-1}; mobile in soil. Toxic to citrus at low levels (>0.075 mg L^{-1}). Acts similar to boron.
Mn (manganese)	0.2	Toxic to a number of crops at a few tenths mg to a few mg L^{-1}, but usually only in acid soils.
Mo (molybdenum)	0.01	Not toxic to plants at normal concentrations in soil and water. Can be toxic to livestock if forage is grown in soils with high levels of available molybdenum.
Ni (nickel)	0.2	Toxic to a number of plants at 0.5 to 1.0 mg L^{-1}; reduced toxicity at neutral or alkaline pH.
Pb (lead)	5.0	Can inhibit plant cell growth at very high concentrations.
Se (selenium)	0.02	Toxic to plants at concentrations as low as 0.025 mg L^{-1} and toxic to livestock if forage is grown in soils with relatively high levels of added selenium. An essential element for animals but in very low concentrations.

Table 7.12. Continued

Element	Recommended Maximum Concentration[a] (mg L^{-1})	Remarks
Sn (tin)	–	Effectively excluded by plants; specific tolerance unknown.
Ti (titanium)	–	(See remark for tin.)
W (tungsten)	–	(See remark for tin.)
V (vanadium)	0.1	Toxic to many plants at relatively low concentrations.
Zn (zinc)	2.0	Toxic to many plants at widely varying concentrations; reduced toxicity at pH >6.0 and in fine-textured or organic soils.

[a] These values are based on potential toxicity problems that may *arise over long-term use* of the irrigation water, especially for sensitive plants in the landscape—turfgrasses can often tolerate higher levels. For fertilization, higher rates than these can be applied as foliar treatment without problems.
[b] Based on Westcot and Ayers[19] and Harvandi.[5]

Nutrients in irrigation water are of a concern because of (a) human health hazard (nitrate); (b) promotion of algae growth (nitrates and phosphates); and (c) nutrient (N, P, K, S, sometimes others) content and their influence on turfgrass and landscape plant growth. These contribute to the overall nutrient additions and must be taken into account in the fertilization program. Huck et al.[7] presented the guidelines in Table 7.13 for nutrient content in irrigation water.

As an example of the use of Table 7.13, assume a turfgrass manager applied 2 acre-feet (i.e., 24 inches, 60 cm) of irrigation water to a site in one year. The water averaged 5 mg L^{-1} NO_3^-. The annual N rate supplied by irrigation water would be:

$$5 \text{ mg L}^{-1} \text{ NO}_3 = 5\left(0.226 \text{ mg L}^{-1} \text{ N}\right) = 1.1 \text{ mg L}^{-1} \text{ N}$$

$$\text{lb of N per acre-foot of water} = \text{mg L}^{-1} \text{ N in water} \times 2.72$$

$$= 1.1 \text{ mg L}^{-1} \text{ N } (2.72)$$

$$= 3.0 \text{ lb N per acre-foot water}$$

$$(2 \text{ acre-feet})(3.0 \text{ lb N}) = 6.0 \text{ lb N per acre}$$

$$= 0.14 \text{ lb N per } 1{,}000 \text{ ft}^2 \text{ per year}$$

Table 7.13. Guidelines for nutrients contained in irrigation water and quantities that may be applied per foot (12 inches, 30.5 cm) of irrigation water. Also, average effluent water quality reported by Stowell[a] and Asano et al.[b]

Nutrient or Element	Nutrient Content in Water in mg L^{-1} (or ppm)				Conversion to lb per 1,000 ft^2 of Nutrient Added for every 12 inches of Irrigation Water Applied	Average	Effluent
	Low	Normal	High	Very High		Stowell, Calif.[a]	Asano et al., Calif.[b]
N	<1.1	1.1–11.3	11.3–22.6	>22.6	11.3 ppm N = 0.71 lb N per 1000 ft^2	–	1.4
NO_3^-	<5	5–50	50–100	>100	50 ppm NO_3^- = 0.71 lb N per 1000 ft^2	–	6
P	<0.1	0.1–0.4	0.4–0.8	>0.8	0.4 ppm P = 0.057 lb P_2O_5 per 1000 ft^2	–	8
PO_4^-	<0.30	0.30–1.21	1.21–2.42	>2.42	1.21 ppm PO_4^- = 0.057 lb P_2O_5 per 1000 ft^2	–	24
P_2O_5	<0.23	0.23–0.92	0.92–1.83	>1.83	0.92 ppm P_2O_5 = 0.057 lb P_2O_5 per 1000 ft^2	–	18
K^+	<5	5–20	20–30	>30	20 ppm K = 1.5 lb K_2O per 1000 ft^2	26	15
K_2O	<6	6–24	24–36	>36	24 ppm K_2O = 1.5 lb K_2O per 1000 ft^2	31	18
Ca^{+2}	<20	20–60	60–80	>80	60 ppm Ca = 3.75 lb Ca per 1000 ft^2	64	59
Mg^{+2}	<10	10–25	25–35	>35	25 ppm Mg = 1.56 lb Mg per 1000 ft^2	23	16
S	<10	10–30	30–60	>60	30 ppm S = 1.87 lb S per 1000 ft^2	65	59
SO_4^{-2}	<30	30–90	90–180	>180	90 ppm SO_4^- = 1.87 lb S per 1000 ft^2	196	180
Mn	–	–	>0.2[a]	–		0.03	–
Fe	–	–	>5.0[a]	–		0.20	–
Cu	–	–	>0.2[a]	–		0.03	–
Zn	–	–	>2.0[a]	–		0.08	–
Mo	–	–	>0.01[a]	–		–	–
Ni	–	–	>0.2[a]	–		–	–

[a] L. Stowell (1999). Average of effluent water used on six golf courses in Southern California. Pace Turf Institute, San Diego, California.
[b] Asano et al.[1]: Average of water quality from six water treatment plants (advanced treatment) in California.

V. REFERENCES

1. Asano, T., R.G. Smith, and G. Tschobanoglous. Municipal wastewater: treatment and reclaimed water characteristics. 1985. In G.S. Pettygrove and T. Asano, Eds. *Irrigation with Reclaimed Municipal Wastewater—A Guidance Manual.* Boca Raton, FL: Lewis Publishers.
2. Ayers, R.S. and D.W. Westcot. 1976. *Water Quality for Agriculture.* Irr. and Drainage Paper 29. Rome: Food and Agric. Organ. of the United Nations.
3. Carrow, R.N. and R.R. Duncan. 1998. *Salt-Affected Turfgrass Sites: Assessment and Management.* Chelsea, MI: Ann Arbor Press.
4. Hanson, B., S.R. Grattan, and A. Fulton. 1999. *Agricultural Salinity and Drainage.* Division of Agriculture and National Resources Pub. 3375. Davis, CA: Cooperative Extension, University of California.
5. Harivandi, M.A. 1994. Wastewater quality and treatment plants. In J.T. Snow, Chair Ed. Comm. *Wastewater Reuse for Golf Course Irrigation.* USGA Publication. Boca Raton, FL: Lewis Publishers.
6. Harivandi, M.A., J.D. Butler, and L. Wu. 1992. Salinity in turfgrass culture. In D.V. Waddington, R.N. Carrow, and R. Shearman, Eds. 1992. *Turfgrass. Agronomy Monograph No. 32.* Madison, WI: Amer. Soc. of Agron.
7. Huck, M., R.N. Carrow, and R.R. Duncan. 2000. Effluent water: Nightmare or dream come true? *USGA Green Section Record* 38(2):15–29.
8. Maas, E.V. 1978. Crop salt tolerance. In G.A. Jung, Ed. *Crop Tolerance to Suboptimal Land Conditions. ASA Spec. Pub. 32.* Madison, WI: Amer. Soc. of Agron.
9. Maas, E.V. 1994. Testing crops for salinity tolerance. In J.W. Maronville, Chair Ed. Comm. *Adaptation of Plants to Soil Stresses.* INTSORMIL Pub. 94-2. Lincoln, NE: University of Nebraska, International Prog. Div., Instit. of Agric. and Nat. Res.
10. Marschner, H. 1995. *Mineral Nutrition of Higher Plants.* New York: Academic Press.
11. Naidu, R., M.E. Sumner, and P. Rengasamy, Eds. 1995. *Australian Sodic Soils: Distribution, Properties, and Management.* East Melbourne, Victoria, Australia: CSIRO Pub.
12. Oster, J.D. and F.W. Schroer. 1979. Infiltration as influenced by irrigation water quality. *Soil Sci. Soc. Amer. J.* 43:444–447.
13. Pessarakli, M. 1994. *Handbook of Plant and Crop Stress.* New York: Marcel Dekker, Inc.
14. Rhoades, J.D. and J. Loveday. 1990. Salinity in irrigated agriculture. In B.A. Stewart and D.R. Nielson, Eds. *Irrigation of Agriculture Crops. Agronomy Monograph No. 30.* Madison, WI: Amer. Soc. of Agron.
15. Rhoades, J.D. and S. Miyamoto. 1990. Testing soils for salinity and sodicity. In R.L. Westerman, Ed. *Soil Testing and Plant Analysis.* Madison, WI: Soil Sci. Soc. of Amer.
16. Snow, J.T., Chair Ed. Comm. 1994. *Wastewater Reuse for Golf Course Irrigation.* USGA Publication. Boca Raton, FL: Lewis Publishers.
17. Sumner, M.E. 1995. Sodic soils: New perspectives. In R. Naidu, M.E. Sumner, and P. Rengasamy, Eds. *Australian Sodic Soils. Distribution, Properties, and Management.* East Melbourne, Victoria, Australia: CSIRO Pub.
18. U.S. Salinity Laboratory Staff. 1954. *Diagnosis and Improvement of Saline and Alkali Soils. USDA Agriculture Handbook 60.* Washington, DC: U.S. Gov. Printing Office.
19. Westcot, D.W. and R.S. Ayers. 1985. Irrigation water quality. In G.S. Pettygrove and T. Asano, Eds. *Irrigation with Reclaimed Municipal Wastewater—A Guidance Manual.* Boca Raton, FL: Lewis Publishers.

Chapter 8

Management of Salt-Affected Sites

PROBLEMS ASSOCIATED WITH SALT-AFFECTED SITES as noted in Chapter 7 are: (a) water deficit or drought stress induced by high total soluble salts; (b) ion toxicities from high levels of Na, Cl, B, HCO_3, or OH; (c) ion imbalances, especially deficiencies in Ca, K, Mg, NO_3, Mn, or P; and (d) soil permeability, where excess Na causes structural degradation leading to poor water infiltration/percolation, low soil O_2, and poor root growth. The type of salt-affected soil (saline, sodic, saline-sodic) determines which of these problems are present on a specific site.

When salt-affected problems are present, they strongly influence most other aspects of turfgrass management. Salt-affected sites* require a *comprehensive management plan* with several components:

- *Assessment* of the site, soil, and irrigation water.
- *Restriction of Salt Additions* where feasible.
- *Grass Selection* to utilize a grass appropriate to the site constraints.
- *Leaching of Salts* which must also encompass *long-term drainage* for salt removal from the site in certain situations. Maximum leaching often requires an intensive *cultivation* program to deal with restrictions to infiltration, percolation, and drainage of water.
- *Amendments* to modify the soil or irrigation water.
- *Adjustment of Cultural Practices* to alleviate nutrient deficiencies, compensate for salt-induced drought, and other aspects.
- *Development of a Monitoring Strategy* to assess the effectiveness of the management program.

Each of these components is elaborated on in the sections that follow.

I. SITE ASSESSMENT

A comprehensive management plan for a salt-affected site cannot be developed without adequate information on soil chemical status, soil physical conditions influencing water movement, irrigation water quality, water table conditions, salt disposal, and other factors affecting salinity. Gathering the necessary information is time-consuming and expensive, but essential.

---

* Chapter 8 contains considerable material from Carrow and Duncan[2] by permission of the authors and publisher.

Soil chemical analyses for salt-affected sites were defined and discussed in Chapter 7. Chemical soil testing is used to determine total salinity, permeability status (Na hazard), specific ion toxicities, and initial nutrient status.

Extent of *soil sampling* is dictated by the nature of the site. Because of greater soil variability some areas require more extensive sampling than others. Also, initial sampling is often more extensive than long-term soil sampling to monitor conditions over time. Initial soil sampling is very important since it establishes baseline conditions and influences management options.

When determining where to sample soil for initial salinity tests, the surface root zone areas are first priority. Sampling to the depth used for routine soil testing will allow the same sample to be used for salinity purposes and normal nutrient/pH evaluations. Turfgrass managers often use a 0 to 3 inch (0 to 7.6 cm) or 0 to 4 inch (0 to 10 cm) depth. Obtaining a representative sample, sampling similar areas together (such as sampling a low area of a fairway separate from a well-drained location), and sampling each green and tee is necessary.

Choice for the next sampling depth may require preliminary evaluation with a field testing unit or kit to locate any zone of salt or Na accumulation. If a high salt content zone is identified and it is within the root zone, then sampling should be within this soil area using a 3 to 4 inch (7.6 to 10 cm) deep sample (for example, sampling at 8 to 12 inches). When a salt accumulation is just below the lower root zone, sampling can be within the lower root zone and measured salinity/Na levels will indicate over time whether the zone is dissipating or rising into the root area.

On some deep well-drained sites that are well irrigated or in a more humid climate, even if irrigation water quality is poor, salts may continuously move deeper into the soil and a surface soil sample would be sufficient. High sand content greens with adequate drainage can also be sampled only within the surface root zone.

Once soil samples are obtained, a complete *chemical analysis for assessing salt problems* should be conducted. A detailed discussion of the most important soil test information is presented in Chapter 7 but essential items include:

- *Total Salinity* determined by electrical conductivity of a soil-water paste extract (ECe).
- *Determination of Sodium Hazard* by ESP or SAR of the soil.
- *Specific Ion Toxicity* of the existing soil can be assessed by testing for Na, Cl, B, and HCO_3 levels.
- *Soil Nutrient Status*

After the first sampling date, the soil chemical analyses data are used along with other necessary information to develop a management strategy to reclaim a site or prevent a salt problem from occurring. If a serious problem already exists, soil testing for monitoring purposes may be required as often as twice per year. In areas with wet and dry seasons, a good practice is to sample at the end of the rainy season and the end of the dry season. This sequence would provide a measure of the extremes of salinity, sodium hazard, or other salt related problems.

Site evaluation should include identifying existing *soil physical conditions*, especially those that influence water movement into the soil (infiltration), through the root zone (percolation), or past the root zone (drainage). The most common hindrances to water movement are: (a) a soil with excessive clay content. For example, a saline condition does not cause structure degradation but a saline soil could exhibit poor water percolation simply because of excessive clay content. Typically, clay soils will contain higher clay content in the B horizon than the A horizon; (b) structure deterioration caused by high Na; (c) soil compaction of the surface or a deeper zone caused by construction or maintenance equipment traffic; and (d) the presence of a layer from natural or man-induced action that limits water movement, such as clay lenses, sand layers, or a cemented horizon.

When evaluating a soil for these factors, soil physical conditions beyond the root zone are important, especially if poor quality irrigation water will be a source of additional salts over a long period of time. Drainage barriers can prevent salt movement deeper into the soil and result in salt buildup above the barrier. This salt may rise back into the root zone, especially during dry periods where leaching is inhibited.

Identification of the *predominant clay type* is very useful, especially if Na is a problem. Nonexpanding or 1:1 clays (kaolinite, Fe/Al hydrous oxides, allophane) are more tolerant of high Na content within the soil or that added by irrigation water than are expanding or 2:1 clays (vermiculite, montmorillonite). Illite is intermediate in Na sensitivity (Table 7.9) and expanding nature.

One positive attribute of expanding clays is that they crack upon drying, which can allow water and amendments to penetrate deeper when applied to the dry soil. However upon wetting, the cracks rapidly seal and water movement greatly diminishes. Openings created by cultivation would exhibit a similar response. While nonexpanding clays do not naturally crack upon drying, any openings created by cultivation tend to remain longer.

Assessment of *irrigation water quality* is just as essential as current soil conditions since water quality influences the future status of soil conditions. Water quality analyses are presented in Chapter 7.

The degree of seasonal variation in water quality parameters is important to know. This is not always easy to determine, especially if wastewater or surface water sources are used. Irrigation water quality should be evaluated annually but if wide variation is present, more frequent monitoring may be necessary, such as monthly until seasonal baselines are determined. If irrigation sources are to be blended or used individually but at separate times, water quality and quantity data will be needed from all sources. As with soil testing, a representative sample using clean utensils is mandatory.

The need for *a drainage system and suitable outlet* can be determined once existing soil chemical and water quality tests are obtained. Continual addition of high salt levels will require extra water to leach salts beyond the root system. Over time, however, any deep restriction to drainage may cause salts to accumulate and then start to salinize the lower root zone during periods when leaching is not occurring or if the water table rises. In other instances there may not be any hindrance to drainage but the natural water table may start to ascend in response to extra irrigation for leaching bringing up the salts.

Any *sources of salt additions* beyond the irrigation water should be measured or estimated. Possibilities include: (a) fill soil containing salts is common along sea coasts; (b) salt water intrusion into the aquifer where water is being pumped; and (c) a sodic or saline subsoil that may cause salts to ascend, especially if a fine-textured horizon is present within a few feet of the surface.

II. RESTRICTION OF SALT ADDITIONS

ON EXISTING SALT-AFFECTED SOILS or ones that may become affected, salt additions should be limited whenever feasible. *Irrigation water options* include: (a) use the best quality irrigation water; (b) blend irrigation waters to dilute undesirable total salinity or Na content in one of the sources. Blending is often achieved by pumping both sources into a holding pond and then irrigating out of the pond; and (c) desalinization of seawater and saline or sodic groundwaters may be economically feasible in some situations. Desalinization processes include evaporation, distillation, and reverse osmosis. Desalinization of irrigation water may not be necessary to the same purity as with drinking water. A suitable means of disposing of the salt brine must be considered in the cost evaluations.

If the source of salts is related to a *high water table and capillary rise into the root zone,* potential management choices are: (a) evaluate water table control for shallow water tables by dikes, ditches, and pumps; (b) consider the use of deep rooted trees and shrubs to root beyond the grass root zone and help lower the water table through extra water extraction; (c) remove any soil barriers within several feet below the root zone that may cause a perched water table (i.e., water table created above the normal water table due to a drainage barrier). Deep cultivation prior to turf establishment may break up layers within 3 or 4 feet (0.90 to 1.25 m) of the soil surface but often perched water table barriers are deeper. Drilling through the barrier into a more permeable zone should be considered; (d) low areas that are poorly drained are most susceptible to salt buildup by runoff or a rising water table. These sites should be assessed for any surface or subsurface drainage barriers as well as location of the water table. Removal of drainage hindrances, lowering of the water table, or filling the area are possible options. If runoff is the source of salts, interception drainage techniques may be useful; and (e) monitoring pipes to follow the water table movement and obtain water samples are valuable for future use.

Options to minimize *salt additions from soil movement* are: (a) avoid the use of fill soil containing undesirable salts; (b) during construction avoid bringing to the surface any subsurface horizons that are high in Na or salts; (c) prior to establishment of the grass, deep ripping of a sodic or saline B horizon will facilitate better leaching and reduce upward movement; and (d) capping a salt-affected soil with a sandy root zone layer, which can be easily leached, is possible at some sites. The soil that is capped may require deep ripping or chemical amendment additions prior to capping to avoid future drainage problems.

Adjusting *fertilizer salt additions* on high sand soils is sometimes necessary where irrigation water contains appreciable salts or Na. Recreational turfgrasses grown on these soils require relatively high K fertilization for wear, cold, heat, and drought tolerance and to compensate for high Na. However, too much K contributes to excessive salinity. Thus, field monitoring of ECe of the surface 0 to 1 inch (0 to 2.5 cm) and 0 to 3 inch (0 to 7.6 cm) zones can aid in adjusting K fertilization or increasing leaching. Relatively inexpensive field conductivity units using a soil:water paste where results are converted to ECe are available.

III. SELECTING SALT TOLERANT PLANTS

IT IS CRITICAL ON SALT-AFFECTED SITES to use grasses and other landscape plants that will tolerate the anticipated salinity levels as well as any specific toxic ions.[4,5,10] In Chapter 7, plant responses to salt related problems were noted as: (a) water deficit or drought responses induced by salts; (b) ion toxicities; (c) ion imbalances; and (d) reduced soil permeability by Na. Plants are classified as to salinity tolerance based on how they respond to increasingly high levels of total salts which include Na and Cl, two ions that contribute to toxicities.

Maas and Hoffman[10] proposed that most crops responded to increasing salinity in a manner that could be represented by two linear lines (Figure 8.1). One is a horizontal line which indicates no yield (or top growth for turfgrasses) response to increasing salinity, and the second depicts yield reduction as salinity increases. This second linear line can be represented by the equation

$$Y = 100 - b(ECe - a)$$

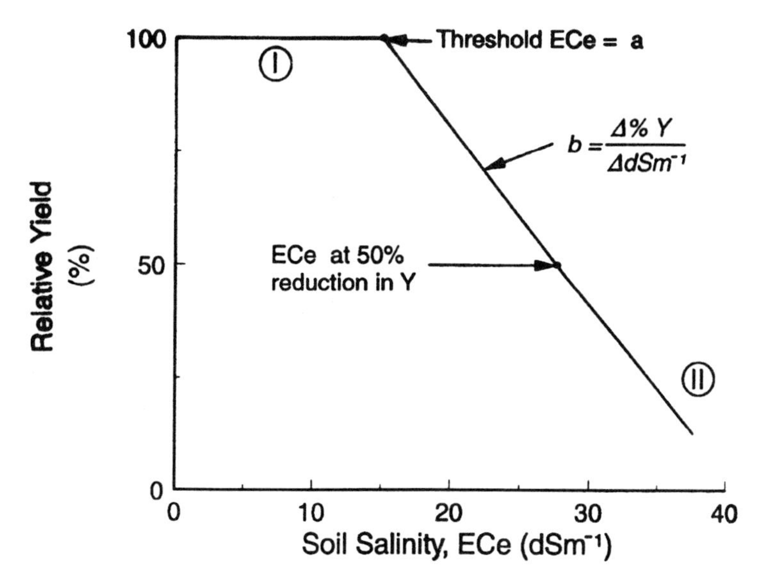

Figure 8.1. The two phase linear response to increasing soil salinity. I. is the horizontal phase where increasing salinity does not cause yield reduction; II. is the linear phase where increasing salinity reduces yield by the rate represented by b (the slope). The threshold salinity is point "a." Line II can be presented as: Y = 100 − b (ECe − a).

where Y represents percent relative yield; a is the salinity threshold in dSm^{-1} defined as the ECe where yield decreases to below a nonsaline condition; b is the slope which indicates the yield reduction per unit increase in ECe. This reduction is expressed in percent per dSm^{-1}; and electrical conductivity is the mean of saturated-soil extracts from the root zone (ECe). When studies are conducted in solution culture the EC_w is assumed to equal ECe. If other measures of EC are used they should be transformed to an equivalent ECe since this is the standard for salinity tolerance data.

Plants are classified as to salinity tolerance based on the threshold ECe (i.e., "a" in Figure 8.1) required to cause a yield reduction below the yield achieved under nonsaline conditions. The classifications of salinity tolerance and threshold ECe levels are found in the footnote of Table 8.1.

Turfgrass salinity tolerances are reported in Table 8.1. For turfgrasses, as well as other plants, the "idealized" relationship of yield versus salinity in Figure 8.1 may be altered based on whether the plant is highly sensitive or insensitive to salinity. *Halophytes* (salt tolerant; like FSP-3 seashore paspalum) plants often exhibit a response nature illustrated by Figure 8.2A where shoot growth actually increases with increasing salinity up to a point and then declines (Jacoby[7]). For example, FSP-3 seashore paspalum demonstrates a 10% increase in shoot growth up to 12 dSm^{-1}.

Common centipedegrass is salt sensitive (*glycophyte*) and shoot growth declines rapidly with salinity (Figure 8.2C). Figure 8.2B is for Kentucky bluegrass, a grass with intermediate salinity tolerance. Within a grass species, cultivar or ecotype salinity tolerance can vary as much as between species. Differences in root growth response to salinity may be even more dramatic than shoot growth.

From the previous discussion on top growth and root growth responses to salinity, it is apparent that several *parameters* can be used *to compare salinity tolerance of grasses.* Ideally, the most tolerant grasses would have:

Table 8.1. Salinity tolerance ranking of turfgrass species based on threshold ECe (from Carrow and Duncan[2]).

Common Name	Scientific Name	General Salinity Tolerance[a]	Threshold ECe		50% Growth Reduction ECe		Grass Type	Comments
			Ave.	Range	Ave.	Range		
			dSm^{-1}					
Seashore paspalum	*Paspalum vaginatum*	T	8.6	0–20	31	18–49	Warm	–
Alkaligrass	*Puccinella* spp.	T	8.5	6–12	25	20–30	Cool	–
Saltgrass	*Distichlis stricta*	T	8.0	6–10	–	–	Warm	Limited data
Kikuyu	*Pennisetum clandestinum*	T	8.0	6–10	–	–	Warm	Limited data
Fairway wheatgrass	*Agropyron cristatum*	T	8.0	6–10	–	–	Cool	Limited data
Western wheatgrass	*Agropyron smithii*	T	8.0	6–10	14	12–16	Cool	Limited data
St. Augustine-grass	*Stenotaphrum secundatum*	T	6.5	0–18	29	22–44	Warm	–
Tall fescue	*Festuca arundenacea*	T	6.5	5–10	11	8–12	Cool	Limited data, new cultivars
Perennial ryegrass	*Lolium perenne*	T	6.5	3–10	9	8–10	Cool	Limited data, new cultivars
Slender creep. red fescue	*Festuca ruba* L. spp. *trichopylla*	T	6.3	3–10	10	8–12	Cool	Limited data, new cultivars
Buffalograss	*Buchloe dactyloides*	MT	5.3	0–10	13	13	Warm	–
Blue grama	*Bouteloua gracilis*	MT	5.2	2–10	–	–	Warm	Limited data

Hard fescue	*Festuca longifolia*	MT	4.5	3–6	–	–	Cool	Limited data, new cultivars
Creeping red fescue	*Festuca ruba* L. spp. *ruba*	MT	4.5	3–6	10	8–12	Cool	Limited data, new cultivars
Bermudagrass, common	*Cynodon dactylon*	MT	4.3	0–12	21	12–32	Warm	–
Bermudagrass, hybrids	*Cynodon* spp.	MT	3.7	0–10	22	11–33	Warm	–
Creeping bentgrass	*Agrostis palustris*	MT	3.7	0–10	8	8	Cool	Limited data, new cultivars
Kentucky bluegrass	*Poa pratensis*	MS	3.0	0–6	14	3–30	Cool	Limited data, new cultivars
Zoysiagrass	*Zoysia* spp.	MS	2.4	0–11	16	4–40	Warm	–
Carpetgrass	*Axonopus* spp.	VS	1.5	0–1	–	–	Warm	Limited data
Centipedegrass	*Eremochloa ophiuroides*	VS	1.5	0–3	8	8–9	Warm	–
Annual bluegrass	*Poa annua*	VS	1.5	0–3	–	–	Cool	–
Colonial bentgrass	*Agrostis tenuis*	VS	1.5	0–3	–	–	Cool	Limited data
Rough bluegrass	*Poa trivialis*	VS	1.5	0–3	–	–	Cool	Limited data, new cultivars

[a] Based on guidelines of Maas[9,10]: VS (very sensitive) <1.5 d Sm^{-1} ECe; 1.6 to 3.0 MS, 3.1 to 6.0 MT; 6.1 to 10.0 T; and >10.1 VT (very tolerant).
[b] – denotes a lack of data.

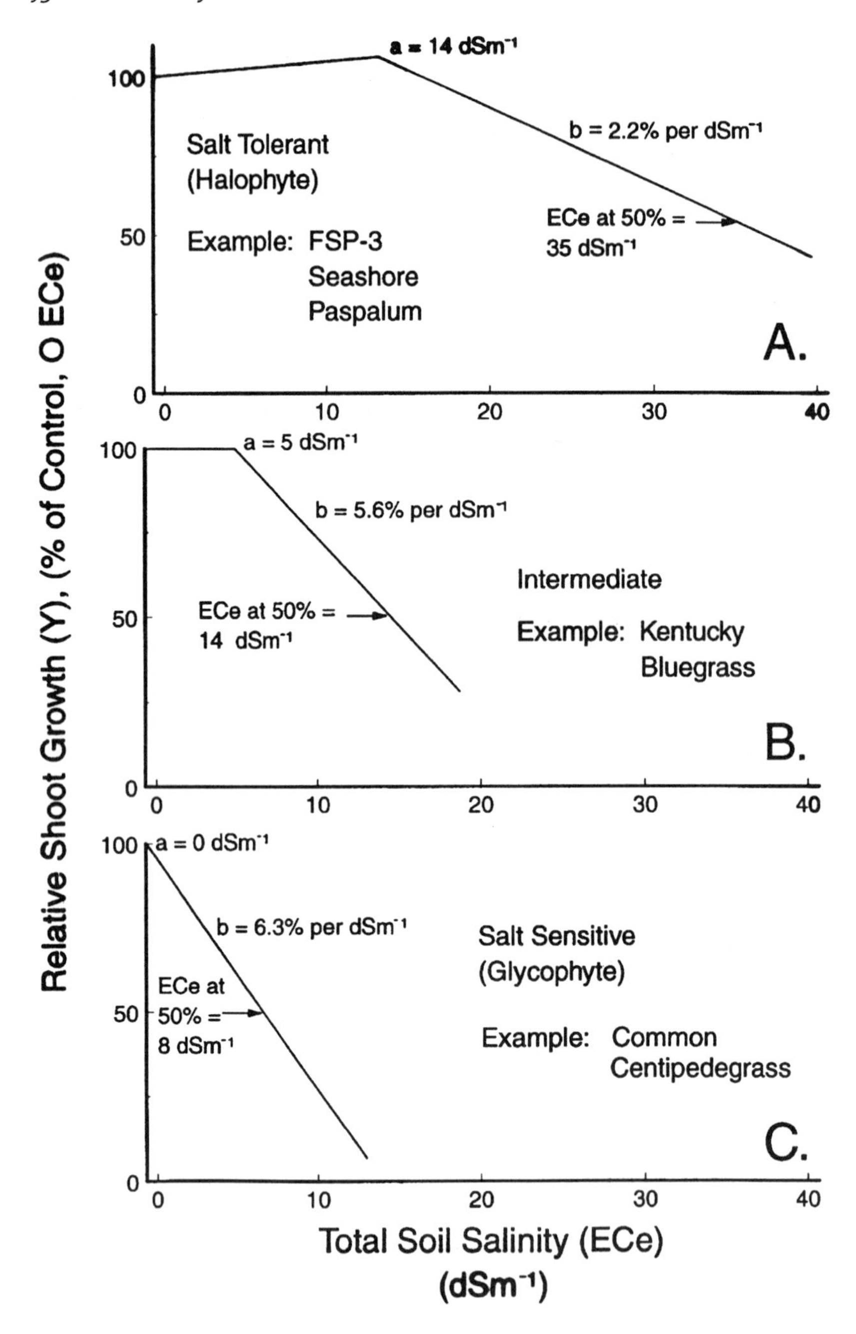

Figure 8.2. Example growth response versus salinity level curves. A. Halophyte (salt tolerant); B. Intermediate salinity tolerance; C. Glycophyte (salt sensitive).

- A high threshold ECe for shoot and root growth. The ability to maintain 100% growth at high ECe greatly expands tolerance to saline sites.
- A slight slope or decrease in growth per unit of ECe increase, which indicates that increasing salinity has only modest influence on growth.

- A high ECe for 50% growth reduction. For turfgrasses this is an important criterion since total yield or 100% top growth is not necessary as in an agronomic crop. Shoot growth must be adequate to withstand wear and maintain quality on a site but does not need to be maximum growth.
- Another important factor that is not revealed in response curves as in Figure 8.2 is total growth rate (i.e., Y, not in percentage but in actual growth). A grass that has an inherently higher growth rate under salinity should be able to tolerate higher salinity and still provide adequate growth. Marcum and Murdoch[11] reported that the two most salt tolerant turfgrasses in a study of six grasses were the ones with the highest growth rates.

If the threshold ECe (a) and slope factors (b) are known for a grass, the linear portion of the salinity equation (where salinity causes reduced growth) can be used to estimate the potential reduction in growth at a particular ECe. For example, the salinity equation (Figure 8.1) for FSP-3 seashore paspalum is:

$$Y = 100 - b\ (ECe - a)$$

where a = 14 dSm^{-1} and b = 2.2% dSm^{-1} from Figure 8.2A. If the current root zone ECe measures 28 dSm^{-1}, the expected Y is:

$$\begin{aligned} Y &= 100 - 2.2\ (28 - 14\ dSm^{-1}) \\ &= 100 - 2.2\ (14\ dSm^{-1}) \\ &= 69\% \text{ of the growth rate at ECe } 0\ dSm^{-1} \text{ (i.e., 100\% growth)} \end{aligned}$$

However, FSP-3 demonstrates a 105% growth rate at the threshold ECe so the actual decrease in growth from the maximum observed is 74%.

Turfgrass breeders are increasingly placing more emphasis on evaluating germplasm for salinity tolerance and improving tolerance. As more data are available, turf managers should utilize the information to make wise grass selection decisions.

Attention to salinity tolerance of trees and shrubs for sites with continual salinity problems is necessary to ensure long-term persistence of plant materials. Maas[9] provides a list of salinity tolerances of 49 ornamental shrubs, trees, and ground covers; plus, Rhoades and Loveday[15] list 38 woody crops that could be used as landscape plants. Countries with significant salt-affected soils often develop lists of salt tolerant plants such as Sen and Mohammed[16] for India and Handreck and Black[6] for Australia.

IV. LEACHING OF SALTS

Leaching of excess salts in saline soils and Na in sodic soils is the most important management component of any comprehensive management plan for all salt-affected sites. If soil salinity levels are not controlled, excessive salinization will eventually lead to crop failure.

Field situations can vary from the extremes of: (a) a salt-affected soil to be planted to a turfgrass and with a good quality irrigation water source. In this case, leaching of excess salts is a one-time event; and (b) a salt-affected soil where a turfgrass is to be established but irrigation water quality is poor. Here, the soil is initially high in salts but future salt additions will also be high. This is obviously a continuing problem of leaching to maintain sufficiently low salinity in the root zone for turfgrass persistence. This latter situation presents *several problems associated with leaching salts,* namely:

- determining the quantity of water, frequency, timing, and procedure to leach salts (i.e., *leaching requirement issues*).
- how to maintain adequate water infiltration, percolation, and drainage to move excess salts beyond the root zone *(irrigation water treatment to maximize infiltration and cultivation issues).*
- whether salts must be removed from the subsoil below the root zone and, if so, how to achieve salt removal in an environmentally acceptable manner (i.e., *drainage requirement issues*).

A. Leaching Requirement

A term that is important to understand is *leaching requirement (LR)* where LR represents the minimum amount of water that must pass through the root zone to control salts within an acceptable level. The LR is presented in terms of a fraction of water applied above that needed to meet turfgrass evapotranspiration (ET) needs. Thus, LR is the quantity of additional water required to maintain salinity within an acceptable range and is called the *maintenance leaching requirement.* Three methods of estimating LR can be used (Carrow and Duncan[2]) but only the Rhoades[14] method is presented.

The formula developed by Rhoades[14] and presented by Ayers and Westcot[1] is:

$$LR = \frac{EC_W}{5\ ECe - EC_w} = \frac{EC_W}{5\ EC_{TS} - EC_w}$$

where ECe is the threshold EC for the turfgrass or the EC the grass can tolerate (EC_{TS}); and EC_w is the EC of the irrigation water. Assuming, for Kentucky bluegrass, the threshold EC_e is 5 dSm^{-1} and the irrigation water has an EC_w of 2 dSm^{-1}:

$$LR = \frac{2\ dSm^{-1}}{5\left(5\ dSm^{-1}\right) - 2\ dSm^{-1}}$$

$$= \frac{2\ dSm^{-1}}{23\ dSm^{-1}} = 0.086$$

which means that the LR is 8.6% more water than ET needs. Water required for the LR can be supplied by irrigation or precipitation. The quantity of water required to reclaim (i.e., *reclamation leaching*) a soil that has been salinized is much greater than for *maintenance leaching.*

Leaching of total soluble salts contributing to high salinity is much more rapid and easy than for removal of Na^+ on CEC sites of a sodic soil. On sodic soils, the Na^+ is chemically held and must be replaced by Ca^{+2} before Na^+ comes into the soil solution where it can be leached. In contrast, soluble salts are already in the soil solution.

B. Irrigation Management

It is easier to visualize irrigation management for salt control if the situation is specified. Common situations include: (a) leaching salts prior to turfgrass establishment; (b) leaching salts after turfgrasses are established using a relatively good quality irrigation water; and (c) salinity control when the irrigation water quality is poor.

Preestablishment

High total salinity has a more adverse effect on grass establishment than does a sodic soil, but sodic soils present more long-term problems. When initial soil salinity levels are sufficiently high to adversely influence turfgrass establishment, leaching prior to attempting establishment is preferred. Irrigation management influences the degree of salt leaching and time requirements.

Ponding of water for leaching is usually not feasible for turfgrass situations except for initial leaching prior to establishment or on established turf sites with level topography. The quantity of water necessary to leach salts by flooding or ponding depends on soil type. As a guideline, about 70% of the total soluble salt will be removed from a sandy soil by 6 inches (15 cm) of water per 12 inches (30 cm) of soil depth; for a medium-textured soil, 12 inches water per 12 inches of soil; and for a fine-textured (clay) soil about 14–18 inches water per 12 inches soil. The quantity of water to leach 70% of the initial soil soluble salts, however, would be greater if the irrigation water quality is poor. Also, on a sodic soil, little Na^+ would be leached by this same quantity of water unless a high quantity of relatively soluble Ca^{+2} had been added with time for Na^+ to be exchanged. Even then, less than 70% Na^+ removal would be expected.

Leaching can be achieved by sprinkler application with one-third to one-half the water required for ponded water leaching but more time will be required. Pulse irrigation is most effective where water is applied and allowed to infiltrate. Additional irrigation events continue at 12 to 24 hr intervals with water applied so as to prevent runoff but maintain infiltration and percolation.

Greater leaching efficiency with less water is possible by intermittent sprinkler irrigation versus ponding because more unsaturated flow occurs in the smaller pores and water films with intermittent sprinkler application. With ponding, water flow is predominantly in the larger pores in the form of saturated flow; thus bypassing salts in the smaller pores.

Postestablishment/Mature Turfgrass

If the turfgrass is established, exhibiting salinity stress, and irrigation water quality is good, the principles and guidelines discussed under "Preestablishment" are appropriate. The focus is a one-time leaching program (i.e., reclamation leaching) to decrease initially high total salinity levels. Until salts are leached, soil moisture should be maintained sufficiently high within the upper root zone to avoid moisture stress—this is elaborated on in the following paragraphs.

The most difficult situation is where initial soil salinity is high and irrigation water quality is medium to very high in salinity. It is in this instance that the LR must be adequate to initially reduce any existing *soil* salinity, and then adjusted to maintain leaching of salts added by the irrigation water. Eventually, soil salinity in the upper root zone will be closely associated with irrigation water salinity as long as salts are not allowed to accumulate.

Plants can tolerate higher salinity levels in the soil if water stress is avoided, such as by high frequency irrigation. For example, high salinity in the deeper root zone can be tolerated if the surface root zone is maintained under frequent irrigation so there is no capillary rise of water and salts, and the salts in the root zone are not concentrated by the soil drying. Since the major influence of high salts is to induce water stress (physiological drought), maintaining high water content aids in counteracting salt induced drought as well as decreasing the concentration of toxic ions.

These principles should, however, be used with a commonsense evaluation of the specific problem on a site since excessive irrigation can also be detrimental. On a site where the initial soil salinity level is high, frequent irrigation may be necessary, but as salinity levels decrease, irrigation can be adjusted. The key to success is a good salinity monitoring program.

Another example of less frequent irrigation would be where a deep-rooted, drought tolerant grass is used that has good salinity tolerance. Under these conditions, less frequent irrigation with a dry-down between irrigations can be done without excessive growth reductions. In contrast, a shallow-rooted, less salt tolerant (or drought tolerant) grass would require a more moist root zone.

It should be emphasized that light, frequent irrigation with a poor quality irrigation water can cause serious buildup of salts in arid regions or during dry periods when ET is high. Sometimes turf managers switch to a light, frequent irrigation regime on bentgrass greens in the summer and do not apply enough water for leaching. Salts will accumulate at the surface from the irrigation water even if salt level in the irrigation water is only moderate. At the same time, capillary rise may bring salts from below the root zone up into the root zone due to lack of leaching. Frequent irrigation can be practiced but the quantity of water must be sufficient to leach salts (i.e., the LR must be adequate).

On sites with a continuous salinity problem due to poor irrigation water quality or water restrictions that limit adequate leaching, additional irrigation at the end of the rainy season can aid in moving salts lower into the profile or into drainage tile for flushing salts. Other beneficial practices are: (a) use multiple pulse irrigation events of 15 to 30 minutes with one or two hours between pulses. This is more effective than a single irrigation cycle of one or two hours. On heavy soils this practice may be conducted on the same site for two or more days (or evenings) to achieve sufficient water movement; (b) allow sufficient time for drainage to occur before greens or tees are to receive play. Control fairway traffic during heavy leaching cycles to prevent rutting and compaction; and (c) when cool-season grasses are present, water management during high temperature periods becomes critical. It is best to apply leaching events that reduce high soil salinity before the high temperature periods. Then, only the LR to maintain adequate salinity levels need be applied during high temperature periods. This practice will reduce problems from salt-induced moisture stress if drying occurs as well as excessive moisture from intensive leaching events.

C. Enhancing Water Movement for Salt Leaching

Leaching of a significant quantity of total soluble salts and Na on sodic soils requires water to enter the soil *(infiltrate),* move through the root zone *(percolate),* and move below the root zone *(drainage).* Sodic and some saline-sodic soils have inherently poor structure due to structure breakdown by slaking, colloid dispersion, and colloid migration. These soils will require the practices presented in this section plus soil amendment application to replace Na ions. Amendments and their use will be discussed in Section 8.V, Amendments and Their Use. Saline soils usually do not require amendments to replace Na but do need to be leached.

In addition to amendments applied directly to sodic or saline-sodic soils to replace Na and thereby improve water infiltration/percolation, irrigation water may be amended: (a) to provide a soluble Ca source to replace Na; and (b) to increase soil surface or irrigation water salinity

(Carrow et al.[3]). Both of these cases can improve permeability. As with amendments applied directly to the soil, irrigation water amendments will be discussed in Section 8.V, Amendments and Their Use.

The primary point is that practices to maximize soil water movement so that leaching occurs are essential. All options should be evaluated, whether chemical amendment of the soil, chemical amendment of the irrigation water, cultivation, or other practices (Carrow and Duncan[2]). Enhancing water movement must include the aspects of infiltration, percolation, and drainage.

In addition to a periodic subsurface cultivation program, a more frequent surface cultivation program is almost always required to: (a) alleviate conditions that limit infiltration; and (b) make the subsurface cultivation program more effective. Percolation will be best when continuous channels or macropore continuity reach the soil surface rather than being sealed off at the surface.

In sodic and saline-sodic soils, and when irrigation water has very low EC_w or high SAR_w, cultivation operations will not last as long as in the same soil without these conditions because of the continuous processes of aggregate slaking, dispersion, and migration of colloids induced by high Na content. As these processes occur, the macropores either collapse or are plugged. As a general rule, surface and subsurface cultivation operations are effective for only one-half the time as the same operation on the same soil but one that is not affected by Na.

Once water moves past the root zone it is considered drainage water. The same soil physical conditions that restrict percolation can hinder drainage. However, deep cultivation to alleviate these conditions is limited once a turfgrasss is established. Individual probes using high pressure air or water may be used to correct some deep problems in limited areas.

Deep cultivation prior to turfgrass establishment can be beneficial when drainage is seriously impeded by heavy clay, sodic, or cemented zones. Agricultural techniques can be used such as deep ripping, paraplowing, and deep moldboard plowing. A version of gypsum slotting underlaid by a mole drain could be feasible prior to turfgrass establishment or even on established turf (Jayawardane and Chan[8]). In this system, slots 4 to 6 inches (10 to 15 cm) wide are spaced 3 to 7 feet (1 to 2 m) apart to 15 to 20 inch (40 to 60 cm) depth with a mole drain below the slot. The soil within the slot is gypsum enriched. Equipment used for slot draining and injection of sand into the slots in turfgrass areas could be modified to achieve a similar purpose if the sand was amended with gypsum.

Mixing gypsum or other amendments to replace Na or create better structure (i.e., fresh organic matter) should be considered whenever any deep cultivation is practiced before turf establishment. These practices will enhance water movement at least during initial phases and are especially important on sites with an existing Na problem B versus, for example, a location that may develop a problem from irrigation with a high SAR_w source.

On sites that contain high salinity within the root zone or will receive high salt inputs from future irrigation, draining salts from the zone below the root zone must be seriously considered. *Resalinization* of the root zone by salts rising in a water table or by accumulation above a drainage barrier is very difficult to remedy once it occurs. Initially, low spots will be affected but if salts continue to rise, all areas will be subject to resalinization. This problem can sometimes occur over a larger geographical area, such as Western Australia, with costly agronomic and social implications.

Resalinization is most likely to happen under the conditions of: (a) a natural water table that rises and carries salts into the root zone. Enhanced water input may be from more frequent irrigation on the site or surrounding landscape, greater runoff into the site, or unusually high rainfall; (b) any impeding barrier that causes a perched water table to develop once irrigation is initiated; or (c) any soil barrier that reduces continuous downward drainage and allows salts to accumulate above the barrier. In the latter two situations, hot and dry climatic conditions in conjunction with insufficient irrigation to maintain leaching can lead to significant capillary rise of salts from these zones of salt accumulation.

The overall design requirements on salt-affected sites should be made in the context of a *water management plan* that encompasses irrigation water quality, irrigation practices, disposal options, and drainage. Limiting unnecessary water inputs will reduce the chances of raising the water table and minimize drainage discharge. Possible *alternatives to limit water input* are: (a) surface drainage to intercept excess saline water or even good quality runoff and prevent it from entering the turfgrass facility; (b) sealing the channels of ditches and ponds that are contributing to water drainage into the water table; (c) using the minimal LR; (d) improving the design efficiency of the irrigation system; (e) using shallower drain lines and closer spacings to prevent drainage into the deeper water table on sites where the natural water table is already high; and (f) practicing no-drainage and drainage cycles for salt control. In this system, LR is kept low so that salts accumulate. As salinity and waterlogging appear within a year or after more than one year, drain tiles are opened (i.e., they are kept closed for the no-drainage cycle) and sufficient water is applied to leach salts. This reduces drainage water volume but salt concentrations are higher in the leachate.

Reuse of drainage water can be beneficial in limiting disposal problems and drainage into the water table where shallow, close-spaced drainage systems are used to intercept water. The drainage water can be used directly or blended with a better quality source. Sometimes the water can be utilized for other purposes such as agroforestry and industrial needs. Eventually, salinity levels increase to where disposal will be necessary when recycling is practiced, but the quantity is greatly reduced.

Disposal options must be consistent with environmental laws since other water users may be affected. Possibilities for disposal include: (a) evaporation ponds; (b) outlet in the ocean or saltwater marshes; (c) dilution into streams, (d) injection into a deep aquifer; or (e) desalinization.

If conditions warrant *subsurface drainage,* potential options are: (a) tile drainage; (b) flexible perforated plastic drainage lines; and (c) mole drains. A drainage engineer who understands saline or sodic conditions should be consulted. Tile depths in arid regions may be at 6 feet (1.8 m) or more to prevent capillary rise of saline water into the root zone. However, tile depth is influenced by tile spacing, soil type, presence of drainage barriers, water table depth, and other factors. Whatever the depth chosen, spacing between lines is important to allow salinity control between lines. In humid regions, tile depth may be at 2 to 4 feet (0.60 to 1.20 m) with appropriate spacing.

Mole drains can be used in some instances, especially when the B horizon has high clay content to stabilize the mole drains. On sodic soils, mole drains tend to be less stable and long lasting. When reclaiming a salt-affected soil prior to turf establishment, mole drains can afford a temporary drainage system.

V. AMENDMENTS AND THEIR USE

SINCE EXCESSIVE NA MARKEDLY REDUCES SOIL PERMEABILITY, the presence of Na in the soil or irrigation water will require chemical amendments be used to add Ca as a replacement ion (Table 8.2). Any salt-affected soil with high Na (i.e., sodic, saline-sodic soils) will need amendment treatment to provide a relatively soluble Ca source. Also, any soil receiving irrigation water with high Na must be amended, even soils that are not initially salt-affected.

When reclaiming a salt-affected soil or preventing a salt problem due to irrigation water quality, several factors must be considered: (a) the particular soil conditions; (b) irrigation

Table 8.2. Summary of soil and irrigation water situations requiring an amendment to provide Ca as a replacement for Na ions.

Current Soil Situation	Irrigation Water Sodium Status	Requirement for an Amendment to Provide Ca to Replace Na
Sodic[a]	High SAR_W	Yes—continuous basis
Sodic[a]	Low SAR_W	Yes—until soil is nonsodic
Saline-Sodic[a]	High SAR_W	Yes—continuous basis
Saline-Sodic[b,c]	Low SAR_W	Yes—until soil is no longer saline-sodic
Saline[a]	High SAR_W	Yes—to prevent sodic condition
Saline[a]	Low SAR_W	No
Nonsalt affected[a]	High SAR_W	Yes—to prevent sodic condition
Nonsalt affected	Low SAR_W	No

[a] All of these situations require leaching to remove Na on a long-term basis.
[b] If a saline-sodic soil has appreciable Ca in the surface horizon, a Ca source may not always be needed when a low SAR_W water is used.
[c] These require leaching until the Na has been removed or high total salts are leached.

water quality as noted in Table 8.2; (c) choice of an amendment or combination of amendments to supply Ca; (d) options for applying amendments, and (e) rates of amendments.

A. The Source of Calcium

The most common chemicals added to the soil to increase the ratio of Ca to Na are gypsum, elemental S, or sulfuric acid with lime required in conjunction with the latter two materials (Table 8.3). Common irrigation water amendments are gypsum and sulfuric acid. Whenever an S amendment is used, there must be lime present in the soil for the S to react with and form gypsum. Other soil or water amendments are sometimes used due to local availability.

Gypsum and Phosphogypsum

Gypsum is widely used as an amendment for sodic and saline-sodic soils. It is mined and found in the forms of dihydrate, $CaSO_4{\cdot}2H_2O$; hemihydrate, $CaSO_4{\cdot}{}^1/_2H_2O$); and anhydrite, $CaSO_4$. Also, phosphogypsum (PG) or flue gas desulfurization gypsum (FGDG) are available as by-products from manufacturing. The most common form of gypsum, $CaSO_4{\cdot}2H_2O$, PG, and FGDG contain 23 to 28% Ca. Solubility of gypsum depends on particle size and degree of crystallization, with mined gypsum often highly crystallized. Higher solubility is related to small particles and less crystallization. Oftentimes, PG and FGDG are 5 to 10 times more soluble than mined gypsum due to fine particle size; however, these materials are not available in all locations. When considering relative costs of materials, determine the purity of the gypsum grade that is available and freight costs. Mined gypsum can be as low as 20% purity.

Soil application is the only method for PG and FGDG, while gypsum can be soil applied and some grades injected through an irrigation system. For soil application, a wide range in particle size of gypsum from 2 mm to fine is preferred over all fine particles, especially on soils with much Na_2CO_3. On these soils, all fine gypsum releases appreciable Ca which can react to form $CaCO_3$ as a coating over the remaining gypsum, thereby reducing further dissolution. Coarser gypsum is not coated to the extent of finer gypsum and provides longer-term Ca release.

Table 8.3. Chemical amendments used to supply Ca for replacement of Na in salt-affected soils or irrigation water. When S materials are used, lime must be present in the soil or added so that gypsum can form.

100% Pure Amendment[a]	Chemical Formula	Pounds Equivalent to 1 lb Gypsum	Soil or Water Amendment
Gypsum (23% Ca)	$CaSO_4 \cdot 2H_2O$	1.00	S, W
Phosphogypsum or	24% Ca to	0.96	S
Flue Gas Desulfuration Gypsum	29% Ca	0.79	S
Elemental S	S	0.19	S
Sulfuric acid[b,c]	H_2SO_4	0.61	S, W
Ferric sulfate	$Fe_2(SO_4)_3 \cdot 9H_2O$	1.09	S
Ferrous sulfate	$FeSO_4 \cdot 7H_2O$	1.61	S
Calcium chloride	$CaCl_2 \cdot 2H_2O$	0.86	S, W
Lime sulfur	9% Ca + 24% S, CaS_x	0.78	S, W
Aluminum sulfate	$Al_2(SO_4)_3$	1.29	S
Ammonium polysulfide	$(NH_4)_2S_x$	1.46	S, W
Ammonium thiosulfate	$(NH_4)_2S_2O_3$	0.62	S, W
Calcium nitrate	$Ca(NO_3)_2 \cdot H_2O$	1.06	S, W
Calcium thiosulfate	CaS_2O_3	–	S, W

[a] Purity. For amendments of less than 100% purity the following formula can be used to calculate an amount equivalent to 1 pound of 100% gypsum:

$$\text{Equivalent amount} = \frac{100\%}{\%\ \text{Purity}} \times \text{Pounds Equivalent}$$

For example, assuming 93% sulfuric acid is to be used:

$$\text{Equivalent amount} = \frac{100}{93} \times 0.61 = 0.66\ lb$$

[b] Sulfur is also spelled as sulphur; sulfate as sulphate; sulfuric as sulphuric.

[c] Sulfuric acid can be purchased as an acid or generated by sulfur dioxide generators from elemental S. Elemental S is oxidized into SO_2, then SO_2 combines with water to generate H_2SO_4 or H_2SO_3.

Surface application is important to maintain permeability of the soil surface for good infiltration. Gypsum, PG, or FGDG can be mixed into the soil prior to establishment but sufficient quantities should be applied to the surface to maintain infiltration and prevent crusting. When high Na is present throughout the root zone or as a sodic B horizon, injection of these products should be considered. This can be achieved by the Yeager-Twose Turf Conditioner, a deep drill device with sand amended with these Ca sources, or a slit drainage device with slits back-filled with amended sand. The Turf Conditioner applies pelletized gypsum at up to 70 to 90 lb per 1,000 ft^2 (3,400 to 4,400 kg ha^{-1}) to a depth of 8 inches (20 cm) at 4 inch (10 cm) spacings, which would be beneficial for ameliorating a sodic B horizon. The other devices result in vertical channels rich in gypsum to enhance water drainage and Na leaching.

When *gypsum is injected through the irrigation system,* a very fine product of high purity is used to saturate water in an agitator tank and then this water is metered into the irrigation line; or a fine grade of gypsum is gravity fed into the irrigation lines. This practice provides a Ca source for replacing Na in the soil and lowering SAR. Second, the Ca increases total salt concentration (i.e., TEC, total electrolyte concentration) of the soil solution, which enhances surface soil stability even at relatively high SAR. A third benefit can occur if EC_w is very low (<0.50 dSm^{-1}). Under these conditions the TEC of the soil surface will be very low and infiltration markedly declines due to surface sealing even when soil SAR (i.e., Na content) is low.

Whether applied as gypsum, PG, or FGDG as a soil or irrigation water amendment, *the mode of action on sodic and saline-sodic soils* is the same. The Ca becomes soluble as these amendments dissolve and Ca replaces Na from soil cation exchange sites, which can then be leached with extra water.

$$\begin{array}{l}Na^+\\Na^+\end{array}\boxed{\begin{array}{c}\text{Soil}\\\text{Colloid}\end{array}}\begin{array}{c}\\Na^+\quad Na^+\end{array} + 2CaSO_4 \rightleftarrows Ca^{+2}\boxed{\begin{array}{c}\text{Soil}\\\text{Colloid}\end{array}} + 2Na_2SO_4(\text{leachable})$$

(lower edge of the second box: Ca^{+2})

At the same time, bicarbonates and carbonates associated with Na are transformed into insoluble $CaCO_3$.

$$2NaHCO_3 + CaSO_4 \rightleftarrows CaCO_3 + \underset{(\text{leachable})}{Na_2SO_4} + CO_2 + H_2O$$

$$Na_2CO_3 + CaSO_4 \rightleftarrows CaCO_3 + \underset{(\text{leachable})}{Na_2SO_4}$$

The major benefit of these reactions is to transform Na associated with HCO_3 and CO_3 into a more soluble and leachable from, while reducing any potential HCO_3 toxicity problems by formation of $CaCO_3$. As these reactions are occurring, Ca enhances TEC to: (a) stabilize structure in the soil surface against high Na permeability hazard; and (b) enhance water infiltration in the case of very pure water with low EC_w.

Elemental S

Elemental S is insoluble and can only be applied as a soil treatment. It does not directly supply Ca but furnishes Ca by reaction with lime ($CaCO_3$) in the soil. Thus when S is applied, lime must be applied or already be present in the soil to generate gypsum over time. Usually a high purity grade of 85 to 99% S is used on turfgrasses but for reclamation purposes grades from 50 to 99% have been mixed into the soil. Finely ground particles (<0.178 mm or preferable <0.150 mm) provide the fastest response. Pelletized granules of fine particles and porous granules of popcorn S (formed from molten S and water) are also available. Other formulations include S plus 10% bentonite as a conditioner; S-slurry a suspension of very fine S in water with 2 to 3% atlapulgite clay conditioner; and agriculture grade S which is a mixture of particle sizes.

When S is applied to a soil containing $CaCO_3$, the *reactions* are:

$$2S + 3O_2 + 2H_2O \xrightarrow{\textit{Thiobacillus}} 2H_2SO_4$$

This sequence requires biochemical oxidation of S by the bacteria genus *Thiobacillus*. In climates where wintertime soil temperatures are <55°F (13°C), this reaction does not occur due to low bacterial activity. Thus, in cool coastal climates where the turfgrass receives high Na inputs from irrigation, salt spray, or flooding in winter months, soil applied S (as well as S from other sources discussed below) may not generate sufficient Ca.

Calcium is derived from an action of H_2SO_4 on $CaCO_3$;

$$H_2SO_4 + CaCO_3 \rightleftarrows \underset{(gypsum)}{CaSO_4} + H_2O + CO_2 \uparrow$$

The gypsum then reacts as discussed in the Gypsum section to replace Na on the cation exchange sites and transform $NaHCO_3$ and Na_2CO_3 into more easily leached Na_2SO_4.

If free $CaCO_3$ is not in the soil or added as lime, elemental S will not produce Ca for Na replacement. Instead the reaction becomes:

$$\begin{array}{c} Na^+ \\ Na^+ \end{array} \boxed{\begin{array}{c} \text{Soil} \\ \text{Colloid} \end{array}}_{Na^+ \quad Na^+} + H_2SO_4 \rightleftarrows \begin{array}{c} H^+ \\ H^+ \end{array} \boxed{\begin{array}{c} \text{Soil} \\ \text{Colloid} \end{array}}_{H^+ \quad H^+} + \underset{\text{(leaches)}}{Na_2SO_4}$$

Under these conditions, Na^+ can be replaced by H^+ and leached but soil structure does not readily improve except when soil pH declines to pH <6.0 and appreciable $Al(OH)_3$ is created. Divalent Ca^{+2} is very effective in flocculating clay colloids together to create structural units; thereby improving soil permeability. Hydrogen ions are less effective in causing flocculation, even though swelling/shrinking may decline, except when the trivalent Al^{+3} becomes prevalent at pH <5.0.

It should be noted that S use on sodic or saline-sodic soils that do not contain $CaCO_3$ will result in lowering pH. A lowering of pH may not be desirable on salt-affected soils of high rainfall areas if the pH is already neutral or acid due to leaching of Ca and Mg. The source of Na for these sites is often from coastal flooding, salt spray, or groundwater high in Na from salt water intrusion. If a turfgrass manager wishes to use elemental S under these conditions, lime should be periodically applied to the soil surface to provide a Ca source and pH should be monitored in the surface 1 inch (2.5 cm) and 4 inch (10 cm) zones.

When poor quality irrigation water high in Na requires continuous use of elemental S, the free $CaCO_3$ near the soil surface may become depleted over time and result in reduced infiltration of water. Yet, sufficient free $CaCO_3$ may be present lower in the profile to allow for gypsum formation and Na leaching in the lower zones. To maintain surface soil permeability, additional lime should be added to the surface.

Gypsum formed by H_2SO_4 reaction with lime has very fine particle size and is thus very active in replacing Na. While it requires 2 to 4 weeks depending on soil temperature for some of the elemental S to be transformed in H_2SO_4 and then for gypsum to start being produced, once the gypsum is created it is fast acting.

Sulfuric Acid (H_2SO_4)

Sulfuric acid can be applied directly to the soil prior to turfgrass establishment with special safety equipment. More commonly it is injected into irrigation water to adjust water pH to 6.5 to 7.0 with lower pH resulting in corrosion of metal irrigation system parts. When injected into irrigation water, equipment to handle high purity liquid sulfuric acid is necessary. Also sulfuric acid can be generated by oxidizing elemental S into SO_3 gas which when combined with water creates H_2SO_4 or H_2SO_3.

Since the S is already in the H_2SO_4 form, *Thiobacillus* bacteria are not needed for oxidization and, therefore, sulfuric acid is not dependent on soil temperature for activity. Outside of these differences, sulfuric acid reacts in the soil in the same manner as elemental S and requires free $CaCO_3$ to create gypsum.

Sometimes irrigation water contains high bicarbonate (HCO_3) or carbonate (CO_3) concentrations. These ions selectively react with Ca and Mg in the irrigation water or in the surface soil solution to precipitate out as $CaCO_3$ or $MgCO_3$. The result is to leave any Na in the irrigation and soil surface in solution to adversely affect structure and possibly cause toxicity problems. Acidification of the irrigation water causes these ions to evolve off as gas (CO_2).

Other Sulfur Based Amendments

Soil application of several sulfate based amendments (ferric sulfate, ferrous sulfate, aluminum sulfate) is possible as preestablishment treatments (Table 8.3). These are not widely used but may be available at reasonable cost in some locations. All react similar to sulfuric acid but are slower reacting due to low solubility.

Lime sulfur (CaS_x) is a liquid containing unoxidized sulfur in the sulfide form. It is also referred to as lime sulfur (Table 8.3) and the Ca serves as a Ca source. Another sulfide is ammonium polysulfide, $(NH_4)_2S_x$, that contains N. Ammonium thiosulfate, $(NH_4)_2S_2O_3$, is also a liquid S source. All three of these materials must be oxidized by *Thiobacillus* to transform the S into sulfuric acid. Their equivalent weights to equal one pound (0.45 kg) of 100% pure gypsum as $CaSO_4{\bullet}2H_2O$ are listed in Table 8.3. While these liquids can be injected into an irrigation system, the N content limits the total for the two ammonium based materials so as not to exceed turfgrass N needs. Lime sulfur is highly alkaline and can be corrosive. Other S containing materials may be marketed and can be used such as potassium thiosulfate (liquid, 25% K_2O, 17% S) or calcium thiosulfate (liquid, 6% Ca, 10% S).

Ammonium sulfate fertilizer applied as a granular or created by ammonia (NH_3) and sulfuric acid injection through the irrigation system can be used as an additional S source. Rate of fertilizer applied is determined by turfgrass needs.

Other Ca Sources

As noted in the preceding section, lime sulfur, CaS_x, is a liquid source for S as well as Ca. Other highly soluble Ca sources are calcium chloride, calcium thiosulfate, and calcium nitrate. Calcium nitrate can be a granular applied fertilizer or added in the irrigation water by a fertigation system. The total quantity of calcium nitrate will be determined by the turfgrass N requirement so it should be considered as a supplemental Ca source. However, because of high solubility, Ca in calcium nitrate is very active in replacement of Na.

Calcium chloride, $CaCl_2$, is expensive unless it is available as a by-product material. But, it has very high solubility and easily increases the TEC of irrigation or surface soil solution water, while adding Ca. Calcium chloride should be considered in the situations of: (a) sodic soils with SAR above 20 in the surface horizon; (b) any soil with a highly sodic B or C horizon of SAR above 20; (c) a saline-sodic or sodic soil where the irrigation water has very low EC_w (<0.50 dSm^{-1}) or a high SAR_w or adjusted SAR_w (<18 mg L^{-1}); or (d) *high salt content irrigation water,* also called the *high salt water dilution method,* can be used on highly sodic soils to affect leaching. The water must be naturally high in Ca or enriched with Ca by $CaCl_2$ or gypsum dissolution so that the EC_w exceeds the electrolyte level (TEC) that inhibits water infiltration at the soil SAR (Figure 7.3). In any of these sodic soil situations, $CaCl_2$ should not be used as a total replacement for gypsum (the primary Ca source), rather as a supplement, due to the total salinity problems that can arise at high rates of $CaCl_2$ use.

Combinations of Amendments

When the irrigation source has high adj SAR_w or the existing soil is highly sodic, a combination of amendments and application procedures may be beneficial. For example, sulfuric acid injected into the irrigation water could remove high bicarbonates and generate gypsum at the soil surface if $CaCO_3$ is present or added. Additional gypsum could be broadcast over the surface, injected at 8 inches (20 cm) in horizontal lines, and applied with sand in vertical holes (via deep drill operation) or slits. Also, the turfgrass manager may include calcium nitrate as a routine fertilizer source. Various other alternatives are possible such as using gypsum applied through an irrigation system. Some turf managers mix very fine gypsum into an irrigation pond just prior to irrigation as a means of applying larger quantities of a very fine particle size gypsum.

As the seriousness of a salt-affected problem increases, more options become cost-effective. In the next section, different types of sodic soil situations are described with comments on management choices.

B. Amendment Application Guidelines

The U.S. Salinity Laboratory, as have others, has developed a formula for estimating the *gypsum requirement.* However, these are only general approximations. In practice, reclamation of a sodic or saline-sodic soil is usually conducted over several years when using a good quality irrigation source. Or, for irrigation water with higher adj SAR_w values, reclamation must be followed by a continuous program to leach added Na. Under these conditions, an initially high amendment rate is followed by lower rates as needed based on monitoring soil ECe and SAR. Thus, an accurate estimation of total gypsum or other amendment is not essential.

As a guide for quantity of gypsum to use, Table 8.4 lists gypsum requirement per 12 inches (30 cm) soil depth by soil texture and initial exchangeable Na content. These broad "ballpark" rates can be adjusted over time. Carrow and Duncan[2] present procedures to calculate more specific rates by accounting for additions of Na versus SO_4, Ca, and Mg in irrigation water and then supplementing with gypsum or other Ca sources to provide adequate Ca to replace Na.

Application guidelines in the following sections are based on 100% gypsum ($CaSO_4 \cdot 2H_2O$) unless otherwise stated. When other amendments are selected, the equivalent quantities are given in Table 8.3. However, a few *precautions* must be observed since gypsum can be safely used at high rates on a mature turfgrass stand but other amendments often must be used at lower rates per application. For example,

- Elemental S, sulfuric acid, and other S based amendments can be applied on a bare soil at high rates as long as they are mixed and a few weeks are allowed for equilibration. During these weeks, the soil should be kept moist and soil temperatures should be above 55°F (12°C) to allow biological conversion of S into H_2SO_4, except for when H_2SO_4 is used.
- Sulfuric acid cannot be applied on a mature turf unless diluted in irrigation water so that pH is at or above 6.0.
- Elemental S and other S sources should not be applied to a mature turfgrass at above 5 lb S per 1,000 ft^2 (245 kg S ha^{-1}) to avoid: (a) foliar burn by soluble S compounds,

Table 8.4. Estimated gypsum requirements per 12 inches (30 cm) of soil depth to reduce ESP to below 10% based on soil texture and initial ESP. These values can vary considerably based on clay type with clays containing high CEC requiring more gypsum.

Soil Texture	Clay Content %	Initial Exchangeable Sodium Percentage				
		15	20	30	40	50
		Tons per acre[a]				
Sand, loamy sand	0–15	0.5–2	0.7–3	1–4	2–5	3–8
Loams	15–55	2–3	3–4	4–6	5–8	7–10
Clays	>55	3–4	4–6	6–8	8–11	10–14(+)

[a] 1 ton = 2,000 lb; 2,000 lb per acre = 2,240 kg ha^{-1}; 1 ton per acre = 46 lb per 1,000 ft^2.

and, more important; (b) excessive acidity in the surface 1 inch (2.5 cm) zone that can cause lower crown damage and root pruning. If the soil contains free $CaCO_3$ in this zone, excessively acid pH (i.e., pH <4.8) will not occur. But, insufficient $CaCO_3$ combined with high S rates can lead to major turfgrass injury. For additional information on S application see Chapter 6.

- All amendments in Table 8.3 except gypsum, phosphogypsum, FGDG, and elemental S have high foliar burn potential when applied to a turfgrass sod as granulars or fluids. This limits the quantity that can be safely applied per application. Turf managers may wish to try out rates in a trial area, starting at 2 to 5 pounds product (but not H_2SO_4) per 1,000 ft^2 (98 to 245 kg ha^{-1}). All materials should be watered into the soil with sufficient irrigation to wash the leaves off.
- Amendments containing N are limited per application and on an annual basis by the turfgrass N requirement.

These limitations on rates of many of the gypsum alternatives in Table 8.3 mean that: (a) many times the alternatives are best used to supplement Ca from gypsum, PG, or FGDG. For example, calcium nitrate used as a routine N-fertilizer could add soluble Ca to supplement gypsum; or (b) the material must be applied through the irrigation system. As an example, a grower may find that elemental S is more cost-effective than gypsum for his location. A couple of applications of elemental S as a broadcast could be made each year but elemental S could also be used to generate SO_3 and, therefore, sulfuric acid for injection via the irrigation system. When making cost comparisons, the cost of application equipment (SO_3 generator) and any required lime should be considered in this example.

Amendment guidelines are best understood in the context of the type of salt-affected problem that exists or is predicted to occur based on the irrigation water being used. As a *sequence for determining amendment application rates and procedures* the following is suggested.

Step 1—Address Irrigation Water Problems

Regardless of the type of salt-affected soil, four potential irrigation water problems should be addressed if they are present (Carrow et al.[3]). *First is the problem of a very pure irrigation water* with EC_w <0.50 dSm^{-1} which leads to poor infiltration. Corrective measures are to add sufficient soluble Ca to the water to raise EC_w or to generate a higher ECe in the surface soil solution by acid injection that reacts with soil lime to form gypsum.

Water soluble Ca can be obtained from calcium chloride, calcium nitrate, or dissolution of very fine gypsum in a device that saturates water in a tank by agitation which is then injected into the irrigation water. For every 1.0 meq Ca L^{-1} added to irrigation water, the EC_w should increase by 0.085 dSm^{-1}. Equivalent rates of calcium salts, acids, and acid forming materials for irrigation water treatment are listed in Table 8.5. As a general guide, amendment rate to increase total Ca to 2.5 meq L^{-1} is at a moderate level while rates to increase to 5.0 meq L^{-1} of Ca are high. As an example from Table 8.5, 234 lb (106 kg) of 100% gypsum dissolved in an acre-foot of irrigation water would raise Ca by 1 meq L^{-1}. This table also contains the quantity of S based amendments required, assuming lime is available in the soil surface.

Second is the problem of high Na content in the irrigation water (high adj SAR). However, this should be considered in conjunction with *a third potential problem—the presence of excessive bicarbonate or carbonate ions* as demonstrated by high adj SAR_w or Residual Sodium Carbonate (RSC). Table 8.5 can also be used to determine the quantity of an acidifying amendment to remove HCO_3 and CO_3 by gas evolution from irrigation water. This prevents reaction of HCO_3 and CO_3 with Ca and Mg and the selective removal of Ca and Mg from the water by lime formation; therefore, making the Ca less active (soluble) while leaving Na in solution. Also, high bicarbonate from irrigation water will reduce soluble Ca in the soil from gypsum, $CaCl_2$, or other sources and convert it to insoluble lime. Some bicarbonate in irrigation water is acceptable since it buffers against a rapid decrease in water pH if too much acid is used. Treated irrigation water with adj SAR_w of 3 to 7 meq L^{-1} or RSC of 0 to 0.50 meq L^{-1} is acceptable.

If the irrigation water has high Na but HCO_3 and CO_3 are low, then the irrigation water could be treated with a Ca source or by acid injection and lime applied to the soil surface. But whenever HCO_3 or CO_3 are excessive acid, injection is preferred.

When determining Ca addition in irrigation water, the turfgrass manager must also consider Na content in the irrigation water (adj SAR_w) or soil surface (SAR) (see Figure 7.1). As adj SAR_w or soil SAR increases, so does the need for irrigation water EC_w to increase, and, therefore, the need for more Ca and associated salts in the irrigation water.

The fourth issue to address in irrigation water is that of *excessively high salinity* as evidenced by a high EC_w. Presence of high salinity does not require any treatment of irrigation water unless HCO_3 or CO_3 are also high. However, it does indicate that extra leaching must be used.

By first dealing with the presence of any of these four irrigation water quality problems, the turfgrass manager will know whether special equipment is needed to acidify irrigation water or to add Ca salts. If such equipment is necessary, then it can be used as part of an overall water and soil management plan.

Step 2—Address Salt-Affected Soil Problems

The specific salt-affected soil problem present on a site is dependent on: (a) the existing soil condition, and (b) the irrigation water quality (Table 8.2). *In terms of the soil,* important factors to consider are:

- Type of salt-affected soil—saline, saline-sodic, and sodic.
- The magnitude of the problem. Soils with very high total salts or Na levels will require more intensive reclamation efforts.
- Location of the problem. A saline or sodic condition only at the surface is much easier to correct than if (a) high salinity or sodicity are throughout the root zone, or (b) distinct sodic B or C horizon exists.
- How widespread or isolated the problem exists (site specific).

Table 8.5. Equivalent rates of calcium salts, acids, and acid forming amendments for irrigation water treatment (Ac-ft = acre foot of irrigation water).

Chemical Name[a]	Trade Name	Pounds per Ac-ft Water to Provide 1.0 meq L^{-1} of Ca or HCO_3	Pounds per Ac-ft Water to Provide 2.5 meq L^{-1} of Ca or HCO_3	Pounds per Ac-ft Water to Provide 5.0 meq L^{-1} of Ca or HCO_3
Sulfur	Sulfur	43.6	109	218
Calcium sulfate dihydrate	Gypsum 100% pure	234	585	1170
Calcium chloride dihydrate	Calcium chloride 27% Ca	201	503	1005
Calcium polysulfide	Lime-sulfur 9% Ca, 24% S	183	458	915
Ammonium polysulfide	Nitro-sul	69–136[b]	172–340	345–680
Potassium thiosulfate	KTS 25% K_2O, 17% S	256–513[b]	640–1283	1280–2566
Ammonium thiosulfate	Thio-sul 12% N, 26% S	110–336[b]	275–840	550–1680
Urea sulfuric acid	US-10 N-Phuric 10/55	148–242[b]	370–605	740–1210
Sulfuric acid	100% Sulfuric acid	133	333	665

[a] Table 8.5. is adapted from p. 112 of *Water Penetration Problems in California Soils,* published by the Kearney Foundation of Soil Science, 1992 and USDA Handbook 60, 1954.

[b] Denotes that the quantity of bicarbonate or lime dissolved by nitrogen containing water amendments is variable and difficult to ascertain. The above ranges in rates are estimates based on number of reasonably assumed soil conditions and reactions.

- The need for cultivation practices to ensure water movement.
- The need for drainage for salt removal and water table control.

In terms of the irrigation water quality, the essential aspects to take into consideration are:

- Quality aspects of total salinity (EC_w), sodium permeability hazard (adj SAR, RSC), presence of toxic ions, and any other factors that may influence turfgrass management and soil conditions. It is the irrigation water that determines anticipated future problems.
- Expected duration of the salt problem. A soil with a serious salinity problem can be reclaimed in weeks while a serious sodic problem may require 1 to 3 years or more for reclamation, if high quality irrigation water is present. But when the irrigation water quality is poor, a continuous, long-term salt management program is necessary. Poor irrigation water quality coupled with a highly sodic soil will require a very intensive initial program of 2 or 3 years followed by a long-term program to maintain adequate soil conditions.
- Opportunities for improving quality through chemical amendment (Step 1) or blending.
- Quantity of water. Is the quantity sufficient to provide plant ET needs and leaching of salts? If not, priorities must be established for which areas to irrigate and leach.

IV. NUTRITIONAL AND PHYSIOLOGICAL PROBLEMS

SALT-AFFECTED SOILS CAN INFLUENCE turfgrass nutritional and physiological relationships that result in problems the turfgrass managers must address.[3,12] The most common problems encountered are: (a) high total salts reduce water uptake and, therefore, uptake of some nutrients. Salt-induced drought stress can limit CO_2 uptake and inhibit cytokinin production in roots. Both of these factors result in reduced photosynthesis; (b) excessively high levels of Na, Cl, B, HCO_3, and OH can cause toxicities. High Na replaces Ca in cell membranes, especially root cells. Calcium is essential for membranes to maintain their integrity and function. Under excessive Na, Ca displacement leads to leakage from membranes including K loss. In addition to leakage of ions, these root cells will be less efficient in taking up nutrients; (c) high salt content, even though not at a toxic level, can induce nutrient imbalances. Common examples of extreme ratios are Na^+ (high ion)/Ca^{+2+} (low ion), Na^+/K^+, Ca^{+2}/Mg^{+2}, and Cl^-/NO_3^-; and (d) salts can cause changes in soil physical properties (i.e., aeration, soil strength) and chemical properties (i.e., pH, redox potentials, chemical forms) that alter nutrient availability. Thus, depending on the situation, certain micronutrients and P nutrition may be adversely affected.

Since there are numerous combinations of salt-affected soil situations and irrigation water quality conditions, the specific nutrient or physiological disorders that occur will vary from site to site. Limited research on nutritional responses of turfgrasses has been conducted under salt-affected conditions. Thus, recommendations are based on the best scientific estimates and growers may wish to try out a particular practice on a trial site as well as talk with experienced growers and agronomists familiar with their unique conditions.

Calcium

Adequate Ca is essential on many salt-affected soils not only as an amendment to replace Na but to maintain cell membrane function against high Na. Improved salinity tolerance is often observed after Ca application on sites where salinity is high but Ca is low. On nonsalt-affected soils, Ca application as a nutrient is very rarely recommended since even moderately acidic soils contain appreciable Ca. The problem with low Ca is due to high Na displacing it from root cell membranes under high Na conditions.

In situations where gypsum or another amendment that generates Ca is being used for soil reclamation or irrigation water improvement, sufficient Ca will be added to address the nutritional needs. The most common conditions that may require Ca application as a nutrient are:

- Acidic to neutral sodic soils.
- Saline or saline-sodic soils that contain low Ca levels. For example, some Canadian Prairie Provinces' soils contain high $MgSO_4$ and Na_2SO_4 but limited Ca.
- Use of irrigation water with high HCO_3 and CO_3 that has not been acidified, especially if Na content is moderate to high.
- Sites where ocean water is used for irrigation and leaching. Ocean water contains a high Mg/Ca ratio that may induce low Ca uptake as well as appreciable Na uptake.

In the above situations, Ca can be applied in a number of ways to the soil or through irrigation water. Acidic sodic soils should receive sufficient lime to raise pH to 6.0 to 6.5. Gypsum applied at 10 to 30 lb per 1,000 ft^2 (490 to 1470 kg ha^{-1}) would supply adequate Ca on an annual basis for more cases where Ca is needed as a nutrient. Use of $Ca(NO_3)_2$ as an N-source will also supply Ca.

Potassium

High Na depresses K uptake and when Na causes membrane leakage, K can be lost from root tissue by this mechanism. For the latter, Ca will alleviate leakage of K. When high Ca levels are applied to replace Na, K uptake can be depressed. Thus, turfgrasses grown on salt-affected soils with either high Na or Ca often require K in greater quantities than a similar nonsalt-affected site, especially when frequent leaching of salts is practiced.

Since K is susceptible to leaching, especially on sandy soils, growers should consider using light, frequent applications. This can be done in conjunction with N fertilization using granular or liquid carriers containing N and K. On sandy soils that are frequently leached, K levels can be added at $N:K_2O$ ratios of 1:1 to 1:1.5.

On fine-textured soils, the K soil test can be used as a guide but recommendations should be increased 25 to 50% above that used for similar nonsalt-affected soils. However, if the fine-textured soil is not receiving adequate water for leaching, K applications should remain at those used for nonsalt-affected soil since added K is a salt. A light, frequent application approach is suggested versus higher, less frequent rates. Application rates per treatment can be 0.25 to 0.50 lb K_2O per 1,000 ft^2 (12.2 to 24.4 kg K_2O ha^{-1}) for a light, frequent program.

In contrast to Ca, applied K does not enhance salinity tolerance but it does improve drought/heat/cold tolerances and wear resistance. With many salt-affected sites susceptible to physiological (salt-induced) drought, K plays a major role in regulating stomatal control and stimulating the development of a finer, more branched root system.

Nitrogen

Nitrogen and salinity relationships are not as pronounced as those for K or Ca. Generally, N applied to a salt-affected soil at the same level considered optimal for a nonsalt-affected soil is adequate. Applying N above this level does not seem to improve salinity tolerance nor growth, even though high Cl often reduces NO_3 uptake. The most probable explanation is that when N is supplied at adequate levels, the most limiting factor is salinity stress. Under N-deficient conditions (i.e., lower N), N is the limiting factor.

Since N-salinity relationships are not readily apparent, practical suggestions to be used on a trial basis are:

- Provide adequate N based on levels used in similar nonsalt-affected sites in most cases (exceptions are presented below).
- When Cl levels are high in the soil from naturally high Cl or by Cl addition in irrigation water, consider increasing N by 10 to 25% in a trial area for comparison to a normal N level. Also, consider using a N-source supplying primarily NO_3 instead of NH_4-N.
- Avoid serious N-deficiency, since under low N the high Cl can inhibit NO_3 uptake. Each stress may accentuate the other stress symptoms.

Other Nutrients

Interactions between salinity and P nutrition are unclear. However, the high rates of Ca required to reclaim many salt-affected soils can reduce P availability by favoring formation of low solubility Ca-P minerals. On soils with inherently low P levels this would be most evident. Since many golf course superintendents tend to maintain sand-based golf greens at minimal P fertilization, these sites could be susceptible to P deficiency. Soil tests are available to assess P needs. Under low P and high Ca additions, additional P should be considered beyond what would be recommended from soil test results for a similar nonsalt-affected soil. As a guideline, annual P could be increased by 25 to 50% above routine (nonsalt-affected soil) levels with the annual rate divided into two to four equal treatments per year.

Magnesium deficiency can occur on acidic sodic soils and on some soils receiving high Ca rates and this could be accentuated by high K applications. One approach would be to use dolomitic lime (contains $CaCO_3$ and $MgCO_3$) when lime is used or applied in conjunction with a S amendment. Several magnesium fertilizers are available that can be used to supply additional Mg with applications split into several treatments favored over a one-time annual fertilization, such as $MgSO_4$ applied at 2 to 4 lb per 1,000 ft^2 (98 to 195 kg ha^{-1}) and watered off the foliage.

In salt-affected soils the solubility of micronutrients is often low, particularly for Mn, Fe, Cu, and Zn, while B and Mo may be higher. Deficiencies of Fe and Mn are most likely to occur on heavily leached sands. Periodic foliar applications or granular formulations can be applied two or three times per year. Salt-affected soils may require somewhat higher micronutrient rates than other soils, due to the potential for greater leaching losses.

Boron Toxicity

The most common sources of B toxicity are from irrigation water, wastewater used for irrigation, composted sewage sludges, and by naturally high B in some arid soils. Boron toxicity in salt-affected soils most often comes from the irrigation water. Boron is associated with clay colloids and organic matter but it can be leached. Leaching is easiest on acidic sodic soils that are sandy. Soil, water, and tissue tests for B can aid in determining whether a problem may occur or be present.

Cytokinins

Cytokinins are plant hormones produced primarily in roots and transported in the xylem to shoot tissues where they apparently regulate photosynthesis activity; aid in maintaining chloroplast membranes; can stimulate chlorophyll accumulation; can increase leaf or shoot initiation; act to delay leaf senescence; and are involved in other plant responses. When turfgrass roots are absent or unhealthy from stress, cytokinin application appears to stimulate photosynthesis, leaf initiation, and lateral root initiation. Salinity stress has been reported to inhibit cytokinin activity in many plant species.

Turfgrasses that are subject to high total salts, toxic ion effects, or poor soil physical conditions induced by high Na may respond positively to cytokinin application. Nabati et al.[13] reported that applied cytokinins improved shoot and root growth of *Poa pratensis* that was under salinity stress. Cytokinin may also reduce salt induced leaf yellowing and senescence, especially if applied in conjunction with foliar Fe treatment. A common observation has been that seaweed based cytokinin products seem to produce better results than a straight synthetic cytokinin. This may be due to the presence of several cytokinins (there are several different natural cytokinins) or other hormones and materials providing a more balanced treatment.

If salinity stress is a continuing problem, such as when using a poor quality irrigation source, cytokinin application on a monthly basis may be beneficial. Less frequent application would be required if a problem is seasonal, such as during the dry season. However, when turfgrass roots are actively growing and not under a salinity stress (or other stress), cytokinin applications should be used with caution. A healthy plant is able to produce adequate cytokinin and maintain a balance between hormones without added cytokinin. Excessive cytokinin is known to inhibit lateral root formation in contrast to applied cytokinin stimulating lateral root initiation when roots are absent or not healthy. An excess level of any one hormone adversely affects the level of other hormones. The implications of many of these hormone imbalances are not well understood due to the complexity of responses.

Silica

As the second most abundant element in the earth's crust, plants grow in an abundance of silicon (Si) with Si in the soil solution as $Si(OH)_2$, monosilicic acid. Grasses take up more Si than most plants with Si contents in shoot tissues of 1 to 3% (by dry weight) and up to 15% for rice. Si moves through the xylem in the transpiration stream with deposition in the outer walls of epidermal cells (upper and lower leaf surfaces) to form a barrier that may limit water loss through the cuticular layer, and impedes fungal infection. Deposition of Si physically strengthens tissues and has been reported to enhance lignin biosynthesis.

Limited research has been conducted on Si-salinity interactions but some growers believe applied Si may be beneficial. Since salinity reduces wear tolerance of grasses, applied Si may improve wear tolerance by imparting greater tissue strength and possibly influencing salt movement in tissues (see Chapter 14). Also, under poor aeration of sodic soils, Si may reduce Mn toxicity. Once aeration improves, however, sodic soils usually exhibit relatively low Mn levels.

For most crops where Si fertilizers are applied, granular materials such as calcium silicate slag ($CaAl_2Si_2O_8$) or calcium silicate ($CaSiO_3$) at 12 to 120 lb material per 1,000 ft^2 (585 to 5,850 kg ha^{-1}) are used to reduce plant lodging. However, foliar applications are possible for turfgrass using silicic acid, H_4SiO_4, or monosilicic acid, $Si(OH)_2$, which are soluble at about 50 to 60 mg Si L^{-1}. As with the use of other materials with very limited research data available, growers are cautioned to use Si on limited trial areas with appropriate nontreated checks, which can be an area protected from application by a sheet of plywood.

VII. MONITORING PROGRESS

SINCE SALT-AFFECTED SOIL PROBLEMS are serious and management is complex, a good monitoring program is recommended. The soil sampling techniques presented in the Site Assessment section can be used as well as the soil tests and water analyses suggested in Chapter 7.

A good seasonal and annual monitoring program is especially important when irrigation water is poor, there is a distinct dry season, or the soil is sandy. Relatively inexpensive equipment can be purchased to enable on-site analysis of soil ECe and irrigation water EC_w.

VIII. REFERENCES

1. Ayers, R.S. and D.W. Westcot. 1976. *Water Quality for Agriculture. Irr. and Drainage Paper 29.* Rome: Food and Agric. Organ. of the United Nations.
2. Carrow, R.N. and R.R. Duncan. 1998. *Salt-Affected Turfgrass Sites: Assessment and Management.* Chelsea, MI: Ann Arbor Press.
3. Carrow, R.N., R.R. Duncan, and M. Huck. 1999. Treating the cause, not the symptoms: Irrigation water treatment for better infiltration. *USGA Green Section Record* 37(6):11–15.
4. Dudeck, A.E. and C.H. Peacock. 1993. Salinity effects on growth and nutrient uptake of selected warm-season turf. *Inter. Turf. Soc. Res. J.* 7:680–686.
5. Dudeck, A.E., S. Singh, C.E. Giordano, T.A. Nell, and D.B. McConnell. 1983. Effects of sodium chloride on *Cynodon* turfgrasses. *Agron. J.* 75:927–930.
6. Handreck, K.A. and N.D. Black. 1994. *Growing Media for Ornamental Plants and Turf.* Randwick, NSW, Australia: Univ. of NSW Press.
7. Jacoby, B. 1994. Mechanisms involved in salt tolerance by plants. In M. Pessarakli, Ed. *Handbook of Plant and Crop Stress.* New York: Marcel Dekker, Inc.
8. Jayawardane, N.S. and K.Y. Chan. 1994. The management of soil physical properties limiting crop production in Australian sodic soils—A review. *Aust. J. Soil Res.* 32:13–44.
9. Maas, E.V. 1978. Crop salt tolerance. In G.A. Jung, Ed. *Crop Tolerance to Suboptimal Land Conditions. ASA Spec. Pub. 32.* Madison, WI: Amer. Soc. of Agron.
10. Maas, E.V. and G.J. Hoffman. 1977. Crop salt tolerance—Current assessment. *J. Irrig. Drainage Div. ASCE* 103(IRZ):115–132.
11. Marcum, K.B. and C.L. Murdoch. 1994 Salinity tolerance mechanisms of six C_4 turfgrasses. *J. Amer. Soc. Hort. Sci.* 119(4):779–784.
12. Marschner, H. 1995. *Mineral Nutrition of Higher Plants.* New York: Academic Press.
13. Nabati, D.A., R.E. Schmidt, and D.J. Parrish. 1994. Alleviation of salinity stress in Kentucky bluegrass by plant growth regulators and iron. *Crop Sci.* 34:198–202.
14. Rhoades, J.D. 1974. Drainage for salinity control. In J. Van Schilfgaarde, Ed. *Drainage for Agriculture. Agronomy Monograph No. 17.* Madison, WI: Amer. Soc. of Agron.
15. Rhoades, J.D. and J. Loveday. 1990. Salinity in irrigated agriculture. In B.A. Stewart and D.R. Nielson, Eds. *Irrigation of Agricultural Crops. Agronomy Monograph No. 30.* Madison, WI: Amer. Soc. of Agron.
16. Sen, D.N. and S. Mohammed. 1994. General aspects of salinity and the biology of saline plants. In M. Pessarakli, Ed. *Handbook of Plant and Crop Stress.* New York: Marcel Dekker, Inc.

Chapter 9

Assessing Chemical/Nutrient Status

I. INTRODUCTION

AN ADEQUATE SUPPLY OF PLANT NUTRIENTS is needed for normal growth of turfgrasses. The practice of liberal fertilization has been used to ensure that turf areas have adequate nutrients. In the past when P and K were relatively inexpensive, they were added in large quantities to obtain high soil test levels, and then N fertilization was used to control growth and color. Considering both economic and environmental effects, unguided, excessive fertilization of turf areas is an unacceptable practice. Moderation in fertilization has become the norm. Visual symptoms on the turfgrass, soil testing, and plant tissue analysis can be used in diagnosing turf problems and in developing guidelines for turfgrass fertilization. Although there are exceptions, soil testing is used primarily as a guide for fertilization programs, and tissue analysis is used primarily as a diagnostic procedure.

Nutrient status is an important consideration in diagnosing problem areas of turf; however, keep in mind that various other factors can affect the appearance of the plant and the results of soil testing and tissue analysis. When diagnosing poor turf areas, consider contributions of other factors such as soil reaction (pH), soil salinity, soil depth, soil water content (excessive or dry), soil compaction, intensity of use (wear), disease or insect damage, pesticide damage, temperature, light, and the adaptation of the turfgrass species for that particular location and use. With some of these factors, visual symptoms may occur days or weeks after the turf has been stressed.

II. VISUAL SYMPTOMS

VISUAL SYMPTOMS INVOLVING COLOR AND GROWTH can indicate nutrient deficiencies and toxicities (see Table 2.4). Nitrogen fertilization is often based on turf color, growth, or both; i.e., light green color and fewer clippings suggest a need for more N. *Chlorosis* (yellowing) of turf could indicate Fe or S deficiency as well as N deficiency. Experienced turf managers, who know the soil and site conditions where they are growing turf, can usually relate chlorosis or other discoloration to a specific nutrient. Since visual symptoms can sometimes be misleading because they can be an indicator of a number of other problems, such as disease, phytotoxicity, environmental stress, etc., it is a good idea to confirm your diagnosis with soil testing or tissue analysis. Another method to confirm deficiencies based on symptoms is to fertilize a small area with the nutrient in question to determine whether it eliminates the deficiency symptom.

III. COMPONENTS OF SOIL TESTING AND TISSUE ANALYSIS PROGRAMS[2,4,9,10,16,19,28]

THE FOUR MAJOR COMPONENTS OF SOIL TESTING AND TISSUE ANALYSIS PROGRAMS are (a) sampling, (b) laboratory analysis, (c) interpretation, and (d) recommendations.

Taking a *representative sample* is the first step toward obtaining meaningful results and recommendations. Therefore, it is important that proper procedures, usually specified by the analytical laboratory, be followed for sampling and sample preparation prior to analysis.

Samples may be submitted to private or public (university, state, provincial) laboratories for the appropriate *chemical analyses* of the samples. Different analytical methods may be used in different laboratories, and numerical results are not always the same. Thus, a turf manager who splits a sample for submission to different laboratories may be confused by reports that list somewhat different nutrient levels.

Interpretation of laboratory results is based on research results and practical experience of soil and plant scientists. Research involves the determination of field responses that can be expected from fertilization, and the appropriate amount of fertilizer required for a given laboratory test value. Thus, research that correlates laboratory results to field response data is required. Interpretation allows for the placement of results into categories such as high, medium, low, deficient, sufficient, or excessive. With agronomic crops, the interpretation is based largely on anticipated yield response and crop quality; however, maximum yield is not of prime importance on turfgrasses, and other turf quality factors such as color, density, stress tolerance, and disease incidence need to be considered. Unfortunately, very little research has been conducted on turfgrasses to provide the necessary information required for precise interpretation. Thus, interpretation may be based on research with forage or other crops, or, in some cases, no research at all.

Recommendations are based on the interpretation of test results, where the experience of the turf manager, lab, or consultant plays a major role in recommendations. If a test level can be placed in a category such as high or low, the recommendation should reflect this placement. The lack of research data for interpretation of turf plant or soil analysis is reflected by the wide range of recommendations sometimes given by different laboratories on the same sample. Different philosophies on fertilization may also contribute to these differences. Sufficient research in the areas of sampling procedures and analytical methods, as well as research dealing with correlation and interpretation of results, will give the most dependable testing programs.

IV. SOIL TESTING

A. Sampling

SAMPLING IS CONSIDERED BY MANY to be the greatest source of error in soil testing programs. Factors to consider when sampling turfgrass areas are: (a) the number of subsamples required to obtain a representative sample; (b) the boundaries of sampling areas as determined by use, slope, soil type, and past fertilization history; (c) sampling depth; (d) time of sampling; and (e) inclusion or exclusion of thatch. Even within a sampling unit (i.e., putting green, athletic field, home lawn), considerable variation in soil fertility can occur. Such variability may be related to soil depth and residues of previously applied fertilizer, which can be affected by nonuniform application of fertilizers and nonuniform mixing of fertilizers during seedbed preparation.

Soil sampling tubes are generally used to sample turf areas. Augers and spades can be used, but they cause more disruption to the surface of established turf areas. If the depth is appropriate, a sample can be obtained by collecting cores of soil during core cultivation of a turf area. However, depth of cores brought to the surface can vary with compaction level, soil moisture, and wear on tines.

Statistical procedures can be used to determine the minimum number of subsamples (cores) required to obtain the mean nutrient value for a soil with a given variability. In general, a composite sample of 20 cores will give a good representation of most turfgrass areas. These cores should be taken in such a pattern that each one represents about one-twentieth of the total area. Note that this is not random sampling of the area; however, sampling within each subarea should be random. Do not sample in straight lines across an area because such sampling could reflect effects of previous fertilizer applications, traffic patterns, or maintenance operations that may have affected the soil differentially. If the above operations are not used in straight lines, then the sampling should not be in alignment with their patterns. Soils on many sites are highly variable. With global positioning systems (GPS) becoming more available, the turf manager will be able to sample soils for specific areas. Knowledge of soil variability can be recorded for site specific fertilization.

On an established turf, sample to a depth of 2 to 4 inches (5 to 10 cm) (Plate 4). If a soil will be tilled prior to turfgrass establishment, sample to a depth of 5 to 6 inches (12 to 15 cm). Ideally, soils should be tested and fertilized and limed prior to turfgrass establishment to ensure adequate nutrients and pH adjustment in the rooting zone. Since some nutrients (such as P and Ca) move only slowly through the soil profile, it is difficult to uniformly adjust soil fertility throughout the profile without adequate mixing. If an area will be reseeded with minimum soil surface disturbance (i.e., core cultivation, raking, slit seeding), sample to 2 to 4 inches (5 to 10 cm) and make adjustments to fertilizer recommendations for turfgrass establishment, which usually assume that the fertilizer will be incorporated by tillage operations.

Be consistent in sampling depth over time for maintenance fertilizer recommendations, because sampling to different depths may give different results. On a fertilized area, nutrient levels are higher near the surface (Table 9.1), and deeper sampling will remove less-fertile soil at lower depths. This change in sampling depth will have the effect of lowering the soil test results. On areas not receiving P or K for a number of years and when clippings are removed, soil test levels may be lower near the surface due to greater rooting and uptake at a shallower depth.

Because sampling depth is so important for long-term use of soil tests in planning a fertilization program, a practical approach is to mark the soil probe at 2 to 3 inch (5 to 7.6 cm) intervals. Small notches can be made on the edge of the probe with a hacksaw. The notches serve as a means of determining more precise depth of the soil sample.

If one desires to monitor nutrient levels over the years, it is best to sample at approximately the same time each year. Available P and K vary throughout the year. Some research has shown levels of both to decrease from spring to fall. Other research has shown K to increase with increased soil water and temperature. Thus, sampling time can affect soil test results.

Thatch may contain considerable amounts of plant nutrients that can be utilized by the turfgrass. Generally, it is recommended that thatch be removed from soil samples. Some feel that thatch deeper than about one inch should be tested separately; however, most laboratories are not set up for this analysis. As thatch depth increases to such depths, perhaps the turf manager should be thinking of thatch removal and control programs as well as soil testing. A major point to remember is that thatch can affect soil test results, and inconsistency in handling of thatch during sample preparation could lead to confusing results. Inclusion of thatch has been shown to increase soil test levels of K, but to a lesser extent when samples were routinely sieved during sample preparation (Table 9.2).

A layer of sand will accumulate on native soil greens (and other turfs) with long-term sand topdressing. At what point should the sand layer be sampled separately? While there is no clear guideline, it seems reasonable to routinely sample to the same depth as previously while the

Table 9.1 Effect of sampling depth on soil test results for P and K on two turfgrass areas (adapted from Turner, et al.[24]).

Sample Depth (inches)	Soil Test Results[a] P (lb/A)	K (lb/A)
	Bentgrass Area (sand to silt loam)	
0–1.5 (0–3.8 cm)	118	86
1.5–3.0	72	78
3.0–4.5	44	78
4.5–6.0	32	78
	Kentucky Bluegrass Area (silt loam)	
0–2 (0–5.1 cm)	143	382
2–4	117	242
4–6	91	226

[a] lb/A × 1.12 = kg/ha.

Table 9.2 Effect of thatch inclusion on soil test results from four turfgrass areas (adapted from Turner et al.[24]).

Type of Sample	Exchangeable Potassium[c] Area I	Area II	Area III	Area IV
	lb/A			
Soil only[a]	86	94	109	202
Soil plus thatch[a]	156	125	117	289
Soil plus unsieved thatch[b]	–	–	226	406

[a] Entire sample sieved through 2 mm sieve.
[b] Soil sieved through 2 mm sieve; thatch broken up and returned to sample.
[c] lb/A × 1.12 = kg/ha.

sand layer approaches 2 inches (5 cm). From that point sample only the sand, or if roots persist into the soil below, collect a separate sample from the native soil as well. Recommendations should be based on the sand layer, especially for cool-season grasses as most roots will be in this layer during stress periods.

Avoid taking samples from unusual areas within the turfgrass area being sampled (i.e., lines on athletic fields, regardless of material used to line the field), and avoid all other forms of contamination that could lead to erroneous results. The subsamples (cores) should be placed in a clean, nonmetallic container to minimize contamination of the sample. After thoroughly mixing the subsamples, withdraw the specified amount for submission to the laboratory. All soil cores should be broken into small pieces during the mixing process.

Most labs provide sample boxes or bags. At least 1/2 pint (0.473) is needed by the lab for analysis. When submitting samples, be sure to label each with an appropriate identification symbol (i.e., green number 16 as G16). Fill out forms supplied by the laboratory, which may request information pertaining to whether an establishment or maintenance recommendation is needed, grass species present or to be planted, use of this area, clipping removal, irrigation, relative quality desired, and any additional testing needed other than the routine soil tests of the particular laboratory. This information is utilized in the interpretation and recommendation phases of soil testing.

B. Laboratory Analysis

Although there have been efforts to establish uniformity in methods used by different soil test laboratories (especially those within a given geographical area), many differences do exist among laboratories. Differences occur in methods to measure pH and to determine lime requirements; in the nutrients that are included with routine testing; in the additional testing for factors such as soluble salts or organic matter content; and in extracting solutions used to extract available plant nutrients from the soil. Extracting solutions often vary due to the type of soil. The effectiveness of extractants used for P can vary with factors related to the form of P present in the soil. Laboratories that analyze samples from a wide range of geographical areas may use several analytical methods, and in some cases, the methods selected are the same as or similar to those used by state or university laboratories in the region where the sample originated.

Routine soil testing does not include tests for N because of the ever-changing levels of the different forms of N in the soil. There have been studies dealing with methods to determine potentially available N, but not with turfgrasses as the test plant. In a turfgrass situation, potentially available N would be in soil organic matter and residual slow-release N sources.

Within the chapters on each nutrient, practical aspects of soil testing and extractants are discussed. But an overview is provided in the following sections.

There is generally not a need for soil testing for S or micronutrients because soils usually contain enough of these elements to meet turfgrass requirements. In areas where deficiencies of these elements occur in turfgrasses, use of appropriate soil testing procedures (often in conjunction with tissue analyses) can be used as a guide for fertilizer recommendations. Sulfur soil tests measure SO_4-S (sulfate). Because of the mobility of this ion in soil, some laboratories recommend deeper sampling to assess its availability. Micronutrients can be tested by various methods, and a measure of extractable nutrient accurately determined. Unfortunately there is a lack of field calibration research to relate test levels to expected turfgrass responses from fertilization. Also, research with field crops has shown that interpretation of test levels should include consideration of other soil properties, including texture, organic matter level, recent lime application, pH, and the amount of other elements that interact with the element in question. The difficulty in interpreting soil test data for micronutrients is one reason to rely on plant analyses to determine whether turfgrasses are obtaining sufficient amounts. Routine soil testing in most labs will include pH and extractable amounts of P, K, Mg, and Ca.

Soil pH is normally measured in a soil suspension using a pH meter equipped with a glass indicating electrode and a calomel reference electrode. Usually the soil is mixed with an equal weight of water or 0.01 M $CaCl_2$ solution to form a soil suspension. After stirring and allowing the suspension to stand a prescribed time, the pH is determined. Portable pH meters with glass electrodes are available for use in the field. Also, field pH kits utilize indicator solutions or indicator paper strips that change color depending on the pH. These kits are not as accurate as pH meters. Lime requirement is usually determined in the laboratory by measuring the effect the soil has on lowering the pH of a buffer solution. Soluble salts are determined by measuring the electrical conductivity of a saturated soil/water paste extract, and are less accurately estimated by measuring the electrical conductivity of a soil/water paste or suspension. The details of these three procedures can vary from one laboratory to another.

Extractants are utilized to remove available forms of nutrients, such as P, K, Ca, and Mg. The amount removed can be determined by appropriate analytical procedures. Again the details can vary among laboratories. Thus, it is not unusual to obtain different laboratory results if different procedures are used. Regardless of the method used, the amount of nutrient extracted should correlate with growth responses; i.e., high and low levels should be associated with greatest and least growth, respectively, or perhaps with least and greatest chlorosis, respectively (Plank[16]).

A good, reputable laboratory participates in proficiency testing programs, in which test results from the same soil can be compared among laboratories using the same procedures or different procedures. Participation in such programs allows the laboratories to assess their performances and make adjustments as needed.

This chapter emphasizes analysis for essential plant nutrients. Many laboratories are capable of other soil chemical tests such as soluble salts (conductivity), other elements such as Al, As, and Na, and calcium carbonate content. Tests are available to determine heavy metals and pesticide residues in soil, tissue, and water. Some laboratories offer water quality testing and sludge analysis, as well as soil and tissue analyses.

C. Interpretation of Laboratory Results

Someone must interpret the nutrient levels found by the soil testing lab. Are nutrient levels excessive, high, medium, or low? At what levels can a response to fertilization be expected? Is the pH in a desirable range? Is the soluble salts level too high? For proper interpretation of laboratory results, correlation and calibration information is needed. Such information results from well-planned research experiments. Correlation research involves comparisons of laboratory results with actual availability or uptake by plants when grown in that soil. Calibration research is used to determine the relationships between soil test values and plant response to fertilization. Thus, calibration research will indicate how much of a nutrient should be added (if any) at various soil test levels to optimize plant growth. Figures 9.1 and 9.2 are examples of response curves obtained in soil test calibration studies conducted in Pennsylvania.[20,23] Such research resulted in the alteration of fertilizer recommendations. Nutrient levels that maximize growth do not necessarily maximize turfgrass quality.[5] More research is needed on soil test calibration for turfgrasses. Such research should include wide ranges of soil types, and should be conducted using various turfgrass species and cultivars.

In some cases, turfgrasses have been placed in a "high" P and K requirement category, while pasture grasses were in a "low" category. This decision was based on economics, not agronomics. The cost of fertilization was not considered of primary importance for turf. Considering current fertilizer prices, scarcity of some fertilizer materials, and the environmental concerns associated with fertilization and soil nutrients, it seems quite appropriate to utilize fertilizer recommendations based on sound research.

Interpretation is affected by various philosophies of laboratories or individuals making recommendations.[2,16] In some cases, the percentage saturation of basic cations (K, Mg, and Ca) is used as a guide to determine whether they are in balance. Then rates of fertilization are made accordingly. For instance, desired ranges could be 2 to 5% K, 5 to 15% Mg, and 60 to 80% Ca. These values indicate the percentage of the total cation exchange capacity (CEC) that is occupied by that cation. Also, ratios of cation saturation percentages are considered. For example, Mg fertilization may be recommended when the Mg/K ratio drops below 2/1, and a Ca/Mg ratio greater than 10/1 would indicate that these nutrients were out of balance. This philosophy is often referred to as the *"basic cation saturation ratio"* (BCSR) concept. A second approach

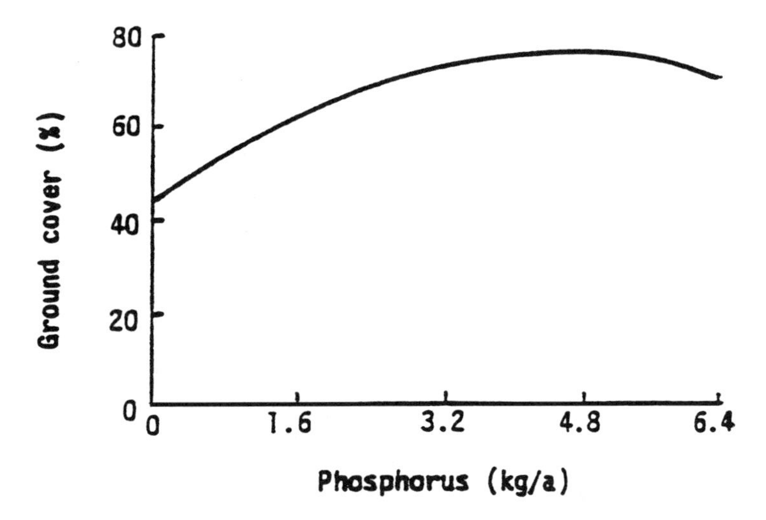

Figure 9.1. Response curve showing the effect of P applications in the seedbed on ground cover of a Kentucky bluegrass-red fescue stand 6 weeks after seeding (1 kg a^{-1} = 2.2 lb per 1,076 ft^2) (Turner, 1980[20]).

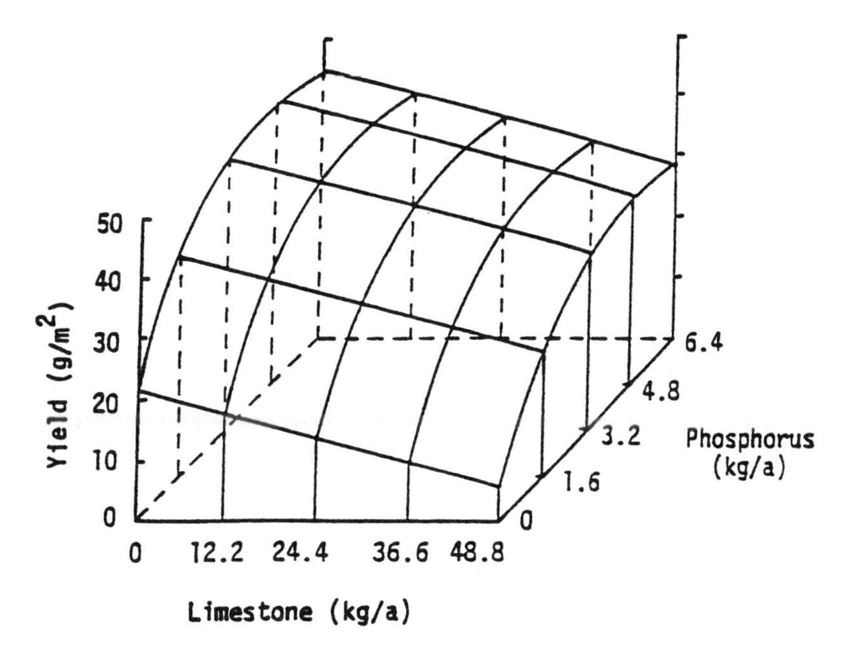

Figure 9.2. Response surface showing the effects of P and limestone applications in the seedbed on initial clipping yield of Kentucky bluegrass-red fescue turf 7 weeks after seeding (1 kg a^{-1} = 2.2 lb per 1,076 ft^2) (Turner, 1980[20]).

is the sufficiency level concept, in which the amount of available nutrient, expressed in pounds per acre (lb/A), parts per million (ppm), or mg/kg, is used to determine the need for fertilization. This concept is often referred to as SLAN, for *"sufficiency level of available nutrients."* Using the SLAN approach, sufficiency levels can be established for P, S, K, Mg, Ca, and the micronutrients. If soil test levels are below the sufficiency level, plant responses to fertilizer are likely. Some laboratories use a combination of these concepts.

With the BCSR method based on percentage data, inadequate levels (i.e., quantities) of a cation could exist even though saturation values and ratios are within acceptable ranges. Such an occurrence would be most likely on low CEC soils such as the sandy media often used on turf areas. In contrast, on fine- and medium-textured soils having higher CEC values, sufficient levels of cations may be present when the criteria of the BCSR method are not met. Due to low buffering capacity, low CEC soils can have large changes in cation saturation and ratios following the addition of cations by fertilization or liming. If sufficiency levels were obtained from research on fine-textured soils, they may not be appropriate for low CEC soils that have less capacity to adsorb nutrients. Regardless of the concepts used in soil test interpretation, the most sound interpretation will be based on results of soil test calibration studies in which plant responses to fertilization and liming are determined on soils having various initial soil test levels.

D. Recommendations

Several approaches can be used in developing recommendations. One approach is to meet the immediate needs of the plant, and the other is to build soil levels to an optimum level as well as meet plant requirements. These approaches are commonly referred to as "sufficiency" and "buildup and maintenance," respectively.[2] Higher recommendations are used if the aim is to build soil levels.

A less appropriate approach to fertilization that is sometimes, although infrequently, suggested is to replenish nutrients removed by the plant. This approach is not based on soil testing but on the weight and nutrient concentrations of the clippings. Such an approach assumes that clippings are removed and neglects nutrient fixation, leaching, and other processes that reduce the availability of applied nutrients. If replenishing nutrients removed was a reasonable option for fertilization, then return of clippings should provide the necessary nutrients. In most cases, this approach would eventually result in inadequate N for color and density desired on most turf areas.

Another difference in approaches to fertilization deals with rate and frequency of application. Light, frequent applications of fertilizer (often termed *"spoon-feeding"*) can be used to keep an adequate supply of nutrients for the plant through the growing season. Advantages offered for spoon-feeding are greater control by the turfgrass manager, fewer periods of excessive growth, less leaching of nutrients, and less fixation of nutrients into unavailable forms. Spoon-feeding is most appropriate on sandy soils where nutrient retention is low due to low CEC values and where frequent irrigation favors nutrient leaching. The spoon-feeding technique contrasts with the methods of one or several fertilizations per year, depending on the N source. Nutrients held in the soil, as well as those added with the fertilizer, provide sufficient amounts of nutrients between the infrequent applications. Combinations of these approaches often are used: i.e., apply P and K in spring, fall, or both, but use a fast-release N source more frequently.

It should be apparent that differences in fertilizer and lime recommendations result from differences in the interpretation of laboratory results. One survey of laboratories[22] showed that the form of recommendation varied from pounds of P_2O_5 and K_2O to pounds of a specific grade to a fertilizer ratio. Recommendations on an annual basis varied by as much as 5 lb P_2O_5, 6 lb K_2O, and 180 lb limestone/1,000 ft^2 for the same soil sent to different laboratories. Some laboratories recommended the same amount of limestone for a soil regardless of whether it was a maintenance or establishment application, while others recommended lower rates for maintenance because the limestone would be surface applied rather than incorporated. Sufficiency levels for P differed among laboratories as did recommended sampling depths.

With so much variation among methods, interpretation, and recommendations, it is apparent that soil testing for turf is not an exact science. Treat the recommendations as a guideline. Achieving exact rates is not critical in most cases. Select a laboratory that uses moderation in recommendations: more toward meeting the turf requirements and less toward building soil levels. Although some factors may have been taken into consideration based on information supplied with samples, fine-tuning of recommendations for your specific situation may be in order. Beard[1] listed the following factors to consider in making recommendations: (1) soil test results; (2) nutrient requirements of species and varieties; (3) fertilizer cost; (4) environmental conditions; (5) turf quality desired; (6) growth rate desired; (7) use of the area; (8) soil physical conditions; and (9) management practices being used (i.e., clipping removal affects fertilizer requirement).

Records of soil test results, fertilization applications (rates and dates), and responses to fertilization should be maintained. They can be useful in future fertilization program planning and in diagnosing problems related to soil fertility. In order to compare soil test results over a period of years, it is best to sample consistently to the same depth and have the testing done at the same laboratory.

E. Commercial Soil Test Kits

Various commercially available soil test kits are available as alternatives to the utilization of soil test laboratories. This do-it-yourself approach gives results quicker than can be obtained by submitting samples to a laboratory and can be used in the field or in indoor facilities near the turf site. Before selecting a soil test kit for either troubleshooting or routine testing, do some checking to determine whether results and recommendations are somewhat in agreement with those from a reputable laboratory. This comparison can be done by obtaining soil samples (at least six) representing a range of pH, P, and K values, from sufficient to deficient (or greens, tees, fairways, and roughs on a golf course or a range of soils and turfs on other sites). Split the samples to obtain subsamples for the soil test kit(s) and laboratory. After analyses are completed, check for agreement.

Compared to common laboratory procedures, soil test kits may use different extractants, and results are determined by the operator assessing color or turbidity in extractants or the color of an indicator solution mixed with soil. Comparisons of results from several soil test kits with results from the soil test laboratory at Virginia Polytechnic Institute and State University indicated significant differences between the kits and VPI & SU for soil P and K levels.[12] Results for soil pH were in agreement with VPI & SU with only one of four kits. These results suggest caution in randomly selecting a soil test kit and also support the recommendation of comparing results before selecting a kit to be used for soil testing.

V. PLANT TISSUE ANALYSIS

A. Types of Analysis

TWO TYPES OF ANALYSIS CAN BE USED to assess the status of nutrients in plants: (a) plant analysis in which the total elemental content of dried tissue is measured; and (b) tissue test in which soluble nutrients in the plant sap are measured. Plant analysis is more quantitative than sap tissue tests and is the preferred method for most plant nutrients.

Plant analysis and tissue testing of turf areas can be used to monitor nutrient levels in the plant and to relate these levels to the need for fertilization or to the response from fertilization. These procedures are also valuable aids in diagnosing nutrient deficiencies, and can identify hidden problems as well as verify a diagnosis based on visual symptoms. On annual crops, a visual symptom, followed by verification by plant analysis or a tissue test, may occur too late in the growing season for effective corrective action; therefore, a combination of these diagnostic methods is more useful on perennials, such as turfgrasses.

B. Tissue Tests of Sap

Tissue tests of plant sap give a rapid determination of nutrient status, but the number of elements that can be tested is limited. Nutrient levels in sap squeezed from tissue is determined by color development or changes on strips of a specific test paper or in special reagents, or by determining ion concentration with battery-operated meters that are specific for a given ion (e.g., NO_3^-, K^+, Na^+). Follow guidelines supplied with tissue testing kits and avoid the use of outdated or contaminated reagents or test papers. Be sure that test kits are calibrated using standard solutions. Various ions can also be extracted under laboratory conditions to assist in diagnoses, but such tests are not a replacement for total plant analysis.

C. Plant Analysis of Tissues[4,6,9]

Sampling

As with soil sampling, care must be used in collecting plant tissue samples. Follow procedures for sampling and handling that are given by the laboratory that will do the analysis. Leaf blades are usually collected, and hand clipping is often preferred to mower clipping to prevent contamination from soil or other foreign matter. Equipment (mowers, clippers, or scissors) used to obtain clippings should be thoroughly cleaned prior to sampling. Reel mowers are preferred to rotary mowers because rotary mowers tend to suck up soil, old clippings, and any debris present or within the turf canopy. If results show excessive amounts of Fe and Al, no doubt the sample was contaminated with soil. Aluminum is not an essential element; however, it can be toxic to turfgrasses, and it is easily determined with other nutrients. Thus, it is sometimes reported with plant analysis results.

Avoid sampling soon after fertilizer or other chemicals have been applied to turf. These contaminants may be particulate matter from dry applications or coatings on leaf tissue from fluid application. A contaminant can increase concentrations of some elements detected because it contains those elements, and also decrease values for others due to the contaminant diluting the sample. Fresh clippings can be placed in a plastic colander and gently and quickly washed, preferably with distilled water, to remove soil and dust contaminants. Contaminants on creeping bentgrass clippings from a putting green have been shown to adversely affect both the consistency and reliability of nutrient concentrations determined for unwashed samples, and washing is considered to be an essential practice on such samples.[13] Sand is a common contaminant in clippings from greens that receive light, frequent topdressing and are closely mowed. Washing should be done immediately after harvest. Washing partially dried or dry clippings can result in some soluble nutrients being washed out. Use of a detergent may be recommended to remove pesticides or fertilizers that stick to foliage; however, it would be better not to sample when these materials are present.

In diagnostic sampling, samples should be taken from both "good" and "bad" areas. Comparisons of results from the good and bad turf can often give more easily interpreted results than comparisons with "standard" deficient, sufficient, or excess levels that may or may not apply to the turf species and varieties that are present.

Avoid sampling areas stressed by drought, wear, diseases, insects, etc., unless your goal is to determine the effect of these stresses on nutrient content. Otherwise, these stresses can interfere with a meaningful assessment of nutrient status. Avoid sampling when seedheads are predominant (a few can be picked out). The analysis is for leaf tissue, not flowers or seedheads.

Nonrefrigerated fresh clippings, especially packed in plastic bags, are very susceptible to decay, which will alter the chemical composition. Do not ship or mail fresh clippings if there is a possibility of decay en route to a testing lab. Shipping in paper bags and delivery within two days is advisable. The lab should be notified to open the samples immediately upon arrival. Clippings can also be spread out to air-dry, dried at 60 to 65°C in an oven, or dried as indicated by the testing laboratory. Send samples in paper bags or envelopes or containers supplied by the laboratory if these are available. Air-dried samples will need to be further dried at 60 to 65°C in the laboratory to prevent any decomposition. After appropriate grinding, the sample is redried and subsamples weighed for analyses.

Laboratory Analyses

Samples either are ashed or digested with strong acids to remove organic materials. Various analytical methods can then be used to determine elemental content of the ash or acid digest. Actual values obtained should be the same regardless of the method employed since the total content of the nutrient is being measured. This is in contrast to soil testing where varying extractants are employed to estimate the plant-available quantities.

Interpretation

To interpret plant analysis results from turf, one should know the relationship between elemental composition and plant yield, growth, quality, or other performance factors. Plant analysis results can be compared to a set of standard values, and then placed into categories such as deficient, critical, adequate, or high. A critical level has been defined as the level below which a 10% reduction in yield may occur due to low nutrient availability. Deficient could be considered to be a level associated with a yield of about 90% or less of maximum growth. These terms are commonly used with crop production where high yields are the goal; however, high yields are not necessarily the goal with turfgrasses. Standard values for turfgrasses need to be established based on density, color, and other components of turf quality as well as growth (yield). More important for turf is how a nutrient level could affect stress tolerance (wear, moisture, temperature, disease). Very little research has been conducted on these relationships. Data obtained for forage grasses could serve as a guide, but forage grasses are usually sampled at a more mature stage and factors such as palatability and nutrient levels for animal health may affect recommendations for some elements. Variation in sufficiency levels among species and even varieties is likely.

There is a need to obtain more data under turf conditions to assist in interpretation of results. Factors such as species, variety, time of season, mowing height, part of plant sampled, and soil moisture need to be considered in establishing standards. Critical values established under greenhouse conditions are often lower than those obtained under field conditions, and the critical

Table 9.3. Differences in P and K tissue concentrations due to variety and species of turfgrasses (from Butler and Hodges[3]) grown under the same conditions.

	Concentration	
Turfgrass	P %	K %
Common Kentucky bluegrass	0.27	1.80
Merion Kentucky bluegrass	0.49	3.08
Creeping red fescue	0.34	2.62

Table 9.4. Differences in tissue P concentration in four turfgrasses grown under the same conditions (from Waddington and Zimmerman[27]).

Turfgrass	P Concentration (%)
Penncross creeping bentgrass	0.76
Norlea perennial ryegrass	0.71
Pennstar Kentucky bluegrass	0.56
Pennlawn red fescue	0.54

value for one element may be dependent on the concentrations of another. Nutrient concentrations in turfgrass are affected by soil type and fertilizer rate and placement,[25] and by season and method of tissue sampling.[7] Examples of differences in concentrations due to variety and species of grass grown under the same conditions are shown in Tables 9.3, 9.4, and 9.5. Many other examples have been included in the review by Turner and Hummel.[21] Differences in K concentrations occur due to fertilization and time of sampling, and chlorosis may or may not be associated with low K concentrations (Table 9.6). These examples indicate why interpretation is a difficult chore. Interpretation is somewhat easier in diagnostic situations where results are available from both good and bad turf. If results are similar, then the bad condition is apparently the result of a factor other than nutrition. If the bad area shows a low concentration of an element, the area can be fertilized with that element and then observed for improvement.

Sometimes interpretation is based on ranges of values obtained from good and poor turf areas, and the assumption is that "good" and "poor" are solely related to fertility. In general, good turf areas have less stress from pests and excessive use than poor turf areas. Differences between areas may be due to shade, topsoil, compaction, and many other nonnutrient factors. In addition, maintenance inputs may vary and include things such as irrigation, cultivation, pest control, and mowing, as well as fertilization. Greater fertilization on good areas can result in higher tissue concentrations of elements, especially N and K, than on less fertilized poor areas. However, lower fertilization rates and lower tissue concentrations on the poorer areas are not necessarily the cause of the poorer turf. If all other maintenance and use factors were equal on good and poor areas, then nutrition would need a closer look.

Within the sufficiency range as soil nutrient levels decrease, tissue nutrient levels generally do not decrease but remain at a reasonably level plateau unless plant growth rate dramatically changes. Obviously this makes monitoring of tissue nutrient content less effective for determining potential oncoming deficiencies. Factors that *concentrate* nutrients and *cause tissue values to increase* above the normal plateau include anything that reduces growth such as low

Table 9.5. Differences in concentrations of macronutrients in bermudagrass varieties grown under the same conditions (from McCrimmon[14]).

Variety	N	P	K	Ca	Mg	S
			%			
Everglades	4.67	0.40	2.71	0.58	0.20	0.48
Tiflawn	3.95	0.37	2.04	0.46	0.17	0.40
Tifway II	4.35	0.40	1.89	0.49	0.16	0.41
U-3	3.70	0.32	1.86	0.47	0.17	0.37

Table 9.6. Differences in K concentration of Penncross creeping bentgrass due to K fertilization and sampling date (from Waddington et al.[26]).

K Treatment	K Concentration on Three Sampling Dates		
	4/73	9/73	4/76
		%	
Not fertilized	1.32[z]	1.26	0.58[a]
Fertilized	2.36	1.80	1.04

[a] Turf was chlorotic.

soil nutrient content of another nutrient; unusually low or high temperatures for the grass species; low rainfall or irrigation creating a moisture stress; PGRs; traffic stress; and/or pest stresses. Sometimes a nutrient content may be greater than the sufficiency range. This can occur after application of a water soluble fertilizer or foliar application. Because turf leaves are routinely mowed off, tissue levels usually are not above the sufficiency range for very long unless growth is very slow.

In contrast, growth stimulation factors that *dilute* tissue nutrient concentrations and *cause tissue levels to decrease* (but still remain in the sufficiency range) are: favorable temperature and moisture for optimum growth; growth stimulation by N; and lack of growth limiting stresses. If a nutrient is truly limiting, tissue levels will eventually reach the critical range, but the change from a fluctuating plateau in the sufficiency range to a decreasing critical value may often be quite sudden rather than a gradual event. For some nutrients, this change is also visible in the form of visual deficiency symptoms.

In climates with prolonged periods of rather consistent weather, less fluctuation in seasonal tissue nutrient levels will be evident. Also, soils with low nutrient retention and high rainfall are sites where tissue nutrient content values can be more predictive of plant needs (and soil nutrient status) than a climate with rapid weather changes.

With the increasing use of effluent water on turfgrass sites, nutrient content in the water must be considered when interpreting tissue tests. Nutrients present in high or very low quantities in the effluent may aid in explaining tissue test results and trends. Also, plant tissue tests are best interpreted when comparing to effective soil test results where soil tests evaluate the plant-available nutrient status of the soil.

Charts showing sufficiency ranges and survey ranges or averages for various turfgrasses are available to help in interpretation.[6,8,10,15] Examples of sufficiency ranges are shown in Table 9.7. It is important to know that general recommendations are not applicable to all turfgrass species and cultivars, growth stages, and sampling times. Ranges for specific cultivars can also vary with factors such as growth stage, sampling time, soil pH, and soil aeration.

Table 9.7. Sufficiency ranges for nutrient concentrations in clippings from turfgrass.

	Sufficiency Ranges for				
Nutrient	Bermudagrass[a]	Creeping Bentgrass[a]	Perennial Ryegrass[a]	St. Augustinegrass[a]	General[b]
N, %	4.00–6.00	4.50–6.00	3.34–5.10	1.90–3.00	2.75–3.50
P, %	0.25–0.60	0.30–0.60	0.35–0.55	0.20–0.50	0.30–0.55
K, %	1.50–4.00	2.20–2.60	2.00–3.42	2.50–4.00	1.00–2.50
Ca, %	0.50–1.00	0.50–0.75	0.25–0.51	0.30–0.50	0.50–1.25
Mg, %	0.13–0.40	0.25–0.30	0.16–0.32	0.15–0.25	0.20–0.60
S, %	0.20–0.50	no data	0.27–0.56	no data	0.20–0.45
Fe, ppm	50–500	100–300	97–934	50–300	35–100
Mn, ppm	25–300	50–100	30–73	40–250	25–150
Cu, ppm	5–50	8–30	6–38	10–20	5–20
Zn, ppm	20–250	25–75	14–64	20–100	20–55
B, ppm	6–30	8–20	5–17	5–10	10–60
Mo, ppm	0.10–1.20	no data	0.5–1.00	no data	no data

[a] Mills and Jones, 1996.[15]
[b] Jones, 1980.[8]

Recommendations

As with soil testing, many factors concerning the turfgrass site conditions, management practices, and intensity of use need to be considered when making fertilizer recommendations. With tissue tests and plant analyses, subsequent testing will indicate whether fertilizer applications were sufficient. Plant tissue testing is not a substitute for soil testing. Consider a case where plant analysis supports that a chlorotic condition on turf is due to low Fe concentration. Iron fertilization would correct the chlorosis; however, if the chlorosis was induced due to overliming, as indicated by a soil test pH value, then a recommendation to use acid-forming nitrogen sources may also be appropriate. Lowering the soil pH by using such N sources would increase iron availability and reduce the chance of chlorosis recurring. Thus, both soil and plant testing should be used along with visual observations to assess fertility status on turfgrass areas. In general, soil testing is used on a routine basis and tissue tests or plant analyses are used to assess problem areas.

Recommendations from plant tissue analysis ultimately are used to make adjustments in the fertility program. Good recommendations depend on accurate and reliable information from quantitative sources *(tissue tests, soil tests, irrigation water quality tests)* and personnel evaluation (*plant visual symptoms and turfgrass performance*). Integrating all these sources of information is always better than reliance on any one technique or source of information.

VI. NEAR INFRARED REFLECTANCE SPECTROSCOPY

Near infrared reflectance spectroscopy (NIRS) is an analytical method in which prepared plant material samples are scanned with monochromatic increments of infrared radiation, and the reflectance of different wavelengths is used to determine chemical composition. NIRS has been effectively used to determine content of protein, moisture, fiber, oil, and other properties of forages, grains, and oil seeds.[11,16,17]

The reflectance is influenced by chemical bonds within the material being analyzed. Statistical procedures (correlation and regression analysis) must be used to relate NIRS results with results of conventional chemical laboratory analysis procedures. If a good correlation exists, NIRS can be used to obtain more convenient, rapid, and inexpensive results than conventional methods.

NIRS has been evaluated for analysis of turfgrass tissue. The method is promising for N, but results with other macronutrients and micronutrients have not been well correlated with those from conventional chemical analyses.[4,18] NIRS has also been used with soils to determine N supplying capability, total N, organic matter, sand, silt, and clay.

VII. SELECTING A SOIL OR PLANT ANALYSIS LABORATORY

When one chooses to send split samples to different laboratories, it is common to receive somewhat different results and recommendations. Which lab is correct? Often both labs are correct. As mentioned earlier, differences in procedures and interpretation often yield different recommendations. So if both are correct, who gets your business? *Consider four C's of lab selection: comfort, confidence, communication, and credibility.* Are you comfortable with the procedures used in the lab and the lab personnel with which you interact? Do you have confidence in the personnel and their interpretation and recommendations? Is there a good line of communication between the lab and clients? Will they respond to questions concerning methods, results, recommendations, and reruns? A laboratory with a good track record will have credibility in the eyes of clients and other laboratories. It can support its credibility by participating in a proficiency testing program. Such programs are available to both soil and plant analytical laboratories. In these programs, samples are sent to participating laboratories for analysis. Results from of all laboratories are statistically analyzed and reported back to the laboratories, with each having their results identified and the others remaining anonymous. Results may be within an acceptable range when compared to other laboratories or they may be too high or too low. If such is the case, the laboratory will check calculations, procedures, reagents, and equipment in an effort to determine the reason for the difference. Thus, participation in proficiency testing programs is good laboratory practice.

Of course you need a lab that is capable of running the specific tests that you want, and that reports results and recommendations in an easy to understand format. Expect reasonably quick results, but not miracles. Do not wait until the last minute prior to seedbed preparation or maintenance fertilization to submit samples.

Cost is another concern when obtaining laboratory services. Do not request or accept unnecessary testing. The fertilizer bill will be less if you select a laboratory that uses moderation in its recommendations. Follow up fertilization with observations of the turf responses, especially with micronutrients other than Fe. Also, another way to assess fertilization results is to leave an unfertilized strip for comparison purposes.

Once you are comfortable with a laboratory and the results you obtain from their recommendations, continue with their services and resist the temptation to split samples for other laboratories. Results of their proficiency testing programs will better tell how they do in comparison to other laboratories. Ask to see the results.

Professional turfgrass managers should insist that the laboratory and any consulting agronomists interpreting their sample results and making recommendations provide: (a) full information so that the professional turf manager is able to make the final decision on recommendations. Necessary information includes: test results; ranges for what is considered low, medium, and high for every nutrient measured; and the extractant used for each measured parameter; and (b) written rationale for recommendations. For example, some laboratories recommend Ca as foliar treatments and/or soil treatments in almost every situation. Since fertilization is one of the three major cultural practices on most turf areas (along with irrigation and mowing) and it has potential environmental impact, professional turfgrass managers should remain directly responsible for fertilizer recommendations.

VI. REFERENCES

1. Beard, J.B. 1973. *Turfgrass: Science and Culture*. Englewood Cliffs, NJ: Prentice-Hall Inc.
2. Brown, J.R., Ed. 1987. *Soil Testing: Sampling, Correlation, Calibration, and Interpretation*. SSSA Special Publ. No. 21. Madison, WI: Soil Science Society of America.
3. Butler, J.D. and T.K. Hodges. 1967. Mineral composition of turfgrasses. *Hort. Sci.* 2:62–63.
4. Carrow, R.N. 2000. Plant tissue analysis as a management tool. Proceedings from the Millennium Turfgrass Conference. 6–9 June 2000. Melbourne, Australia. AGCSA: Waverly, VIC, Australia.
5. Christians, N.E., D.P. Martin, and J.F. Wilkinson. 1979. Nitrogen, phosphorus, and potassium effects on quality and growth of Kentucky bluegrass and creeping bentgrass. *Agron. J.* 71:564–567.
6. Duble, R.L. 1977. Leaf analysis—A back up to soil testing. *Turf-Grass Times* 13(1):14–17.

7. Hall, J.R. and R.W. Miller. 1974. Effect of phosphorus, season, and method of sampling on foliar analysis of Kentucky bluegrass. pp. 155–171. In E.C. Roberts, Ed. *Proc. Second Int. Turfgrass Res. Conf.* Madison, WI: Amer. Soc. Agron.
8. Jones, J.B., Jr. 1980. Turf analysis. *Golf Course Mgt.* 48(1):29–32.
9. Jones, J.B., Jr. 1994. *Plant Nutrition Manual.* Athens, GA: Micro-Macro Publ., Inc.
10. Jones, J.B., Jr., B. Wolf, and H.A. Mills. 1991. *Plant Analysis Handbook.* Athens, GA: Micro-Macro Publ., Inc.
11. Marten, G.C., J.S. Shenk, and F.E. Barton II, Eds. 1989. *Near infrared reflectance spectroscopy (NIRS): Analysis of forage quality.* Agric. Handbook 643. Washington, DC: USDA-ARS.
12. McCoy, D.E. and S.J. Donohue. 1979. Evaluation of commercial soil test kits for field use. *Commun. Soil Sci. Plant Anal.* 10:631–652.
13. McCrimmon, J.N. 1994. Comparison of washed and unwashed plant tissue samples utilized to monitor the nutrient status of creeping bentgrass putting greens. *Commun. Soil Sci. Plant Anal.* 25:967–988.
14. McCrimmon, J.N. 1998. Effect of nitrogen and potassium on the macronutrient content of fifteen bermudagrass cultivars. *Commun. Soil Sci. Plant Anal.* 29:1851–1861.
15. Mills, H.A. and J.B. Jones, Jr. 1996. *Plant Analysis Handbook II.* Athens, GA: Micro-Macro Publ., Inc.
16. Owen, P. 2001. Soil Testing-Turf. Web-site at www.GeorgiaTurf.org.
17. Shenk, J.S., J.J. Workman, Jr., and M.O. Westerhaus. 1992. Application of NIR spectroscopy to agricultural products. In D. Burns and E. Ciurczak, Eds. *Agricultural Handbook of Near-Infrared Analysis.* New York: Marcel Dekker.
18. Stowell, L., C. Mancino, and A. Maricic. 1995. Comparison of near infrared reflectance spectroscopy and conventional chemistry methods for turfgrass tissue analysis. In L.J. Stowell and W.D. Gelernter, Eds. *PTRI Turfgrass Research Report.* San Diego, CA: Pace Turfgrass Institute.
19. Thomas, J.C. 1994. Soil and tissue testing for turf management. *Texas Turfgrass.* Fall Issue, pp. 15–22.
20. Turner, T.R. 1980. *Soil Test Calibration Studies for Turfgrasses.* Ph.D. thesis, Pennsylvania State University, University Park, PA.
21. Turner, T.R. and N.W. Hummel, Jr. 1992. Nutritional requirements and fertilization. pp. 385–439. In D.V. Waddington, R.N. Carrow, and R.C. Shearman, Eds. *Turfgrass. Agronomy Monograph No. 32.* Madison, WI: Amer. Soc. Agron.
22. Turner, T.R. and D.V. Waddington. 1978. Survey of soil testing programs for turfgrass. *Commun. Soil Sci. Plant Anal.* 9:71–87.
23. Turner, T.R. and D.V. Waddington. 1983. Soil test calibration for establishment of turfgrass monostands. *Soil Sci. Soc. Amer. J.* 47:1161–1166.
24. Turner, T.R., D.V. Waddington, and J.M. Duich. 1978. The effect of sampling depth and thatch on soil test results of turfgrass areas. *Commun. Soil Sci. Plant Anal.* 9:89–104.
25. Waddington, D.V., A. E. Gover, and D. B. Beegle. 1994. Nutrient concentrations of turfgrass and soil test levels as affected by soil media and fertilizer rate and placement. *Commun. Soil Sci. Plant Anal.* 25:1957–1990.
26. Waddington, D.V., T.R. Turner, J.M. Duich, and E.L. Moberg. 1978. Effect of fertilization on Penncross creeping bentgrass. *Agron. J.* 70:713–718.
27. Waddington, D.V. and T.L. Zimmerman. 1972. Growth and chemical composition of eight grasses grown under high water conditions. *Commun. Soil Sci. Plant Anal.* 3:329–337.
28. Walsh, L.M. and J.D. Beaton, Eds. 1973. *Soil Testing and Plant Analysis.* Madison, WI: Soil Sci. Soc. of Amer.

Chapter 10

Nitrogen

AMONG THE FERTILIZER NUTRIENTS PRESENT IN TURFGRASSES, nitrogen (N) is present in greatest quantities, ranging from a low of around 2% to well over 5% in dry leaf tissue[9] (Table 2.1). Nitrogen has a major impact on a number of factors involved in turf management. Among these are: (a) effects on plant growth and metabolism, influencing grass response to a number of stress conditions; (b) potential environmental implications; (c) for a quality stress-tolerant turf, it must be routinely applied; and (d) it accounts for the highest cost of a turfgrass fertilization program. It is obvious that a good understanding of how N is involved in both plant and soil is essential for the turf manager to most effectively utilize this nutrient in a turf management program.

I. PLANT RELATIONSHIPS

A. N Compounds in the Plant

NITROGEN IS FOUND IN NUMEROUS COMPOUNDS IN THE PLANT. Some are relatively simple, others are highly complex. As N is taken up by the plant it is assimilated into *amino acids* that provide the basis for formation of key N compounds basic to plant growth and metabolism.[6–8] Amino acids, characterized by the presence of the *amino group* ($-NH_2$), are the building blocks of these N compounds. There are about 20 amino acids involved in plant growth and metabolism. Other low molecular weight N compounds are amides, peptides, and amines. These along with the amino acids serve as precursors for the more complex compounds: proteins, chlorophyll, enzymes, hormones, osmoregulators, and nucleic acids.

Proteins are combinations of amino acids. Each protein has a distinct structure and unique chemical properties. In plants they serve a number of functions including being used in structural components, for N storage, for ion channels in membranes, and in enzymes. The latter serve to catalyze various biochemical processes in the plant, providing greater efficiency in metabolic reactions. The enzymes needed for metabolic processes contain N; some are present in fairly high concentrations.

Chlorophyll, found in chloroplasts, contains N as a constituent. Chlorophyll is essential for the plant to capture light energy through photosynthesis in order to form the carbon compounds necessary for growth of new cells. These new cells require amino acids and proteins. When nitrogen is limited, the reduced levels of chlorophyll result in a loss of green color, reduced growth, and a number of other responses.

Hormones regulate plant growth and development. Those containing N include auxins, cytokinins, and ethylene. They can be synthesized in roots and/or shoots.

Nucleic acids are vitally important as they function in duplication and transfer of genetic information that determines plant characteristics. *Deoxyribonucleic acid (DNA)* is present in the nucleus and in mitochondria. DNA duplicates genetic information of the parent cell chromosomes for the daughter cells. *Ribonucleic acid (RNA)* is found in the nucleus and cytoplasm, carrying out the instructions coded by the DNA molecules.

Glycine betaine and proline are N-containing compounds that serve as *osmoregulators* that help the plant adjust to stress from high soluble salt levels, heat, or moisture stress. They protect against inactivation of enzymes or destabilization of cell membranes.

Plant available forms of N (*nitrate,* NO_3^-*; ammonium,* NH_4^+; and *urea*) can be taken up by plant roots or absorbed by shoots. Root uptake is primarily as nitrate (NO_3^-) or ammonium (NH_4^+). In well-aerated soils, nitrate uptake predominates. Urea can also be taken up by roots in small amounts where it can be hydrolyzed to NH_3 or it can be translocated to the shoots for hydrolysis. Absorption of N by shoots is usually associated with foliar fertilization from solution fertilizers.

In the plant, nitrate (NO_3^-) must be reduced to ammonia (NH_3) or ammonium (NH_4^+) so the N can be used to fulfill various functions in the plant. The first step reduces nitrate to nitrite (NO_2^-) for which the enzyme nitrate reductase is required. Nitrate reduction can occur in the cytoplasm of either roots or shoots.

$$\underset{\textit{Nitrate}}{NO_3^-} \rightarrow (\text{nitrate reductase}) \rightarrow \underset{\textit{Nitrite}}{NO_2^-}$$

The second step in nitrate reduction occurs in chloroplasts (leaves) or proplastids (roots). This involves reducing nitrite to ammonium utilizing nitrite reductase.

$$\underset{\textit{Nitrite}}{NO_2^-} \rightarrow (\text{nitrate reductase}) \rightarrow \underset{\textit{Ammonium}}{NH_4^+}$$

Significant quantities of both enzymes are necessary for nitrate reduction for which high amounts of energy are required. Warm-season grasses (C4) are much more efficient in nitrate reduction than cool-season grasses (C3). *Nitrogen use efficiency* (NUE) refers to the amount of carbon dioxide fixed per unit of N. Well-fertilized cool-season grasses typically have N concentrations of 4 to 4.5% while warm-season grasses more commonly contain 2 to 3.5% N (see Table 2.1 for typical N concentrations). The higher N in cool-season grasses reflects their lower NUE. This diversity in NUE is due to differences in the enzymes involved in fixing carbon dioxide and the plant organs in which the enzymes involved are active.

Nitrate reduction begins in the root shortly after absorption. At higher rates of fertilization there are not sufficient levels of the enzymes to reduce all of the nitrate. Since nitrate is mobile in the xylem tissue of the plant it can translocate to leaves where it can be reduced or stored in the vacuoles for nitrate reduction at a later time. There it can serve in osmoregulation to help maintain a proper cation: anion balance in the plant. The proportion of nitrate reduced in roots increases with temperature, age of the plant, and the accompanying cation. When potassium (K) levels are high there is greater tendency for both K and nitrate to translocate to the shoots. Since high levels of K are utilized on many turfs the tendency for this to occur is greater than when lower K is available. If calcium (Ca) in the plant is high, less nitrate will translocate to the shoots.

When N is taken up by roots as ammonium, it must be incorporated into organic N compounds in the root. Ammonium, and especially ammonia, is toxic to plant tissues at fairly low concentrations. Fortunately, the plant usually assimilates ammonium quickly, provided there are sufficient levels of carbon skeletons (from photosynthesis) in the root. Assimilation of ammonium into amino acids is done by specific enzymes. This assimilation of ammonium requires about 5 mols of ATP energy. In contrast, 15 mols are required to reduce nitrate to ammonium.

Once more complex proteins have been formed in plant tissue, the plant cannot convert the N in proteins back into ammonium or nitrate. However, when N is limited, the plant can convert complex proteins into simpler, low molecular weight N compounds (amides, ureides, amino acids) that are more soluble and can move from one part of the plant to another. This permits the plant to generate new leaf tissue where N demand is high. The result is that under low N older leaves begin to lose color and senescence begins.

When nitrate levels are high, the capacity for nitrate reduction in the root can be exceeded. It then is translocated to the shoots where the carbohydrates from photosynthesis are predominantly allocated to production of amino acids. Under high N conditions, less of the carbohydrate is allocated to sugars that can be translocated to the roots. The net result is a stimulation of top growth and a depletion of roots. This effect is most noticeable for cool-season grasses during periods of higher temperatures.

B. Turf Responses to N

Nitrogen has a major influence on a number of plant responses among which are: (a) color; (b) shoot growth; (c) shoot density; (d) root growth; (e) rhizome and stolon growth; (f) carbohydrate reserves; (g) high temperature stress; (h) cold tolerance; (i) drought resistance; (j) compaction and wear tolerance; (k) thatch accumulation; and (l) recuperative potential.[2,3] These responses are graphically depicted in Figures 10.1 and 10.2. The curves shown are generalized to provide an indication of typical responses to rates of N. The shape of these response curves will vary with species, cultivars, use of the turf, environmental conditions, and management practices utilized. Other responses to nitrogen include effects on diseases (Table 2.5) and the species of plants that dominate a given turf (Plates 5–8).

Visual symptoms of grass response at low levels of N are easily identified. As N levels decrease there is a gradual loss of green color (*chlorosis*) that first appears in older leaves. New (upper) leaves remain green as the plant is able to convert complex N compounds to more soluble N compounds that can be translocated to new leaves. Any uptake of N is also sent to the new leaves (Plate 1). As N becomes more limiting, all leaves can become chlorotic, growth is stunted, and there is a gradual loss of leaves, tillers, and entire plants, resulting in thinning of turf. Deficiency symptoms and conditions that contribute to N deficiency are given in Table 2.3.

As nitrogen rate is increased from significantly deficient levels there is an increase in the content of chlorophyll, providing the linear *color* response in Figure 10.1A. At very high N levels there is no further improvement in color. When excessive N has been applied there may be some loss of color because growth rate is so high that some dilution of chlorophyll may occur and shading results in yellowing of lower leaves, a condition that is especially apparent after mowing.

Shoot growth rate (Figure 10.1B) follows much the same curve as color. Growth depends on the production of new cells for which amino acids and proteins are needed. The more rapid growth rate at higher N necessitates more frequent mowing. Leaf width and length increase

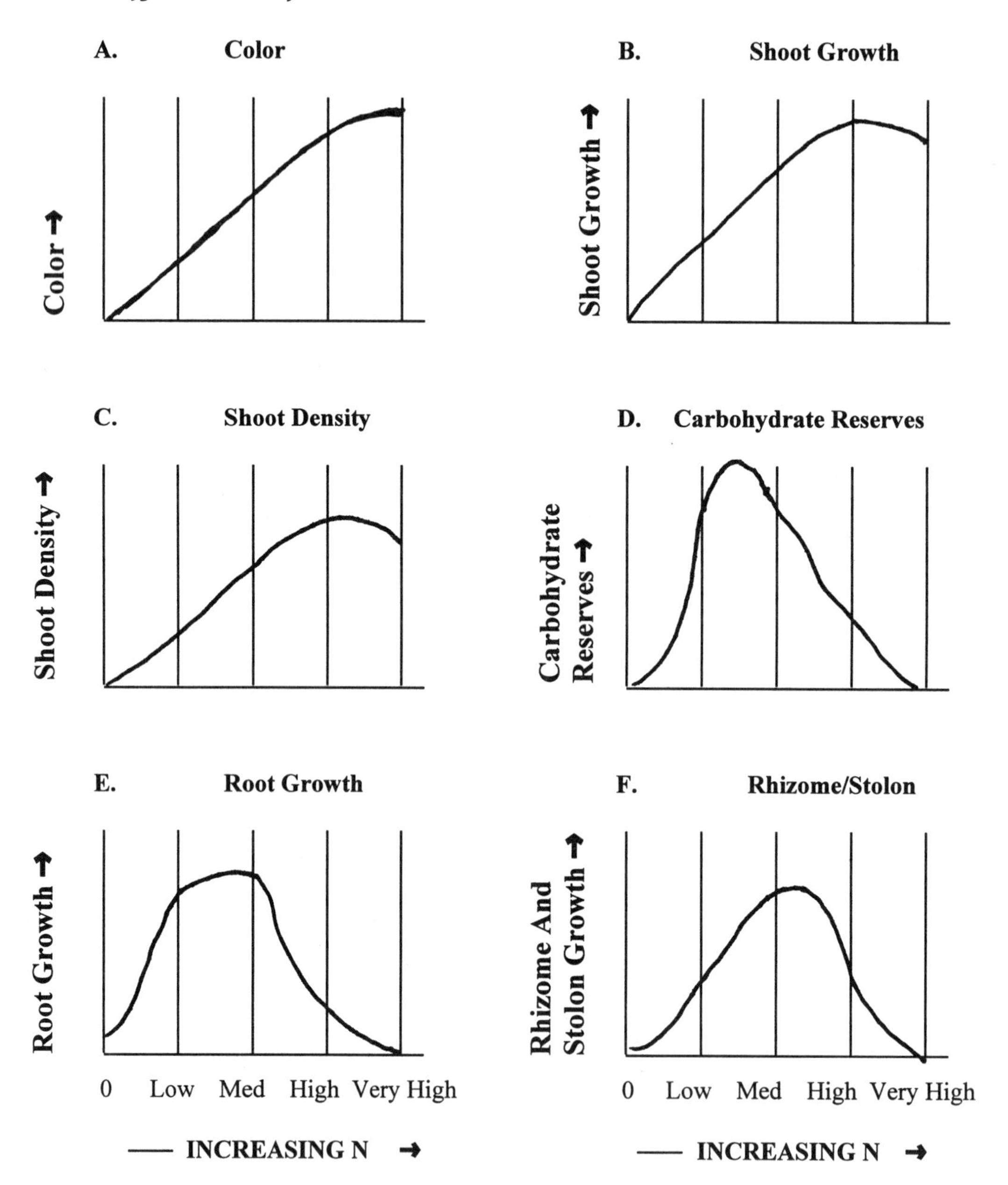

Figure 10.1. Turfgrass responses to increasing N: color, shoot growth, shoot density, root growth, rhizome and stolon growth, and carbohydrate reserves. Adapted from Beard.[2,3]

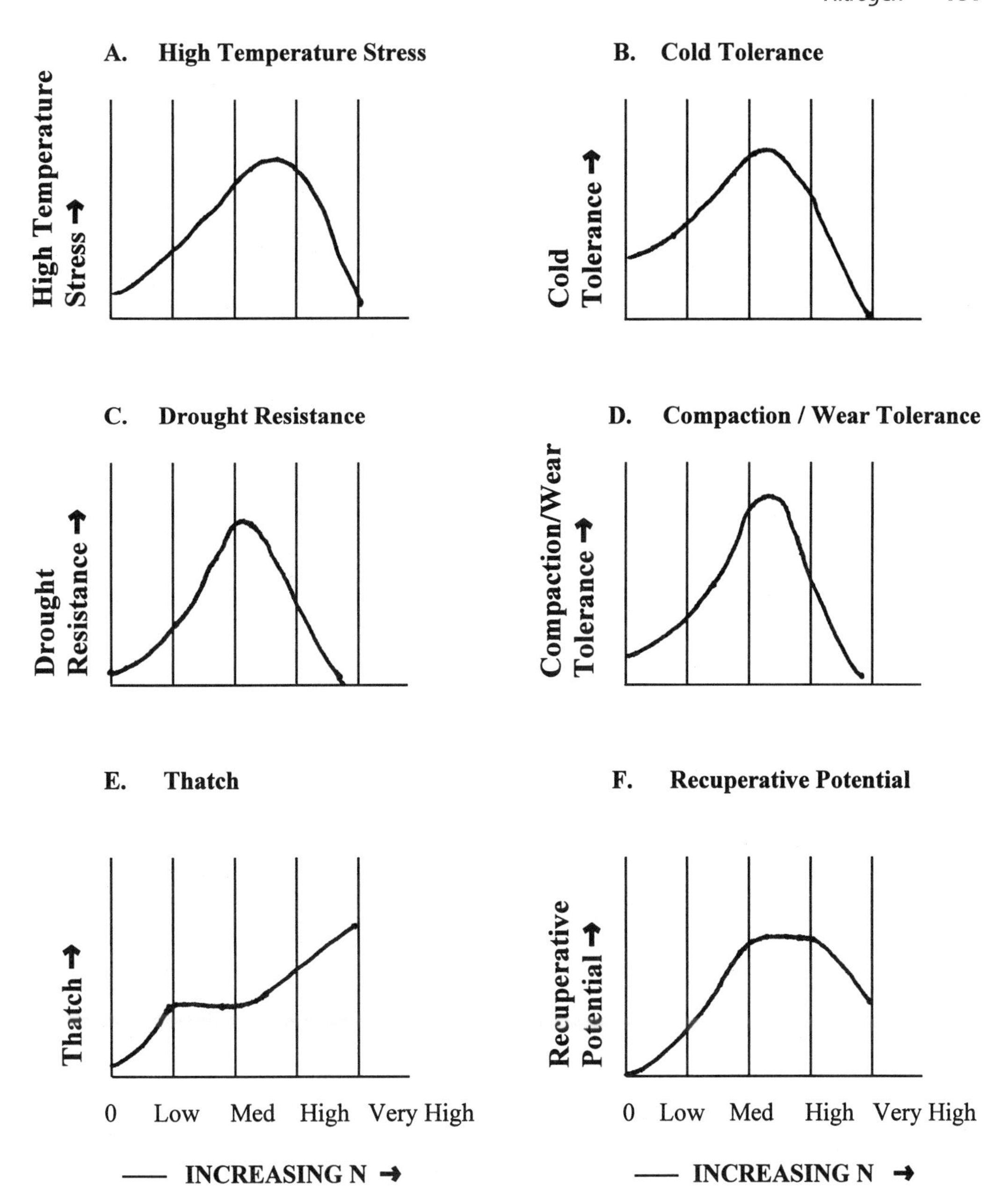

Figure 10.2. Turfgrass responses to increasing N: high temperature tolerance, cold temperature tolerance, drought resistance, compaction/wear tolerance, thatch accumulation, and recuperative potential (adapted from Beard[2,3]).

with N rate. At excessive N levels there may be additional growth response, but cells become large with thin cell walls. Light reception may be less efficient. During periods of warm, wet, cloudy conditions the enhanced growth rate may contribute to loss of color at more modest N levels because of leaf shading effects. Mowing frequency should be increased under these conditions.

The *shoot density* (Figure 10.1C) response curve is similar to shoot growth. At lower N levels the plant responds with more tillers and increased leaf width. As additional N is applied there is a linear response, but at higher N levels tillering and leaf width create a shading effect. When N is very high there can be a decline in numbers of tillers and turf density, partly due to shading, inadequate mowing frequency, and limited carbohydrates.

Carbohydrate reserves are very important for survival during dormant periods, turf regrowth, and tolerance to various stresses. These reserves are predominantly fructosans in cool-season grasses and starch in warm-season grasses. As N is increased from very low to medium levels there is a very rapid increase in carbohydrates in plant tissues (Figure 10.1D). Carbohydrate reserves can be stored in roots, stolons, rhizomes, stem bases, and leaf bases. However, above moderate N levels there is a rapid loss of carbohydrate reserves in cool-season grasses with increasing N. Higher levels of N in the plant cause a shift of allocation of the products of photosynthesis to shoot growth and with rapid leaf production, carbohydrate reserves can become depleted. Cool-season grasses are particularly susceptible to this loss of carbohydrates during the peak of the growing season. Warm-season grasses are somewhat less susceptible to this response during the heat of summer, but there is still the possibility of depletion of carbohydrates if N is consistently applied at high rates. Nitrogen use on warm-season grasses should cease during the fall before dormancy begins.

Root growth is dependent on a continuous supply of carbohydrates from the shoots to root tissues. As a result, the rooting curve reflects the carbohydrate reserves curve. When N is limiting (Figure 10.1E) the plant produces sugars that are transported to the roots. Although the turf may be light green to yellow in color, root growth of cool-season grasses will usually be very good to excellent. At higher N levels, carbohydrates are utilized in shoot growth with reduced translocation to roots. During summer stresses, carbohydrate reserves for cool-season species become depleted and roots can become deprived of adequate carbohydrates. Excess N causes a further depletion of carbohydrates for roots by stimulating extra shoot (leaf) production. Thus, during summer stress periods, root decline is typical for cool-season grasses but excess N will deplete roots even further. This loss of roots may result in an accumulation of dead root material in the surface layer of soil, potentially contributing to a sealing of the surface of sand root zone mixes. Warm-season grasses need N during the summer when photosynthesis is greatest, and with these grasses there is not a significant loss of carbohydrates and roots at higher N levels as occurs with cool-season grasses. Still, excess N should be avoided for practical (mowing requirements), physiological (stress tolerance), and environmental reasons.

Rhizome and stolon growth in response to N (Figure 10.1F) is very similar to root growth. Carbohydrates are necessary to develop these storage organs. Rhizomes of cool-season grasses are particularly susceptible to carbohydrate loss under high N applications. Stoloniferous grasses need extra N to encourage spreading so stolon response will be somewhat less susceptible than rhizomes to loss at modest and high N levels. At excessive N levels, leaves will be produced on stolons, but the rate of spread for filling by rhizome/stolon elongation in the turf may be reduced due to reduced carbohydrate levels as the majority of carbohydrates are allocated to leaf production. The reduction in rhizome and stolon production is most often observed when warm-season grasses are plugged, sprigged, or stolonized and then maintained under very high N for two or three months.

The response to nitrogen in *high temperature tolerance, low temperature tolerance, drought resistance,* and *compaction/wear tolerance* are all quite similar (Figures 10.2 A–D). This similarity in response should be expected since they are all related to carbohydrate levels in the plant and higher carbohydrates provide better stress tolerance. These carbohydrates are needed to produce the protoplasmic compounds that protect key proteins, bind water, and produce soluble sugars that increase cell osmotic potential. The result is less succulence and greater hardiness. One exception is that cold temperature tolerance is reasonably good at low N levels, particularly for warm-season grasses. The tolerance to these stresses drops significantly at higher N levels, again as a result of lower carbohydrate levels. Drought resistance is highest at medium to low N levels as a result of higher root: shoot ratios, adequate water uptake, and good levels of soluble carbohydrates.

A different curve applies to *wilting tendency* (curve not shown) with a general linear increase in susceptibility to wilting as N level increases. Causes for this response include: (a) development of large cells with thin cell walls; (b) stomata that close more slowly when N is high in the plant; (c) water is less likely to be bound to carbohydrates, making the plant more susceptible to loss through stomates; (d) loss of roots reduces the volume of soil from which they can extract water; and (e) high N increases water use.

There will be little *thatch* in most turfs when no N is applied to thatch-forming species. As N increases to low levels a modest rate of thatch will develop (Figure 10.2E). Beyond that there is not complete agreement on how much thatch will develop. Other factors exert a major influence on thatch accumulation including grass species or cultivar; irrigation management; soil conditions including pH and compaction; environmental conditions that influence plant growth and microbial activity; and mowing height and management practices. Overwatering rapidly enhances thatch accumulation. Our understanding of N influence on thatch is complicated by the highly variable composition and structure of thatch.

From low to medium N there is a tendency for no further thatch accumulation. Then at high N levels thatch increases again. Since thatch is an accumulation of roots, stems, and crown tissue (could also include rhizomes and stolons), an increase in thatch would be expected as turf density increases with increasing N. This may occur in cool climates where soil temperature is below 55°F (13°C) much of the year, discouraging microbial activity that could decompose thatch. In warmer climates, including subtropical and tropical regions, high soil temperatures are conducive to rapid organic matter decomposition by soil microbes. Thatch accumulation may not be a problem even at relatively high N. Some have suggested that at higher N rates the C:N ratio will be narrow enough to enhance microbial activity that could decompose thatch. That would significantly change the shape of this curve (Figure 10.2E). However, in cases where high N rates contribute to greater soil acidity, the acid condition can slow thatch decomposition. In practice, turf managers should lime when required to maintain an optimum pH for decomposition (i.e., pH 6.0 to 7.0).

When turf density is lost due to weed competition, damage by pests, traffic, moisture stress, or other environmental stresses, additional N is needed to improve turf density (Figure 10.1C). At excessive N levels carbohydrates are used to promote shoot growth by leaf production and tillering, but may reduce the potential for stolons and rhizomes to fill in open areas as noted previously. Adequate moisture is also needed in conjunction with additional N in order to increase turf density.

Another turf response to N rate is the species that predominates in a mixed turfgrass stand. The relative percentage of different species can be referred to as *turf community composition.* Depending on turf use, soil conditions, and management there is a general level at which a given grass will compete effectively with other plant species. As an example, in a mixed stand of Kentucky bluegrass (*Poa pratensis*) and fine fescues (*Festuca* spp.), Kentucky bluegrass will dominate the mixture if high rates of N are applied over a period of years. Low N rates will favor the fine fescues.

Another example is the effect of N on competition between the desired grass and weedy species. If nitrogen rates are too low for adequate turf density, weedy species may predominate. One plant that competes very favorably with underfertilized turfgrasses is dandelion (*Taraxacum officinale*). A high density of yellow seedheads in the spring is a common observation on unfertilized turfs. Many other broadleaf weeds will give a similar response although the result is not as visible. Higher N tends to enhance *Poa annua* at the expense of other cool-season grasses, especially when applied in early spring.

Fertilization at establishment of a mixture of grasses can affect species predominance. New seedings that are underfertilized may be overcome with weedy species, especially when seeded at less than optimum conditions. A key example is when seeding a mixture of perennial ryegrass (*Lolium perenne*) and Kentucky bluegrass. If the turf receives a heavy application of N shortly after the perennial ryegrass germinates, this species will dominate the stand because the Kentucky bluegrass seedlings germinate and establish much more slowly and will not compete effectively with the rapidly growing perennial ryegrass.

A common problem on turf sites is the competition of annual grasses with the desired species. For a species like crabgrass (*Digitaria* spp.) that requires light for germination, a dense turf as a result of more aggressive late fall and early spring applications of N can result in less opportunity for crabgrass to germinate and get established. By contrast, once annual grasses have germinated, N applied subsequently will cause the weedy grass to grow and compete more aggressively. Thus nitrogen fertilizer programming serves an important role in an integrated approach to weed management.

Fertilization rate, time of application and carrier play major roles in how quickly an overseeded grass gets established into a warm-season grass or how quickly the transition back to the warm-season grass occurs in the spring.

Nitrogen rate, timing, and even carrier can have an impact on *disease susceptibility* of the turf. Reported effects of N on turf diseases are given in Table 2.5. Those relationships that are the most consistent and strongest are noted in the table. There are many variables that influence which disease attacks a given turf and how severely the turf is damaged. Some disease organisms are responsive to N applications since they utilize N as a nutrient. The various effects of N level on the plant metabolism and morphology can make it more or less susceptible to a given disease organism.

For example, under high N the plant will have thinner cell walls, more succulent tissue, and low carbohydrate levels, making it more susceptible to *Pythium* spp. or brown patch (*Rhizoctonia* spp.). In contrast, low N results in slow growth, senescence of leaves, and thin, weakened plants, making the plant more susceptible to dollar spot (*Sclerotinia homeocarpa*), rust (*Puccinia* spp.), red thread (*Laetisaria fuciformis*), or pink patch (*Limonomyces rosiepellis*).

For many diseases the impact of N fertilization is minimal, but with some diseases N fertilization can be used in a disease management program. Examples are necrotic ring spot (*Leptosphaeria korrae*) on Kentucky bluegrass, and anthracnose (*Colletotrichum graminicola*) on *Poa annua*. For these diseases, modest rates of N applied monthly as a slow-release carrier have proved effective in disease management.[13] Nutrition alone is seldom sufficient to adequately control most diseases but proper nutrition, including avoidance of extreme deficiencies or excesses of N can minimize activity of certain diseases. Certainly, N management should be a key part of an *integrated disease management program*.

Nitrogen can also influence a disease indirectly by influencing nonpathogenic activity. Applications of N, particularly from organic carriers, may spawn rapid increases in populations of some microorganisms. These nonpathogens can sometimes suppress the activity level of pathogens.

Another impact of N fertilization is the potential for most carriers to decrease pH of the thatch or surface layer of soil. This increase in acidity could in turn change microbial numbers, activity, and balance; and thus influence thatch degradation or occurrence of some diseases.

Fortunately, most turfgrasses are not subjected to excessive N nutrition due to many adverse effects that can occur. One exception is during grow-in. Warm-season grasses being established from plugs, stolons, or springs are often fertilized at much higher rates than would be needed for established grasses. Applying too much N for too long can actually slow the rate of establishment as carbohydrates go to producing shoot growth (primarily leaves and some tillers), thus slowing rhizome and stolon growth as was discussed earlier.

Another example of very high N use is on mature *Cynodon* spp. used for intensively maintained recreational turfs in regions with long growing seasons and where sandy soils exist. Sometimes very high annual N rates of 20 to 24 lb N per 1,000 ft^2 (958 to 1,170 kg ha^{-1}) are applied due to the long growing season, clipping removal, etc. Under these conditions the turf could have a limited root system, be susceptible to pests, and have low recuperative capacity.

Given the range of effects of N on both warm- and cool-season grasses, it is obvious that proper N fertilization is basic to maintaining a healthy, stress tolerant, attractive turf. An understanding of the soil and environmental factors influencing N relationships is important when developing a N fertilization program.

II. SOIL AND ENVIRONMENTAL RELATIONSHIPS

A. Soil and Atmospheric Forms of N

THE NITROGEN CONTENT IN SOILS ranges from nearly zero in clean sands to more than 2.5% by weight in some peats and other organic soils. The higher the organic matter content of a soil, the higher the amount of nitrogen in a soil. A very small percentage of nitrogen found in soils is present in the available forms, nitrate (NO_3^-) or ammonium (NH_4^+). By far the greatest amount of nitrogen in the world occurs in the lithosphere in the forms of coal and ammonium fixed in various minerals. About 2% of the world's supply of nitrogen is found in the atmosphere, mostly as N_2 gas (about 78% of air) with small amounts of nitric oxide (NO) and nitrous oxide (N_2O).

Nitrogen management is the most important aspect of an effective turf fertilization program. Understanding the processes that influence what can happen to nitrogen in the soil and with fertilizer sources is essential.

Most of the N taken up by plants is in the nitrate form although ammonium is readily absorbed by most grasses when present in appreciable quantities. Excessive levels of either can contribute to a soluble salt problem, but unusually high levels of ammonium can be toxic to the plant. In soils with good microbial activity, the amount of ammonium is usually small. Other forms of nitrogen found in the soil are nitrite (NO_2^-), nitrous oxide, and nitric oxide. Nitrite is seldom present in high quantities because of rapid conversion to nitrate. Nitrous oxide and nitric oxide are also normally present in low quantities because as gases, for the most part they escape into the atmosphere. Both nitrous oxide and nitric oxide as well as N_2 gas result from denitrification of nitrate nitrogen.

There are many organic forms of nitrogen in soils, ranging from simple amino acids to highly complex compounds that are not well understood. The simpler compounds are decomposed readily by soil microbes, releasing nitrogen for grass and/or microbe use. By contrast, complex organic matter compounds like lignin are highly stable and resistant to microbial degradation. These sources contribute little to the available nitrogen pool. The rate of conversion of organic nitrogen to available nitrogen may be a few days for simple N compounds to 100 years or more for highly complex sources. Nitrogen in grass clippings could be recycled within days to a few weeks.

B. Soil Nitrogen Cycle

Transformations among the various forms of nitrogen in the soil are influenced by soil organisms as well as by soil environmental conditions. Perhaps the easiest means of describing soil nitrogen transformations is through the *soil nitrogen cycle* (Figure 10.3). This diagram includes the various forms of nitrogen that can be found in the soil that affect N for the plant, the processes that convert N from one form to another, as well as where additions and losses fit into the cycle. The turf manager must understand the N cycle well both to manage N fertilization for good plant health and to minimize potential loss of N to the environment.

Most of the transformations of N in the soil are accomplished by soil organisms. Several factors influence biological activity among which are soil temperature, soil moisture, oxygen status and other gases, and soil pH (see Chapter 15).[5,11]

While all these factors influence microbial activity, *soil temperature* has the greatest influence on nitrogen transformations, particularly on *mineralization*—conversion of N in organic matter into mineral forms (ammonium and nitrate). The impact of temperature on N transformations by soil microbes can be illustrated by the temperature impact on nitrification. At temperatures below freezing there is very little nitrification. As soil temperature increases from 32° to 41°F (0° to 5°C), a very gradual increase in nitrification occurs. From 41° to 95°F (5° to 35°C), a doubling of nitrification occurs with every increase of 18°F (10°C). Maximum nitrification occurs at 86° to 95°F (30° to 35°C). Above 104° to 113°F (40° to 45°C) nitrification rates are reduced, but soils under turf seldom reach those temperatures unless the turf is dormant due to lack of water.

A minimum soil temperature of 50° to 55°F (15° to 17°C) is considered necessary for sufficient biological activity to enhance release of nitrogen for plant use from organic nitrogen carriers. As soil temperatures increase above 55°F the rate of N release from organic fertilizers or soil organic matter increases accordingly. Below 50° to 55°F release rates are low. Soil temperatures lag behind air temperatures during seasonal change. In spring when soil temperatures remain cool, nitrification rates will be low. As air temperatures cool in the fall, soil temperatures are still warm, enhancing nitrification somewhat more than one might predict based on air temperature.

If *soil moisture* is adequate for good turf growth, there is adequate moisture for high levels of microbial activity. Even in soil that is fairly dry for turf, nitrification rates are quite high. Nitrifiers are classified as obligate autotrophic aerobes, meaning oxygen is necessary. For this reason soil aeration is essential for optimum rates of nitrification to occur. Nitrification is high when soil oxygen is in the range of 10 to 20% by volume. Below 5% oxygen, nitrification drops rapidly.

Soil pH has a limited influence on nitrification. There is little change over the range of pH 5.5 to 10, with highest rates at about 8.5. Under pH 5.5, nitrification declines.

A balance of *nutrients* that is adequate for grass growth should also be sufficient for soil microbial activity. The most limiting nutrient for maximum nitrification is N, followed by P.

In surface soils the majority of the nitrogen is present in organic matter. Potential losses of soil organic matter include: (a) by erosion of soil by flooding; or (b) decomposition by soil microbes that can release N for plant use. Additions to the soil organic matter pool include topdressing materials or accumulations from plant growth (clippings, roots, stems). Any addition of organic matter would include a certain amount of nitrogen. The amount of organic

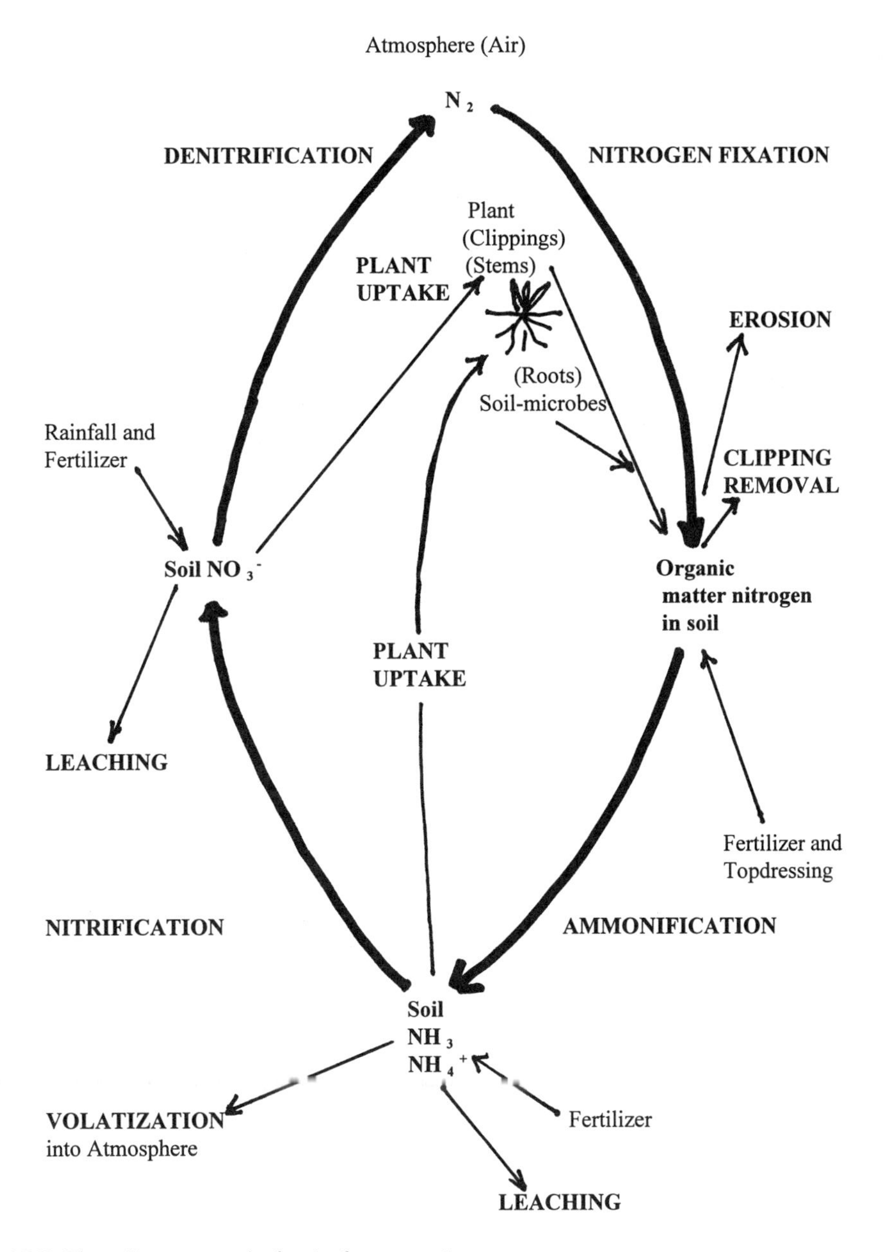

Figure 10.3. The nitrogen cycle for turfgrass systems.

matter added in the form of organic fertilizers is negligible compared to the amount of organic matter in a soil. Thus, the use of such fertilizers has an insignificant effect on total soil organic matter levels in most soils.

The conversion of organic matter nitrogen into available mineral forms is termed *mineralization.* The first step in this process, sometimes referred to as *aminization,* produces amines and amino acids. The next step produces ammonia (NH_3) and is referred to as *ammonification.* Many different heterotrophic soil organisms contribute to ammonification, including fungi, bacteria, and actinomycetes.

Ammonification may be represented by:

$$R\text{–}NH_2 + HOH \rightarrow NH_3 + R\text{–}OH + \text{energy}$$

In this equation, R represents organic matter that contains the amine group (NH_2). With addition of another molecule of water, ammonia then forms ammonium:

$$NH_3 + HOH \rightarrow NH_4^+ + OH^-$$

Ammonia/ammonium can be: (a) nitrified to nitrate; (b) taken up as ammonium by the grass plant or soil microbes; (c) attracted as the ammonium cation to the cation exchange sites; (d) fixed as ammonium in a relatively unavailable form in certain clay minerals; (e) volatilized as ammonia into the atmosphere; or (f) leached, particularly from sands.

The rate that ammonification takes place is affected by the C:N ratio in the organic matter. Grass clippings, for example, have a narrow C:N ration of less than 10:1 and are readily decomposed, releasing ammonium into the soil. Any material with a ratio well above 20:1 results in soil microbes competing with the grass for available nitrogen. When available N (NO_3^- or NH_4^+) becomes part of the soil microbial biomass or plant tissue, this process is called *immobilization.* Immobilized N must be released by microbial action before it is once again available for plant or microbe uptake.

The final step in mineralization is *nitrification* in which ammonium is converted to nitrate. This is a two step process, the first of which converts ammonium to nitrite:

$$2NH_4^+ + 3O_2 \rightarrow 2NO_2^- + 2\ H_2O + 4H^+$$

The primary organisms responsible for this first step are thought to be the autotrophic bacteria, *Nitrosomonas* and *Nitrospora,* although there is evidence to suggest several different heterotrophs may be involved as well. *Nitrosomonas* spp. are more active in ammonium-rich soils.

The second step in nitrification is the conversion of nitrite to nitrate:

$$2NO_2^- + O_2 \rightarrow 2NO_3^-$$

The group of microbes causing this conversion are *Nitrobacter* spp., although several different types of microbes may play some role. Nitrate can be taken up by plants or microbes, lost by denitrification, or lost by leaching.

Associated with nitrification are some very practical observations. One is that in the first step there is a release of hydrogen into the soil. This released H^+ has potential to contribute to soil (or thatch) acidification, with the intensity of the effect depending on a number of factors including: (a) N carrier; (b) rate of N applied; (c) soil pH; (d) presence of free calcium carbonate in the soil; (e) cation exchange capacity; and (f) chemicals in irrigation water.

Any *nitrogen carrier* (i.e., fertilizer) that contains ammonium or produces ammonium (such as urea) will result in release of some hydrogen upon nitrification. Ammonium carriers (like ammonium sulfate, ammonium phosphate) are the most acidifying because all of the nitrogen is in the ammonium form. Higher *rates of nitrogen* will obviously have greater acidification potential. Soils with higher *pH* or *higher cation exchange capacity* will be less affected by any acidity produced in nitrification due to greater buffering.

The amount of acid produced by nitrification will have no practical effect on soil pH when there is any appreciable amount of *free calcium carbonate* present in the soil. Some *irrigation water* sources contain sufficient calcium carbonate to offset any acidity contributed by nitrification. The amount of acid produced by nitrification of nitrogen fertilizers is normally low and will have an impact only on the thatch and perhaps the surface inch of soil. However, in acid soils with low cation exchange capacity and when high rates of ammonium forming carriers are used it is possible to significantly reduce soil pH.

A second important point with nitrification is that *oxygen* is required. In heavily compacted soils or when the surface is kept too wet the rate of nitrification could be reduced. In fact, under these soil conditions denitrification is possible.

C. Losses of N from the Turf/Soil Ecosystem

An understanding of N losses from turf and soil is helpful in N fertilizer management proper fertilization for healthy turf and environmental protection. Most turfgrasses require at least a minimal amount of N to provide a reasonable quality of turf. On many sites clippings are returned but the N needs are reduced only 20 to 35% compared to clipping removal. This level of N recovery from turf tissue suggests there is appreciable loss of N from turf sites. Among the potential losses of N beyond clipping removal are denitrification, leaching, volatilization, run-off, and rarely, erosion.[1,5,10,11]

Denitrification

Denitrification results in loss of N in gaseous form as nitrous oxide (N_2O), nitric oxide (NO), or N_2 gas. All forms are easily lost to the atmosphere. The primary reaction involves reduction of nitrate by the following sequence:

$$NO_3^- \rightarrow NO_2^- \rightarrow NO \rightarrow N_2O \rightarrow N_2$$

Several different groups of soil microbes can cause denitrification; most are anaerobic, but a few can function in the presence of oxygen. Conditions that influence denitrification include: (a) presence of readily decomposable organic matter; (b) soil moisture and oxygen content; (c) soil temperature; (d) soil pH; (e) plant growth; and (f) nitrate level.

In turf soils there are high levels of *easily decomposable organic matter.* This organic matter comes from clippings returned to the turf, from organic matter that accumulates in thatch, or from dead roots in the surface layer of soil.

Highly maintained turf sites are well-watered, reducing oxygen content in the soil. Compaction of the surface soil and the accumulation of organic matter in the surface soil can also contribute to low rates of aeration. Soil oxygen levels must be very low (less that 2%) for significant denitrification. Wet soils are subject to greater denitrification. Microsites in the soil, such as the internal areas of aggregates, can hold water near saturation and, therefore, have soil O_2 levels below 2% even when the bulk soil O_2 is higher. These sites can have sufficiently low oxygen levels that are conducive to high denitrification rates.

As *soil temperature* rises the rate of denitrification increases rapidly, but there is also evidence to suggest denitrification can take place at low rates in both late fall and early spring when soils are cold. Limited denitrification occurs in highly acid (pH below 5.0) soils because the denitrifiers are sensitive to H^+ ions. In moderately to slightly acid soils most of the gaseous N loss occurs as nitrous oxide. In slightly acid to alkaline (pH above 6.5) soils, the loss of N by N_2 gas will predominate.

Activity of plant roots has an influence as well. As roots take up nitrate and water there is less potential for denitrification. By reducing nitrate concentrations in the soil, less is available for denitrification. Uptake of water by plants decrease soil water content around the roots and makes conditions less conducive for denitrification. On the other hand, turfgrasses have an active root system that produces root exudates, a ready source of organic matter that could enhance denitrification. Also, root respiration, as well or microbial respiration, lowers O_2 levels in the soil, especially in warm weather. Obviously, application of high rates of nitrate can enhance the potential for denitrification that occurs. This could be one reason why golf course superintendents who apply most of their nitrogen through spoon-feeding find they can maintain adequate turf at somewhat lower annual or total N rates. Light and frequent rates of N are utilized quickly by the plant, making nitrate less susceptible to denitrification.

The contribution of denitrification to loss of N from the turf/soil ecosystem has received limited study. One report suggests as high as 85% of applied N was lost through denitrification, but most research data suggest rates of 5% or less. For many turf situations with adequate soil oxygen levels, denitrification losses are probably very low. Still, conditions in the root zone of some turfs (compaction, surface soils sealed due to high organic matter or algae, poor drainage, wet soils, high soil temperatures) are conducive to denitrification losses. Further study is needed to determine the ultimate fate of N applied to turf.

Volatilization

Another potential loss of N from the turf/soil complex is *volatilization* as ammonia. Most of this loss is related to the use of N fertilizers that contain urea although potentially there could be small volatilization losses from other carriers. The enzyme *urease* is necessary for the following hydrolysis reaction to take place:

$$\underset{Urea}{CO(NH_2)} + H_2O - (urease) \rightarrow 2NH_3 + CO_2$$

Both ammonia and carbon dioxide can be lost to the atmosphere as gases. Studies have revealed volatilization of ammonia from foliar applications of urea can range from nil to as high as 40% of that applied.

Urease is ubiquitous in soils so it is seldom limiting for urea hydrolysis. A number of soil microorganisms contain urease. The rhizosphere has very high urease activity. It is also found on fresh organic matter, including on grass leaves. Some of the ammonia volatilization from spray applications of urea likely occurs directly from leaf surfaces on grass.

As with other N transformations in the soil a number of factors influence the potential for volatilization: (a) level of urea and ammonium present; (b) temperature; (c) soil pH; (d) soil moisture; (e) cation exchange capacity, and (f) application management.

Since urease is ubiquitous, *higher applications of urea* increase the amount of ammonia developed, increasing the potential rate of volatilization. The more ammonia or ammonium present (either already present or resulting from high rates of hydrolysis of urea), the more ammonia will be lost.

Urea hydrolysis is relatively slow at *temperatures* below 50°F (10°C), and increases with increasing temperature to about 77°F (25°C). Above 77°F there is no appreciable rate increase.

When ammonia (NH_3) gains a hydrogen (H^+) ion (proton), an ammonium cation (NH_4^+) that can be held on the cation exchange capacity is formed. Acid soils, having more H^+, are less susceptible to volatilization. When urea is hydrolyzed an alkaline environment is created in the area around the granule, increasing potential for volatilization.

There is less volatilization when *soil moisture* is high and there is less volatilization from soils that have higher *cation exchange capacity or organic matter content.* Losses are markedly reduced if application of urea is followed by irrigation.

Leaching

The fate of nitrogen that has received more attention than any other is the potential of *leaching of nitrates.* As an anion, nitrate (NO_3^-) is not attracted to soil colloids so it is susceptible to leaching. Factors that influence leaching are: (a) N rate and carrier; (b) soil texture; (c) amount of water that passes through the root zone; and (d) use by the grass. Higher *N rates* result in more nitrate in the soil solution. Nitrate *carriers* or those that convert readily to nitrate increase the possibility of leaching. More leaching can occur in *sands* than in soils with some silt and clay. Since nitrate is so water soluble, it moves readily with soil water. When excess *water from irrigation and/or rainfall* passes through the root zone, more leaching occurs. Once beyond the root zone it will move to groundwater if additional water passes through the profile.

Most studies reveal that with proper management, leaching of nitrates from established turfs is minimal. But other studies have revealed significant leaching of nitrates can occur under poor fertility management. Low concentrations of nitrates (less than 2 ppm) are typically found in leachates from mature turfs. However, during establishment of a new turf when root systems are being generated is the time of greatest potential for leaching.

A key factor in limiting leaching is the ability of *grasses* to readily utilize nitrates. Deeper rooted grasses can take up nitrates that may have moved below the surface where the highest percentage of roots are located. If the plant is physiologically active (including an active root system) it can take up appreciable levels of nitrates within a day or two. Because of environmental concerns, it is essential that turf managers utilize N fertility and irrigation programs that minimize nitrate leaching.

Leaching of ammonium is normally very small. Ammonium is usually taken up by the plant or soil microbes, held on the cation exchange sites, or nitrified before it is leached. In sands with extremely low cation exchange capacities, a modest amount of ammonium could be leached, depending on management.

Runoff

Loss of nitrogen from turf sites in *runoff* water can occur.[1] On sites with good turf cover and high infiltration rates, loss of N is negligible. However, there can be significant water runoff from compacted soils with low infiltration rates. Organic fertilizers are more susceptible to runoff losses due to lower density of particles. When intensive rainfall is possible, an environmentally sound approach is to irrigate after fertilization to help move the fertilizer into the thatch and upper layer of soil. Proper fertilizer management is necessary to prevent any appreciable loss of N in runoff.

Erosion

One additional potential loss of N from soil is *erosion.* Loss of topsoil and associated organic matter would remove the N from the site. A major benefit of turf is protection against erosion provided by the sod, so such loss is not a factor except in serious flooding situations or during establishment when the turf stand is limited.

Clipping Removal

There is significant *removal of nitrogen when clippings are routinely removed,* usually 25 to 60%. Nutrient deficiencies have developed when clippings have been regularly removed without nutrients being replaced by fertilization. Higher rates of N enhance the rate of depletion of other nutrients. Because of low native fertility sands or subsoils are most susceptible to nutrient depletion by clipping removal. When clippings are removed, greater attention should be given to soil and/or tissue testing to assess nutrient status.

D. Additions of N to the Turf/Soil Ecosystem

In addition to N added to the turf/soil system by N fixation, N fertilizers, topdressing materials, and deposition of fixed atmospheric sources contribute to the N pool (Figure 10.3). Fertilizers (Chapter 17) enter the cycle at appropriate points as organic or mineral sources. Understanding of both the N cycle and the characteristics of individual N carriers is necessary for wise fertilizer management.

The amount of N contributed by *topdressing materials* is very small compared to the amount of N already in the soil. Use of *composts* on turfgrass soils will contribute a limited amount of N. The amount of N in any soil material added to a site should be considered in planning a fertilizer program.

Ammonium, nitrate, nitrite, nitrous oxide, and some simple organic compounds are added in *rainfall.* Most of the mineral sources come from regions where there is intense industrial activity. It is estimated that only 10 to 20% of the nitrate contribution results from electrical storms, depending on the relative amount of industrial contribution in a region. Organic matter additions are likely from dust storms. The amount of N added from atmospheric sources ranges from 1 to 50 lb N per acre (1.1 to 56 kg ha^{-1}) annually. Most N fertilization programs are based on turf response so atmospheric sources are often too low to be considered in determining annual N rates.

Most *irrigation water* is low in N; however, effluent water can add appreciable N with 1 to 11 ppm N normal. At 11 ppm N, every 12 inches (30 cm) of irrigation water would apply 0.71 lb N per 1,000 ft^2 (37 kg N ha^{-1}). Turf managers using effluent should adjust their N program according to the N added by irrigation.

Nitrogen fixation plays a minor role in most turf systems. The exception is when clover is present in the turf. *Rhizobium* spp., living in a symbiotic relationship with leguminous plants, fix N_2 in nodules on clover roots. Leakage of N compounds (amino acids and other compounds) from the clover can be utilized by microbes. *Rhizobium* spp. living in a symbiotic relationship with leguminous plants fix N_2 in nodules on the roots. Typically, grass in areas where clover is present is greener than in surrounding areas. Applying nitrogen at higher N rates will usually result in a decrease of clover populations in turf.

Small amounts of *N are fixed by other organisms in the soil.* In the rhizosphere, free-living (asymbiotic) *Azotobacter* and *Clostridium* species take advantage of root exudates as an energy source and provide limited amounts of N from fixation for grass use. Some *Azospirillum* species may also be active in N fixation. Blue-green algae are known to fix some N more effectively under moist soil conditions. They need light for best growth, and algae are considered a pest on putting greens and other turf surfaces. Attempts at encouraging nonsymbiotic N, associative fixation in turf situations have not proved practical. Such fixation is not sufficient to support good quality turfgrasses. Additions of fertilizer N to obtain the desired turfgrass quality also supplies N for the microorganisms, and they fix less atmospheric N.

II. PRACTICUM

A. Determining N Needs

Soil Testing

WHILE SOIL TESTS CAN BE USED TO DETERMINE the level of *available N* at a given point in time, they are not widely utilized to predict how much N will be available over time for a healthy, stress tolerant turf. Quantitative tests for both soil NO_3^- and NH_4^+ are quite accurate when conducted by a qualified soil testing lab. However, levels of both can fluctuate from week to week and even during the day. Soil microbial activity can release available N in both forms and can utilize either during the day or night. Actively growing plants can utilize high amounts of both, particularly nitrate.

A soil test for either form of available N provides only a picture of what is available at the time of sampling. Some soil testing labs provide nitrate test results on a routine basis, but more typically for an additional cost. Because of variability, nitrate tests have limited value as a predictive tool for developing N fertilization programs.

A few laboratories conduct a *nitrification test* in which a soil sample is incubated under appropriate conditions. This test predicts the amount of nitrate that can be generated in a soil. This technique has been utilized for estimating how much N will become available for a given crop, but it has not been widely used for turfgrasses.

For accurate tests, both available N and nitrification potential must be conducted by a soil testing lab. Time needed to conduct the tests may delay receipt of test results until after N is needed. Unfortunately, there is not a consistent basis for interpretation of what are high, medium, or low test results. Testing for predicting potentially available N for field crops has been studied for many years with limited success. Much more research is needed before N soil tests will become routine in turf management.

Tissue Testing

The use of *tissue testing* for predicting N needs for high maintenance turfs has gained recent popularity. Routine chemical tests in a laboratory are expensive, but very accurate. As with soil testing, the time needed for analysis is a limitation when quick decisions are desired. Near infrared (NIR) procedures provide a quick analysis of dry grass clippings. Analysis for N content is reasonably dependable. Turf managers may purchase NIR equipment to monitor N in the turf on a regular basis or can send samples to a lab for NIR analysis. Turf managers who have gained experience with this procedure have used it effectively for their nitrogen management program. Cost of equipment is a major factor when utilizing NIR technology. For more details on soil and tissue testing, see Chapter 9.

Turf Growth Patterns and N Needs

Most turf managers have developed N fertilization programs based on observation, knowledge of local turf conditions, and experience.[3,4,7,12] Many factors influence the N needs of a given turfgrass. Adequate N should be available at times when the grass needs it and can utilize it most effectively and efficiently. Actually the grass needs N whenever it is growing; however, amounts being utilized vary with time of year (i.e., seasonal and weather effects) and management strategies that use N to achieve some growth objective (i.e., recovery, color, disease susceptibility). Perhaps the most important factor in determining the appropriate timing of N application is an understanding of the growth cycle of the grass and how the plant responds to N applied at various growth stages during the year. The typical growth cycle of warm-season grasses is considerably different from that for cool-season grasses (Figure 10.4). These growth cycles will vary in length depending on species of grass, climate, and specific weather conditions for a given year, but some general observations can be made regarding the timing of N use by the grasses.

Warm-season grasses. Comments on seasonal N use by warm-season grasses are given in Table 10.1. During *late winter to early spring* the grass is breaking winter dormancy and utilizing stored carbohydrates. Applying N too early or at too high rates to promote spring green-up should be avoided during this time. Since carbohydrates are needed for both breaking dormancy and the additional growth encouraged by N fertilization, applying N too early can deplete carbohydrate levels, jeopardizing plant health, especially under conditions of: (a) wet, cloudy, cool spring weather; (b) warm weather that encourages growth followed by frosts in repeated cycles; or (c) conditions favoring intracellular or intercellular freezing.

From *midspring through midsummer* is prime weather for growth of warm-season grasses. They respond to applied N with enhanced growth and color. Increased turf density permits excellent competition with weedy species.

Proper timing of N applications on overseeded grasses is significantly affected by weather conditions. Cool weather following N application encourages the cool-season grass to persist longer than desired and may endanger recovery of the warm-season grass. Once past the danger of frost, the warm-season grass can be encouraged by N fertilization. High temperatures during this time may be detrimental to the cool-season grass, further enhancing the rate of reestablishment of the warm-season species.

In some years, the roots of warm-season grasses may be physiologically pruned at the crown in the early to midspring at about the same time that 50 to 70% green-up occurs. Forcing shoot growth at this time with high N levels is not recommended. However, at two to three weeks after full green-up, higher N can be applied as needed.

Late summer to early fall is the time when warm-season grasses begin the process of hardening in preparation for winter dormancy. In areas where intracellular or extracellular freezing may occur in the winter, N rates should be reduced while still allowing adequate growth for recovery from wear. Sites to be overseeded should also receive less N during this period to permit slower growth of the warm-season grass and a more competitive opportunity for the overseeded grass.

Nitrogen is avoided in *midfall through winter* as it may decrease cold hardiness in later winter. Winter weed problems will increase with N applied at this time. Overseeded grasses will require additional N, varying with intensity of use of the turf and length of season. Timing of N may have impact on disease susceptibility of overseeded cool-season grasses as well as spring deadspot on bermudagrass.

Cool-season grasses. Like warm-season grasses, cool-season grasses must break winter dormancy to begin spring growth utilizing stored carbohydrates. A review of seasonal responses to N applications is presented in Table 10.2. As air and soil temperatures warm in *early spring,* growth is initiated. Nitrogen applied during this period results in rapid growth. Warm spring rains enhance growth even more, often resulting in the need for increased mowing. Although early spring is a time for major root growth, heavy rates of N applied at this time result in carbohydrates being utilized in top growth at the expense of root growth.

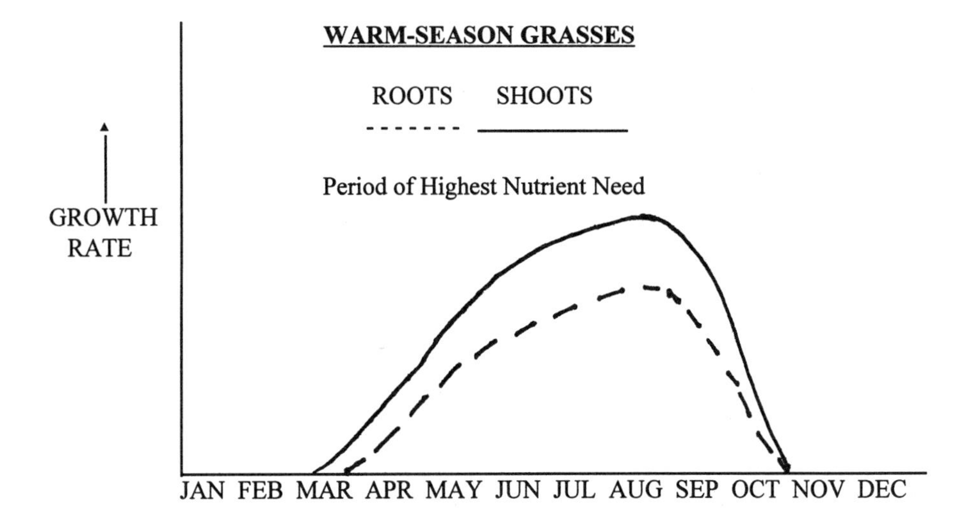

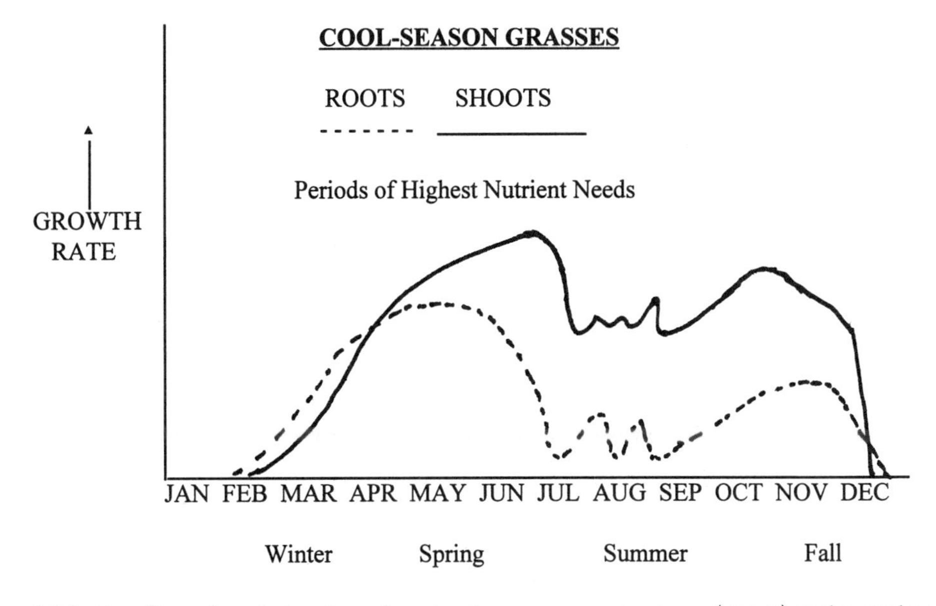

Figure 10.4. Growth cycles of shoots and roots of a warm-season grass (upper) and a cool-season grass (lower) in North America. Shape of curves and length of the growing season will vary with location and yearly weather patterns.

Depletion of carbohydrate reserves due to excessive top growth makes the turf more susceptible to summer stresses. Succulent turf tissues suffer greater moisture and temperature stress, as well as wear injury. This effect from early spring N may also contribute to greater summer disease problems in which moisture stress is a major factor. Increased pink snow mold (*Microdochium* spp.) may result from early spring N applications.

Table 10.1. Nitrogen use on warm season-grasses where winter dormancy occurs.

Time of Year	Comments
Late winter to midspring	Stored carbohydrates are needed for turf to break dormancy; avoid applying N too early or at too high rates; use N to encourage/discourage overseeded grass.
Midspring to midsummer	Prime growth period for shoots and roots; grass should compete very effectively with weedy species.
Late summer to early fall	Modest growth needed for wear areas; use modest N to permit effective overseeding and/or beginning of hardening process.
Midfall to winter	N is avoided as it may decrease cold hardiness in late fall; N encourages winter weeds; overseeded turfs need N on cool-season grass.

Table 10.2. Nitrogen use on cool-season grasses.

Time of Year	Comments
Early spring	Stored carbohydrates are needed for turf to break dormancy and initiate new root and shoot growth; rapid growth as soil warms, frequent mowing; good color response; enhances turf density; competition with weeds; tends to deplete carbohydrate reserves; increases susceptibility to summer stresses; variable disease effects. Little to no N will be needed if turf density and color are acceptable. If turf density is poor, N will be needed.
Late spring to early summer	N needed for growth, wear recovery, turf density; responses less dramatic than in early spring, depending on weather. Grass should compete very effectively with weedy species.
Summer	Modest N needed for wear recovery, modest color; monitor effect on summer diseases, moisture stress. Root growth slow and roots often die back.
Fall	Important time to increase turf density and for accumulation of carbohydrates. May be the most important time of year for N application.
Midfall	Avoid N as it may decrease cold hardiness in late fall and increase snow mold.
Late fall	Foliar growth has slowed or ceased, but roots are still active; plant is physiologically active with little or no top growth, carbohydrates accumulate; initiation of new roots. N applied appropriately can enhance carbohydrate accumulation.

On the positive side, early spring N provides good color response and enhances turf density (Plate 13). High turf density reduces space for weedy species to get established and this is especially important for competition with spring germinating grass and broadleaf weeds as well as winter annuals and perennial weeds. When there has been significant injury from snow mold diseases, additional N in the spring will enhance recovery of turf density.

If N was applied in late fall there may be no need for N during early spring or, at most, at a reduced rate. But for a turf that did not receive late fall N, N at a modest rate could be applied at this time.

During *late spring to early summer* modest N rates are needed for continued growth, modest color, recovery from wear injury, or continued improvement in low density turf. The key is to apply enough N for a reasonable quality turf but to avoid maintaining a dark green color.

On higher quality turfs, some N will be necessary in *summer* to prevent N deficiency and to promote some growth for recovery from traffic and other injury effects. Emphasis should be placed on the minimum acceptable turf color. Excessive N will dramatically enhance moisture and high temperature stresses. In an integrated management program for certain diseases, some N will be helpful in reducing disease effects. For other diseases, increased disease activity may result. Using low N rates will minimize an adverse effect while still providing adequate N. Do not use N on non-irrigated turf that has gone into dormancy.

Early fall is an important time for recovery from thinning caused by summer stresses, by increasing turf density. Nitrogen is needed for enhanced carbohydrate production when fall respiration is less than in the warmer summer. The increased turf density increases competition against fall germinating weeds. Some recovery of roots will occur if excessive N is not applied.

An early fall application of N should provide sufficient N needs for the *midfall* period. Avoid additional N in mid-fall unless a clear N deficiency is apparent. As temperatures cool, more of the carbohydrates are stored, enhancing root growth and permitting the turf to "harden off." Increased snow mold disease on cool-season grasses often results from applications in midfall.

In *late fall* shoot growth has essentially ceased and limited or no additional mowing is required. The plant is still physiologically active, especially root growth as photosynthesis continues (Plate 7). Soil temperatures are warmer than air temperatures and roots continue to be active in uptake of N and other nutrients. Nitrogen applied in late fall stimulates a rapid accumulation of carbohydrates, benefiting root growth and carbohydrate storage. The turf has excellent fall color and some enhancement of turf density by tillering may occur, depending on low temperatures that occur.

There may be a small increase in mowing during late fall compared to no late fall application. Spring growth of grass is increased as a result of late fall N, but there is much less growth than would result from applying N in early spring.

Some have suggested that late fall N may increase susceptibility to winter hardiness of cool-season grasses, but this has not been observed in research when N is applied at appropriate rates. Increased carbohydrate levels in the plant should theoretically result in greater tolerance to low temperatures. Nor has greater desiccation injury been reported in research studies. Most low temperature injury occurs in late winter/early spring as the plant breaks dormancy, not during the winter.

Perhaps the most significant negative effect of late fall N is increased susceptibility to snow mold diseases. Although increased disease is commonly observed with late fall N, spring recovery is often enhanced because of increased carbohydrates in the plant as long as total kill of crown tissues by disease has not occurred. Another response to late fall N is increased *Poa annua* seedhead production in certain years. Higher rates of N in early fall and late fall can cause an increase in seedhead production likely related to increased carbohydrate levels in the plant. Another response to late fall N on *Poa annua* turfs is increased seedhead production the following spring. This response occurs sporadically with little effect some years and significantly more seedheads other years. If a highly effective plant growth regulator (PGR) is used for seedhead control on *Poa annua* turfs, late fall N can be considered. However, application of a less effective PGR or if no PGR is used, late fall N should be eliminated.

Fertilizers should not be applied to turfs that are dormant (not physiologically active) nor on frozen turfs. Runoff of fertilizer nutrients is possible with dormant turf and highly likely when there is frost on the ground.

Timing of N application also plays a key role in competition between the desired grass species and weeds. Early spring N should increase turf density, reducing space and light needs for weed seed germination. Late spring/early summer N applied after germination of weeds could actually increase weed growth, particularly with annual grass weeds like crabgrass (*Digitaria* spp.) or goosegrass (*Eleusine indica*). Summer N or slow release carriers applied in the spring can supply N for these grassy weed species, increasing their competition with the desired species.

B. Rate of N Applications

Nitrogen should be applied at the rate necessary for the degree of response needed for healthy grass. Too much emphasis is often placed on color when determining N rates for grass. The best control of N response is provided by light and frequent applications of soluble N sources. This approach may be possible on many recreational turf sites such as putting greens, but it is not practical for general turf areas. The appropriate rates of N should be based on turf conditions, knowledge of how a given turf responds, and N carrier for a given grass. Recommendations for N rates are usually given in lb or kg of N per growing month or per year. Table 10.3 gives some suggested guidelines for warm- and cool-season grasses under low, medium, and high maintenance levels. A range is given since the turf manager adjusts the appropriate rate based on turf and site conditions and experience.

Most grasses require a minimal amount of N to maintain a reasonable turf density. Some species that are reasonably competitive at low N levels are fine fescues (*Festuca* spp.), centipedegrass (*Eremochloa opiuroides*), carpetgrass (*Axonopus* spp.), bahiagrass (*Paspalum notatum*), and buffalograss (*Buchloe dactyloides*). The differences in N requirements among species is well documented, but there are also differences among cultivars of a given species that are not as well documented with research.

Low maintenance turfs could include some grounds and lawns where minimal turf quality is acceptable. High maintenance turfs include putting greens, bowling greens, intensively maintained tees, and some athletic fields. All other turfs receive medium maintenance fertilization.

One example of adjusting N management on golf courses is the importance of applying adequate N for recovery of divots on fairways and tees. Increasing N enhances growth rate and provides faster healing of divots, but the amount of N applied should be balanced with potential negative effects of higher N on the grass during stress periods. Similar concerns apply to sports fields (i.e., soccer, football) and other grounds subjected to concentrated heavy traffic where increased N is needed to enhance recovery.

For sports fields and other turfs that periodically receive heavy wear, N applications should be timed for adequate recovery of turf density. Late fall N applied on cool-season grasses at the end of the football playing season has proven very effective in enhancing turf quality. Emphasis can be placed on higher N for turf recovery during the off-season while only enough N is applied during the playing season to maintain modest growth.

On putting greens the pressure to achieve high green speeds dictates the use of very low N rates with emphasis on spoon-feeding during the major portion of the golfing season. Some bentgrass greens are maintained at rates of 2 lb N per 1,000 ft^2 (98 kg ha^{-1}) annually or even less. But greens that receive very heavy play will need higher N to provide adequate recovery from wear effects. The most appropriate rate for a green varies with the individual green. Other management practices should be an integral part of managing green speeds, including mowing height, verticutting, grooming, topdressing, and irrigation.

C. Selection of N Carrier

While factors influencing selection of N carrier will be covered in greater detail in Chapter 17, Fertilizer Carriers, and Chapter 19, Developing Fertilizer Programs, a few comments will be made here regarding choice of N carrier.

Table 10.3. Nitrogen requirements for warm- and cool-season turfgrasses.

	Pounds of N per 1,000 ft^2 per Time Period[b]		
Maintenance Level	**per month**	**per 6 months**	**per 12 months**
		Warm-Season Grasses	
Low	0.15–0.25	0.9–1.5	1.8–3.0
Medium	0.25–0.50	1.5–3.0	3.0–6.0
High	0.5–1.0	3.0–6.0	6.0–12.0
		Cool-Season Grasses	
Low	0.15–0.25	0.9–1.5	1.8–3.0[a]
Medium	0.25–0.50	1.5–3.0	3.0–6.0[a]
High	0.50–1.0	3.0–6.0	6.0–8.0[a]

[a] Growing season for cool-season grasses grown in warm climates may approach 12 months; however, low or no N used in summer months results in somewhat lower annual N rates.
[b] 1 lb N per 1,000 ft^2 = 49 kg ha^{-1}; 0.10 lb N = 4.9 kg.

Most turf managers use a granular fertilizer as the basis for the fertilization program. For many, only granulars are applied. Some of these contain totally or mostly soluble N sources; others have a high percentage of slow release carriers. There are many ways to combine different N sources in fertilizing turf.

For those turf managers who prefer a spoon-feeding approach during stress periods, a typical program is to apply a granular in spring and fall, often with some slow release N; then use a carrier that is mostly or totally soluble in a light, frequent program.

There are various philosophies regarding what N carriers to apply for late fall fertilization on cool season grasses. Historically, golf course superintendents in northern climates have applied a natural organic fertilizer just before the ground freezes in northern climates. Sufficient time should be allotted to permit movement of the fertilizer product into the turf so there is reduced potential for runoff. Most of the N becomes available to the plant the next spring.

Another approach for late fall fertilization is to use a predominantly soluble N source about the time growth ceases. As described in the preceding section on timing of N for cool-season grasses, the root system is still active and capable of taking up soluble N. Since the grass plant is still capable of photosynthesis, application of soluble N that the plant can use at this time enhances photosynthesis and carbohydrates storage.

If a slow-release fertilizer is applied in the late fall there would be a limited amount of N available for the plant because of cool soil temperatures. Applying a 100% slow-release N carrier earlier in the year for a late fall response could result in N release rates that are too fast or too slow for utilization in the late fall period due to variable weather patterns that can occur during this season. For these reasons, a fertilizer with predominantly soluble N and from 15 to 25% slow-release N seems to work best. The soluble portion is taken up and utilized by the plant while the slow release source will be available for utilization by the plant the following spring.

Questions have been raised about the environmental impact of late fall applications. Field research using large lysimeters has verified that there is no difference in the amount of leaching of nitrates that occurs from either a more traditional program that applies more N in the spring compared to one that utilizes a late fall application. In both cases, very low levels of nitrates have been detected.

IV. REFERENCES

1. Baird, J.H., N.T. Basta, R.L. Huhnke, G.V. Johnson, M.E. Payton, D.E. Storm, C.A. Wilson, M.D. Smolen, D.L. Martin, and J.T. Cole. 2000. Best management practices to reduce pesticide and nutrient runoff from turf. In J.M. Clark and M.P. Kenna, Eds. *Fate and Management of Turfgrass Chemicals.* Washington, DC: Am. Chem. Soc. Symp. Series 743.
2. Beard, J.B. 1987. Apply less more often? *Grounds Maint.* 22(6):26, 28, 30.
3. Beard, J.B. 1973. *Turfgrass: Science and Culture.* Englewood Cliffs, NJ: Prentice-Hall, Inc.
4. Beard, J.B. 2001. *Turfgrass Management for Golf Courses.* Chelsea, MI: Ann Arbor Press.
5. Foth, H.D. and B.G. Ellis. 1997. *Soil Fertility,* 2nd edition. Boca Raton, FL: CRC Press, Inc.
6. Hull, R.J. 1992. Energy relations and carbohydrate partitioning in turfgrasses. In D.V. Waddington, R.N. Carrow, and R.C. Shearman, Eds. *Turfgrass.* Agronomy Monograph 32. Madison, WI: Amer. Soc. Agron.
7. Hull, R.J. 1996. N usage by turfgrass. *Turfgrass Trends* 5(11):6–15.
8. Marschner, H. 1995. *Mineral Nutrition of Higher Plants.* New York: Academic Press.
9. Mills, H.A. and J. Benton Jones, Jr. 1996. *Plant Analysis Handbook II.* Athens, GA: Micromacro Publ.
10. Petrovic, A.M. 1990. The fate of nitrogenous fertilizers applied to turfgrass. *J. Env. Qual.* 19:1–14.
11. Tisdale, S.L., W.L. Nelson, and J.D. Beaton. 1985. *Soil Fertility and Fertilizers,* 4th ed. New York: Macmillan Publ. Co.
12. Turner, T.R. and N.W. Hummel, Jr. 1992. Nutritional requirements and fertilization. In D.V. Waddington, R.N. Carrow, and R.C. Shearman, Eds. *Turfgrass.* Agronomy Monograph 32. Madison, WI: Amer. Soc. of Agron.
13. Vargas, J.M., Jr. 1994. *Management of Turfgrass Diseases.* Boca Raton, FL: CRC Press, Inc.

Chapter 11

Phosphorus

PHOSPHORUS (P), ALONG WITH N AND K, is one of the primary nutrients that most often require fertilization to meet turfgrass nutrient needs. Provision of adequate P is complicated by low total quantities of P in soil, very low P concentration in soil solution, and the highly reactive nature of P in the soil environment. Additionally, leaching or runoff of P into aquatic environments is of environmental concern because algae and aquatic plants are greatly stimulated by P. This can lead to eutrophication and a decline in dissolved O_2 in water.

I. PLANT RELATIONSHIPS[4,5,10]

PHOSPHORUS IS PRESENT IN THE SOIL SOLUTION in very low concentrations and uptake is primarily as $H_2PO_4^-$ (pH <7.0), HPO_4^{-2} (pH >7.0), or certain soluble organic phosphates. Once in the plant, P can remain in the inorganic form or be incorporated into various organic P forms. It is very mobile within the plant and is involved in almost all metabolic processes, especially for energy storage and transfer.[4–6]

Phosphorus forms high energy (energy-rich) pyrophosphate bonds in adenosine diphosphate (ADP), adenosine triphosphate (ATP), and other phosphates. These compounds serve to store and transfer readily available energy within the plant. Carbohydrates derived from photosynthesis and metabolized in respiration result in available energy in the form of high energy ATP bonds to supply energy for most other metabolic processes (examples are protein biosynthesis, phospholipid biosynthesis, nucleic acid synthesis, lipid synthesis, active membrane transport, etc.). The energy-rich phosphate molecules in ATP can be transferred to energy-requiring substances in the process called phosphorylation. Thus, P deficiency can adversely affect a number of metabolic activities by reducing available energy required for these biochemical processes, and thereby, result in substantially reduced growth.

Phosphorus also is a structural constituent in a number of biochemicals such as phospholipids, phosphoproteins, nucleic acids, sugar phosphates, nucleotides, and coenzymes. Phosphorus is a bridge molecule between adjacent units of DNA and RNA where it aids in maintaining structural organization of these macromolecules responsible for storage and transfer of genetic information. Likewise, P functions as bridge molecules in phospholipid membranes.

In photosynthesis, P is involved: (a) as ATP to provide energy for several of the steps; (b) as a constituent of 3-phosphoglycerate (3-PGA), the first stable product of photosynthesis that is a precursor of other sugars. Formation of 3-PGA comes from addition of atmospheric CO_2 to the 5 carbon sugar ribulose-1,5-bisphosphate (RuBP) which is unstable and splits into two 3-PGA molecules; and (c) as a constituent of several other sugar phosphates that lead to starch formation.

Additionally, P is a coenzyme involved in several metabolic processes. Usually, inorganic phosphate acts with an enzyme to stimulate a given process. With adequate P nutrition, plants can store extra P as inorganic P in cell vacuoles and as phytate in seeds. The phytate is very important during seed germination as a ready source of P for phospholipid membranes, nucleic acids, and energy transfer.

Phosphorus content of turfgrass shoot tissues may range from 0.10 to 1.00% by dry weight, with a sufficiency range of 0.20 to 0.55% (Table 2.1).[10] Below 0.20% is considered deficient and above 1.00% excessive. The highest P requirement is in new leaves and meristematic tissues. While P is very immobile in soils, it is accumulated in plant tissues at 100 to 1,500 times soil solution concentrations due to active uptake and high mobility within the plant.

Visual symptoms of P deficiency are initially reduced shoot growth and a dark green color (Plate 11). Stunted growth is in response to reduced leaf expansion caused by limited P for energy transformations and structural requirements. Photosynthesis can eventually be depressed but reduced shoot growth happens before this occurs. The dark green color is due to chlorophyll concentration increasing per unit leaf area. Lower leaves may exhibit a more dark green coloration than the younger upper leaves.

As P deficiency continues, lower leaves may turn reddish at the leaf tips and then progress down the blade (Plates 1, 10, 12, and 13). The reddish color is from anthocyanin pigment accumulation. When low P inhibits shoot growth, photosynthesis can still produce starch which: (a) is translocated to the roots to maintain root growth; and (b) accumulates in leaf tissues and stimulates anthocyanin synthesis. If P deficiency continues to where photosynthesis declines, root growth will then be adversely affected, but until that occurrence, root growth continues. During establishment, however, low P can cause reduced root growth much more readily (Plate 9 and 14). The reddish or purple coloration from P deficiency does not occur until after shoot growth inhibition and the dark green coloration.

Phosphorus deficiency is most likely to occur (Table 11.1):

(a) When available soil P is very low. This can be determined by soil testing.
(b) During turfgrass establishment when rooting is limited, especially for seedlings (Plate 19). During seeding or overseeding, a starter fertilizer high in P is often used to provide sufficient P at the surface for shallow rooted seedlings.
(c) During cool spring periods when root growth is slow and root metabolic activity is relatively low for active P uptake. Warm-season turfgrasses may undergo spring root dieback after shoot green-up is initiated in some years and can be susceptible to P deficiency because of limited roots, cool soil temperatures, and a reduced tissue pool of P. Also, some of the older bentgrass cultivars contained biotypes that exhibited considerable purpling or discoloration in the spring and fall, which may have been due to pigment changes more than P deficiency.

Many turfgrass fertilizers contain little or no P. One reason is the belief that high P favors *Poa annua* invasion of creeping bentgrass.[5,10] However, researchers have not always observed this response. It seems reasonable that the true annual forms of *Poa annua*, which are prolific seed producers, may produce seeds that are more competitive for germination and establishment if P levels are sufficient to allow phytate to accumulate in seeds.

Initially, P content of turfgrass fertilizers was reduced in the 1950s and 1960s when tricalcium arsenate was widely used to selectively control *Poa annua* in other cool-season grass stands. Since high P can counteract the phytoxic effects of As due to their similar chemistry, turf growers did observe that high P favored *Poa annua* survival. But this was only in the presence of high As.

Table 11.1. Soil, climate, and management conditions associated with phosphorus (P) deficiency and toxicity/excess levels.

Deficiency Associated with	Toxic/Excessive Levels Associated with
• P deficiency is often greater on sandy, low CEC, irrigated soil, due to low P content. • Under acidic pH (<5.5) due to fixation as Fe, Al, and Mn compounds. • Under high pH (>7.5) from fixation with Ca. • On soils containing hydrous oxides of Fe and Al, Mn, or kaolinite clay, due to high P fixation capacity. • During turfgrass establishment, when P demand is high but roots are limited. • Cold soils where P uptake is restricted. • Soil low in P content or available P.	• No true toxicity problem. • Excessive P may induce Fe deficiency.

More recently, a number of fertilizers with higher P contents have become available as turf managers realized that adequate P is needed, especially on high sand greens. Phosphorous fertilization continues to be maintained at adequate (i.e., low-to-medium, medium soil test levels) but modest levels because of concern over P leaching or runoff. Phosphorus can enhance algae growth and eutrophication of surface water. While P is relatively immobile in soils, excessive P use or misapplication can result in leaching in certain soil conditions (e.g., sands with shallow water table) or surface runoff. Restrictions on P use near "sensitive" wetland areas have been imposed in some locations.

Adequate P has been reported to enhance cold tolerance of warm-season turfgrasses, drought recovery, and water-use efficiency.[5] The drought responses may be due to improved rooting compared to severely deficient P situations. Once P is within the sufficiency range, rooting would not be expected to improve. However, grasses with reduced root viability, such as a cool-season grass under high temperature stress of summer, may respond to higher P at the surface simply because of the inability to obtain P deeper in the root zone with unhealthy roots. Adequate P to maintain shoot growth and provide energy needs will improve turfgrass stress tolerance compared to deficient P, but once P is ample, further addition would not be expected to be beneficial.

Some plants can exhibit P toxicity but little evidence exists for this in turfgrasses grown on soils. Phosphorous toxicities are more readily produced in solution cultures where solution P can be raised to levels above those that occur with soil solutions. Growth of bermudagrass has been reported to decline in Florida under excessive P, but cool-season grasses can tolerate very high levels. High P may induce Fe deficiency in some situations where plant-available Fe is low, but this is not a toxicity. Rather it is a case of an excessive level of one nutrient (P) causing the deficiency of another (Fe).

Some diseases have been reported to be suppressed by P application, but data are not always consistent (Table 2.5). Also, interaction with other nutrients, especially N and K, are sometimes evident. Any nutritional program that induces a P deficiency, either directly by low P or indirectly by promoting rapid growth by N, could alter a plant's ability to resist or recover from a disease. This occurs because injured plants require adequate P to use in energy processes for synthesis of metabolites in regrowth as well as structural P. Thus, P is most likely to influence diseases indirectly rather than in a primary mode of action.

II. SOIL AND ENVIRONMENTAL RELATIONSHIPS[1,3,8]

THE TOTAL CONTENT OF P IN MOST SOILS is about 0.02 to 0.10%. Plants absorb P mainly as $H_2PO_4^-$ and HPO_4^{-2}, which are in soil solution at low concentrations from 0.003 to 0.5 mg L^{-1}. Plant available P in the soil solution can be: (a) taken up by turfgrasses; (b) utilized by microorganisms; (c) leaches; (d) removed by clippings; or (e) chemically reacted with Fe, Al, Mn, and Ca to form various insoluble inorganic compounds. HPO_4^{-2} and $H_2PO_4^-$ are highly reactive, which results in considerable chemical *fixation* of P into insoluble forms (Figure 11.1). As a result, turfgrasses take up a small percent of P added as fertilizer with an uptake efficiency of 10 to 40% in most instances and the remainder becomes fixed into inorganic forms or is taken up by microorganisms and incorporated in organic forms *(immobilization).*

A. Inorganic Soil P

Soluble P released from fertilizer into the soil solution, if not taken up by the turfgrass or soil microorganisms, can be adsorbed onto mineral surfaces or precipitated as Fe-P, Al-P, Mn-P, or Ca-P compounds (Figure 11.1). In acid soils, P adsorption occurs on the surface of Al and Fe oxide and hydroxide minerals, and on the edges of kaolinite clays. Within calcareous soils, surface adsorption is on $CaCO_3$.

Precipitation of soluble P in acid soils is by chemical reaction with soluble Fe, Al, and Mn ions. The inorganic compounds that are formed are initially somewhat plant available but gradually they become more crystaline and less soluble.

Regardless of which type of reaction (surface adsorption on Fe/Al minerals, kaolinitic clay, $CaCO_3$; or, precipitation with Fe, Al, Mn, and Ca), soluble P is converted to less soluble and less plant available inorganic P forms. These processes are called *fixation* (Figure 11.1).

The influence of soil pH on fixation processes is illustrated in Figure 11.2. Plant-available P from inorganic P sources contributes 50 to 90% of the total available P. The pH range of 6.0 to 7.0 is most favorable for maximum concentration of P from these less soluble inorganic forms by *slow dissolution.*

In addition to soil pH, several other factors affect P fixation and, therefore, the degree that P fertilizers are fixed into less available inorganic P compounds.

These include:

- Clay type and content. Fixation of P is greater in soils containing kaolinite than other silicate clays. As clay content increases, P fixation increases.
- Quantity of Al/Fe oxides and hydroxides. Since $H_2PO_4^-$ can react directly with Fe and Al on the surface of these insoluble hydrous oxides, P fixation increases with higher quantities of these minerals, which are commonly found in weathered, acid soils.
- Quantity of soluble Fe, Al, or Mn in the soil. Under highly acid conditions, soluble Fe, Al, and Mn levels may increase. Any soluble P ions from fertilizer or other sources will quickly react to form less soluble Fe, Al, or Mn phosphates. Initially, these will be amorphorous with some P plant available, but over time they become more crystalline and less soluble.
- Quantity of $CaCO_3$ and soluble Ca present. Phosphorus can be adsorbed on the surface of precipitated $CaCO_3$ and can react directly with Ca in the soil solution. Thus, calcareous soils and sites receiving appreciable Ca as amendments or from irrigation water can exhibit high P fixation.

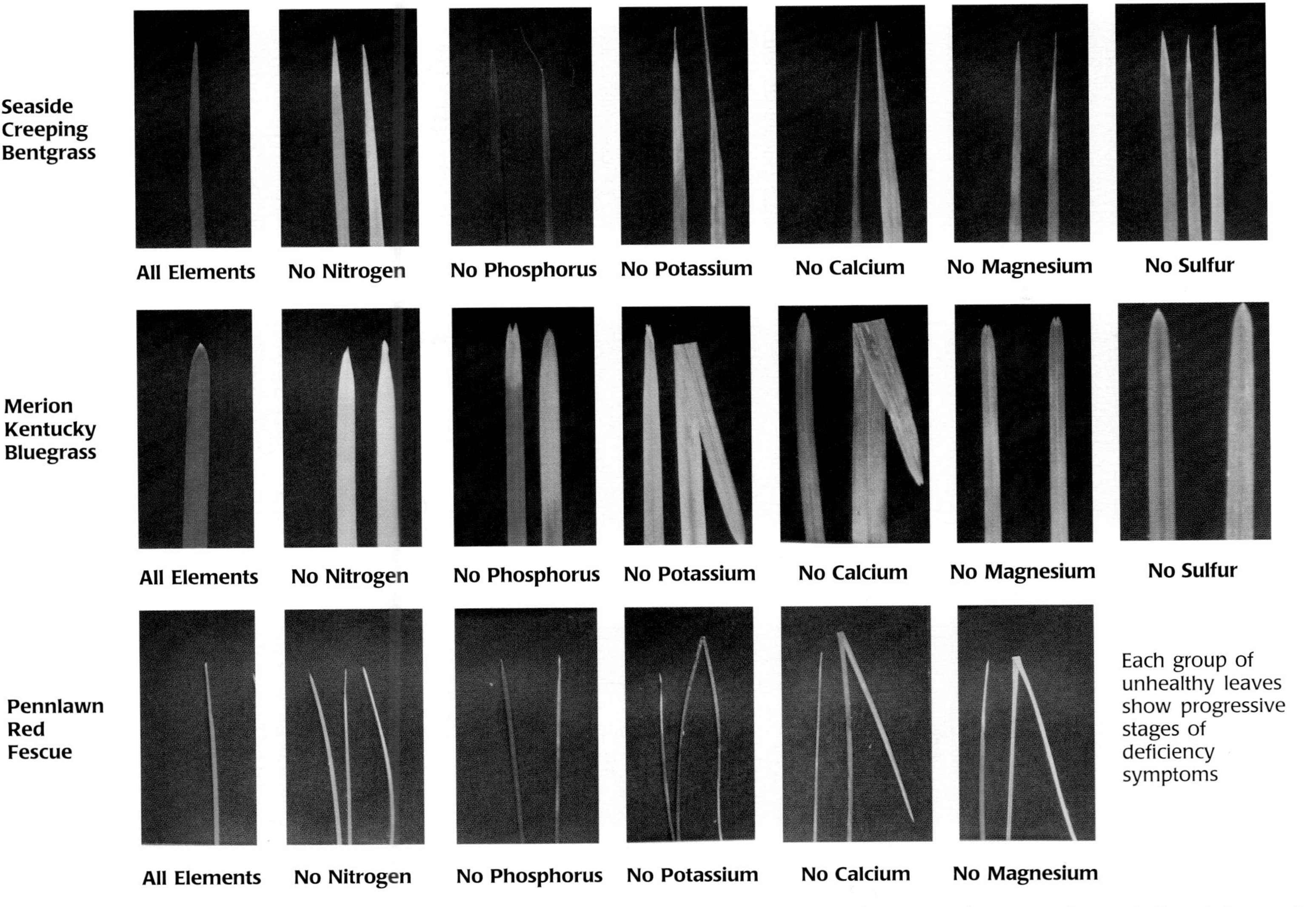

Plate 1. Foliar symptoms of six essential nutrient deficiencies in three cool-season turfgrasses. (Courtesy of O.J. Noer Research Foundation and Milorgonite–MMSD)

Plate 2. Saline (white salt accumulation areas) and sodic soil (black areas).

Plate 3. Sodic soil with poor drainage and aeration.

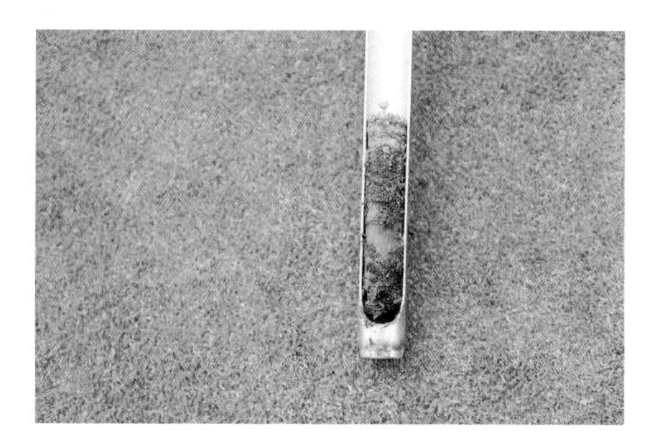

Plate 4. Soil sampling turfgrass to a depth of 2 to 4 inches.

Plate 5. Young turfgrass seedlings need adequate N for establishment.

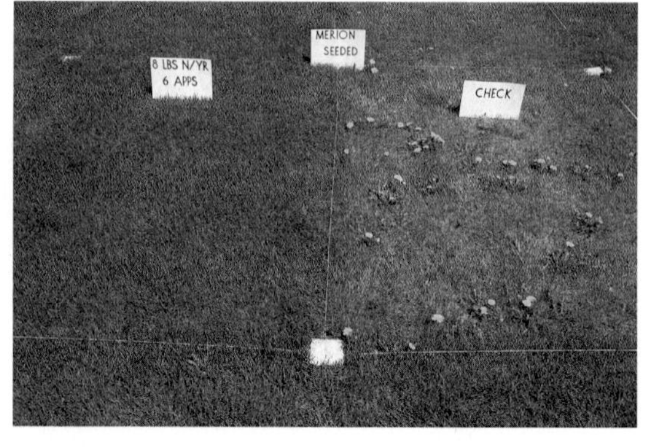

Plate 6. Most grasses require a minimum amount of N to compete with weedy species.

Plate 7. Fall response to N applied to creeping bentgrass in the late fall at the time shoot growth ceased.

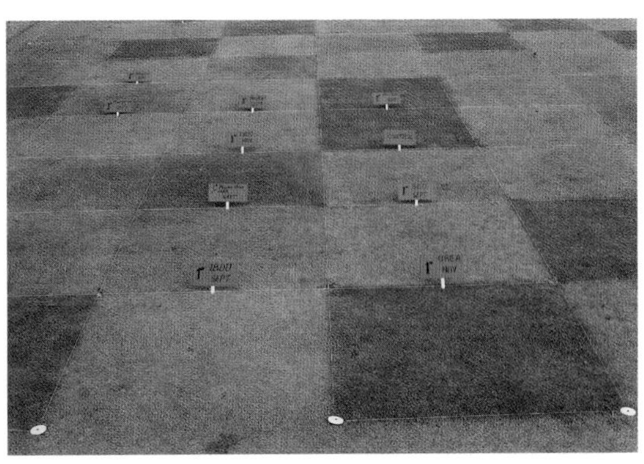

Plate 8. Spring response to N applied to creeping bentgrass in the late fall.

Plate 9. Phosphorus response on a new stand of Kentucky bluegrass. Phosphorus favors seedling growth.

Plate 10. Phosphorus deficiency on Kentucky bluegrass.

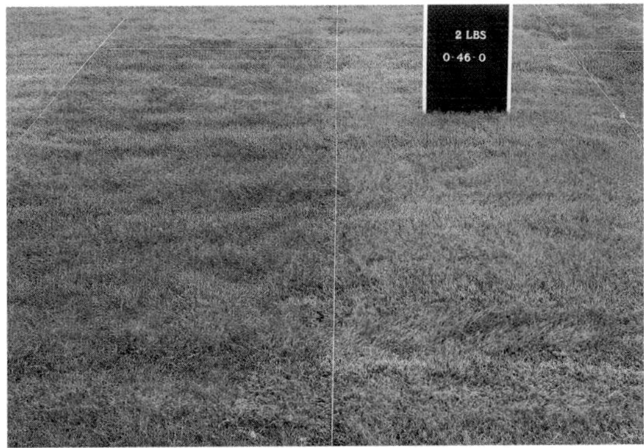

Plate 11. Phosphorus deficiency limiting growth (left) and adequate (right) on Kentucky bluegrass. Initially a P deficiency may cause a darker green color (left).

Plate 12. Phosphorus deficiency on creeping bentgrass.

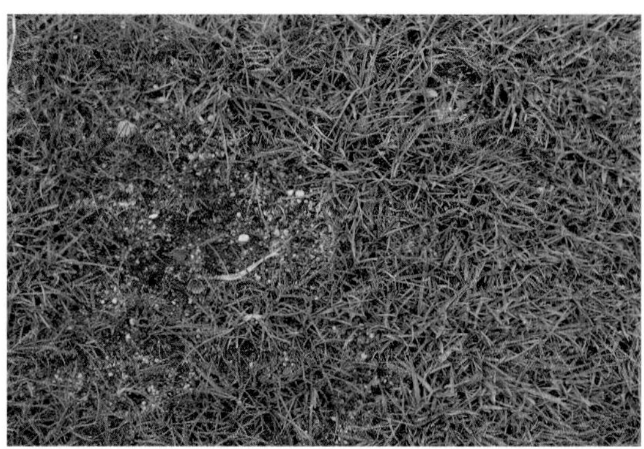

Plate 13. Phosphorus deficiency on creeping bentgrass (close-up).

Plate 14. Adequate K (left) and deficient (right) on Kentucky bluegrass.

Plate 15. Potassium deficient Kentucky bluegrass exhibits wilting (darker color), while barely adequate K results in a lighter green color and no wilt.

Plate 16. Sulfur response on bermudagrass. Chlorotic area did not receive S application (M. Goately).

Plate 17. Iron deficient Kentucky bluegrass. Symptoms often resulted in a mottled canopy appearance, sometimes mistaken for disease activity.

Plate 18. Iron deficient Kentucky bluegrass cultivars (J. Butler).

Plate 19. Iron chlorosis on a soccer field turf where limestone had been used to line the field. considered to be lime induced Fe deficiency.

Plate 20. Iron toxicity on centipedegrass, a species sensitive to foliar Fe applications. (a) iron toxicity (left), untreated (right). (b) close-up of Fe toxicity.

Plate 21. Zn toxicity on seedling Kentucky bluegrass (left) corrected by foliar application of Fe (right).

Plate 22. Excess S applications contributed to formation of black layer. Condition was corrected by adequate oxygen in the soil as show around the aerifier holes (reddish soil).

Plate 23. Black layer on a golf green.

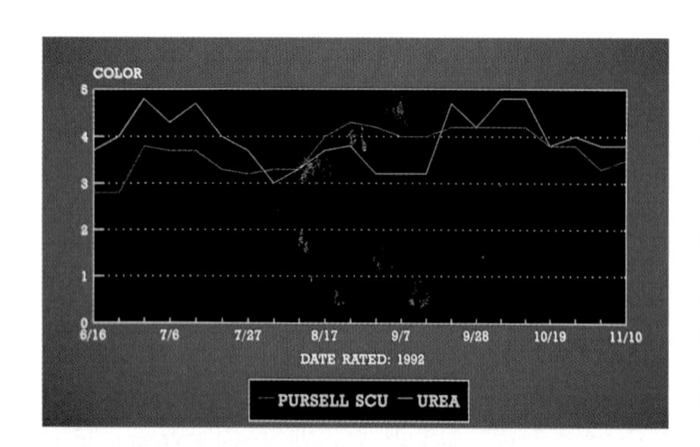

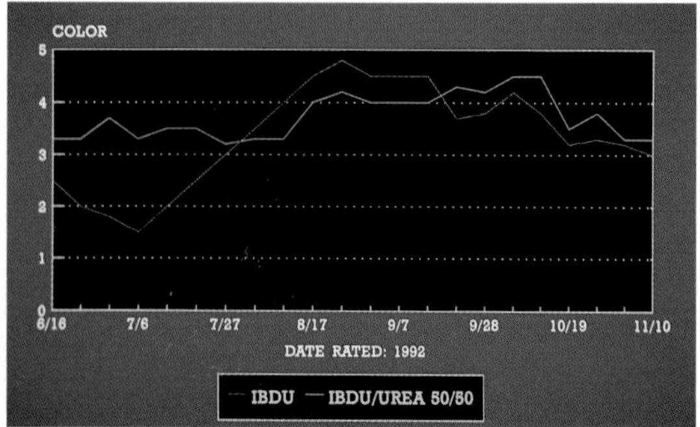

Plate 24. Color response curves illustrate differences in release patterns of N sources: (a) greater response from urea than sulfur-coated urea following fertilization in spring and fall, but greater response from the slow-release sulfur-coated urea in the summer. (b) a combination of 50% urea-N and 50% IBDU-N gives greater responses that IBDU-N after spring and fall fertilization; however, the slow-release IBDU exhibits greater residual response in the summer.

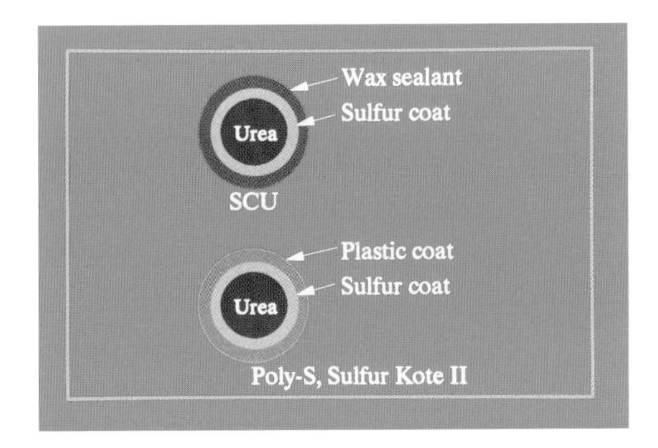

Plate 25. Coated N sources. SCU—sulfur coated urea (top); PSCU—polymer sulfur coated urea (bottom).

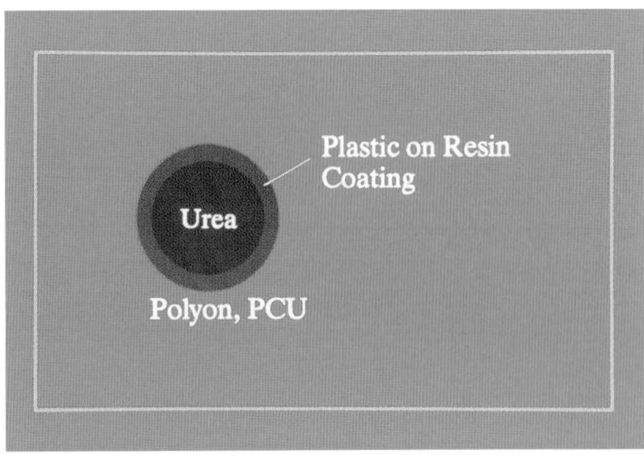

Plate 26. Plastic coated urea (PCU).

Plate 27. Foliar fertilizer burn on turfgrass.

Plate 28. Drop-type fertilizer spreader (P. O'Brien).

Plate 29. Rotary walk behind fertilizer spreader (P. O'Brien).

Plate 30. Tractor driven pendulum spreader (P. O.'Brien).

Plate 31. Proper spreader calibration for *rate of product delivery* and for *uniformity of delivery* are important. Weight of fertilizer in each container provides a measure of uniformity of distribution (P. Landschoot).

Plate 32. To prevent fertilizer application skips/ misses or excessive overlap of application, each pass should be clearly identified (P. O'Brien).

Plate 33. Fertilizer misapplications with a drop-type spreader resulting in a non-uniform pattern of growth and color.

Plate 34. Fertilizer granules visible on top of a turfgrass. If these do not easily integrate into the turf canopy, they can be picked up by mowers.

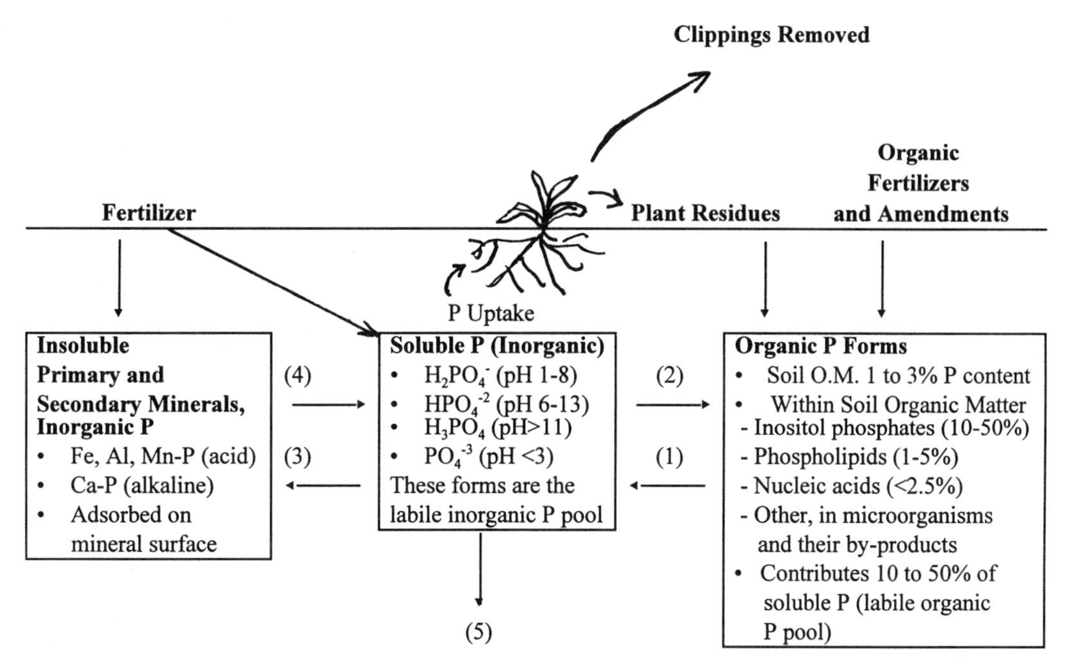

Figure 11.1 The phosphorus (P) cycle in soil, where (1) represents mineralization, (2) immobilization, (3) fixation, (4) dissolution, and (5) loss due to erosion or leaching. Labile P is readily available for plant uptake.

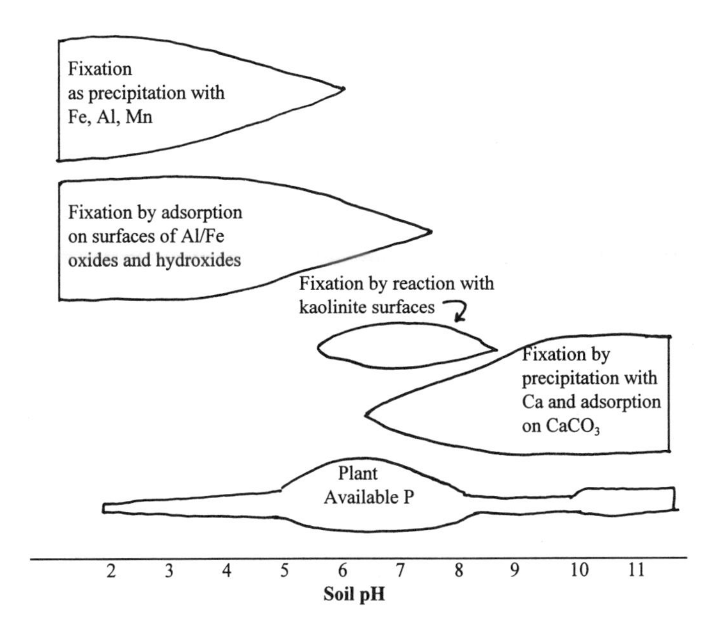

Figure 11.2. Influence of soil pH on fixation of P into insoluble inorganic P forms by: (a) adsorption onto surfaces of Al/Fe minerals, $CaCO_3$, and kaolinite clay; and (b) precipitation with Fe, Al, Mn, and Ca in soil solution. Plant-available P includes soil soluble P and relatively soluble compounds available within a year. The greatest quantity of plant-available P occurs at pH 6.0 to 7.0 because fixation tends to be less within this range (after Brady[1]).

- Ion effects. Phosphorus fixation is greater on clays with high Ca or Al saturation. Also, high levels of the anions Cl or SO_4 may compete for adsorption sites with P and result in somewhat greater P availability. Organic anions, such as oxalate and citrate in wastewater, can cause similar results.

B. Organic Soil P

Phosphorus contained in organic forms can make up from 15 to 80% of total P in the soil. However, much less is known about the organic P fraction than the inorganic P forms (Figure 11.1). Various soil test extractants used to determine plant-available P (labile P) concentrate on measuring the labile inorganic P rather than the labile organic P pool.

Inositol phosphates are the most abundant organic P compounds, contributing about 10 to 50% of total organic P. These are believed to be due to microbial degradation of plant residues. Nucleic acids also occur in microorganisms and plant residues, and account for less than 2.5% of organic P. Another 1 to 5% of total organic P occurs as phospholipids. The remaining organic P compounds are unknown.

Mineralization is the transformation of organic P into soluble inorganic P (Figure 11.1). The transformation of inorganic soluble P into organic P is called *immobilization,* because of the loss of plant-available P. Phosphatase enzymes of a wide variety of soil microorganisms can degrade plant residues to mineralize organic P forms into soluble inorganic P.

Mineralization is favored by: (a) P content >0.3% in the organic residue; (b) high soil organic matter contents; and (c) factors stimulating microbial activity. Addition of organic matter may also enhance P availability by reacting with soluble Fe and Al ions to limit P fixation; and by some organic compounds reacting with the surfaces of hydrous oxides and silicate clays to hinder fixation of P.

III. PRACTICUM

PHOSPHOROUS IS A MACRONUTRIENT but P additions into turfgrass systems are often limited due to: (a) many fertilizers used on mature turfgrasses have a low P analysis; (b) concern for stimulating *Poa annua* invasion by P has reduced P fertilization rates; (c) concerns about enhancing P runoff or leaching into wetlands and surface waters; (d) normally the P content of irrigation water and various chemicals used on turfgrasses is low; and (e) P removal in clippings where clippings are not returned. By contrast, older turf sites where clippings have been returned may have very high P levels, or if the sites received high P content fertilizers that were common years ago. Limited additions of P coupled with several soil conditions that can reduce P availability (Table 11.1) suggest that turfgrass managers should carefully evaluate their P fertilization programs. Visual symptoms of P deficiency are easily overlooked and many turf managers allow plant-available P levels based on soil tests to remain in the low range. The combination of these factors often results in overly conservative P fertilization.

A. Soil and Tissue Testing[1,3,8]

Soil testing is valuable for determining plant-available P status. Extractants used to provide a measure of available P must determine the ability of a soil to replenish soil solution P after plant uptake. Replenishment of readily available P in the soil solution comes from slowly available P

Table 11.2. Extractable P and the rankings of Bray P1, Mehlich III, and Olsen soil P tests often used for turfgrass.

	P Sufficiency Level[a]			
Extractant	Very Low	Low	Medium	High
	ppm P			
Bray P1	0–4	5–15	16–30	>31
Mehlich III	0–12	13–26	27–54	>55
Olsen	0–6	7–12	13–28	>29

[a] These are representative P sufficiency levels and may vary somewhat from laboratory to laboratory.

forms such as amorphorus (freshly precipitated) Fe, Al, Mn, and Ca compounds; surface adsorbed phosphates that are still somewhat soluble; and somewhat soluble P compounds in P fertilizers.

The Bray P1, extractant (0.03M NH_4F + 0.025 M HC1) has been widely used to assess plant-available P.[8] The weak acid dissolves some of the more soluble Ca-P, Al-P, and Fe-P, while the F anion complexes Al in soil solution that results in dissolution of some of the $A1PO_4$. Recently, the Mehlich III extractant (0.015 M NH_4F + 0.2 M CH_3 COOH + 0.25 M NH_4NO_3 + 0.013 M HNO_3 + EDTA) has been widely used. It also relies on dilute acids and F to extract P. Originally, Bray P1 was designed for acid soils, while the Olsen extractant (0.5M $NaHCO_3$ at pH 8.5) was recommended for neutral, alkaline, or calcareous soils. In calcareous and alkaline soils, Ca-P slowly dissolves to replenish solution Ca and supplying P. Actually, Bray P1 and Mehlich III extractants have worked well on nonacid soils as well. Typical extractable P sufficiency levels of these extractants are in Table 11.2.

Tissue testing can be used to help diagnose a true P deficiency (Table 2.1). However, the sufficiency range may vary with species, cultivar, and growing conditions. Treating a small area with a foliar application of soluble P to test for P deficiency may not provide immediate results since P deficient grass normally has good green color but limited growth. Enhanced growth rate should occur over several days depending on climatic and soil moisture conditions.

B. Fertilization Guidelines[2,5,7,10]

Recreational turfgrasses grown on low CEC, acid sands are most susceptible to P deficiencies (Table 11.1). In high rainfall climates, acidic, silica sands may have most of the soluble Fe and Mn fractions leached out. Thus, it is difficult to build up soil test P levels without promoting P leaching. The use of a spoon-feeding approach of P fertilization on mature turf is especially important for these conditions, where P is applied at two to six times per year at low rates of 0.25 to 0.50 lb P_2O_5 per 1,000 ft^2 (5.3 to 10.6 kg P ha^{-1}). Higher of these rates will be needed until soil test levels increase. Building of P soil tests in sands may require several years. One application should be made at the time of any overseeding operation as well.

On low CEC calcareous sands, P is less likely to leach even in humid climates because of fixation as Ca-P. Soil test sufficiency levels of P may be able to be raised to a low-medium range without leaching concerns. This would allow somewhat less frequent P applications than silica sands at 0.50 to 1.00 lb P_2O_5 per 1,000 ft^2 rates (10.6 to 21.2 kg P ha^{-1}). Generally, a total of 2 or 3 lb P_2O_5 per 1,000 ft^2 per year (42.6 to 64.0 kg P ha^{-1}) is adequate for either acid or calcareous sands exposed to high irrigation and rainfall. Over time, soil P tests should increase.

Under semiarid or arid climates, the P soil test can be a good guide for P fertilization of sands with a low-medium level as adequate and P fertilization adjusted to stay within this range. Fertilization may be from one (general turf, short growing season) to three times per year (recreational sites, long growing season). Alternatively, a fertilizer with a wide N:P ratio could be used throughout the growing season to reach the same level of total P to be applied. If soil test P levels continue to increase beyond the low-medium range, then P rates can be reduced or P fertilization omitted for a period of time.

For sandy loams and finer-textured soils, soil testing is the best guide for P needs. Since turfgrasses are generally efficient in P acquisition, maintenance of a P sufficiency level of medium-low to medium is a good target. Fine-textured soils with high P fixation capabilities will require greater P fertilization to maintain this level than soils with less P fixation. Using two or four applications per year of P at 0.50 to 1.0 lb P_2O_5 per 1,000 ft^2 is preferred over one high rate of fertilization on these soils.

Except during initial establishment, P fertilization should remain at 1.0 lb P_2O_5 per 1,000 ft^2 (21.2 kg P ha^{-1}) or less per single application to minimize potential for leaching, runoff, or excessive fixation. If annual recommendations exceed the 1.0 lb P_2O_5 per 1,000 ft^2 level, the total should be split into two or more applications.

At initial establishment by seeding, stolonizing, or plugging, a starter fertilizer high in P content is often used during this period to support developing roots and tillers. On sites where soil P may be limited at establishment, such as those noted in Table 11.1, and in the absence of recommendations based on soil tests, P may be mixed into the root zone to a depth of 2 to 4 inches at a rate of 2.0 lb P_2O_5 per 1,000 ft^2, with an additional 1 to 2 lb P_2O_5 per 1,000 ft^2 applied to the surface just prior to or after seeding and just prior to vegetative planting. The advantage of mixing P into soil is less potential for runoff. Starter fertilizers containing preemergence herbicides are often applied just after seeding. Lower rates of P can be used for establishment on soils with a medium soil test level or where P deficiency is not expected. In these situations, 1.0 lb P_2O_5 per 1,000 ft^2 applied to the soil surface is adequate. When a cool-season grass is overseeded into a warm-season turf, a starter fertilizer applied at 0.50 to 1.0 lb P_2O_5 per 1,000 ft^2 is often used, especially when seeding rates are high.

Timing of P fertilization should be adjusted to optimize P availability. As noted in the previous paragraph, one important time for P fertilization is at establishment whether as a new turf or for overseeding. In climates where warm-season grasses have a winter dormancy, P application at the time of initial green-up is important. It is not unusual for warm-season turfgrasses to exhibit spring dieback of roots at this period and P at the surface aids in green-up and may enhance regrowth of roots. In cool, wet springs, some warm-season grasses demonstrate a period of P deficiency until the soil warms. Spring P fertilization helps prevent this occurrence. In late winter, cool-season grasses may exhibit a similar response on cold soils or on sites where low soil P exists (Table 11.1). The slow growth may be mistaken for inadequate soluble N when it is lack of P that limits growth. Thus, the late winter or early spring (cool-season grasses) and midspring (warm-season grasses) periods are important P fertilization times.

Whenever a grass loses its root system is another key period for P application. For example, by late summer, cool-season grasses may lose considerable roots. Phosphorus at this time can aid in maintaining physiological health in warm weather and root regrowth as cooler temperatures occur. Another example could be after nematode, disease, or insect damage to roots.

In tropical climates, P applications before and after monsoon seasons are appropriate, especially on sands or where soil P tests are low. Even when a true monsoon season does not occur but there are wet and dry cycles, P needs will be greater during and after the wet periods, on such sites.

Irrigation water, especially effluent sources, may contain P. This P should be considered in the overall P fertilization program as well as potential for eutrophication.

On salt-affected areas, especially sodic conditions, P nutrition can be adversely affected by: (a) high leaching required to remove soluble salts or Na can enhance P deficiency, particularly on sandy soils; (b) high content of anions (Cl^-, SO_4^{-2}) may somewhat hinder P uptake; and (c) high rates of lime plus S or gypsum can result in P fixation as Ca-P compounds.[2] As a guideline, annual P can be increased by 25 (fine-textured soils) to 50% (sands, low CEC sites) above routine (nonsalt-affected soil) levels and divided into several applications per year.

Besides the above mentioned specific times of year for P fertilization, timing should be adjusted to supply adequate P over the whole growing season. Several applications per year are important whenever: the soil fixes appreciable P; the growing season is long; on sandy soils or infertile soils with low fixation potential; when winter overseeding is practiced; when monsoon seasons occur; and on salt-affected soils. The physiological importance of P in plant energy relations demonstrates that a good fertilization program is needed for this macronutrient to maintain adequate P throughout the growing season.

Means of maximizing use of soil P or P in fertilizers are rather limited beyond careful timing of application. Use of granular P-sources results in less fixation than would be obtained with fine or pulverized materials. Large particles result in less surface area, thus less surface contact with the soil. On acidic soils, adjusting pH to 6.0 to 7.0 will aid in soil P availability. Fertilizer placement does not seem to be an issue for P uptake except when too much thatch is present. While it is beneficial to mix P into the root zone for establishment, mature turfgrasses do seem to be able to effectively use surface-applied P except when thatch retains most of the P. Even with thatch, roots can acquire P as long as the roots are viable. Uptake of P would be most limited from thatch whenever it dried, such as on unirrigated sites or dry seasons, primarily by inhibiting dissolution. In contrast, P content in thatch may become low under irrigated situations, due to ease of P leaching in organic media (Chapter 16). Incorporation of organic matter into root zones during establishment often aids in P availability, especially on soils where the organic matter improves rooting.

Clipping removal can result in a decline in soil P levels over time. More frequent soil testing should be practiced to monitor P levels.

C. Fertilizers[1,7,9]

A number of P fertilizers can be used. The most common P sources are MAP (monoammonium phosphate) and DAP (diammonium phosphate) (Table 11.3). Both are used in homogeneous fertilizers and in fertilizer blends. While several P carriers are water soluble, once they are applied to the soil, P availability is controlled by soil chemical conditions that influence P-fixation and other processes in the P cycle (Figure 11.1).

IV. REFERENCES

1. Brady, N.C. 1990. *The Nature and Properties of Soils,* 10th ed. New York: Macmillan Publishing Co.
2. Carrow, R.N. and R.R. Duncan. 1998. *Salt-Affected Turfgrass Sites: Assessment and Management.* Chelsea, MI: Ann Arbor Press.

Table 11.3. Phosphorus fertilizers with potential for use in turfgrass management.[a]

Source	Analysis		Application Form[c]
	P_2O_5	Other	
Ammonium phosphates	%		
Monoammonium phosphate (MAP)	48–62	11–13N	G, L
Diammonium phosphate (DAP)	46–53	18–21N	G, L
Basic slag	15–25	–	G
Bone meal	15–30	3–5N	G
Calcium metaphosphate	62–63	Ca	G
Phosphogypsum[b]	4–7	Ca	G
Phosphoric acid	52–54	–	L
Potassium phosphate			
Monopotassium phosphate	51	$35K_2O$	G, L
Dipotassium phosphate	41	$54K_2O$	G, L
Potassium polyphosphate	51	$40K_2O$	G, L
Rock phosphate	25–40	–	G
Superphosphates			
Ammoniated normal SP	18–21	3–6N; 9–11S	G
Ammoniated triple SP	44–52	4–6N; 0–1S	G
Triple superphosphate	44–53	1–1.5S	G

[a] Also, see Chapter 17, Table 17.6.
[b] Phosphogypsum is primarily used to treat salt-affected soils and acidic soils due to its Ca content but PG does contain P as an added benefit.
[c] G = granular; L = liquid.

3. Fixen, P.E. and J.H. Grove. 1990. Testing soils for phosphorus. In R.L. Westerman, Ed. *Soil Testing and Plant Analysis,* 3rd ed. Madison, WI: Soil Science Society of America, Book Series No. 3. SSSA.
4. Hopkins, W.G. 1995. *Introduction to Plant Physiology.* New York: John Wiley & Sons, Inc.
5. Hull, R.J. 1997. Phosphorus usage by turfgrasses. *Turfgrass Trends* 6(5):1–12.
6. Marschner, H. 1995. *Mineral Nutrition of Higher Plants.* New York: Academic Press.
7. McCarty, L.B., J.B. Sartain, G.H. Snyder, and J.L. Cisar. 1993. *Plant Nutrition, Fertilizers and Fertilization Programs for Florida Golf Courses.* University of Florida Bulletin 282. University of Gainesville, FL.
8. Plank, C.O. 2001. Soil testing-turf: Extraction. Web-site www.georgiaturf.com. Athens, GA: University of Georgia, College of Agriculture and Environmental Science.
9. Tisdale, S.L, W.L. Nelson, J.D. Beaton, and J.L. Havlin. 1993. *Soil Fertility and Fertilizers,* 5th ed. New York: Macmillan Publishing Co.
10. Turner, T.R. and N.W. Hummel, Jr. 1992. Nutritional requirements and fertilization. In D.V. Waddington, R.N. Carrow, and R.C. Shearman, Eds. *Turfgrass Monograph No. 32.* Madison, WI: Amer. Soc. of Agron.

Chapter 12

Potassium

POTASSIUM (K) IS OFTEN CONSIDERED AS SECOND IN IMPORTANCE behind N as a nutrient in turfgrasses. It does not influence growth to a great degree but strongly influences turfgrass tolerance to drought, cold, high temperature, wear, and salinity stresses. In many sandy soils, K can easily be leached. These factors contribute to the high degree of interest in maintaining adequate K in turfgrass systems.

I. PLANT RELATIONSHIPS[3,5,6,11]

UPTAKE OF K FROM THE SOIL SOLUTION IS AN ACTIVE PROCESS. Once K is in the plant, it is highly mobile but highly regulated by K-channels in plasma, vacuole, and chloroplast membranes. Potassium is the only nutrient that is not a constituent of any plant compound. Yet it is the most abundant primary nutrient after N with concentrations in shoot tissues of 1.0 to 3.0% by weight (Table 2.1). Sufficiency levels range from 1.5 to 3.0% but vary with grasses.[7,11]

Potassium is required for activation of many enzymes and, therefore, influences the processes that the enzymes are involved in catalyzing. Enzymes are proteins and enzyme function depends on the particular protein configuration. Potassium concentrations in the cytosol (cytoplasm not included in one of the organelles like a vacuole) of cells and stroma of chloroplasts that are in the sufficiency range are also optimal for maintaining enzyme conformation (i.e., therefore, enzyme activity). One enzyme requiring K as a catalyst is starch synthase, which transforms soluble glucose into the starch storage form.

Potassium is also the most important inorganic solute in the vacuole involved in osmoregulation and, thereby, water regulation in plants. Osmoregulation and K-induced water regulation involves: (a) enhancing water transport in the xylem as high solute levels in the root cause water uptake; (b) maintaining of high cell turgor pressure that allows metabolic processes and photosynthesis to continue under the daily moderate water stress that grasses are exposed to in summer afternoons. Turgor pressure also aids in wear tolerance; (c) cell extension of new cells that depends on accumulation of sufficient K in the vacuole to maintain water intake into the cell; and (d) stomatal control that regulates transpirational cooling, leaf water potential, and adequate stomata openings for CO_2 intake required for photosynthesis.

Potassium is thought to be involved in the genetic translation steps of protein synthesis including the enzyme RuBP carboxylase that catalyzes CO_2 fixation into ribulose biphosphate in photosynthesis. Potassium also appears to be required for nitrate reductase synthesis and activity, the enzyme required to reduce NO_3^- into the NH_2 form prior to incorporation into amino acids and proteins.

Besides the role of K in CO_2 fixation in photosynthesis, it is required for synthesis of ATP used in this process. Also, K is needed to maintain chloroplast hydration during drought and salinity stresses. High K in chloroplast stroma allows photosynthesis to continue. High K also decreases respiration rates.

Sucrose loading into the phloem and its transport is affected by K. Under low K, photosynthate transport declines to areas requiring sugars. Translocation of sugars requires energy in the form of ATP, which requires K for synthesis. With so many physiological roles, it is not surprising that plants require appreciable K.

Visual symptoms of K deficiency are: interveinal yellowing of older leaves (lower), followed by dieback at the leaf tip, scorching or firing of the margins, and total yellowing of the leaf blade including the veins. The turfgrass plants may appear weak and spindly. Also, under high evaporative demand, wilting and leaf firing may be accelerated as well as wear injury around the cup on greens and other high traffic areas (Plates 1, 14, and 15).

Except under true deficiencies, K does not have a dramatic influence on turfgrass quality, color, or density—unless the plant is exposed to certain stresses, then physiological health of the grass is affected by K status. Potassium nutrition is especially important on grasses grown on sites where soil K levels are consistently low due to leaching and clipping removal, particularly low CEC sand soils (Table 12.1). Maintenance of adequate K on these sites requires a *"spoon-feeding"* approach where small quantities (0.10 to 0.50 lb K_2O per 1,000 ft^2, 0.04 to 0.21 kg per K 100 m^2) are applied on a relatively frequent basis. This could be as a true foliar feeding (<0.10 lb K_2O per 1,000 ft^2), drench, or granular application.

A second situation where K nutrition is important is when turfgrass is exposed to periodic severe stresses such as wear, cold, heat, and drought. Sometimes research results on K have not shown an influence on these stresses. In most cases the lack of apparent response appears to be due to one or more of the following factors: (a) a sufficiently high level of K was in the soil so that all treatments were at a sufficiency level or above; (b) plants were not exposed to sufficient stress; (c) use of various plant parts by researchers to assess response (field-obtained cores, rhizome tissue, crown tissue, crown plus shoot, etc.). For example, a rhizome in the field is likely to tolerate colder temperatures than shoot tissues used by another scientist; and (d) grasses exposed to stressful conditions such as close mowing, traffic, shade, high N, or excessive moisture are more likely to reveal K relationships with wear, cold, heat, and drought stresses. This is because these situations weaken the plant by depleting carbohydrates, reducing roots, or making tissues more succulent. Stresses are additive and a physiologically weak plant is more responsive to K, the physiological "health" nutrient.

As K becomes limiting in field situations, the most common problem is adverse water relationships and drought stress, which can easily escalate into high temperature stress in summer months (Plate 15). Under low K, the stomatal control mechanism becomes less efficient and ET increases as stomata remain open. This results in higher water use, more rapid onset of drought stress and wilting, greater high temperature stress, and loss of cell turgor pressure. If the turf is exposed to traffic, wear injury is increased several fold.

On sand soils, K has been found to promote a more extensive fibrous or branched root system on creeping bentgrass. A well-developed root system is important on sands for maximum water availability since unsaturated flow of water to roots is very slow in sands.

Low K increases the potential for low temperature injury, particularly in late winter when carbohydrates are low. Adequate K aids in maintaining cell moisture under prolonged cold temperatures (intercellular freezing) and helps buffer intracellular freezing in the late winter when dormant tissues start to hydrate. Whether in dormant or actively growing turf, K is the most important inorganic solute for maintenance of cell osmotic-turgor pressure.

Table 12.1. Factors associated with K deficiencies or toxicity/excess problems.

Deficiency Associated with	Toxicity/Excessive Levels Associated with
• High rainfall or irrigation • Sandy or low CEC soils • Acidic soil (pH <5.5) • Sites receiving high inputs of Ca, Mg, or Na • Clippings are removed and high N fertilization • Soils high in vermiculite, illite, or smectite clays at high pH that "fix" K into less available form	• Excess K can contribute to total salinity stress • High K can suppress Mg, Ca, or Mn uptake • Excess K can cause fertilizer burn to foliage, roots, and/or crown tissues.

Once a K-deficient turfgrass is injured by drought, heat, or other stresses, recovery will be slowed by reduced protein synthesis, inhibition of the activity of many enzymes, decreased rate of glucose to starch conversion, high transpiration, reduced photosynthesis, and increased respiration. Soluble N compounds (amino acids, nitrate) may accumulate in shoot tissues as well as soluble carbohydrates. Translocation of soluble sugars in the phloem can decline. While none of these responses are initially fatal, the plants are progressively less healthy and vigorous.

A third field situation where K nutrition becomes especially important is with the presence of high Na from irrigation water or within the soil. High Na^+ suppresses plant K^+ uptake. While Na in the vacuole can replace to some extent the osmoregulation function of K, it cannot substitute for K as an enzyme catalyst or in other metabolic roles in the cytosol (also call hyaloplasm). Under high salinity stress from Na, adequate K does not necessarily enhance salinity tolerance, but it will maintain critical K metabolic roles and enhance turfgrass tolerance to stresses from cold, heat, drought, and wear that often occur while plants are under salinity stress. A spoon-feeding approach is useful for supplying K, particularly if the soil is sandy and irrigation water contains appreciable Na. Sometimes application of other cations (Ca^{+2}, Mg^{+2}) at high and frequent levels as fertilizer or irrigation water inputs can limit K uptake. This results from other cations displacing K from the soil CEC sites into the soil solution and increasing the possibility for loss by leaching.

Potassium and N often interact. Adequate levels of each are important for optimum plant health. High levels of N tend to enhance K problems. Thus, growers using high N should provide sufficient K, especially when conditions favoring low K are present, such as leaching, low CEC soils, acid soils, sandy sites, presence of high Na^+, etc. However, caution should also be exercised under high N regimes not to provide excessive K since both N and K fertilizers can contribute to total salt accumulation. This is important when leaching is limited. Maintaining a proper N and K balance is also important for optimum heat, cold, high temperature, and wear tolerances.

Several diseases have been reported to be influenced by K nutrition (Table 2.5). However, the responses have not been consistent or strong. Certainly, no presently known disease can be controlled or even greatly reduced by K alone.

Over the past decade, turfgrass managers have generally used higher annual K on recreational sites than on lawns or general grounds. This additional K is required due to various combinations of conditions causing K loss (clipping removal, leaching) or presence of stresses (close mowing, traffic, higher N, etc.) that enhance the need for K as a stress conditioning element. While true K toxicity is not a problem, excess K accumulation in the soil can contribute to total salinity buildup (Table 12.1). This is most likely to occur in arid regions, in humid climates during periodic drought, and with continued high K application as fertilizer when leaching does not occur.[2] Actual K toxicity from K accumulation in leaf tips is not a problem on turfgrasses due to mowing and removal of leaf tips but can occur on other landscape plants.

The symptoms of excessive salinity from K are the same as K deficiency in terms of drought, heat, and wear stresses but for a different reason. Excessively high K in the soil solution decreases the osmotic potential of soil water (i.e., the water becomes less available for root uptake because it is attracted to salt molecules). Plants exhibit wilting and are more susceptible to injury from high temperature and wear. Thus, turfgrass managers should avoid K deficiency and excessive K.

II. SOIL AND ENVIRONMENTAL RELATIONSHIPS[1,2,4,10]

TOTAL K CONTENT OF MANY SOILS ranges from less than 1% to 2.5% and is often present in higher quantities than Ca and Mg. A high percentage of K, however, occurs in primary minerals (feldspars like orthoclase, microcline; micas like muscovite, biotite, phlogopite) and secondary minerals (clay) such as illite, vermiculite, and chlorite. The very low availability of K from these sources in combination with potential losses of K from turfgrass systems (leaching, clipping removal) and higher K needs of recreational turfgrasses, often necessitates fertilizer K in quantities similar to N, depending on soil texture.

A. Soil Forms of K

Soil K resides in four forms that differ substantially in their availability for plant uptake (Figure 12.1). In most soils, 90 to 98% of total K is as a *constituent of primary minerals* such as feldspars and micas. The K may be very slowly released over many years and this fraction contributes little to plant K needs during a year.

The next largest pool at 1 to 10% of total soil K is the *nonexchangeable K* associated with 2:1 clay minerals. Potassium (and NH_4^+) ions can fit between the layers of these crystalline clays where they are protected from normal ion exchange reactions such as occurs on the surfaces. This K fraction is called *nonexchangeable, fixed, or reserve K.* The term fixed denotes that K added as fertilizer may enter the clay interlayers and become "fixed" by electrochemical attraction to clay. Over several weeks or a year, some of this may be slowly released and become available for plant use, especially in soil with high contents of these clays. Clays with high potential for K fixation are illite (a hydrous mica), vermiculite, chlorite, and smectite (montmorillonite).

The third fraction is the *readily available K* at 1 to 2% of total K, which consists of exchangeable K and soil solution K. Exchangeable K resides primarily on cation exchange sites on clay surfaces as well as some K from the interlayers at the edges. About 90% of readily available K is in the exchangeable form with only 10% in soil solution at any one time. Soils with higher CEC can retain more exchangeable K than those with low CEC such as sands, or soils in which kaolinitic clays are dominant.

Soil solution K is easily taken up by plants and then replenished by exchangeable K. Thus, there is a rapid equilibrium between soil solution K and exchangeable K on CEC sites. On a sand soil with low CEC, fertilizer K may increase the soil solution K to high levels if there are few CEC sites for K to be retained. The solution K can: (a) be readily taken up by turfgrass;

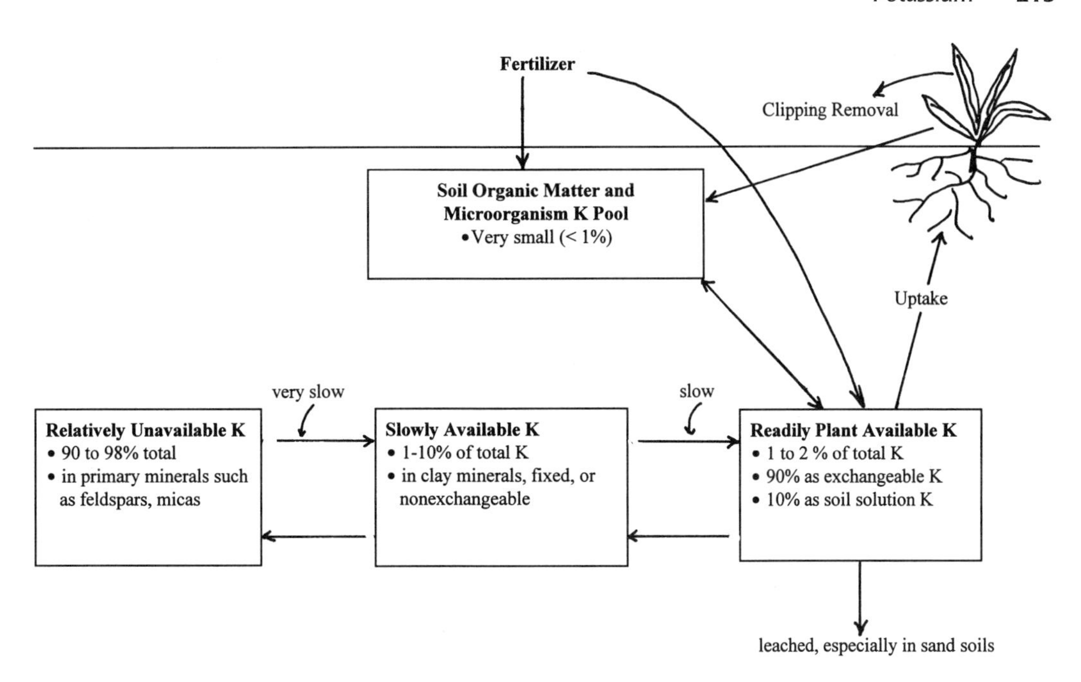

Figure 12.1. Potassium cycle with representative percentage of K in different forms in the soil.

(b) contribute to total salinity stress; or (c) be readily leached with a heavy rain or irrigation. In contrast, a soil with higher CEC will retain more of the applied K on CEC sites where K is somewhat protected from leaching, does not contribute to high salt concentrations in the soil solution, and is readily available for plant use or to be fixed.

Only a very small amount of K is contained in soil organic matter and within the soil microbial population. While K can be retained on organic matter CEC sites, it is loosely held and can be leached over time. The portion of K on organic matter CEC sites is reported as exchangeable K since extracts can remove this fraction at the same time as K is removed from inorganic CEC sites. The remaining K content of soil organic matter is low. On humid, tropical sites with weathered soils, much of the potentially available K may be in the living plants. As these sites are cleared to establish turf, the K is removed with the plant debris. Thus, K fertilization is often necessary to meet plant needs after one or two years.

B. Factors Affecting Soil K Availability[1,4,10]

Several soil, climatic, and management factors influence soil K availability (Table 12.1) under turfgrass culture.

Clay Type and Content

Since the majority of readily available K for turfgrasses is in the exchangeable form, increasing CEC increases the quantity of available K. Thus, as clay content increases so does the CEC associated with the clay and organic matter bound to the clay. Kaolinite clays have low CEC relative to other clays and thus can hold less exchangeable K.

In addition to K on clay CEC sites, soils with K-fixing clays (vermiculites, illite, smectite, chlorite) will contain higher levels of slowly available K from the interlayers. However, the fixation abilities of these clays may necessitate high K fertilization, if not present from previous cropping practices, especially for the first few years after turfgrass establishment.

Soil Reaction (pH) and Cation Type

Acidic, leached soils contain less K as well as other basic cations (Ca, Mg). Both Al^{+3} and H^+ can easily displace K^+ from the CEC sites as a soil becomes more acidic. As pH increases from a highly acid condition to pH 6.5 to 7.0, there is less competition from H and Al and total CEC often increases due to pH dependent CEC sites (Chapter 4). This aids in retaining more K on CEC sites.

As pH increases above 7.0, high content of Ca and Mg may result in less available K and suppressed uptake of K. This can also occur whenever high Ca or Mg levels are added to an acid soil or during treatment of sodic soils with Ca amendments. Sometimes, high additions of Ca or Mg from irrigation sources have the same effect.

High Na applications from irrigation water or high natural Na levels in soils can displace K from CEC sites and suppress K uptake. High applications of Ca on sodic soils are used to displace Na from CEC sites, followed by leaching to remove the Na. Such treatments also displace K^+ from these sites. Thus, K as well as Na is removed by subsequent leaching aimed at correcting a sodic condition. K displaced by Na from irrigation water is also subject to leaching loss.

Soil Physical Conditions

The most rapid uptake of K occurs on warm, moist and well-aerated soils. Soil moisture near field capacity facilitates K transport by diffusion to roots. On sand soils, water films are thinner than in fine-textured soils and the pathway to roots is longer due to the larger particle size. This limits K diffusion. One of the plant responses to adequate K nutrition is a more branched, finer root system. This is important on sands to enhance K uptake, since roots will contact more of the soil particle surfaces and soil solution.

Probably the greatest influence of soil moisture on K activity is by leaching. Sandy soils with low CEC are especially susceptible to K leaching losses. Sands most likely to exhibit very high K leaching are: (a) ones with low inherent organic matter content and therefore lower CEC. Often tropical and subtropical climates result in considerable soil organic matter loss by decomposition due to the continuous high day/night soil temperatures. The CEC sites in the organic matter are also lost. During establishment and grow-in on sand soils is another period when CEC from organic matter is low and K leaching is likely to be higher. Peats utilized in sand mixes will add some CEC; (b) acidic sands; (c) sands receiving higher inputs of Ca, Mg, or Na; and (d) sands subjected to high rainfall or irrigation.

In contrast, sand soils in semiarid or arid climates (or dry periods in any climatic zone), can easily exhibit high total salinity stress as salts (including K) accumulate (Chapters 7, 8). Lack of leaching plus low CEC sites for removal of added K from soil solution can cause K to become a potentially toxic ion problem contributing to physiological drought and K accumulation in landscape plants.

Uptake of K increases as soil temperatures rise. This is likely a result of higher metabolic activity by the plant, more rapid root growth, and greater K diffusion in the soil. Under low soil

O_2 root respiration decreases and active K uptake declines. Also, rooting is restricted under waterlogged and compacted conditions. Thus, alleviation of waterlogged or compacted soil conditions will enhance K uptake.

III. PRACTICUM[2–4,7–9]

A. Assessing K Needs

Soil Testing

SOIL TESTING IS A GOOD MEANS TO ASSESS PLANT AVAILABLE SOIL K (see Chapter 9). Some turfgrass managers have been disillusioned when their K soil tests always are very low on heavily leached sands of low CEC. Actually, the soil test is accurate but under these conditions K is easily leached and plant-available levels remain low. For these conditions, other means of determining K fertilization requirements will be necessary and these are discussed in the next section. However, for all other soils, soil testing is the best method for assessing K needs. This includes sands that are not heavily leached.

Various extractants have been used with neutral (pH 7.0) 1M NH_4OAc (ammonium acetate) the most widely used.[4,9] This extractant removes exchangeable K on soil CEC sites as well as solution K and has been well calibrated against plant responses. In soils with high total salts where appreciable K may be in the soil solution (such as after a dry season), this method and other extractants will overestimate plant-available K since the solution K can easily be leached (during a wet period) and be unavailable for plant uptake. On saline soils, a saturated paste extract can be made and K content determined, which simulates soil solution conditions. This amount can be subtracted from the total exchangeable plus solution K extraction with the NH_4OAc to obtain a better estimate of exchangeable K availability. On nonsaline soils this correction is not necessary.

The quantity of extractable K is then ranked as low to high with respect to providing sufficient K for the crop. Recreational turfgrasses require more K than most plants so the ranking should be specific to the use of turfgrasses (Table 12.2). Sufficiency rankings for K in Table 12.2 may vary somewhat with laboratory. The sufficiency (SLAN-*sufficiency level of available nutrients*) approach is based on estimating the nutrient supplying power of the soil and then ranking whether this is sufficient to meet the plants' needs.[9] It is, therefore, based on estimating a "quantity" of available nutrient, which relates to plant needs because a plant requires a certain quantity of nutrient during a growing season. A moderate ranking indicates approximately 50% of the plant nutrient need will come from the soil and the remainder from fertilizer.

Other extractants are used such as Mehlich I (0.05 M H_2SO_4 + 0.05 M HC1), and Morgan (0.72 M NaOAc + 0.52 M CH_3COOH). In recent years the Mehlich III extractant (0.2 M CH_3COOH + 0.25 M NH_4NO_3 + 0.015 M NH_4F + 0.013 M HNO_3 + 0.001 M EDTA) has become popular as a universal extractant. It extracts about 20% more K than the NH_4OAc procedure but is well correlated to K removed by the latter method. The higher quantity of K extracted is from the nonexchangeable fraction due to the weak acid action of the Mehlich III.

The K sufficiency levels in Table 12.2 require several comments: (a) the rankings for "sands/most soils" can be used for soils with high K fixation properties due to high content of 2:1 clays; (b) various laboratories may use somewhat different rankings. Labs may also use somewhat different soil to solution ratios or shaking times, resulting in some variation in sufficiency rankings; and (c) for home lawns and general turfgrass sites the "moderate" range is normally acceptable. But for high maintenance recreational sites, the "high" range is desirable.

Table 12.2. Common K sufficiency ranges for several extractants for recreational turfgrasses (see Chapter 9).

Extractant	K Sufficiency Rankings[a]			
	Very Low	Low	Moderate	High[b]
	ppm			
1M NH_4OAc (pH 7.0)				
Sands/most soils	0–40	41–75	76–175	>176
Fine-textured[c]	0–55	56–100	101–235	>235
Mehlich III				
Sands/most soils	0–25	26–50	51–116	>116
Fine-textured[c]	0–40	41–75	76–175	>176
Mehlich I				
Sands/most soils	0–30	31–60	61–140	>140
Fine-textured[c]	0–45	46–90	91–200	>201

[a] 1 ppm = 2 lb/A.
[b] High maintenance recreational turf sites would use the High level as a target, while general turf areas would use the Moderate range as acceptable.
[c] Soils with higher K retention/fixing abilities that contain >35% clay.

In addition to being reported as a sufficiency level in ppm or pounds per acre, K is often reported as *percent K saturation on the CEC.* This value is useful in monitoring whether the percent of K in the soil CEC is changing over time in response to fertilization or irrigation. Also, a target of 2 to 7% K saturation on the CEC is often used as a reasonable range to maintain. Cation ratios of K with Ca and Mg based on percent saturation of each ion has also been used by some to make fertilizer recommendations.[9] This procedure of using ratios based on *percent values is called the BCSR (basic cation saturation ratio)* and: (a) it usually increases fertilizer recommendations that are unnecessary relative to the SLAN procedure; (b) the use of *percentage* ignores the importance of *quantity* of K or other nutrients present. A sand with a low CEC may exhibit a 10% K saturation but have very little extractable K. In contrast, a fine-textured soil of higher CEC may only have 3% K saturation but moderate levels of extractable K; and (c) when appropriate K is applied based on sufficiency data, the percent levels adjust naturally to what are reasonable for the soil type.

Guidelines for Mg:K and Ca:K ratios based on saturation percentages on the soil CEC have some value if they are supported by extractable levels of these nutrients. Common guidelines are:

- Ca:K below 10:1, Ca deficiency may occur
  above 30:1, K deficiency may occur
- Mg:K below 2:1, Mg deficiency may occur
  above 10:1, K deficiency may occur
- Ca:Mg below 3:1, Ca deficiency may occur
  above 3:1, Mg deficiency may occur

These guidelines are very broad and whether nutritional problems arise depends on the "extractable" levels of nutrients more than "percent" based ratios. Thus, the above ratios are often not of much practical use.

Another problem with use of cation saturation percentages is that errors in determining CEC alters the percent values. For example, 1M NH_4OAc (pH 7.0) is a common extractant to determine extractable K (and other cations). The quantities of all cations are often totaled to determine CEC of a soil. Since this extractant has a pH of 7.0 when it is used on highly acid soil, the CEC is overestimated because pH-dependent CEC sites are "counted" that are not present at the actual field soil pH. The overcounting usually occurs as H^+ ions but when these are factored into the percent calculations the cation saturation percentages will be lower than they actually are for K, Ca, and Mg.

Percent K saturation can also be underestimated on soils containing appreciable soluble salts or free $CaCO_3$ regardless of the extractant. These salts become totaled with exchangeable levels of cations to overestimate CEC. This generally underestimates the cations that are at low levels in the soluble salt, while increasing estimates of those present in the soluble salts. If K is present in the excess soluble salts in the soil solution, then it becomes extracted as "exchangeable K" as noted earlier and should be corrected by saturation paste extract data.

A summary of the main implications on soil testing for assessing soil K status is:

- A number of extractants are available for estimating K sufficiency levels (SLAN approach). The SLAN is the best procedure for evaluating the K supplying power of a soil.
- If data on % K saturation are used directly or as ratios with Ca and Mg, the CEC must be accurately determined for the percent values to be accurate. The 1M NH_4OAc (pH 7.0) procedure is often inaccurate on acid soils (Chapter 4).
- If high levels of soluble salts are present and dissolved by K soil test extractants, these will give erroneous data on whatever cations are extracted, including K. This can be corrected in soil test labs by determination of K (or other cations) in a saturated paste extract. The saturated paste extract levels of K, Ca, and Mg are not accurate predictive soil tests because they ignore the exchangeable quantities which account for most of the plant available cations. This is true even on low CEC sands.
- Soil testing is the best means of determining K fertilization requirements except on heavily leached, low CEC, sand soils.

Leached Sands and N:K_2O Ratios

Potassium can easily be leached from sands, especially under one or more of these situations: (a) high rainfall; (b) high irrigation rates to leach total salts or Na on salt-affected turfgrass sites; (c) where appreciable additions of soluble Na, Ca, or Mg that displaces K from exchange sites into the soil solution where it is susceptible to leaching; (d) low CEC soils, especially at CEC values of <4 cmol kg^{-1} (Chapter 4); (e) acid pH conditions; and (f) low organic matter content typical of grow-in situations, sandy subsoils, and soils in tropical climates. Often, several of these factors are present on a site as well as clipping removal losses of K.

Due to the low CEC and high leaching, K cannot be built up in these soils but must be maintained by a spoon-feeding approach. The exchangeable fraction where most plant-available K resides for other soils is low in these sands, and soil tests reflect this reality. In Chapter 4, the case of low CEC sands is discussed with respect to enhancing CEC and management of various nutrients including K. In Chapter 4 are guidelines for using N rates (i.e., N:K_2O ratios) and application timing to determine K rates and times of application. In Section C, Potassium Fertilization, of the current chapter, N:K_2O ratios are further discussed. Spoon-feeding of K is also discussed later in this chapter.

Tissue Testing

Tissue tests can determine true K deficiencies because the values will be low, continue to be low, and visual symptoms of K deficiency will start to be expressed. Obtaining samples from a site with visual symptoms and an adjacent site with the same grass but without symptoms aid in interpretation (Chapter 9). Soil tests from these areas will be helpful as well.

Use of tissue tests to monitor K leaf status can provide some useful information for understanding plant responses to K fertilization and weather conditions. However, reliance on tissue K levels for the purpose of K fertilization is questionable because: (a) K levels can increase or decrease within the sufficiency range in response to many factors besides soil K status such as N applications, plant growth regulators, temperature conditions, and rainfall or irrigation. A decrease does not mean K is limiting but usually indicates better growing conditions and K becomes diluted in rapidly growing tissues; (b) when K levels do become deficient then adverse physiological effects of K deficiency are already acting on the turfgrass. It is better to avoid this condition; (c) K tissue content does not usually respond very much to added K unless very low levels are present in the tissue and in the soil. Turfgrasses seem to take up K to a point and then are rather unresponsive as far as changes in tissue K levels to additional K additions (Miller[8]). The ideal of "charging" the plant with additional K (i.e., luxury consumption) is unrealistic for turfgrasses where leaves are mowed; (d) there isn't a universal K tissue sufficiency level even within a species. For example, seashore paspalum (*Paspalum vaginatum*) ecotypes vary in K tissue content from 1.2 to 3.9% K at the same modest soil K level. A turfgrass manager can determine an approximate sufficiency range for a given grass and location by tissue testing over time, and watching turfgrass response to stress; and (e) results using methods for rapid field K tissue tests may not be well correlated to the accurate laboratory plant analyses. The NIRS method (Chapter 9) has a significant but very low correlation to accurate wet lab procedures. Thus, a single NIRS test value can be very inaccurate but the average of several samples from a site will be closer to a true value.

B. Potassium Fertilizers

A number of K fertilizers are available with many in either granular or liquid forms (Table 12.3). Muriate of potash (KCl) is the most commonly used K fertilizer but K_2SO_4 is widely used on recreational turfgrasses. On sands, KNO_3 is often used as a K source, but N needs must be properly balanced with other N sources to maintain a proper N:K_2O balance. In recent years, several slow-release K products have been developed using sulfur, polymer, or resin coatings and different K sources. Unless very high rates of potash are needed, most of the K_2O is applied in fertilizers with ratios like 4-1-2, 5-1-5, 1-0-1, 2-1-1, etc.

C. Potassium Fertilization

Annual K

On fine-textured soils or sandy soils where leaching is minimal, soil testing provides a good indication of plant-available K in the soil. In many locations, state extension services or turfgrass institutes have developed annual K recommendations based on soil test results. Table 12.4 lists typical annual K recommended rates for recreational turfgrass sites based on soil test result, soil type, and length of the growing season. These rates are further adjusted within the

Table 12.3 Potassium fertilizers with potential for use on turfgrasses (also see Table 17.7).

Source	Approx. Formula	Usual K_2O Content[a]	Application Form[b]
Coated, *slow release* K carriers. Coatings;	KCl, K_2SO_4, KNO_3 are used as the K source for most	%	
– Sulfur coated		VAR	G
– Polymer coated		VAR	G
– Resin coated		VAR	G
Potassium bicarbonate	$KHCO_3$	46	L, G
Potassium carbonate			
Solid	K_2CO_3	48	G
Liquid	K_2CO_3	34	L
Potassium chloride (muriate of potash)	KCl	60–62	G,L
Potassium hydroxide	KOH	83	L
Potassium magnesium sulfate	$K_2SO_4 \cdot 2\ MgSO_4$	22;22S,11Mg	G
Potassium nitrate	KNO_3	44;13N	G,L
Potassium phosphates			
Potassium metaphosphate	KPO_3	39;59 P_2O_5	L
Monopotassium phosphate	KH_2PO_4	35;51 P_2O_5	L, G
Dipotassium phosphate	K_2HPO_4	54;41 P_2O_5	L, G
Potassium polyphosphate	$K_3HP_2O_7 \cdot KH_2PO_4$, others	40;51 P_2O_5	L, G
Potassium-metal ion-phosphate, *slow release.* M=Mg, Mn or Zn	$KMPO_4$	17–22;27–37 P_2O_5; 13–24% M	G
Potassium polysulfide	KS_x	22;23S	L
Potassium sodium nitrate	$KNO_3/NaNO_3$	14; 15N	L
Potassium sulfate (sulfate of potash)	K_2SO_4	50–52;17S	G, L

[a] % K = 0.83 K_2O; % P = 0.437 P_2O_5

[b] G = granular; L = liquid. Analysis of the liquid formulation can vary depending on dilution.

range where higher K is required for longer growing seasons, high intensity of use, clipping removal, or high rainfall/irrigation.

Fine-textured soils with appreciable quantities of K-fixing clays require high K fertilization if the K soil test is low. However, at moderate or higher K soil test levels, little K is required since these soils contain considerable nonexchangeable K that does contribute appreciably over a season to the plant-available K. While the suggested annual K levels in Table 12.4 are for recreational turfgrasses, the table can be used for amenity or general grounds areas by reducing K rates by about 30% (sands) to 50% (fine-textured soil) at a given soil test ranking.

For frequently leached sandy soils, annual K requirement is based on the total N applied per year. Suggested N:K_2O ratios for recreational turfgrass areas as listed in Table 12.5. A higher N:K_2O ratio (i.e., more K_2O per unit of N) is recommended when annual N is low to be sure there is adequate K percent to enhance wear tolerance under conditions where turf growth rate will be minimal. At high N conditions, the total K will be high but the N:K_2O ratio should be less than 1:1. This practice avoids application of too many soluble salts on these sandy soils.

Table 12.4. Recommended annual potassium fertilization requirements for recreational turfgrasses. General grounds and home lawns would require 30 to 50% less K on an annual basis (see Table 12.5 for recommendations for heavily leached sand soils).

Soil Type and Soil Test Ranking	Length of Growing Season	
	5 to 11 Months	12 Months or Warm-Season Grass with Winter Overseeding
	pounds K_2O per 1,000 ft^2	
Sands with Minimal Leaching; Fine-Textured Soils Containing Kaolinite, Fe/Al Oxides and Other Highly Weathered Clays. Soil test of:		
Very low	3–6[a]	4–7
Low	2–5	3–6
Moderate	1–4	2–5
High	0–2	1–3
Very high	0	0–1
Fine-Textured Soils Containing Appreciable 2:1 Clays with High K-Fixation Abilities (illites, vermiculite, montmorillonite). Soil test of:		
Very low	4–7	5–8
Low	3–6	4–7
Moderate	1–2	2–3
High	0–1	0–2
Very high	0	0

[a] Within the range of K recommended, higher K would be used for longer growing months, high intensity of traffic use, clipping removal, and high rainfall or irrigation. 1 lb K = 0.83 lb K_2O; lb per 1,000 ft^2 ÷ 2 = kg per 100 m^2.

Table 12.5. Use of $N:K_2O$ ratios to determine annual K requirements on recreational turfgrasses when the sand root zone is subjected to frequent leaching from rainfall or irrigation (see Table 12.4 for recommendations for fine-textured soils and sand soils not subjected to heavy leaching by irrigation or rainfall).

Annual N Applied[a]		Nitrogen to Potassium Ratio to Use[b]	
Pounds per 1,000 ft^2	kg N ha^{-1}	$N:K_2O$	N:K
<3	<167	1:1.75	1:1.45
3–7	168–342	1:1	1:0.83
7–12	343–585	1:0.75	1:0.62
>12	>586	1:0.50	1:0.42

[a] Total annual N includes N applied for any winter overseeding grasses.
[b] For nonrecreational turfgrasses (general grounds, home lawns) growing on sandy soils subjected to frequent leaching, a ratio of 1:0.75 is suitable for most situations regardless of the annual N applied.

The problem of excessive salts results if rainfall or irrigation becomes limited so that leaching does not occur. High rates of N plus excessively use of K can rapidly contribute to total salinity buildup and cause physiological drought and associated wilt, scalping, and wear stress. When high rates of K are used, K_2SO_4 or slow-release forms are the preferred sources because they have a lower salt index than KCl. Additionally, high K fertilization without leaching may contribute to cation imbalances with Ca and, especially, Mg.[8]

Rates of K Per Application and Frequency

The basic fertilization approach for K on many recreational sites should be a spoon-feeding program where lighter but more frequent applications are made. This approach helps ensure adequate K in the soil solution regardless of high leaching conditions (on sands or low CEC soils) or high K fixation (2:1 clays). Spoon-feeding is especially important on recreational turfgrasses with high traffic; grasses exposed to high/low temperature and moisture extremes; and sites where clipping removal prevents K recycling. However spoon-feeding does not need to be practiced on lawns or general grounds (especially when fine-textured soils are present), where leaching is limited, or when soil tests are medium or above.

Many individuals assume that spoon-feeding means liquid applications. However, granular products can be incorporated into this approach whether they are water-soluble K products or slow-release K carriers. Typical single application rates for various types of products are:

- Liquid K-carrier as a foliar application in 1 to 3 gallons water per 1,000 ft^2 (4 to 12 L per 100 m^2) can be applied at 0.10 to 0.33 lb K_2O per 1,000 ft^2 (4.0 to 13.2 kg K ha^{-1}). At higher rates, the chance for foliar burn increases unless the water rate is increased or the fertilizer is washed off the leaves.
- Mini-size particles of granular, salt-type K-carriers applied to close out turf (<0.25 inch; 0.64 cm) is usually at 0.33 to 0.50 lb K_2O per 1,000 ft^2. At less than 0.33 lb K_2O per 1,000 ft^2 there may not be enough particles per unit area of turf for good coverage. Irrigation should follow to wash materials off leaves, and dissolve fertilizer granules. Normally, 0.10 to 0.15 inch (0.25 to 0.38 cm) of irrigation is adequate.
- Granular, salt K fertilizers on turf mowed above golf green height is usually applied at 0.50 to 1.0 lb K_2O per 1,000 ft^2 on sandy or fine-textured soils. Irrigation should follow.
- Slow-release K fertilizers, whether of mini-size particles or larger, can be applied at 0.50 to 2.0 lb K_2O per 1,000 ft^2 per application except on greens where the range is 0.50 to 1.0 lb K_2O per 1,000 ft^2. For slow-release materials, return clippings for 1 or 2 mowings.
- Salt-type K fertilizers applied as a drench through the irrigation system (i.e., *fertigation*) can be applied as 0.10 to 1.5 lb K_2O per 1,000 ft^2 since ample water prevents foliar burn.

Many K sources are water-soluble salts with a moderate to high salt index (Chapter 17). To prevent foliar burn, it is always wise to irrigate immediately after any granular, salt type K fertilizer is applied at over 0.33 lb K_2O per 1,000 ft^2 (13.2 kg K ha^{-1}) on close-cut, dense turfgrass or above 0.50 lb K_2O per 1,000 ft^2 on higher-cut, more open turf. Foliar burn is most likely to occur when temperatures are warm and the grass is physiologically active. Slow-release K sources have lower salt indexes but irrigation aids in integrating them into the soil surface to avoid mower removal or damage to coated particles.

As indicated above, the form of K fertilizer influences the rate per application, but a second factor is soil type. Turfgrasses on sandy, frequently leached sands respond best to salt-type K carriers when applied in the summer months at 0.10 to 0.66 lb K_2O per 1,000 ft^2 (4.0 to 26.7 kg K ha^{-1}) for warm-season grasses at a two to four week schedule. During cooler periods, the single application rate can be higher. Higher and somewhat less frequent applications of K can be made using slow-release sources on these sands. When a sandy soil is not subjected to frequent leaching, then applied K remains in the root zone and frequency of application can be extended to four to six weeks using these same general rates of application. Higher K rates per application can be used on fine-textured soils since they have adequate CEC to retain more K.

Other conditions that require more frequent, light K applications, include: (a) the presence of clay types that have high K fixation characteristics and exhibit low K soil test values; (b) situations where the irrigation water (such as some effluent water) is adding appreciable Na, Ca, or Mg but little K. Typical K concentration in wastewater sources is 5 to 20 ppm (mg L^{-1}) where 5 ppm is equivalent to adding 0.37 lb K_2O per 1,000 ft^2 per acre-foot of irrigation water (18 kg K_2O ha^{-1} per 30.5 cm irrigation water). Many water resources contain less K than this amount but relatively high Ca, Mg, or Na contents. Seawater contains about 380 ppm K which would be equivalent to 28.4 lb K_2O per 1,000 ft^2 for every 12 inches of seawater applied. But even in this extreme case, K content of the water is $<1\%$ of total cations applied; (c) instances where high rates of Ca or Mg amendments are added, such as by lime or gypsum, on a routine basis. Sodic soils receiving irrigation water high in Na require frequent and high rates of Ca (gypsum, lime plus S, soluble Ca sources), plus heavy leaching is necessary. Under these conditions, K should be applied on a frequent basis; and (d) turfgrasses subjected to intense traffic in conjunction with clipping removal, irrigation, and high N use require frequent K additions.

In order to eliminate the labor requirements of applying light, frequent K treatments, application is usually done in conjunction with N. Fertilizers are selected with N:K_2O ratios that provide sufficient quantities of these nutrients for use in a spoon-feeding program. For example, a 23-0-23 fertilizer (N-P_2O_5-K_2O) would provide a 1:1 ratio of N:K_2O.

Timing

Since K is important for cold, heat, drought, and wear stresses, it is essential to provide adequate K when these stresses are present. It is often difficult to increase leaf tissue content of K above the moderate sufficiency level for the particular grass species and cultivar, especially if the grass is actively growing and regularly mowed.[8] Thus, K cannot usually be "built up" in leaf tissue for future use. Instead, the goal is to maintain tissue K in the moderate sufficiency range with ample available soil K for rapid replenishment of tissue K lost by clipping removal. For sandy soils with low CEC where the plant-available soil K pool is often limited, the best approach is to make frequent, light K treatments to supplement the limited amount in the soil.

Stresses, such as high temperature, drought, and wear, usually occur over a prolonged period, requiring a spoon-feeding approach to maintain ample soil K throughout the stress period (as long as the grass is growing and not dormant). Adequate K should be applied prior to the stress occurring (i.e., as a "hardening" application) and during the period of continued stress. For high-use recreational sites, wear may be present as a stress for the whole growing season; thus, regular spoon-feeding is appropriate on sand soils.

In climates with a winter dormancy period, an ample soil K level determined by soil test or a moderately high application of K prior to winter dormancy can aid in increasing tissue K content to the moderate sufficiency range and supply some soil K for potential future use. Conflicting results have been reported by researchers as to the influence of K prior to dormancy. Some of the differences are due to use of different plant parts (rhizomes, stolons, crowns) and freezing techniques (field, cold chambers). In field situations, the most dramatic positive response to applied K for cold temperature tolerance has been for instances of close-mowed recreational grasses, often in conjunction with other stresses such as crown hydration for intracellular freezing, soil compaction, or shade. It is when these stress conditions occur along with unusually cold temperatures that K does make a positive difference. High K applications should not be made prior to freezing weather conditions to avoid damage to turf as freezing concentrates K in the soil solution.

As grasses start to green up after winter dormancy is also a critical time for K availability. This is particularly important in climates where warm-season grasses may demonstrate root dieback after initial greenup. Ample soil K aids in maintaining sufficient tissue K contents to harden the plant against an unexpected freeze or wear injury.

Another important period for K application is after unusually heavy, prolonged rainfalls. On low CEC sands, even one heavy rainfall may deplete considerable plant-available K, especially K in the soil solution. Even fine-textured soils with kaolinitic type clays that exhibit relatively low CEC can have appreciable K lost by leaching over a monsoon season.

Sometimes turfgrass managers follow a program for K fertilization that is appropriate for replenishment of K under high rainfall but do not adjust the program for dry periods. This can lead to overapplication of K that leads to salt accumulation. On sandy soils where salt accumulation from K may occur rather rapidly, K fertilization programs must be adjusted for unusually wet or dry periods that alter leaching patterns.

On sands susceptible to K leaching, timing of K relative to applying other cations can affect the magnitude of K leached. Since K can be displaced from CEC sites rather easily by Ca or Mg, applying a K fertilizer after addition of amendments containing these cations will help maintain K on exchanges sites in contrast to adding K beforehand. This practice is especially important for sites where periodic heavy applications of gypsum, lime, or Mg fertilizers are made. On very low CEC root zone mixes (i.e., <1 cmol kg^{-1}), applying compounds with cations other than K (i.e., $CaSO_4$, $MgSO_4$) at the time of K fertilization may favor greater K leaching.

D. Enhancing K Retention in Soil

Beyond the means already addressed in this chapter for maintaining adequate K in the root zone (i.e., use of spoon-feeding; use of slow-release of K carriers; appropriate timing of K to minimize leaching), turfgrass managers may be able to enhance CEC of the soil so that more total K can be retained in the exchangeable form. Chapter 4 includes different methods to increase CEC, but adjusting acidic pH to a pH of 6.0 to 7.0 and incorporation of zeolite are most practical.

IV. REFERENCES

1. Brady, N.C. 1990. *The Nature and Properties of Soils,* 10th ed. New York: Macmillan Publishing Co.
2. Carrow, R.N. and R.R. Duncan. 1998. *Salt-Affected Turfgrass Sites: Assessment and Management.* Chelsea, MI: Ann Arbor Press.
3. Christians, N.E. 1998. Potassium fertilization. *Turfgrass Trends* 7(3):9–13.
4. Haby, V.A., M.P. Russelle, and E.O. Skogley. 1990. Testing soils for potassium, calcium, and magnesium. In R.L Westerman, Ed. *Soil Testing and Plant Analysis,* 3rd ed. Madison, WI: Soil Science Society of America, Book Series No. 3., SSSA.
5. Hopkins, W.G. 1995. *Introduction to Plant Physiology.* New York: John Wiley & Sons, Inc.
6. Marchner, H. 1995. *Mineral Nutrition of Higher Plants.* New York: Academic Press.
7. McCarty, L.G., J.B. Sartain, G.H. Snyder, and J.L. Cisar. 1993. *Plant Nutrition, Fertilizers, and Fertilization Programs for Florida Golf Courses.* University of Florida Bulletin 282. University of Florida, Gainsville.

8. Miller, G.L. 1999. Potassium application reduces calcium and magnesium levels in bermudagrass leaf tissue and soil. *Hort. Science* 34(2):265–268.
9. Plank, C.O. 2001. Soil testing-turf: Extraction. Web-site http://www.georgiaturf.org, Univ. of Georgia, Coll. of Agric. and Enviro. Sci., Athens, GA.
10. Tisdale, S.L., W.L. Nelson, J.D. Beation, and J.L. Havlin. 1993. *Soil Fertility and Fertilizers,* 5th ed. New York: Macmillan Publishing Co.
11. Turner, T.R. and N.W. Hummel, Jr. 1992. Nutritional requirements and fertilization. In D.V. Waddington, R.N. Carrow, and R.C. Shearman, Eds. *Turfgrass Monograph No. 32.* Madison, WI: Amer. Soc. Agron.

Chapter 13

Calcium, Magnesium, and Sulfur

THE MACRONUTRIENTS CALCIUM (CA), MAGNESIUM (MG), AND SULFUR (S) are *secondary nutrients* that are applied less frequently as fertilizers compared to the primary nutrients (N, P, K).[3,10,12] However, turfgrasses contain about as much Ca, Mg, and S on a dry weight basis as P. Deficiencies of Mg and S are sometimes observed, especially on intensively managed turfgrasses grown on high sand root zone mixes, while Ca deficiencies are much less common.

I. CALCIUM

A. Plant Relationships[5,6,9]

UPTAKE OF CA BY TURFGRASS ROOTS is in the Ca^{+2} form and is primarily a passive process. However, the outer cell wall surfaces form voids or intercellular spaces (apoplasm) where the soil solution can enter between root cells. These outer cell wall surfaces contain carboxyl groups ($R\text{-}COO^-$) that impart cation exchange properties to the roots. Calcium is preferentially attracted to these sites which greatly increases Ca content in the root cortex and facilitates Ca uptake.

Functions of Ca

After translocation to shoot tissues in the xylem, some of the Ca^{+2} binds on the exterior wall surfaces in the leaf tissue apoplasm where cation exchange sites also exist. Considerable Ca is located within cell wall structures where Ca^{+2} links pectin chains in the middle lamella. This Ca-pectin linkage strengthens cell walls and the plant tissue formed by the cells.

Calcium also is localized on the outer surfaces of the plasma membrane where it aids in membrane function. Apparently, Ca organizes membrane proteins into complexes by linking proteins together that are then more active in function.

Inside cells, Ca concentration is highest in vacuoles, chloroplasts, and the endoplasmic reticulum (ER) membrane system. Within vacuoles, it serves as an inorganic solute to counteract inorganic and organic anions for maintenance of osmotic balance. Calcium in the ER functions to stabilize the membrane and serves a similar role in thylakoid membranes in chloroplasts. Calcium levels are maintained at low concentrations in the cytosol (portion of cytoplasm not part of a cell organelle such as a vacuole) by active Ca pumps in the plasma membrane and tonoplasts. High Ca concentrations in the cytoplasm would likely precipitate inorganic P and compete with Mg^{+2} for binding sites.

While Ca is involved in cell division, it influences root extension in a more pronounced manner. As noted, Ca enhances cell strength. Since root cell walls must expand for growth or extension, some of the Ca is displaced by H ions stimulated by auxin acting on plasma membrane H transport. This allows pectin chains to expand, the cell elongates, and then Ca replaces the H to regain cell wall stability.

Calcium is necessary for secretion of mucilage around root caps. It is also required for formation of secretory vesicles that lead to cellulose precursors used in cell walls and callus formation on plants in response to injury.

In recent years, Ca has been identified as a signal messenger to indicate when and how a plant should respond to certain stimuli—such as mechanical injury, pathogen infection, hormones, light or temperature. Also, Ca has been identified as a stimulant for some membrane-bound enzymes and amylase in germinating seeds.

Deficiencies and Excesses

Calcium is present in grasses in about the same concentrations as P, 0.50 to 1.25% with <0.50% considered deficient (Table 2.1). However, cultivars within a species can vary considerably as to Ca requirements.

Visual deficiency symptoms for Ca on turfgrasses are very rare in field situations. From solution culture studies, reported symptoms are distorted appearance of new leaves; reddish brown to rose leaf blades; leaf tips and margins may wither and die; and roots may be stunted and discolored (Plate 1). Calcium is very immobile in the plant so symptoms appear on new leaves.

One reason Ca deficiency is so rare on grasses is that monocots (grasses) have a considerably lower Ca requirement than dicots—as much as 40-fold lower. The fibrous root system of grasses also allows for considerable contact with soil minerals in solution and thereby, good nutrient uptake efficiency. Also, turfgrass sites often receive appreciable Ca input applied as lime, gypsum, and irrigation water. This latter aspect is often overlooked where rainfall at 8 ppm or mg L^{-1} Ca would add 0.50 lb Ca per 1,000 ft^2 which is equivalent to 1.25 lb $CaCO_3$ per 1,000 ft^2 (61 kg $CaCO_3$ ha^{-1}) per acre-foot of rain. Irrigation water often has 25 to 50 mg L^{-1} Ca and would add 1.6 to 3.2 lb Ca per 1,000 ft^2 (78 to 156 kg Ca ha^{-1}) per acre-foot of water. Wastewater (effluent) Ca levels may range from <20 (low) to >80 (very high) mg L^{-1} where ratings refer to nutrient levels.[2]

High external (soil solution) concentrations of Al^{+3}, H^+, Mn^{+2}, or Na^+ can result in replacement of appreciable Ca^{+2} by cation exchange on the root exchange sites in the root apoplasm (Table 13.1). Even under these conditions, shoot symptoms of Ca deficiency are rarely reported. But added Ca often does improve turfgrass growth when these ions are present at extremely high levels in the root zone. Displacement of Ca from root exchange sites would be expected to reduce root cell wall formation and stability without Ca to react with pectin. Also, root cell plasma membranes may become less stable and leak solutes under these conditions. The net result would be a less viable root system that appears brown/black, thin, and spindly, especially near the root tips. It may be that reported cases of ion toxicities from high Na^+, Al^{+3}, Mn^{+2}, and H^+ are more accurately an induction of Ca deficiency in new root tip cells.

Calcium has been reported to influence disease susceptibility (Table 2.5) with low Ca levels enhancing *Phythium* blight and some other diseases. Acidic thatch (see Chapter 5), could potentially be sufficiently low in Ca to affect disease relationships even when soil pH is not excessively acidic.

Table 13.1. Soil, climate, or management factors associated with calcium (Ca) deficiency or toxicity/ excess levels.[1,10,11]

Deficiency Associated with[a]	Toxic/Excessive Levels Associated with
• Acidic pH (< pH 5.5) on low CEC soils soils under high leaching. High soluble levels of Al^{+3}, Mn^{+2}, and H^{+} may induce Ca^{+2} deficiency. • High Na^{+} levels, especially on low CEC soils that are neutral to acidic.	• High soil Ca content may induce Mg, K, Mn, or Fe deficiencies.

[a] Deficiencies associated with these situations are not likely to cause visual shoot deficiency symptoms but can result in root deterioration.

Calcium toxicities have not been reported for turfgrasses except as a foliar burn when a soluble salt form of Ca (i.e., $CaCl_2$, $CaNO_3$) has been applied at an excessive rate. However, this response is not due to Ca toxicity, but "salt" toxicity or fertilizer burn that can occur from any soluble salt applied at a sufficiently high rate on foliage. High soil Ca levels can suppress Mg and K uptake. This is most likely to be observed following the application of high rates of a Ca amendment (i.e., $CaCO_3$, $CaSO_4$) without sufficient Mg or K to maintain cation balance. Thus, on acid soils where the lime requirement is high, dolomitic limestone ($CaCO_3$ plus $MgCO_3$) is often recommended to maintain adequate Mg. On sodic soils receiving high $CaSO_4$ additions, Mg balance can be achieved by periodic use of Mg fertilizers such as $MgSO_4$, MgO, or $MgSO_4$ plus K_2SO_4 combinations. Dolomitic limestone applied in conjunction with an S source to convert the lime to sulfate forms is another means of applying considerable Mg without burn problems.

B. Soil and Environmental Relationships[1,3,10,11,13]

Calcium content of soils can vary from less than 0.5% by weight for leached sands to more than 25% in calcareous soils with most soils containing 0.7 to 1.5%. Total Ca content of 3.0% or more indicates that free $CaCO_3$ is likely to be present. Calcium is present in various native soil minerals (anorthite, calcite, dolomite, among others), on CEC sites, and from materials added as amendments such as $CaCO_3$ (free calcium carbonate), $CaMg(CO_3)_2$ (dolomite), and $CaSO_4$ (gypsum). In the soil solution, Ca^{+2} is present in equilibrium with Ca^{+2} on the CEC sites (exchangeable Ca^{+2}). In soils containing $CaCO_3$, $CaMg(CO_3)_2$, or $CaSO_4$, solution Ca^{+2} will also be increased by these chemicals. Soil factors that influence plant-available Ca are total quantity of Ca present, soil pH, CEC, clay type, and the presence of other cations (Table 13.1).

Total Quantity of Ca Present

In contrast to most nutrients, the total quantity of Ca present in a soil is related to plant-available Ca. All Ca on CEC sites is readily available for plants but since many of the Ca containing compounds have intermediate solubilities they also contribute appreciable Ca for plant use.

Soil Reaction (pH)

As a basic cation, Ca is more prevalent as pH increases, but under acidic conditions, Ca can be replaced by H and Al on the CEC sites. At excessive acidity (pH <5.0), high H activity can suppress plant Ca uptake as well as replace it on the soil CEC sites. Lime is applied on acid soils to raise pH (Chapter 5, Soil pH Concepts and Acidity Problems) and one of the benefits is to increase Ca saturation on the CEC and provide a pool of slowly available Ca as the lime dissolves.

Cation Exchange Capacity and Ca Saturation

Soils with high CEC potentially have more plant-available Ca but this depends on the percent Ca saturation on the CEC. As the percent Ca saturation increases, Ca becomes more readily available for plant use. Thus, a soil with low CEC but high Ca saturation may provide as much Ca as one with higher CEC but lower Ca saturation.

Tisdale et al.[11] indicate that many crops respond to added Ca if the Ca saturation is <25%. Thus, adequate Ca can be present for plant growth even at low Ca (e.g., 30–50% Ca) saturations. On turfgrasses, it is not so much the lack of total Ca that is a problem, instead it is the excess quantity of other cations such as Na (in salt-affected soils) or Al/Mn (acidic soils at pH <5.0) that results in these being present at higher than normal cation saturation percentages on the CEC sites. Irrigation water high in Mg can also reduce Ca saturation on the soil CEC. Seawater has a relatively high Mg content (about 1,300 mg L^{-1}) relative to Ca (about 400 mg L^{-1}) and can cause this condition when it is used for irrigation.

Sometimes the Ca saturation percentage of 65 to 80% on the soil CEC sites is presented as the "ideal." But as long as Na, Al, or Mn are not predominant ions on the soil CEC, the percent Ca can be appreciably lower without any anticipated Ca deficiencies.[13] However, when Na, Al, or Mn are present at levels to cause root toxicity, then additional Ca would be required to displace these ions regardless of the percent Ca saturation.

The ratios of Ca to Mg and K are sometimes used to evaluate Ca needs or more importantly, Mg and K requirements. Ratios are usually based on percent cation saturation values on the soil CEC but extractable cation values (such as Mehlich III extractable cations) can be used to generate ratios. Cation ratios vary substantially from the proposal "ideal" levels without nutritional problems but they still provide a very general guide to cation balance. Generally the ratios used are: $\leq$ 8.5:1 for Ca: Mg; $\leq$ 15:1 for Ca:K. Fertilizer and lime applications based on soil pH and soil extractable Mg and K will adjust the Ca: Mg and Ca: K ratios to an appropriate balance.

Other Factors

Clay type can influence Ca activity with 2:1 clays requiring higher Ca saturation on soil CEC than 1:1 clays to maintain the same level of Ca activity. This fact plus the greater tendency of 2:1 clays to exhibit deterioration of soil structure in response to Na than 1:1 clay types demonstrates that: (a) percent Ca saturation on soils with 2:1 clays should be maintained relatively high on Na affected sites; and (b) a lower Ca saturation percentage may be acceptable on 1:1 clays that have high Na levels.

In previous sections it was noted that high levels of K, Mg, Mn, Na, or Al may suppress Ca uptake to some extent. Also, Al and Na can decrease Ca content of root tissues and cause root injury, but without visual shoot symptoms of Ca deficiency. In contrast, NO_3^--N has been observed to enhance Ca uptake in many plants.

C. Practicum[1,6,10,11,13]

Soil nutrient status is normally assessed by extracting a soil sample with a chemical extractant that removes the plant-available portion of the nutrient. Then the extractable nutrient level is rated as low, medium, or high. Since Ca is the dominant cation on the CEC sites of most soils and is also widely found in precipitated salts ($CaCO_3$, $CaSO_4$) and minerals, extractable Ca levels are sufficient to meet turfgrass growth needs. Thus, Ca deficiency symptoms on shoot tissues have not been reported in field situations. This is in contrast to Mg and K which can often exhibit low soil extractable levels and may exhibit field deficiency symptoms. However, applications of Ca amendments are still necessary for specific problem situations.

Situations Requiring Ca

One common situation is acidic soil conditions where Ca as lime ($CaCO_3$) is applied to increase soil pH by Ca^{+2} replacing H^+ on CEC sites and the H^+ and Al^{+3} reacting with HCO_3^- and OH^- to form H_2O, $Al(OH)_3$, and CO_2 gas. The net result is to decrease H^+ concentration and increase Ca saturation on the CEC sites. The cation component (usually Ca^{+2}) of liming materials displaces H^+ on the CEC sites, but the anion component (CO_2^{-2}), which forms HCO_3^- and OH^- in water; OH–; or SiO_3^{-2} is responsible for neutralizing acidity by reacting with H^+ and Al^{+3}. On excessively acid soils (pH < 5.0) where Al^{+3}/Mn^{+2} toxicities can occur, liming results in Ca^{+2} displacing Al^{+3} and Mn^{+2} from CEC sites; and with the increase in pH, Al and Mn form less soluble compounds, thereby reducing their concentrations in soil solution. Calcium, also, replaces Al/Mn that may be on root cation exchange sites and contributing to root deterioration. The quantity of lime to apply in acid situations is determined by a lime requirement test. This topic is addressed in a more comprehensive manner in Chapter 5, Soil pH Concepts and Acidity Problems.

A second situation requiring a relatively soluble or active Ca amendment is when *high* Na^+ causes: (a) sodic or saline-sodic situations with deterioration of soil physical conditions. In this case, Ca^{+2} is required to displace Na^+ from the soil CEC for improved soil structure; or (b) Na^+ root toxicity, which sometimes occurs on sodic or saline sodic soils but can also occur in saline soils. Calcium is required to displace Na^+ from the root cells. This can occur on grasses but is often observed on other landscape plants before root deterioration is seen on turf plants. In these salt-affected sites, Ca needs depend on the quantity of Na^+ already present in the soil, quantity of Na^+ added by irrigation, soil CEC, and amount of Ca added by the irrigation water. Chapters 7 and 8 present an expanded discussion of salt-affected sites and their management as well as the book by Carrow and Duncan.[2]

A third situation where Ca addition may be necessary is when appreciable water is being applied to the turfgrass and the *water has a low EC* (electrical conductivity). Such low salt content water may be from snow melt irrigation sources or as continuous, heavy rainfall from a monsoon weather pattern. As salts are leached from the soil surface zone of a few millimeters thickness, Na is left on the CEC sites causing deterioration of structure and crusting. Application of Ca salts to the irrigation water or soil surface can prevent this problem.

Other Considerations

Sometimes Ca has been recommended for sites that do not exhibit any of the problem situations just discussed. These recommendations generally arise from: (a) use of a percent Ca saturation range as being "ideal," such as 60–85%, and the percentage is somewhat less for the soil on the site; (b) use of an "ideal" Ca:Mg or Ca:K ratio based on extractable levels of these cations or percent saturation levels on the CEC sites, where Ca is recommended to adjust the ratio; or (c) use of an "ideal" extractable Ca level that increases as CEC increases in contrast to a consistent acceptable extractable Ca range.

Traditionally a single extractable range for Ca has been used to assess Ca levels in the soil for turfgrass.[13] It is a very adequate procedure since turfgrasses require much less Ca than Ca sensitive plants (peanuts, celery, tomatoes) and Ca sensitive plants are normally used to establish the soil sufficiency ranges. The other methods noted in the prior paragraph for producing a Ca recommendation will generate much more frequent "requirements" for Ca when there is not a demonstrated response to Ca. Such recommendations result in Ca fertilization that is unnecessary, but more important, the unneeded Ca may induce Mg or K deficiencies in some situations. Thus, by undue attention to a cation seldom if ever deficient (unless associated with excess Al, Mn, or Na), nutrient deficiencies may be induced for cations (Mg, K) that could become deficient for turfgrasses.

The extractable Ca level most often used to determine Ca nutritional needs is: 200 to 400 ppm (400 to 800 lb A^{-1}) and 500 to 1,000 ppm are considered moderate for Mehlich I and 1M ammonium acetate at pH 7.0 extractants, respectively.[13] For Mehlich III extractant, 375 to 750 ppm (750 to 1,500 lb A^{-1}) is considered moderate with <375 ppm being low. Since low Ca levels are almost always associated with acidic (pH <4.5) sands of low CEC, application of lime to increase pH provides sufficient Ca for nutritional needs.

Ca Sources

When Ca is required, the choice of Ca source depends on: the particular problem, application equipment available (granular, fertigation, equipment to treat irrigation water), costs, and fertilizer availability. Often more than one Ca carrier may be incorporated in a treatment program for excessively acid soils, sodic soils, and where Na^+ ion root toxicities are present. In these situations, Ca materials with relatively high solubilities can aid in alleviating problems deeper in the root zone due to greater mobility. A general ranking of common Ca carriers based on solubility is shown in Table 13.2. (See also Table 17.8 in Chapter 17.)

Since the less soluble Ca sources are generally lower in cost and often more available, they are more commonly used. More soluble forms can be incorporated into a program to supply additional, high solubility Ca. The last three Ca carriers can be applied as granular or water soluble formulations. Gypsum is the most widely used Ca source in high Na situations.

Calcium does not lend itself to foliar application since it is the least mobile of the essential nutrients. If a true Ca deficiency was to be noted on shoot tissues based on visual symptoms, foliar Ca could be used. But, since the true need for Ca is almost always in root tissues, especially root tips, Ca must be moved within the soil to the roots. One situation where foliar Ca may potentially be beneficial would be where water very high in Na is consistently applied to the turf, such as seawater irrigation or seawater blends. In such cases some displacement of Ca in shoot tissues by Na would be possible.

II. MAGNESIUM

A. Plant Relationships[3,5,7,9,10,12]

MAGNESIUM UPTAKE is as the Mg^{+2} ion. As with Ca and other cations, Mg is attracted to exchange sites on the root cortex apoplasm. However, other cations (Ca^{+2}, K^+, Mn^{+2}) will easily displace Mg and, therefore decrease Mg uptake, which is believed to be passive. In contrast to

Table 13.2. Calcium carriers based on solubility (see also Table 17.8).

Ca Material	Solubility
$CaCO_3$ (lime) (coarse)	Low Solubility
$CaCO_3$ (fine particles)	
$CaSO_4$ (gypsum, coarse)	
$CaSO_4$ (fine)	
Phosphogypsum (PG) or	
Flue Gas Desulfurization	
Gypsum (FGDG)	
CaS_x (lime sulfur)	
$CaNO_3$	
$CaCl_2$	Highly Soluble

Ca, Mg is very mobile within the plant both upward (xylem) and downward (phloem) so foliar applications are effective.

Functions of Mg

Magnesium is the central atom in the chlorophyll molecule and 6% to 25% of total plant Mg can be for this function. For chlorophyll synthesis, Mg is also required for activation of two enzymes. Within chloroplasts, Mg enhances the activity of the enzyme RuBP carboxylase that allows addition of CO_2 to RuBP in photosynthesis. After sucrose synthesis, Mg is required for an enzyme necessary for sucrose loading of the phloem, which supplies roots with carbohydrates. Without phloem loading, sucrose is transformed to starch and accumulates within chloroplasts even when photosynthesis is reduced under Mg deficiency.

Magnesium serves to link ATP to the active sites of enzymes for maximum energy transfer. Enzymes with the MgCATP requirement are involved in energy transfer in many plant processes including photosynthesis.

During protein synthesis, Mg acts as a bridging agent to bring ribosome (complexes of RNA and protein that are the site for protein synthesis) units together and stabilize them. Considerable Mg is stored in cell vacuoles where it aids in turgor regulation and maintenance of cell anion to cation balance. Magnesium binds with cell wall pectate and assists in strengthening cell walls but to a much lesser degree than Ca.

Deficiencies and Excesses

Leaf tissue content of Mg is usually within the range of 0.15 to 0.50% (dry weight) with less than 0.15% considered deficient (Table 2.1). The deficiency limit may vary with grass species or cultivar. *Deficiency symptoms* start as a general loss of green color on older (lower) leaves. Since Mg is mobile in the plant, translocation from old to new leaves occurs under deficient conditions. Color may progress from pale green to cherry red with leaf margins exhibiting blotchy areas of red (Plate 1). Leaf veins remain green and some light yellow striping may occur between veins. Leaves will start to die.

Magnesium deficiency on turfgrasses is relatively common (Table 13.3). Situations where Mg deficiency is most likely to occur are: (a) acidic soil with deficiency potential increasing as

Table 13.3. Soil, climate, and management aspects associated with magnesium deficiency and toxicity/excess levels.[1,10–13]

Deficiency Associated with	Toxic/Excessive Levels Associated with
• acidic pH (pH <5.5) on low CEC soils subjected to leaching • high additions of Ca as lime, gypsum, or from irrigation source • high addition of Na from irrigation • soils naturally high in Na • high K fertilization • high leaching condition	• high Mg can induce K, Mn, or Ca deficiencies • seawater irrigation, since Mg is relatively high compared to Ca content, may induce K or Ca deficiencies.

acidity increases due to replacement of base cations by Al^{+3}, H^+, or Mn^{+2}; (b) acid, saline soils where acid cations and Na^+ displace Mg^{+2}; and (c) soils on which high rates of Ca have been applied. When high Ca rates are used, it is generally beneficial to use dolomitic lime (contains $MgCO_3$) or an Mg source such as $MgSO_4$ or MgO. As with Ca, irrigation water may contain Mg and should be considered a potential source. A water source containing 20 ppm or mg L^{-1} Mg would supply 1.25 lb Mg per 1,000 ft^2 (61 kg Mg ha^{-1}) per acre-foot of water. Common Mg levels in wastewater are <10 (low) to >35 (very high) mg L^{-1} with ratings referring to nutritional needs, especially the potential to apply too much Mg and cause problems associated with excessive Mg levels (Table 13.3).[2] High K fertilization may also contribute to Mg deficiency but usually only where very high K applications are made on sands.

Due to the onset of chlorosis, a deficiency of Mg in the field will be readily evident. However, Mg may not be recognized as the cause since other nutrients (N, Fe, Mn, S) and some environmental stresses also cause chlorosis. A foliar application of $MgSO_4$ in a test area at 0.10 lb Mg per 1,000 ft^2 (5 kg ha^{-1}) in 1 to 2 gal water (378 to 756 L) will provide a rapid indication of whether chlorosis was due to low levels of Mg, S, or both. Magnesium is more often deficient than S but a K_2SO_4 source could be applied to an adjacent area to resolve whether Mg or S provides the greening response.

If a true deficiency is not corrected, chlorosis will continue and photosynthesis will decline, but leaf sugars may actually increase. The sugar increase is due to reduced loading of sucrose into the phloem for translocation. The combined effect of reduced photosynthesis and limited sucrose translocation to growing sites is particularly detrimental to maintaining roots.

Toxicity of Mg is not a problem (Table 13.3). However, excessively high Mg levels can induce K or Ca deficiencies, especially on low CEC sands. Seawater normally contains about 100 to 105 meq L^{-1} of Mg and 18 to 22 meq L^{-1} Ca. So, areas receiving seawater by irrigation, flooding, spray, or other means may exhibit suppressed Ca and K uptake because of high Mg and Na in the water.

B. Soil and Environmental Relationships[1,3,11,13]

The total content of Mg can vary from less than 0.5% for sandy soils in humid regions to 5.0% in some fine-textured soils. Magnesium may exist as a constituent of primary minerals (biotite, dolomite, others); as precipitated $MgSO_4 \cdot 7H_2O$ (esponsite), $MgCO_3$, and $Na_2Mg(SO_4)_3 \cdot 4H_2O$ (bloedite); in secondary 2:1 clay minerals as part of their lattice structure; and as exchangeable Mg on soil colloid CEC sites. Magnesium in the soil solution and exchangeable Mg are the predominate plant-available sources but some slowly available Mg can come from other sources.

Factors that affect the level of plant-available Mg are soil pH, rainfall, soil CEC and Mg saturation, and levels of other cations (Table 13.3).

Soil Reaction (pH)

As with the other basic cations such as Ca and K, exchangeable Mg levels decline as pH decreases. With increasing acidity, H^+ and Al^{+3} become more predominant and displace the Mg^{+2} on CEC sites, enhancing the leaching of Mg and the potential for Mg deficiency.

Rainfall

Magnesium can be leached from soils by rainfall or intensive irrigation. Sandy soils with high percolation rates and low CEC are most susceptible to leaching of Mg. High irrigation rates to induce leaching of total salts or Na on salt-affected sites can result in Mg losses. However, irrigation with seawater can result in Mg accumulation on the soil CEC sites due to a high Mg to Ca content.

Cation Exchange Capacity and Mg Saturation

For turfgrasses, Mg saturation on the soil CEC sites of 10 to 20% is normal. For low CEC sands or soils (i.e., CEC less than 4 meq per 100 g), the extractable quantity of Mg should be at least 30 to 60 ppm (Mehlich I), 70 to 140 ppm (Mehlich III), or 80 to 140 ppm (1 M NH_4OAc, pH 7.0) with the extractable Mg a better indicator of Mg availability than percent CEC saturation.[13] For finer-textured soil with CEC greater than 4 meq per 100 g, extractable Mg should be approximately double those of sands.

Ratios of Mg to Ca and K are sometimes used to assess Mg needs in conjunction with extractable Mg and percent Mg saturation on CEC. Ratios are very general guidelines and can vary widely without any apparent Mg deficiencies. Typical guidelines for Mg ratios based on percent cation saturation on the CEC or extractable cation levels are: ≤ 8.5 for Ca:Mg; $\leq 5{:}1$ for Mg:K. When Mg or K fertilizers are applied based on extractable (i.e., sufficiency) levels of these cations, the Ca:Mg and Mg:K ratios usually adjust to within these guidelines.

Other Cations

High levels of other cations can induce Mg deficiencies since these can replace Mg on CEC sites and cause Mg leaching losses over time. The most common situations where this may occur are: (a) high Ca applications from lime, gypsum, or irrigation water; (b) high Na^+ application in irrigation water; (c) high Al^{+3} and H^+ under excessive acidity of pH <5.5; (d) frequent application of K^+ or NH_4^+ fertilizers, and (e) combinations of these factors.

C. Practicum[1,3,7,11–13]

When assessing soil Mg status, the most important aspect is extractable Mg levels. For sandy, low CEC soils typical extractable soil test levels (moderate range) were presented in the previous section on Cation Exchange Capacity and Mg Saturation. When Mg fertilizer is recommended, turfgrass managers should consider any Mg addition made through irrigation. For

Table 13.4. Magnesium (Mg) fertilizer sources (see Table 17.9 in Chapter 17).

Source	Formula	Approx. Percent Mg	Usual Application Form[a]
Dolomitic limestone	$CaCO_3 + MgCO_3$	8–20	S
Epsom salts	$MgSO_4 \cdot 7H_2O$	9.9;13S	F, S
Potassium magnesium sulfate	$K_2SO_4 \cdot 2MgSO_4$	11.2; 22S, 18K	S
Magnesium oxide	MgO	55	S
Magnesium carbonate (magnesite)	$MgCO_3$	29	S
Magnesium nitrate	$Mg(NO_3)_2 \cdot 6H_2O$	9.5; 10.9N	F, S
Chelates—natural or synthetic	–	2 to 9	S

[a] F = foliar applied; S = soil applied.

example, irrigation water obtained from limestone aquifers often contains appreciable Ca and Mg, as do many effluent sources. Imbalances in Ca:Mg or Mg:K can often be explained by looking at the water quality tests for the quantities and balances of Ca, Mg, and K.

Acidic, low CEC sands subjected to high rainfall or irrigation leaching can receive appreciable Mg from dolomitic lime applications (Table 13.4). Additional Mg from other sources may still be required to maintain adequate levels but the $MgCO_3$ in dolomitic lime acts as a slow-release Mg source. On sodic soils where S plus lime is used to generate gypsum, dolomitic lime can be used so that $MgSO_4$ is formed over time. The Mg can be effective in replacement of Na^+ on CEC sites and provide Mg for plant nutritional needs.

Granular applications of soluble salt forms of Mg (i.e., Epsom salts, potassium magnesium sulfates, and magnesium nitrate) are limited to 0.20 to 0.40 lb Mg per 1,000 ft^2 (9.8 to 19.5 kg Mg ha^{-1}) due to burn potential and these materials should be watered into the soil. Soluble Mg carriers can be applied at 0.05 to 0.10 lb Mg per 1,000 ft^2 in 3 to 5 gallons of water (2.5 to 5 kg Mg ha^{-1} in 1,130 to 1,890 L), for foliar treatment.

III. SULFUR

A. Plant Relationships[3–5,8–10,12]

SULFUR IS TAKEN UP BY TURFGRASSES as the SO_4^{-2} (sulfate anion) by an active process involving a SO_4^{-2} transporter to carry the ion across the plasma membrane and into the cytoplasm. There, most SO_4^{-2} is further transported across cell membranes into the xylem. Some SO_4^{-2} can be reduced in the roots during formation of cysteine, an amino acid. Sulfur is readily mobile in the xylem as SO_4^{-2} for movement to shoot tissues; but, once it is reduced into other forms, it is relatively immobile. Some S can be remobilized to the SO_4^- form by oxidation but this is limited.

Functions of S

Most plant SO_4 is assimilated into cysteine in roots and leaves with SO_4 reduction rates in chloroplasts of leaves much higher than in roots. Cysteine is the first stable product of assimilation and is a precursor for synthesis of all other compounds containing reduced S. In cysteine, S resides in the -SH group (*sulfhydryl group*). Two cysteine molecules can be bound by formation of a -C-S-S-C- *disulfide bond* to form cystine, another amino acid. Methionine, a third amino acid containing S is produced from cysteine. These three S-containing amino acids are essential building blocks for many proteins.

The various types of sulfhydryl and disulfide bonds affect protein structure and function, especially in enzyme proteins. During dehydration of tissues, disulfide bond formation increases at the expense of -SH groups. This leads to protein aggregation and denaturation. Plants resistant to protein denaturation during cold, heat, and drought stresses have mechanisms to protect -SH groups.

Cysteine is a precursor for other metabolites such as coenzymes (i.e., coenzyme A) and the vitamins thiamine (B_1) and biotin. In a second pathway where SO_4^{-2} is not reduced, sulfate esters instead of cysteine are formed. Sulfate esters are used as precursors for other plant compounds (i.e., sulfolipids). Sulfolipids are important in thylakoid membranes of chloroplasts.

Cysteine and glutamate combine in a third pathway to form glutathione (GSH) which is needed for phytochelatin synthesis. Phytochelatin can bind heavy metal cations and detoxify them, especially Cd, but also Zn and Cu.

GSH is also an *antioxidant. Oxygen radicals* are toxic oxygen species that can damage plant tissues. In removing free radicals, hydrogen peroxide (H_2O_2) is produced but it is also destructive, particularly in the chloroplasts. GSH is involved in transport of electrons to H_2O_2 to degrade it into water. This reaction is very important during stress periods when oxygen radicals are most likely to form.

Another very important role of S is involvement in electron transfer. During biosynthesis of many important plant compounds, electrons from reduced electron carriers (NADH, ferredoxin, etc.) must be transferred to specific metabolites. Ferredoxin requires S and is important in nitrite and sulfate reduction cycles.

Sulfur is not a constituent of chlorophyll but is required for chlorophyll stabilization, which occurs by it binding to proteins in the chloroplast membranes. Under deficient S, protein synthesis decreases and stable chlorophyll-protein binding is impaired. As a result, chlorophyll degrades and chlorosis is exhibited.

Deficiencies and Excesses

Tissue content of S in turfgrasses generally ranges from 0.15 to 0.50% by dry weight with >0.20% often considered sufficient (Table 2.1).[8] Grasses have a lower S requirement than many other plants.

Visual deficiency symptoms associated with low S levels include a reduced shoot growth rate. This stage can occur without appreciable yellowing. As the deficiency is prolonged, yellowing of new leaves becomes apparent with the leaf tip and margins showing symptoms first. Once SO_4^{-2} is reduced in the plant, S is not very mobile from older to younger leaves. Thus, with low soil SO_4, the new leaves exhibit deficiencies earlier than older ones but eventually older leaves can show chlorosis in the interveinal areas as S is slowly translocated out of these tissues (Plate 1). These symptoms can easily be confused with those produced by N, K, and Fe deficiencies and some environmental stresses that cause chlorosis (Plate 16). Turfgrasses grown under high N are most susceptible to S deficiency (Table 13.5).

By the time chlorosis has been observed, chlorophyll degradation will have caused reduced photosynthesis. Prior to this event, however, injury from S deficiency is most likely to be a combination of the following:

a. Greater susceptibility to wear damage from reduced growth.
b. Enhanced injury from any environmental stresses or other stresses that may create oxygen radicals. Injury would be from the stress plus any oxygen radicals that are not dissipated by the S-containing compound GSH.
c. Possible greater disease infection from *Fusarium* patch or take-all patch (Table 2.5). Application of S has been reported to suppress these pathogens but the pH change when S is added may also be involved.

Direct toxicity from S by excessive uptake in the plant is not a problem, probably because plants can remove excessive S as H_2S gas from leaves. But, granular, flowable, or liquid materials applied at rates greater than 2 to 5 lb product per 1,000 ft^2 (98 to 245 kg ha^{-1}) may cause leaf burn depending on the carrier and the S compound. Burn potential varies with S source and environmental conditions. Elemental S does not appear to cause leaf burn and any injury comes from creating an excessively acid zone at the surface over a period of weeks. Flowable or liquid S fertilizers do have potential to burn.

High S levels in the soil may become a problem if reducing conditions occur, leading to: (a) production of H_2S, which can be phytotoxic; and (b) formation of iron and magnesium sulfides that create the black coloration in black layer. Black coloration is likely due to FeS and MnS_2. This condition further enhances low soil O_2 conditions (see Chapter 16, Unique Soil Problems). Also, high rates of elemental S applied to a well aerated soil may cause lower crown or root damage from creation of an excessively acid layer in the thatch or at the soil surface. In the case of soils, injury may result from Al or Mn toxicities as these compounds become more soluble under acidic conditions created by the S.

Sulfur application has been reported to reduce *Poa annua* encroachment into creeping bentgrass. This occurrence was in a region where S deficiencies were relatively common and may reflect a preferential response for S by the bentgrasses. Also, bentgrass may tolerate greater acidity than annual bluegrass.

B. Soil and Environmental Relationships[1,2,4,11,13]

Sulfur is widely found in nature and is present in minerals such as $CaSO_4 \bullet 2H_2O$ (gypsum), $MgSO_4 \bullet 7H_2O$ (epsomite), $Na_2SO_4 \bullet 10H_2O$ (mirabilite), FeS_2 (pyrite), elemental deposits of S, and many other minerals. In ocean water, SO_4^{-2} content is approximately 2,700 mg L^{-1}. Within soils, organic and inorganic forms occur (Figure 13.1). In arid, semiarid, or other calcareous soil situations there may be sulfate minerals present that provide most of the plant-available SO_4^{-2}. However, in noncalcareous soils, most of the plant-available S comes from the organic S pool, unless SO_4^{-2} additions are made. In many turfgrass situations, S-containing compounds are added and these contribute to plant-available S. Examples would include sulfur coated urea (SCU) fertilizers; SO_4 forms of K, Mg, and Ca compounds; SO_4^{-2} in irrigation water or rainfall; and S contained in composts.

Figure 13.1 is a simplified version of the *S cycle* illustrating the most important interactions. Various conditions influence the activities of different organic and inorganic S forms to make them more (or less) available for turfgrass use.

Sulfate (SO_4) Forms

Solution or soluble SO_4 is especially important because this is the form that plants use for uptake. Generally, 3 to 5 mg L^{-1} of SO_4 in soil solution is adequate for turfgrass growth. The presence of K, Ca, or Mg sulfate compounds, occurring naturally or added, markedly increases

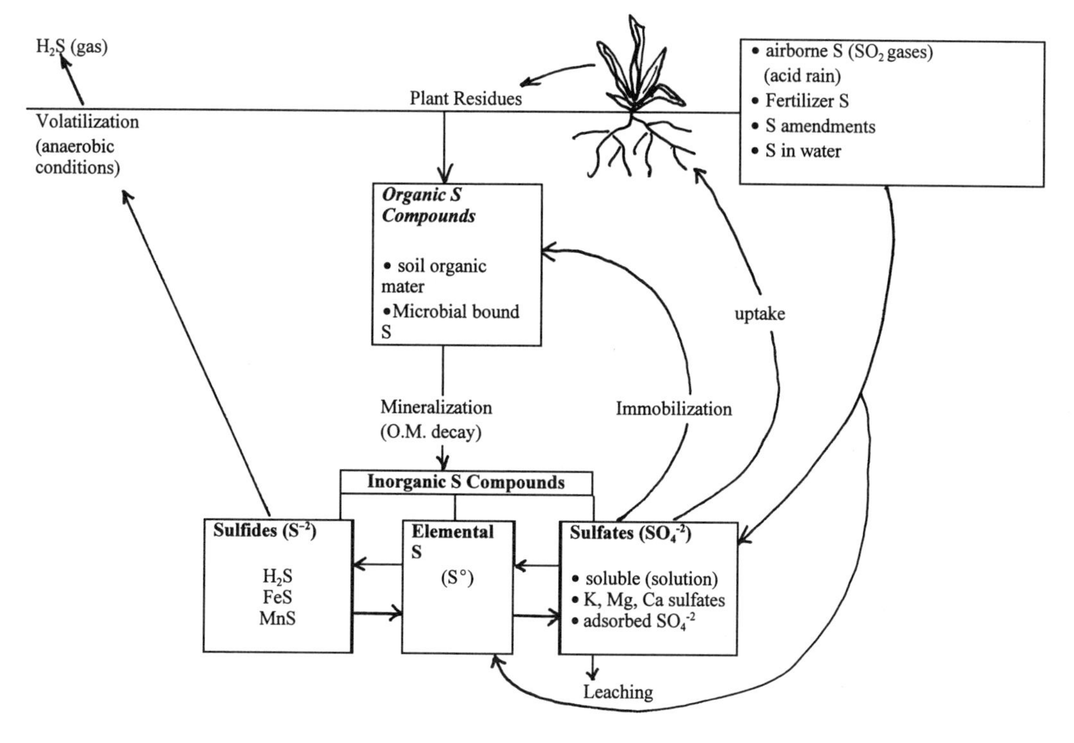

Figure 13.1. The sulfur cycle illustrating the major transformations.

soluble SO_4. Also, soil solution SO_4 may come from: (a) atmospheric deposition; (b) microbial mineralization of organic matter converting reduced S organic compounds into the oxidized form of SO_4; (c) release from various soil minerals in addition to the K, Ca, and Mg sulfates previously noted; and (d) irrigation water, especially wastewater sources. Soluble SO_4^{-2} (i.e., sulfate) can be easily leached, especially on sandy soils (Table 13.5). High quantities of monovalent cations (K^+, Na^+) cause greater leaching than Ca^{+2} or Mg^{+2} since the K^+ and Na^+ sulfates are more soluble.

Another form of sulfate is *adsorbed* SO_4^{-2} that is particularly important on Al and Fe oxide soils. These soils occur in high rainfall regions and are highly weathered. Adsorbed SO_4^{-2} is negligible above pH 6.5 but can be a significant source of readily available S for plants at pH <6.5.

Reduced Inorganic S Forms

Sulfide (S^{-2}) is a reduced form of S that can occur in anaerobic waterlogged soils by organic matter decay. It can react with H^+, Fe^{+2}, or Mn^{+2} (reduced forms) to form H_2S (hydrogen sulfide), FeS (iron sulfide), FeS_2 (iron pyrite), MnS and MnS_2 (manganese sulfides). In turfgrass situations, the black coloration of *black layer* (Chapter 16) is due to reduced forms of FeS and MnS, while a rotten egg odor comes from H_2S. On seacoast marsh areas where a ready source of decaying organic matter is present along with ample SO_4 from the seawater, Fe sulfides can accumulate. If these sites are drained and the FeS_2 starts to oxidize, H_2SO_4

Table 13.5. Soil, climate and management aspects associated with sulfur deficiency and toxicity/excess levels.[1,10,11,13]

Deficiency Associated with	Toxicity/Excessive Levels Associated with
• sandy soils subjected to leaching • high rainfall and leaching conditions • areas not receiving atmospheric deposition of S • associated with high N use and clippings are removed • low soil organic matter content, especially sandy, leached soils with <1.5% o.m. by weight	• high foliar rates of some sources can cause foliar burn • high granular rates of some sources can cause fertilizer burn • excessive acidity (pH <4.8) may occur in the surface zone when high element S rates are applied to a soil without free $CaCO_3$ and cause root/lower crown injury • excess S can contribute to black layer and anaerobic conditions

forms and creates an excessively acid (pH <3.5) condition. These *acid sulfate soils* are discussed in Chapter 5.

Elemental S (S°) is another reduced form of S in the inorganic S pool. The most common source of elemental S is by addition as an amendment but it can arise by oxidation of the sulfides. Elemental S may be added in turfgrass management: (a) as a pH reduction agent; (b) along with $CaCO_3$ to form gypsum ($CaSO_4 \cdot 2H_2O$) when treating sodic soils; (c) as a S-fertilizer; and (d) in a sulfurous generator to acidify irrigation water. In this latter use, the S is chemically transformed to SO_3 by burning (an oxidation process). Therefore, the S is added in the SO_3 form. Upon the addition of water (H_2O) to SO_3, sulfuric acid (H_2SO_4) is formed.

Within the inorganic S pool, shifts between sulfide (S^{-2}), sulfur (S°), and sulfate (SO_4^{-2}) forms occur by oxidation and reduction reactions (Figure 13.1). Under anaerobic conditions (i.e., low soil O_2) bacteria of the *Desulfovibrio* and *Desulfotomaculum* genera reduce S into sulfide forms, which rapidly react with H, Fe, and Mn to form H_2S (gas), FeS, and MnS_2. These reactions and their role in black layer formation are discussed in Chapter 16.

Oxidation of reduced forms of S into SO_4 can occur by chemical means but at a slow rate. Biochemical transformation is more prevalent and rapid. Three microorganism populations are involved in S oxidation. The first are chemoautotrophic bacteria of the genera *Thiobacillus* that use energy released by S oxidation for fixation of CO_2. The general reaction is:

$$CO_2 + S^\circ + 1/2\,O_2 + 2H_2O \rightarrow \underset{\substack{\textit{microbial}\\ \textit{organic matter}}}{\left[CH_2O\right]} + SO_4^{-2} + 2H^+$$

Various *Thiobacillus* species may use other reduced S forms besides S°, such as thiosulfates ($S_2O_3^{-2}$). These are considered the most important S-oxidizing microorganisms. Many heterotrophic micrganisms can also oxidize S° (i.e., elemental S) especially in the rhizosphere. Also, green bacteria *(Chlorobium)* and purple bacteria *(Chromatium)* can use H_2S for photosynthetic C fixation as photoautotrophs in anaerobic muds or water exposed to light.

As S° is oxidized by *Thiobacillus,* H^+ ions are produced that can acidify the soil. Thus, high elemental S and some additions (acid rain, S amendments, etc.) can decrease soil pH. However, SO_4 alone, such as in irrigation water or fertilizers, does not acidify soil except as H_2SO_4, where H^+ is contributed from H_2SO_4, or from $(NH_4)_2SO_4$, where H^+ ions result from oxidation of NH_4^+ in the $(NH_4)_2SO_4$. The presence of free $CaCO_3$ (Chapter 6) will prevent a pH decline.

Rate of S° (elemental S) oxidation is influenced by soil and climatic conditions. Turfgrass managers that are adding S° should consider the influence of these factors on rate of conversion into the SO_4 form. For example, S° added to the soil would not be converted to SO_4 at a rapid rate at soil temperatures <55°F (13°C). The optimum range for most S°-oxidizing organisms is 75 to 103°F (25 to 40°C).

Since most S°-oxidizing microorganisms are aerobic, a well-aerated, moist soil is ideal. At low O_2 conditions, such as waterlogging or a compacted soil, S° oxidation rapidly declines. Also, oxidation rates are decreased at soil moisture levels somewhat drier than field capacity. Other soil properties, including pH, have only minor influence on S° oxidation rates. High soil levels of NO_3 and Cl anions are reported to decrease *Thiobacilli* activity.

Organic S Compounds

Sulfur present in soil organic matter is the major source of plant-available S in noncalcareous soils and can represent >90% of the total S pool in these soils. Similar to N, there is a close relationship with the organic C in soil organic matter with many topsoils exhibiting a C/N/S ratio of about 100:7.7:1.

Conversion of organic S into inorganic SO_4 as soil microorganisms break down the organic matter is called *mineralization*. Factors influencing S mineralization are similar to those affecting N mineralization, such as:

- Between 50 to 104°F (10 to 40°C) mineralization of S increases with increasing temperature. Below 50°F (10°C) and above 140°F (40°C) mineralization declines.
- Gradual changes in soil moisture between field capacity to about 60% field capacity have little effect on S mineralization. Excessively wet or dry soil inhibits mineralization.
- Nature of the organic matter is important. Organic residues containing >0.15% S usually result in SO_4 release by mineralization as do residues with C/S ratios of <200/1. However, at <0.15% S or C/S ratios of >200/1, *immobilization* of inorganic SO_4 into organic S is likely. Since microorganisms require S for their metabolic activities, low S content or high C/S ratios result in microbial uptake of any soluble SO_4 into microbial cells and eventually into soil organic matter.
- Often an increase in mineralization occurs with a pH increase, but the opposite effect has been observed. Mineralization of S should not be severely limited at pH values suitable for turfgrass growth.

C. Practicum[1,2,4,8,11–13]

Sulfur deficiencies are most prevalent on sandy soils subjected to frequent leaching and in conjunction with low inherent soil O.M (such as tropical, semitropical climates), high N use, and clipping removal (Table 13.5). If these sites do not receive atmospheric deposition of S, high rainfall, deficiencies can be common. Near some industries annual deposition may be as high as 3.4 lb S per 1,000 ft^2 (168 kg S ha^{-1}) but normal rates are <0.30 lb S per 1,000 ft^2.

Grasses are efficient in uptake of SO_4. Also, turfgrass sites often receive S additions as a component of: (a) N-fertilizers like SCU, $(NH_4)_2SO_4$; (b) K-fertilization as K_2SO_4, potassium magnesium sulfate; (c) P-fertilization in ordinary superphosphate which is 0-20-0 (12% S); (d) $CaSO_4$ added to alleviate sodic soils; (e) S plus $CaCO_3$ to create gypsum in sodic soil remediation; (f) Mg fertilizers like $MgSO_4$ and micronutrients applied as sulfate forms; (g) use of S to reduce pH of alkaline, noncalcareous soils; and (h) in irrigation water that has been acidified or is from a wastewater or seawater source. Thus, S deficiencies are observed less often on turfgrasses than would be expected. As clean air practices are used, less SO_2 deposition may occur and S deficiencies may increase. Routine removal of clippings could also deplete SO_4^{-2} levels in some soils.

When assessing a site for S deficiency, extractable SO_4 may be determined by water extraction, salt solutions, weak acids and others. For the extractants NH_4OAc (pH 7.0) and Mehlich III, moderate ranges often used are 30 to 60 and 15 to 40 ppm SO_4, respectively. However, there has not been agreement on the best extractant to determine plant available SO_4. The extractants $Ca(H_2PO_4)$ or $NaHCO_3$ have been the most widely used for measuring plant-available S. In semi- and/or arid regions, soil tests seem to be more reliable than humid areas. In humid areas, SO_4^{-2} can easily leach over time, whether as soil solution SO_4 or precipitated SO_4^{-2} salts. Thus, most potentially plant-available S resides in the organic S pool which is more difficult to determine and depends on mineralization to be transformed into the inorganic form of SO_4.

Probably the most reliable method to determine a potential S deficiency is a combination of tissue testing (Table 2.1) and a trial application of a SO_4 containing fertilizer (Table 13.6). Since S deficiency can result in chlorosis, the use of K_2SO_4 as a foliar or granular treatment (or $CaSO_4$ as a granular) for a trial area is preferred over a Mg or N carrier containing SO_4 to avoid confusion over possible chlorosis from potential lack of Mg or N. A foliar application of 0.05 lb S per 1,000 ft^2 as K_2SO_4 in 3 to 5 gallons of water should provide a greening response within 1 to 3 days if S is deficient. This is equivalent to 2.4 kg S ha^{-1} or 0.28 lb of K_2SO_4 (18% S grade) per 1,000 ft^2. For a higher rate with granular materials, 2 to 4 lb per 1,000 ft^2 (98 to 196 kg K_2SO_4 ha^{-1}) of K_2SO_4 or $MgSO_4$ can be applied with ample water to prevent fertilizer burn (Table 13.6). Or, 10 to 40 lb $CaSO_4$ per 1,000 ft^2 (488 to 1952 kg $CaSO_4$ kg^{-1}) provides a higher rate and a more slow-release pattern of SO_4 release.

When S is applied as a nutrient to prevent S deficiency, 0.50 to 2.0 lb S per 1,000 ft^2 per year (24 to 98 kg S ha^{-1}) is usually sufficient. Sulfate (SO_4) fertilizers will provide S in the form turfgrasses can immediately use, while sulfide or elemental S forms require time for microbial oxidation to occur. On sites where sandy soils and high rainfall cause leaching of solution SO_4^{-2}, the use of $CaSO_4$ or elemental S as part of the S fertilizer provides moderately slow-release of S and helps protect against leaching.

Research in the Northwest (U.S.) indicated that 3 to 4 lb elemental S per 1,000 ft^2 per year (150 to 200 kg ha^{-1}) would reduce *Poa annua.*[12] These results have often not been observed in other locations possibly due to different *Poa annua* ecotypes, a positive bentgrass response to S as a nutrient since S deficiency is fairly common in the Northwest, or a pH reduction suppressing P availability under low P conditions where annual bluegrass requires higher P than bentgrass. The latter response illustrates that whenever elemental S is added to a turfgrass site as a fertilizer or for some other reason (pH reduction, amending sodic soils, etc.), the surface 1.0 inch (2.5 cm) of soil or thatch should be monitored for any major pH reduction (Chapter 6). At annual S rates above 2 lb per 1,000 ft^2 (98 kg S ha^{-1}) on sandy soils without free $CaCO_3$, the potential for creating an excessively acid layer at the surface is high, given sufficient time. Monitoring pH in the surface inch of soil or thatch should be done at least annually.

Sulfur application at 0.5 to 2.0 lb S per 1,000 ft^2 per year (24 to 98 kg S ha^{-1}) is reported to suppress take-all patch and *Fusarium* patch on creeping bentgrass (Table 2.5). Also, summer patch and spring-dead spot are less prevalent at lower pH (Table 2.5). Suppression of these diseases is probably a combination of S affecting the pathogen or more likely the resulting acidic conditions.

Table 13.6. Common S fertilizer sources (see Table 17.10 in Chapter 17).

Source	Formula	Approx. Percent S	Usual Application Form
Ammonium sulfate	$(NH_4)_2 SO_4$	24, 21N	Granular
Elemental S			
Wettable S	S	90–100	Granular[a]
Flowable S	S	52–70	Suspension[a]
Flowers of S	S	90–100	Granular[a]
Gypsum Suspension[a]	$CaSO_4 \cdot 2H_2O$	17, 22 Ca	Granular[a]
Magnesium sulfate (Epsom salt)	$MgSO_4 \cdot 7H_2O$	14, 10 Mg	Granular Liquid
Polysulfides			
Ammonium	NH_4Sx	45, 20N	Liquid
Potassium	KSx	23, $22K_2O$	Liquid
Potassium magnesium sulfate	$K_2SO_4 \cdot 2\ MgSO_4$	22, $22K_2O$, 11 Mg	Granular
Potassium sulfate	K_2SO_4	18, $50K_2O$	Granular Liquid
Sulfuric acid	H_2SO_4	20–33	Liquid in irrigation water
Thiosulfates			
Ammonium	$(NH_4)_2S_2O_3$+H_2O	26, 12N	Liquid
Potassium	$K_2S_2O_3$	17, $25K_2O$	Liquid
Urea-Sulfuric acid	$CO(NH_2)_2 \cdot H_2SO_4$	9–18, 10–28 N	Liquid in irrigation water

[a] Since these require microbial oxidation or are less soluble sulfates, these S fertilizers exhibit slow-release properties.

Beyond the nutritional uses of S discussed in this chapter, S is used for other purposes. These are presented in Chapter 6 (pH reduction), Chapters 7 and 8 (salt-affected sites), and Chapter 16 (waterlogged/anaerobic conditions).

IV. SELECTED REFERENCES

1. Brady, N.C. 1990. *The Nature and Properties of Soils*. New York: Macmillan Publishing Co.
2. Carrow, R.N. and R.R. Duncan. 1998. *Salt-Affected Turfgrass Sites: Assessment and Management*. Chelsea, MI: Ann Arbor Press.
3. Handreck, K.A. and N.D. Black. 1994. *Growing Media for Ornamental Plants and Turf*. Randwick, NSW, Australia: University of NSW Press.
4. Harivandi, A. 1988. Sulfur in action: Lowering soil pH. *Golf Course Management* 56(8):38–48, 89–91.
5. Hopkins, W.G. 1999. *Introduction to Plant Physiology*. 2nd ed. New York: John Wiley & Sons, Inc.
6. Hull, R.J. 1998. Calcium usage by turfgrasses; the nutrient forgotten by turf managers. *Turfgrass Trends* 6(10):6–12.
7. Hull, R.J. 1998. Magnesium usage by turfgrasses. *Turfgrass Trends* 7(8):7–14.
8. Hull, R.J. 1998. Sulfur usage by turfgrasses. *Turfgrass Trends* 7(2):1–9.
9. Marschner, H. 1995. *Mineral Nutrition of Higher Plants*. New York: Academic Press.

10. McCarty, L.B., J.B. Sartain, G.H. Snyder, and J.L Cisar. 1993. *Plant Nutrition, Fertilizers and Fertilizer Programs for Florida Golf Courses.* University of Florida Bulletin 282. University of Florida, Gainesville.
11. Tisdale, S.L., W.L. Nelson, J.D. Beaton, and J.L. Havlin. 1993. *Soil Fertility and Fertilizers.* New York: Macmillan Publishing Co.
12. Turner, T.R. and N.W. Hummel, Jr. 1992. Nutritional requirements and fertilization. In D.V. Waddington, R.N. Carrow, and R.C. Shearman, Eds. *Turfgrass Monograph No. 32.* Madison, WI: Amer. Soc. Agron.
13. Westerman, R.L., J.V. Baird, N.W. Christensen, P.E. Fixen, and D.A. Whitney. 1990. *Soil Testing and Plant Analysis. SSSA Book Series 3.* Madison, WI: Soil Sci. Soc. of Amer.

Chapter 14

Micronutrients and Other Elements

MICRONUTRIENTS REQUIRED FOR TURFGRASS GROWTH AND DEVELOPMENT are Fe, Mn, Zn, Cu, Mo, B, Cl, and Ni.[2,4,6,7,10,11] While all are essential nutrients, *deficiencies* of most are very rarely observed (Zn, Cu, Mo, B) or never reported on turfgrasses (Cl, Ni) under field situations. Iron (Fe) deficiencies are relatively common, while Mn deficiencies are less often observed but still not unusual. *Toxicities* from excessive levels have been reported for B, Mn, Fe, and Cl (as a salt) with certain soils and climates. Toxicities of other micronutrients (Zn, Cu, Mo, Ni) can occur but are usually confined to localized areas contaminated by heavy metals from added soil amendments, airborne deposits from nearby industries, or overapplication of micronutrient containing fertilizers.

Some *nonessential elements* are commonly found in turfgrass culture and may influence growth under certain conditions. Sodium (Na) as a salt ion is the most prevalent. Another receiving some attention in recent years is silicon (Si). These elements are discussed later in the chapter.

Plant nutrition aspects of each micronutrient and nonessential element (Na, Si) that are presented include: forms taken up by plants; role of each nutrient or element in plant metabolism; and plant deficiency and toxicity symptoms. Soil fertility facets of interest include: soil conditions affecting deficiencies or toxicities; and management of soil conditions to reduce deficiencies or toxicities. In this chapter, the emphasis is on turfgrass situations. For a more basic overview, readers are directed to Glendinning,[2] Mortvedt,[6] Peverill et al.,[7] and Tisdale et al.[10] for soil and environmental factors affecting micronutrient availability in soils and Marschner[4] or Hopkins[3] for plant aspects.

I. IRON

A. Plant Relationships

PLANTS CAN TAKE UP Fe^{+2} and Fe^{+3} forms but the ionic concentration of these in the soil solution is normally very low. However, several natural occurring plant *organic chelates* complex with Fe to increase its availability. Chelates are soluble organic compounds (citric and oxalic acids are examples) that bond with Fe, Zn, Cu, and Mn (as well as Ca, Mg), but the bound metal is available for root uptake. These compounds arise from microbial activity and root exudates, and occur naturally in soil organic matter.

Under Fe-deficient conditions, grasses synthesize *phytosiderophores* such as mugineic acid that can form very stable complexes with Fe^{+3}.[4,6,12] Phytosiderophores are released into the microrhizosphere adjacent to roots where they complex with Fe^{+3}. Uptake by the root includes the phytosiderophore plus Fe^{+3} by active transport across the plasma membrane of root cells and into the cytoplasm. Phytosiderophores also complex with Zn, Cu, and Mn but they are not actively transported into root cells by the transport system used for Fe. This means of acquiring Fe under Fe-deficient conditions is called Strategy II and is found in grasses.[4] Once inside the root, regardless of the means of uptake, Fe transport in the xylem is as Fe bound with or associated with other compounds.

Iron is required for biosynthesis of chlorophyll pigment but also influences chloroplast size and function. Thylakoid membranes, which contain the chlorophyll pigment and are the site of light-dependent photosynthesis reactions, require considerable Fe for structural and functional integrity. Chloroplast protein content depends on Fe for biosynthesis and low Fe affects chloroplast protein content much more than total plant protein. Additionally, Fe is necessary for activity of ferrodoxin, an important electron transfer agent for photosynthesis, and several other plant processes. Cytochromes are also electron transfer compounds that are heme proteins with Fe as part of their structure. Cytochromes are components of chloroplast redox systems along with ferrodoxin, a nonheme protein coordinated with S.

Iron is a constituent of other heme and nonheme proteins involved in plant processes besides photosynthesis. Heme enzymes include catalase and peroxidases, both involved in detoxification of H_2O_2. Peroxidase also plays a role in cell wall lignin formation. Aconitase is a nonheme Fe-S protein that is a catalyst in the citric acid cycle (tricarboxylic acid cycle) of respiration.

Iron is associated with other enzymes as a component of the redox reactions for electron transfer or as a bridging agent for the enzyme and substrate. One class of enzymes is lipoxygenases that are involved in membrane stability. Another Fe-containing enzyme is associated with biosynthesis of ethylene.

Visual deficiency symptoms for Fe occur first on younger leaves, due to immobility of Fe in the plant, as interveinal yellowing. Continued deficiency will result in leaves turning pale yellow to white; exhibiting a thin, spindly growth; and older leaves exhibiting chlorosis (Plates 17 and 18). The turfgrass area often appears mottled with areas showing symptoms and others without symptoms. In contrast, N deficiency appears initially on older leaves and is more uniform over a turfgrass stand.

Tissue concentrations of Fe are usually within 100 to 500 ppm. The critical deficiency content varies with bentgrasses <100 ppm and bermudagrasses <50 ppm.[4,5] Plants can store Fe in plastids as phytoferritin. Correlations of leaf Fe content (i.e., total Fe) is not always well correlated to chlorophyll content, especially on calcareous soils with high P. Under these conditions, some Fe may precipitate within the leaf apoplasm and be nonactive. Iron extracted from leaf tissues by dilute acids or chelating agents has been termed "active" iron[4,12] and is often better correlated with chlorophyll content. However, the source of active iron is not well defined.

As Fe becomes limiting in field situations, chlorosis appears and photosynthesis rapidly declines because of the many functional roles of Fe that influence photosynthesis reactions and constituents. Iron deficiency is most prevalent for turfgrasses that are Fe sensitive and grown on calcareous, high P soils in arid and semiarid regions (Table 14.1). Warm-season grasses can exhibit temporary Fe chlorosis during the spring green-up period, especially on cold, wet soils. Cool-season turfgrasses that develop thatch may demonstrate Fe chlorosis in the summer as roots deteriorate. Irrigation water high in HCO_3^- can induce Fe chlorosis, particularly on calcareous soils (Plate 19).

Actual direct toxic effects of Fe on turfgrasses can occur with excessive foliar Fe application (Table 14.1) (Plate 20).[12] High Fe application may also induce Mn deficiency. Under acidic (pH <4.8) conditions with poor aeration, soluble Fe may contribute to root injury, but, more often, it results in formation of reduced compounds that contribute to black layer and a further reduction in aeration (see Chapter 16).

Table 14.1. Soil, climate, or management conditions associated with iron (Fe) deficiency and toxicity/excess levels.

Deficiency Associated with	Toxic/Excessive Levels Associated with
• Cultivars that are susceptible to Fe deficiency. • Deficiencies are most likely at pH >7.0. • Under poor rooting or root viability.[a] • Presence of excess thatch. • Cold, wet soils in the spring, especially on warm-season species. • Presence of high P, especially at high pH. • On high pH calcareous soils in arid regions. • With irrigation water high in HCO_3^-, Ca, Mn, Zn, P, or Cu. • Low organic matter soils. • Heavy metals (Cu, Zn, Mn) from some sewage sludges.	• High foliar Fe can blacken leaves and, if sufficiently excessive, cause tissue injury. • Grasses (centipedegrass) sensitive to foliar Fe. • High Fe can induce Mn deficiency. • Acidic, poorly drained soils can produce toxic levels of soluble Fe. • Poorly drained or anaerobic soil conditions can favor soluble Fe (reduced) that reacts with S to increase black layer. This is not a toxicity or excess so much as a physical problem.

[a] Poor rooting from pest or soil stresses.

Considerable foliar Fe is applied to high quality turfgrass areas that are not Fe deficient but still exhibit a greening response.[12] In other cases, Fe as a foliar spray may be used to reduce herbicide or plant growth regulator induced chlorosis. Also, foliar Fe in conjunction with cytokinin has been used to alleviate chlorosis from various stresses and prolong greening of warm-season grasses in the fall.

B. Soil and Environmental Relationships

Total Fe concentration in soils can vary from <1% to more than 50% by weight but comprises an average of 5% of the earth's crust. Most of the Fe is in very insoluble forms such as oxides, hydroxides, clay minerals, and other primary or secondary minerals. Soil solution Fe is primarily as $Fe(OH)_2^+$ or Fe^{+3} for aerobic conditions in very low concentrations. Under anaerobic conditions, Fe^{+3} is reduced to the more soluble Fe^{+2} form (see Chapter 16, Waterlogged Soils, section). Plant-available Fe can be found in natural organic chelates. Several soil factors influence Fe availability.

Soil Reaction (pH)

Both Fe^{3+} and Fe^{2+} forms are more available under acidic conditions. As pH increases, concentrations of both forms in the soil solution decrease dramatically; therefore, Fe deficiencies are more prevalent in high pH soils. At pH >6.0 inorganic Fe compounds cannot maintain sufficient soluble Fe in solution to meet plant needs. Thus, turfgrass plants must rely on production of root chelates (phytosiderophores), Fe in natural organic chelates, reduction of Fe^{+3} to more available Fe^{+2}, or applied Fe (foliar or soil applied) to meet their Fe needs.

Calcareous soils, which contain free $CaCO_3$, generally have a pH between 7.3 to 8.5 and these are especially prone to causing Fe deficiency (Plate 19). Bicarbonate (HCO_3^-) ions can form in calcareous soils by the reaction:

$$CaCO_3 + CO_2 + H_2O \rightleftarrows Ca^{2+} + 2HCO_3^-$$

Available Fe levels may be reduced due to Fe reacting with HCO_3^- to form $FeCO_3$ precipitates. Also, irrigation water high in HCO_3^- can induce Fe deficiency by the same mechanism. Lime-induced Fe chlorosis is caused by the same mechanism. Iron can also react with OH^- to form insoluble $Fe(OH)_3$ under alkaline pH.

Aeration and Soil Moisture

As soil O_2 decreases due to a waterlogged or compacted situation, anaerobic conditions cause reduction of Fe^{+3} into more soluble Fe^{+2}. This reduction of Fe is especially prevalent in acid soils where Fe^{+2} can reach toxic or excessive levels. However, in calcareous or recently limed soils, CO_2 accumulates under poor aeration and can enhance Fe chlorosis by $FeCO_3$ formation as noted previously. This reaction is most likely to occur in cool, wet weather.

Soil Temperature

Soil temperature can influence Fe chlorosis through effects on plant activity and soil Fe availability (Mortvedt[6]). Low soil temperatures may: (a) promote HCO_3^- accumulation in the soil solution and cause $FeCO_3$ formation in soils with free $CaCO_3$ or receiving irrigation water high in HCO_3^-; (b) reduce root growth and/or cause spring root dieback or pruning in warm-season grasses. Both responses limit Fe uptake, especially if in conjunction with wet, fine-textured soils that are slow to warm up in the spring; and (c) may limit root activity in terms of phytosiderophere production necessary for increasing Fe mobilization.

High soil temperatures may also enhance Fe chlorosis by: (a) causing root dieback and reduced root viability, especially for cool-season grasses in the summer. Thus, some cool-season grasses may exhibit more Fe chlorosis as the summer progresses. Turfgrasses with excessive thatch are more likely to exhibit this problem; (b) enhancing microbial degradation of root-produced phytosiderosphores; and (c) increase soil HCO_3^- production in response to higher microbial activity causing CO_2 to accumulate.

Organic Matter

A number of natural organic compounds in soils are able to react with Fe as chelating agents. The Fe can be exchanged for other metals and the Fe taken up by plant roots. Organic *chelates* arise from microbial degradation of organic matter and as root exudates. Two common natural chelates are citric acid and oxalic acid. Thus, soils with high organic matter content exhibit better Fe availability. Under acidic, waterlogged conditions, high organic matter can further increase Fe solubility and potential toxicity.

Nutrient Interactions

Excessive levels of other metal cations (Cu, Mn, Zn) can inhibit Fe uptake. In return, high levels of available Fe may cause reduced uptake of these cations, especially Mn. Sometimes high P levels can enhance Fe chlorosis, particularly at high pH. Various mechanisms have been proposed such as formation of Fe-P compounds that precipitate out either in the soil or plant tissue. Application of quick-release N can sometimes increase Fe chlorosis by encouraging more rapid growth that accentuates any Fe chlorosis that is already present.

C. Practicum

Many times Fe chlorosis on turfgrasses is a seasonal occurrence in response to loss of a root system or reduced root viability. Management practices to improve root growth and viability can correct the Fe chlorosis in these instances. Increasing water drainage on fine-textured soils often improves Fe availability for warm-season grasses in the early spring when their roots are limited. The decrease in Fe deficiency symptoms associated with better drainage in the early spring is believed to be in response to warmer soil temperatures. Cool-season grasses that demonstrate Fe chlorosis in late summer often have excessive thatch resulting in root deterioration by late summer. Thatch control may help prevent the Fe deficiency or choosing a cultivar less susceptible to root loss. Controlling root diseases or nematodes that are affecting the health of the root system may be an appropriate action. Another example would be acidification of irrigation water high in HCO_3^- to remove the HCO_3^- and improve Fe availability.

Iron contained in soil-applied Fe carriers (Table 14.2) is often rapidly precipitated as very insoluble $Fe(OH)_3$ under alkaline pH. One approach is to include an acidifying material that causes pH to decrease at least on a micro-site basis. On calcareous soils where Fe chlorosis is most prevalent, pH reduction of the bulk soil is not feasible but pH may be reduced around a granule of FeS_2 or elemental S enough to increase Fe solubility. As the acidifying material dissipates, Fe from the other components of the Fe fertilizer would be less available.

Another approach is to use a natural or synthetic organic chelate that protects the Fe from precipitation. Soil pH can influence longevity of soil-applied Fe chelates. On calcareous soils, Ca^{2+} can displace Fe from the chelate over time and expose the Fe to precipitation. The chelate Fe EDDHA is most resistant to this reaction at pH >7.0. Application of natural organic fertilizers or composts can supply plant-available Fe complexed with organic chelates. Milorganite, an organic N carrier, is relatively high in Fe due to Fe addition during conditioning of this activated sewage sludge and it often reduces Fe chlorosis.

A number of water-soluble Fe carriers are available for foliar application (Table 14.2). For a rapid test to determine if a chlorosis is due to lack of Fe, foliar treatment can be made to a small area at a rate equivalent to 1 lb Fe per acre (0.025 lb Fe per 1,000 ft^2 in 1 to 3 gal water; 1.12 kg Fe ha^{-1} in 184 to 550 L water). Color improvement should be apparent within four hours. This procedure can also be used on a limited site to determine the Fe sensitivity of a grass. Most turfgrasses can receive at least 1 lb Fe per A without foliar burn but some grasses may exhibit blackening at this rate (centipedegrass often does). Bermudagrasses and zoysiagrasses may tolerate higher rates. Inclusion of 0.10 lb N per 1,000 ft^2 (4.4 lb N per acre; 4.9 kg ha^{-1}) with the Fe often provides a synergistic response in greening and duration of color response. Also, a number of fertilizers with N, P, and K contain Fe.

The primary problems with foliar Fe applications are (a) potential for blackening of turfgrass leaves and the upper thatch tissues of more open grasses if Fe rate is excessive for the particular grass (Plate 20); (b) duration of response varies (see Chapter 2, section on Foliar Nutrient Uptake) with climatic conditions, but it is essentially a short-term solution; and (c) Mn deficiency can sometimes be induced. This can be corrected by adding supplemental Mn.

If a chronic Fe deficiency problem exists even after other associated management practices have been corrected, turfgrass managers may wish to conduct an on-site trial of several foliar and soil materials to determine the best product for magnitude and longevity of response. Foliar materials can be applied at a 1 lb Fe per acre rate, while soil materials should be at a uniform Fe

Table 14.2. Iron (Fe) fertilizer forms with potential for use in turfgrass management (see Table 17.11 in Chapter 17).[a]

Fe Source	Formula	Approx. Percentage Fe	Usual Application Form[b]
Ferrous sulfate	$FeSO_4 \cdot 7H_2O$	20	F, S
Ferric sulfate	$Fe_2(SO_4)_3 \cdot 4H_2O$	23	S, F
Ferrous sulfide	FeS_2	45	S
Ferrous oxide	FeO	77	S
Ferric oxide	Fe_2O_3	69	S
Ferrous ammonium phosphate	$Fe(NH_4)PO_4 \cdot H_2O$	29	F, S
Ferrous ammonium sulfate	$FeSO_4 \cdot (NH_4)SO_4 \cdot 6H_2O$ or no H_2O	14–22	F, S
Iron ammonium polyphosphate	$Fe(NH_4)HP_2O_7$	22	F, S
Iron chelates, synthetic	• Fe DPTA	10	
	• Fe EDTA	5–14	
	• Fe EDDHA	6	F, S
	• Fe citrate	1–4	F, S
	• Fe-orthophosphate	5–8	F, S
Natural organic chelates	• Digested sewage sludges or composts	5–10	S
	• Fe polyflavonoid[c]	9–11	F, S

[a] Adapted from Mortvedt[6] and Tisdale et al.[10]
[b] F = foliar applied; S = soil applied. The most common method is listed first.
[c] A by-product from the wood processing industry.

rate chosen by converting product rates to obtain the same level of Fe per unit area. The various manufacturers' suggested rates can be used as a starting point in determining an appropriate soil or foliar application rate to use to compare products.

When assessing soil Fe levels, the most common extractant used is Fe-DTPA (diethylene triaminepentaacetic acid) because it chelates with Fe as well as other micronutrients (Mn, Cu, Zn) (Table 14.3).[2,6,7,10] Some laboratories may use weak acid extracts. Recently the Mehlich-III extractant has become popular as a more universal extractant and it contains the chelate EDTA. Additional information on soil testing is found in Chapter 9, Assessing Chemical/Nutrient Status.

II. MANGANESE

A. Plant Relationships

TURFGRASS ROOT UPTAKE of Mn is primarily as Mn^{+2} but it can be absorbed as an organic chelate. Once Mn is translocated to shoot tissues, it is immobile.

Manganese is involved in photosynthesis, including O_2 evolution in PS II (Photosystem II component of photosynthesis process) where Mn influences the ultrastructure of thylakoid membranes in chloroplasts. When Mn is deficient, disruption of the thylakoid membrane can rapidly decrease photosynthesis, but this effect quickly reversed with Mn addition. However, a more severe, prolonged Mn deficiency results in reduced chlorophyll content and alterations in the thylakoid structure that are not easily corrected. Chlorosis would be evident at this time. As

Table 14.3. DTPA and Mehlich III extractable Fe, Zn, Cu, and Mn levels used by many laboratories for micronutrient availability.[a]

Micronutrient	Low (Deficient)	Medium	High (Sufficient)[b]
DTPA[c]		ppm	
Fe	<2.5	2.6–5.0	>5.0
Mn	<1	1–2	>2
Zn	<0.5	0.6–1.0	>1
Cu	<0.2	0.2–0.4	>0.4
Mehlich III[c]			
Fe	<50	50–100	>100
Mn	<4.0	4.0–6.0	>6.0 (pH 6.0)
	<8.0	8.0–12.0	>12.0 (pH 7.0)
Zn	<1.0	1.1–2.0	>2.0
Cu	<0.3	0.3–2.5	>2.5

[a] After Tisdale et al.[10] and Mortvedt.[6]

[b] Extractable micronutrient levels are preferred to be within the High range for high maintenance, recreational turfgrass sites but within the Medium range for nonrecreational grasses.

[c] Rankings for micronutrients are more accurate for plants sensitive to a particular micronutrient, such as vegetable crops than for turfgrasses, which are not sensitive to micronutrients.

photosynthesis is decreased due to Mn deficiency, root growth can be severely depressed by lack of soluble carbohydrates for maintenance and growth. Reduced root growth is also a result of a combination of inhibition of cell division, reduced cell elongation, and stoppage of lateral root formation induced by low Mn.

Manganese is a cofactor that activates at least 35 different enzymes but is a structural component of only two enzymes. One of these enzymes transmits electrons for the water splitting reaction of PS II and this enzyme is sensitive to Mn deficiency. The second Mn-containing enzyme is one of the enzymes that removes free oxygen radicals from plants. Where Mn^{+2} is a cofactor, Mg^{+2} can often replace it, but Mg^{+2} is not always as efficient as Mn^{+2}.

Lignin biosynthesis depends on Mn in several of the pathway enzymes as a cofactor. Reduced lignin content in Mn deficient roots may make them more susceptible to take-all patch (Table 2.5) since lignification causes root cell walls to be thicker.

Tissue concentrations of Mn are usually within 20 to 500 ppm (mg kg^{-1}) with <20 ppm considered deficient. This value seems to be reliable for many plant species. Deficiencies in turfgrasses are most often observed on heavily leached acidic sandy soils, high pH calcareous soils, or on soils where high applications of Fe or Na have induced the deficiency (Table 14.4).

As Mn levels become critical, net photosynthesis, chlorophyll content, and shoot/root growth decline rapidly. *Visual deficiency symptoms* beyond reduced growth rate and chlorosis may be small, distinct greenish-gray spots on leaves. Chlorosis occurs on the youngest leaves, since Mn is immobile, as interveinal yellowing with veins green to light green. Leaf tips may turn grey or white and exhibit drooping or withering. The turfgrass stand may appear mottled and not respond to N fertilization.

Manganese deficiencies are sometimes observed on turfgrasses grown on acid sandy soils and calcareous sands, especially in Florida or similar climates with high rainfall. The frequent use of foliar Fe contributes to deficiencies by suppressing Mn uptake. Areas receiving high Na inputs may also be more prone to Mn deficiency.

Table 14.4. Soil and climatic factors associated with manganese (Mn) deficiency and toxicity/excess occurrences.

Deficiency Associated with	Toxic/Excessive Levels Associated with
• High pH soils, calcareous soils • Acid, heavily leached sand • Peat and muck soils at pH >7.0 • Dry, warm weather • High soil levels of Cu, Zn, Fe, or Na, especially on low CEC soils that are heavily leached	• Acid soils of pH <4.8 • Anaerobic soils, especially if acidic • High Mn may induce Fe, Mg or Ca deficiencies • Plant tolerance to Mn toxicity may increase under high temperatures and high Si

Toxicities of Mn are also relatively common where excessively acid soils (pH <4.8) contain high soluble Mn levels that cause direct root injury or replace Ca in root cells to cause root tissue deterioration. Anaerobic conditions on these soils further enhance Mn solubility and toxicity. In other cases, high Mn application or soil levels may induce Mg or Fe deficiencies.

B. Soil and Environmental Relationships

Manganese that is unavailable for plant uptake in the soil occurs as Mn in various minerals and as tightly chelated Mn in organic matter. Plant-available Mn consists primarily of Mn^{+2} in the soil solution and Mn^{+2} chelates containing exchangeable Mn^{+2}, with some Mn-chelates being water soluble. Manganese deficiencies and toxicities are influenced by soil and climatic factors (Table 14.4) but soil pH and aeration status are the most important.

Soil Reaction (pH)

A number of Mn minerals increase in solubility as pH decreases, particularly at pH <5.5, regardless of the aeration status. Thus, excessive or toxic Mn problems are relatively common on highly acidic soils. On acidic sands in high rainfall regions, however, the soluble Mn can become leached and result in low Mn levels even with acidic pH. Solubility of Mn minerals decreases rapidly as pH increases. Deficiencies of Mn are most often associated with high pH soils or recently limed soils. This response is most prevalent for low CEC soils subjected to frequent leaching.

Aeration (Redox)

Under waterlogged or low aeration conditions, Mn is reduced and solubility increases. Some soils may exhibit excessive or toxic Mn levels under waterlogged conditions even at pH 6.0 to 7.0. But at pH <6.0, the combination of low pH and low aeration can result in excessive or toxicity problems on many soils (see Chapter 16, Waterlogged section).

Soil Temperatures

In general, Mn availability and uptake are lower in cold, moist (not waterlogged) soils in the spring. Part of this response may be due to reduced plant metabolism for Mn uptake under these situations. As soil temperatures increase, Mn availability usually is enhanced. However, high temperatures and dry soil conditions may enhance Mn deficiency in some instances, probably due to low Mn mobility in the soil or less root growth.

Organic Matter

As soil pH increases, Mn forms increasingly more stable complexes with organic matter. The Mn in these complexes is primarily unavailable. Thus, high organic matter soils at pH >7.0 are likely to exhibit Mn deficiency, especially mucks or well decomposed peats. Addition of less-decomposed organic matter often increases Mn availability due to Mn complexes with relatively soluble organic chelates. On acidic, poorly drained sites, the addition of less-decomposed organic matter may enhance excess Mn problems.

Nutrient Interactions

High soil levels of available Fe, Cu, or Zn can reduce Mn uptake, especially on alkaline, sandy, leached soils. Application of frequent soil or foliar Fe treatments has been observed to suppress Mn uptake in turfgrasses under these conditions. High Na has been reported to reduce Mn uptake, possibly due to root toxicity from the Na. Acidifying N-carriers may increase Mn availability on alkaline sites by enhancing Mn solubility. On some plants, high Si content in tissues has been found to cause redistribution of Mn in leaf tissues or cell organelles, with a resulting decrease in toxicity. The presence of high Mn may suppress uptake of Fe, Mg, and Ca.

C. Practicum

Most soil-applied micronutrient package fertilizers contain Mn as one of the nutrients. Especially on intensively managed turfgrasses grown on sandy soils, a micronutrient package fertilizer may be applied one or more times per year. However, the soil treatment of a Mn fertilizer alone is not common in turfgrass culture. Instead, Mn is usually included as a component in various micronutrient package fertilizers for foliar application in one of the forms listed in Table 14.5.

Foliar application of Mn is the most common method of supplying Mn in situations where Mn deficiency may occur or to prevent potential deficiency conditions. It is often included with a foliar Fe treatment at a rate equivalent to 0.5 to 1 lb Mn per acre (0.0125 to 0.025 lb Mn per 1,000 ft^2 in 1 to 3 gal water; 0.56 to 1.12 kg Mn ha^{-1} in 407 to 1,222 L) per 1,000 ft^2. If a turfgrass manager is unsure whether an existing deficiency symptom of chlorosis is from lack of Fe or Mn, then only Mn would be applied. If Mn is deficient, enhanced greening should be apparent in one to two days. Higher foliar Mn rates should be avoided to prevent foliar injury. As with Fe, Mn may be included as a micronutrient in N-P-K fertilizers.

In situations where soil pH reduction is feasible, Mn availability would be expected to increase as pH declines except on heavily leached acid sands. More typical is Mn toxicity at low soil pH. In this instance, lime application would reduce Mn levels. However, when excessive acidity in the B horizon or a subsurface horizon is the location of Mn toxicity, lime would best be injected into this zone. Surface applied lime may require several years to decrease Mn in a subsurface horizon.

The DTPA and Mehlich III extractants are the most often used to determine plant-available Mn status (Table 14.3).[2,6,7,10]

Table 14.5. Manganese sources used in micronutrient packages or for foliar treatment (see Table 17.12, Chapter 17).[a]

Mn Source	Formula	Approx. Percentage Mn	Usual Application Form[b]
Manganese sulfate	$MnSO_4 \cdot 4H_2O$	26–28	F, S
Manganese oxide	MnO	41–68	S
Manganese frits	Fritted glass	10–35	S
Manganese chloride	$MnCl_2$	17	F, S
Mn chelates	MnDTPA	8–10	F, S
Mn EDTA		5–12	F, S
Manganese lignosulfonate[c]	–	5–9	F, S
Manganese polyflavonoid[c]	–	5–9	F, S

[a] Adapted from Mortvedt[6] and Tisdale et al.[10]
[b] F = foliar applied; S = soil applied. Most common is listed first.
[c] By-products from the wood industry, other organic Mn carriers.

III. ZINC

A. Plant Relationships

Zinc (as well as Cu and Mo) is very rarely deficient on turfgrasses. When a deficiency has been noted, it is almost always associated with high levels of other micronutrient metals. There are crop plants (corn, rice, soybeans) that are much more sensitive to Zn than turfgrasses. Uptake of Zn is primarily as Zn^{+2} and possibly as $ZnOH^+$ at high soil pH. Chelating exudates from roots can enhance Zn uptake. Once in the plant and translocated, it remains somewhat mobile for phloem movement.

Many enzymes require Zn as a structural component. One of these is the CuZnSOD (superoxide dimutase) antioxidant that detoxifies free O_2 radicals generated in photosynthesis. It is found in chloroplasts, mitochondria, and glyoxysomes. Increased membrane permeability and leakage associated with Zn deficiency is believed to arise from lack of this enzyme and, therefore, greater O_2 radical injury to membranes. Oxidative stress from O_2 radicals may be expressed as chlorosis, necrosis, and greater membrane permeability. Additionally, O_2 free radical degradation of indoleacetic acid (IAA) is believed to explain the stunted growth from shortened internodes (rosetting) and reduced leaf size ("little leaf") at least in dicotyledons under Zn deficiency.

Protein synthesis requires Zn through several means. DNA replication and transcription involves Zn metalloproteins. Ribosomes, the site of protein synthesis, have a structural requirement for Zn that influences their function. Also, Zn deficiency can induce high RNAase activity that degrades RNA. The combination of these Zn influences results in low protein content and high amino acid content of Zn deficient plants.

Carbohydrate metabolism is affected by Zn through several Zn dependent enzymes, such as carbonic anhydrase that hydrates CO_2 into HCO_3^-. In C_4 plants, the lack of carbonic anhydrase activity under Zn deficiency is believed to account for reduced photosynthesis rate. However, the influence of Zn on carbohydrate metabolism appears to be less important under deficient conditions than the role of Zn in protein synthesis and O_2 radical detoxification to maintain membrane integrity.

Zinc tissue concentrations in turfgrasses are usually between 20 to 70 ppm with <20 ppm considered as deficient and 20 to 55 ppm as sufficient.[11] On grasses, Zn *deficiency symptoms* are chlorotic leaves with some mottling, stunted leaves, leaf margins may roll or appear crinkled. Generally, symptoms first appear on younger leaves and are more pronounced on young versus older leaves.

Conditions associated with Zn deficiencies are noted in Table 14.6. The P-Zn relationship is a relatively common one on some crops—but not necessarily turfgrasses. High soil P is often associated with Zn deficiency due to a combination of factors such as: reduced availability of soil Zn; decreased solubility and mobility of Zn within the plant; Zn deficiency enhances P uptake and translocation to shoot tissues where P may interfere with Fe metabolism; and Zn may impair P translocation in the phloem and, therefore, enhance P shoot concentrations.

Excessive Zn levels are of more concern than deficiencies on turfgrasses, especially if composts containing high Zn are used. High Zn may induce Fe, Mn, or Mg deficiencies. Root and rhizome inhibition by high Zn have been observed on turfgrasses with cultivar differences in response to Zn.[11]

B. Soil and Environmental Relationships

Zinc level in soil is usually relatively low with Zn found as: solution Zn^{+2} with part of this as natural organic chelates; Zn^{+2} on clay CEC sites; a constituent of various minerals; tightly complexed with highly decomposed humus; and associated with carbonates. Plant-available Zn levels are influenced primarily by soil pH but other soil and climatic factors can affect availability.

Soil Reaction (pH)

As soil pH increases, Zn availability decreases; thus, Zn deficiency is most common at alkaline pH. At high pH, various insoluble compounds of Zn (also Fe, Al, and Mn) hydrous oxides can form. In calcareous soils, Zn adsorption to Ca and especially Mg carbonates can also reduce availability.

Organic Matter

Organic matter and Zn relationships depend on the predominant form of organic matter. Abundant, well-decomposed organic matter (mucks, peat humus, lignin) can form insoluble complexes with Zn. Soluble organic acids or fulvic acids can increase Zn availability by forming soluble chelates similar to chelates in root exudates. These chelates are more prevalent in less decomposed organic matter.

Nutrient Interactions

High plant tissue or soil levels of Fe, Mn, or Cu can inhibit Zn uptake (Plate 21). High P can increase the occurrence of Zn deficiency in many sensitive plants, as was noted earlier. Plants on a borderline Zn deficiency may exhibit deficiency symptoms after application of N that increases growth, and dilutes Zn concentration in plant tissue while increasing demand for Zn.

Table 14.6. Factors that induce deficiencies or toxicity/excess nutrient problems for certain micronutrients (Zn, Cu, B, Mo, Cl, Ni).

Nutrient	Deficiency Occurrence	Toxicity or Excessive Occurrence
Zn	Deficiencies more common on alkaline soils; high levels of Fe, Cu, Mn, P, N; high soil moisture; cool, wet weather and low light intensity; highly weathered acid, coarse textured soils.	Some mine spoils and municipal wastes may be high in Zn. High Zn may cause chlorosis by inducing Fe or Mg deficiencies.
Cu	Deficiencies are most often observed on organic soils due to strong binding of Cu; heavily leached sands; high levels of Fe, Mn, Zn, P, and N; high pH.	Toxic levels can occur from some sewage and industrial sludges, mine spoils or pig/poultry manures; use of high Cu content materials.
B	High pH can induce deficiencies, especially on leached, calcareous sandy soils; high pH; high Ca can restrict B availability; dry soils; high K may increase B deficiency on low B soils.	B toxicity is much more likely than deficiencies due to irrigation water high in B; soils naturally high in B; overapplication of B; use of some compost amendments.
Mo	Deficiencies are usually on acid, sandy soils; acid soils high in Fe and Al oxides; high levels of Cu, Mn, Fe, S suppress uptake.	Mo toxicities are important for grazing animals and are associated with high pH soils that are wet.
Cl	Cl^- uptake is suppressed by high NO_3^- and SO_4^{2-}.	Cl^- is a common salt ion that can be directly toxic to leaf tissues and roots; more often it reduces water availability by enhancing total salinity.
Ni	Conditions associated with Ni deficiency are not clear due to the rare occurrence of Ni deficiency.	Ni toxicity can arise from use of some high Ni industrial or sewage sludges.

Other Factors

In contrast to Fe and Mn, anaerobic soil conditions do not increase Zn solubility. Zinc deficiencies on Zn sensitive plants have been noted to be more apparent under cool, moist, cloudy weather common in spring periods of temperate climates. While Zn solubility may be depressed by cool temperatures, limited root activity may also account for reduced Zn uptake. Since Zn-containing minerals are less abundant in coarse-textured soils, Zn deficiencies are more likely on these soils. Acidic, highly leached, sandy soils may result in Zn deficiency due to leaching of the available Zn over time without mineral-bound Zn to replenish the available Zn fraction.

Zinc toxicity on turfgrasses is rare but excessive use of Zn-containing materials should be avoided since Zn is difficult to leach. Some organic composts may contain high Zn levels. Of more concern than direct toxicity is depression of Fe or Mn uptake, thereby inducing deficiencies of these nutrients (Plate 21). If high Zn is present, liming may decrease Zn solubility, but it can also reduce Fe and Mn solubility. It is not unusual for a soil test to list Zn as high where this is based on Zn sensitive plants and not turfgrasses.

C. Practicum

Zinc is commonly found in certain fertilizers or pesticides applied on turfgrasses. Application of a micronutrient package fertilizer (i.e., contains some or all micronutrients) once or more per year adds ample Zn for almost all situations without causing excess Zn problems. While a number of Zn fertilizers are available for soil application (Table 14.7), these should not be applied as soil treatments unless: (a) a true Zn deficiency has been determined; (b) Zn in the micronutrient package fertilizer is insufficient to correct it; and (c) foliar treatment does not resolve the deficiency to a sufficient degree. This approach minimizes the chances of applying too much Zn. The particular compounds containing Zn in turfgrass micronutrient package fertilizers will usually be one or more of those listed in Table 14.7. A well-formulated micronutrient package fertilizer will avoid excessive levels of any one nutrient and provide ample bulk to uniformly apply granular products.

A suspected Zn deficiency should be investigated by foliar application to a small area at 0.44 lb Zn per acre (0.01 lb Zn per 1000 ft^2; 0.49 kg Zn ha^{-1}) in a low volume of water (see Fe Practicum section). If a deficiency is present, then two approaches are: (a) increase the use of micronutrient package fertilizer application rate or frequency; or (b) use foliar treatment at the above rate.

While the DPTA and Mechlich-3 extractants are often used to assess available Zn levels (Table 14.3), the ranges (low, medium, etc.) are not well correlated to grasses which are insensitive to Zn.[2,6,7,10] These ranges are designed to predict Zn availability for sensitive crop plants. It is not unusual for: (a) a soil test to report a low Zn level but no Zn response occurs; or (b) a Zn level may be reported as very high because of Zn-containing chemicals used in turfgrass culture C or a galvanized pail or rubber material contacting a soil sample prior to analysis.

IV. COPPER

A. Plant Relationships

PLANT UPTAKE OF Cu is as Cu^{+2}, $Cu(OH)^+$, and Cu chelated to soluble organic compounds. Copper has intermediate mobility within the plant (Table 2.1) and most Cu is present in complexes with various compounds.

The Cu-protein plastocyanin is involved in electron transport of PS I in photosynthesis.[3,4] Copper polypeptides are thought to maintain membrane-based electron transport in the chloroplast membrane. Another role of Cu in photosynthesis is the CuZnSOD isoenzyme antioxidant that detoxifies O_2 free radicals in photosynthesis that can cause structural damage to chloroplasts. Under severe Cu deficiency, several Cu dependent enzymes in photosystem II may exhibit depressed activity that reduces PS II. All of these functions of Cu contribute to plant responses observed in Cu-deficient conditions—reduced photosynthesis, low carbohydrate levels, leaf chlorosis, and poor root growth.

Copper is a component of other Cu-proteins such as diamine oxidase, integral to processes that do not involve photosynthesis. This enzyme functions in lignification and suberization of cell walls. With low Cu, lignification is impaired and young leaves may be distorted and have weaker cell walls.

Copper-containing enzymes are involved in mitochondria (site of cell respiration) electron transport. However, respiration is less affected than photosynthesis by Cu deficiency.

Table 14.7. Fertilizer sources for Zn, Cu, B, and Mo (see Tables 17.13 to 17.16 in Chapter 17).[a]

Micronutrient and Sources	Formula	Approx. Percentage Element	Usual Application Form[b]
Zinc			
Zinc sulfates	• $ZnSO_4 \cdot H_2O$	35	F, S
	• $ZnSO_4 \cdot 7H_2O$	23	F, S
Zinc carbonate	$ZnCO_3$	53	S
Zinc chloride	$ZnCl_2$	48–50	F, S
Zinc frits	Fritted glass	10–30	S
Zinc oxide	ZnO	50–80	S
Basic Zn sulfate	$ZnSO_4 \cdot 4Zn(OH)_2$	55	S
Zinc nitrate	$Zn(NO_3)_2 \cdot 6H_2O$	22	F, S
Zinc chelates	• Zn EDTA	14	F, S
	• Zn lignosulfonate	5–8	F, S
	• Zn polyflavonoid	5–10	F, S
Copper			
Copper sulfates	• $CuSO_4 \cdot 5H_2O$	25	F, S
	• $CuSO_4 \cdot H_2O$	35	F, S
Copper chloride	$CuCl_2$	47	F, S
Copper chelates	• Cu EDTA	13	F
	• Cu lignosulfonates	5–8	F
	• Cu polyflavonoids	5–7	F
Cupric oxide	CuO	7–8	S
Boron			
Boric acid	H_3BO_3	17	F, S
Boron frits	Fritted glass	2–6	S
Borax	$Na_2B_4O_7 \cdot 10H_2O$	11	F, S
Sodium pentaborate	$Na_2B_{10}O_{16} \cdot 10H_2O$	18	F, S
Sodium tetraborates	• $Na_2B_4O_7 \cdot 5H_2O$	14–15	F, S
	• $Na_2B_4O_7 \cdot 5H_2O$ + $Na_2B_{10}O_{16} \cdot H_2O$	20–21	
Molybdenum			
Sodium molybdates	• Na_2MoO_4	47	F, S
	• $Na_2MoO_4 \cdot 2H_2O$	39	F, S
Ammonium molybdate	$(NH_4)_6Mo_7O_{24} \cdot 4H_2O$	54	F, S
Molybdenum frits	Fritted glass	2–3	S
Molybdenum trioxide	MoO_3	66	S

[a] Adapted from Mortvedt[6] and Tisdale et al.[10]

[b] F = foliar treatment; S = soil applied. Turfgrass *micronutrient package fertilizers* (i.e., contains all or most micronutrients) are usually formulated as granular materials using any of these sources along with sufficient carrier or filler to allow granular application in a uniform manner. Sprayable products with combinations of micronutrients are also available. *Individual micronutrient sources* (except Fe) are seldom applied as a soil treatment to turfgrasses but foliar applications can be applied.

Turfgrass leaf tissues normally contain 10 to 50 ppm Cu with <5 ppm considered as the critical deficiency level.[5,11] Turfgrasses grown on heavily leached sands and receiving high rates of Fe, Mn, or Zn are the most likely sites to exhibit Cu deficiency (Table 14.6). *Visual deficiency symptoms* appear on the youngest to middle leaves as yellowing and chlorosis of leaf margins; white to bluish leaf tips that wither, turn yellow, and die; and stunted growth with leaves rolling or twisting.

Copper toxicities can arise from application of materials containing high Cu levels such as some manures or sludges. Excessive Cu can suppress uptake of Fe, Mn, Zn, and Mo, as well as inhibit rooting.

B. Soil and Environmental Relationships

Total Cu content of most soils is between 1 to 40 ppm as compared to 10 to 300 ppm for Zn, 0.7 to 50% by weight for Fe, 20 to 3,000 ppm for Mn, 2 to 200 ppm for B, and 0.2 to 5 ppm for Mo (Tisdale et al.[10]). However, only a small quantity of Cu is plant-available as Cu^{+2} or $CuOH^{+}$ in soil solution or on CEC sites and as organically complexed Cu. Soil factors affecting Cu availability are soil pH, organic matter content, soil texture, and nutrient interactions. As with Zn, low aeration or waterlogging does not cause Cu to be reduced and become more soluble.

Soil Reaction (pH)

As a soil becomes more acid from an initial pH of 7.0, solubility increases for most Cu minerals; therefore, plant-available Cu increases. Much of this Cu is adsorbed to clays, organic matter, and Fe/Al/Mn oxides. Thus, Cu deficiencies are more prevalent at high pH.

Organic Matter

Copper deficiencies are more common on peat and muck soils than mineral soils. Total Cu is often lower in these soils and Cu can form insoluble complexes with organic matter. However, in mineral soils, organic complexes with Cu may enhance availability since the association seems to be less strong.

Soil Texture

Copper can be on clay CEC sites and chemically adsorbed by Fe/Al/Mn oxides with some of the Cu being available for plants. Thus, heavily leached sands, including calcareous sands, are more likely to be deficient in Cu due to low clay and hydrous oxide content.

Nutrient Interaction

On Cu-sensitive plants, high available levels of Fe, Zn, Mn, and P have been associated with enhanced Cu deficiency. Plants that are low in Cu may exhibit a greater degree of deficiency symptoms after N application.

Copper toxicities on turfgrasses are rare but may occur near Cu smelters or from application of amendments excessively high in Cu. Liming may decrease Cu solubility, and increased levels of Fe, Mn, and Zn may reduce Cu toxicity.

C. Practicum

The same precautions noted for Zn should be applied to Cu. While a number of Cu fertilizers are available (Table 14.7) for soil application, this should not be attempted unless a true deficiency has been identified. The probability of a true deficiency on turf is very low. The Cu contained in various N-P-K fertilizers and pesticides supplies some Cu and periodic use of a micronutrient package fertilizer will supply additional Cu. With the small quantity of Cu required by the plant, additional soil-applied Cu is not recommended due to the potential for uneven application or excessive levels. If a Cu deficiency is expected, a foliar application at 0.13 lb (i.e., 59 grams) of Cu per acre (0.003 lb Cu per 1,000 ft^2; 0.146 kg Cu ha^{-1}) can be made to a small test site. Typical soil test levels and rankings for DTPA and Mechlich III extractants are found in Table 14.3.[2,6,7,10] As with the other micronutrients in this table, the rankings are more accurate for plants sensitive to Cu deficiencies than turfgrasses.

V. BORON

A. Plant Relationships

AT PH <9.0, H_3BO_3 IS THE PREDOMINANT FORM FOR PLANT UPTAKE with $H_2BO_3^-$ present at pH >9.0. Uptake of B increases with increasing soil solution B concentrations, but plant species vary greatly in their uptake, indicating genetic-based mechanisms of control that are currently not well understood. Boron accumulates in leaves, especially leaf tips, as it is carried in the transpiration stream, but some redistribution can occur by phloem transport. Factors influencing B availability are noted in Table 14.6.

Plant functions of B are less understood than other nutrients. Boron forms strong complexes with polyhydroxyl compounds (sugar alcohols, uronic acids) that are important constituents of hemicellulose and pectic substances of cell walls. Grasses have a lower B requirement than dicots probably because of fewer pectic and hemicellulose materials in their cell walls. In addition to cell wall synthesis, B can form cross-links with esters that break and reform during cell elongation.

Lignin formation requires B and, when B deficient conditions occur, phenolics, precursors of lignin, accumulate. Accumulation of phenols can lead to excessive free O_2 radical formation with the potential for damage to the plasma membrane. Boron can influence the plasma membrane by acting as a stabilizing agent through complex formation with membrane glycoproteins and glycolipids and, therefore, enhancing membrane function. Low B can also inhibit plasma membrane activity by reducing membrane-bound H^+ pumping ATPase activity.

These effects of B lead to a substantial role in cell wall and plasma membrane structure and integrity. Root cell elongation and activity are especially inhibited by B deficiency. Xylem differentiation may be decreased by low B. Other effects of B are believed to be secondary.

Turfgrass critical deficiency range is <5 to 10 ppm B with a sufficiency range of 10 to 60 ppm.[5,11] Other landscape plants may be more sensitive to B toxicity than turfgrasses and mowing of grasses aids in plant removal of B which tends to accumulate in leaf tips. *Visual symptoms of B deficiency* occur initially on younger leaves as leaf tip chlorosis, followed by interveinal chlorosis of young and older leaves, and curling of leaves. Roots may be stunted and thickened. Plants are stunted and appear bushy or rosette in appearance.

Boron deficiencies are very rare on turfgrasses but B toxicities are much more likely, especially in arid regions on soils with high levels of B and Ca or on sites receiving irrigation water high in B (Table 14.6). Boron toxicity is expressed as leaf tip and margin chlorosis on older leaves followed by death of tissue (necrosis). Plants, including turfgrasses, vary in B uptake, and high uptake has been observed for creeping bentgrass.[11] Toxicity levels of B in grasses is from 100 to 1,000 ppm dry weight.

B. Soil and Environmental Relationships

In most soils, the total B content is from 2 to 200 ppm, primarily as borosilicate minerals. Plant-available B is present as H_3BO_3 (soil solution) and complexed with organic matter (slowly available). Unavailable B is found in minerals and adsorbed on the surfaces of clays and Fe/Al oxides. Toxicity from B is more common than deficiencies for turfgrasses. Soil factors influencing plant-available B level are soil pH, soil type, organic matter, soil moisture, and nutrient interaction.

Soil Reaction (pH)

The most important soil property affecting B availability is soil pH. As pH increases, B availability decreases with a sharp decrease between pH 6.3 to 7.0 as B is adsorbed by clay and Al hydroxy surfaces. Sometimes liming an acid soil to pH >6.5 can result in a temporary B deficiency as B becomes adsorbed by freshly precipitated $Al(OH)_3$. When soil B is excessive, a light lime application may aid in reducing its solubility.

Soil Type

Since the predominant soluble form of B (H_3BO_3) has a neutral charge, it is easily leached from coarse-textured soils. Fine-textured soils with higher clay content and Fe/Al oxides are less likely to exhibit B deficiency resulting from B leaching. Due to these relationships, excessive B can be leached much more readily in sandy than fine-textured soils.

Organic Matter

Boron is not adsorbed onto organic matter to any great extent. The B associated with organic matter is as a constituent of various compounds or in the microbial biomass. As these compounds degrade, B becomes available for plant uptake. Thus, increasing organic matter content of mineral soils often enhances B availability. However, B is often deficient in peats or mucks, especially after liming.

Soil Moisture

Flooded or anaerobic conditions do not appreciably influence B level. However, low soil moisture enhances B deficiency by limiting B uptake and B release from organic matter.

Nutrient Interactions

High Ca content in calcareous soils or recently limed soils to pH >6.5 reduces B availability. High K can enhance B deficiency on low B soils as well as increase B toxicity under high B. The reasons for these responses are not clear.

Boron toxicities may arise from: (a) application of irrigation water high in B; (b) soils naturally high in B which is most common in arid or semiarid climates; or (c) overapplication of B-containing fertilizers or some compost amendments. Leaching of excess B can be achieved on sandy soils but is difficult on fine-textured ones due to greater adsorption to clays and Fe/Al oxides and more limited water percolation. Light to moderate lime application may also aid in reducing soluble B levels.

C. Practicum

Most grasses are relatively insensitive to B deficiencies and toxicities. The most common extractant used for a B soil test is hot-water-soluble B with a critical range of 0.1 to 2.0 mg B kg^{-1} (ppm) for most crops. At above 5.0 mg kg^{-1}, toxicities are likely on many plants including Kentucky bluegrasses. These values illustrate the narrow range in soluble soil B between deficiencies and toxicities. Thus, soil B applications should not be attempted unless a true B deficiency has been determined based on soil test, tissue test, and turfgrass response to foliar treatment of a test area with a control. Application of a foliar treatment can be at 0.09 lb B per acre (0.002 lb per 1,000 ft^2 in 3 to 5 gal water; 0.10 kg ha^{-1} in 550 to 920 L water) (Table 14.7). If a soil application is necessary, B can be applied at 0.5 to 2.0 lb per acre (0.56 to 2.24 kg ha^{-1}). Sources of B are listed in Table 14.7. Because B can be toxic at very low levels, uniformity of application is essential. The B must be mixed with other fertilizer materials to achieve this uniformity. Grass sensitivity to B toxicity has been reported as: creeping bentgrass > perennial ryegrass > 'Alta' fescue > Kentucky bluegrass > zoysiagrass > bermudagrass.[11]

VI. MOLYBDENUM

A. Plant Relationships

MOLYBDENUM IS REQUIRED BY GRASSES in very low quantities, while legumes and other plants that depend on N_2 fixation have a higher requirement. Uptake of Mo is as MoO_4^{-2} and $HMoO_4^-$. It is readily mobile once in the plant.

Molybdenum is required for structural and catalytical functions in a small number of enzymes where it is involved in redox reactions. The most important is nitrogenase, a very important enzyme for N_2 fixing plants but not for turfgrasses. In turfgrasses and other plants, Mo is a cofactor for nitrate reductase, sulfite oxidase (other enzymes can replace its function under low Mo), and an oxidase/dehydrogenase that catalyzes purines to uric acid (this is much more important in legumes than grasses).

Typical tissue levels of Mo are 1 to 4 ppm with the critical deficiency level believed to be <1 ppm. While the range from deficiency to toxicity is narrow for Mn and B (about 10-fold), it is very wide for Mo (about 1,000-fold) and Mo toxicity is rare.

Due to its involvement in N metabolism, Mo *visual deficiency symptoms* are similar to N deficiency—chlorosis of older leaves and stunted growth. Some mottling and interveinal yellowing of leaves may appear.[5] These are the only field expressions of Mo that would be expected. Application of N as NO_3^- would not be expected to improve greening and may cause more chlorosis. However, N applied as NH_4^+ may cause a greening response since nitrate reductase activity would not be required.

B. Soil and Environmental Relationships

A typical range for soil Mo content is 0.2 to 5 ppm.[10] Most Mo is not plant-available in the form of primary or secondary minerals. Molybdenum is strongly adsorbed by Fe/Al oxides with availability depending on soil pH. The primary factors influencing Mo plant availability (Table 14.6) are: (a) *soil pH* with Mo availability increasing with increasing pH. This is the opposite of other micronutrients. At low pH (acidic), Mo is tightly adsorbed to Fe/Al oxides but adsorption declines as pH increases. Thus, liming can enhance Mo availability. The influence of pH and Fe/Al oxides explain the observation that Mo deficiency is most common on acidic, sandy soils and acidic soils high in Fe/Al oxides; (b) *nutrient interactions* may affect Mo uptake with suppression reported when SO_4, Cu, Mn, and Fe levels are high. In contrast, high Mg, P, and NO_3 may enhance uptake; and (c) *climatic conditions*. Uptake may be reduced under dry soil conditions, while humid, high rainfall climates are conducive to acidic, leached sands which can induce Mo deficiency. Toxicity from Mo on plants is very rare but toxicity in grazing animals can occur under low Cu conditions.

C. Practicum

The soil extractant (ammonium oxalate, pH 3.3) most often used for Mo is only a very general guide with a critical range of about 0.1 to 0.3 mg kg^{-1}. If a Mo deficiency is expected based on soil and tissue tests, a test area can be treated with 0.044 lb per acre of Mo (0.001 lb per 1,000 ft^2) as a foliar application in 3 to 5 gal water per 1,000 ft^2 (0.049 kg ha^{-1} in 550 to 920 L water). On some crops, Mo seed treatment supplies ample nutrient. While liming may increase Mo availability, it may be much less costly to apply Mo periodically as part of a micronutrient package.

VII. CHLORINE

A. Plant Relationships

CHLORINE IS WIDELY FOUND IN NATURE and is a very common component of salt as the Cl ion.[1] Plants take up Cl as Cl^-, which is very mobile in plants. Additional discussion of Cl is in Chapters 7 and 8 on salt-affected sites with respect to its influence on water uptake (total salinity) and ion toxicity.

Chlorine deficiency reduces leaf size and dry weight due to a reduction in cell division and elongation, especially on plants with a higher Cl requirement such as kiwi fruit and palm trees. The mechanisms for these responses are not known. The most widely recognized need for Cl is in the water-splitting of Photosystem II in photosynthesis where O_2 is evolved. Chloride is thought to act as a stabilizing agent for reactants in PS II. Reduced plant growth under low Cl is initially due to the influence on cell division and extension more than photosynthesis suppression.

A proton-pumping ATPase at the tonoplast is sensitive to Cl levels and results in Cl accumulation in vacuoles. There Cl acts as a major inorganic osmotically active solute that is particularly important in roots to maintain turgor pressure as well as to maintain electrical neutrality with cationic solutes (i.e., K^+ or Na^+) in the vacuole. In a similar manner, Cl^- may be involved in stomatal regulation of some plants as a counter ion for K^+.

Typical tissue concentrations of Cl in turfgrasses are 1,000 to 6,000 ppm (0.10 to 0.60% by dry weight) but the critical deficiency level is only 200 to 400 ppm for most plants. *Deficiency symptoms* on turfgrasses have not been described but on other plants they are expressed as chlorosis of new leaves; wilting, especially at leaf margins; leaf curling; and eventually necrosis. Growth is stunted, including root growth.

Excessive levels of Cl can cause several problems that commonly occur on turfgrasses, with reduced water uptake from high salt concentrations (i.e., total salinity stress) the most prevalent (Table 14.6). Within the plant, excessive Cl can induce severe leaf chlorosis and reduce photosynthesis by inhibiting enzyme activities. Also, tissue dehydration, loss of turgor pressure, and tissue desiccation can contribute to toxicity. Turfgrass and other plants vary greatly in their tolerance to high Cl with woody species often very sensitive. Sensitive plants may exhibit toxicity at 0.30 to 0.50% by weight in leaves (3,000–5,000 ppm), while tolerant species may tolerate 2.0% by weight or more.

B. Soil and Climatic Conditions

While Cl deficiency is not a problem on turfgrasses, excess and toxicity problems are relatively frequent on salt-affected sites (Chapters 7 and 8).[1] The most common causes of high Cl in soils are:

- high Cl content in irrigation water
- salt water intrusion, flooding, or spray. Seawater has high Cl levels.
- upward movement of Cl from the subsoil by a high water table or capillary action
- insufficient leaching of salts due to lack of sufficient water or poor soil conditions for drainage

Excess and toxicity Cl levels must be corrected by leaching to remove it from the root zone.

VIII. NICKEL

ONLY RECENTLY HAS Ni been classified as an essential nutrient for higher plants but there is no direct evidence of a Ni deficiency observed on any higher plant grown in a field soil.[3] In carefully controlled greenhouse studies, Ni deficiency has been demonstrated. Plant uptake is as Ni^{+2}.

Urease is the only Ni-containing enzyme found in higher plants. It catalyzes the transformation of urea, $CO(NH_2)_2$, to NH_3. Nickel is a metal component of the enzyme necessary for proper structure and activity of urease.

Data on turfgrasses are lacking but crop plants often contain 1.0 to 10.0 ppm Ni by weight in vegetative tissues. The critical deficiency level in barley is 0.1 ppm. A visual deficiency symptom on barley is a partial chlorosis as interveinal yellowing with eventual necrosis and failure of the leaf tip to unfold.

Some industrial sludges are high in Ni and Ni toxicities have been observed (Table 14.6). Tissue concentrations for toxicities have been observed that range from 10 to 50 ppm (sensitive plants) to 50 to 110 (moderately tolerant plants).

IX. NONESSENTIAL ELEMENTS (Si, Na)

TWO ELEMENTS WIDELY FOUND IN TURFGRASSES that are nonessential but can influence growth and plant performance are silicon (Si) and sodium (Na).

A. Silicon

Silicon is not found free in nature, but occurs primarily as the oxide (SiO_2) and as silicates. Silica is silicon dioxide (SiO_2), which is found in nature as sand, quartz, and other minerals.

Many species of Gramineae (grasses) can accumulate Si, such as rice (10 to 15% by weight) and dryland Gramineae (1 to 3%), while many dicots contain <0.5%.[8,9] Silicon accumulators take up $Si(OH)_4$ (silicic acid, $H_4SiO_4°$) which moves in the xylem with deposition in the walls of xylem cells and outer walls of epidermal cells on both sides of leaves. This deposition creates a barrier that may inhibit fungal infection, reduce cuticular transpiration, and mechanically strengthen tissues. In grasses, Si deposition also occurs in "silica cells" in leaves, especially zoysiagrass and bahiagrass. Silicon may also play a role in promoting lignin biosynthesis and in increasing cell wall elasticity during elongation—followed by strengthening of wall tissues.

The potential benefits of Si in field situations (research on turfgrasses is limited) may be: (a) greater leaf erectness that reduces adjacent leaf shading and increases radiation absorbance; (b) enhanced leaf and stem tissue strength for reduced lodging and potentially greater wear tolerance of grasses; (c) reduced incidences of root and leaf pathogens; and (d) reduced the potential for Mn or Fe toxicities by suppressing uptake or allowing more uniform distribution in tissues.

Total Si content in soils ranges from 23 to 40% as the second most abundant element.[10] Silicon in the soil solution ($H_4SiO_4°$) may vary from <1 to 37 ppm Si but as concentrations become too high it precipitates as SiO_2 (quartz). Solution Si arises from dissolution of various minerals and alumino-silicates.

Soil pH does not have an appreciable influence on Si availability. On plants that require Si for optimum performance such as rice, low Si levels are associated with: (a) highly weathered soils low in total Si; (b) adsorption from soil solution by reaction with Fe/Al oxides; and (c) liming may reduce uptake in some cases. Consistently, moist soil conditions enhance Si availability and uptake.

While soil applications of granular Si fertilizers are used on sugarcane and rice, the rates are high at 2,000 to 5,000 lb material per acre (2,240 to 5,600 kg ha^{-1}) with materials containing 18 to 31% Si. The most common granular materials are:

Calcium silicate ($CaSiO_3$)	31% Si
Calcium silicate slag ($CaAl_2Si_2O_8$)	18 to 21% Si
Sodium metasilicate ($NaSiO_3$)	23% Si

Potassium silicate (20.8% SiO_2, 8.3% K_2O), a liquid potassium salt of silicic acid, was used by the author (R.N. Carrow,[1] R.R. Duncan, and L. Trenholm, personal communication) at 2 lb Si per acre (foliar) and 20 lb Si acre (drench) on *Paspalum vaginatum* to assess the influence on wear tolerance. After three treatments at two-week intervals and under good moisture conditions, the drench rate resulted in a minor increase in wear tolerance. However, this appeared to be due to the K and not Si. In fact, Si reduced K uptake. Researchers at North Carolina State University (personal communication) have recently reported 18 to 30% reduction in dollar spot, minor influence on brown patch, and no influence on *Pythium aphanidermatum* using the same liquid Si source. Thus, effects of Si on turfgrasses have to date been very modest or nonexistent.

B. Sodium

Sodium is widely found in nature and can easily be taken up by turfgrasses as Na^+. It is not an essential nutrient for turfgrasses but is considered essential for some C_4 species such as sedges.

Chapters 7 and 8 contain considerable discussion of Na as a component of salt and potential adverse effects on turfgrasses due to: (a) ion toxicity of high Na^+ levels in tissue; (b) ion imbalance where Na^+ may inhibit K^+, Ca^{+2}, Mg^{+2}, Mn^{+2} uptake; (c) sodic influence on soil structure deterioration (Na permeability hazard); and (d) Na contributing to total salinity.[1]

Even though not an essential nutrient, Na can result in positive growth responses in many turfgrasses, especially halophytes (salt tolerant) species. Marschner[4] describes four general classes of plants as:

Group A. Most salt tolerant (*halophytes*); *natrophillic* or salt includers that readily transport Na to shoots; Na can provide significant additional growth that cannot be achieved by increasing K; Na can replace a high portion of K functions without reducing growth.

Group D. Least salt tolerant (*glycophytes,* nonhalophytes); *natrophobic* or salt excluders that usually exclude Na by removing Na from the xylem and retransporting it downward. No additional growth is achieved with Na and Na cannot replace K functions.

Groups B and C are intermediates. These four groups are a general classification, and plants exhibit a wide array of Na tolerance mechanism and growth responses to Na. Most agricultural crop plants are in groups C and D. Turfgrass species can be found in all categories.

Group A plants can accumulate large quantities of Na in the shoots but maintain it largely in the cell vacuole where it allows the shoot to osmotically adjust to the high soil osmotic stress, thereby maintaining turgor pressure and physiological activity of leaf cells. To counter the high solute concentration in the vacuole, organic osmolites, such as glycine betaine, are synthesized in the cytoplasm. Additionally, high K may be selectively maintained in the chloroplasts for maintenance of photosynthesis. Other mechanisms could come into play, such as partial inhibition of Na uptake by a thick Casparian strip in roots; higher solute concentrations in cells for optimal protein synthesis and activity; Na could substitute for K as a solute for maintaining osmotic adjustment; Na may substitute for K in some metabolic roles like the translation step of polysomes; and enhanced photosynthesis by higher cytoplasm solute concentrations.

Sodium, therefore, can have many potential means of influencing halophytes and positive growth responses may result over a fairly wide salinity range for some grasses—depending on the specific mechanisms involved. Part of the growth enhancement on halophytes may be due to greater solute concentrations (salt and organic solutes), while greater photosynthesis or protein synthesis at moderate salinity may account for some of the increased growth. Increased succulence caused by Na may enhance growth, since Na is more effective than K in being selectively accumulated in the vacuole to stimulate water uptake. With the advent of grasses with very high salinity tolerance (i.e., some *Paspalum vaginatum* ecotypes do well with seawater irrigation), it may be advantageous to apply Na as a fertilizer to these halophytes when they are grown on nonsalt affected sites.

Tissue concentrations of Na in turfgrasses can vary substantially but may be 0.05 to 2.00% by weight. Salt-sensitive grasses and landscape plants may exhibit toxicities at 0.25 to 0.60% by dry weight. Excessive Na can cause toxicities by the same mechanisms that Cl does as an excess salt ion. An additional means of Na toxicity is by excessive replacement of Ca from root cell walls which causes deterioration of cell activity, elongation, and differentiation. Also, high Na can reduce uptake of K, Ca, Mg, and Mn.

X. REFERENCES

1. Carrow, R.N. and R.R. Duncan. 1998. *Salt-Affected Turfgrass Sites: Assessment and Management.* Chelsea, MI: Ann Arbor Press.

2. Glendinning, J.S., Ed. 2000. *Australian Sail Fertility Manual.* Collingwood, VIC (Australia): CSIRO Publishing.
3. Hopkins, W.G. 1999. *Introduction to Plant Physiology,* 2nd edition. New York: John Wiley & Sons, Inc.
4. Marschner, H. 1995. *Mineral Nutrition of Higher Plants.* New York: Academic Press.
5. McCarty, L.B., J.B. Sartain, G.H. Snyder, and J.L. Cisar. 1993. *Plant Nutrition, Fertilizers and Fertilizer Programs for Florida Golf Courses.* University of Florida Bulletin 282. University of Florida, Gainesville, FL.
6. Mortvedt, J.J. (Ed.). 1991. *Micronutrients in Agriculture.* Second edition. Madison, WI: Soil Sci. Soc. of Amer., Inc.
7. Peverill, K.I., L.A. Sparrow, and D.J. Reuter, Eds. 1999. *Soil Analysis and Interpretation Manual.* Collingwood, VIC (Australia): CSIRO Publishing.
8. Savant, N.E., G.H. Korndörfer, L.E. Datnoff, and G.H. Snyder. 1999. Silicon nutrition and sugarcane production. *J. Plant Nutrition* 22(12):1853–1903.
9. Schmidt, R.E., X. Zhang, and D.R. Chalmers. 1999. Response of photosynthesis and superoxide dismutase to silica applied to creeping bentgrass grown under two fertility levels. *J. Plant Nutrition* 22(11):1763–1773.
10. Tisdale, S.L., W.L. Nelson, J.D. Beaton, and J.L. Havlin. 1993. *Soil Fertility and Fertilizers.* New York: Macmillan Pub. Co.
11. Turner, T.R., and N.W. Hummel, Jr. 1992. Nutritional requirements and fertilization. In D.V. Waddington, R.N. Carrow, and R.C. Shearman, Eds. *Turfgrass Monograph No. 32.* Madison, WI: Amer. Soc. Agron.
12. Wehner, D. 1993. Utilizing iron in turfgrass management. *Golf Course Mgt.* 61(3):44–47.

Chapter 15

Biochemical Aspects and Amendments

SOIL BIOLOGICAL PROPERTIES CAN INFLUENCE plant nutrition and soil fertility, especially through the types and quantity of *microorganisms* present in the soil, and by the presence or absence of certain chemicals that are biologically derived (i.e., *biochemicals*), such as *biostimulants, humates, humic acids,* and *composts.* The purposes of this chapter are: (a) to review the climatic and edaphic (soil) factors that influence microorganism activity and, therefore, their specific functions; and (b) to discuss various biochemicals, either applied to soils or produced within the soil by plants, that may potentially stimulate plant growth and development. Organic chemicals that are classified as plant growth regulators (PGRs) or herbicides are not discussed.

I. SOIL MICROORGANISMS[1,5,10]

SOIL MICROORGANISMS have a number of important functions that influence turfgrass growth and persistence. *Primary functions are:*

- Responsible for nutrient transformations from one chemical form to another, especially N, P, S, Fe, and Mn.
- Degradation of organic matter, which includes altering the types of organic matter present in a soil. Some of these forms of organic matter are important in soil fertility due to possession of CEC sites, chelating abilities (humic acids), or the nutrients contained in the compounds that are potentially plant available as degradation continues.
- Degradation of pesticides.
- Enhancement of soil structure through the production of polysaccharides and humic substances that bind mineral components together into aggregates.
- As a source of biochemicals that may influence plant growth (i.e., hormones, biostimulants), as they are excreted into the rhizosphere or released as microorganisms die.
- Fixation of N_2 into N forms that plants can use by free-living bacteria, blue-green algae, and microorganisms in symbiotic associations with a higher plant (i.e., legume-*Rhizobium* association).
- Suppression of pathogenic organisms by beneficial microorganisms through competition or production of growth suppressing products.
- As pathogens that cause turfgrass diseases.

Several of these microorganism functions directly impact soil fertility and plant nutrition. Thus, a basic appreciation of different soil microorganism populations and the soil factors that influence their activity aids in understanding soil fertility and plant nutrition. Many of these aspects and other soil microbiology topics are discussed in detail by Alexander[1] and Tate.[10]

Bacteria are the most abundant soil microorganisms in number but not necessarily in mass due to their small size as single-cell organisms. Bacteria are able to increase rapidly in numbers under a favorable environment. While bacteria are most abundant under aerobic conditions, certain populations are highly active under anaerobic situations.

Fungi predominate in terms of mass due to their larger, often-filamentous nature. *Molds* and *mushroom fungi* are the most important soil fungi. A wide variety of organic residues are decomposed by various fungal populations. Certain fungi called mycorrhiza form mutually beneficial (symbiotic) associations with plant roots, either as *ectomycorrhiza* on the surface of roots and stimulated by root exudates or *endomycorrhiza,* where the fungi forms within the root cells.

Algae are most prevalent near the soil surface under moist and light conditions. Many algae are capable of photosynthesis under these conditions. Different algae groups are blue-green, green, yellow-green, and diatoms.

Soil *actinomycetes* are unicellular but can form mycelial-like molds. They are important for organic matter decomposition, especially for breakdown of very resistant compounds such as chitin and cellulose.

Protozoa are small, single-celled animals that feed on bacteria and other microorganisms. Their numbers can be almost as high as bacteria and they are generally low in mass.

As the soil microenvironment changes, microorganism populations (and their particular functions) also are altered. The most important soil properties that affect microorganisms are: energy/nutrient source; temperature; oxygen status; moisture; pH; competitive/antagonistic relations with other soil microorganisms; and soil applied chemicals that repress a population (i.e., fungicides, algaecides, etc.). Within soils, these factors may vary over time and spatially within the soil from the surface to deeper. Also, microsite variations in soil properties, such as aeration/moisture on the inside of an aggregate versus the outside, can result in differences in microbial populations in small distances.

A. Energy/Nutrient Sources

Soil microorganisms can be classified on the basis of their sources of energy and carbon (C). For microorganisms to grow and maintain life, energy is required and they must obtain C. Two strategies have developed: (a) *autotrophic* which obtain energy from sunlight (*photoautotrophic;* through photosynthesis) or from oxidation of inorganic elements such as N, S, and Fe (*chemoautotrophs*). Autotrophs assimilate CO_2 as their C source. Photoautotrophs include higher plants (i.e., photosynthesis is required), soil algae, and some bacteria. Chemoautotrophs are limited to a few bacteria, but these are very important for soil fertility; and (b) *heterotrophic* organisms that obtain energy and C from the breakdown of soil organic matter with C obtained from C fixed in the organic matter. Heterotrophic soil organisms are the most abundant and include protozoa, fungi, actinomycetes, and most bacteria.

Oxidation reactions result in the energy production required for cellular functions. As microorganisms oxidize their specific substrate (organic matter; inorganic N, S, Fe), electrons are generated and must be transported to an electron acceptor. During this process, energy is derived (trapped as high energy chemical bonds) for use by the organism to maintain cell activities. Terminal electron acceptors vary with the type of organism but include O_2 (where the H^+ electron combines to form H_2O), NO_2^-, NO_3^-, SO_4^{-2}, fixed C (acetate, pyruvate), and CO_2.

The most common electron acceptor in soil is O_2, which is most available in aerobic conditions, to form water. *Aerobes* are soil microorganisms that must have adequate O_2. *Anaerobes* are of two types: (a) *facultative anaerobes* that develop either in the presence of O_2 or in its absence, when they use another electron acceptor, or (b) *strictly anaerobic organisms* that require organic C acceptors such as organic acids.

The relationships between energy sources, C sources, and terminal electron acceptors are summarized in Table 15.1. Regardless, of the organism in question, one principle applies—the abundance of available energy source and source of C strongly influence the activity of specific microorganism populations. The majority of soil microorganisms use soil organic matter (SOM) for their energy source as the SOM undergoes decomposition. During decomposition, nutrients are released from the SOM and organic compounds can be formed that act as chelating agents or contain cation exchange sites for nutrient retention. The chemoautotrophs are not present in large numbers but are very important for N and S transformations. Under anaerobic conditions, certain microorganism populations may increase and become active in reducing several nutrients into such forms as N_2, H_2S, FeS, and Mn^{+2}. Thus, the presence of an appropriate energy source, C source, and other environmental conditions (such as O_2, pH, etc.) can result in a number of biologically induced reactions that influence soil nutrient status.

B. Nutrients and Growth Factors

As living organisms, soil microorganisms require: (a) mineral nutrients—the same macro- and micronutrients essential for higher plants; and (b) growth substances, some of which a particular species may not be able to synthesize and thus would not grow in environments where that required growth factor is not present. Common growth factors for soil microorganisms are certain amino acids, vitamins, or organic structural compounds. Soil microorganism compete with turfgrasses for nutrients and growth factors.

The *carbon to nitrogen (C/N or C:N) ratio* is especially important in soils and when composting. The C:N ratio of organic matter in most soils is 8:1 to 15:1 and within the bodies of microorganisms 4:1 to 9:1. While adding N to a turfgrass can increase organic matter production, it may also enhance microorganism activity by resulting in a narrower C:N ratio. Organic amendments added to soils can limit N availability to turfgrasses if their C:N ratio is large, and additional N will be required until the C:N ratio stabilizes. Generally, organic amendments with C:N greater than 25 will require some N to enhance more rapid breakdown. For composting, C:N ratios of 25 to 40 provide adequate decomposition rates. In addition to N, the most common nutrients required for microorganism proliferation are P and S.

C. Moisture

As soil moisture changes, the total microbial activity varies from very low under dry conditions (–30 to –50 bar soil water potential; permanent wilting point is –15 bar for many higher plants where 1 bar = 0.1 MPa); to a maximum between –2 to –20 bar where arid soils have a maximum at about –10 to –20 bar and consistently moist sites at –2 to –10 bar. Then activity declines under increasing anaerobic conditions of 0 to –2 bar (at –2 bar, any anaerobic sites would likely be as microsites within soil aggregates). While total microbial activity changes with soil moisture, the populations also change. At soil moisture consistently above field capacity, algae and anaerobic bacteria predominate while other population groups decline, especially actinomycetes and filamentous fungi which are primarily strict aerobes. As soil moisture dries below

Table 15.1. Soil microorganism groups and their respective energy source, carbon (C) source, and primary electron acceptors that are important in turfgrass soil fertility (adapted from Tate[10]).

Soil Microorganism Group	Energy Source[a]	Carbon Source	Terminal Electron Acceptors	Primary Products	Examples
Heterotrophs					
• Aerobes (oxic)	Decomposition of SOM	SOM	O_2	Less complex organic matter, CO_2, H_2O	Many bacteria fungi, actinomycetes, and protozoa
• Facultative anaerobes (anoxic)	Decomposition of SOM	SOM	NO_3^-	NO_2^-, N_2O, N_2	Denitrifiers[b]
	Decomposition of SOM	SOM	Fe^{+3}	Fe^{+2}, FeS,	*Bacillus polymyxa, Enterobacter aerogens,* others
	Decomposition of SOM	SOM	Mn^{+4}	Mn^{+2}	Several bacteria
• Obligate (strict) anaerobes (anoxic)	Decomposition of SOM such as organic acids	SOM	SO_4^{-4}	S, FeS, H_2S	Sulfate reducers such as *Desulfovibrio desulfuricans*
	Decomposition of SOM such as cellulose	SOM	Organic compounds like organic acids	Organic compounds like organic acids, CO_2, H_2O	*Clostridium* spp.
Autotrophs					
• Chemoautrophs aerobes (oxic)	Inorganic NH_4^+	CO_2	NO_2^-	NO_2^-	*Nitrosomonas*
	Inorganic NO_2^-	CO_2	NO_3^-	NO_3^-	*Nitrobacter*
	Inorganic S	CO_2	O_2, NO_3^-	SO_4^-	*Thiobacillus*
• Chemoautotrophs anaerobes (anoxic)	H_2	CO_2	CO_2	CH_4	*Methanogens bacteria*
• Photoautotrophs	Light	CO_2	–	$C_6H_{12}O_6$	Algae[c]
	Light	CO_2	–	$C_6H_{12}O_6$	Photosynthetic bacteria

[a] SOM = soil organic matter, also called fixed carbon.
[b] Some soil microbiologists classify denitrifiers as heterotrophic aerobes because they can use O_2 as a terminal electron acceptor. Some denitrifier organisms are chemoautotrophs using H or S as energy sources but most are facultative anaerobes.
[c] Blue-green algae and photosynthetic bacteria can also fix N_2.

50% field capacity, actinomycetes and fungi are most prevalent, followed by bacteria. Within the normal soil moisture range of irrigated turfgrasses, bacteria, fungi, actinomycetes, and protozoa dominate. Many are aerobes; but, even in a relatively dry soil, microsites can be anaerobic. Anaerobic microsites are numerous in frequently irrigated turfgrass soils.

D. Oxygen

Microbial population shifts as soil moisture increases are primarily due to change in O_2 status as gas exchange decreases. Turfgrass sites usually have abundant decomposable organic matter as an energy source for heterotrophic aerobes and facultative anaerobes. Thus, when gas exchange becomes limited, soil O_2 can rapidly be depleted by microbial and turfgrass root tissue respiration.

As air-filled porosity (macropores) decrease below about 20% total, soil microbial activity starts to decrease. At approximately 10% and below, there is a shift from aerobic to predominantly anaerobic populations. As anaerobic microorganisms dominate, the by-products of their metabolism also become more prevalent, including reduced forms of inorganic compounds (S, FeS, H_2S, Mn^{+2}, Fe^{+2}, N_2, and organic compounds (organic acids, CH_4) (Table 15.1) (see Chapter 16).

E. Temperature

Soil microorganisms are classified into three groups for temperature tolerances: (a) *psychrophiles* with optimum temperature for growth at less than 68°F (20°C), (b) *mesophiles* with an optimum temperature range of 77° to 95°F (25° to 35°C) but with growth over 59° to 113°F (15° to 45°C), and (c) *thermophiles* exhibiting temperature optimum within the 113° to 149°F (45° to 65°C) range. Most microorganisms in turfgrass soils are mesophiles, with some psychrophiles also present.

Total soil microbial activity is often highest at 77° to 95°F (25° to 35°C), decreases to very low activity at 32°F (0°C), and also declines at temperatures above the optimum. Warm temperatures (>90°F) favor bacteria, actinomycetes, fungi, and algae (if moisture and sunlight are present). Protozoa prefer cool, damp environments, while actinomycetes exhibit little growth below 41°F (5°C).

For every 18°F (10°C) rise in temperature between 32°F and 95°F, soil microorganism activity increases by 1.5 to 3.0 fold in general. Using the 3-fold value and assigning microbial activity at 32°F (0°C) as 1, the influence of temperature is illustrated shown in Table 15.2. The temperature of 55°F (12.7°C) is often given as a value below which microorganism activity becomes increasingly limited for several important soil processes: nitrification, organic matter decomposition, N-release from organic compounds (mineralization), and S oxidation.

F. Soil Reaction (pH)

Specific microorganism populations have preferences for certain pH ranges. Bacteria are favored by pH 6.0 to 8.0 and decline under high acidity or alkalinity. Actinomycetes prefer pH 6.5 to 8.0 and rapidly decline at pH less than 5.0. Fungi are present over a wide pH range but the specific fungi populations will vary as pH changes. Under low pH of less than 5.5, fungi dominate as the bacteria and actinomycetes decline. Algae can also be present over a wide pH range

Table 15.2. Influence of temperature on soil microorganism activity.

°F	°C	Relative Microbial Activity	
32	0	1	(4%)[a]
50	10	3	(11%)
55	12.7	4.6	(17%)
68	20	9	(33%)
86	30	27	(100%)

[a] Numbers in parentheses are percentages of maximum activity as measured at 86°F.

but populations shift with primarily *Chlorophyceae* (green algae) present below pH 5.2 and mixed algae populations above 5.2. Protozoa seem to tolerate a wide pH range.

Nitrification is sensitive to soil pH and is markedly reduced at acidic pH with a decline starting at pH 6.0 and becoming very low at pH 5.0. Since nitrification is favored by an abundance of basic cations, especially Ca, the depression at low pH may be in part due to low Ca. Organic matter decomposition is reduced under acidic (pH <5.5) conditions due to suppression of bacterial and actinomycete populations.

G. Competition/Antagonistic Organisms

Microbial populations compete with other populations for energy substrates and growth factors. Species will be more competitive if they can use alternative energy substrates, require fewer growth factors from the surrounding environment, or are mobile. However, a change in the environment that favors one population over another has a major influence on competitive ability. The environmental change could be temperature, O_2, moisture, pH, or other factors. Some soil organisms may be able to synthesize *antibiotics* that suppress other organisms, or produce organic acids or *chelating agents (siderosphores)* that enhance nutrient availability. Also, predator and parasitic organisms can prey on other soil organisms. These include protozoa and certain bacteria and fungi. Microbial populations can be altered by applied chemicals such as fungicides that are specific to certain fungal pathogens.

II. BIOCHEMICALS

CERTAIN BIOLOGICALLY DERIVED CHEMICALS (i.e., biochemicals) can stimulate plant growth through: (a) presence of nutrients that can be released for plant uptake; (b) nutrient retention by cation exchange or chelating abilities; or (c) growth stimulating factors such as hormones. The latter aspect is not a true soil fertility/plant nutrition topic but is discussed because growth stimulation by biostimulants is often viewed by turfgrass managers as a nutritional-type of response.

Several categories of biochemicals will be discussed but they are not mutually exclusive. Instead, there is considerable overlap since many of these materials contain a diversity of biochemical substances rather than a single compound. Also, many of these substances may have some influence on soil physical and biological factors as well as soil fertility or plant nutrition.

We will emphasize only the soil fertility/plant nutrition or growth stimulation responses. Reference readings that focus on some of these compounds are MacCarthy et al.[8] and Wallace.[12,13]

A. Composts[5,14]

The oldest "biochemical" used on turfgrasses is compost derived from composting a variety of organic materials—peats; manures; organic waste products such as sewage sludge, cotton seed meal, rice hulls, leaf clippings, etc.; marine algae; seaweed meal; and mixtures of these and other organics. By definition, organic composts contain organic matter that had been composted in contrast to raw undecomposed organic matter. Mined peats can range from well-decomposed peats to some that are altered very little by decomposition. If a compost contains sufficient nutrients, it may be sold as an organic fertilizer rather than as compost and the nutrient content influences the quantity applied.

While peats often contain 80% or more organic matter by weight, man-made organic composts can vary from 25 to 60% organic matter content by weight. Common types of organic composts are leaf/yard waste, manure, sewage sludge, and spent mushroom soil based. Wilkinson[14] provides a good overview of compost use on golf courses and the quality aspects that are of interest.

Composts may vary from partially decomposed to well-decomposed materials. After addition to the soil, decomposition continues. Organic matter in composts (or soils) includes: (a) relatively simple organic substances such as simple sugars and amino acids; (b) more complex organic materials of higher molecular weight like polysaccharides and proteins; and (c) *humic substances* that are very complex organic compounds that cannot be classified into any of the discrete categories used above.[8] Humic substances are further categorized as:

- *Humic acids.* The humic substance fraction that is not soluble (i.e., precipitates) in water under very acid (pH <2) conditions but can be extracted from soil with dilute alkali or other extractants.
- *Fulvic acids.* The fraction of humic substances that is soluble in water under all pH conditions.
- *Humin.* The fraction of humic substances that is not soluble in water at any pH.

In most soils, the *nonhumic substance* organic matter (i.e., less complex and easier to decompose) comprises 20 to 30% of the total organic matter, while the *humic substance* organic matter makes up 60 to 80%. For turfgrasses under irrigated, high maintenance conditions, a higher percentage of nonhumic organic matter content than 20 to 30% would be anticipated. Nevertheless, humic substances are dominant in native soil organic matter and increasingly in composts as they decompose. The percentage nonhumic substances in composts will usually vary from 60 to 80% for relatively fresh organic matter to 20 to 30% for well-composted material.

Of the humic substances, fulvic acids are the lowest in molecular weight, humic acids are intermediate, and humin has the highest molecular weight and complexity. When fresh plant residues are added to the soil:[7]

- About 60 to 80% of the total residue is decomposed (oxidized) by microorganisms in one year with 90% of the simple organic substances oxidized.
- Approximately 30% of the lignin (contains phenols and quiones) from plant residue is degraded in one year but lignin-like phenol compounds in microbial biomass are slower to decompose (i.e., melanins).

- Of the 20 to 40% total residue not decomposed within one year, 15 to 35% is classified within the humus fraction, primarily as humic acids and fulvic acids.
- The humus fraction is subject to continued microbial degradation but at a much reduced rate. Total decomposition of the fulvic acid fraction would require 15 to 50 years, the humic acid compounds several hundred years, and the humin substances over 1,000 years. It is estimated that 2 to 5% of the total humus fraction decomposes each year.

Soil chemical related benefits of adding organic composts to a turfgrass site include: (a) release of the nutrients in the compost during degradation for turfgrass and microorganism growth; (b) enhanced cation exchange capacity for nutrient retention and chemical buffering; and (c) increased microbial activity especially if the organic matter is readily decomposable due to a favorable C:N ratio. Since the native soil organic matter contains appreciable humic acid and fulvic acid fractions, the potential benefits attributed to these materials in added humates/humic acid amendments may already be present in the soil. These potential benefits are the topic of the next section.

Enhanced CEC from composts comes mainly from the humus (humic) fraction which is composed of very complex polyphenols, polyquinones, polyuronides, and polysaccharides that are bound with each other and clays. The complex organic compounds contain many negative charge sites from various functional groups such as:

$$\text{— OH (hydroxyl)} \longrightarrow \text{— OH}^- + H^+$$

$$\text{— COOH (carboxyl)} \longrightarrow \text{— COO}^- + H^+$$

$$\text{-⌬-OH (phenolic)} \longrightarrow \text{-⌬-O}^- + H^+$$

B. Humates/Humic Acids[3,4,7,8,11]

The term *"humates"* is often used for any humic substance, but technically it should refer only to naturally occurring deposits of humic substance. *Humic acids* are products that contain some content of humic acid as defined in the preceding section on "Composts." *Commercial humates or humic acids* come from a variety of sources such as: (a) humates derived from natural deposits of coal, lignite, leonardite, or well-decomposed peats; (b) composted sewage sludge humic substances, which relative to natural humates, are higher in N content and percent fulvic acid versus humic acid, but have lower C/N ratios; (c) sea plants like brown marine algae (Knotted Wrack seaweed) that are harvested and then composted; and (d) essentially any organic waste material can be composted and used as a source of humic substances. Thus, there is considerable overlap in "composts" and "humates/humic acids." In the previous section on "Composts," this variation is emphasized as the different organic matter components are discussed—from fresh organic matter to the humic substances composed of fulvic acids, humic acids, and humin.

Granular humic substances can vary considerably with respect to percent organic matter (15 to 95% range), percent humic acid (1.5 to 75%), and nutrients. Materials with the highest organic matter and humic acid contents are preferred. Also, knowledge of the mineral (ash) component is useful, especially if it contains clay or silt.

Liquid humic acids normally contain both humic acid and fulvic acid, where fulvic acid is often the more active component, especially for foliar applications. Typically, the term "humic acids" is used to include both humic and fulvic acid. The total (humic acids) content of liquids generally varies from <1 to 12% by dry weight. The liquid extracts can contain suspended solids with a low percent preferred (<5%), especially if clogging of spray nozzles becomes a problem. Various nutrients are also usually present.

Since granular and liquid humic substances can be derived from a wide range of natural deposits and composted materials, there is wide diversity in their composition. This diversity is further complicated by addition of other materials such as N, surfactants, micronutrients, and readily decomposable organic matter. The sea plant based humic substances often contain a substantial portion of nonhumic organic matter, which can provide a more evident plant response from released nutrients; potential hormones or other materials in the relatively fresh organic matter fractions; and stimulation of microbial activity.

Chen and Aviad[3] and Varshovi[11] have reviewed plant responses to humic substances, while Liu and Cooper[7] discuss the limited research on turfgrass. Organic amendments in general (whether classified as composts, peats, or humic substances) may potentially provide beneficial responses from:

- enhanced soil nutrient content
- increased CEC
- stimulation of the soil microbial population if C:N ratios are sufficiently low (<30) and the C source is relatively easily decomposed
- soil structure improvement, primarily if soil microorganism activity is stimulated
- increased moisture holding capacity

The magnitude or degree that these aspects are exhibited depends on the characteristics of the amendment and the rate. For example, in high sand golf greens, tees, or athletic fields, organic amendment/additions must be made at 1 to 4% by weight (i.e., about 5 to 15% by volume) to provide sufficient beneficial responses as listed above. A 1% by weight of organic matter mixed or blended to an 8 inch (20 cm) depth represents about 460 lb per 1,000 ft^2 or 22, 400 kg ha^{-1}.

In addition to these soil or plant responses, humic substances may cause other unique but desirable plant responses in some situations. The types of effects reported in the literature are:[3,7,8,11]

- Solubilization of microelements (Fe, Mn, Zn) and some macroelements (P, Ca, K).
- Chelation of micronutrients for higher plant availability. If toxic metals are present, the solubilization and chelating properties may enhance toxicity, while CEC properties of the humin fraction normally would decrease metal ion toxicity. The fulvic acid fraction is most active as a chelating agent.
- Increase in membrane permeability that enhances ion uptake. One theory is that protein associated with fulvic acid may become embedded in cell membranes and act as nutrient carriers across the membranes.
- Photosynthesis or chlorophyll content are sometimes enhanced by humic substances in nutrient solutions or foliar applications.
- Enhanced protein synthesis, especially synthesis of certain enzymes.
- Plant hormone-like activity, especially *auxin* (indole-3-acetic acid, *IAA*) responses. This may be due to inhibition of IAA-oxidase, an enzyme that breaks down plant produced IAA. Other hormone-like responses may occur in sea plant derived humic substances, since these often contain relatively easily decomposable organic matter from plants that could contain *cytokinins* or other hormones. In these cases, the

hormone-like materials would not be from the humic substances but from less decomposed organic fractions. Cytokinins will be discussed in the next section.
- Enhanced root respiration.

The net effect of the above potential effects of humic substances on overall plant growth and development has been:

- Seed germination rate may increase as well as seedling growth at humic acid concentrations up to 100 mg L^{-1}.
- Stimulated root growth and root initiation have commonly been observed in nutrient solution at fulvic acid concentrations up to 300 mg L^{-1}, followed by a decline at higher rates. Foliar application of humic and fulvic acids up to 300 mg L^{-1} produces similar results.
- Shoot stimulation also can often occur from foliar spray or in nutrient solutions at concentrations from 50 to 300 mg L^{-1}, with growth declining at higher concentrations.

While the above plant responses from humic substances appear impressive, very few results have been reported in actual field studies. Chen and Aviad[3] demonstrate that to achieve a 100 mg L^{-1} concentration of soluble humic substances in a typical root zone of a field soil would require 1.54 lb soluble humic and fulvic acid per 1,000 ft^2 (75 kg ha^{-1}). Many soils already contain up to 400 mg L^{-1} of soluble humic substances and would not be expected to demonstrate a beneficial response with further addition.

However, soils that are very low in organic matter content may benefit. Examples would be: (a) during grow-in, especially on sandy soils, before the turfgrass and soil microorganisms produce appreciable organic biomass; (b) in hot, humid climates where native organic matter rapidly decomposes due to good moisture and high soil temperatures; and (c) in warm semi- and arid climates where organic matter production is limited—this may not be the case for irrigated turfgrasses. Soluble organic matter in these soils may only be 20 to 30 mg L^{-1}.

Under these conditions, foliar treatment may produce similar results to soil application (at 1.54 to 3.10 lb per 1,000 ft^2 water-soluble humic/fulvic acids equivalent). Foliar rates to achieve similar responses would be approximately 10.0 to 20.0 grams per 1,000 ft^2 of water-soluble humic/fulvic acids.

It is important to understand that humic substances applied at the above low soil or foliar rates are far below those required to achieve the typical responses of organic amendments when incorporated at 1 to 4% by weight as in a high sand green. At such low rates, micronutrient chelation and solubilization responses may not occur, but micronutrients already chelated in the humic substances could provide some short-term responses. Also, it is not unusual for companies to add N, Fe or other nutrients to a humate or humic acid material. Thus, the observed response may not be due to the humic acid or humate which a turf manager may assume is the "active ingredient" when purchasing these materials.

C. Biostimulants[9,15]

Plant hormones are organic compounds synthesized in one part of a plant and translocated to another part, where they have a regulatory or controlling effect—i.e., to stimulate or inhibit physiological or morphological processes. *Biostimulants* are natural plant extracts or synthetic chemicals that have hormonal properties when applied to a plant. Normally, compounds that stimulate or promote a process are listed in this category; however, the same materials may cause inhibitory responses if applied at high concentrations or in a manner that causes imbalance with other hormones.

The five major natural plant hormones (also called *phytohormones*) are *auxin (IAA), gibberellins (GA), cytokinins, ethylene,* and *abscisic acid (ABA).*[6,15] Plant hormones can influence a number of growth and development processes (dormancy, cell elongation, cell division, root initiation, flowering, senescence, and many other processes). Many of these processes are affected by more than one hormone. For example, auxins inhibit axillary bud formation (buds from which tillers, rhizomes, or stolons can arise) but cytokinin application to the shoot can remove this inhibition. Additionally, ABA and ethylene can influence axillary bud inhibition. Thus, plant hormone reactions and interactions are very complex[6] and beyond the scope of this chapter. Instead, the focus will be on situations where applied biostimulants may potentially influence turfgrass growth and development.

Humic acids are sometimes reported to exhibit hormonal activity similar to auxin. However, this response may be an indirect effect where humic acids inhibit IAA-oxidase, an enzyme that inactivates IAA.[8] Without inactivation, high IAA levels may occur and induce such responses as stimulation of root initiation or shoot elongation.

Cytokinins have been increasingly used as biostimulants in turfgrass management.[4,7,9,15] These include: (a) natural cytokinins such as kinetin and zeatin; (b) synthetic cytokinins—like benzyladenine (BA) and benzylamenopurine; (c) cytokinins derived from seaweed (*Ascophyllum nodosum,* knotted wrack or brown marine algae) that is naturally high in cytokinins. Seaweed meal (granulars) and seaweed extracts (liquids) can be formulated; (d) cytokinin extracted from *Yucca* plants; and (e) triazole fungicides, which can produce cytokinin-like responses. These include triademefon, propiconazole, and fenarimol.

Healthy plants are able to synthesize, break down, and/or translocate hormones to the sites necessary to control growth and development. That is why the plant is "healthy"—i.e., the plant's own natural system of controlling growth and development events by chemical messengers (hormones) is functioning. The processes controlling synthesis, degradation, balance among hormones, and translocation are very complex and not well understood.[6] However, if a stress inhibits hormone production, it seems likely that application of the hormone may then produce beneficial effects. This decrease in hormone production is most likely the reason why cytokinin responses are more prevalent than responses from other hormones.

Cytokinins are synthesized in the roots, especially active root tip cells, and then transported to the shoot tissues. If roots are absent, undergoing root dieback, or are under a stress where they are less viable (low soil O_2; high salinity; indirect high temperature induced carbohydrate deprivation; drought stress; high soil strength; toxicities—Al, Mn, Na, Cl; nematodes; root pathogens; root feeding insects), then synthesis may be limited or lacking. Under these conditions, applying cytokinin as a substitute for naturally produced cytokinins appears to often provide beneficial response.[15]

Cytokinin-induced responses reported for turfgrasses have been inhibition of leaf senescence and inhibition of chlorophyll loss. These responses have been widely reported on other plants but the mechanism is not clear. Possibly, cytokinin stimulates metabolism in senescencing leaves and results in mobilizing nutrients to these tissues. Cytokinins do not seem to cause recovery as much as delaying further chlorosis or leaf senescence. Best "greening" results on turfgrasses have come from applying foliar Fe to increase green coloration along with cytokinin to stabilize against senescence and chlorophyll loss.

Cytokinin applied to shoot tissues when roots are absent or limited seems to induce tillering. This response is consistent with the observation that cytokinin can remove inhibition by auxins of axillary bud formation where tillers arise. Increased tillering has been reported on seedlings treated with foliar cytokinins—where young seedlings have a limited root system of only the primary root.

Enhancement of photosynthesis following cytokinin treatment has been noted,[15] and could be in response to greater photosynthetically active leaves and greater leaf area from delayed senescence, stoppage of chlorophyll loss, and increased tillering. However, when roots are absent or limited, applied cytokinin seems to stimulate the photosynthesis process beyond that anticipated from the above responses.

Turfgrasses under high salinity stress often exhibit depressed cytokinin production in roots and reduced photosynthate (carbohydrate) production by photosynthesis. Glycophytes (salt-sensitive plants) exhibit this response more than salt-tolerant halophytes. Application of cytokinin on consistently salt-stressed grass may enhance photosynthesis and improve salt tolerance.

Under a variety of stresses, plants produce more toxic *free oxygen radicals* which are directly toxic to tissues and degrade chlorophyll. While plants have several systems to deactivate free oxygen radicals, the excess production during stress essentially creates an additional stress unless they are rapidly deactivated. Cytokinin application appears to prevent formation of some free oxygen radicals, stimulates *antioxidant* systems, and deactivates free oxygen radicals directly.[15]

In turfgrass culture, much emphasis has been placed on cytokinin application to enhance root growth. This enhancement can occur under the conditions when turfgrass roots are absent, stressed, or limited. Under these situations, the various shoot responses previously mentioned occur first to enhance leaf area, chlorophyll content, and photosynthetic efficiency. The net result is more carbohydrate production, which allows greater root growth. However, stimulation of turfgrass root growth seems to occur only when roots were removed (cut sod), or very limited (new seedling or newly planted vegetative material), or stressed (salt). When cytokinins were applied under these conditions, shoot response improvements were often followed by a secondary response of better rooting.

Based on the level of research information available on turfgrasses and other plants, some recommendations are suggested for growers to try on their sites or at least on trial areas:

- Cytokinins applied as foliar treatment or in seaweed materials may enhance turfgrass establishment regardless of the method of planting on sandy soils or low organic matter soils. The primary benefit expected would be somewhat better rooting following top growth improvement.
- Cytokinins may aid in maintaining turfgrass roots undergoing stress such as low soil O_2 stress, high salinity, indirect high temperature stress on cool-season species in the summer, and high nematode populations. In these cases, application prior to the anticipated stress or as it is initially occurring should be best for maintaining viability.
- Root regrowth after root death or removal may be enhanced by cytokinins treatment since normal plant cytokinin synthesis will be limited until roots regenerate. Examples would be in early fall for cool-season grasses; after spring root-dieback on warm-season grasses; after root pruning or damage by root pathogens, insects, nematodes; or low soil O_2.
- To delay discoloration associated with senescence such as to delay cold-induced color loss on warm-season grasses in midfall or on any grass exhibiting chlorosis.

While cytokinins can be a tool in modifying some stresses and aiding in turfgrass recovery, they will not prevent or eliminate the stress; and, if a stress is severe enough, it will override benefits from cytokinin application. Or, to put it in other terms—neither cytokinins, as well as other biochemicals, cannot substitute for good, preventative turfgrass management targeted to the primary stress causing turf injury.

The question often arises about application of cytokinins (or any other hormone) on a routine basis whether the turfgrass is healthy with a viable root system and is not stressed. Caution is urged concerning cytokinin application on a turfgrass that is sufficiently healthy to produce and regulate its own cytokinin or hormone supply. This statement is based on: (a) the lack of research to support any benefits under nonstressed conditions, especially root enhancement which is a secondary response occurring primarily when roots are absent; (b) applied cytokinins can stay within the turfgrass system for several weeks; and (c) the complexity of natural plant hormone interactions and control suggests that we "tread only where we feel the ground is firm." It is possible to create undesirable responses by providing excessive cytokinin that may interfere with normal plant metabolism.

One possible response on turfgrasses has been shown on other plants—loss of stomatal control by high cytokinin levels suppressing the regulatory role of ABA. When plants are drought stressed, ABA is rapidly synthesized and carried in the transpiration stream to stomatal guard cells where it induces stomatal closure (or partial closure) to regulate water loss. At the same time, high tissue ABA reduces cell elongation to slow shoot growth. Drought stress also causes natural cytokinin levels in shoot tissues to decline. This is most likely part of the stomatal control system of plants because low cytokinin tissue levels cause stomatal closure. Thus, if treatment by cytokinin results in higher levels than normal, two responses are possible: (a) high cytokinin causing open stomata, and (b) high cytokinin suppressing ABA and stomata remain open. Under drought conditions, cytokinin-treated barley and wheat have been reported to perform poorly, possibly for these reasons.

D. Other Amendments

The popular literature contains many references to materials applied in turfgrass situations to modify the plant, soil (physical, chemical, biological properties) and/or thatch. Various terms are used, such as *soil amendments, soil conditioners, biostimulants, enhancers, soil modifiers, biocontrol agents, turf conditioners,* etc. Often these terms are not well defined and they are used interchangeably in many cases. Some materials are new, while others have been available for many years or have "reappeared" in a cyclic fashion. Thus, confusion exists among turf managers concerning which products are beneficial and when/how to use the materials.

One caution is to not get caught up in the latest magic cure-all or "silver bullet"—i.e., the one thing that does all, cures all. Turfgrass management requires an integrated approach where many inputs are required in the proper balance. The nearest materials we have to a silver bullet are water, nitrogen, oxygen, and sunlight. Many times a new product or technology has a place in turfgrass management, but it is important to understand the proper use and economics involved.[2]

Eight questions that can aid a turfgrass manager in determining whether a new soil amendment, piece of equipment, or technology is beneficial in their situation are:[2]

- Is this product *needed* in my situation? Does the material specifically address a problem that is important? Much of turfgrass management consists of alleviating or preventing climatic, soil, use, and pest stresses that limit turfgrass growth. Thus, does the material alleviate one of these stresses? In some instances, the material may already be present or is being added to the turfgrass system—examples are Ca or Mg in irrigation water; humic acids produced from plants as they add soil organic matter.
- Are *independent test results* available? The main reason for turfgrass research scientists at the public university is to conduct unbiased research, and this includes product

testing. Since society (i.e., taxpayers) already support universities, those with a financial interest in testing a product are also expected to bear some of the cost. Testimonials may bear some credence if the individual is known by the turf manager and considered as knowledgeable and honest. But testimonials, while costing no research money or little money, can be misleading. Not only should reliable research be expected but also access to the full data (results) and information on the specific source of information rather than carefully selected data.

- What is the *magnitude* of response? Many materials can potentially have *some* influence in a system. Almost anything you add to soil, including "water," has the potential to influence soil physical, chemical, and biological properties. However, what is important is the magnitude of the response. Is the response sufficient to truly result in a significant benefit? As noted, bottled "water" could be marketed as a secret ingredient that would positively affect soil chemical, physical, and biological properties. But what would the "magnitude" of response be for bottled water applied at a liter per ha? Also, some products contain sufficient N or Fe to produce a turfgrass color or growth response but what the buyer may be paying for is the "*in*active ingredient." Check the active ingredients on the label and if they are not specifically listed—buyer beware.
- What is the *duration* of response? A material may cause a short-term response while another provides benefit over a long period. Addition of simple sugars can markedly enhance microorganism activity on a moist soil and create aggregation, but the response is of short-term duration. When a turfgrass sod is present, the aggregation effect is very seldom if ever observed because the turf is excreting natural sugars into the root zone at higher quantities than can be added.
- What is the *consistency* of results? Is the product consistent in producing the expected result or does it work in only some instances?
- Are there better *alternatives*? Sometimes other materials can produce the same result at higher magnitude, duration, and consistency; and possibly at a lower cost.
- Do *benefits* justify cost? Costly materials should bring higher expectations for results.
- Should I try this on a *trial* area? Certainly, trying a new material on their specific site is one way to help answer the previous questions for a turfgrass manager. However, this testing should be done with some sense of good science—use replicated treatments, include nontreated controls, carefully watch for plant responses, use a uniform area that is managed uniformly except for the specific treatments and control of interest, and keep records of the treatments and results.

III. REFERENCES

1. Alexander, M. 1977. *Soil Microbiology*. New York: John Wiley & Sons, Inc.
2. Carrow, R.N. 2000. Purchasing new products and technologies: An ethical and common sense approach. *USGA Green Section Record* 38(3):17–20.
3. Chen, Y. and T. Aviad. 1990. Effects of humic substances on plant growth. In P. MacCarthy, C.E. Clapp, R.L. Malcolm, and P.R. Bloom, Eds. *Humic Substances in Soil and Crop Sciences: Selected Readings*. Madison, WI: Amer. Soc. of Agron., Soil Sci. Soc. of Amer.
4. Cooper, R.J. 1999. Humic substances and their potential for improving turfgrass growth. *Turfgrass Trends* 7(6):9–13.
5. Elliott, M.L. and E.A. Des Jardin. 1999. Effect of organic nitrogen fertilizers on microbial populations associated with bermudagrass putting greens. *Bio. Fertil. Soils* 28:431–435.

6. Hopkins, W.A. 1999. *Introduction to Plant Physiology,* 2nd edition. New York: John Wiley & and Sons, Inc.
7. Liu, C. and R.J. Cooper. 1999. Humic substances: Their influence on creeping bentgrass growth and stress tolerance. *Turfgrass Trends* 7(8):6–12.
8. MacCarthy, P., C.E. Clapp, R.L. Malcolm, and P.R. Bloom, Eds. 1990. *Humic Substances in Soil and Crop Sciences: Selected Readings.* Madison, WI: Amer. Soc. of Agron., Soil Sci. Soc. of Amer.
9. Nus, J. 1993. Biostimulants. *Golf Course Mgt.* 61(3):76–86.
10. Tate, R.L. 1995. *Soil Microbiology.* New York: John Wiley & Sons, Inc.
11. Varshovi, A. 1996. Humates and their turfgrass application. *Golf Course Mgt.* 64(8):53–56.
12. Wallace, A., Ed. 1997. *Soil Conditioner and Amendment Technologies. Vol 1.* Jefferson City, MO: Micro Macro Publishing.
13. Wallace, A., Ed. 1997. *Soil Conditioner and Amendment Technologies. Vol 2.* Jefferson City, MO: Micro Macro Publishing.
14. Wilkinson, J.F. 1994. Applying compost to the golf course. *Golf Course Mgt.* 62(3):80–88.
15. Zhang, X. and R.E. Schmidt. 1999. Biostimulating turfgrasses. *Grounds Maint.* (11):14–32.

Chapter 16

Unique Soil Problems (Waterlogged, Pollutants, Organic)

CERTAIN UNUSUAL OR UNIQUE SOIL CHEMICAL PROBLEMS have been discussed in previous chapters such as soils exhibiting low CEC, excessively acid, excessively alkaline, salt-affected, or infertile conditions. Chemical constraints that may arise from three other field problem situations are the focus of this chapter, namely:

- waterlogged or low aeration soils
- soils that are contaminated with heavy metals
- organic soils.

I. WATERLOGGED SOILS[4,7,8,11,12,16]

IT IS NOT UNUSUAL FOR MANY TURFGRASS SITES to contain *waterlogged* or *low aeration* (low soil O_2) areas. Some of the most common causes of waterlogged conditions are:

- high water table resulting in saturation of the root zone
- low spots that accumulate water such as "pocket areas" on greens that are not surface drained off the green
- compacted soils with low infiltration and percolation rates exhibit waterlogging in low areas but even level sites can retain excess soil moisture at the expense of soil aeration
- seepage areas where water seeps to the surface
- perched water tables due to a layer that slows or impedes drainage, thereby ponding water above the layer
- soils containing too many fines (clay, silt) or organic matter may retain excess moisture due to a high content of micropores but few macropores for water drainage and aeration. These soils are often prone to soil compaction which further reduces aeration.
- sites subjected to periodic flooding
- soils where structure has been destroyed by high Na content.

Waterlogging or low soil aeration is essentially a result of: (a) lack of macropores to allow rapid water drainage and gas exchange; and/or (b) movement of excess water onto a site, whether by surface or subsurface movement of water. Some of these situations may cover large acreage, while others are confined to relatively small landscape areas. Also, it is not unusual for more than one of the above factors to be present on the same site. The long-term management goal is to remove the underlying cause for poor soil aeration or excess moisture. Specific management practices depend on the particular problem but often include cultivation, soil modification, or drainage techniques.

Until the primary factor(s) causing low aeration is corrected, turfgrass managers must deal with the adverse effects that occur in the soil and turfgrass plant. Limited soil oxygen can range from: (a) *hypoxia* conditions with varying degrees of oxygen stress or depletion; to (b) *anoxia,* where the O_2 molecule is not present. The general term *anaerobic* includes both conditions, while *aerobic* indicates that O_2 is not limited. Low aeration problems may be a chronic problem in turfgrass soils with few macropores, high water table, perched water table from an undesirable layer problem, or a low area. In the case of flooding, an acute, rapid anaerobic condition results.

Lack of O_2 causes adverse soil chemical, turfgrass plant, and soil microorganism responses. The magnitude of a particular response depends on many conditions, such as degree of low O_2 stress, soil and air temperatures, soil pH, type of grass, longevity of O_2 stress, and other aspects.

A. Soil Chemical and Biochemical Responses to Low Aeration

Soil chemical and biochemical (chemical reactions involving microorganisms) reactions of C, N, S, Fe, and Mn often are oxidation and reduction in nature. An *oxidation-reduction reaction* involves the transfer of electrons from one molecule or ion to another, where an *electron acceptor is called an oxidizing agent* while an *electron donor is a reducing agent.* Oxygen is the strongest electron acceptor generally present in soils.

Aerobic, heterotrophic soil microorganisms obtain their energy and carbon for growth and metabolic activities from oxidation of soil organic matter. This process is called *microbial respiration.* Similarly, a turfgrass root cell obtains energy for growth and metabolism by oxidation of carbohydrates (derived from photosynthesis) in *cell respiration.* The general reaction for both microbial and cell respiration is (see Chapter 2, Section IV.B):

$$\underset{\substack{\textit{Soil O.M.}\\ \textit{or plant}\\ \textit{carbohydrates}}}{(CH_2O)_x} + \underset{\substack{\textit{The}\\ \textit{electron}\\ \textit{acceptor}}}{6O_2} + 6H_2O \rightarrow 6CO_2\uparrow + 12H_2O + \underset{\substack{\textit{For use}\\ \textit{in plant}\\ \textit{functions}}}{\text{energy}}$$

Energy is trapped in the form of high energy bonds, especially in adenosine triphosphate (ATP) as the organic compounds are broken down into more simple forms. In the above reaction, it appears as if O_2 is liberating energy when it acts on the organic matter or carbohydrate. In reality, degradation of these organic compounds (electron donor) releases electrons which must be removed. Oxygen is the terminal electron acceptor in aerobic respiration, whether in microorganisms or root cells. Maximum energy production occurs under aerobic conditions.

When soil O_2 starts to become limited, other electron acceptors become important in chemical and biochemical soil reactions. However, turfgrasses and other higher plants can only use O_2 as an electron acceptor in their respiration processes. While other electron acceptors can be used by certain soil microorganism populations under limited aeration (see Chapter 15), the energy production is much less.

Thus, as soil O_2 becomes limited, several important changes are induced in soils:

- Soil microbial populations shift from primarily aerobic and facultative anaerobic organisms to facultative anaerobic and strict anaerobic organisms (see Chapter 15).

These anaerobic organisms utilize different electron acceptors than O_2 and alternative energy sources to organic matter. Thus, new sets of biologically induced reactions are initiated as well as accumulation of end products of these reactions.

- Important biochemical reactions that are initiated under various degrees of anaerobic conditions are listed in Table 16.1. The chemical forms produced under reducing (low O_2) conditions are in the right-hand side of the reaction. The *redox potential* is a measure of the tendency for reduced forms of elements or molecules to be present with lower (including negative values) potentials indicating greater reducing conditions. The general time frame for reactions to be initiated or completed after initiation of waterlogging at 25°C (77°F) is listed in Table 16.1, but these vary greatly with severity of reducing conditions, temperature, pH, and other factors.
- Some of these reducing compounds can combine to create even worse aeration conditions in the future such as formation of FeS and MnS precipitates that contribute to plugging soil pores and the black coloration in *black layer*.
- Anaerobic conditions and anaerobic respiration by soil microorganisms and plant roots can cause certain chemicals to accumulate such as organic acids (acetic, butyric, formic, lactic, and others), ethylene, ethanol, phenolic substances, methane, and others. Some of these chemicals can be root toxins. Carbon dioxide (CO_2) also accumulates to a much higher percentage (i.e., 1 to 10% or more).

Soil fertility and plant nutrition are influenced by many of these anaerobic-induced, soil chemical and biochemical changes. Primary nutritional effects are: (a) alternating the chemical form of nutrients into less available forms (N, S) or into a more available form (Fe, Mn) where the latter may increase to toxic levels in some cases; and (b) creating a more hostile environment for root viability and persistence through lack of O_2 and presence of root toxins.

In most cases, these adverse soil chemical conditions are improved by enhancing soil physical properties, especially by the creation of macropores (>0.12 mm diameter) for water movement, gas exchange, and root growth channels. Macroporosity is enhanced by cultivation procedures or soil modification. Additional excess water must be removed through surface and subsurface drainage methods. However, the black layer condition also requires supplemental practices.

B. Black Layer[2,8,11,12]

Black layer has been observed on high sand content root zone mixes such as golf greens as well as fine-textured soils (Plates 22 and 23). It is characterized by a continuous or discontinuous black colored subsurface layer that often exhibits a rotten egg or other odor.[11] Anything that impedes water percolation to create a waterlogged zone can initiate a black layer condition. This includes migration of colloidal particles (clay or organic in nature), salt deposition, natural occurring layers, and other factors. Cyanobacteria (blue-green algae) can produce gel-like substances that help induce anaerobic conditions.[11] *Biofilms* produced by bacteria can also plug pores.[8,12] Impeded water movement may occur before any black layer symptoms appear.

Regardless of the initial or primary cause of excess moisture/low aeration, anaerobic chemical and biochemical reactions will follow. Sulfur seems to be especially important as a secondary factor that contributes to additional anaerobic conditions and the "black layer symptoms" in many of the turfgrass situations due to the use of a number of S-containing materials in management programs or high S in irrigation water (Plate 22). Thus, H_2S, FeS, and MnS compounds can follow reduction of SO_4^{-2} to S^{-2} by *Desulfovibrio desulfuricans* and create more sludge-like

Table 16.1. Redox reactions in soils as related to redox potential and the general time period after a flooding event that selected reactions are initiated or completed.[a]

Redox Reaction Equations: Left Side Oxidized Form[b] = Right Side Reduced Forms[b]	Redox Potential[c] mV		Time after Flooding for Chemical Change to Appear in Soil (days)
$O_2 + 4H^+ + 4e^- = 2H_2O$	850 to 1230	aerobic[d]	–
$Fe^{+3} + e^- = Fe^{+2}$ (onset of reaction)	770		4–22
$NO_3^- + 2H^+ + 2e^- = NO_2^- + H_2O$ (onset of denitrification process)	420 to 550		–
$Mn^{+4} + 4e^- = Mn^{+2}$ (onset of Mn^{+2} formation)	350 to 450		1–12
Absence of free O_2	330		1–10
$SO_4^{-2} + 10H^+ + 8e^- = H_2S + 4H_2O$ (onset of sulfate reduction)	310		5–20
NO_3^- conversion to N_2 completed	222 to 280		4–16
Mn^{+4} conversion to Mn^{+2} completed	222 to 280		–
Fe^{+3} conversion to Fe^{+2} completed	150 to 180		–
SO_4^{-2} conversion to S^{-2} completed	−120 to −180		–
CO_2 conversion to CH_4 (methane) completed	−200 to −280	anoxic[d]	>100

[a] After Marschner,[15] Brady,[4] and Setter and Belford.[16]
[b] Reduced forms occur under anaerobic conditions, and oxidized forms under well aerated situations.
[c] Redox potential of soil is a measure of the oxidation or reduction potential. The lower the redox potential, the greater the tendency for reducing conditions and the presence of reduced forms of elements or molecules.
[d] Aerobic = soil O_2 is not limited; anoxic = no soil O_2 present. In between aerobic to anoxic conditions the soil is anaerobic (some O_2 is present but O_2 is limiting).

materials to further reduce water percolation and gas exchange.[2] *Important components of black layer management are:*

- Most important are preventative measures to avoid creation of anaerobic conditions. To provide adequate macropores for water infiltration/percolation/drainage and to avoid excess water accumulation requires a site-specific soil modification, drainage (surface, subsurface), irrigation and/or cultivation program(s).
- Improve drainage to remove excess water from the site.
- Establish a cultivation program to enhance air exchange and water percolation, while breaking up any subsurface layers that impede water drainage.
- Irrigate at rates and frequencies that will help to avoid excess moisture. Limiting water applied to affected area of greens to permit drier conditions while hand syringing the other areas needing water can be beneficial.
- Use wetting agents to increase infiltration and percolation.
- Avoid composts and organic fertilizers to reduce a readily available C source.
- Check the irrigation water for S, cyanobacteria, and fines. When irrigation water has high SO_4^{-2} levels, periodic light applications of lime will help convert solution SO_4^{-2} into $CaSO_4$ (gypsum). This essentially removes soluble SO_4^{-2} so that it cannot be readily reduced if anaerobic conditions occur.
- Reduce S use from such sources as S-containing fertilizers, elemental S, topdressing materials, and gypsum until black layer symptoms disappear.
- Fertilize lightly and frequently.

Turfgrass species and ecotypes/cultivars within a species can vary in tolerance to flooded conditions (standing or moving water), waterlogged soils, compacted soils, and other anaerobic situations. It is beyond the scope of this book to present the various tolerance mechanisms plants may exhibit. But, good overviews are provided on plant responses to oxygen stress/waterlogging (Marschner,[13] Setter and Belford[14]) and tolerance mechanisms (Crawford and Braendle[6]).

II. POLLUTANTS[1,5,6,9,10,17,18]

THE MOST COMMON SOURCES OF inorganic or organic chemical pollutants on turfgrass sites are from some sewage sludges (also termed *biosolids*), industrial sludges, composts, effluent irrigation water, chemical spills, airborne pollutants, or contaminants present before grass establishment. There are many different potential chemical pollutants including:

Inorganics

1. Nutrient elements. Toxic levels of N, B, Cu, Zn, Mo, Fe, Mn, Ni.
2. Heavy metals: Heavy metals are metallic elements that have densities greater than 5 Mg m^{-3} (5g cm^{-3}). When present in soils in sufficient amounts, they can pose long-term environmental hazards. They can cause toxicity in plants, and animal and human health problems when in the diet. In soils these metals include As, Cd, Co, Cr, Cu, Fe, Hg, Mn, Mo, Ni, Pb, Se, V, and Zn, some of which are also classified as essential elements for plants. Heavy metals in commercial organic fertilizers or microelements applied at normal rates should pose no problem on turfgrass sites. Most products do not contain sufficient heavy metals to pose a problem for turfgrasses. Checking the product label is suggested.
3. Other metals and nonmetals. Al, F.

Organics

1. Petroleum products or by-products.
2. Chlorinated organics. Polychlorinated biphenyls (PCBs), pentachlorophenol (PCP), chlorobenzenes (CBs), and trichloroethylene (TCE).
3. Nitroaromatic compounds (TNT).
4. Organic pesticides.

Sewage sludge (biosolids) quality can be assessed prior to approval for land application. Quality factors include:[17,18] (a) concentration of pollutants, (b) processes used to reduce human pathogens and amount of reduction, and (c) processes used to reduce sewage sludge characteristics that attract disease vectors (e.g., rodents, insects). Regulations of the U.S. Environmental Protection Agency (EPA) define two categories of sewage sludge:[17,18] (a) exceptional quality (EQ sludge) and (b) nonexceptional quality (non-EQ sludge). Sewage sludge not meeting requirements of EQ or non-EQ cannot be land applied, and must be incinerated or placed in landfill areas. To qualify as an EQ sludge, the sludge must meet requirements for pollutant contents, pathogen reduction, and vector attraction limits. It must be a nonliquid; such sludge is largely free of regulatory restraints for land application. A non-EQ sludge must meet requirements for each of the quality factors, but requirements are less strict than for EQ sludge. Extensive regulatory requirements apply to non-EQ sludge land application.

Table 16.2. Concentration limits used to classify sewage sludge for land application.[17]

Pollutant	EQ Sludge[a]	Non-EQ Sludge	Sludge Not To Be Land Applied
	mg/kg based on dry weight		
Arsenic	<41	41 to 75	>75
Cadmium	<39	39 to 85	>85
Copper	<1,500	1,500 to 4,300	>4,300
Lead	<300	300 to 840	>840
Mercury	<17	17 to 57	>57
Molybdenum	<75	75	>75
Nickel	<420	420	>420
Selenium	<100	100	>100
Zinc	<2,800	2,800 to 7,500	>7,500
PCBs	<4	4 to 8.6	>8.6

[a] EQ = Exceptional Quality.

Table 16.3. Cumulative loading limits for pollutants in land-applied non-EQ sewage sludge.[a]

Pollutant	Cumulative Pollutant Loading Rate (lb A^{-1})
Arsenic	36
Cadmium	34
Copper	1,320
Lead	264
Mercury	15
Nickel	370
Selenium	88
Zinc	2,464

[a] EQ = exceptional quality.

The EPA regulations on sewage sludge for land application apply to 10 pollutants; nine elements and polychlorinated biphenyls (PCBs). Concentration limits of these pollutants are shown in Table 16.2. The EPA regulations also place limits on the cumulative amount of pollutants for a given application site. These limits (Table 16.3) apply only to non-EQ sludge.

Various problems can arise from chemical pollutants. Primary potential problems include: (a) human health considerations; (b) inhibition of plant rooting and growth (Breckle[5]); (c) toxicity to soil microorganisms and their processes (Giller et al.[10]); and (d) odors. Due to the diversity and complexity of chemical pollutant situations, it is beyond the scope of this book to provide an in-depth treatment of this subject. Additional suggested readings are Brady (Chapter 18, Soils and Chemical Pollution),[4] Cunningham et al.,[9] Beck et al.,[1] and Clapp et al.[6] Toxicities from nutrient elements are discussed in the chapters of this book pertaining to the specific element.

III. ORGANIC SOILS[3,13,14]

ORGANIC SOILS CONTAIN at least 20% organic matter (weight basis) for coarse-textured soils to 30% or more for soils containing more than 50% clay. Also, organic soils (Histosols soil order in the U.S. soil taxonomy system) normally contain organic soil materials in more than half of the surface 32 inch (80 cm) layer. Thus, soil chemical and physical properties are dominated by the organic fractions. Histosols comprise only about 1% of the total soil area in the world but these soils: (a) are important sod production soils; (b) are often found on limited areas of golf courses and other turfgrass sites either under turfgrass culture or in adjacent wetlands; (c) exhibit some unique soil chemical or fertilization problems; and (d) are often the source of mined (peat) organic soil amendments.

Organic soils are often classified based on their fiber content and state of decomposition into: (a) *peats* which vary from slightly decomposed to moderately well decomposed but where plant parts are still identifiable, and (b) *mucks,* which are highly decomposed. *Fiber content* refers to the percentage of undecomposed or partially decomposed plant fibers that do not pass through a particular sieve opening. The *degree of decomposition* refers to the amount of decomposed (humified) plant material. There is not a worldwide standard for fiber content or decomposition state but common standards are discussed by Malterer et al.[12] Bethke[2] presents information on classification and characteristics of peats often used as turfgrass soil amendments.

Mucks are organic soil materials in which the original plant parts are not recognizable. In a muck soil the sum of thickness of organic layers is usually greater than the sum of thickness of mineral layers. In their natural field locations, mucks can be productive for sod production and vegetable crops. Mucks are sometimes called *peat humus.* Peat humus is a term used to describe decomposed peats and can be defined as peat material in which the oven-dried peat contains less than 33-1/3% fiber by weight. Fibers are defined as the plant materials remaining on a No. 100 or 0.15 mm (150 mm) sieve after wet sieving. Peat humus or muck used to modify soils on turf areas should, in general, contain less than 25% ash by dry weight. A rather wide range of physical properties exists with peat humus materials. More fibrous peats than peat humus are usually classified according to origin and fiber content (i.e., *sphagnum moss peat, hypnum moss peat,* and *reed-sedge peat*).

Sedimentary peats come from the bottom of peat bogs and often contain appreciable mineral matter and salt. They have physical properties that are difficult to manage and are seldom used for turfgrass or other horticultural purposes. Woody peats develop from trees and shrubs. These peats are not fibrous and have relatively low water retention capacity. They are satisfactory field soils, but are inferior to other peats for horticultural uses.

Organic soils have high cation exchange capacity (CEC), often within the 100 to 200 cmol kg^{-1} (100 to 200 meq per 100 g of dry soil) range. However, since organic soils have bulk densities of only 20 to 30% that of mineral soils, expressing CEC on a mass basis (the usual way to report CEC) is misleading. Plants grow in a volume of soil, thus reporting CEC of organic soil on a volume basis is a better means of determining the CE sites actually present in a root zone volume. For example, a comparison of an organic soil (bulk density 0.30 Mg m^{-3}) and a mineral soil (bulk density 1.25 Mg m^{-3}) for CEC on volume and mass basis reveals the differences in reporting (Table 16.4). While CEC of an organic soil is appreciably lower on a volume than on a weight basis, it is still high compared to most mineral soils.

When reported on a dry weight basis, the water holding capacity of organic soils is considerably greater than that for mineral soils. However, using the same reasoning as with CEC, we should be more interested in the volume of water retained within a volume of soil. The product of % H_2O (wt. basis) times the bulk density gives the % H_2O (vol. basis). The differences in weight and volume expressions for reporting water content are illustrated in Table 16.5.

In the above comparison (Table 16.5), the mineral soil holds more available water in an 8 inch (20 cm) depth than the organic soil (1.36 vs. 1.12 inches; 3.45 vs. 2.84 cm), although water contents at saturation, field capacity, and wilting point are higher with the organic soil. Differences between the two soils are greater when water content is reported on a weight basis.

Table 16.4. Comparison of organic soil and mineral soil on volume and mass.

CEC	Organic Soil	Mineral Soil
Mass (cmol kg^{-1})	250	9
Volume (cmol L^{-1})	75	11

Table 16.5. Comparison of water content determinations on an organic and mineral soil when reported on a weight (wt.) versus volume (vol.) basis.

Soil	Bulk Density (g cm^{-3})	Water Content: Saturation (% wt.)	Saturation (% vol.)	Field Capacity (% wt.)	Field Capacity (% vol.)	Wilt Point (% wt.)	Wilt Point (% vol.)	Plant Available Water[a] (% wt.)	Plant Available Water[a] (% vol.)
Organic	0.30	283	85	120	36	73	22	47	14
Mineral	1.30	39	51	24	31	11	14	13	17

[a] Available Water = Field Capacity – Wilt Point. Available water (% vol.) × soil depth (inches) = available water (inches) held in that soil depth.

Total N content in organic soils will be much higher than mineral soils, but much of the N is held in various organic compounds and ranges from relatively available to unavailable for plant use. The C:N ratio of organic soils is generally about 20:1 but appreciable mineralization can occur to release plant available N. Organic soils normally must be drained for turf use. The improved oxygen status of the soil permits microbial degradation of organic matter with loss of mass and release of N. Thus, N fertilization can often be reduced to some extent, especially during mid to late summer when soil temperatures are high.

Phosphorus is typically very low in organic soils and P application often improves growth, especially rhizome, stolon, and root development in sod production fields. Potassium is also usually low and turfgrass plants exposed to cold, heat, drought, or wear stresses may benefit from supplemental K.

Organic soils often exhibit acidic pH within the pH 4.5 to 5.5 range. However, the optimum range for plant nutrient availability in organic soils is at pH 4.8 to 5.6 versus pH 6.5 to 7.0 for mineral soils. As pH increases to >5.0, nutrients that may become deficient are Mn, Fe, Cu, Zn, B, and K. Organic soils exhibit higher Ca saturation on CEC at low pH than do mineral soils. Magnesium can be deficient on organic soils and, if lime is applied, dolomitic lime is preferred. Sulfur is ample in organic soils due to the quantity of S in plant constituents forming organic deposits. Due to the availability of nutrients within the pH 4.5 to 5.0 range, organic soils may not need liming unless to adjust pH to within this range.

Since organic soils invariably are located in sites that may become waterlogged, water table adjustment is important. Excessive water can cause any of the soil chemical reactions characteristic of waterlogged soils discussed earlier in this chapter. Also, excessive application of P and N should be avoided to minimize leaching of these nutrients into the groundwater.

IV. REFERENCES

1. Beck, A.J., R.E. Alcock, S.C. Wilson, M.J. Wang, S.R. Wild, A.P. Sewart, and K.C. Jones. 1995. Long-term persistence of organic chemicals in sewage sludge-amended agricultural land: A soil quality perspective. *Adv. in Agron.* 55:345–391.

2. Berndt, W.L. and J.M. Vargas, Jr. 1992. Elemental S lowers redox potential and produces hydrogen sulfide in putting green sand. *Hort. Sci.* 27:1188–1190.
3. Bethke, C.L. 1988. A guide to the selection of peat for use in turf. *Golf Course Management* 1(3):100–111.
4. Brady, N.C. 1990. *The Nature and Properties of Soils.* New York: Macmillan Publ. Co.
5. Breckle, S.W. 1991. Growth under stress—Heavy metals. In Y. Waisel, A. Eshel, and V. Kafkafi, Eds. *Plant Roots: The Hidden Half.* New York: Marcel Dekker, Inc.
6. Clapp, C.E., W.E. Larson, and R.H. Dowdy. 1994. *Sewage Sludge: Land Utilization and the Environment.* Madison, WI: SSSA Misc. Pub. ASA, CSSA, and SSSA Pubs.
7. Crawford, R.M.M., and R. Braendle. 1996. Oxygen deprivation stress in a changing environment. *J. Exper. Botany* 47(295):145–159.
8. Cullimore, D.R., S. Nilson, S. Taylor, and K. Nelson. 1990. Structure of black plug layer in a turfgrass putting sand green. *J. Soil and Water Conservation.* Nov.–Dec.:657–659.
9. Cunningham, S.D., T.A. Anderson, A.P. Schwab, and F.C. Hsu. 1996. Phytoremediation of soils contaminated with organic pollutants. *Adv. in Agron.* 56:55–114.
10. Giller, K.E., E. Witter, and S.P. McGrath. 1998. Toxicity of heavy metals to microorganisms and microbial processes in agricultural soils: A review. *Soil Biol. Biochem.* 30(10/11):1389–1414.
11. Hodges, C.F. and D.A. Campbell. 1997. Nutrient salts and the toxicity of black-layer induced by cyanobacteria and *Desulfovibrio desulfuricans* to *Agrostis palustris. Plant and Soil* 195:53–60.
12. Lindenbach, S.K. and D.R. Cullimore. 1989. Preliminary in vitro observations on the bacteriology of the black plug layer phenomenon associated with the biofowling of golf greens. *J. Applied Bact.* 67:11–17.
13. Lucas, R.E. 1982. *Organic soils (Histosols). Formation, distribution, physical and chemical properties, and management for crop production.* Mich. State Univ. Res. Report 435. East Lansing, MI.
14. Malterer, T.J., E.S. Verry, and J. Erjavec. 1992. Fiber content and degrees of decomposition in peats: Review of national methods. *Soil Sci. Soc. Am. J.* 56:1200–1211.
15. Marschner, H. 1995. *Mineral Nutrition of Higher Plants.* New York: Academic Press.
16. Setter, T. and B. Belford. 1990. Waterlogging: How it reduces plant growth and how plants can overcome its effects. *W. Aust. J. Agric.* 31:51–55.
17. Stehouwer, R.C. 1999. Land application of sewage sludge in Pennsylvania: A plain English tour of the regulations. *Penn State Cooperative Extension Pub.,* University Park, PA: Pennsylvania State University.
18. Stehouwer, R.C. 1999. Land application of sewage sludge in Pennsylvania: Use of biosolids in crop production. *Penn. State Cooperative Extension Pub.,* University Park, PA: Pennsylvania State University.

Part III

Fertilizers and Fertilization

Chapter 17

Turfgrass Fertilizers

I. INTRODUCTION

Fertilizers are materials that are added to a soil or plant to supply one or more elements that are essential for plant growth. Turfgrass fertilizers are comprised of organic or inorganic substances of natural or synthetic (man-made) origin. They are used to obtain some level of turf quality; to increase soil fertility levels; and to replenish nutrient elements lost from the area due to clipping removal, leaching, runoff, erosion, or gaseous losses such as volatilization and denitrification.

The *fertilizer requirement* for a turfgrass area is the amount of nutrient elements needed in addition to the amount supplied by the soil to provide the desired level of growth, color, or other component of turfgrass quality. The fertilizer requirement decreases as available nutrient levels in the soil increase. Fertilizer recommendations may vary between soil testing laboratories due to differences in the philosophies of fertilization.[11] Some recommendations are based on providing the plant with needed nutrients, whereas others, calling for higher rates, are based on increasing the soil levels as well as supplying the plant. Fertilizer requirements may also be affected by different philosophies on fertilizer application: frequent, low rates vs. infrequent, high rates. Although more time-consuming, the frequent applications may require less total fertilizer due to reductions in losses or unavailability due to factors such as leaching, luxury uptake, or fixation in less available forms.

Turfgrass fertilizers are "specialty fertilizers," a category of fertilizers manufactured and distributed for use on turfgrass, flowers, shrubs, house plants, and other nonfarm areas. Turfgrass fertilizers used on established turf areas differ from most farm or crop fertilizers by having higher N contents than P_2O_5 and K_2O and by usually containing some form of slow-release N. This chapter covers terminology and physical and chemical properties that are useful in understanding the characteristics and components of turfgrass fertilizers.

II. TERMINOLOGY

Definitions and explanations of common terms used with fertilizers follow:

Fertilizer material—a substance or compound containing one or more essential elements. Fertilizer materials may be used alone as fertilizers or combined to produce a mixed fertilizer. Examples of fertilizer materials are urea, superphosphate, diammonium phosphate, and potassium chloride.

Mixed fertilizer—a fertilizer containing two or more fertilizer materials. Mixed fertilizers may be dry mixtures of materials, granular mixtures in which chemical reactions have occurred, and fluids.

Compound fertilizer—a mixed fertilizer containing at least two of the fertilizer elements: N, P, and K.

Complete fertilizer—a mixed fertilizer containing each of the fertilizer elements: N, P, and K. Examples are 20-4-10 and 32-3-5, but not 22-0-16, which contains only N and K.

Slow- or controlled-release fertilizer—a fertilizer containing one or more plant nutrients in forms that delay the availability of a nutrient for plant uptake.

Blended fertilizer—a mixed fertilizer produced by mechanically mixing solid fertilizer materials. For example, diammonium phosphate, urea, sulfur-coated urea, and potassium chloride can be blended to produce a complete fertilizer such as a 32-4-8. In some cases, sulfur-coated or polymer-coated ureas are blended with a granular homogeneous fertilizer base that supplies the soluble N, P, and K for the final product. Blends are marketed in bulk (bulk blends) or as bagged or other packaged product. A disadvantage of blends is the potential for segregation of materials. Segregation can occur in piles of fertilizer, bags, trucks transporting bulk blends, and during spreading. Materials used in a blend should have similar sizes and densities to minimize segregation. Most producers of blends for turfgrass fertilization have done a commendable job in selecting materials with appropriate particle sizes; however, the segregation problem continues in blends of fine, lightweight organic materials with denser, granular materials. Such blends are best spread with drop-type spreaders rather than broadcast spreaders, which give a narrower spreading pattern with the light particles than with the larger, more dense particles.

Bulk fertilizer—fertilizer, either solid or liquid, distributed in a nonpackaged form.

Granular homogeneous fertilizer—a mixed fertilizer produced by creating granules from the fertilizer materials. Although a number of granulation methods exist, the most common manufacturing process is the ammoniation granulation in which ammonia or ammonia-containing N solutions are reacted with phosphoric and/or sulfuric acids. Dry, solid ingredients such as KCl and superphosphate are mixed, acids are added, and then ammonia as the mixing continues. The ammonia reacts with the acids to form ammonium sulfate and/or ammonium phosphates. Granulation of the mixture is favored by the heat produced by the chemical reaction and a wet, but stiff, consistency (a slurry resembling a concrete/water mixture, somewhat on the dry side). The newly formed salts and the added solid materials are thoroughly mixed and homogeneous granules form. The mixture is discharged into a dryer (large rotating drum), where granulation continues as heated air passes over the fertilizer to remove excess moisture. Granules then pass through a cooler (another large rotating drum) and then are screened to obtain the desired particle sizes. Fines are returned to the granulation stage and oversized particles are crushed and returned to the screening or other stage of the process. Uniform particle size is desirable for broadcast spreading. These fertilizers are called *homogeneous* because each granule contains all the nutrients that were formulated into the product. As with blends, these fertilizers are distributed in bulk and in bags.

Granulation can also be accomplished by: (a) a process in which a melt, formed by the reaction of ammonia with sulfuric acid, phosphoric acid, or both, granulates dry materials to form N, P, K fertilizers; (b) a process in which dry materials are mixed and then treated with steam, water, or both in a granulator where granules are formed; and (c) a process called roll compaction in which mixed components are compacted to form aggregates, which are blocky or angular rather than round as those produced in granulators. Granules produced by each method are screened to obtain appropriate sizes for the final product.

Granular fertilizer—a fertilizer that has at least 95% of its particles in the range of 4.75 to 0.85 mm (passing a No. 4 and retained on a No. 20 sieve).[1] The granular fertilizer may be a blend, homogeneous, or combination product. Some granular fertilizers produced for application to greens and other close-cut turf are finer than these commonly defined size limits.

Lightweight fertilizer—fertilizer in which nutrients are impregnated in or carried on lightweight, bulky materials, such as expanded vermiculite, ground corncobs, peat, compost, and synthetic foam. A relatively high N content in these fertilizers allows for the use of a low weight, and the carrier adds bulk to ensure ease and uniformity of application. Lightweight fertilizers have densities in the range of 20 to 30 lb ft^{-3} (0.32 to 0.48 g cm^{-3}) whereas the more conventional granular products generally have densities ranging from 45 to 75 lb ft^{-3} (0.72 to 1.20 g cm^{-3}).

Fertilizer grade—the nutrient content of a fertilizer expressed as the percentages of N, P_2O_5, and K_2O. The grade coincides with the minimum guaranteed analysis of the fertilizer. Note that P and K are expressed as oxides of these elements. P_2O_5 (phosphorus pentoxide, a compound not used in fertilizers) is referred to as *"available phosphate"* on fertilizer labels. Previous to the use of "available phosphate," a more descriptive term adopted by Association of American Plant Food Control Officials (AAPFCO) in 1993, the term "available phosphoric acid" had been used on labels and may still appear on some labels. K_2O (potassium oxide, a compound not found in fertilizers) is referred to as *potash* and is listed as *"soluble potash"* on fertilizer labels. Reporting of elements as oxides is a carryover of reporting analyses by early chemists. Conversion factors for P_2O_5 and P and for K_2O and K are as follows:

$$P_2O_5 \times 0.437 = P; \; P \times 2.29 = P_2O_5$$

$$K_2O \times 0.83 = K; \; K \times 1.20 = K_2O$$

Thus, a 20-10-10 grade would contain 20% N, 4.4% P, and 8.3% K.

Fertilizer analysis—the nutrient content of a fertilizer as determined by chemical analyses. Such analyses are routinely conducted in quality control laboratories of fertilizer manufacturers and in laboratories of state or other regulatory agencies that monitor fertilizers for accuracy in guaranteed analysis.

Guaranteed analysis—the minimum percentage of plant nutrients, which is displayed on the fertilizer label. Content of any given nutrient could be higher but only the minimum is guaranteed. Examples follow:

Country Club 16-8-8

Guaranteed Analysis

Total nitrogen (N) 16%

16.0% Ammoniacal nitrogen

Available phosphate (P_2O_5) 8%

Soluble potash (K_2O) 8%

Sulfur (S) combined 15.0%

Nutrient sources: ammonium phosphate, ammonium sulfate, and potassium chloride.

ProTurf Fairway Fertilizer 32-3-10

Guaranteed Analysis

Total nitrogen (N) 32%

0.5% Ammoniacal nitrogen

24.8% Urea, methylene ureas nitrogen

6.7% Water insoluble nitrogen

Available phosphate (P_2O_5) 3%

Soluble potash (K_2O) 10%

Sulfur (S) combined 3.4%

Derived from monoammonium phosphate, urea, methylene ureas, and potassium sulfate.

ProTurf Super Turf Fertilizer 26-4-12

Guaranteed Analysis

Total nitrogen (N) 26%

0.8% Ammoniacal nitrogen

25.2% Urea nitrogen*

Available phosphate (P_2O_5) 4%

Soluble potash (K_2O) 12%

Sulfur (S) (Total) 12%

7.8% Sulfur (S) (Free)

4.2% Sulfur (S) (Combined)

Derived from monoammonium phosphate, potassium sulfate, and polymer-encapsulated sulfur-coated urea.

*All of the urea has been coated to provide 20.1% coated slow-release nitrogen.

Country Club 21-3-18

Guaranteed Analysis

Total nitrogen (N) 21%

0.6% Ammoniacal nitrogen

5.5% Water insoluble nitrogen

6.1% Urea nitrogen

8.8% Other water soluble nitrogen*

Available phosphate (P_2O_5) 3%

Soluble potash (K_2O) 18%

Total magnesium (Mg) 0.6%

0.6% Water soluble magnesium (Mg)

Total sulfur (S) 5.6%

5.6% Combined sulfur (S)

Total iron (Fe) 0.4%

0.4% Water soluble iron (Fe)

Total manganese (Mn) 0.2%

0.2% Water soluble manganese (Mn)

Nutrient sources: ammonium phosphate, ammonium sulfate, isobutylidene diurea, methylene ureas, urea, sulfate of potash, sulfate of potash magnesia, iron sulfate, manganese sulfate.

*8.8 slowly available nitrogen from methylene ureas.

The AAPFCO indicates that nutrients other than P and K should be guaranteed on the elemental basis and that nutrients other than N, P, and K should be listed in the following order, and has suggested minimum percentages that will be accepted for registration for most products.[1] Minimum percentages are shown after each element: Ca (1.0%), Mg (0.5%), S (1.0%), B (0.02%), Cl (0.1%), Co (0.0005%), Cu (0.05%), Fe (0.1%), Mn (0.05%), Mo (0.0005%), Na (0.1%), and Zn (0.05%).[1]

Fertilizer ratio—the relative proportions of N, P_2O_5, and K_2O in a fertilizer grade. For example, a 32-4-8 has a ratio of 8-1-2; an 18-4-10, a 9-2-5 ratio; and a 12-4-8, a 3-1-2 ratio.

Fertilizer formulation—a list of materials, their nutrient content, and the amounts to produce a given weight of fertilizer. For example, the following formulation in Table 17.1 is for one ton (2,000 lb; 909 kg) of a 32-4-10 fertilizer with one-half of the N derived from sulfur-coated urea.

Few turfgrass managers will ever formulate a fertilizer; however, the same procedures can be used in determining amounts of fertilizer required to meet annual goals (ideally based on soil test recommendations). If annual requirements are 4 lb N, 2 lb P_2O_5, and 2 lb K_2O per 1,000 ft^2, various options exist. Three are shown in Table 17.2. Of course, application timings and rates will be dependent on N sources. In options II and III, materials would usually be applied separately, not mixed. Amounts of fertilizer required per 1,000 ft^2 should be adjusted for the total area to be fertilized.

Table 17.1. Example of a fertilizer formulation or components for a 32-4-10 fertilizer.

		Nutrients Supplied (lb)		
Fertilizer Material	**lb**[a]	**N**	**P_2O_5**	**K_2O**
Urea (46-0-0)	628	289	–	–
Sulfur-coated urea (37-0-0)	868	321	–	–
Diammonium phosphate (18-46-0)	178	32	82	–
Potassium chloride (0-0-62)	326	–	–	202
Totals	2,000	642	82	202
Formulated Percentages [(lb nutrient/2,000) x 100]	–	32.1[b]	4.1	10.1

[a] 1 pound (lb) = 0.45 kg.
[b] Slightly overformulated to protect from errors due to off-grade materials. Overformulation can also protect against deficiencies caused by sampling products in which segregation has occurred.

Table 17.2. Examples of formulating fertilizer needs for an annual program.

		Nutrients Supplied (lb)		
Fertilizer Material	**lb**[a]	**N**	**P_2O_5**	**K_2O**
Option I				
16-8-8	25	4	2	2
Option II				
20-4-10	20	4	0.8	2
Superphosphate (0-46-0)	2.6	–	1.2	0
Option II				
Ammonium sulfate (20-0-0)	20	4	–	–
0-25-25	8	–	2	2

[a] 1 pound (lb) = 0.45 kg.

Filler—A substance added to fertilizer to provide bulk, to condition (prevent caking), or to accomplish a purpose other than providing nutrients. In formulating mixed fertilizers, the amount of materials needed to obtain the desired weight of N, P_2O_5, and K_2O for a ton of fertilizer is often less than 2,000 lb. The additional weight is obtained by adding a filler, usually limestone. For example, a formulation for a 32-4-10 blended fertilizer with all soluble N could be as presented in Table 17.3.

Nutrient carrier vs. fertilizer carrier—Fertilizer materials are nutrient carriers. Materials such as vermiculite or ground corncobs act as fertilizer carriers in lightweight fertilizers. Fertilizers can serve as carriers for pesticides in fertilizer-pesticide products.

Additional terms are defined in the text of this and other chapters dealing with fertilizers and fertilization. Excellent sources of definitions related to fertilizers are the "Official Fertilizer Terms and Definitions" published annually by AAPFCO,[1] the "Fertilizer Dictionary" in annual editions of the *Farm Chemicals Handbook,*[9] the *Glossary of Soil Science Terms,*[12] and the *Fertilizer Manual,*[8] which was prepared by the United Nations Industrial Development Organization (UNIDO) and the International Fertilizer Development Center (IFDC), and ASTM publications.[2]

Table 17.3. Example of fertilizer and filler components in a 32-4-10 blended fertilizer.

		Nutrients Supplied (lb)		
Fertilizer Material	**lb[a]**	**N**	**P_2O_5**	**K_2O**
Urea (46-0-0)	1,326	610	–	–
Diammonium phosphate (18-48-0)	178	32	82	–
Potassium chloride (0-0-62)	326	–	–	202
Limestone (filler)	170	–	–	–
Totals	2,000	642	82	202
Formulated percentages		32.1	4.1	10.1

[a] 1 pound (lb) = 0.45 kg.

III. PHYSICAL FORMS OF FERTILIZERS

BOTH SOLID AND LIQUID FERTILIZERS can be used to fertilizer turfgrasses; however, most turfgrass fertilizers are solid, granular products. Solid fertilizers include granular, nongranular, and water soluble products.

A. Solid Fertilizers

Granular Fertilizers

Granular fertilizers generally contain particles that fall within the size range of 0.85 to 4.75 mm. Granular fertilizer particles may be agglomerates formed by granulation processes, granular or crushed fertilizer materials, salt crystals, and/or prills, all screened to obtain desired particle size. *Prills* are spherical particles formed when molten material called a solution melt is sprayed into the top of a prilling tower and then solidifies as it falls through an upward draft of cool air. Materials that can be prilled include urea, ammonium nitrate, and potassium nitrate.

To ensure size uniformity within a product, the largest particle in a granular fertilizer should not be greater than four times the opening size in the sieve that retains 95% or more of the product. Good quality turfgrass fertilizers will have narrower ranges of sizes. Manufacturers' specification sheets usually indicate information on particle sizes; however, methods of expressing sizes varies. Sizes are reported by: the percentages (by weight) that pass various sieves (screens); the cumulative percentages retained on a series of sieves; the percentage retained on each sieve; and by indicating the sieve sizes between which the particles fall [e.g., –8 + 12 mesh indicates that the particles pass through an 8 mesh sieve and are retained on a 12 mesh sieve (see Appendix F). Such a size would be appropriate for many turf areas; however, fertilizers designated for close-cut turf would be smaller, perhaps –12 + 16 mesh.]

To further complicate the matter, different *sieve designations* are used (see Sieve Designations in Appendix F). Sieves are designated by opening size, a numbering system, and by a mesh number (the number of openings per linear inch). The United States Standard Sieve Designations are the same as recommended by the ISO (International Standards Organization) and ASTM (American Society for Testing and Materials), and sieve designations may be in millimeters and microns (standard designation) or in inches above one-quarter inch and by sieve number for smaller sieves (alternate designation). AAPFCO recommends the use of sieve numbers; however, some manufacturers use mesh designations. The Tyler Screen Series uses mesh size. In some cases, the sieve number and mesh number are the same for a sieve with a given opening, and in other cases they are different. For example, a 3.35 mm sieve is a No. 6 and a 6 mesh, but a 2.0 mm sieve is a No. 10 and a 9 mesh. The same fertilizer could have particle size described as demonstrated in Table 17.4.

Another designation used to characterize the size of fertilizers is the *Size Guide Number (SGN)*. To obtain the SGN, the median size (the size below which 50% of the particles occur) in millimeters is multiplied by 100. The SGN for a product having a median size of 1.9 mm is 190. If two products were both –8 +12 mesh, but had different SGNs of 190 and 210, the product with 190 is finer. SGN is discussed in more detail in Chapter 18. In spite of confusion that may occur in the expression of granule sizes, this characteristic needs to be considered when selecting a fertilizer.

Another choice when selecting granular fertilizers is that of *blended or homogeneous fertilizers*. The segregation problem with blended fertilizers has been addressed, and it should not be an issue if uniformly sized blends are used (see Chapter 18 for more detail on uniformity of particle sizes). The fact that each particle of homogeneous fertilizer contains all guaranteed elements, whereas those of blends do not, is of little importance if uniformity of spread is obtained with the blend. Considering the movement of nutrients after dissolution of the fertilizer, the widely spread root system of turfgrasses, the existing soil fertility, the ability of a portion of the root system to supply enough of a nutrient for the entire plant, it is really unimportant that a granule of one nutrient source is an inch or two from a granule of another nutrient source. Subsequent applications of blends should eventually get every square inch covered with each nutrient, to the satisfaction of those concerned about coverage. Smaller granular size will help with uniformity of coverage when low rates are used. Also, a lower N analysis would result in more particles.

Choice of nitrogen source may dictate the selection of a blend. Sulfur-coated urea, polymer/sulfur-coated urea, and polymer-coated urea are altered by the various physical and chemical conditions associated with the manufacture of homogeneous fertilizers. Thus such N sources are limited to blending with other fertilizer materials or a homogeneous base fertilizer that supplies additional N plus the P and K components. Methylene ureas can be made "in situ" during granulation processes and are commonly used as slow-release N sources in homogeneous fertilizers. Methylene ureas and isobutylidene diurea are included as components in some granulation processes. They are also used in blends.

Nongranular Fertilizers

Nongranular fertilizers, also called pulverized and powdered fertilizers, are not made for a dry application to turf. In the past, when such fertilizers were available for turf, they posed a dust problem, were difficult to spread with broadcast spreaders, were susceptible to caking in the bag, and had a more severe potential for fertilizer burn because more material was retained on the foliage. Powdered forms of ureaform, methylene ureas, and isobutylidene diurea have been used in fluid applications of fertilizer.

Soluble Fertilizers

Soluble fertilizers supplied in solid form but dissolved in water for liquid applications as solutions include relatively pure fine granules, crystals, or powders of single fertilizer materials or

Table 17.4. Examples of particle size descriptions of a fertilizer by several methods.

Sieve Designation[a]			Size Description			
Std.	Alt.	Mesh	Cumulative Percentage Retained	Percentage Passing	Percentage Retained	Maximum and Minimum
4.75 mm	No. 4	4	0	100	0	
2.36 mm	No. 8	8	0	100	0	2.36 to 1.18 mm
1.70 mm	No. 12	10	25	75	25	or
1.40 mm	No. 14	12	85	15	60	−8 + 14 mesh
1.18 mm	No. 16	14	100	0	15	or
1.00 mm	No. 18	16	–	–	–	– No. 8 + No. 16
0.85 mm	No. 20	20	–	–	0	

[a] See Appendix F.

mixed fertilizers. These fertilizers can be applied alone and, in some cases, with fungicide applications by the professional, and certain formulas are available for hose-end sprayers used by the home owner.

B. Fluid Fertilizers

Fluid fertilizers, sometimes referred to as *liquid fertilizers,* may be in solution, suspension, or slurry form. Fluid fertilization of turfgrasses increased greatly with the early growth of the lawn care industry. The terms fertilizer material, mixed fertilizer, and complete fertilizer apply to fluid as well as solid fertilizers.

Solutions

Solutions are clear fluids in which all materials are dissolved. Some terminology reserves the term liquid fertilizers to describe these true solutions, and uses fluid as an overall heading. Solutions used as N sources for turfgrasses include various urea, methylol urea, and methylene urea combinations and a urea/triazone product. Various grades of mixed fertilizers are available.

Suspensions

Suspensions contain both dissolved and undissolved materials. The undissolved component may remain in suspension due to its own properties or a suspending agent such as clay may be used to stabilize the suspension. Suspended methylene urea products are used for turf fertilization, and various grades of mixed fertilizers are available.

Slurries

Slurries contain both dissolved and undissolved materials and require continuous mechanical agitation to keep undissolved materials from settling, thus maintaining uniformity of the product as it is applied. *Powdered slow-release sources* fall into this category.

IV. NUTRIENT SOURCES

THIS DISCUSSION IS NOT MEANT TO BE ALL-INCLUSIVE FOR NUTRIENT SOURCES, and emphasis is placed on sources that are or have been used both commercially and experimentally for turfgrass fertilization. For additional detail on nutrient sources and production methods, see the references listed at the end of the chapter.[4–6,8,10,13,14]

A. Nitrogen

Nitrogen sources used for turfgrass fertilization encompass a wide variety of chemical and physical properties and release characteristics (Table 17.5). Physical forms range from gran-

Table 17.5. Typical properties of selected nitrogen sources used for turfgrass fertilization.

Physical Form	Material	Grade	Total N	Water-Insoluble N	Other Nutrients
			%	%	
Soluble Solids	Ammonium nitrate	34-0-0	34	0	–
	Ammonium sulfate	21-0-0	21	0	24% S
	Diammonium phosphate	18-46-0	18	0	–
	Monoammonium phosphate	10-50-0	10	0	–
	Calcium nitrate	15-0-0	15	0	20% Ca
	Potassium nitrate	13-0-44	13	0	–
	Sodium nitrate	16-0-0	16	0	–
	Urea	46-0-0	46	0	–
Slow-Release Solids	Urea-formaldehyde products				
	• ureaform	38-0-0	38	27	–
	• methylene ureas	40-0-0	40	14.5	–
	Isobutylidene diurea				
	• coarse	31-0-0	31	27.9	–
	• fine	31-0-0	31	26.4	–
	Polymer-coated urea	variable	39–44	–	–
	Sulfur-coated urea	variable	31–38	–	12–20% S
	Polymer/sulfur-coated urea	variable	39–40	–	10–11% S
	Activated sewage sludge	6-2-0	6	5.5	various
	Other natural organics	variable	1–12	variable	various
Solutions	Methylol urea + urea	30-0-0	30	0	–
	Methylene ureas + urea	28-0-0	28	0	–
	Triazones + urea	28-0-0	28	0	–
	Ammonium polyphosphate	10-34-0	10	0	–
	Ammonium thiosulfate	12-0-0	12	0	26% S
Suspensions	Methylene ureas + urea	18-0-0	18	4.5	–
Sprayable Powders	Methylene ureas	41-0-0	41	12	–
	Ureaform	38-0-0	38	25	–
	Isobutylidene diurea	31-0-0	31	21	–
Fluids Used in Manufacture of Ammoniated Granular Fertilizers	Anhydrous ammonia	82-0-0	82	0	–
	Ammoniating nitrogen solutions	variable	37–49	0	–
	Urea-formaldehyde concentrate	11-0-0	11	0	–

ules for dry applications to powders, suspensions, and true solutions for fluid applications. Nitrogen sources can be used alone or in mixed fertilizers. Release of N is rapid with some sources and slow with others (Plate 24). Intermediate release rates are obtained with some N sources and with mixed fertilizers containing both quick- and slow-release sources. Knowledge of the properties and release characteristics of N sources is of great importance when one is developing a fertilizer program.

Various trade names have been used in this chapter to indicate examples of some types of N sources. Where trade names are listed, no discrimination or endorsement of a product is intended. Ownership of the rights to a product or a product name often changes among companies in the fertilizer industry. Trade names and company names for some products are updated annually in the *Farm Chemicals Handbook,*[9] and more current changes may be obtained from trade magazines and company representatives.

Quick-Release vs. Slow-Release Sources

Quick-release sources are also called quickly available, fast-acting, soluble, readily available, and other terms that indicate rapid availability of N after application. Slow-release sources may also be referred to by terms such as controlled release, slowly available, slow acting, delayed release, and insoluble. Compared to quick-release sources, slow-release N sources have lower potentials to cause turfgrass injury from fertilizer burn, can be applied at higher N rates, require fewer applications, provide a longer lasting release of N, and are less prone to leaching losses. Disadvantages associated with slow-release sources are higher cost per unit of N, slow initial response following application, and, with some, a much lower recovery of N by the turf during the first year or two of use, especially for those products with the slowest release materials. Of course, slow-release sources vary in their relationships to these characteristics. Methylene ureas and coated ureas will generally give greater response than ureaform, isobutylidene diurea, or natural organics following application. Efficiency of N utilization from slow-release sources (as measured by recovery in the plant) on a short-term basis and up to several years tends to be highest with methylene ureas and coated ureas, and higher with isobutylidene diurea than with ureaform and natural organics, both of which have greater long-term slow-release than the others. Also responses will vary with the formulation of methylene ureas and the coating material and weight (thickness) of coated ureas or other coated soluble salts. Most mixed fertilizers manufactured for use on turfgrasses contain both quick- and slow-release N sources. The quick-release sources provide a quick response and help to keep costs down, while the slow-release sources give a longer lasting effect and provide safety from the standpoint of fertilizer burn.

It has been our experience that some N sources that are claimed to have slow-release properties actually release N quite rapidly. Of course "slow" is a relative term, and if two quick-release N sources do not give identical release rates, one must be slower than the other. The Soil Science Society of America (SSSA) *Glossary of Soil Science Terms*[12] defines slow release as "a fertilizer term used interchangeably with delayed release, controlled release, controlled availability, slow acting, and metered release to designate a rate of dissolution (usually in water) much less than is obtained from completely water-soluble compounds." The AAPFCO definition for slow or controlled release fertilizer is "a fertilizer containing a plant nutrient in a form which delays its availability for plant uptake and use after application, or which extends its availability to the plant significantly longer than a reference 'rapidly available nutrient fertilizer' such as ammonium nitrate or urea, ammonium phosphate, or potassium chloride. Such delay of initial availability or extended time of continued availability may occur by a variety of mechanisms. These include controlled water solubility of the material (by semipermeable coatings, occlusions, or by inherent water insolubility of polymers, natural nitrogenous organics, protein materials, or other chemical forms), by slow hydrolysis of water soluble low molecular weight compounds, or by other unknown means."[1]

Concerning slowly-released plant nutrients, AAPFCO[1] has adopted the following policy: "No fertilizer label shall bear a statement that connotes or implies that certain plant nutrients contained in a fertilizer are released slowly over a period of time, unless the slow release components are identified and guaranteed at a level of at least 15% of the total guarantee for that nutrient(s)." Thus, a statement such as "contains long-lasting nitrogen" must be backed up with the source of N and the guaranteed amount. Such a statement could be used on a number of products; however, the user must read the label to determine the N source and the amount in the product.

The term "Enhanced Efficiency" has been selected by AAPFCO to refer to slow-release and stabilized fertilizers, which are fertilizers that have the potential to provide more efficient use of nutrients by plants and to enhance environmental protection by reducing nitrate leaching and gaseous losses of N by denitrification and volatilization. The term "stabilized" refers to products that have been amended with an additive that slows the rate of transformation of fertilizer compounds, resulting in an extended time of availability in the soil. Examples of stabilizing additives are nitrification inhibitors and urease inhibitors (see Section IV.A, Stabilized N Fertilizer, in this chapter).

In the following discussion, N sources are categorized based on responses obtained in our field research experiments, not on the claims of product literature.

Quick-Release N Sources

Quick-release N sources include urea [a synthetic organic made by reacting ammonia (NH_3) and carbon dioxide (CO_2)], inorganic salts containing ammonium (NH_4) or nitrate (NO_3) ions, and a group of low molecular weight, water soluble urea-formaldehyde reaction products. Some urea-formaldehyde reaction products contain enough water soluble N so that they give responses closer to those obtained with urea or soluble salts than with slow-release sources such as ureaform, activated sewage sludge, isobutylidene diurea, and most coated ureas. The quick-release sources are divided into two groups for discussion.

Inorganic Salts and Urea. These materials are water soluble, have N contents ranging from 15 to 46%, and are less expensive than slow-release sources. Being water soluble, they may be applied in solution as well as in dry form. These sources have high salt indexes and thus have high potentials for fertilizer burn. They give a rapid response and frequent applications at low rates are recommended to minimize overstimulation of growth and fertilizer burn.

The *ammonium and nitrate salts* readily dissolve in water and dissociate into their cation and anion components: e.g., ammonium nitrate (NH_4NO_3) dissociates into ammonium ions (NH_4) and nitrate ions (NO_3); and ammonium sulfate [$(NH_4)_2SO_4$] dissociates into NH_4 and sulfate (SO_4) ions. In the soil, nitrifying bacteria convert NH_4 to NO_3 in an oxidation process called nitrification. Plants may utilize nitrogen in either the NH_4 or NO_3 form, but most is taken up as NO_3. The NO_3 is readily leached, but NH_4 is less susceptible to leaching because it can be adsorbed on soil colloids. Ammonium phosphates and potassium nitrate (KNO_3) are primarily sources of P and K, respectively; however, they also provide quickly-available N. Ammonium phosphates are seldom applied alone on turfgrasses, but are frequently utilized in mixed fertilizers produced for turfgrass fertilization. Calcium nitrate is used in some countries with acid soils and for *Paspalum vaginatum* (seashore paspalum).

Urea (NH_2-CO-NH_2) is water soluble, and is quickly hydrolyzed (reacts with water) in the presence of adequate moisture and the enzyme urease to form NH_4^+ (Plate 24). Under favorable conditions, more than 60% of the applied urea can be expected to hydrolyze in one day, and hydrolysis should be complete in about 7 to 10 days. Under alkaline conditions gaseous loss of N as ammonia may occur from urea and ammonium compounds. This process, called volatilization, is also favored by low soil cation exchange capacity, drying of moist soil, and high temperature. Losses are usually greatest with urea; and on grass areas, losses as high as 30% of the applied N have been reported. Watering-in fertilizer will minimize such losses.

Urea-Formaldehyde Reactions Products. A well-known urea-formaldehyde fertilizer is ureaform, which is a slow-release source of N with about 70% of the total N being water insoluble. By altering the ratio of urea to formaldehyde, reaction products with considerably less water-insoluble N (WIN) can be produced. The water soluble nitrogen of these products contains compounds such as unreacted urea, *methylol urea*, and *methylene ureas.*[7] The amount of each is largely dependent on the urea/formaldehyde ratio and the conditions under which the reaction takes place. These N sources are more expensive than the conventional solubles, but they are safer from the standpoint of fertilizer burn.

Methylol urea is the first compound formed when urea and formaldehyde are chemically combined. As the reaction continues, short-chain and, later, long-chain methylene urea polymers are formed. The short-chain molecules are water soluble and the longer-chain molecules are water insoluble. *RESI-GROW® GP-4340* (30-0-0) and *GP-4341* (30-0-2) are clear aqueous solutions containing methylol urea and unreacted, or free urea, which supplies about 50% of the N. Other water-soluble urea-formaldehyde reaction products are *Formolene®-Plus* (30-0-0) and *CoRoN®* (28-0-0). They are solutions that contain water soluble methylene ureas and some unreacted urea (also referred to as free urea). About 25 to 30% of the N is from unreacted urea. *N-SURE®* is a solution that differs from the previously mentioned solutions in that it contains N primarily in the forms of triazones and urea. *Triazones* are cyclic N compounds that form when the fertilizer is manufactured by reacting urea, formaldehyde, and ammonia. Each of these solutions has a lower burn potential than urea, and can be used more safely than urea at higher rates or on heat or water stressed turf. Definitions of AAPFCO indicate that some slowly available nitrogen is present in the above-mentioned solutions. However, turfgrass response (growth and color) to these N sources is similar to and sometimes slightly less than that obtained with urea.

FLUF®, *Homogesol-27, Slo-Release,* and *RESI-GROW® 4318* are flowable urea-formaldehyde reaction products that contain water-insoluble as well as water-soluble methylene ureas. Quick response is obtained with these materials, but the intensity of response is not as great as with urea and the previously discussed solution fertilizers.

Slow-Release N Sources

Slow-release N sources used for turfgrass can be classified according to the release mechanism: (a) microbial activity is required for decomposition and release of N from natural organics and urea-formaldehyde reaction products (ureaform, methylene ureas); (b) low water solubility and a very slow rate of dissolution gives the slow-release characteristic of isobutylidene diurea (magnesium ammonium phosphate, 8-40-0, is in this category, but it is used primarily for horticultural plants); and (c) coatings on soluble N sources act as physical barriers that delay the dissolution of N from sources such as sulfur-coated urea, polymer-sulfur-coated urea, polymer-coated fertilizers, and urea coated with magnesium ammonium phosphate (Plates 25 and 26). Slow-release sources used on turfgrass include various natural organic materials; synthetic organic materials, which are urea-aldehyde reaction products (ureaform, methylene ureas, isobutylidene diurea, and crotonylidene diurea), melamine (a triazine), and oxamide; and coated fertilizers.

Natural Organics. For the most part, these materials are by-products from the plant and animal processing industries or waste products. The term *biosolids* is used in reference to primarily organic, solid materials produced by wastewater treatment processes that have value as nutrient sources or soil amendments. Considerable variation exists in the properties of different organic materials, and even within a given material. The natural organics can be characterized by relatively low N content; the presence of water-insoluble N (WIN); slow N release, which varies among the different sources; and the presence of other essential plant nutrients. Examples include hoof and horn meal, fish scrap and meal, seed meals (cottonseed, linseed, castor pomace), dried and composted manures, composted poultry waste, processed paper waste, sewage sludge, and process tankage.

Release of N is dependent on microbial activity. Factors influencing release are the chemical composition of the material (form of N and C:N ratio) and environmental conditions that influence microbial activity. Environmental conditions that affect breakdown of natural organics include temperature, soil moisture and oxygen, soil pH, and available minerals. *Milorganite®* is an activated sewage sludge and has been the most popular natural organic N source used on turf. Recovery of N tends to be low in initial years of use, perhaps only 25 to 30% of the applied N, compared to 50 to 65% with soluble N sources. However, the N that builds up in the soil slowly becomes available in future years. Other sludge products (e.g., *Actinite®*) and various poultry manures and wastes are processed for the turfgrass fertilizer market. Other natural organic sources of N that may be in turf fertilizers include materials such as: dried blood, bone meal, meat meal (tankage), leather tankage (e.g., *Hynite®*), fish meal, hydrolyzed feather meal, and various seed meals. Unlike N in most natural organics, N in dried blood is quickly available. Because of different chemical composition, the N release rates and N recovery values vary among natural organic fertilizers. In some cases, the use of natural organics has been related to disease suppression on turfgrasses. Odors, small particle sizes, and/or dust associated with some of these materials may be considered objectionable, and the low nutrient content necessitates the handling and/or storage of greater amounts of fertilizer than would be required with inorganic salts, urea, and the synthetic organic N sources.

Urea-Formaldehyde Reaction Products. These synthetic organic N sources are formed when urea (NH_2-CO-NH_2) and formaldehyde (CH_2O) are reacted under controlled conditions.[7] A variety of reaction products can be produced, and the mole fraction of urea/formaldehyde (U/F), pH, temperature, and time of the reaction affect the final product. In these reactions methylol urea is first formed, followed by methylene urea polymers of increasing length. The reactions can be depicted as follows:

1. NH_2-CO-NH_2 + CH_2O → NH_2-CO-NH-CH_2-OH
   urea (U) + formaldehyde (F) → methylol urea (MU)
2. NH_2-CO-NH-CH_2-OH + NH_2-CO-NH_2 → NH_2-CO-NH-CH_2-NH-CO-NH_2 + H_2O
   MU + U → methylene diurea (MDU) + water
3. MU + MDU → NH_2-CO-NH-CH_2-NH-CH_2-NH-CO-NH_2 + H_2O
   dimethylene triurea (DMTU)
4. MU + DMTU → trimethylene tetraurea (TMTU) + H_2O
5. MU + TMTU → tetramethylene pentaurea (TMPU) + H_2O
6. MU + TMPU → pentamethylene hexaurea (PMHU) + H_2O

Based on solubility, the N in the U-F reaction products can be divided into three fractions. *Fraction I* is soluble in cold water (25°C), and contains unreacted urea and the short-chain methylene ureas: methylene diurea and dimethylene triurea. Availability of N in this fraction is similar to that of soluble sources, but is not as quickly available. *Fraction II* is made up of slow-release, intermediate length polymers (trimethylene tetraurea and tetramethylene pentaurea). It is insoluble in cold water, but soluble in hot water (100°C). *Fraction III* is insoluble in both hot and cold water and is made up of pentamethylene hexaurea and longer chain polymers. It is the fraction most resistant to decomposition. In a study by Kaempffe and Lunt[7] (University of California) the breakdown of these fractions was studied over a period of 26 weeks. After this time period, 4% of fraction I, 25% of fraction II, and 84% of fraction III remained in the soil. Products made by this technology vary in the amounts of each fraction. Those with little or no

N in fraction III are more efficient over a single growing season, and those having primarily fraction I N give greater initial responses following application. Granular U/F materials include ureaform and various methylene urea products, and methylene ureas are indicated as a N source in mixed fertilizers in which the U/F component is made in situ during the manufacturing process. *The water-insoluble N (WIN)* indicated on labels of these products refers to cold-water-insoluble N (i.e., fractions II and III).

Ureaform is made using a U/F mole fraction of about 1.3/1 and contains 38% N, with about 71% of the N as water-insoluble N. Release of N from ureaform is dependent on microbial activity and the same environmental factors that affect release from natural organics also affect release from ureaform. Because of low N recovery (efficiency) in initial years of use, it is usually necessary to use higher rates or supplement ureaform with soluble sources in these years. This low recovery and slow response during cool periods support the concept of fertilization with combinations of ureaform and quick-release N sources. The relatively high amount of N in fractions II and III contributes to the low efficiency of ureaform in the initial years of use. With continued use and buildup of ureaform, recovery of N improves. Some turf managers have been able to significantly reduce N inputs on areas with a long history of fertilization with ureaform.

According to the AAPFCO, ureaform should contain at least 35% N, with at least 60% of the total of N being water insoluble N (WIN), and the WIN should have an *activity index (AI)* of at least 40%. The AI represents the amount of cold water insoluble N that is soluble in hot water (commercially available material has an AI of about 55%).* *Nitroform® Blue Chip, Blue Granular,* and *Powder Blue* meet these criteria. Urea-formaldehyde reaction products not falling within these guidelines are referred to by other terms such as methylene urea, methylol urea, and flowable ureaform.

Methylene ureas are made with various amounts of water-insoluble N (WIN). A U/F mole fraction of approximately 1.9/1 is used to manufacture methylene ureas that have about 35% of the N as WIN. *Nutralene®* is a granular product containing 40% N and 14% WIN (representing 35% of the total N). The SGN (size guide number) for greens, fairway, and general purpose *Nutralene* are 100, 125, and 215, respectively. Similar products are *Scotts MU 40* (in products with SGNs of 80 to 90 and 140 to 150) and *METH-EX 40* Granular (SGN 220) and Chip (SGN 135). These granular products have produced turfgrass response similar to that obtained with fertilizers having 50 and 60% of their N from ureaform (38% N; 27% WIN, which is equal to 71% of the total N). There has been a sprayable methylene urea having 30% of the N as WIN. Urea-formaldehyde concentrates can be used to form methylene ureas during the production of ammoniated granular homogeneous fertilizers. The *Triaform™* process uses a U/F mole fraction of about 2.0/1 and produces fertilizers having a methylene urea component that is primarily water soluble methylene diurea and dimethylene triurea, both considered sources of slowly available N by AAPFCO. These water soluble methylene ureas contribute to residual response over several weeks, and approximately 95% of *Triaform* N is released over a 12-week period. Thus the differences in U/F nitrogen sources give the turfgrass manager a range of release patterns to choose from.

---

* The AI is calculated as follows using values for cold water insoluble N (CWIN) and hot water insoluble N (HWIN):

$$\mathrm{AI} = \frac{\%\ \mathrm{CWIN} - \%\ \mathrm{HWIN}}{\%\ \mathrm{CWIN}} \times 100$$

In a relatively new process to manufacture U/F reaction products, ammonia is introduced at an appropriate time in the reaction to inhibit the polymerization process. The resulting U/F product has been termed *aminoureaformaldehyde*, and it has the advantage of a higher AI value; that is, a greater percentage of the cold-water soluble N exists as fraction II (soluble in hot water). Aminoureaformaldehyde is used as a nitrogen source and bonding agent in *NOVEX* T™ fertilizers.

Isobutylidene Diurea. This material is a synthetic organic N source made by reacting urea and isobutyraldehyde:

$$\underset{\text{isobutyraldehyde}}{\begin{matrix}CH_3\\CH_3\end{matrix}\!>\!CHCHO} + \underset{\text{urea}}{2NH_2-CO-NH_2} \rightarrow \underset{\text{isobutylidene diurea}}{\begin{matrix}CH_3\\CH_3\end{matrix}\!>\!CHCH\!<\!\begin{matrix}NHCONH_2\\NHCONH_2\end{matrix}} + H_2O$$

This N source, which contains 31% N, is marketed as *IBDU*® in several size ranges. A fine grade (SGN = 85) has 26.4% WIN (equivalent to 85% of the total N), a mid-size grade (SGN = 150) has 27.0% WIN (equivalent to 87% of the total N), and a coarse grade (SGN = 230) has 27.9% WIN (equivalent to 90% of the total N). An extra-coarse or oversize product with an SGN of approximately 350 is available and in the past a spray grade (<0.25 mm) was available. Isobutylidene diurea is used as a N source alone, in homogeneous fertilizers, and in blends. Nitrogen release is slow due to low solubility; but once in solution, isobutylidene diurea is readily hydrolyzed to form urea and isobutyraldehyde (Plate 24). Particle size has a large effect on release of N, with smaller particles releasing more quickly and large particles giving a greater residual effect. Release also increases with increased soil water content. Release is also affected to some extent by temperature and pH. Hydrolysis is faster under acidic conditions. The rate of release also increases with temperature, but low temperature does not affect isobutylidene diurea as much as it does those sources dependent on microbial activity for release. Greater cool-season response occurs with isobutylidene diurea than with ureaform or *Milorganite.*

A 3 to 4 week delay often occurs before response is noted from isobutylidene diurea applications. With continued use and release of residual N this effect becomes less apparent. It can be used with a quick-release N source to prevent such delays in response. Early spring greening from residual isobutylidene diurea often occurs on areas where it had been used in the previous growing season. The plant recovery of N during initial years of use is greater with isobutylidene diurea than with ureaform and *Milorganite.*

Polymer-Coated N Sources. Soluble N sources are coated with various polymers to slow the release of N (Plate 26). Urea is commonly coated and potassium nitrate is also coated to obtain slow-release K as well as N. In some cases, polymers are used to coat K salts, ammonium phosphate, and NP, NK, and NPK compound fertilizers. *"Resin-coated"* and *"plastic-coated"* are terms sometimes used in place of *"polymer-coated."* Materials used to coat fertilizers include polyurethane, polyolefin, and an alkyd resin. The polymers may be applied in a solvent that evaporates after application or by alternate application of monomers that react on the fertilizer to form the polymer coating.

The second method, used to make *POLYON*® fertilizers, is known as the Reactive Layers Coating process, and urea coated by this method is referred to as *RLCU*™. Other polymer coated products include *Osmocote*®, *Sierra*®, *Agriform*®, *ProKote*®, *Scottkote*®, *Meister*®, *V-Cote*®, and *MultiCote*®. Compared to typical coatings on sulfur-coated urea, thinner coatings (less weight) are required with polymers, and polymer coated ureas have higher N contents (39 to 44% N) than do sulfur coated ureas (32 to 38% N). For N release to occur, water or water vapor passes through the coating and dissolves the encapsulated N source. The coating acts as a semipermeable membrane through which water moves from a dilute solution to a concentrate solution within the coating (a process called osmosis). As the internal pressure increases, the polymeric shell (capsule) swells, and the dissolved N source diffuses out through enlarged pores in the coating. Unless broken, each particle slowly releases N. Empty shells or shells filled with various concentrations of salt or urea solutions can often be found by close inspection of turfgrass areas fertilized with these products.

Different coating thicknesses are used to obtain different release patterns. As coating thickness increases, release is slower and N content is lower. Coating thickness is regulated by the length of time the particles are exposed to spray applications of the coating materials. Release increases with increased temperature. If coatings are ruptured or cracked by mechanical damage or due to prolonged, excessive drying, released rate increases. The release rate is not significantly influenced by soil water levels (from wilting point to field capacity), volume of water applied, soil pH, or microbial activity.

In the past, the relatively high cost of polymer-coated products was a deterrent to their use on turfgrasses. They have been widely accepted for greenhouse, container, and nursery plants. With newer technology, reduced production costs, and proven performance, current polymer coated products and blends containing such products are receiving increased acceptance. A range of release patterns are available from different producers and from products produced by a single manufacturer. A selection of particle sizes is available, with the finest product being suitable for putting greens. Applied particles should settle to points below the mowing height to minimize breakage during mowing operations or removal with clippings.

Sulfur-Coated Urea. Sulfur-coated urea (SCU) is made by spraying preheated urea prills or granules with molten sulfur (Plate 25). A sealant, such as wax or a mixture of oil and polyethylene, is usually applied to seal pores and imperfections in the sulfur coating, and a conditioner (diatomaceous earth) is used to decrease stickiness. Polymer sealants on sulfur-coated fertilizers have resulted in a relatively new category of slow-release fertilizers: polymer/sulfur-coated products, which are described in the following section. Nitrogen content of SCU is usually in the range of 32 to 38% and is dependent on coating thickness (weight). Sulfur (S) content ranges from 12 to 22%, depending on release rate desired and on the size of urea being coated. Increasing the coating thickness decreases the rate of release, and smaller particles, having greater surface area per unit weight, require more coating to obtain a given thickness. Sealants make up about 2 to 3% and conditioner about 2% of the final product weight.

For N release to occur, water vapor or liquid water enters the particle through pores or imperfections in the coating. Increased pressure from the solution within the shell causes N to be released due to degradation of the coating and/or diffusion of soluble nitrogen through pores in the coating. Release rate increases as coating thickness decreases and as temperature increases. The formation of ferrous sulfide on SCU under waterlogged conditions slows release of N. As with the plastic-coated materials, breakage of the coating increases release. The 7-day dissolution rate in 38°C water (laboratory determination) is commonly used to characterize different formulations of SCU. Most commercial products for turf have had dissolution rates within the range of 25 to 35%. One product had a rate approaching 65%. These values can be used to roughly estimate the amount of N that will be readily available. The remaining N will have some degree of slow release. A much wider range of dissolution rates has been used in experimental SCU. A product with an 11% dissolution rate was somewhat slow for 3 years under central Pennsylvania conditions, but it was quite satisfactory in tests conducted in the warmer climate of Alabama. An experimental SCU with a dissolution rate of 83% gave results similar to those obtained from soluble sources. Although this material was a SCU, it could hardly be called slow-release. It would, however, offer less potential for fertilizer burn than straight urea.

Particles within an SCU product are not identical. If they were, one might expect all of them to release N at the same time. Quickest release occurs from imperfectly coated particles; particles in which a sealant has covered imperfections release N at an intermediate rate (such particles are not present in SCU products manufactured without a sealant); and the greatest delay in release occurs with the thicker coated and more perfectly coated particles having no imperfections. Once release begins from a given particle, it is quite rapid. Thus, the slow-release property of SCU comes from the variability in coatings among the individual particles and the various delay times before a particle degrades to release N. The slowest releasing particles may not release N for several years. This is the fraction referred to by the term "lock-off," meaning unreleased. Long-term studies show that the "locked-off" product does eventually release N.

Various sized particles have been available, including a fine grade for putting greens. Sulfur-coated urea is available as straight material and as a slow-release N source in blends.

Polymer/Sulfur-Coated Fertilizer. These fertilizers are also called *polymer-coated sulfur-coated* and *polysulfur coated* (Plate 25). The primary N source coated by this process is urea. The urea is first coated with sulfur, the thickness of which influences release rate, and then a thin layer of polymer is applied. The function of the polymer is to act as a sealant and delay water entry into the sulfur coating; thus, the sulfur and polymer characteristics jointly determine release properties. The use of the polymer coating has also produced a product that is less susceptible than conventional sulfur-coated urea to breakage or abrasion during handling and spreading. Various release patterns are available and typical products contain 39 or 40% N. Polymer/sulfur-coated urea has replaced sulfur-coated urea in most product lines. Examples of polymer/sulfur coated ureas are *Poly Plus®*, *Poly-S®*, *TriKote®*, *Poly-X PRO®*, and *Poly NS-52®*.

Other Coated Fertilizers. Magnesium ammonium phosphate and magnesium potassium phosphate are slightly soluble salts and are sources of slowly available nutrients. These compounds can be manufactured in processes that allow them to serve as a coating. Such compounds are utilized in the production of *Luxa Cote®*, a coated urea that provides slow release of P, K, and Mg as well as N.

Crotonylidene Diurea. Crotonylidene diurea is manufactured by reacting urea and crotonaldehyde or acetaldehyde and is marketed as *Crotodur®* and *CDU®*. Release of N occurs slowly as this material dissolves in water and gradually decomposes to form urea and crotonaldehyde. Release is due to hydrolysis and microbial decomposition and is affected by environmental conditions that influence microbial activity. Release rate decreases as particle size increases. This material is not generally used in North America, and is more common in Europe and Japan, where it is usually formulated into complete, granular fertilizers.

Other N Sources. In the past, a number of N sources have been included in N source evaluation research and some have had periods of commercial availability. Such sources include materials with various mechanisms of release including slow dissolution, microbial degradation, coatings, and matrixes, in which soluble N was mixed with wax or other materials to slow dissolution. Several of these sources are described in this section.

Oxamide is a synthetic organic N source that has been known for over 70 years. High production costs have kept it from being produced commercially as a fertilizer. A renewed interest in this material as a slow-release N source has resulted in recent studies on turfgrass. Oxamide contains 31.8% N, and the chemical formula is NH_2-CO-CO-NH_2. Release of N is by hydrolysis reactions and more rapid release is favored by finer particle size and warm temperatures. Turfgrass responses to this material have shown a similarity to that obtained with IBDU. A delay in response has been observed following application (especially with larger granule sizes) and adequate release occurs in cool weather to promote good green color. Fine oxamide (less than 0.25 mm) has given quicker response than granular oxamide (1–3 mm), but release from the fine material is slower than with soluble sources.

Another older slow-release source is melamine. *Melamine* (2,4,6 triamino-1,3,5-triazine) is a long lasting, insoluble N source containing 66% N. The combination of powdered melamine (*Nitrazine*® 66N) and molten urea in a rotating drum granulator has been used to produce *Nitrazine*® fertilizers. Three formulations were made by utilizing various ratios of melamine and urea. Ratios of 1:3, 1:1, and 3:1 yield 50-0-0, 55-0-0, and 60-0-0, respectively. The lowest N content (50%) reflected the highest amount of urea used, and this product gave the greatest initial response. The initial response with each was due to the urea component. Melamine begins to release N after a delay of several months. The *Nitrazine*® fertilizers could be applied dry as granules or in water. In fluid applications, the urea dissolved and the melamine was a suspended solid.

Organiform is a N source made by reacting urea and formaldehyde in the presence of a natural organic N source. Organiform contains about 24 to 25% N, of which about 70% is WIN. Organiform is a copolymer of a natural organic N source and methylene ureas. It has been produced using leather tankage and sewage sludge. Release of N is dependent on microbial activity, and N release is quite slow. Organiform faded from the market when the manufacturer could no longer obtain an adequate supply of leather tankage. A venture into production with sewage sludge was short-lived.

Stabilized N Fertilizer

Nitrogen stabilizers are materials that are added to fertilizers to increase the time that N remains in the urea or NH_4^+ form after application. By delaying the conversion of N to the NO_3^- form, reduced losses of N by leaching or denitrification may be realized. Two types of N stabilizers are *nitrification inhibitors* and *urease inhibitors.* Nitrification inhibitors delay the conversion of NH_4^+ to NO_2^- (nitrite) in the nitrification reaction process by inhibiting the activity of *Nitrosomonas* bacteria, which are responsible for this conversion. Examples of nitrification inhibitors are nitrapyrin [2-chloro-6-(trichloromethyl)-pyridine] which is marketed as *N-Serve*® and *DCD* (dicyandiamide), which is marketed as *Didin*®. Urease inhibitors slow the activity of the enzyme urease, which is required for the conversion of urea-N to NH_4-N. Examples are NBPT [N-(n-butyl) thiophosphoric triamide] and PPD (phenyl phosphorodiamidate). The four products mentioned have been evaluated on turfgrasses and their activity documented; however, when compared to nonstabilized N, turfgrass responses to these products were slight or absent. Lack of color and growth responses with nitrification inhibitors could be explained by uptake of N as NH_4^+, and soil and management conditions that were not conducive to either leaching or denitrification losses of N. Urease inhibitors have the potential to decrease volatilization losses of NH_3, as urea is hydrolyzed to form NH_3, and lack of turfgrass responses due to these products would indicate that less than favorable conditions existed for volatilization losses.

B. Phosphorus

Phosphorus sources include a number of materials that can be used alone or in mixed fertilizers to supply the P needs of turfgrasses. They are listed in Table 17.6. Phosphorus is not very mobile in soils, and leaching is seldom a problem. The fertilizer P is usually "fixed" in the soil by sorption or precipitation reactions, and thus, is converted to less available forms. Some fixed P is relatively unavailable; thus, the use of practices such as using granular P sources and localized placement such as banding P fertilizer will reduce the contact of the fertilizer with the soil and reduce fixation. Descriptions of some common P sources follow.

Table 17.6. Typical properties of phosphorus fertilizer sources.

Material[b]	Formula	Grade	Other Nutrients
		(N-P_2O_5-K_2O)	
Rock phosphate (Fluorapatite)	$Ca_{10}F_2(PO_4)_6$	0–5 to 17[a]–0	
Ordinary superphosphate	$Ca(H_2PO_4)_2 + CaSO_4 \cdot 2H_2O$	0-20-0	20% Ca; 11% S
Concentrated superphosphate	$Ca(H_2PO_4)_2$	0-46-0	13% Ca
Phosphoric acid	H_3PO_4	0-55-0	–
Superphosphoric acid	$H_3PO_4 + H_4P_2O_7$	0-72-0	–
Monoammonium phosphate	$NH_4H_2PO_4$	11-48-0	–
Diammonium phosphate	$(NH_4)_2HPO_4$	18-46-0	–
Ammonium polyphosphate	$NH_4H_2PO_4 + (NH_4)_3HP_2O_7$	10-34-0 (solution)	
Ammoniated ordinary superphosphate	–	3-19-0	19% Ca; 11% S
Ammoniated concentrated superphosphate	–	5-44-0	13% Ca
Magnesium ammonium phosphate	$MgNH_4PO_4 \cdot H_2O$	8-40-0	14% Mg

[a] 27 to 41% total P_2O_5.
[b] See also Table 11.3.

Phosphate Rock. Phosphate rock, a naturally occurring rock material, is the major source of P found in commercial fertilizers. The phosphorus is in the mineral *apatite* and is insoluble in water. Phosphate rock, also called *rock phosphate,* is relatively inefficient as a P source for plants. Heat treatment or acid treatment of phosphate rock converts the P to forms that are more readily available. Available phosphate, as indicated on fertilizer labels, is the sum of water soluble and citrate-soluble phosphate, which is insoluble in water but soluble in a solution of ammonium citrate. Phosphate that is soluble in water or ammonium citrate solution is closely related to the plant availability of P in a product. For example, "available P_2O_5" in rock phosphate ranges from 5 to 17%, depending on the product, while "total P_2O_5" would range from 27 to 41% P_2O_5 (Table 17.6).

Superphosphates. Superphosphates are made by reacting phosphate rock with either sulfuric acid (H_2SO_4) or phosphoric acid (H_3PO_4). During these reactions, the relatively unavailable form of PO_4^{-3} is changed to forms of P that are more available to plants. Close to 100% of the total P in superphosphates is available phosphate. Ordinary (also called normal) superphosphate is formed when sulfuric acid is used. It contains 16 to 22% P_2O_5, but is typically 20%. Gypsum ($CaSO_4$) is also formed in this reaction, and the S content in ordinary superphosphate is about 11%. When phosphate rock is reacted with phosphoric acid, a higher concentration of P_2O_5 results (44 to 52%, but typically 46%), and this product is referred to as concentrated, double, or triple superphosphate. Superphosphate may be used alone or in mixed fertilizers to supply the plant's P needs.

Ammoniated Superphosphates. During the manufacture of ammoniated fertilizers, anhydrous ammonia can react with superphosphates. Compounds of this type vary in composition and act as sources of both P and N. N contents vary from 2 to 6% with higher amounts in ammoniated concentrated superphosphates.

Phosphoric Acid. Phosphoric acid is manufactured using phosphate rock. It contains 55% P_2O_5 and is used to manufacture triple superphosphate and ammonium phosphates. It can be used in fluid fertilizers and is sometimes applied directly to soils. Superphosphoric acid is a concentrated phosphoric acid made by evaporating water from phosphoric acid. These products are highly acidic and must be handled with extra care by trained personnel.

Ammonium Phosphates. Monoammonium phosphate (MAP) and *diammonium phosphate (DAP)* are produced by reacting anhydrous ammonia with phosphoric acid and are sources of both P and N. The fertilizer grades of DAP and MAP products can vary, but they are similar within each material. Ammonium phosphates can be used alone or in mixed fertilizers, and all of the P contained is available phosphate.

Ammonium Polyphosphates. Ammonium polyphosphates are made by ammoniating superphosphoric acid, and are primarily used in fluid fertilizers. The grades 10-34-0 and 11-37-0 are representative of ammonium polyphosphate solutions. A polyphosphate contains two or more orthophosphate (PO_4) ions joined together. If two are joined, the polyphosphate is pyrophosphate. Longer chains are called tripolyphosphate, tetrapolyphosphate, etc. Polyphosphate fertilizers contain some orthophosphates as well as polyphosphates. Polyphosphates in the soil can be fixed, transformed to orthophosphate forms, and taken up by plants.

Other P Sources. Other P sources include magnesium ammonium phosphate, nitric phosphates, urea-ammonium phosphate, various potassium phosphates, bone meal, various organic wastes and by-products, and coated sources of MAP. Due to its slow dissolution rate, magnesium ammonium phosphate (8-40-0) can serve as a slow-release source of Mg, N, and P.

C. Potassium

Potassium found in fertilizers is primarily obtained by mining underground deposits of K salts, in particular, potassium chloride (KCl). Several processes can be used to separate KCl from sodium chloride (NaCl) and other salts. Various chemical reactions involving KCl can be used to produce other potassium salts that are used for fertilization. Typical properties of K sources are shown in Table 17.7. Potassium salts used in turf fertilizers are typically granular products; however, various sizes can be obtained using appropriate screens.

Potassium Chloride. This salt is often called *muriate of potash* in the fertilizer industry. It is the least expensive of K sources, but also has the greatest potential for fertilizer injury (burn) due to a relatively high salt index. Pure KCl is white; however, fertilizer grades of KCl vary in color from white to pink to a dark red color. The red coloration is due to iron oxide impurities.

Potassium Sulfate. This salt is produced by reacting KCl with sulfuric acid or other sulfate (SO_4) containing or producing substances. It is also known as *sulfate of potash.* KCl and K_2SO_4 are the major K sources used in turfgrass fertilizers.

Potassium Magnesium Sulfate. Also known as sulfate of potash magnesia, this salt is formed through a refining process in which chloride salts are removed from langbeinite ($K_2SO_4 \cdot 2MgSO_4$) ore. Langbeinite can also be used as a source of K, Mg, and S, or refined in another process to form K_2SO_4.

Potassium Nitrate. This salt (KNO_3) is produced by reacting KCl with nitric acid (HNO_3). It is also known as nitrate of potash.

Other Potassium Sources. Other K sources used to a much lesser degree are potassium carbonate, potassium hydroxide, and potassium phosphates. Polymer/sulfur-coated and polymer-coated K salts are also available.

D. Calcium and Magnesium

In most turfgrass soils there is seldom a need to fertilize with Ca or Mg to meet the plant's nutrition needs. Adequate levels are usually present in the soil. Sandy, acid soils with low cation exchange capacities (due to low clay and organic matter contents) are the most likely candidates for Ca or Mg fertilization. In soils with pH values conducive for plant growth, adequate amounts

Table 17.7. Typical properties of potassium fertilizer sources.

Material[a]	Formula	Grade	Other Nutrients
		(N-P_2O_5-K_2O)	
Potassium chloride	KCl	0-0-62	45% Cl
Potassium sulfate	K_2SO_4	0-0-52	17% S
Potassium magnesium sulfate	$K_2SO_4 \cdot 2MgSO_4$	0-0-22	11% Mg; 22% S
Potassium nitrate	KNO_3	13-0-44	–

[a] See also Table 12.3.

of Ca and Mg usually are present. Besides being added with liming materials, Ca is added with applications of various fertilizers such as superphosphates and $Ca(NO_3)_2$. If calcium is needed and no pH change is desired, as would occur with liming materials, gypsum can be used. Gypsum is often used on soils high in Na. Various chelated forms of Ca are also available. Magnesium is added to soils when liming materials containing Mg are used and with fertilizers such as magnesium ammonium phosphate and potassium magnesium sulfate. Magnesium can also be added by using magnesia and magnesium sulfate. Agricultural limestones contain various quantities of calcium carbonate ($CaCO_3$) and dolomite [$CaMg(CO_3)_2$], and can be classified according to the content of magnesium carbonate.[2] Dolomitic limestone contains from 35 to 46% $MgCO_3$, magnesium limestone contains from 5 to 35% $MgCO_3$, and high-calcium limestone contains from 0 to 5% $MgCO_3$.[2] Magnesium fertilization of forage grasses is often aimed at increasing Mg in the tissue to prevent grass tetany in cattle that consume the grass. Thus, Mg fertilizer recommendations, based on critical plant tissue levels for forage grasses, may not be appropriate for nutrition of turfgrasses. Typical properties of Ca and Mg sources are shown in Tables 17.8 and 17.9, respectively. The concentrations of nutrients given for limestone in these tables are for pure carbonate. Actual percentages are usually lower due to natural impurities.

E. Sulfur

As with Ca and Mg, S is seldom applied as the primary reason for fertilization. In the past, two major sources of S were sulfur dioxide (SO_2) from the atmosphere and ordinary superphosphate. With regulations aimed at reducing industrial air pollution and concentrated superphosphate largely replacing ordinary superphosphate, additions from these sources of S have been reduced. Sulfur is added as a component of many materials used to supply other nutrients; for example, N sources: ammonium sulfate and S-coated urea; P source: ordinary superphosphate; K sources: potassium sulfate, potassium magnesium sulfate; and sulfates of the following essential elements: Ca, Cu, Fe, Mg, Mn, and Zn. Elemental S and aluminum sulfate are sometimes used to lower soil pH. In addition to lowering the pH, these materials supply S that can be utilized by turfgrasses. Gypsum, sulfuric acid, and acid-forming sulfur compounds used in the reclamation of sodic soils also act as S sources. Properties of selected S-containing fertilizers are listed in Table 17.10.

F. Iron

Of the microelements, only iron is routinely applied as the primary nutrient in turfgrass fertilization. Iron fertilization is used to correct iron deficiencies in turf, which are indicated by chlorotic turf or tissue analyses. Iron chlorosis may result from either low Fe levels or immobi-

Table 17.8. Typical properties of calcium sources.

Material[a]	Calcium Content Formula	%	Other Nutrients
Limestone: pure calcite (calcium carbonate)	$CaCO_3$	40	–
Limestone: pure dolomitic (calcium-magnesium carbonate)	$CaMg(CO_3)_2$	21.6	13.1 Mg
Agricultural limestones (mixtures of calcite and dolomite)	$CaCO_3 + xCaMg(CO_3)_2$	18 to 39	0.04 to 12.7% Mg
Hydrated lime (pure calcium hydroxide)	$Ca(OH)_2$	54	–
Gypsum (calcium sulfate)	$CaSO_4 \cdot 2H_2O$	23	19% S
Calcium nitrate	$Ca(NO_3)_2$	24	15% N
Ordinary superphosphate	$Ca(H_2PO_4)_2 + CaSO_4 \cdot 2H_2O$	20	20% P_2O_5, 11% S
Concentrated superphosphate	$Ca(H_2PO_4)_2$	13	46% P_2O_5

[a] See also Table 13.2.

Table 17.9. Typical properties of magnesium sources (see also Table 13.4).

Material	Formula	Magnesium Content %	Other Nutrients
Limestone: pure dolomite (calcium-magnesium carbonate)	$CaMg(CO_3)_2$	13.1	21.6% Ca
Agricultural limestones (mixtures of calcite and dolomite)	$CaCO_3 + xCaMg(CO_3)_2$	0.04 to 12.7	18 to 39% Ca
Hydrated lime: from pure dolomite (calcium-magnesium hydroxides)	$Ca(OH)_2 + Mg(OH)_2$	18	30% Ca
Magnesia (magnesium oxide)	MgO	55	–
Potassium magnesium sulfate	$K_2SO_4 \cdot 2\,MgSO_4$	11	22% K_2O, 22% S
Magnesium ammonium phosphate	$MgNH_4\,PO_4 \cdot H_2O$	14	8% N, 40% P_2O_5
Magnesium sulfate			
(Epsom salt)	$MgSO_4 \cdot 7H_2O$	10	13% S
(Kieserite)	$MgSO_4 \cdot H_2O$	18	23% S

lization of Fe in plant tissue. Iron fertilization is also used to darken nondeficient turf, a practice which in some cases decreases the amount of N required to create and maintain a darker green color. Thus, the grower has darker color without the increase in growth associated with N fertilization. Iron chlorosis in turfgrass is favored by high soil pH and sandy soils. Chlorosis is also favored by high levels of Mn, Cu, and other cations that create an imbalance of metal ions, and by excessive P or Mo. When Fe chlorosis occurs on calcareous soils, Fe fertilization is a more appropriate choice than trying to lower soil pH. On overlimed, noncalcareous soils, the use of acidifying materials such as S, $Al_2(SO_4)_3$, and acidifying N sources as well as Fe fertilization are appropriate measures to reduce chlorosis. Iron sulfate and chelated iron formulations are commonly used on turf areas. Properties of these and other Fe sources are shown in Table 17.11. Iron chlorosis can be corrected by foliar applications as well as soil applications. Ferrous sulfate works better as a foliar spray, because once in the soil the ferrous ion (Fe^{+2}) is converted to the much less available ferric ion (Fe^{+3}). Fe chelates are more effective than ferrous sulfate for soil applications. A *chelate* is an organic compound formed when a cation or anion is bound

Table 17.10. Typical properties of S-containing fertilizers (see also Table 13.6).

Material	Formula	Sulfur Content %	Other Nutrients
Ammonium sulfate	$(NH_4)_2SO_4$	24	21% N
Ammonium thiosulfate solution	$(NH_4)_2S_2O_3 + H_2O$	26	12% N
Sulfur-coated urea		12–20	31–38% N
Polymer/sulfur-coated urea		10–11	39–40% N
Ordinary superphosphate	$Ca(H_2PO_4)_2 + CaSO_4 \cdot 2H_2O$	11	20% Ca; 20% P_2O_5
Potassium sulfate	K_2SO_4	17	52% K_2O
Potassium magnesium sulfate	$K_2SO_4 \cdot 2\ MgSO_4$	22	22% K_2O; 11% Mg
Gypsum (calcium sulfate)	$CaSO_4 \cdot 2H_2O$	19	23% Ca
Epsom salt (magnesium sulfate)	$MgSO_4 \cdot 7H_2O$	13	10% Mg
Sulfur	S	90–100	
Ferrous sulfate (copperas)	$FeSO_4 \cdot 7H_2O$	12	20% Fe
Manganese sulfate	$MnSO_4 \cdot 4H_2O$	15	25% Mn
Copper sulfate	$CuSO_4 \cdot 5H_2O$	12	25% Cu
Zinc sulfate	$ZnSO_4 \cdot H_2O$	17	36% Zn
Aluminum sulfate	$Al_2(SO_4)_3 \cdot 18H_2O$	14	–

Table 17.11. Typical properties of iron sources (see also Table 14.2).

Material	Formula	Iron Content %
Ferrous sulfate (copperas)	$FeSO_4 \cdot 7H_2O$	20
Ferric sulfate	$Fe_2(SO_4)_3 \cdot 4H_2O$	23
Ferrous ammonium phosphate	$Fe(NH_4)PO_4 \cdot H_2O$	29
Ferrous ammonium sulfate	$(NH_4)_2SO_4 \cdot FeSO_4 \cdot 6H_2O$	14
Iron chelates	NaFe DTPA	10
	NaFe EDDHA	6
Ferrous oxide	FeO	77
Ferric oxide	Fe_2O_3	69

by a ring structure of either naturally occurring or artificial chelating agents. Examples of chelating agents, with common abbreviations, are diethylene triamine pentaacetic acid (DTPA), ethylene diamine tetraacetic acid (EDTA), ethylene diamine di(*o*-hydroxy-phenylacetic acid) (EDDHA), hydroxyethyl ethylene diamine triacetic acid (HEDTA), citric acid (CIT), and oxalic acid (OX). The polyphosphoric acids, pyrophosphoric acid (P_2O_7), and triphosphoric acid (P_3O_{10}), are better described as complexing agents rather than chelating agents. The stability of chelates in the soil varies with the chelating agent, chelated ion, and soil pH.

Micronutrients such as Fe, Mn, Zn, and Cu can also be supplied in natural organic complexes called polyflavonoids. Such complexes typically contain 5 to 10% of the microelement. The advantage of these metals being in natural or synthetic complexes is that they are not tied up in unavailable forms as rapidly as unprotected ions, and thus, remain available for a longer period of time.

G. Other Micronutrients

Occasions on which fertilizer micronutrients other than Fe are deficient in turf are quite infrequent. In some areas where Mn deficiencies occur, Mn is routinely added to turf fertilizers.

Table 17.12. Typical properties of manganese sources (see also Table 14.5).

Material	Formula	Mn Content %
Manganese sulfate	$MnSO_4 \cdot 4H_2O$	27
Manganese oxide	MnO	41–68
Manganese chelate	Na_2Mn EDTA	12

Table 17.13. Typical properties of zinc sources (see also Table 14.7).

Material	Formula	Zn Content %
Zinc sulfate	$ZnSO_4 \cdot H_2O$	35
Zinc sulfate	$ZnSO_4 \cdot 7H_2O$	23
Zinc oxide	ZnO	78
Zinc chelate	Na_2Zn EDTA	14

Table 17.14. Typical properties of copper sources (see also Table 14.7).

Material	Formula	Cu Content %
Copper sulfate	$CuSO_4 \cdot H_2O$	35
Copper sulfate	$CuSO_4 \cdot 5H_2O$	25
Copper oxide	CuO, Cu_2O	75, 89
Copper chelate	Na_2Cu EDTA	13

Microelements are required by turf in very small quantities, and sufficient levels usually occur in turf soils. Frequently irrigated sandy soils are most likely to exhibit deficiencies. Micronutrients are applied as impurities in various materials used as macronutrient sources, as added nutrients to mixed fertilizers used primarily for N, P, and K application, and as micronutrient fertilizers (a single material or mixture of micronutrient sources). Some are also added as components of pesticides and as impurities in limestone.[3] Sources of Mn, Zn, Cu, Mo, B, and Cl are shown in Tables 17.12 through 17.17. Some of the micronutrient sources also contain macronutrients: e.g., S in sulfates and N in chelates, such as EDTA, that contain amine groups in their structure. When such sources are used at rates recommended for a micronutrient, the rate of macronutrient applied is quite small in relation to the normal requirements for the macronutrient. Not listed in the tables are *fritted micronutrients* in which nutrients are contained in a glass product produced after nutrient sources and glass raw products are mixed together. The number of micronutrients and contents vary in fritted products. Release of nutrients from frits is slow, and the rate of release is dependent on the composition and size of the frits.

H. Organic Sources of Nutrients

Natural organic sources of N were mentioned in the section on nitrogen sources. These organic materials serve as sources of other nutrients in various amounts. Other elements may be listed in the guaranteed analysis if their contents meet minimum percentages required for registration by regulatory agencies. *Milorganite* (6-2-0) was mentioned previously as a N source. It

Table 17.15. Typical properties of molybdenum sources (see also Table 14.7).

Material	Formula	Mo Content %
Sodium molybdate	$Na_2MoO_4 \cdot 2H_2O$	40
Molybdenum trioxide	MoO_3	66
Ammonium molybdate	$(NH_4)_6Mo_7O_{24} \cdot 2H_2O$	54

Table 17.16. Typical properties of boron sources (see also Table 14.7).

Material	Formula	B Content %
Sodium borate (Borax)	$Na_2B_4O_7 \cdot 10H_2O$	11
Other sodium borates	Various	14 to 21
Boric acid	H_3BO_3	17

Table 17.17. Typical properties of chlorine sources.

Material	Formula	Cl Content %
Potassium chloride	KCl	45
Other chloride salts	Various	Varies

also supplies P_2O_5 and Fe, which are listed on the label at 2% and 5%, respectively. Not guaranteed, but present, are: K, Ca, Mg, S, Mn, Zn, Cu, B, and Mo. A composted poultry manure product, *N-HANCE*™, (4-5-4) also guarantees Mg, Fe, Mn, and Zn at 0.60, 0.15, 0.05, and 0.05%, respectively, while a processed paper waste (8-2-0) guarantees N and P_2O_5 only.

Not only are organic sources used alone, but they are combined with other organic and inorganic materials in mixed fertilizers. For instance, an 8-3-5 product is derived from hydrolyzed feather meal, meat meal, bone meal, poultry meal, blood meal, fish meal, and langbeinite, and Ca, Mg, S, and Fe are guaranteed as well as N, P_2O_5, and K_2O.

When assessing the amounts of secondary nutrients and micronutrients contained in a fertilizer, one should consider the rate of application as well as content. Turf fertilizers are usually applied based on N requirement, and a greater amount of natural organic fertilizer than higher analysis manufactured or blended products will be required to obtain the same amount of N. For example, compare a 4-5-4 containing 0.15% Fe with a 20-5-10 containing 0.20% Fe. In fertilizing to obtain 1 lb N/1,000 ft^2, 25 lb of 4-5-4 or 5 lb of 20-5-10 would be required. Although the 4-5-4 contains less Fe, more would be applied with the 4-5-4 in this example: 0.0375 vs 0.01 lb Fe/1,000 ft^2.

V. REFERENCES

1. AAPFCO. 2000. *Official Publication No. 53. Association of American Plant Food Control Officials.* West Lafayette, IN: AAPFCO, Inc.
2. American Society for Testing and Materials. 1996. Standard terminology relating to lime and limestone (as used in the industry). (Designation C51-95). In *Annual Book of ASTM Standards*, Vol. 04.01:55-56. West Conshohockon, PA: ASTM.

3. Chichilo, P. and C.W. Whittaker. 1961. Trace elements in agricultural limestones of the United States. *Agron. J.* 53:139–144.
4. Engelstad, O.P., Ed. 1985. *Fertilizer Technology and Use,* Third Edition. Madison, WI: SSSA.
5. Hignett, T.P., Ed. 1979. *Fertilizer Manual.* Reference Manual IFDC—R-I. Muscle Shoals, AL: International Fertilizer Development Center.
6. Jones, J. Benton, Jr. 1994. *Plant Nutrition Manual.* Athens, GA: Micro-Macro Publishing, Inc.
7. Kaempffe, G.C. and O.R. Lunt. 1967. Availability of various fractions of urea- formaldehyde. *J. Agric. Food Chem.* 15:967–971.
8. Lee, R.G. and J.A. Kopytowski, Eds. 1998. *Fertilizer Manual.* Dordrecht, The Netherlands and Norwell, MA: Kluwer Academic Publishers.
9. Meister, R.T., Ed. 1999. *Farm Chemicals Handbook.* Willoughby, OH: Meister Publ. Co.
10. Mortvedt, J.J., P.M. Giordano, and W.L. Lindsay. 1972. *Micronutrients in Agriculture.* Madison, WI: SSSA.
11. Plank, O.C. 2000. *Soil Testing-Turf.* Web-site http://mars.cropsoil.uga.edu/turf/ Athens, GA: University of Georgia, Coll. of Agric. and Enviro. Sciences.
12. Soil Science Society of America. 1997. *Glossary of Soil Science Terms 1996.* Madison, WI: SSSA.
13. Tisdale, S.L., W.L. Nelson, and J.D. Beaton. 1985. *Soil Fertility and Fertilizers.* New York: Macmillan Publ. Co.
14. Trenkel, M.E. 1997. *Improving Fertilizer Use Efficiency: Controlled-Release and Stabilized Fertilizers in Agriculture.* Paris: International Fertilizer Industry Association.

Chapter 18

Factors in Selecting a Fertilizer

I. INTRODUCTION

A WIDE RANGE OF PRODUCTS IS AVAILABLE FOR TURFGRASS FERTILIZATION. The variety of fertilizers exists within manufacturers' product lines as well as between different manufacturers. Also, similar products can be obtained from a number of manufacturers. For example, most product lines include a starter fertilizer; and although grades may not be exactly the same, all such products have a relatively higher P content compared to either N or K. The *chemical and physical properties of fertilizers* play an important role in the suitability of a fertilizer for a particular response goal on a given turf area. If suitable fertilizers are available from several manufacturers or distributors, then cost and service may influence the final selection.

II. FERTILIZER CHEMICAL FACTORS

A. Ratio and Grade

IDEALLY THE RATIO OF N, P_2O_5, and K_2O desired will be based on soil test results. The fertilizer ratio should be similar to the ratio of nutrients in the fertilizer recommendation if that fertilizer will be used exclusively. Quite often two (or more) different ratios can be used to meet the recommended amounts of nutrients. For example a 6-1-1 ratio of nutrients could be obtained by using applications of products having ratios of 3-1-1 and 1-0-0; 2-1-1 and 1-0-0; or 1-1-1 and 1-0-0. The selection of ratios should be such that the annual fertilizer recommendation is met within reason. If available fertilizers do not have ratios close to the ratio of recommended nutrients, then select appropriate ratios from fertilizers and nutrient sources to meet the requirement. For instance, a ratio requirement of 2-2-1 could be obtained using a 4-1-2 or 2-1-1 ratio fertilizer plus superphosphate (0-1-0). If soil test results are not available, select a ratio ranging from 3-1-2 to 7-1-3 for maintenance fertilization and a ratio close to 1-2-1 for seedbed fertilization.

Usually a desired ratio can be obtained from several fertilizer grades. For example, both 20-4-12 and 25-5-15 have a 5-1-3 ratio. Not all grades are easily converted to a simple ratio. An 18-4-10 has an exact ratio of 9-2-5, but in most cases it would be accepted in lieu of a 4-1-2 ratio fertilizer, as would an 18-5-9 or 18-4-9. Both 12-4-8 and 18-6-12 have a ratio of 3-1-2. Aside from the usual chemical and physical properties that would influence the choice of the 12-4-8 or 18-6-12, it should be remembered that the lower analysis material will require more material to obtain a given amount of nutrients, and selecting it will result in greater shipping costs, more handling, and, if stored prior to application, more storage space. Because an 18-6-12 has 1.5 times the nutrient content as a 12-4-8, only two-thirds as much material would be required: e.g., 150 lb 12-4-8 is equivalent to 100 lb 18-6-12.

B. Potential for Turfgrass Injury Due to Osmotic Effects

Injury to turfgrass plants can occur when fertilizer concentrations in the soil solution or in solutions on aboveground parts are high enough to cause dehydration of plant cells due to osmosis. *Osmosis* is a process in which a solvent (water in a plant/soil system) moves from a low concentration solution through a semipermeable membrane into a more concentrated solution, thus tending to equalize the concentrations of the two solutions. The pressure that would be required to stop movement of water through the semipermeable membrane is called the osmotic pressure. All things (solutes) in solution exert an osmotic pressure. The osmotic pressure is not dependent on the nature of the solute molecules, but is dependent on and proportional to the number of solute molecules per unit volume (solute concentration). Solutions of different substances but with the same molar concentration have the same osmotic pressure. In solutions, electrostatic attraction between ions can cause ions to stick together briefly and behave as a single particle or ion pair, thus reducing the osmotic pressure below an anticipated value. Ion pairing is less with lower charged ions and in lower concentration solutions.

As an example of how different N sources could have different osmotic pressures, consider the choice between urea and sodium nitrate for application in a solution. One urea molecule (NH_2-CO-NH_2) provides two nitrogens. In solution sodium nitrate dissociates and results in two molecules (one Na^+ and one NO_3^-) and provides one nitrogen. Thus, for sodium nitrate to match the two nitrogens in a urea molecule, four molecules (two Na^+ and two NO_3^-) would be required; and for an equal amount of N, the osmotic pressure would be four times greater in the sodium nitrate solution than in the urea solution. The greater the osmotic pressure in solutions in contact with plants, the greater the potential for plant injury. During the osmotic process, plant cells become dehydrated, wilting symptoms often occur, and plants die under severe conditions. The damage to turf is often referred to as *fertilizer burn* (Plate 27). Injury due to osmotic effects is not limited to fertilizers. Improperly diluted wetting agents or pesticides could cause similar injury.

The *salt index* of fertilizers is a measure of the osmotic pressure created in the soil solution by the addition of fertilizers. Salt index values are based on applications of equal weights of the materials, and are expressed relative to the osmotic pressure produced by sodium nitrate, which has an assigned value of 100 (Table 18.1). Salt indexes can be calculated for mixed fertilizers by using index values and amounts of each component. The second column of values in Table 18.1 gives an indication of the relative potential for plant injury for the same amount of plant nutrient from the various N, P, and K sources. The higher osmotic pressures in soil solution are associated with N and K sources. Of the soluble N sources shown in Table 18.1, urea causes the lowest osmotic pressure. Also, of the two major K sources in turfgrass fertilizers, KCl presents a greater potential for injury than K_2SO_4. Due to low solubility, materials such as natural organics, ureaform, and isobutylidene diurea do not create appreciable osmotic pressures.

Although salt index refers specifically to osmotic effects in soil solution, the values are sometimes used to assess the potential for injury from direct contact with aboveground parts. With equal fertilizer additions, osmotic pressure measured in soil solution is lower than measured in a solution made with pure water, and the difference between soil solution and water solution is not the same for all materials. Lower values in the soil solution are attributed to cation exchange, phosphate fixation, and other reactions in the soil. While osmotic pressures measured in water alone may not be appropriate for soil applied fertilizer, they would be of value in solutions or suspensions applied directly to turfgrass foliage.

The term salt index has been applied to nonsalt fertilizer materials (e.g., urea, methylene ureas, isobutylidene diurea, and natural organics) as well as fertilizer salts. Perhaps a more appropriate term to describe this characteristic of fertilizers would be osmotic index.

Table 18.1. Relative potential for injury from various fertilizer materials (adapted from Rader et al., 1943[11]).

Material	Salt Index: Based on Equal Amounts of Material[a]	Salt Index: Based on Equal Amounts of Plant Nutrient[b]
N Sources		N
Sodium nitrate	100	6.06
Potassium nitrate	74	5.34
Ammonium sulfate	69	3.25
Ammonium nitrate	105	2.99
Monoammonium phosphate	30	2.45
Urea	75	1.62
Diammonium phosphate	34	1.61
Ammonia	47	0.57
Natural organic (5% N)	3.5	0.70
P Sources		P_2O_5
Diammonium phosphate	34	0.64
Monoammonium phosphate	30	0.49
Ordinary superphosphate	8	0.39
Concentrated superphosphate	10	0.22
Monopotassium phosphate	8	0.16
K Sources		K_2O
Potassium magnesium sulfate	43	1.97
Potassium chloride	116	1.94
Potassium nitrate	74	1.58
Potassium sulfate	46	0.85
Monopotassium phosphate	8	0.24

[a] Relative to sodium nitrate = 100.
[b] Value obtained by dividing first column value by percent nutrient.

Damage due to osmotic effects of fertilizers occurs in several ways. In the seedbed, seed or seedlings may be adversely affected, with the result of a reduced stand population. Such effects would be more severe under drier conditions, and, assuming the same fertilization rate, more severe with surface application than with incorporation. Rainfall and irrigation of seedbeds will move salts downward; however, if the area is allowed to dry, salts are brought to the surface by evaporation of soil water. Excessive fertilization of turfgrass can cause soil salt levels high enough to cause injury to the roots and crowns of turfgrass plants as well as reduce water uptake. Under such cases, the turf can wilt and die without the typical symptoms of foliar turfgrass burn. Even when applied dry, the deliquescent nature (tendency to absorb moisture from the air and form a liquid) of these salts can lead to very concentrated solutions on the plant tissue surfaces. Use of granular materials and watering-in fertilizers will help to minimize foliar damage due to fertilizers. In mild cases of burn, most of the injured foliage is removed in the next few mowings. On occasion, leaf tip burn may occur from concentrated guttated water. One mowing usually removes this effect. In slightly more severe cases of fertilizer burn, foliage may die, but recovery occurs from crowns that survived. In the most severe cases, revegetation will be required. Plant stresses due to high osmotic pressure cannot always be visually observed in the form of wilt or fertilizer burn. Soil water availability decreases as the osmotic pressure increases, and plant growth could be slowed without any visual symptoms to indicate this osmotic effect.

Table 18.2. Effect of material, rate of N, and foliage wetness on fertilizer burn of Kentucky bluegrass turf (adapted from Moberg, 1969[7]).

	Injury Rating[a]					
	Dry Turf[c] lb N/1,000 ft²			Wet Turf[c] lb N/1,000 ft²		
Material	**1**	**2**	**4**	**1**	**2**	**4**
Urea	0	15	20	15	35	65
18-6-12[b]	0	20	25	10	35	55
Isobutylidene diurea (IBDU)	0	0	0	0	0	0
Ureaform	0	0	0	0	0	0
Activated sewage sludge	0	0	0	0	0	0
Plastic-coated urea	0	0	0	0	0	0

[a] Rating scale: 0 = no injury, 100 = complete foliar injury.
[b] Contained 5.2% cold water insoluble N from isobutylidene diurea.
[c] N rates equivalent to 49, 98, and 195 kg ha^{-1}, respectively.

Osmotic pressure is proportional to temperature and concentration. Thus potential for injury is greater in warmer weather and when higher rates of fertilizer are used. Also, freezing concentrates solutes in soil water and influences the potential for injury. Thus, fertilizer materials, application rates, temperature, soil water levels, rainfall and irrigation, and amount of water used to apply fluid applications are factors to consider when assessing potential for injury due to fertilizer applications. Also, foliar damage from the same rate of granular fertilizer is often greater on denser turf stands because fewer particles fall through the turf to the soil or thatch layer. Having no fertilizer on the foliar portion of the plant does not preclude fertilizer injury to turf. Fertilizer salts at the soil surface or in the thatch layer can cause injury to crown and root tissues.

Results of tests to determine the effects of N sources on turfgrass injury are shown in Table 18.2. Note the safety associated with slow-release sources, increases in injury with higher rates, and greater injury when these materials were applied to wet turf.

When applied at recommended rates, turfgrass fertilizers seldom present a burn problem. However, if applied at excessive rates, if overlapped during application, or if applied under environmental conditions such as high temperature or low soil moisture causing wilt, the osmotic effects of fertilizer sources become more important.

C. Acidity or Basicity of Fertilizers

Fertilizer materials, in particular, N sources, can alter the soil pH. Ammonium salts and natural and synthetic organic N sources, which produce NH_4^+ as a result of mineralization, contribute to soil acidity when NH_4 is converted to NO_2^- by *Nitrosomonas* bacteria during the *nitrification* process:

$$2\ NH_4^+ + 3\ O_2 \rightarrow 2\ NO_2^- + 2\ H_2O + 4\ H^+$$

Nitrates of basic cations, such as Ca^{+2}, K^+, and Na^+, can have a basic effect because these cations persist in the soil longer than NO_3^-. P and K sources do not have a residual effect on soil reaction unless they also contain N. Pierre[10] developed a method to estimate the influence of *acidic or basic effect of fertilizers.* The method takes into account factors such as N form, the other ion in NH_4 and NO_3 salts, relative plant uptake of involved ions, and leaching of ions.

Table 18.3. Equivalent acidity and basicity for various fertilizer materials (adapted from various sources[6,10,14]).

Material	Calcium Carbonate Equivalent per	
	100 lb Material	1 lb Nutrient
	lb	
N Sources		**N**
Ammonium sulfate	110	5.4
Monoammonium phosphate	56	5.1
Diammonium phosphate	64	3.6
Sulfur-coated urea (37% N, 16% S)	119	3.2
Polymer/sulfur-coated urea (40% N, 10% S)	105	2.6
Polymer-coated urea (44% N)	80	1.8
Urea	84	1.8
Ammonium nitrate	59	1.8
Anhydrous ammonia	148	1.8
Ureaform	68	1.8
IBDU	57	1.8
Activated sewage sludge	10	1.7
Calcium nitrate	20 B[a]	1.3 B
Sodium nitrate	29 B	1.8 B
Potassium nitrate	26 B	2.0 B
P Sources		**P_2O_5**
Monoammonium phosphate	56	1.2
Diammonium phosphate	64	1.4
Ordinary superphosphate	0	0
Concentrated superphosphate	0	0
K Sources		**K_2O**
Potassium chloride	0	0
Potassium sulfate	0	0
Potassium magnesium sulfate	0	0
Potassium nitrate	26 B	0.6 B
Other Materials		
Sulfur (pure)	313	–
Limestone (pure $CaCO_3$)	100 B	–
Dolomite (pure $CaMg(CO_3)_2$)	109 B	–

[a] B indicates a residual basicity. All other values refer to acidic effects.

Thus, the fate of ions plays an important role in these estimates. For example, the difference in the fate of NO_3 and SO_4 in the soil explains why KNO_3 and $Ca(NO_3)_2$ have a basic effect, while K_2SO_4 and $CaSO_4$ have no effect on soil reaction.

The acidic or basic effects are expressed as *equivalent acidity or basicity* using the pounds of pure $CaCO_3$ that it would take to: (a) neutralize the acidic effect; or b) equal the basic effect. Equivalent acidic and basicity values are usually expressed relative to the effects of 100 pounds of material or one pound of nutrient element (Table 18.3). These values can also be used to calculate the *potential acidity* of mixed fertilizers. In the past, these values were sometimes listed on the label by statements such as "Potential acidity 400 lb calcium carbonate equivalent per ton," meaning that in this case the acidifying effects of one ton of the fertilizer would require 400 pounds of pure $CaCO_3$ or its equivalent to neutralize the acidic effect. However, such statements are not in general use at present. Because field conditions can vary considerably, the actual effect of a given fertilizer on acidity can also vary. The values in Table 18.3 give an indication of the relative effect among fertilizers. Ammonium sulfate and the ammonium phosphates have greater potentials for increasing acidity than other N sources. These materials or a mixed fertilizer containing one or more of them would be a good choice when one is trying to decrease the soil pH. Elemental S has a very acidic effect on soils, and when used to coat urea or other materials, it contributes to the equivalent acidity. Due to the slower availability of N (acidification from slow-release N sources), it is not as rapid as with ammonium salts and urea.

Because fertilizers are applied to the surface of established turfgrass stands, the acidifying effects are greatest near the surface. The same holds true for basic effects from fertilizers and liming materials. Soil sampling to a depth of several inches may not reveal the magnitude of soil pH changes near the surface that result from various N sources.

It should be apparent that most turfgrass fertilizers will decrease the soil pH. This change can be monitored by checking the soil pH, and then corrected by applying recommended rates of liming materials if the pH becomes too acid. Results from four N sources in Table 18.4 show a greater acidifying effect with sulfur-coated urea and a lower pH near the surface. The sampling depth effect has also been shown with surface applications of S to reduce soil pH (Table 18.5).

D. Nutrient Sources

Knowledge of nutrient sources in a fertilizer can help one make judgments on factors such as burn potential and acidifying effects, but there are also other considerations. Perhaps of greatest importance is the presence and type of slow-release N sources. The N component in a fertilizer can vary from 100% fast-release N to 100% slow-release N, and expectations of responses are related to this information (Plate 24). Determine whether elements other than N, P, and K are guaranteed. A mere look at the fertilizer grade will not reveal this information about other nutrients and N sources. Check the label (see label examples in Chapter 17) as well as specification sheets prepared by the manufacturer. Another chemical property of fertilizers that may affect selection is odor. Some organic materials (e.g., fish, manure, or sludge products) have odors that may be objectionable to some users.

E. Fertilizer-Pesticide and Other Combinations

In some instances, it may be appropriate to use a combination product. Combination products may contain fertilizer plus one of the following: preemergence herbicide, postemergence herbicide, insecticide, fungicide, growth regulator for *Poa annua* control, or wetting agent. Compared to turf fertilizers, the range of fertilizer ratios and N sources is limited in combination products; however, manufacturers do offer a choice of grade and amount of slow-release N with some combinations. Fertilizer-pesticide combination products should be considered pesticide-containing fertilizers and always should be applied in accordance with pesticide application regulations.

These products offer several advantages over individual applications of fertilizer and a pest control product or wetting agent. There is a labor savings in making one rather than two applications. In some cases there is an appreciable savings in cost of materials. For example, a fertilizer may be a less expensive carrier for a control chemical than a conventional carrier, such as ground corncobs or clay products. The turf responses of stimulated growth and darker color due to the fertilizer may mask the injury from a pest, and improved growth will speed fill-in of turf where weeds were eradicated or where turf was damaged by pests.

Table 18.4. Effect of N source and sampling depth on soil pH after three years of fertilizing with 5 lb N per 1,000 ft² per year (adapted from Hummel, 1982[3]).

	Original pH	pH Three Years Later	
N source	0–2 inches[a]	0–0.25 inches	0.25–2 inches
	pH		
Sulfur-coated urea	6.9	5.4	6.2
Isobutylidene diurea	6.9	5.6	6.4
Ammonium nitrate	6.8	5.7	6.4
Ureaform	6.8	5.7	6.4

[a] 1 inch = 2.54 cm.

Table 18.5. Effect of S application after sixteen months on soil pH at four sampling depths (adapted from Rieke, 1969[12]).

Sampling Depth inch	lb S per 1,000 ft²	
	0	59[a]
	pH	
0–2[b]	7.3	5.4
2–4	7.3	6.9
4–6	7.4	7.2
6–8	7.4	7.2

[a] Equivalent to 2,880 kg ha^{-1} of S.
[b] 2 inches = 5.1 cm.

Before selecting a fertilizer-pesticide combination product, one should be sure that both components are needed and that the timing is appropriate for both the fertilizer and the pesticide. Spring fertilization and preemergence herbicide application is usually a good match; however, if late fall or winter fertilization has been used on cool-season grasses, more fertilizer may not be needed when it is time for preemergence herbicide. In such cases, a combination product with no fertilizer N or a low rate of N could be used.

The rate of application must be based on the control product. Do not adjust application to receive more or less N. Doing so will also alter the pesticide rate and possibly result in no control, injury to turf instead of acceptable control, or higher cost than needed. The recommended rate for some products varies with turfgrass species or target weeds or insects. For instance, a fertilizer-insecticide product may be recommended at one rate for surface insects and twice that rate for soil insects. Thus, in the case of the soil insects, such as grubs, twice as much N will also be applied. A precaution to be taken when using fertilizer-herbicide combinations is to avoid spreading material into garden areas adjacent to the turf where vegetables, flowers, or shrubbery may be damaged. Also, prevent these products from reaching hard surfaces where they could run off to surface waters.

In addition to fertilizer-pesticide combinations, there may be conditions under which a fertilizer-wetting agent combination could be utilized. If water repellent surfaces are a problem, consider such a product if fertilization is also appropriate at that time. Other types of combination products include mulching material impregnated with fertilizer and turfgrass seed coated with fertilizer. Seeding blankets can provide both seed and fertilizer within the blanket, which acts as a mulch. Use of such products would assure that some fertilizer was also applied to a seedbed.

III. FERTILIZER PHYSICAL FACTORS

A. Solid vs. Fluid Fertilizer

BOTH SOLID AND FLUID FERTILIZERS ARE USED FOR TURFGRASS FERTILIZATION. *Solid turfgrass fertilizers* include granular products, either bagged or bulk, made for direct application using fertilizer spreaders, and various finer grades and powders prepared specifically for application with water. *Fluid fertilizers* include solutions and suspensions that are applied in various manners to turfgrass areas.

The choice of solid or fluid fertilizer for turfgrass fertilization is largely influenced by ease of transport, handling, storage, and application. The use of fluid fertilizers and fluid applications on turfgrass increased greatly as the lawn care industry became established. Some advantages of fluids are ease of storage in tanks, less labor for handling of bags, convenience of obtaining various nutrient ratios when mixing materials in spray tanks, and the uniformity of pesticide mixing with fertilizer in the spray tank. Agitation is required in spray tanks containing suspension or slurries to minimize settling that could affect pump performance and flow of the material. The storage of some fluids may be a problem if crystallization or polymerization occurs, which could affect chemical properties as well as physical properties related to handling and application. Some liquids, especially strong acids or bases can be harmful to equipment and cause injury to humans if not properly handled.

Solid granular fertilizers allow for the inclusion of a greater variety of slow-release N sources than can be obtained with fluid fertilizers. When storage is required, bagged goods require more handling than either bulk or fluid materials. Portable bins have been used effectively for brief storage of bulk fertilizer at some turfgrass facilities.

The selection of solid or fluid fertilizer will ultimately be decided on the capability of the user to uniformly apply the fertilizer. This capability is related to application equipment available and the ability of personnel to properly calibrate and use the equipment.

Dry vs. Fluid Application

The attributes of dry and fluid applications have been widely discussed within the lawn care industry. However, decisions on dry vs. fluid are also faced by other professionals and even homeowners. Dry, granular fertilizers can be applied using rotary, pendulum, and drop-type spreaders (Plates 28 through 30). Fluid applications can be made using spray guns, such as used by lawn care companies; spray booms, such as used on golf courses and other professionally maintained turf areas; hose-end sprayers, a homeowner option, and other proportioners; and injection into irrigation systems (i.e., *fertigation*). With irrigation system injection, uniformity of fertilization is dependent on the uniformity of the water application. Uniformity of other types of application is dependent on the condition and calibration status of the equipment and the ability of the operator (Plates 31 through 33).

Application method influences the ways in which flexibility in materials applied is obtained in lawn care operations. A single spray tank operation limits flexibility as different clients are serviced. Multiple tanks and pesticide injection capabilities at the spray gun increase options. With dry application programs, flexibility is obtained by using bagged products of different compositions that can provide options in grade or ratio, N source, the inclusion of pesticides, or other properties. The greater the flexibility desired for dry applications, the larger the inventory of products that must be maintained by the lawn care company.

Turfgrass responses to dry and fluid application of the same nutrient sources are essentially the same. The water used to deliver nutrients in fluid applications evaporates and formerly dissolved components are then in a dry form. The use of granular fertilizer or sufficient water with fluid applications minimizes the amount of fertilizer retained on foliage, which in turn minimizes fertilizer burn and removal of fertilizer if clippings are removed. Removal of fertilizer as granules is more apparent visually in the removed clippings than is removal of fluid applied materials that are residues on the leaf surface.

Fluid Application vs. Foliar Fertilization

Fluid applications of turf fertilizers have the primary objective of distribution of nutrients to the turfgrass area. Rates of water used may vary from 2 to 10 gallons water per 1,000 ft^2 (815 to 4,075 L ha^{-1}) depending on the type and amount of N and K sources used and the type of turfgrass. Foliar fertilization is also a fluid application, but at a much reduced rate of nutrients and rate of water (see "Foliar nutrient uptake" in Chapter 2). Some foliar absorption of nutrients can occur from conventional fluid applications, but the amounts will be low. Water rates and droplet size used with fluid applications are usually calculated to minimize retention on foliage and thus minimize foliar injury due to fertilizer burn. Lower rates of water are necessary for fertilizer/herbicide combination products when the herbicide must reside on leaf surfaces.

B. Particle Size and Uniformity of Granular Fertilizers

Particle size and uniformity of dry fertilizers and fertilizer materials are important physical characteristics from standpoints of material selection for blends and spreading properties of fertilizers.[1,2,5] However, granule size may also be of concern for other reasons. Release of N by slow dissolution from slow-release sources such as ureaform, IBDU, oxamide, and magnesium ammonium phosphate increases as particle size decreases because of greater surface area exposure. Availability of soluble N and K salts is not significantly influenced by granule size; however, as size becomes smaller, potential for burn increases due to greater retention on foliage. Larger granules of P sources slow the fixation of P in the soil, thus keeping more P available for plant uptake. Particle size is quite important in agricultural limestone. The finer the particles, the quicker the reaction. Coarse, ground limestone produced to provide improved spreading characteristics on lawns and gardens is less efficient than the usual ground agricultural limestone. Fine agricultural limestone can be pelletized, to provide a product that more easily flows and spreads using common fertilizer spreaders, without sacrificing its neutralizing power.

Granule size also affects pickup during mowing and removal of fertilizer if clippings are removed (Plate 34). Finer grades are made for application to putting greens and other close-cut turf to minimize pickup. Even with the finer fertilizers, it may be appropriate to skip clipping removal for a mowing or two until most of the fertilizer dissolves or moves into the turf canopy.

Particle size distribution of materials used for blending should be closely matched to minimize segregation. Not only should materials fall within upper and lower limits, their particle size distribution should be similar. If particle size distribution curves (accumulative percentages retained on sieves plotted against decreasing size of sieve openings) are prepared for each material, the difference between all materials in percentage retained at any size should not exceed 10% to ensure a good match of materials. The same comparison can be made if curves are based on percentage passing sieves (% passing = 100 – % retained).

The *size guide number* (SGN) and *uniformity index* (UI) are two measures developed by the Canadian Fertilizer Institute for use in assessing materials proposed for blending. The values are also useful to define size characteristics of final fertilizer products. The SGN is a calculated number obtained by: (a) determining the average particle size to the nearest 0.01 mm; and (b) multiplying that value by 100. Another way to define SGN is $d_{50} \times 100$, where d_{50} = the particle size below which 50% of the mass of particles occurs. The UI is the ratio of particle sizes representing the smallest 10% and the largest 5% times 100. Thus, it is the ratio of d_{10}/d_{95} times 100, where d_{10} = the size below which 10% of the particle mass occurs and d_{95} = the size below which 95% of the particles occur. The greatest value possible for UI is 100 (maximum uniformity with this method). A value of 50 would indicate that the largest size of the finest 10% of particles (d_{10}) is 50% of the value representing the smallest size of the largest 5% of particles (d_{95}).

Materials and products used on turfgrasses generally have an SGN range of 80 to 350. Values for the finest materials used on greens range from 80 to 100. Other products for greens and close-cut turf range from 125 to 150. Fertilizers for lawns and other higher cut turf range from 210 to 240, with a value as high as 350 for oversize products. UI values range from 35 to 60, and a value of 50 is typical. Considering the wide range of materials and fertilizers available, not all will fall within the listed ranges.

The SGN and UI values can be determined from a graphic plot showing the cumulative percentage of fertilizer particles passing various sieve sizes (openings). After the sieve analysis, data can be plotted on 2 cycle semilogarithmic graph paper. Percentage is plotted on the rectangular scale and particle (sieve) size on the logarithmic scale (Figure 18.1). A d_{50} value can be obtained by reading horizontally from the 50% point to the curve, and then vertically down to determine the size below which 50% of the particles occur. Determine d_{95} and d_{10} in a similar manner (see Figure 18.1 for examples). Should an accumulation curve be based on percentage retained as opposed to percentage passing, these values are still easily determined.

Segregation occurs because particles of unequal size tend to segregate during various handling processes. Segregation can occur during shipment, both in bulk and in bags or other containers during filling of the spreader, and even in a spreader during the spreading operation. Size is considerably more important in segregation than shapes (rounded to angular) or densities (1.27 to 2.12 g cm^{-3}) that are typical of fertilizer materials. If a blend segregates, chemical uniformity is affected. If a well-granulated, homogeneous mixed fertilizer segregates, chemical uniformity remains good; however, in an imperfectly granulated mixed fertilizer product, segregation may cause chemical nonuniformity. Chemical uniformity is of concern when fertilizer products are sampled to test whether the nutrient concentrations meet the guaranteed analysis. Thus, a deficiency in nutrient concentration may result from a lack of uniformity in a product as well as a lack of that nutrient being added in sufficient amounts.

Segregation of particles is caused by vibration during transportation by truck or rail and also in a spreader during spreading. The vibration causes finer particles to move downward through void spaces between larger particles. Fertilizer may be stored in conical piles, prior to delivery, bagging, or spreading. During placement in piles, segregation occurs during the flow of the fertilizer. Larger particles flow further down the sides of the pile than finer particles before coming to rest.

Ballistic segregation has been used to describe the segregation that can occur when fertilizer particles are propelled through the air by pendulum or rotary spreaders. Larger particles travel a greater distance from the spreader than do finer particles. An assessment of segregation during spreading as well as uniformity of spread can be obtained from placing a series of collection pans or boxes across the spreading width to collect material from a moving spreader or, in some cases, a stationary spreader with the spinning or pendulum mechanism being operated. For details on methods and results in studies dealing with distribution patterns, refer to Karnok,[4] Parish,[8,9] and Reed and Wacker.[13]

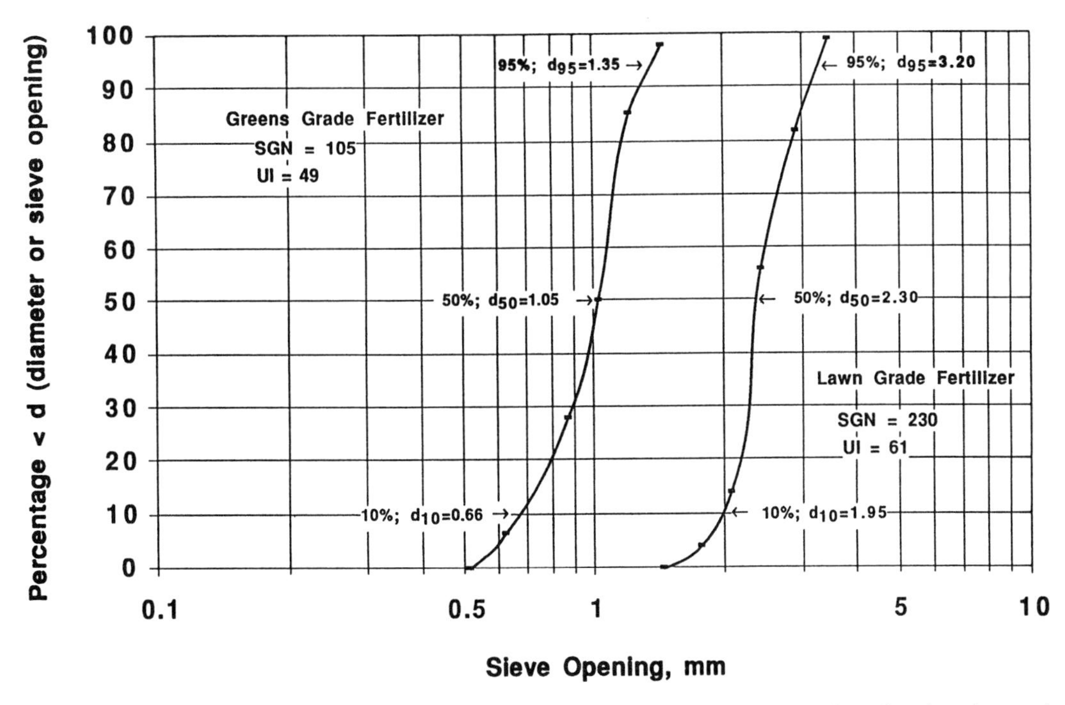

Figure 18.1. Particle size accumulation curves for two fertilizers showing values for d_{95}, d_{50}, and d_{10}. The SGN ($d_{50} \times 100$) for the green and lawn fertilizers are 105 and 230, respectively; and the UI [$(d_{10}/d_{95}) \times 100$] values are calculated as follows: $(0.66/1.35) \times 100 = 49$ for the greens fertilizer and $(1.95/3.20) \times 100 = 61$ for the lawn fertilizer.

C. Other Properties of Granular Fertilizers

Granule hardness, bulk density, dustiness, and caking potential are other physical properties that may be considered in selecting a fertilizer product.[2,5]

Hardness

Specific properties related to hardness that can be assessed are crushing strength, abrasion resistance, and impact resistance. Impact resistance relates to impacts received during the spreading operations. Sufficient granule hardness helps prevent the production of fines and dust during handling and spreading. Also, hardness should be such that there is stability in the size of materials in which release is size dependent. Manufacturing processes of coated fertilizer sources should provide coatings that resist damage due to the above forces of crushing, abrasion, and impact.

Bulk Density

The *bulk density* of a fertilizer is the weight per unit volume. It may be expressed in lb ft^{-3}, kg m^{-3}, or g cm^{-3}. Values for granular fertilizers range from 45 to 75 lb ft^{-3}, while values for lightweight fertilizers may be in the range of 20 to 30 lb ft^{-3}. Bulk density affects the space required for storage and shipping of fertilizers. Also, spreading width with rotary and pendulum spreaders is less with lightweights. Average bulk density (apparent specific gravity) values for various fertilizers, fertilizer materials, and fillers are listed in the Fertilizer Dictionary in the *Farm Chemicals Handbook.*[6]

Dustiness

Dustiness contributes to the discomfort of spreader operators, drift of materials, and unevenness of distribution. Granular products should be essentially dust free. If dust occurs in such products, it may be the result of inefficient screening during production, breakage of particles, poor adherence of anticaking conditioner dusts, or formation of surface crystals on granules that abrade to dust size particles. Dust particles can cake and collect on spreader parts, possibly changing flow and distribution.

Hygroscopicity and Deliquescence

Hygroscopicity of fertilizers refers to the absorption of water from the air. Water soluble materials exhibit some degree of hygroscopicity, which is affected by chemical composition, moisture content, particle size, relative humidity, temperature, and duration of exposure. Both single nutrients and mixed materials can be affected. The critical relative humidity (CRH) of a fertilizer is the relative humidity at which the fertilizer absorbs atmospheric moisture. Water is not absorbed at humidities below the CRH. The CRH for a mixed fertilizer is often lower that CRH for individual nutrients used in the fertilizer. The CRH for individual nutrient at 30°C is as follows:[5] ammonium nitrate 55 to 60%; ammonium sulfate 75 to 85%; DAP 65 to 75%; MAP 70 to 75%; triple superphosphate 75 to 85%; potassium chloride 70 to 80%; potassium sulfate 75 to 80%; and urea 70 to 75%. A 16-0-30 composed of urea and potassium chloride has a CRH of 45 to 55%. Moisture penetration into fertilizer particles varies among fertilizers and is often more important than CRH in affecting storage and handling properties.

Deliquescence is the process of soluble solids adsorbing water, becoming visibly wet, and then dissolving in the water. Calcium chloride is effective in decreasing dust on non-paved roadways due to its deliquescence nature.

The hygroscopicity and deliquescence nature of some fertilizers affects caking, handling, storage, and spreading. To minimize such effects store fertilizers in a dry place and in unbroken bags that resist moisture uptake.

Caking

During storage in bulk or bags, some fertilizer may exhibit *caking* or formation of lumps that affect handling and spreading. If caking is noticed in a granular product prior to opening a bag, a gentle drop to the floor will often restore an acceptable physical condition. Caking is usually caused by the growth of crystals on granules that bond particles together. Caking is favored by moisture present in the fertilizer following manufacture, fine products (pulverized or powdered), and the presence of fines in a granular product. Caking is also favored by high storage temperature of some products, by pressure during storage in piles or stacks of bags, and by inadequate curing time (for continued chemical reactions after production).

Conditioners can be added to fertilizers to maintain good flow characteristics. Materials such as ground corncobs, vermiculite, and perlite have been used to prevent caking of pulverized fertilizers. Externally applied materials such as diatomaceous earth, kaolin clay, talc, and chalk can be used to condition granular products. Also, "internal" conditioners added during the manufacture of some fertilizer materials reduce caking (e.g., 0.2 to 0.5% formaldehyde or urea-formaldehyde in urea).

There are no regulations regarding physical properties as there are with chemical properties of fertilizers. Many manufacturers of turfgrass fertilizers list sizes on product information sheets and screen products to different sizes according to their intended use (finer products for putting greens and other close-cut turf).

Perhaps some inappropriate physical properties will not be discovered by the user until after purchase when the product is being applied. Should segregation, dustiness, or caking be a problem, look for a manufacturer that produces products that are free of these problems.

For additional information on physical and chemical properties of fertilizers, consider the following references: Engelstad,[1] Hoffmeister,[2] Lee and Kopytowski,[5] Meister,[6] and Tisdale et al.[14]

IV. REFERENCES

1. Engelstad, O.P., Ed. 1985. *Fertilizer Technology and Use,* 3rd ed., Madison, WI: Soil Science Society of America, Inc.
2. Hoffmeister, G. 1979. *Physical Properties of Fertilizers and Methods for Measuring Them.* Bul. Y-147. Muscle Shoals, AL: National Fertilizer Development Center, Tennessee Valley Authority.
3. Hummel, N.W., Jr. 1982. *Evaluation of Sulfur-Coated Urea for Fertilization of Turfgrasses.* Ph.D. Thesis. The Pennsylvania State University, University Park, PA.
4. Karnok, J.K. 1986. The segregation of homogenous and blended granular fertilizers from a rotary spreader. *Agron. J.* 78:258–260.
5. Lee, R.G. and J.A. Kopytowski, Eds. 1998. *Fertilizer Manual.* Dordrecht, The Netherlands and Norwell, MA: Kluwer Academic Publishers.
6. Meister, R.T., Ed. 1999. *Farm Chemicals Handbook.* Willoughby, OH: Meister Publ. Co.
7. Moberg, E.L. 1969. *Evaluation of Nitrogen Sources for Turfgrass Fertilization.* M.S. Thesis. The Pennsylvania State University, University Park, PA.
8. Parish, R.L. 1987. The effect of speed on performance of a rotary spreader for turf. *Applied Engineering in Agriculture* 3:14–16.
9. Parish, R.L. 1995. Pattern skewing with a pendulum spreader. *Applied Engineering in Agriculture* 11:511–512.
10. Pierre, W.H. 1933. Determination of equivalent acidity and basicity of fertilizers. Analy. Ed., *Ind. and Eng. Chem.* 5:229–234.
11. Rader, L.R., Jr., L.M. White, and C.W. Whittaker. 1943. The salt index—A measure of the effect of fertilizers on the concentration of the soil solution. *Soil Sci.* 55:201–218.
12. Rieke, P.E. 1970. Soil pH for turfgrasses. pp. 212–220. In *Proc. 1st Int. Turfgrass Res. Conf.,* Harrogate, England. 15–18 July 1969. Bingley, England: Sports Turf Res. Inst.
13. Reed, W.B. and E. Wacker. 1970. Determining distribution patterns of dry fertilizer applicators. *Trans. ASAE* 13:85–89.
14. Tisdale, S.L., W.L. Nelson, and J.D. Beaton. 1985. *Soil Fertility and Fertilizers,* 4th ed. New York: Macmillan Publishing Co.

Chapter 19

Developing Fertilizer Programs

FERTILIZATION IS ONE OF THE MAJOR MANAGEMENT PRACTICES on most turfgrass sites. The purpose of this chapter is to focus information from the previous chapters onto *development of site-specific fertilizer programs* that are sound from the aspects of science, environmental concerns, and practical turfgrass management. This approach results in some overlap of material discussed in previous chapters where a more detailed presentation of each nutrient and fertilizer is made.

In the current chapter, we discuss the components of a good fertilization program and the various factors that should be considered. The primary components are:

- determining the total annual N requirement
- determination of dates of application, carriers, and rates per application for N
- formulating programs (rates, carriers, timing) for nutrients other than N
- considerations for adjusting the target fertilization program to meet seasonal changes.

I. DETERMINING ANNUAL N NEEDS

WHILE SOIL NO_3 and NH_4 levels can be measured, they fluctuate widely over relatively short time periods. Thus, measured NO_3 and NH_4 in the soil are not very useful for predictive purposes such as a P soil test would be where a high P test would predict high plant-available P over the growing season. To determine an estimate of *total annual N requirement* (i.e., pounds of N to apply per unit area per year), turfgrass managers that have limited experience at their sites generally rely on information provided by:

- extension or institute publications that focus on the particular region's climate, soils, grasses, and turfgrass use conditions.
- turfgrass agronomists such as USGA Green Section agronomists, private consultants, commercial/industrial agronomists affiliated with manufacturers and distributors of fertilizers, turfgrass institute agronomists, and university/regional extension specialists with experience relative to local conditions.
- fellow turfgrass managers, especially those in the same general location.

Incorporated into total annual N recommendations from these sources are adjustments for the grass species and cultivar (i.e., common types versus improved or hybrids); climatic conditions such as rainfall, temperature, and length of the growing season; soil conditions such as sandy or fine-textured soils; site-specific conditions such as shade, high wear areas, pest problems; and turfgrass use such as for lawns or general turfgrass sites versus recreational areas.

Lacking these local information sources, an approximate annual N rate can be determined by use of tables that list N requirements per growing month for a particular grass (Tables 19.1 and 19.2). Since the N rate is given in terms of rate per growing month, the total annual N requirement is adjusted for the number of *growing months,* which are those months when the grass is actively growing and not dormant or semidormant.

Recommendations for total annual N are normally given as a range such as "4 to 6 pounds of N per 1,000 ft^2 per year." The suggested annual N rate is determined by making adjustments for:

- *Quality expectations.* Grasses on sites where the clientele desires high quality will require more N, especially if dark green color is a high priority.
- *Clipping removal.* As much as one-third the annual N needs can be met by returned clippings as they degrade and release N.
- *Use of the turfgrass site.* Recreational turfgrass areas require higher N as demonstrated in Table 19.1 and 19.2 to recover from wear and other stresses.
- *Irrigation frequency.* Irrigation promotes more growth and nutrient use.
- *Rainfall.* High rainfall enhances turfgrass growth rates and increases the potential for greater leaching losses, while unusually dry periods may result in lower N use.
- *Soil type.* Sandy or infertile soils will require higher N due to lack of inherent N and potential for leaching losses.
- *Overseeding.* Overseeding of a warm-season turfgrass with a cool-season species will increase total N requirement since the growing season is extended.
- *Shade.* Less N is generally required on shaded sites unless tree and shrub roots compete for nutrients. Deep injection of nutrients for the tree or shrub will help avoid competition with the grass.
- *Disease problems* may require adjustment of N.
- *Recuperative needs.* Higher N may be needed to obtain recovery from injuries such as wear, pests, core aeration, etc.
- *Organic soils.* Less N is usually needed due to release of N from organic matter when these soils are drained.

Sites where the extremes of most of these factors are present, (high rainfall, sand soils, 12-month growing season, high quality requirements, etc.) such as south Florida golf courses, will necessitate annual N rates that are at the high end of the range and may in some cases exceed the normal ranges listed in Table 19.1 and 19.2.

II. DETERMINATION OF DATES OF APPLICATION AND N-RATE PER APPLICATION

THE ANTICIPATED CALENDAR DATES FOR N to be applied to a turfgrass are based primarily on the *growth cycle of the grass.* When shoot and root tissues are actively developing, nutritional needs are greatest.

Temperature is the climatic factor that most affects seasonal growth of turfgrasses. Temperature optimums (the temperature for highest sustained growth rate) and minimums (where active growth ceases) are noted in Table 19.3 for cool- and warm-season grasses. Temperature optimums and minimums for shoot responses are based on air temperatures while those for roots are based on soil temperatures at a 4 inch (10 cm) depth.

Table 19.1. Approximate nitrogen requirements for warm-season turfgrass species per growing month.[a]

Warm-Season Turfgrass		Nitrogen Requirement[b]				
		Pounds N per 1,000 ft^2 per Growing Month		Kilograms per hectare per Growing Month		
Common Name	Scientific Name	General Turf	Recreational	General Turf	Recreational	General N Requirement
Bahiagrass	*Paspalum notatum*	0.0–0.2	0.1–0.5	0.0–9.8	4.9–24.4	Low
Bermudagrass	*Cynodon* spp.					
• common types		0.2–0.4	0.4–0.7	9.8–19.5	19.5–34.2	Low–Med.
• hybrid types		0.4–0.6	0.6–1.5	19.5–29.3	29.3–73.2	Med.–High
Blue grama	*Bouteloua gracilis*	0.0–0.2	0.2–0.4	0.0–14.6	9.8–19.5	Very low
Buffalograss	*Buchloe dactyloides*	0.0–0.2	0.2–0.4	0.0–14.6	9.8–19.5	Very low
Carpetgrass	*Anonopus* spp.					
Centipedegrass	*Eremochloa ophiuroides*	0.0–0.3	0.3–0.4	0.0–14.6	14.6–19.5	Very low
Kikuyu	*Pennisetum clandestinum*	0.2–0.3	0.3–0.6	9.8–14.6	14.6–29.3	Low–Med.
Saltgrass	*Distichlis stricta*	0.0–0.2	0.1–0.4	0.0–9.8	4.9–19.5	Very low
Seashore paspalum	*Paspalum vaginatum*	0.2–0.4	0.4–0.8	9.8–19.5	19.5–39.0	Low–Med.
St. Augustinegrass	*Stenotaphrum secundatum*	0.3–0.5	0.4–0.6	14.6–24.4	19.5–29.3	Low–Med.
Zoysiagrass	*Zoysia* spp.					
• common		0.1–0.3	0.3–0.5	4.9–14.6	14.6–24.4	Low–Med.
• improved		0.2–0.3	0.3–0.6	9.8–14.6	14.6–29.3	Low–Med.

[a] Growing month is when the grass is actively growing and not dormant or semidormant.
[b] Nitrogen requirement rates per month are for determining total N needs based on the number of growing months per year. General turf = lawns, amenity turf, general grounds; Recreational turf = turfgrasses used for golf courses, bowling greens, and sports fields.

Table 19.2. Approximate nitrogen requirements for cool-season turfgrass species per growing month.[a]

Cool-Season Turfgrass		Nitrogen Requirement[b]				
		Pounds N per 1,000 ft^2 per Growing Month		Kilograms per hectare per Growing Month		
Common Name	**Scientific Name**	**General Turf**	**Recreational**	**General Turf**	**Recreational**	**General N Requirement**
Alkaligrass	*Puccinellia* spp.	0.0–0.2	0.2–0.4	0.0–9.8	9.8–19.5	Very low
Annual bluegrass	*Poa annua*	0.3–0.5	0.4–0.8	14.6–24.4	19.5–39.0	Low–Med.
Canada bluegrass	*Poa compressa*	0.0–0.2	0.2–0.4	0.0–9.8	9.8–19.5	Very low
Colonial bentgrass	*Agrostis tenuis*	0.3–0.5	0.4–0.8	14.6–24.4	19.5–39.0	Low–Med.
Creeping bentgrass	*Agrostis palustris*	0.3–0.6	0.3–1.0	14.6–29.3	14.6–48.8	Low–High
Fine Fescues	*Festuca* spp.					
• Chewings		0.2–0.4	0.3–0.5	9.8–19.5	14.6–24.4	Low
• Creeping red		0.2–0.4	0.3–0.5	9.8–19.5	14.6–24.4	Low
• Hard		0.2–0.4	0.3–0.5	9.8–19.5	14.6–24.4	Low
• Slender		0.2–0.4	0.3–0.5	9.8–19.5	14.6–24.4	Low
Kentucky bluegrass	*Poa pratensis*					
• Common		0.1–0.3	0.2–0.6	4.9–14.6	9.8–29.3	Low–Med.
• Improved		0.3–0.4	0.4–0.8	14.6–19.5	19.5–39.0	Medium
Perennial ryegrass	*Lolium perenne*	0.2–0.4	0.4–0.7	9.8–19.5	19.5–34.2	Low–Med.
Rough bluegrass	*Poa trivialis*	0.2–0.4	0.4–0.7	9.8–19.5	19.5–34.2	Low–Med.
Tall fescue	*Festuca arundinacea*	0.2–0.4	0.3–0.7	9.8–19.5	14.6–34.2	Low–Med.
Velvet bentgrass	*Agrostis canina*	0.3–0.5	0.4–0.8	14.6–24.4	19.5–39.0	Low–Med.
Wheatgrass	*Agropyron* spp.	0.1–0.2	0.2–0.5	4.9–9.8	9.8–24.4	Low

[a] Growing month is when the grass is actively growing and not dormant or semidormant.

[b] Nitrogen requirement rates per month are for determining total N needs based on the number of growing months per year. General turf = lawns, amenity turf, general grounds; Recreational turf = grasses for golf course, bowling greens, and sports fields.

Table 19.3. Optimum and minimum air temperatures for shoot growth and optimum and minimum soil temperatures at 4-inch (10 cm) soil depths for root growth.

Grass Type	Shoot Growth		Root Growth	
	Minimum	Optimum	Minimum	Optimum
	air temp		soil temp at 4 inches	
Cool-Season	40°F	60° to 75°F	33°F	50° to 60°F
	4°C	15° to 24°C	1°C	10° to 15°C
Warm-Season	55°F	80° to 95°F	50° to 60°F	75° to 85°F
	13°C	27° to 35°C	10° to 15°C	24° to 29°C

As the north or south distance away from the equator increases, warm-season grasses reach a zone where a winter dormancy or semidormant state is achieved. At a further distance, cool-season grasses also exhibit a winter dormancy period. For Atlanta, GA conditions, Figure 19.1 illustrates typical root/shoot seasonal growth cycles for warm-season and cool-season turfgrasses when light and soil water are not limiting.

A. Cool-Season Grass Growth Cycle

For cool-season grasses (Figure 19.1A), the winter dormancy period of the northern hemisphere (late December to mid-February) would be shorter during a warmer winter. In fact, the grass may go into and out of dormancy as weather fluctuates. At a somewhat more southern zone than Atlanta, Georgia, or on the coastal areas of Georgia, a cool-season grass may grow year-round unless a summer dormancy results from limiting soil water content and high soil temperatures. In more northern (cooler) climates or with increasing altitude in mountains, the cool-season growing season becomes shorter.

These temperature responses of a cool-season grass have a major influence on timing of N and other nutrients as well as rates of N per application. Important considerations on cool-season grasses relative to N application at different times of year are denoted in Table 19.4.

B. Warm-Season Grass Growth Cycle

The warm-season turfgrass growth cycle illustrated in Figure 19.1B for Atlanta, Georgia (northern hemisphere) would be more constricted under somewhat cooler climates due to more northern locations or higher altitudes. Under subtropical conditions warm-season grasses may undergo a winter dormancy. Important considerations relative to timing and rate of N application during different seasons are summarized in Table 19.5. If winter or early spring temperatures are sufficiently cold to potentially cause low temperature injuries, N applications should be adjusted to minimize possible injury.

Near the equator, warm-season turfgrass seasonal influences related to temperature are minimal (Figure 19.2). However, *wet and dry seasons or rainfall intensity* become more important for N application. For example, prior to an expected rainy season, N rates or applications may be decreased to avoid excessive growth and mowing as the rain occurs. During the rainy season, N may need to be applied at low rates and/or with use of a slow-release N material to provide sufficient N for growth and to compensate for possible leaching. Cloudy weather (i.e.,

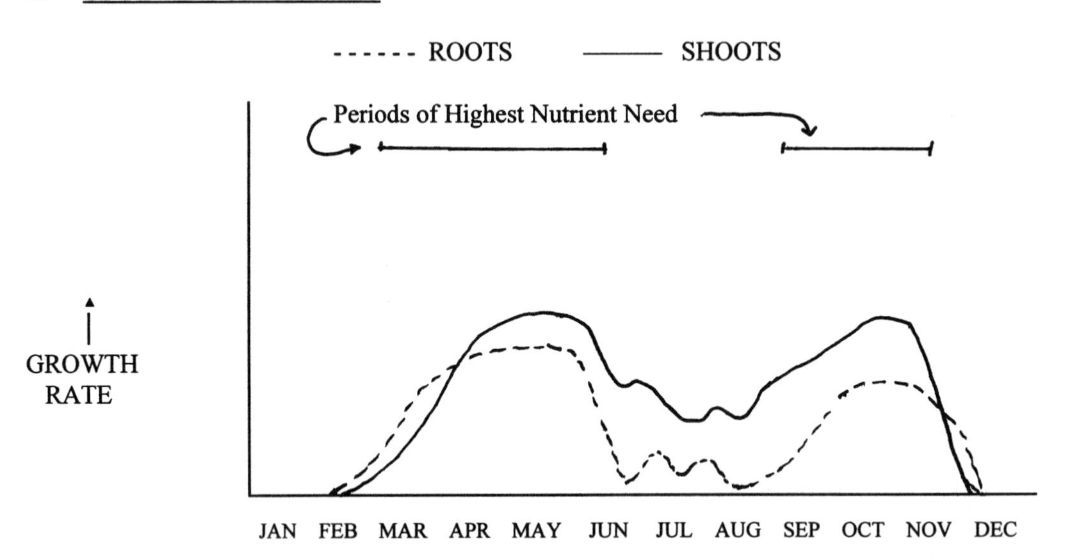

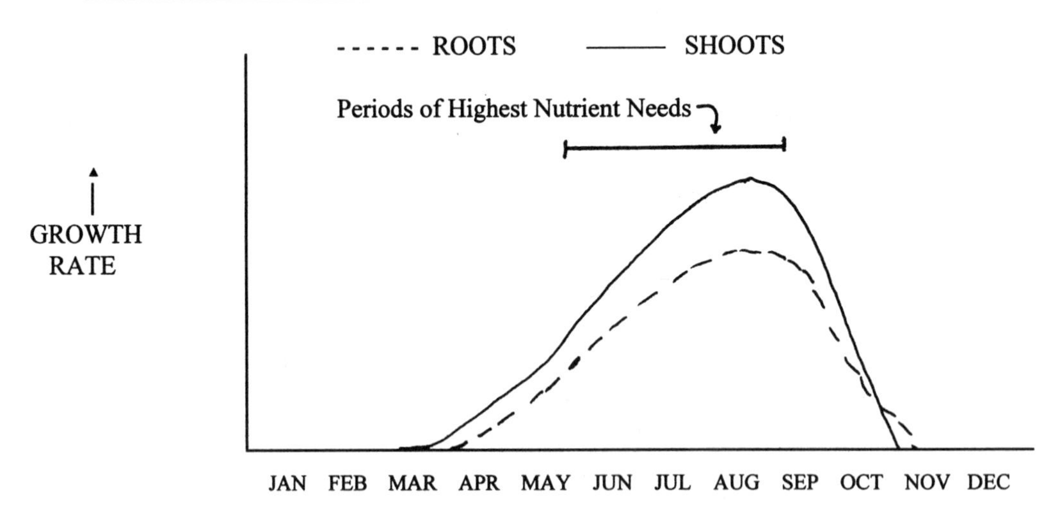

Figure 19.1. Growth cycles for shoots and roots of warm-season and cool-season turfgrasses in Atlanta, Georgia (northern hemisphere).

Table 19.4. Comments on N application at different seasons for a cool-season turfgrass.

Time of Year	Comments on N Application	Relative N Rate Per Application[a]
Early Spring	This is a period of growth; greater mowing; good color response; good recovery of shoot density; good competition with weeds. Too much N will deplete carbohydrates; reduce rooting; increase turf susceptibility to some diseases (Table 2.6) and summer drought/high temperature stress. If a late fall N application was made, additional N may not be needed or could be applied at a reduced rate. If no late fall application, then adequate but not excessive N is important.	0 to **
Mid- to Late Spring	This is an optimum time for shoot growth so excessive N can easily stimulate shoot growth over root development. Only low to modest N rates should be applied if the grass is exhibiting low N stress. In climates with long springs, N may become depleted from early spring or previous late fall applications and require a modest application.	* to **
Summer	Some N may be required to prevent N deficiency; promote some growth for recovery from or prevention of wear and stresses (pest or climate); and maintain color. Excessive N will substantially enhance drought and high temperature stresses. In climates with long summers, some N may become necessary to prevent serious N deficiency by late summer. Withhold N if turf is allowed to go into a summer dormancy. Some N may be needed for an integrated disease management program for certain diseases.	0 to *
Early Fall	Nitrogen needed for recovery from summer stresses in terms of increased shoot density, color, growth, and carbohydrate; also, some recovery of root growth. However, too much N will stimulate excessive leaf growth without other positive benefits.	** to ***
Mid-fall	An early fall N application is usually sufficient to provide adequate N in midfall. Avoid additional N unless N deficiency is apparent or root recovery and buildup of carbohydrate reserves for winter hardiness will decline. N during this period can enhance snow mold diseases in some regions.	0 to *
Late Fall	After vertical shoot growth has stopped but the grass is still green and the plant is physiologically active is a primary time to add N. This timing stimulates rapid accumulation of carbohydrates, root growth, shoot density, and color. Oftentimes some of the N is available in soil organic matter, plant tissues, and soil for early spring N responses. On sites susceptible to leaching, avoid overapplication of N. Snow mold disease may be enhanced by N at this time. Also, annual bluegrass may be enhanced at the expense of creeping bentgrass.	***
Winter	Avoid N application of readily available N or winter annual weeds will be favored. Slow-release N sources are sometimes applied in winter on frozen soil for convenience, however, such practices increase the potential for runoff losses of nutrients.	0 to *

[a] More *(s) indicate higher N per application or total N during the season.

Table 19.5. Comments on N application at different seasons for a warm-season turfgrass.

Time of Year	Comments on N-Use on Warm-Season Grasses	Relative N Rate per Application[a]
Late Winter to Midspring	Excessive N and/or applying N too early to promote spring green-up are problems where the following conditions may occur: cold, wet spring, warm weather but the chance of repeated frosts, conditions favoring intracellular or extracellular freezing.	* to **[b]
Midspring to Midsummer	Prime growth period but excessive N should not be applied at any one time or by too frequent N applications. Once the danger of frost is past, overseeded bermudagrass can be favored by moderate N application sufficient to produce good bermudagrass growth. In some years, the roots of warm-season grasses may be sloughed or physiologically pruned at the crown in early to midspring, about the same time that green-up occurs. Forcing shoot growth at this time with high N levels is not recommended. However, at 2–3 weeks after full green-up, higher N can be applied if needed.	***
Late Summer to Early Fall	In areas where intracellular or extracellular freezing may occur in the winter, warm-season grasses must be allowed to "harden off" in late summer to early fall. Reduce N to minimal levels but sufficient to maintain adequate growth where wear occurs and to maintain adequate quality. On sites that are to be winter overseeded with a cool-season species in midfall, N application is often reduced in the late summer up to the time of overseeding to decrease the growth rate of the warm-season grass and ensure a more competitive overseeded grass.	*
Midfall to Late Winter	Nitrogen is avoided since it may decrease cold hardiness in late winter, as well as promote winter weed problems. In overseeded situations, the cool-season species is fertilized with N as needed for the cool-season grass, but by light applications of N.	0 to *[c]

[a] More *(s) indicate high N per application or total N during the particular season.
[b] Limited N is applied in climates where low temperature injuries may occur but higher N can be used in more moderate climates.
[c] If no overseeded cool-season grasses are used, then no N would be applied to assist recovery from core aeration or verticutting used for overseeding.

low light intensity for photosynthesis) of a monsoon season may further restrict N use, which illustrates a *solar radiation or light* influence. As the rainy season ends, N may be adjusted upward for an initial application to compensate for N removal and leaching in the wet period. Afterward, N is adjusted to the turfgrass growth rate which is usually a reflection of irrigation intensity.

C. Other Factors

In addition to the seasonal growth cycle of the turfgrass as influenced by temperature, rainfall, and light conditions, *use of the site* influences N fertilization programing. Recreational use of turfgrass imposes: (a) wear stress on the shoot tissues through pressure, abrasion, and tearing

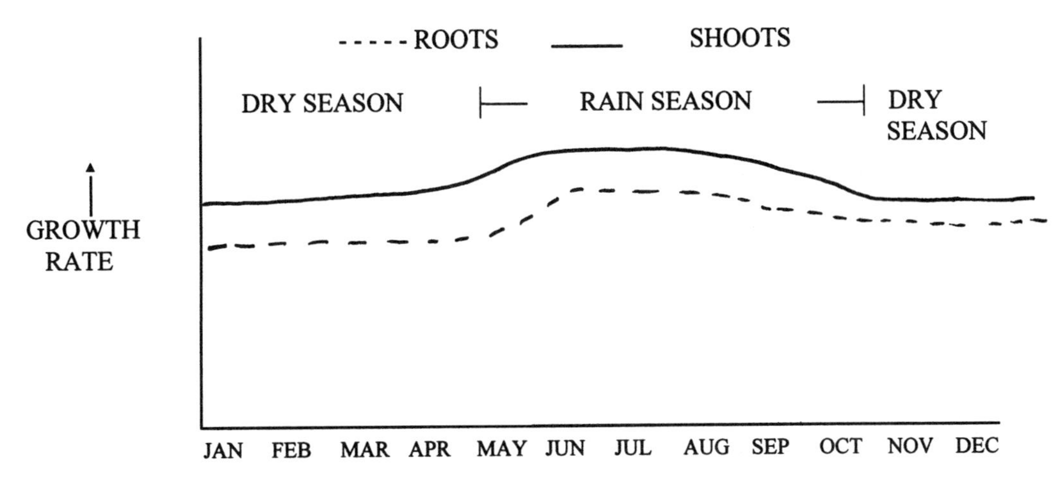

Figure 19.2. Example of a warm-season turfgrass annual growth cycle for near the equator and with wet/dry seasons and irrigation during the dry season.

action by foot and vehicle traffic; (b) soil compaction where traffic pressures compact the soil to alter water, oxygen, and soil strength relations, which in turn adversely affect turfgrass root development and viability, and ultimately shoot growth and quality; (c) rutting from vehicle traffic during wet weather; (d) sometimes planned events may require stages or covers that inhibit light and temperature exchange; and (e) supplemental N may be needed to heal the surface after core aeration.

Routine sports events and extra use of recreational fields do not necessarily coincide with the natural growth cycles of the grasses. Thus, N fertilization may be adjusted to provide: (a) continual enhanced growth to compensate for wear injury to shoot tissues; and (b) recovery from sports field damage or special event injury to the grass. Nitrogen rates can be increased and the normal application periods extended to provide adequate growth for wear or for recovery enhancement. However, there are limits on how effective additional N can be to provide positive benefits. For example, quick-release N may result in a somewhat longer growth period in the fall for a warm-season turfgrass and early spring green-up. But, sufficiently cool temperatures will induce dormancy regardless of the N rate. The increased year-round use of sports fields with many activities occurring during prime (optimum) times for renovation has severely limited the renovation efforts of turfgrass managers. Instead, additional N (as well as other practices such as cultivation, irrigation, etc.) is used to attempt recovery during use. Again, there are limits to this practice where further N will not achieve additional recovery and may decrease turfgrass quality, and there are potential detrimental reactions whenever a living plant is pushed to grow beyond normal limits by additional N. As an example, extending the growth period of a warm-season grass in the cool periods enhances the potential for low temperature injury.

D. Spoon-Feeding Approach

Whenever recreational use forces turfgrass managers to apply additional N outside of the normal growing season or primary growth periods for the species, a spoon-feeding approach will buffer against undesirable responses better than high rates of N with fewer applications. Spoon-feeding of N is discussed in the following paragraphs as a scheduling philosophy.

In addition to the seasonal growth cycle of the turfgrass as influenced by temperature, rainfall, light conditions, and use of the site, another factor that influences timing of N applications and N rate per application is the scheduling philosophy preferred by the turfgrass manager. Some managers prefer to apply N at the higher rates but less frequently, while others use a *"spoon-feeding" approach* with lower N rates per application and more frequent applications.

The spoon-feeding philosophy first gained favor in warm-season areas where N leaching could easily occur due to sandy soils and high rainfall as well as in regions where this approach helped to reduce susceptibility to stresses by cool-season grasses. The objective is to provide a relatively uniform and low to moderate N level while avoiding excessive N that may result in a less hardy grass, too much growth, or substantial leaching. With increased environmental concerns for N leaching and the success of this approach in allowing control over N availability, spoon-feeding on high maintenance turfs is now widely used under the following conditions:

- in climates with high rainfall periods and sandy soils with low nutrient retention
- on many sand-based golf greens and sports fields regardless of the climate
- where a cool-season grass is used and it is exposed to consistent summer high temperature stresses such as creeping bentgrass in the transition zone of the United States.
- in climatic zones where frequent rainfall or a prolonged wet period occurs regardless of the soil type (i.e., both fine-textured and sandy soils) and control of N availability is desired
- on sites with fertigation systems.

Spoon-feeding is not limited to use of water soluble fertilizers or fertigation. The latter is just one form of spoon-feeding where nutrients (including N) are applied at low, frequent rates through the irrigation system. Another approach could be by application at low, frequent levels in a sprayer. However, granular N carriers with rapid release or slow-release characteristics can be used. Typical N application rates per application in a spoon-feeding program are:

- Fertigation rates range from 0.05 to 0.20 lb N per 1,000 ft^2 (2.5 to 9.8 kg N ha^{-1}) depending on the grass needs and frequency of application.
- Sprayer applications (i.e., foliar) are usually in 3 gal or less water per 1,000 ft^2 (1,222 L ha^{-1}) and at 0.10 to 0.20 lb N per 1,000 ft^2 (4.9 to 9.8 kg N ha^{-1}), which may provide sufficient N for 1 to 3 weeks. At low water rates (i.e., 1 gal per 1,000 ft^2) and higher N rates a foliar burn could occur in hot, dry weather.
- Granulars with quick-release N forms are applied at 0.15 to 0.33 lb N per 1,000 ft^2 (7.3 to 16.1 kg N ha^{-1}). Especially on close-cut turfgrass, the fertilizer particle size should be small when low application rates of granulars are used to prevent green spots. With small particle size, there are more particles per unit area and less N concentrated per particle (Plate 34). Repeat application may be needed after 2 to 4 weeks. Fertilizer must be watered-in immediately after application.
- Granulars with slow-release N forms often are incorporated into a spoon-feeding program at 0.20 to 0.50 lb N per 1,000 ft^2 per treatment (9.8 to 24.5 kg N ha^{-1}). As with quick-release N granulars, small particle sizes are necessary on close-cut turfgrasses. After 3 to 6 weeks, a repeat application may be required.
- Combination programs that use both quick-release (granular or foliar) and slow-release N carriers are common. Rates of N are typically at 0.20 to 0.40 lb N per 1,000 ft^2 (9.8 to 19.6 kg N ha^{-1}) applied at 2 to 5 weeks.

The use of slow-release granular N carriers as a sole source of N in a spoon-feeding regime is based on applying these materials at lower rates per treatment than normal but more often than a more traditional slow-release program. This practice buffers against excessive N release in a relatively short time period if conditions are ideal for maximum rate of N release from the product. When using this approach for spoon-feeding, it is best to focus on a low N base level and supplement with foliar N rather than to apply too much N.

E. Slow-Release N-Programs (Traditional Approach)

A complete *slow-release N source program* with high N rates per application which is to provide N for extended time periods is the opposite of a spoon-feeding regime. Use of slow release N carriers in this manner has been the *traditional approach.* However, the basic idea behind both programs is to provide sustained but adequate N for plant uptake while minimizing potential leaching losses. In arid climates or dry periods in other climates, N release from various slow-release forms is controlled in a manner that normally prevents too much N becoming available at any one point in time. (**The most basic rule of N fertilization is never to lose control of N release so that too much N is released at any one time period.**) Rates and times of application of slow-release fertilizers should be planned for "typical weather conditions" such that release of N occurs at appropriate times for grass needs. This requires a good understanding of fertilizer characteristics and environmental conditions that affect release of N. In nonirrigated turfgrasses, N availability is controlled primarily by soil moisture, with N being released when there is adequate rainfall or irrigation and limited N release under low soil moisture conditions. After a prolonged dry period, some N is still available for release and plant uptake when soil moisture increases. With arid, irrigated sites, N availability from slow release materials is a function of soil moisture and temperature. But, unusually rapid N release is not a problem unless the site is exposed to excess irrigation.

It is in humid climates or in wet seasons under adequate temperatures that N release from various slow-release carriers may occur in a more rapid manner than normal, thereby resulting in excessive N. This potential problem is usually associated with prolonged high temperatures in conjunction with moist soil surface conditions. Occurrences of unexpected and undesirable release of excessive N in relatively short time periods rather than in an extended manner has damped the use of single high application of slow-release N to provide long-term N availability except for:

- climates that are consistently arid for prolonged periods or year-round
- on sites where one application is desired to provide long-term N and uncertainties in release patterns are acceptable, such as on lawns, general grounds, or amenity turf, but usually not on intensively used recreational turfs or where uniform, high quality turf is expected.

Practical use of slow-release N carriers on recreational sites has been achieved by: (a) carefully choosing the carrier to provide the desired release pattern under the climatic and soil conditions of the site; (b) using more modest N rates per application with more applications, yet less frequent than for quick-release sources. This spreads out N release and buffers against excessive spikes of N release; and/or (c) using a slow-release fertilizer containing sufficient quick release to provide good initial response. Thus, an N fertilization program can be developed even on a golf green that would utilize only slow-release N carriers. When slow-release carriers are the sole N sources, typical rates per application are:

- 0.50 to 1.5 lb N per 1,000 ft^2 (24.4 to 73.2 kg N ha^{-1}) on general or amenity grasses, golf course fairways, and most sports fields.
- 0.20 to 0.80 lb N per 1,000 ft^2 (9.8 to 39.1 kg N ha^{-1}) on greens.

Many turfgrass managers develop N fertilization programs that incorporate spoon-feeding and slow-release components. With the diversity of quick-release and slow-release N carriers available to the turfgrass grower, good programs can be formulated for a particular site using solely quick-release spoon-feeding (granular or foliar), only slow-release carriers, or combinations. In fact, many fertilizers are available with both quick- and slow-release N materials combined together.

Understanding the characteristics of different N carriers is very important for selection of appropriate N fertilizers with special attention to factors that influence their N release. One example would be the use of slow-release N sources for the late fall application on cool-season turfgrasses. The desired goal is to provide available N at the time vertical shoot growth stops but the grass is green with active photosynthesis. Quick-release N sources would provide immediate N availability but on sandy sites or in humid regions the potential for N leaching exists. If a slow-release N source is selected, it should be applied early enough to provide available N at the expected period of vertical growth slowing or stoppage. Slow-release carriers that do not depend on soil microorganisms will release N at a somewhat slower rate in cool weather than warm but application at 10 to 14 days prior to anticipated need is normally acceptable—i.e., in the summer 5–10 days may be sufficient. Those N carriers requiring soil microbial activity for N release must be applied 3 to 6 weeks earlier, while in the summer, N availability may occur in 7 to 14 days. Because of variations in temperature and rainfall during late fall, the N release pattern from slow-release sources is somewhat less predictable. For this reason, turf managers often use quick-release N at this particular time.

Turfgrass managers are encouraged to develop an N fertilizer program for each different type of situation; for example, greens, tees, fairways, and roughs on a golf course. The program should be written with: (a) target dates of application; (b) rate of N application, usually as a range to allow for adjustments; and (c) type of N carrier which could be very specific as to the particular carrier or general, such as quick-release or slow-release. The formal program should include other nutrients that are to be applied. Several example programs that include N, P, K and other nutrients to be applied (Table 19.5) are discussed later in this chapter.

III. FORMULATE PROGRAMS FOR OTHER NUTRIENTS (P, K, ETC.)

A. Phosphorus

PHOSPHORUS NEEDS ARE BEST BASED ON SOIL TEST RESULTS with interpretation and recommendations specific for turfgrass sites. On recreational turf, the trend has been to use very little P since *Poa annua,* normally considered as undesirable, responds to P by producing more viable seeds. In cool-season turfgrasses, *Poa annua* infestation is especially important because it is a year-round problem and can easily dominate the stand; however, it is difficult to keep *Poa annua* out of recreational turfgrass sites, regardless of P level. Also, it is appropriate to minimize P use from an environmental viewpoint so to reduce the chances of leaching or runoff, but adequate P must still be available for turfgrass growth.

Cool-season turfgrasses grown on sand-based root zone mixes with lower P-fixation abilities often require some supplemental P. High sand root zones such as a USGA green are somewhat less prone to *Poa annua* infestation than more fine-textured soils and they are also more likely to exhibit P deficiencies if adequate P is not supplied. But they are more susceptible to P leaching if too much P is added. On these sites, a moderately low to moderate soil test would suggest the need to apply about 0.5 to 1.5 lb of P_2O_5 per 1,000 ft^2 per year (24.4 to 73.2 kg P_2O_5 ha^{-1}). With continuous use, the P soil test level will likely increase. Keeping a record of soil test results will help determine how P levels are changing and will serve as a basis for adjusting annual P needs.

For warm-season turfgrass, there is less concern over *Poa annua* infestation except as a winter annual but leaching and runoff concerns remain. A soil test of moderately low to medium would suggest 1.0 to 2.0 lb P_2O_5 per 1,000 ft^2 per year as a reasonable average within most of the United States but 2.0 to 3.0 lb P_2O_5 per 1,000 ft^2 where there is a 12-month growing season. Root zone mixes that contain some clay (i.e., sandy loams to clays) may require somewhat less P than sand root zones.

Phosphorus soil test rankings (i.e., very low, low, etc.) are best correlated to establishment situations where P needs are greatest. Thus, a very low soil test would imply a high probability of P deficiency for establishment unless supplemental P is added. Many mature turfgrasses may obtain sufficient P even when the soil test is low but the chances of incurring P deficiency is still present. Grasses growing on sandy sites with aggressive growth or being forced to grow to recover from wear are the most likely to exhibit deficiencies. Cool-season grasses seem especially prone to exhibit P deficiency in early spring when it may not be recognized because: (a) growth tends to be slow from cool temperatures; and (b) turf that is deficient in P can still have dark green color, but a very slow growth rate that does not respond to applied N. In climates where warm-season grasses go dormant in the winter, the period after spring green-up has started is a prime period for P deficiency to develop.

Assuming some P is to be applied to a cool-season turfgrass, the most important times of application are:

- late winter or early spring when P activity in the soil is low due to cool soil temperatures
- early fall or late summer when roots are less active in response to summer stresses.

If more than 1.0 lb P_2O_5 per 1,000 ft^2 is recommended per year, it can be divided into split applications at these times. However, P can be applied at any time of the year.

For warm-season turfgrasses, the most important times of application for P are:

- Midspring at the time of initial spring green-up since P availability may be low due to cold soil temperatures and it is not unusual for warm-season turfgrasses to exhibit spring root dieback as green-up occurs. Thus, surface applied P would be available as new roots develop.
- late summer to early fall on nonoverseeded grasses
- at the time of winter overseeding for warm-season grass sites that are to be overseeded to provide adequate P for establishment of the cool-season grass. As long as the warm-season turf is not dormant, it will also take up P.

Especially on sandy soils and for climates with a long growing season for warm-season grasses, split applications are desirable versus one higher application.

When clippings are routinely removed from a site, soil P tests should be monitored more closely, particularly for turfs grown on sands or low P subsoils. Higher N rates increase growth, increasing the potential for a P deficiency when clippings are removed.

B. Potassium

On most turfgrass sites, K soil test recommendations are the best approach for determining annual K needs. For cool- and warm-season grasses subjected to intense traffic and close mowing, turf managers should attempt to maintain a high K soil test level. On medium to lower maintenance turfs, a moderate K-soil test is acceptable.

Sandy, low CEC soils in any climate are susceptible to K leaching if overirrigated. Turf managers should adjust irrigation to prevent unnecessary K leaching. *On very sandy, low CEC soils subjected to frequent high rainfall,* K easily leaches and routinely measures low on the soil test. In this situation, the following guidelines can be used for cool- and warm-season grasses that are based on relating the K application to the N applied.

- Use a 1:1.5 N:K_2O ratio (i.e., 1.5 lb K_2O applied for every 1.0 lb N) for annual N programs of 1 to 3.0 lb N per 1,000 ft^2 (48.8 to 146.4 kg N ha^{-1}). A 1:1.5 N:K_2O ratio = 1:1.25 N:K ratio.
- Use a 1:1 N:K_2O ratio (1:0.83 N:K) for grasses grown under 3 to 7 lb N per 1,000 ft^2 (146.4 to 342 kg N ha^{-1}). Above 6 lb N use a 1:0.75 or 1:0.50 N:K_2O ratio up to a maximum of 7 to 12 lb K_2O per 1,000 ft^2 per year (253 to 434 kg K ha^{-1}). When high N plus high K are applied, total soluble salt levels within the soil may become high enough to induce salinity injury exhibited as greater wilt, reduced water uptake, and more scalping. Thus, a lower N:K_2O ratio is suggested under high N regimes (see Table 12.5).

These guidelines are for conditions of actual leaching occurring over time that removes K from the root zone. Even in normally humid, high rainfall environments, prolonged dry periods may occur. Also, some climates have a wet or monsoon season followed by a long dry period. Whenever dry periods do occur and irrigation is not sufficient for leaching of salts, high K applications can contribute to buildup of total salts (high salinity). Thus, K rates should be adjusted downward to avoid excess salt accumulation under nonleaching periods. Some turf managers use KNO_3 to avoid adding extra salt ions (Cl, SO_4) that the plant does not take up at high rates and which contribute to soil salt levels.

On sites with high Na inputs, irrigation is normally recommended to be increased so that greater leaching occurs and there is a net downward movement of Na—either in saline, sodic, or saline-sodic soils. Three factors occur in these situations that suppress K uptake: (a) leaching removes K; (b) the presence of soil solution Na inhibits K uptake; and (c) Na often displace some of the K on CEC sites. Thus, in situations where high Na is present, the N:K_2O may be adjusted toward more K such as 1:1 instead of 1:0.50 or 1:0.75, common under high N regimes.

Appropriate *application timing* on cool-season grasses depends on the situation. General/amenity and recreational turfgrasses growing on fine-textured soils (loams or higher in clay), may require only one or two applications of K per year if the soil test recommends K. If the total annual K_2O recommendation exceeds 1.0 lb K_2O per 1,000 ft^2, it is preferred to split applications into equal increments of 0.50 to 1.0 lb K_2O per 1,000 ft^2 application (20.3 to 40.6 kg K ha^{-1}). Split applications are often accomplished by using a fertilizer with an appropriate N-K_2O analysis so that both nutrients are applied at the same time. Heavier applications of K (and N) would be in cool periods, while summer applications should be avoided except on high use recreational sites where one or two summer applications at 0.25 to 0.50 lb K_2O per 1,000 ft^2 can be made. Salt effects on turfgrasses can be minimized by using K_2SO_4 rather than KCl in these warm and often dry months. For cool-season grasses susceptible to summer stresses (temperature, drought, wear), adequate soil K levels are especially important. However, avoid applying K fertilizers to wilted turf or turf in summer dormancy.

When the cool-season turfgrass root zone is coarse-textured (i.e., sand to sandy loam), K applications are best approached on a more frequent but lighter rate basis. This practice buffers against leaching losses if high rainfall occurs and against excessive salt accumulation in dry periods. Consideration should be given to the use of coated K sources on these areas where leaching may be a problem.

As noted above, the frequency and rates of K fertilization vary with intensity of culture for cool-season turfgrasses. For example:

- General grounds and lawns may benefit from two to four applications divided into increments of 0.33 to 1.00 lb K_2O per 1,000 ft^2, with the lower rates used in summer.
- Sports field managers often divide the total annual K needs into four to six applications of 0.25 to 1.0 lb K_2O per 1,000 ft^2 with a three to five week interval and somewhat lower rates used in summer (0.25 to 0.50 lb K_2O per 1,000 ft^2 per treatment).
- Golf course greens, bowling greens, and some golf tees under intense use can benefit from four to eight applications with treatment intervals of three to four weeks. The total annual K requirement should be applied in increments of 0.25 to 0.75 lb K_2O per 1,000 ft^2 but with 0.25 to 0.50 lb K_2O per 1,000 ft^2 used in the summer months.
- Cool-season grasses grown in climates conducive to winter injury should receive K in the late fall period about the time growth ceases at the rate of 0.50 to 0.75 lb K_2O per 1,000 ft^2 (20.3 to 30.4 kg K ha^{-1}).

Timing of K fertilization on warm-season turfgrasses is adjusted for soil conditions and intensity of management, just as for cool-season grasses. Important periods of application in climates where winter dormancy occurs are:

- Midspring as spring green-up occurs. The specific rate of application will vary with soil test recommendation or N:K_2O used (for sandy sites with active leaching) but applications of 0.50 to 1.0 K_2O per 1,000 ft^2 (20.3 to 40.6 kg K ha^{-1}) are typical.
- Midspring to midfall. When the soil is fine-textured, K may be applied once or twice at 0.33 to 1.00 lb K_2O per 1,000 ft^2 per treatment for general turf sites, and two to three times at 0.33 to 0.75 lb K_2O per 1,000 ft^2 on sports areas. Rates are typically adjusted downward on more sandy sites to 0.33 to 0.50 lb K_2O per 1,000 ft^2 at two to six weeks apart.
- Midfall to late fall. Prior to dormancy, an application of 0.50 to 1.0 lb K_2O per 1,000 ft^2 is useful, assuming the K soil test demonstrates a need or the site is a sandy, leached soil. This application can enhance winter hardiness especially if native soil K levels are low, the grass is under intensive maintenance, and low temperature stresses are severe.

Warm-season turfgrasses grown in areas without a winter dormancy period can receive K fertilization year-round with higher rates applied when higher N is needed. As with N, the primary factors influencing rates are wet or dry seasons, intensity of irrigation and culture, soil type, and degree of use. Rates per application are usually 0.33 to 1.0 lb K_2O per application (fine-textured soils) or 0.33 to 0.75 lb K_2O per 1,000 ft^2 (sandy soils) with the total annual K requirement applied in six to 12 increments. If slow-release K fertilizers are used, rates would typically be somewhat higher per application than a readily available K carrier but at a less frequent application schedule. Periods following monsoon seasons are when K deficiencies are most likely, while the potential for K-induced salt accumulation increases with duration of the dry season.

Ranges of application rates for K are given in the preceding discussion. The turf manager should select rates that will result in an annual rate similar to the annual recommendation based on soil test results.

C. Other Nutrients

On almost all turfgrass areas, routine, annual fertilization of N, P, and K are necessary. Whether other nutrients are required on a routine, annual basis depends on the soil and turfgrass conditions. Readers are referred to the chapters that discuss these secondary macronutrients or micronutrients and their use on turfgrasses. However, some general observations can aid in enhancing programs for these nutrients when they are required.

Magnesium

Magnesium deficiencies are infrequent but seem to be more prevalent in recent years, especially on recreational sites, for a combination of reasons such as: (a) tendency for some turfgrass managers to allow soil pH to reach relatively acid conditions of pH 4.7 to 5.4; (b) increasing use of sand root zone mixes with low CEC; (c) the use of relatively high K fertilization on recreational turf which can induce more Mg leaching; and (d) some consulting agronomists recommend Ca as a nutrient on acid soils and even some alkaline soils based on a supposedly low extractable Ca level or low % Ca saturation percentage on the CEC. Traditionally, when pH was low, lime was recommended to adjust pH, and dolomitic lime (contains Mg) was suggested if Mg levels were low. However, Ca is sometimes being recommended from sources that do not increase pH ($CaSO_4$, $CaCl_2$) nor supply Mg. One of the side effects is to suppress Mg as well as K availability. Thus, turfgrass managers are encouraged to give attention to extractable Mg levels on soil tests (which are more reliable than extractable Ca soil test levels which are not well correlated to grass needs). Magnesium fertilizers and fertilization are discussed in Chapter 13, Calcium, Magnesium, and Sulfur.

Iron

Iron fertilization can be used on cool- and warm-season grasses in the following situations:

(a) *Nondeficient Fe* conditions for color enhancement of grasses, especially those that are genetically lighter green. Foliar application of Fe is used for nondeficient Fe conditions, usually at rates of 0.5 to 1.0 lb actual Fe per acre (i.e., 0.012 to 0.024 lb actual Fe per 1,000 ft^2 or 0.56 to 1.12 kg Fe ha^{-1}). Addition of 0.05 to 0.10 lb N per 1,000 ft^2 (2.44 to 4.88 kg N ha^{-1}) enhances Fe uptake (some Fe carriers contain N already in the formulation). The Fe and N are applied in 1 to 5 gallons of water per 1,000 ft^2 (400 to 2,000 L ha^{-1}). Frequency of application is usually once every 3 to 4 weeks.

Many turfgrasses can tolerate higher foliar Fe rates than 0.024 lb Fe per 1,000 ft^2 (i.e., 2 to 3 times these rates) without foliar burn or blackening. Excessive rates of Fe can cause significant turf injuries, especially when applied under stress conditions. New products should be tested on a small area before using over a whole site. Some grasses, however, like centipedegrass are very sensitive to excess Fe and will turn black. For centipedegrass or other sensitive grasses, use $\leq$0.024 lb Fe per 1,000 ft^2 on days where air temperatures do not exceed 85°F (29°C). On days with air temperatures >85°F, reduce the rate to $\leq$0.012 lb Fe per 1,000 ft^2. Color responses from foliar application of Fe can be highly variable in intensity of color and duration. Best color responses in magnitude of greening and duration vary with weather conditions, with responses in the order of: cool, dry conditions > cool, moist > warm, dry > warm, moist.

(b) *Deficient conditions* where Fe has been demonstrated to be deficient by soil tests or past history of Fe deficiency symptoms. Fe deficiency is most common under the following conditions:

- alkaline soils, especially if high in P
- sites receiving irrigation water high in bicarbonates
- sites having cultivars that are more susceptible to iron chlorosis.

Foliar applications can be used as often as needed at the rates noted for nondeficient Fe situations. Granular Fe fertilizers are also used at higher Fe rates than for foliar Fe. Granular materials may work better on some soils than others so the turf manager may wish to apply granular materials on a trial area. On greens, Milorganite can be used 1–3 times per year since it contains about 5% naturally chelated Fe. Also, some turfgrass fertilizers are formulated with Fe as well as the main fertilizer element.

Manganese (Mn)

Manganese can be deficient on sandy soils that are subjected to high rainfall and contain little organic matter. Frequent foliar Fe application may enhance Mn deficiency. Manganese can be applied as a foliar material (for example, as $MnSO_4 \bullet H_2O$ at 0.025 lb actual Mn per 1,000 ft^2 or 1.22 kg Mn ha^{-1}) or granular at higher rates. Manganese is also present in some maintenance turfgrass fertilizers.

Other Micronutrients

Fertilization with micronutrients other than Fe and Mn is rarely needed on turf except under intensive culture. *"Micronutrient packages"* are fertilizers containing all or most of the micronutrients. These products contain a range of micronutrients that are usually sufficient for turf needs. Generally, the fertilizers are high in Fe, medium in Mn, and low in other micronutrients. Many other materials applied to turf contain micronutrients—some N, P, K fertilizers, pesticides, irrigation water, dust deposition, etc. Overuse of micronutrients can lead to toxicity. However, application of a micronutrient fertilizer 1 to 4 times per year is a common practice, especially on sandy soils.

IV. OTHER FERTILIZER PROGRAMING CONSIDERATIONS

THE CENTRAL FOCUS OF FERTILIZER PROGRAM DEVELOPMENT is to formulate agronomically sound programs for each site with respect to all necessary nutrients. In the previous sections, the most important factors to consider relative to developing a formal program for each site were presented. These were agronomic factors. However, other considerations can be important but will only be listed here since they are addressed in more detail in other chapters, especially Chapter 18, of this book.

Factors in Selecting a Fertilizer

- spreadability; uniformity of particle size and density
- granulated vs. blended
- presence of dust

- foliar burn potential
- bulk vs. bags vs. liquid; equipment availability
- cost of fertilizer vs. cost of application
- type of nitrogen; rate and longevity of response
- ratio; relate to soil test
- pH effects
- storage characteristics
- availability of particular carrier
- corrosion potential; effect on equipment
- hygroscopicity and deliquescence
- impurities
- fertilizer-pesticide combination products
- cost per unit of nutrient
- salinity effects

Fertilization and Environmental Protection[1,2]

Fertilization of turfgrass sites has received considerable criticism from some groups as a source of nonpoint pollution of surface and groundwaters. Nitrates and phosphorus are of particular concern because of the potential to enhance weed and algae growth in surface waters and their impact on wetlands. Leaching of nitrates into groundwaters can affect drinking water quality.

Recent research[1,2] has been helpful in identifying which concerns are real and where fertilizer management practices may need to be adjusted to provide protection of water and wetland resources. When N fertilization on mature turf follows sound practices, leaching of nitrates has been found to be minimal. Similar results have occurred for P fertilization. During grow-in on sands is the time of greatest concern for leaching. Runoff during grow-in can occur when bare soil is exposed to loss of both N and P with the water and in the eroded soil. Research on runoff of nutrients from mature turfs was found to be essentially zero on soils with excellent soil structure, but has raised concern on highly compacted, sloping soils.

Basic to good fertilizer management are an understanding of plant needs, characteristics of the carrier, and what happens to nutrients in the soil as discussed elsewhere in this book. *The following guidelines include a number of practical suggestions for protecting against loss of nutrients from turf sites.*

1. Apply N only at rates and times when the turf can utilize it efficiently.
2. Use slow-release carriers at modest rates on sensitive sites, considering the factors that enhance N release rates (temperature, moisture). Lightweight slow-release fertilizers can be susceptible to movement with surface water flow.
3. Establish a buffer zone around surface waters and wetlands. A very conservative approach would include a zone of trees and shrubs, a practice that is not practical in some situations. Using higher mowing heights as a grass buffer zone adjacent to sensitive sites can slow runoff water flow, reducing nutrient runoff potential.
4. Plant low-N-requiring grasses or ones with high uptake efficiencies adjacent to sensitive sites or simply apply less fertilizer in these areas.
5. Follow a spoon-feeding approach during periods when runoff or leaching events are likely to occur. This will help provide good stress tolerance as well.
6. Utilize soil tests for P fertilization planning. For areas adjacent to sensitive sites, use zero-P fertilizers unless P deficiency symptoms develop.

7. Irrigate following fertilization to move nutrients into thatch and soil, reducing the possibility for runoff of nutrients with the water.
8. Do not fertilize just before a significant rainfall event is likely to occur.
9. Use modest irrigation to reduce leaching and runoff. Maintaining drier soil conditions reduces potential for both runoff and leaching when major rainfall events occur.
10. Never apply fertilizers in such a way that they reach hard surfaces or surface waters. Proper use of a drop spreader can prevent this from occurring. Runoff from hard surfaces such as parking lots, streets, and sidewalks can reach surface waters, especially through storm sewers or on sloping sites adjacent to surface waters.
11. Remove clippings near sensitive areas. As much as possible, prevent tree leaves from dropping into surface waters.
12. Divert runoff water originating on turfgrass sites from reaching surface waters through the use of berms, etc. This practice is seldom practical since surface waters occupy the lowest part of the landscape. As an alternative it may be practical to divert the water into a holding pond or a constructed wetland where nitrates can be denitrified and P can be tied up in organic matter.
13. When feasible, prevent or divert runoff water from hard surfaces that drain across turf sites to reduce potential for nutrient runoff.
14. Divert drainage tile lines from greens into a low-lying area or grassed holding pond rather than into a highly sensitive stream.

Soil and site conditions are major factors in potential loss of nutrients from turfs. For good environmental stewardship, turf managers should have a good understanding of soil and site in order to develop sound fertilization programs.

V. PLAN THE PROGRAM

AFTER DECIDING ON ANNUAL RATES OF N, P_2O_5, and K_2O, and the type of N (slow-release, fast-release, or combination) to be applied, a turf manager has the option of applying individual nutrient sources or selecting a mixed fertilizer with a ratio of N-P_2O_5-K_2O that approximates the annual needs. Most turfgrass fertilizer manufacturers have a product line that includes many fertilizer grades, different N sources, and different combinations of quick- and slow-release forms. Check manufacturers' literature or consult with their representatives to determine whether they have a product that will meet your needs. In some cases, the use of two or more products during the growing season will enable the manager to more closely meet the N-P_2O_5-K_2O needs. If it has been determined that micronutrients are needed, options are to use: (a) a single micronutrient fertilizer; or (b) a mixed micronutrient fertilizer containing two or more micronutrients, or a conventional mixed fertilizer that also contains a guaranteed level of one or more micronutrients.

The final product of fertilization programing should be a formal program in table form for each type of site with dates, carriers, rates, and additional notes. Table 19.6 illustrates two program versions for the same site to illustrate programing principles and how widely different programs can be developed for the same site.

It is best to make recommendations in terms of reasonable ranges of dates and fertilizer rates for a specific time during the season. The use of ranges in planning is a reminder that adjustments in planned timing or rates are normal. The example program format in Table 19.6 is a very basic one. Ultimately, the turf manager must add more specific information such as the fertilizers to be used since this provides a basis for what should be ordered. An example of such records

Table 19.6. Two potential fertilization programs for a bermudagrass (hybrid) golf green in the coastal area of Georgia in the Southeast United States that is overseeded with perennial ryegrass in midfall (October 10) and with a suggested total annual N rate of 5 to 8 lb N per 1,000 ft^2 (244 to 390 kg N ha^{-1}); K recommendations based on an approximate 1:1 N:K_2O ratio since this is a site with sandy soils and frequent leaching; P soil test is low (P_2O_5 recommended is 2.0 to 2.5 lb per 1,000 ft^2); pH 5.7. Conversion: 1 lb per 1,000 ft^2 = 49 kg ha^{-1}.

	Nitrogen		lb per 1,000 ft^2		
Date of Application	lb N per 1,000 ft^2	N-Source Type	P_2O_5	K_2O	Other
Quick-Release, Spoon Feeding Program[a]					
Jan 1–10	0.25–0.5	Quick release	0	0.25–0.5	
Feb 1–10	0.25–0.5	" "	0	0.25–0.5	
Mar 1–10	0.25–0.5	" "	1.0	0.25–0.5	
Apr 1–10	0.5–0.75	" "	0	0.5–0.75	Micros, Mg[e]
May 1–10	0.75–1	" "	0	0.5–0.75	
Jun 1–10	0.75–1	" "	0.25	0.5–0.75	
Jul 1–10	0.75–1	" "	0	0.5–0.75	Micros, Mg[e]
Aug 1–10	0.5–0.75	" "	0	0.5–0.75	
Sep 1–10	0.25–0.5	" "	0	0.25–0.5	Micros, Mg[e]
Oct 10[b]	0.25–0.5	" "	1.0	0.25–0.5	
Nov 1–10	0.25–0.5	" "	0	0.25–0.5	
Dec 1–10	0.25–0.5	" "	0	0.25–0.5	
	5.0–8.0		2.25	4.25–7.25	
Slow-Release Program		(QR:SR)[c]			
Feb 1–10	1–1.25	50:50[d]	0	0.75–1	
Apr 1–10	1–1.25	50:50	1.0	0.75–1	Micros, Mg[e]
Jun 1–10	1–1.5	30:70	0.25	0.75–1	Micros, Mg[e]
Aug 1–10	1–1.5	30:70	0	0.75–1	
Oct 10[b]	1–1.25	50:50[d]	1.0	0.75–1	Micros, Mg[e]
Dec 1–10	1–1.25	50:50[d]	0	0.75–1	
	6.0–8.0		2.25	4.5–6.0	

[a] These two programs represent the "extremes" of quick release versus slow release. Programs that are intermediate and adopt both quick-release and slow-release fertilizers are often used.
[b] Winter overseeding date for perennial ryegrass. Supplemental quick-release N may be needed 1–2 weeks after germination.
[c] QR = quick-release; SR = slow-release carrier.
[d] SR N-carrier must not be based on microbial N release on these dates.
[e] Mg based on a low Mg soil test.

is Table 19.7, where data relate to applying nutrients outlined in Table 19.6 using two commercially available water soluble fertilizers and Epsom salts. Amounts and dates do not exactly match those in Table 19.6 but represent a realistic effort at closely matching the planned needs.

VI. ADJUST THE PROGRAM DURING THE YEAR

EVEN THOUGH A TURFGRASS MANAGER HAS DEVELOPED a good formal fertilizer program for a site, many factors can alter the program, especially for N applications. Ultimately the best

Table 19.7. Example of records showing dates, materials, and rates to achieve objectives shown in Table 19.6 (spoon-feeding program) using two water soluble spray grade fertilizers and Epsom salts.

Date of Application	Fertilizer Applied		Nutrients Applied				
	Material	Rate	N	P_2O_5	K_2O	Mg	Micros
			lb per 1,000 ft^2				
Jan 3	20-20-20[a]	13	0.26	0.26	0.26	–	yes
Jan 31	20-20-20	13	0.26	0.26	0.26	–	yes
Feb 28	20-20-20	13	0.26	0.26	0.26	–	yes
Mar 28	20-20-20	25	0.50	0.50	0.50	–	yes
	Epsom salts[a]	3	–	–	–	0.3	–
Apr 24	26-0-26[a]	30	0.78	–	0.78	–	Fe
May 24	26-0-26	30	0.78	–	0.78	–	Fe
Jun 29	26-0-26	30	0.78	–	0.78	–	Fe
	Epsom salts	3	–	–	–	0.3	–
Jul 31	20-20-20	25	0.50	0.50	0.50	–	yes
Aug 28	20-20-20	13	0.26	0.26	0.26	–	yes
	Epsom salts	3	–	–	–	0.3	–
Oct 10	20-20-20	13	0.26	0.26	0.26	–	yes
Nov 6	26-0-26	10	0.26	–	0.26	–	Fe
Dec 4	26-0-26	10	0.26	–	0.26	–	Fe
	Total Nutrients =		5.16	2.3	5.16	0.9	

[a] 20-20-20 is soluble spray grade with B, Cu, Fe, Mn, Mo, Zn; Epsom salts is 10% Mg; 26-0-26 is soluble spray grade with 0.10% Fe.

guide for adjusting the timing or rate of N per application is the *visual condition of the turfgrass plant,* growth rate, and understanding of stress and disease problems. As N becomes limited, the initial turf response is a reduced growth rate which may be noted as fewer clippings removed per unit area. Chlorosis also starts, gradually becoming apparent on the lower leaves. These plant responses are visually apparent even before a tissue test for N may start to reveal N deficiency.

If a turfgrass is exhibiting good color, growth, and shoot density at the time of a planned N application, the N treatment should be reduced, delayed, or omitted unless a slow-release source with a delayed response is being utilized. Conversely, the early appearance of N deficiency symptoms would suggest applying N fertilizer prior to the planned date and possibly at a higher rate.

Anticipated *disease activity* or existing disease infections can alter N programing. Quick-release N may increase brown patch (*Rhizoctonia* spp.) and *Pythium* spp. blight if they are active at the time of application (Table 2.6). Rust (*Puccinia* spp.) or dollar spot (*Schlerotonia homeocarpa*) infection, however, can be reduced with quick-release N. Management of N can play a major role in an integrated disease management program (see Chapter 10, Nitrogen).

Turfgrasses recovering from disease injuries or other *injuries* can benefit from supplemental N. For example, core aeration or dethatching a site can cause damage to the desired turfgrass species. An additional application of quick-release N just previous to or immediately after these operations can enhance recovery. Typical rates are 0.33 to 0.50 lb N per 1,000 ft^2 (16.1 to 24.4 kg N ha^{-1}). If an N application was already planned based on the routine N program, additional N treatment would not be required but perhaps a slightly higher N rate should be considered.

Forecasted or prolonged, *weather conditions* can alter N programs. Unseasonably warm and wet weather would imply adjusting N downward or using a slow-release form to avoid excessive clipping growth and mowings. However, the influence of warm, wet conditions on N release from the slow-release N carrier should be taken into account. These adjustments would be in the planned routine program but wet periods can often occur outside the normal seasonal cycles. Extensive dry periods causing turf dormancy may result in reduced N or K needs on unirrigated turfs.

Program adjustments may be required for other nutrients. Some common examples are:

- Any nutrient may be required outside the planned program dates of application if deficiencies are detected.
- Additional K may be necessary on sandy soils if unseasonable rainfall occurs, or K may be reduced during unexpected dry periods.
- If a turfgrass has its roots pruned from insects, nematodes, or other causes, supplemental P may be useful for recovery.
- High applications of lime or gypsum may induce Mg or K imbalances or deficiencies. Thus, supplemental treatment with these nutrients at the time of lime or gypsum application may be warranted.
- During extended periods of wet, cloudy weather, foliar Fe may help improve turf color.

VII. FERTILIZATION DURING GROW-IN

FERTILIZATION DURING THE ESTABLISHMENT *(grow-in)* period is different than on an established, mature turfgrass, especially on sandy soils. Thus, sandy soils and fine-textured soils will be discussed separately. As with mature grasses, a variety of different fertilization programs can be used for establishment. Those suggested in the following sections are formulated based on experience; consideration to minimizing leaching and runoff losses; attention to providing rapid turf coverage; and achieving stabilization of nutrient fluctuations inherent in established grasses, particularly on high sand sites.

A. Coarse-Textured (Sandy) Soils

High sand content sports fields, fairways, tees, and golf greens, such as a USGA green, present real challenges for maintaining adequate nutrition during the first year of establishment. Primary reasons are: (a) the nutrient retention capability of the root zone media is very low. Nutrient retention is a result of cation exchange capacity (CEC) which resides in the clay and organic matter fractions; (b) most organic matter sources added during construction are low in nutrient content, low in CEC, and sands are basically infertile; (c) new greens exhibit high infiltration and percolation rates that contribute to the potential for greater leaching losses; and (d) sufficient nutrients must be added to develop a turfgrass stand and build microbial populations up to the levels inherent in a mature turf stand.

As a new turfgrass stand "matures" over the first year, the organic fraction consists of the original organic matter that has not decomposed, as well as a continual supply of fresh, more nutrient-rich organic matter from the grass-produced roots, clippings (if returned), and dead shoots. These "fresh" sources can more easily decompose composed to organic matter in the original mix and release nutrients for plant uptake. Since the roots generally grow throughout the surface 6 to 8 inches for cool-season grasses (deeper for warm-season turfgrass) during the first year, they help maintain a supply of new organic matter that not only adds nutrients during decomposition, but also begin to contribute to CEC properties. As these roots fill much of the pore space in the surface few inches, infiltration and percolation decline, thereby leaching potential decreases.

As these changes occur, the turfgrass site starts to stabilize in nutrient needs toward that of a mature turfgrass. The time frame for the transition varies with soil, grass, climate, management, and type of establishment method but generally requires 6 to 12 months. While the turfgrass may achieve full cover from seeding, sprigging, plugging, or stolonizing well before this time, the sod is still maturing and *nutrient stabilization* requires a longer period.

From shortly after seed germination or vegetative establishment until about one year has elapsed, the following conditions often occur: the turf will appear healthy with adequate color and growth rate, but within a 1- to 3-day period, shoot growth declines and yellowing typical of N-deficiency starts to appear; as N is applied, color and growth resumes and the cycle repeats after a period of time. Initially, these cycles are closer together but become less frequent over time. Other nutrient levels, such as K, can exhibit similar cycles but visual symptoms are less evident than with N. Also, sodded turfgrass is less susceptible to such rapid fluctuations since sod has more biomass already developed that contains considerable nutrients in addition to soil-based nutrients.

Nitrogen

The addition of a natural organic N-carrier to the rooting medium by surface application and tilling to a depth of 4 to 6 inches provides a good source of N that does not readily leach and also adds micronutrients. Milorganite® at equivalent to 2 lb N per 1,000 ft^2 is often used (i.e., 33 lb material per 1,000 ft^2; 1,600 kg ha^{-1}) but other natural organic fertilizers can be used. This practice will provide some buffering against rapid fluctuations in N levels for a couple of months after establishment. The N release rate is dependent on soil temperatures. If soil temperatures remain below 55°F (13°C), some additional soluble N may be needed.

Nitrogen contained in a starter fertilizer applied at establishment will provide N for only a short period. Often the N-rate for a starter fertilizer (examples: 5-20-20; 13-25-12; 18-24-8) is about 1.0 lb N per 1,000 ft^2 (48.8 kg N ha^{-1}) when surface applied. The N rate for incorporated preestablishment fertilizer may be as high as 2 lb N per 1,000 ft^2; however, deeper than 4 to 6 inches placement subjects much of the soluble N to leaching before roots grow into the entire fertilized depth.

From midspring through midfall of temperate or subtropical climates, when soil temperatures are high enough to allow microbial release of the N in natural organic or long-chain ureaformaldehyde (UF) fertilizers, these materials should be included in your N-program at about 0.30 to 0.60 lb N per 1,000 ft^2 per month (14.6 to 29.3 kg ha^{-1}). Natural organic fertilizers should be used for at least half of these applications to provide supplemental micronutrients, and are best applied in late spring or early fall. Summer applications may promote algae growth if the turfgrass has not fully covered the soil surface. Additional micronutrient fertilizer may be applied two or three times per year for the first year. In some places, Fe and Mn may be needed because of true deficiencies, especially with the high irrigation intensity during establishment. Foliar Fe and Mn can be applied to grass from four weeks after germination at monthly intervals for improved color and growth. Granular micronutrient packages could also be applied, most typically with chelated sources to reduce fixation in the sand.

By applying natural organics and/or UF in small amounts over the warmer growing months, the N in these compounds is gradually released for plant uptake and aids in moderating wide growth and color fluctuations. Turf managers should avoid applying too much slow-release N at any one application or excessive N may be released, creating lush growth. Also, these two N carriers should not be used when soil temperatures are below 55°F (13°C) because they will not release N, which could cause an accumulation from two or more applications releasing N in a short time period in the spring. The primary reason for suggesting natural organic N-carriers and UF is that they tend to exhibit a wider (i.e., longer) time period for N-release than other sources; however, other slow-release N carriers of moderately long-term release characteristics can be used in place of F, but the natural organic fertilizer component should still be periodically incorporated into your program to provide micronutrients. Natural organics may promote microbial activity during establishment on sandy soils.

In the cool periods when soil temperatures are <55°F, a monthly application of slow-release N fertilizer can be applied at about 0.50 lb N per 1,000 ft^2 (24.4 kg ha^{-1}) as any slow-release product not dependent upon microbial activity for release of N, e.g., coated sources and IBDU. This, again, is to act as a baseline level of fertility but without the chance of too much N becoming available at any one time.

Besides the base level of N applied through the use of slow-release N carriers, additional N may be necessary. This additional N should be primarily in the form of quick-release N. Carriers that have some slow-release N (one-third or less of the N as slow-release) can also be used but the purpose of these N applications is to provide rapid color and growth responses.

Quick-release N applications are made on an "as-needed" basis. Just as soon as N-deficiency symptoms are apparent, N fertilization should occur. Such applications are similar to the "spoon-feeding" approach used by many turf managers on mature grass stands. One difference is that N rate needs are somewhat higher during grow-in than typically used for mature turf, because of the lack of residual N and high leaching potential in new sand root zone soils. Slow-release N will help provide some residual, but the N present in decaying plant materials will be initially limited. Nitrogen rates per application can be 0.33 to 0.75 lb N per 1,000 ft^2 (16.1 to 36.6 kg N per ha^{-1}) with irrigation immediately afterward to prevent foliar burn. Sodded turfgrass requires little N just after laying compared to that needed for seeded or other types of vegetatively established turf.

Following germination the quick-release N fertilization may be needed once every two weeks. After a time, these N applications can be less frequent but are appropriate whenever the turf demonstrates a need, which may be indicated. This is often observed by a decline in the quantity of clippings, even before a color difference occurs. The high N rates or frequency will be during the more favorable environments for the grass species being used—i.e., cool periods for cool-season grasses and warm periods for warm-season turfgrasses. However, fairly high N may be required for cool-season grasses in the summer to enhance establishment.

Total annual N requirement during the first year is about 1-1/2 times the mature rate if the above approach to fertilization is used. Grow-in by the use of all quick-release N applications often results in more total N required due to leaching losses from the irrigation regimes necessary for establishment on high sand soils. Also, the stabilization of N level may be delayed under a high N regime using only quick-release formulations compared to one using some slow-release types.

Sometimes a turfgrass manager may attempt to force growth by continual use of high N such as 1.0 lb N per 1,000 ft^2 (48.8 kg ha^{-1}) every week or two. Grasses initially respond with more leaf growth and some stolon or rhizome growth. However, after a while, stolon and rhizome growth slows and may actually decline. Grasses with high N requirements (Tables 19.1 and 19.2) will respond the longest before these adverse effects occur, while grasses such as *Zoysia* spp. exhibit detrimental responses much more rapidly.

Excessively high N during grow-in can have other undesirable consequences such as: (a) development of too much thatch, especially if proper mowing and a good topdressing program are not begun immediately. Rapid thatch accumulation occurs with higher mowing heights and can result in high organic matter content or a layer that inhibits water movement and gas exchange after the grass matures. If soil pH declines below 5.5 due to high N and irrigation (leaching), thatch will accumulate more readily. A thatch layer buried by sand topdressing may become in subsequent years, a zone where black layer develops; (b) restricted root development that can cause future problems such as drought or winter desiccation; (c) a succulent turfgrass that is more prone to traffic injuries once use is allowed; (d) increased chance of *Rhizotonia* and *Pythium* diseases, and (e) low carbohydrate reserves necessary for dormancy periods, cold/high temperature/drought tolerance, and recovery from injuries.

Sometime during the 12- to 18-month time period, the N in the root zone and sod will begin to stabilize and the manager will no longer see rapid onset of N-deficiency symptoms characteristic of newly planted sandy sites. Instead of a rapid onset of N-deficiency symptoms as N becomes limiting, the turf goes gradually (over 1 to 2 weeks versus 1 to 3 days) into the slow growth and discoloration phases caused by lack of N. This buffering from rapid changes in turf nutrient status is provided by slow-release N and a buildup of residual N held in live and decaying turfgrass tissues and soil microorganisms. Greens often take the longest to stabilize the N level due to clipping removal.

From this point, the turf manager can go into a normal N fertilization program for mature grass. It is important for a superintendent to recognize when this change occurs because it often happens rather rapidly instead of on a gradual basis. After 12 to 18 months of frequent, heavier fertilization, it is easy to get into a habit of fertilizing by the calendar instead of by the appearance of the grass. Continuing to apply grow-in rates of N beyond the transition period will rapidly lead to excessive N problems, including potential leaching of nitrates. For new sand greens, it may be necessary to gradually lower annual N rates over 2–3 years before full stability occurs.

Potassium

With low cation exchange capacity of USGA greens and other sandy soils, potassium (K) is easily leached. Also, appreciable K may be carried off with clippings and many sands test very low in soil K. Maintenance of an adequate K supply is important since K deficiency results in lower carbohydrates in the plant; thin spindly plants; some degree of yellowing, especially as leaf tip burn; greater wilt; reduced wear, cold, and disease tolerance; reduced growth rate; greater tendency for scalp damage; and reduced rooting.

A starter fertilizer applied at seeding normally contains some K that is usually sufficient for 3 to 4 weeks. Shortly after seeding emergence, additional K should be applied at 0.25 to 0.50 lb K_2O per 1,000 ft^2 every 2 to 3 weeks (12.2 to 24.4 kg K ha^{-1}). In the summer months on cool-season grasses, it would be preferable to use twice per month applications at 0.25 to 0.40 lb K_2O per 1,000 ft^2 rates rather than one application due to the greater chance for fertilizer burn at this time of year. An alternative would be to apply K at 1:1 ($N:K_2O$) ratio with each N treatment. Both granular and water-soluble spray grades are available in a 1:1 ratio.

The preferred K-sources would be KNO_3, slow-release K, or K_2SO_4; the latter provides S, another essential nutrient used by grasses in appreciable quantities. Also, adverse effects of fertilizer salt injury are less likely to occur from K_2SO_4 versus KCl or KNO_3.

Potassium will stabilize somewhat as N does. However, as discussed in K fertilization programing on mature turf, a residual pool of K does not develop in sands that are leached due to heavy irrigation or high rainfall. Thus, light, frequent K applications are necessary to maintain a uniform supply.

Phosphorus

Most USGA golf greens or other high sand soils are low in P. Prior to final grading of the seedbed, it is a good idea to incorporate a 5-20-20 fertilizer and Milorganite® (or similar products) into the root zone mix. When applied to the surface and rototilled twice into the surface 2 to 4 inches (5 to 10 cm), typical rates of product would be 10 lb 5-20-20 per 1,000 ft^2 and 17 lb 6-2-0 per 1,000 ft^2 to provide 2.34 lb P_2O_5 per 1,000 ft^2 (49.8 kg P ha^{-1}). Also, at the time of seeding, a starter fertilizer such as 5-20-20 can be applied to the soil surface at 5 lb fertilizer per 1,000 ft^2 (0.50 lb P_2O_5 per 1,000 ft^2; 10.7 kg P ha^{-1}). These practices will ensure ample P during the early establishment phase, as well as some residual P deeper in the profile for long-term needs. Periodic use of natural organic N-sources during the grow-in months will supply additional P. Application of the P-containing fertilizers and the rates suggested above for the grow-in period will not induce more *Poa annua* but will enhance grass establishment. Grasses have high P needs during establishment.

Phosphorus deficiency can occur on grass during establishment and not be readily recognized. Initial symptoms of P deficiency are reduced shoot growth rate, a darker green color, and eventually the shoots become more spindly. Such turfgrasses will not be very responsive to additional N, Fe, or irrigation.

Micronutrients

Turfgrasses are very efficient in obtaining nutrients from the soil, including micronutrients. Micronutrients are required in only very small quantities. Just about any material added to turfgrasses contains small quantities of some micronutrients—often as impurities. These additions plus natural soil levels are sufficient for good growth in many instances. Required nutrients are iron (Fe), manganese (Mn), zinc (Zn), copper (Cu), molybdenum (Mo), boron (B), chlorine (Cl), and nickel (Ni). Only Fe and Mn have occasionally been found to be deficient on bentgrass greens but more frequently on warm-season grasses in high rainfall areas.

Iron deficiency occurs primarily in arid and semiarid regions in association with pH levels above 7.5, calcareous soils, high bicarbonate irrigation water, and sometimes with high P levels. Sometimes calcareous sands are used for construction of turfgrass root zone mixes even in humid regions. In these situations Fe deficiency may occur. Also, silica or calcareous sand sites in high rainfall climates with intensive turf management can exhibit Fe and Mn deficiencies. Other factors that may cause Fe deficiency are excessive thatch and high Mn or Zn applications.

Many golf course superintendents use 0.5 to 1.0 lb Fe per acre (0.56 to 1.12 kg Fe ha^{-1}) as foliar applications on a monthly basis. This provides better color, especially in cool dry periods, and alleviates any true Fe deficiencies.

Manganese deficiency is sometimes observed on alkaline soils (such as calcareous sands) subjected to intense leaching. High soil P and heavy use of foliar Fe may be associated with Mn deficiency. Most occurrences on Mn deficiency in the United States are in Florida or other humid regions where calcareous sands are present and the manager uses frequent foliar Fe. Use of the natural organic based N-carriers and twice annual micronutrient applications should be sufficient to prevent Mn deficiencies in most instances. But, where Mn deficiencies are more common, foliar applications of $MnSO_4$ or Mn chelate can be used once per month at 0.25 to 0.50 lb Mn per acre (0.28 to 0.56 kg Mn ha^{-1}). Some turf fertilizers include Mn at a low concentration that will provide adequate Mn.

Application of a complete micronutrient fertilizer every 3 to 4 months during grow-in in addition to the Fe and Mn treatments will help ensure adequate levels. Overapplication of complete micronutrient fertilizers or any one micronutrient should be avoided since toxicities or imbalances can occur. The most frequent (though rare) imbalance is for a high level of Fe, Mn, Cu, or Zn to result in deficiency of one of the others.

Other Nutrients

Sulfur (S) deficiency has been reported on turf growing on sandy soils, low in organic matter, under high leaching conditions, and in areas not receiving S by atmospheric deposition. If the K is applied at appropriate rates as K_2SO_4, adequate S should be present. Magnesium (Mg) deficiency can occur during grow-in, especially if one or more of the following conditions are present: (a) a high application of Ca from gypsum or $CaCO_3$ lime; (b) the irrigation source is high in Ca or Na; (c) soil pH is too acidic; and (d) high K rates are being used. If lime is needed, the use of dolomitic lime will supply Mg. Otherwise, periodic application of Mg may be necessary. The quantity of Mg (a macronutrient) in most micronutrient fertilizers is insufficient to supply all the Mg required.

While true Ca deficiency is very rare, grasses do respond during grow-in (as well as when mature) to Ca when: (a) irrigation water is high in Na or Mg; or (b) soil pH is acidic enough to induce Al or Mn toxicities. In this case, Ca addition aids in reducing toxicities of other elements (i.e., Al, Mn) rather than correcting a true Ca deficiency. However, high Na in the root zone can cause true Ca deficiency in root tissues. Foliar Ca will not be translocated to the roots, so a relatively soluble soil Ca fertilizer applied to the soil will be required to address root toxicities in a timely fashion.

B. Fine-Textured Soils

Grow-in of turfgrasses on fine-textured soils is much less complicated than on coarse-textured ones due to: (a) better inherent nutrient levels; (b) less leaching potential; and (c) better moisture retention. Nutrient stabilization and the transition to a mature turfgrass stand fertilization program is much more rapid especially when there is adequate organic matter present in the topsoil. Soil testing is a more useful guide to K status and estimated fertilizer needs than for sandy soils.

Nitrogen does not need to be premixed into the root zone of fine-textured soils but can be added at establishment at 0.50 lb N per 1,000 ft^2 (24.4 kg N ha^{-1}) as part of the starter fertilizer. Quick-release N carriers can be applied at 0.50 to 1.0 lb N per 1,000 ft^2 at 1 or 2 weeks after seed germination or vegetative planting (except sod) and every 2 to 4 weeks thereafter until coverage. Use of a slow-release N source in addition to the quick-release N should give a longer N response and reduce the need for fertilization equipment on a still soft seedbed. Excess N should be avoided since on fine-textured soils the N is usually not leached but produces excessive clipping growth and succulence while root growth and lateral shoot growth decline. Runoff of N and P can occur on sloping sites with intensive rainfall events. These sites are more prone to excess N problems than are sandy ones. Usually grow-in N needs are 1-1/4 to 1-1/2 times the mature turfgrass stand requirements.

Sodded sites: (a) may not need the starter N if the sod exhibits a good color with no apparent N deficiency symptoms; and (b) the first N application after sodding should be at a relatively low N rate of 0.33 to 0.50 lb N per 1,000 ft^2 (16.1 to 24.4 kg N ha^{-1}) to avoid inhibiting root development. Excess N can force top growth at the expense of good root establishment. Usually a normal N fertilization program can be initiated at 4 to 6 weeks after sodding.

Even fine-textured soils with a low or moderate P soil test can benefit from a starter P fertilizer, especially for seeding. Also, vegetatively established grasses, including sod, are often responsive to an initial P treatment, especially if the soil test P level is low. Other nutrients can be applied as would be required on a mature grass on the same site.

C. Special Problems of Grow-In

As with coarse-textured soils, toxic elements are sometimes present in the soil surface. Newly established grasses are more sensitive to potential toxicities than are mature grasses since the roots are near the surface and new tissues are more succulent in nature. If *toxic elements* are present, steps should be taken to reduce levels within at least the surface 2 to 3 inch (5.1 to 7.6 cm) zone during establishment. The most common toxicity problems are: (a) *high total salts* (see Chapter 8). Small seedlings are highly susceptible to salt injury. Extra irrigation prior to establishment can leach salts deeper into the profile. Once irrigation is started, the site should not be allowed to become too dry or salts will rise back into the surface in capillary water. It is best to leach salts, dry the site enough for establishment, and then continue light, frequent irrigation. The goal is to add sufficient water to maintain a net leaching but not allow a waterlogged soil; (b) *soils with pH <5.0 may exhibit Al or Mn toxicities* (see Chapter 5). If economics do not allow liming of the root zone, turf managers can select acid tolerant grasses. However, even acid tolerant plants are more sensitive to these toxicities during establishment. A relatively light application of either lime (preferred) or gypsum at 2 to 5 lb material per 1,000 ft^2 (97.6 to 244 kg ha^{-1}) will reduce toxicity problems within the surface. Such applications should be surface applied and mixed into the top 1 to 2 inches (2.5 to 5.1 cm). Maintaining good moisture will also minimize potential problems; and (c) the third potential toxicity during grow-in is *B in soils* with high natural levels. Approaches to reducing B in the surface few inches for establishment would be: (a) application of extra water to promote leaching; (b) addition of sufficient lime to raise pH to above 7.5; and (c) maintaining a moist soil surface since drying enhances B toxicity.

Another surface problem that can occur that hinders establishment is poor soil physical conditions due to a *sodic soil surface.* On sodic soils water infiltration is low and, once a soil is wet, it becomes waterlogged with poor aeration. Thus, application of gypsum will be beneficial at 2 to 4 weeks prior to establishment with irrigation to allow the gypsum to dissolve and replace Na, and to leach out of the surface. Addition of 20 to 80 lb $CaSO_4 \cdot 2H_2O$ per 1,000 ft^2 (976 to 3,903 kg $CaSO_4 \cdot 2H_2O$ ha^{-1}) to the surface may be required to provide adequate soil physical conditions for establishment. After establishment the site should be kept moist with continued leaching of Na to prevent reformation of sodic conditions at the surface.

VIII. REFERENCES

1. Balogh, J.C. and W.J. Walker. 1992. *Golf Course Management and Construction: Environmental Issues.* Boca Raton, FL: Lewis Publishers.
2. Marshall, C.J. and M.P. Kenna. 2000. *Fate and Management of Turfgrass Chemicals.* Am. Chem. Soc. Symp. Series 743. Am. Chem. Soc., Washington, DC.

Appendixes

A. Units of Measure
B. Common Fertilizer Calculations
C. Symbols and Atomic Weights of Selected Elements
D. Symbols and Valences of Selected Cations and Anions
E. Commonly Used Acronyms
F. Sieve Designations and Nominal Openings for U.S. Standard Sieve Series and Equivalent Tyler Screen Designations

Appendix A

Units of Measure

Units of measurement related to the plant and soil sciences may be in the English, metric, or SI (International System of Units) systems. In some cases, measurements or rates of application are given using two systems (e.g., g/1,000 ft^2). The SI system is similar to the metric system but has added physical units and does not include all commonly used metric units. Although the SI system (with exceptions for some units) is required in much of the scientific literature, English and metric units remain commonly used in the popular press, commercial literature, soil and tissue test results, product labels, and by turfgrass management professionals. Equivalents within and between systems follow.

Fertilizer

lb P_2O_5 (0.437) = lb P
lb P (2.29) = lb P_2O_5
lb K_2O (0.830) = lb K
lb K (1.20) = lb K_2O

Length

1 inch (in.) = 25.4 mm (millimeter) = 2.54 cm (centimeter)
1 foot (ft) = 12 in. = 30.48 cm = 0.3048 m
1 yard (yd) = 3 ft = 0.914 m
1 mile (mi) = 5,280 ft = 1,760 yd = 1,609.3 m (meter) = 1.6093 km (kilometer)
1 micrometer (μm) = 1 micron (μ) = 0.001 mm
1 millimeter (mm) = 1,000 μm = 0.03937 in.
1 centimeter (cm) = 10 mm = 0.3937 in.
1 decimeter (dm) = 10 cm = 3.937 in.
1 meter (m) = 10 dm = 100 cm = 1,000 mm = 39.37 in. = 3.281 ft = 1.094 yd
1 kilometer (km) = 1,000 m = 0.62137 mi

Area

1 $in.^2$ = 6.4516 cm^2
1 ft^2 = 144 $in.^2$ = 929.03 cm^2 = 0.0929 m^2
1,000 ft^2 = 92.9 m^2
100 m^2 = 1,076.4 ft^2
1 yd^2 = 9 ft^2 = 0.83613 m^2
1 acre = 43,560 ft^2 = 4,840 yd^2 = 0.4047 ha
1 cm^2 = 100 mm^2 = 0.15500 $in.^2$

1 dm^2 = 100 cm^2 = 15.500 $in.^2$ = 0.10764 ft^2
1 m^2 = 100 dm^2 = 10,000 cm^2 = 10.764 ft^2 = 1.1960 yd^2
1 are = 100 m^2 = 0.01 ha = 1076.4 ft^2 = 119.6 yd^2
1 hectare (ha) = 10^4 m^2 = 0.01 km^2 = 100 are = 2.471 acre
1 km^2 = 10^6 m^2 = 100 ha = 0.3861 mi^2

Volume (Cubic)

1 $in.^3$ = 16.387 cm^3
1 ft^3 = 1,728 $in.^3$ = 0.028317 m^3
1 yd^3 = 27 ft^3 = 0.76455 m^3
1 cm^3 = 1,000 mm^3 = 0.0610 $in.^3$
1 dm^3 = 1,000 cm^3 = 61.023 $in.^3$
1 m^3 = 1,000 dm^3 = 10^6 cm^3 = 35.03 ft^3 = 1.3079 yd^3

Volume (Liquid)

1 fluid ounce (oz) = 29.573 mL
1 quart (qt) = 2 pints = 32 oz = 0.94635 L = 946.35 mL
1 gallon (gal) = 4 qt = 128 oz = 3.7854 L
1 milliliter (mL) = 1 cm^3 = 0.033814 oz
1 deciliter (dL) = 100 mL = 3.3814 oz
1 liter (L) = 1,000 mL = 1.0567 qt = 0.26417 gal

Mass/Weight

1 ounce (oz) (avoirdupois) = 28.350 g
1 pound (lb) = 16 oz = 453.59 g = 0.45359 kg
1 ton (short ton) = 2,000 lb = 907.18 kg
1 gram (g) = 1,000 mg = 0.035274 oz
1 kilogram (kg) = 1,000 g = 2.2046 lb
1 quintal (q) = 100 kg
1 megagram (Mg) = 1 tonne (t) = 1 metric ton = 1,000 kg = 2,204.6 lb
1 short ton = 2,000 lb = 0.907 metric ton
1 long ton = 2,240 lb = 1.016 metric ton

Rate and Yield

Considerable variation occurs in the expression of rates and yields. A "base" unit of 1,000 ft^2 is typically used for turfgrass areas. Lime, fertilizer, and seed recommendations for roadsides are sometimes given for a unit of 1,000 yd^2. In some cases when metric units were required in a scientific publication, rates were expressed in terms of 92.9 m^2 instead of 1,000 ft^2. Also, it is not uncommon in some literature to find metric units of mass or liquid per English unit of area.

The conversion values in this section have enough significant figures to yield sufficiently accurate conversions for most cases. The converted value is no more precise than the original value, and should be rounded off to the same number of significant digits as in the original value.

1 pound/1,000 ft^2 (lb 1,000 ft^{-2}) = 43.56 lb $acre^{-1}$ = 48.8241 kg ha^{-1} = 0.488 kg are^{-1} = 0.488 g m^{-2}
1 lb $acre^{-1}$ = 1.121 kg ha^{-1}
1 oz 1,000 ft^{-2} = 2.7225 lb $acre^{-1}$ = 3.0515 kg ha^{-1}
1 oz $acre^{-1}$ = 0.07005 kg ha^{-1} = 70.053 g ha^{-1}
1 short ton (2,000 lb) $acre^{-1}$ = 2.242 Mg ha^{-1} = 2.242 tonne ha^{-1}
1 g m^{-2} = 100 g are^{-1} = 10^4 g ha^{-1} = 10 kg ha^{-1} = 3.2771 oz 1,000 ft^{-2} = 8.9218 lb $acre^{-1}$
1 kg ha^{-1} = 0.01 kg are^{-1} = 0.1 g m^{-2} = 0.89218 lb $acre^{-1}$ = 0.02048 lb 1,000 ft^{-2}
1 Mg ha^{-1} = t ha^{-1} = 0.4461 short ton (2,000 lb) $acre^{-1}$
1 g are^{-1} = 100 g ha^{-1} = 0.100 kg ha^{-1} = 0.089218 lb $acre^{-1}$
1 kg are^{-1} = 100 kg ha^{-1} = 89.218 lb $acre^{-1}$ = 2.048 lb 1,000 ft^{-2}
1 gal $acre^{-1}$ = 9.3537 L ha^{-1}
1 L ha^{-1} = 0.1069 gal $acre^{-1}$
1 gal 1,000 ft^{-2} = 43.56 gal $acre^{-1}$ = 407.45 L ha^{-1}

Pressure

1 atmosphere (atm) = 14.7 lb $in.^{-2}$ = 29.12 in. or 760 mm of mercury = 1,033 cm of H_2O = 1.0132 bar = 1013.2 millibar = 0.101 megapascal (MPa) = 101 kilopascal (kPa)
1 bar = 1,000 mb = 100 kPa = 0.1 MPa = 0.98697 atm = 1,020 cm of water
1 millibar (mb) = 0.1 kPa = 1.02 cm of H_2O
1 cm of H_2O = 0.098 kPa = 0.98 mb
1 MPa = 10 bar = 10,000 mb = 1,000 kPa
1kPa = 0.01 bar = 10 mb = 10.2 cm of H_2O
1 lb $in.^{-2}$ = 6,900 pascal (Pa)
1 lb ft^{-2} = 47.9 Pa
1 pascal (Pa) = .0209 lb ft^{-2} = 1.45×10^{-4} lb $in.^{-2}$

Soil water potential may be expressed in atmospheres, bars, cm of water, or millibars. The former two units are approximately equivalent, as are the latter two. In the SI system, soil water potential is reported using the units megapascal and kilopascal.

Electrical Conductivity

1 millimho per centimeter (mmho cm^{-1}) = 0.1 siemen per meter (S m^{-1}) = 1 deciSiemen per meter (dS m^{-1})

Cation Exchange Capacity

1 milliequivalent per 100 grams (meq 100 g^{-1}) = 1 centimole per kilogram (cmol kg^{-1})

Concentration

1 percent = 10,000 ppm = 10 gram per kilogram (10 g kg^{-1}) = 1 part per hundred
1 part per million (ppm) = 1 milligram per kilogram (mg kg^{-1})
1 g kg^{-1} = 0.1%
1 mg kg^{-1} = ppm

Temperature

°C (Celsius) = 5/9 (°F –32)
°F (Fahrenheit) = (9/5 °C) + 32
K (Kelvin) = °C + 273

°F	°C
0	–17.8
32	0
50	10
68	20
86	30
104	40

Water (assuming 1 g/cm^3)

1 cm^3 = 1 mL = 1 g
1 L = 1,000 mL = 1,000 g = 1 kg = 2.20 lb
1 qt = 946 g = 2.086 lb
1 gal = 8.34 lb
1 ft^3 = 7.48 gal = 62.4 lb
1 m^3 = 1 Mg = 10^6 g
1 acre-inch = 27,154 gal = 0.0103 hectare-meter
1 acre-inch = 102.8 m^3
1 hectare-meter = 10^5 m^3 = 8.11 acre-foot

For other measurement equivalents and conversions, see the latest edition of K.J. Karnok, Ed., *Turfgrass Management Information Directory,* Chelsea, MI: Ann Arbor Press; publication style manuals; encyclopedias; dictionaries; and chemistry and physics reference books.

Appendix B

Common Fertilizer Calculations

Example 1

(a) A 50 lb bag of fertilizer has an analysis of 25-5-10 (N-P_2O-K_2O). How much N, P_2O_5 and K_2O does the bag contain?

The analysis of the fertilizer indicates that it contains 25% N, 5% P_2O_5, and 10% K_2O. Percentages expressed on a decimal basis would be 25/100 or 0.25, etc; that is, 25% N would use 0.25 for calculation purposes.

(50 lb)(0.25 N) = 12.5 lb N
(50 lb)(0.05 P_2O_5) = 2.5 lb P_2O_5
(50 lb)(0.10 K_2O) = 5.0 lb K_2O

(b) How much P and K does the bag contain? See Appendix A for conversion factors.

(2.5 lb P_2O_5)(0.44) = 1.1 lb P
(5.0 lb K_2O)(0.83) = 4.15 lb K

Example 2

(a) A 25 kg bag of fertilizer has an analysis of 25-2-5 (N-P-K). How much N, P, and K does the bag contain?

The analysis of the fertilizer indicates that it contains 25% N, 2% P, and 5% K.

(25 kg)(0.25 N) = 6.25 kg N
(25 kg)(0.02 P) = 0.50 kg P
(25 kg)(0.05 K) = 1.25 kg K

(b) How much P_2O_5 and K_2O does the bag contain? (see Appendix A for conversion factors).

(0.50 kg P)(2.29) = 1.14 kg P_2O_5
(1.25 kg K)(1.20) = 1.50 kg K_2O

Example 3

For most turfgass sites, the turf manager is interested in how much fertilizer material to apply to a given area of turfgrass to achieve a specific fertilizer rate.

Problem: How much 25-5-10 ($N\text{-}P_2O_5\text{-}K_2O$) fertilizer should be applied to a 160 ft wide × 360 ft long football field to achieve a rate of 1.0 lb N per 1,000 ft^2?

- *Field size:*

  (160 ft)(360 ft) = 57,600 ft^2

- *Pounds of fertilizer to apply per 1,000 ft^2.* Often fertilizer calculations are first made on a basis of quantity of fertilizer required per 1,000 ft^2. Then the quantity needed for the whole area is determined. The quantity of actual N desired per 1,000 ft^2 is 1.0 lb N. The fertilizer contains 25% N. The formula used for a 1,000 ft^2 area is:

$$\frac{\text{lb of N desired}}{\text{percent of N in fertilizer on a decimal basis}} =$$

$$\frac{1.0\text{ lb N}}{0.25} = \begin{array}{c}\text{4.0 lb 25-5-10 fertilizer}\\ \text{required per 1,000 ft}^2\text{ of turf}\end{array}$$

- *Pounds of material to apply to 57,600 ft^2 of area.* The ratio method is used.

$$\frac{\text{X lb 25-5-10}}{57{,}600\text{ ft}^2} = \frac{\text{4.0 lb 25-5-10}}{1{,}000\text{ ft}^2}$$

$$(X)(1{,}000) = (4.0)(57{,}600)$$

$$X = \frac{(4.0)(57{,}600)}{1{,}000} = \begin{array}{l}\text{230.4 lb 25-5-10 applied to 57,600 ft}^2\\ \text{will provide 1.0 lb actual N per 1,000 ft}^2\end{array}$$

Example 4

When the units are in metric terms, the problem of how much fertilizer material to apply to a given area of turfgrass to achieve a specific fertilizer rate is similar to the approach in Example 3.

Problem: How much 25-2-5 (N-P-K) fertilizer should be applied to a 69 m (wide) x 100 m (long) rugby field to achieve a rate of 0.50 kg N per 100 m^2 ?

- *Field Size:*

$$(69 \text{ m})(100 \text{ m}) = 6{,}900 \text{ m}^2$$

- *Kilograms of fertilizer to apply per 100 m^2.* Fertilizer calculations are often based on a 100 m^2 area basis when using metric units in contrast to a 1,000 ft^2 basis for English units (1,000 ft^2 = 92.9 m^2; 100 m^2 = 1,076 ft^2).

$$\frac{\text{kg of N desired}}{\text{percent of N in fertilizer on a decimal basis}} =$$

$$\frac{0.50 \text{ kg N}}{0.25} = 2.0 \text{ kg fertilizer (i.e., 25-2-5) per } 100 \text{ m}^2$$

- Kilograms of fertilizer to apply to 6,900 m^2.

$$\frac{\text{X kg 25-2-5}}{6{,}900 \text{ m}^2} = \frac{2.0 \text{ kg N}}{100 \text{ m}^2}$$

$$\text{X} = \frac{2(6{,}900)}{100}$$

$$\text{X} = 138 \text{ kg of 25-2-5 required to provide 0.50 kg N per } 100 \text{ m}^2 \text{ to the } 6{,}900 \text{ m}^2 \text{ area.}$$

Example 5

A golf green is 6,500 ft^2 in size and a turfgrass manager desires to apply 1.0 lb actual Fe per acre to the site using a sprayer unit that delivers 3.0 gallons water per 1,000 ft^2. The iron carrier is a liquid formulation with 8.0% Fe and 1.0 gallon of product weighs 11.5 pounds.

- *Determining the Fe rate on a 1,000 ft^2 basis.*

1 acre = 43,560 ft^2

$$\frac{\text{W lb Fe}}{1{,}000\ \text{ft}^2} = \frac{1.0\ \text{lb Fe}}{43{,}560\ \text{ft}^2}$$

$$(\text{W})(43{,}560) = (1.0)(1{,}000)$$

$$\text{W} = 0.023\ \text{lb Fe per}\ 1{,}000\ \text{ft}^2$$

- *Determining the quantity of product (i.e., 8% Fe) to use per 1,000 ft^2.*

The analysis (i.e., 8% Fe) has the same meaning for liquids as it does with granular fertilizers, which is the "percent by weight." Since 1.0 gallon weighs 11.5 lb according to the label (if this is not listed on the label, a gallon should be weighed):

$$(\text{weight of gallon})(\%\ \text{Fe}) = \text{lb Fe per gallon}$$

$$(11.5\ \text{lb per gal})(0.08) = 0.92\ \text{lb Fe per gallon}$$

$$\frac{\text{X gal}}{0.023\ \text{lb Fe}} = \frac{1\ \text{gal}}{0.92\ \text{lb Fe}}$$

$$(\text{X})(0.92) = (1)(0.023)$$

X = 0.025 gal product required per 1,000 ft^2 of green to apply the 1 lb Fe per acre.

- *Determining the product required per 6,500 ft^2 green.*

$$\frac{\text{Y gal}}{6{,}500\ \text{ft}^2} = \frac{0.025\ \text{gal}}{1{,}000\ \text{ft}^2}$$

$$(\text{Y})(1{,}000) = (0.025)(6{,}500)$$

$$\text{Y} = 0.163\ \text{gal product per}\ 6{,}500\ \text{ft}^2$$

- *Determining the final spray mix.* Since the sprayer delivers 3.0 gal water per 1,000 ft^2, the total quantity of water required will be:

$$\frac{\text{Z gal water}}{6{,}500\ \text{ft}^2} = \frac{3.0\ \text{gal}}{1{,}000\ \text{ft}^2}$$

$$(\text{Z})(1{,}000) = (3.0)(6{,}500)$$

$$\text{Z} = 19.5 \text{ gallons water required to cover the } 6{,}500\ \text{ft}^2 \text{ green.}$$

To the 19.5 gallons water would be added the 0.163 gal (21 fluid ounces or 620 mL) product (i.e., 8% Fe product) to provide 0.023 lb actual Fe per 1,000 ft^2 for the green. The answer in fluid ounces is obtained by multiplying 0.163 gal times 128 fl oz per gal ($0.163 \times 128 = 20.9$ fl oz). For mL: 0.163 gal × 3785.4 mL per gal = 617 mL.

Additional examples of fertilizer and area calculations are presented by N. Christians and M.L. Agnew. 1997. *The Mathematics of Turfgrass Maintenance,* 2nd edition. Chelsea, MI: Ann Arbor Press.

Appendix C

Symbols and Atomic Weights of Selected Elements[a]

Element	Symbol	Atomic Weight	Element	Symbol	Atomic Weight
Aluminum	Al	26.98	Lithium	Li	6.94
Arsenic	As	74.92	Magnesium	Mg	24.31
Barium	Ba	137.33	Manganese	Mn	54.94
Boron	B	10.81	Mercury	Hg	200.59
Bromine	Br	79.90	Molybdenum	Mo	95.94
Cadmium	Cd	112.41	Nickel	Ni	58.69
Calcium	Ca	40.08	Nitrogen	N	14.01
Carbon	C	12.01	Oxygen	O	16.00
Chlorine	Cl	35.45	Phosphorus	P	30.97
Chromium	Cr	52.00	Potassium	K	39.10
Cobalt	Co	58.93	Silicon	Si	28.09
Copper	Cu	63.55	Silver	Ag	107.87
Fluorine	F	19.00	Sodium	Na	22.99
Hydrogen	H	1.01	Strontium	Sr	87.62
Iodine	I	126.90	Sulfur	S	32.07
Iron	Fe	55.85	Vanadium	V	50.94
Lead	Pb	207.2	Zinc	Zn	65.39

[a] For information on other elements, consult chemistry books or *CRC Handbook of Chemistry and Physics*, Boca Raton, FL: CRC Press Inc.

Appendix D

Symbols and Valences of Selected Cations and Anions

Cations		Anions	
Aluminum	Al^{+3}	Acetate	$C_2H_3O_2^-$
Ammonium	NH_4^+	Amide	NH_2^-
Barium	Ba^{+2}	Arsenate	AsO_4^{-3}
Cadmium	Cd^{+2}	Arsenite	AsO_3^{-3}
Calcium	Ca^{+2}	Bicarbonate	HCO_3^-
Cobalt	Co^{+2}	Borate	$B_4O_7^{-2}$
Copper I (Cuprous)	Cu^+	Bromide	Br^-
Copper II (Cupric)	Cu^{+2}	Carbonate	CO_3^{-2}
Hydrogen	H^+	Chloride	Cl^-
Iron II (Ferrous)	Fe^{+2}	Citrate	$C_6H_5O_7^{-3}$
Iron III (Ferric)	Fe^{+3}	Hydroxide	OH^-
Lead	Pb^{+2}	Molybdate	MoO_4^{-2}
Magnesium	Mg^{+2}	Nitrate	NO_3^-
Manganese II (Manganous)	Mn^{+2}	Nitrite	NO_2^-
Manganese IV	Mn^{+4}	Oxalate	$C_2O_4^{-2}$
Mercury I (Mercurous)	Hg_2^{+2}	Oxide	O^{-2}
Mercury II (Mercuric)	Hg^{+2}	Phosphate	PO_4^{-3}
Potassium	K^+	Phosphate	HPO_4^{-2}
Silicon	Si^{+4}	Phosphate	$H_2PO_4^-$
Silver	Ag^+	Silicate	SiO_4^{-4}
Sodium	Na^+	Silicate	$Si_3O_8^{-4}$
Strontium	Sr^{+2}	Sulfate	SO_4^{-2}
Zinc	Zn^{+2}	Sulfide	S^{-2}
		Sulfite	SO_3^{-2}

Appendix E

Commonly Used Acronyms

Organizations

AAPFCO	Association of American Plant Food Control Officials
ASA	American Society of Agronomy
ASTM	American Society for Testing and Materials
CSSA	Crop Science Society of America
FAO	Food and Agriculture Organization of the United Nations
ISO	International Standards Organization (International Organization for Standardization)
SSSA	Soil Science Society of America
USDA	United States Department of Agriculture
USGA	United States Golf Association

Biochemical

ABA	Abscisic acid
ADP	Adenosine diphosphate
AMP	Adenosine monophosphate
ATP	Adenosine triphosphate
DNA	Deoxyribonucleic acid
GA	Gibberellins, Gibberlic acid
IAA	Indoleacetic acid
NAD^+	Nicotinamide adenine dinucleotide
RNA	Ribonucleic acid

Other

BC	Buffer capacity
CCE	Calcium carbonate equivalent
CE	Cation exchange
CEC	Cation exchange capacity
DAP	Diammonium phosphate
ECa	Bulk soil electrical conductivity
ECe	Electrical conductivity in a saturated soil paste extract
ECp	Electrical conductivity of a saturated soil:water mixture
ECsw	Electrical conductivity of soil water
ECw	Electrical conductivity in water (solution)
ESP	Exchangeable sodium percentage
FGDG	Flue gas desulfurization gypsum
IBDU	Isobutylidine diurea
LR	Leaching requirement
M	Molar
MAP	Monoammonium phosphate
NIRS	Near infrared reflectance spectroscopy
NUE	Nitrogen use efficiency

PCU	Polymer coated urea
PG	Phosphogypsum
PGR	Plant growth regulator
RSC	Residual sodium carbonate
SAR	Sodium adsorption ratio
SARw	Sodium adsorption ratio of irrigation water
SCU	Sulfur coated urea
SGN	Size guide member
SI	International system of units (System Internationale)
TDS	Total dissolved salts (sometimes also refers to total dissolved solids)
TEC	Threshold electrolyte concentration
TSS	Total soluble salts
UF	Ureaform, ureaformaldehyde
UI	Uniformity index

Appendix F

Sieve Designations and Nominal Openings for U.S. Standard Sieve Series and Equivalent Tyler Screen Designations

U.S. Sieve Series[a]				
Sieve Designation		Sieve Opening		
Standard[b]	Alternate[d]	mm	inch (approximate equivalent)	Tyler Screen Scale Equivalent Designation[e]
125 mm	5.0 inch	125	5.00	–
106 mm	4.24 inch	106	4.24	–
100 mm[c]	4.0 inch[c]	100	4.00	–
90 mm	3.5 inch	90	3.50	–
75 mm	3.0 inch	75	3.00	–
63 mm	2.5 inch	63	2.50	–
53 mm	2.12 inch	53	2.12	–
50 mm[c]	2.0 inch[c]	50	2.00	–
45 mm	1.75 inch	45	1.75	–
37.5 mm	1.5 inch	37.5	1.50	–
31.5 mm	1.12 inch	31.5	1.25	–
26.5 mm	1.08 inch	26.5	1.06	1.050 inch
25 mm[c]	1.0 inch[c]	25	1.00	–
22.4 mm	0.875 inch	22.4	0.875	0.883 inch
19.0 mm	0.75 inch	19.0	0.750	0.742 inch
16.0 mm	0.625 inch	16.0	0.625	0.624 inch
13.2 mm	0.530 inch	13.2	0.530	0.525 inch
12.5 mm[c]	0.5 inch[c]	12.5	0.500	–
11.2 mm	0.4375 inch	11.2	0.438	0.441 inch
9.5 mm	0.375 inch	9.5	0.375	0.371 inch
8.0 mm	0.3125 inch	8.0	0.312	2.5 mesh[f]
6.7 mm	0.265 inch	6.7	0.265	3 mesh
6.3 mm[c]	0.25 inch	6.3	0.250	–
5.6 mm	No. 3 1/2	5.6	0.223	32 mesh
4.75 mm	No. 4	4.75	0.187	4 mesh
4.00 mm	No. 5	4.00	0.157	5 mesh
3.35 mm	No. 6	3.35	0.132	6 mesh
2.80 mm	No. 7	2.80	0.111	7 mesh
2.36 mm	No. 8	2.36	0.0937	8 mesh
2.00 mm	No. 10	2.00	0.0787	9 mesh
1.70 mm	No. 12	1.70	0.0661	10 mesh
1.40 mm	No. 14	1.40	0.0555	12 mesh
1.18 mm	No. 16	1.18	0.0469	14 mesh
1.00 mm	No. 18	1.00	0.0394	16 mesh
850 μm	No. 20	0.850	0.0331	20 mesh
710 μm	No. 25	0.710	0.0278	24 mesh
600 μm	No. 30	0.600	0.0234	28 mesh

U.S. Sieve Series[a]				
Sieve Designation		Sieve Opening		
Standard[b]	Alternate[d]	mm	inch (approximate equivalent)	Tyler Screen Scale Equivalent Designation[e]
500 μm	No. 35	0.500	0.0197	32 mesh
425 μm	No. 40	0.425	0.0165	35 mesh
355 μm	No. 45	0.355	0.0139	42 mesh
300 μm	No. 50	0.300	0.0117	48 mesh
250 μm	No. 60	0.250	0.0098	60 mesh
212 μm	No. 70	0.212	0.0083	65 mesh
180 μm	No. 80	0.180	0.0070	80 mesh
150 μm	No. 100	0.150	0.0059	100 mesh
125 μm	No. 120	0.125	0.0049	115 mesh
106 μm	No. 140	0.106	0.0041	150 mesh
90 μm	No. 170	0.090	0.0035	170 mesh
75 μm	No. 200	0.075	0.0029	200 mesh
63 μm	No. 230	0.063	0.0025	230 mesh
53 μm	No. 270	0.053	0.0021	270 mesh
45 μm	No. 325	0.045	0.0017	325 mesh
38 μm	No. 400	0.038	0.0015	400 mesh
32 μm	No. 450	0.032	0.00125	450 mesh
25 μm[c]	No. 500[c]	0.025	0.0010	500 mesh
20 μm[c]	No. 635[c]	0.020	0.0008	635 mesh

[a] The openings (and standard numbering) in standard series sieves are based on an approximate $\sqrt[4]{2}$ (fourth root of 2) ratio with the base opening being 1.00 mm. An increase of two series sizes results in an approximate doubling of opening area; e.g., 1.00 mm sieve has opening area of 1.00 mm^2 and a 0.710 mm sieve has an opening of 0.504 mm^2.

[b] The standard designations correspond to those recommended by the International Organization of Standardization (Geneva, Switzerland).

[c] Sieve is not the standard $\sqrt[4]{2}$ series, but it is commonly used.

[d] Alternative designations No. 10 to No. 400 are the approximate number of openings per linear inch.

[e] W.S. Tyler Inc., Mentor, Ohio.

[f] Mesh refers to the number of openings per 1 linear inch and is a function of opening size and wire diameter.

Index

A

E

F

G

H

W

Y

Z